European Sports Law

Collected Papers

Asser International Sports Law Series

Editors

Robert C.R. Siekmann and Janwillem Soek

ISSN 1874–6926

This publication was realised with the cooperation of the

International Olympic Committee

FIFPro

Partners of the ASSER International Sports Law Centre

Larrauri & López Ante Abogados

LNA Legal Netlink Alliance — Lawyers Worldwide

LCA avvocati e commercialisti d'impresa studio associato

TOLUN Consulting Sport Law Center — With Us, The Solution Is Well Within Reach...

DF Advocates — Deguara Farrugia Advocates

C/M/S/ Derks Star Busmann — Attorneys at Law Civil Law Notaries Tax Advisers

TaylorWessing

De Keersmaeker Vromans — The Brussels Office of the Asser International Sports Law Centre

WILKENS c.s. — Translators & Interpreters

T.M.C. ASSER INSTITUUT
ASSER INTERNATIONAL SPORTS LAW CENTRE

EUROPEAN SPORTS LAW

COLLECTED PAPERS

by

Stephen WEATHERILL

T•M•C• ASSER PRESS

Published by T·M·C·ASSER PRESS
P.O. Box 16163, 2500 BD The Hague, The Netherlands
<www.asserpress.nl>

T·M·C·ASSER PRESS' English language books are distributed exclusively by:

Cambridge University Press, The Edinburgh Building, Shaftesbury Road,
Cambridge CB2 2RU, UK,
or
for customers in the USA, Canada and Mexico:
Cambridge University Press, 100 Brook Hill Drive, West Nyack, NY 10994-2133, USA
<www.cambridge.org>

ISBN 978-90-6704-243-7
ISSN 1874-6926

Cover photograph: Pyke Koch, "Soccer Players V", 1959. Tempera on paper on wood.
Collection Scheringa Museum of Realist Art, The Netherlands.

The Scheringa Museum of Realist Art (formerly Frisia Museum) was founded by Dirk and Baukje Scheringa-De Vries. They began collecting work by Magic Realist Carel Willink in the 1980s, as well as various contemporaries of the artist. In the mid-1990s the idea developed of opening their private collection to the public and in 1997 the museum was opened. Apart from focusing on Magic Realism, the Scheringa Museum of Realist Art also presents Dutch and international realist art of the interwar years as well as of the postwar period. www.scheringamuseum.nl

T.M.C. Asser Instituut – Institute for Private and Public International Law, International Commercial Arbitration and European Law

Institute Address: R.J. Schimmelpennincklaan 20-22, The Hague, The Netherlands; Mailing Address: P.O. Box 30461, 2500 GL The Hague, The Netherlands; Tel.: +3170 342 0300; Fax: +3170 3420 359; Internet: www.asser.nl.
Over fourty years, the T.M.C. Asser Institute has developed into a leading scientific research institute in the field of international law. It covers private international law, public international law, including international humanitarian law, the law of the European Union, the law of international commercial arbitration and increasingly, also, international economic law, the law of international commerce and international sports law.
Conducting scientific research, either fundamental or applied, in the aforementioned domains, is the main activity of the Institute. In addition, the Institute organizes congresses and postgraduate courses, undertakes contract-research and operates its own publishing house.
Because of its inter-university background, the Institute often cooperates with Dutch law faculties as well as with various national and foreign institutions.

FOREWORD

I am deeply honoured and very pleased to have been invited by Dr Robert Siekmann, the Director of the ASSER International Sports Law Centre in The Hague, The Netherlands, to contribute this Foreword to Professor Stephen Weatherill's collection of writings on European Union law and sport.

We have one important thing in common: we are both, in our respective ways, humble pioneers in this evolving field of law. He is a distinguished academic and I am an enthusiastic practitioner. As such, we are, in a sense, in a symbiotic relationship. In practising before the European Court of Justice as a sports lawyer, I am always pleased to draw on his insights and ideas in testing my arguments; and he, of course, draws on the actual decisions of the Court itself, to provide a coherent and critical legal analysis of how sport is being regulated at the European level and a European sports law policy is emerging, despite the fact that the present Treaty does not – at least as yet – contain any so-called 'sport article'. For this reason – and indeed many others – I very much welcome the opportunity that this book offers me and others with an interest in sports law of being able to have access in one place to his scholarship, insight and learned writings, which I am pleased to acknowledge have contributed to my knowledge and understanding of the development of European Union law in the field of sport. As a lawyer practising in the civil law tradition, I would remind readers of the fact that the opinions of textbook writers and academics, such as Stephen Weatherill, are one of the sources of the law – and an important one at that!

I would also like to congratulate Robert Siekmann, who is also a pioneer in the field of international sports law, having set up and continuing to lead with distinction the International Sports Law Centre at the prestigious T.M.C. Asser Institute in The Hague, for having had the constructive idea for this book and organising its publication through Philip van Tongeren, Publisher of T.M.C. Asser Press. And, last, but by no means least, I would like to salute and warmly congratulate Stephen Weatherill for providing us with such interesting, thought-provoking and compelling reading.

This book will, I am sure, quickly establish itself as a leading work on European law and sport and become a *vademecum* for all those involved in a variety of ways and functions, as administrators, managers, researchers, academics, marketers, broadcasters, advisers and practitioners, in the exciting field of international sport and the ever unfolding challenges that the interface between European Union law and sport provides in daily life, especially now that sport is big business accounting for 2 per cent of the combined gross national product of the enlarged European Union of 27 Member States.

Belgium, March 2007

Maître Jean-Louis Dupont
Avocat

TABLE OF CONTENTS

Foreword by Jean-Louis Dupont V

List of Abbreviations and Acronyms XIII

Introduction by Stephen Weatherill 1

Where lies the interest in 'EC sports law'? 1
The European Court sets the scene 2
The papers contained in this book 5
Concluding remarks 12

Discrimination on Grounds of Nationality in Sport 15

I. Introduction 15
II. The discriminatory player restrictions 15
III. Is there a breach of the Treaty? 17
A. Sport and the Treaty of Rome 17
B. Article 48 EEC 18
(a) Are the rules within the scope of the Treaty? 20
(b) Are the Treaty rules horizontally directly effective? 23
(c) Justification 25
(d) Discrimination internal to a single Member State 26
C. Articles 85 and 86 EEC 27
(a) Are the rules within the scope of the Treaty? 28
(b) Are the Treaty rules horizontally directly effective? 33
(c) Justification 33
(i) The straightforward application of Article 85(3) 34
(ii) The straightforward application of Article 85(3) doubted 35
(iii) Making a special case for sport 36
(iv) The special case for sport – the argument redefined 36
(d) Discrimination internal to a single Member State 38
D. Conclusion 39
IV. Enforcement by the Commission 39
A. Article 48 39
B. Articles 85 and 86 41
(a) The Commission's Enforcement Powers 41
(b) Why has the Commission not initiated such proceedings? 41
C. Remedies against the Commission 42
V. Enforcement by private parties before national courts 44
VI. Concluding remarks 46
A. General 46
B. The overlap between Article 48 and Article 85 47
C. A solution 48
(a) Demarcation at Community level 48
(b) Accepting the overlap 49

European Football Law 53

I. Introduction 53

II. Jean-Marc Bosman 54
A. The Transfer System – the Road to Litigation 54
B. Nationality Restrictions in Football 56
C. Access to Justice in the Football Industry 57
III. Jurisdictional Questions 59
A. Is Sport Within the Scope of Application of Community Law? 59
B. Application to Private Parties 60
IV. The Nationality Restrictions 61
A. National Representative Football 61
B. Club Football 62
C. Residual Issues 63
D. Adjusting Practices in the Football Industry 64
V. The Transfer Rules 65
A. The Basis of the Court's Objection to the System 65
B. Players still under Contract 66
C. Adjustments in the Game 68
VI. The Scope of the Law of Free Movement 69
VII. Justification 73
A. Law 73
B. Application to Football 73
C. Adjusting Football 74
D. Fostering Competitive Equality 75
E. Encouraging Young Players 78
VIII. A Transfer System within a Domestic League 79
A. Reverse Discrimination 79
B. Economic Pressures 80
C. Legal Issues 81
IX. Conclusion 84

Annotation [*Bosman* Case] 87

1. Introduction 87
2. The factual background 88
2.1. The structure of the football industry 88
2.2. The transfer rules 89
2.3. The nationality restrictions 90
2.4. Jean-Marc Bosman, the footballer 90
2.5. Jean-Marc Bosman, the litigant 91
3. The Opinion of the Advocate-General 92
4. The Judgment of the Court 94
4.1. The application of Article 48 EC to the transfer rules 94
4.1.1. Sport and the Economy 94
4.1.2. EC law and the private sector 94
4.1.3. An obstacle to free movement 95
4.1.4. Justifying the rules 96
4.2. The application of Article 48 EC to nationality restrictions 97
4.2.1. Trade restriction and nationality discrimination 97
4.2.2. Jurisdiction under Article 177 97
4.2.3. Defending the rules 99
5. Comment 101
5.1. Bosman and the reorganization of the football industry 101
5.1.1. The transfer system 101
5.1.2. The nationality restrictions 105

5.2. The limits of the *Bosman* ruling and prospects for future litigation 106
5.2.1. Domestic transfer systems 106
5.2.2. Players who are not EU nationals 111
5.2.3. Players whose contract has not expired 112
6. Conclusion 114

0033149875354: Fining the Organisers of the 1998 Football World Cup 117

Introduction 117
The facts 117
The decision 118
Comment 121
Conclusion 125
Letter from Stephen Weatherill to the EC Commission, June 17, 1997 125
Reply from the EC Commission (DG IV – Competition) to Stephen Weatherill, September 25, 1997 126
Reply from Stephen Weatherill to the EC Commission, October 14, 1997 127
Reply to Stephen Weatherill from the EC Commission, November 21, 1997 128
Reply to the EC Commission from Stephen Weatherill, December 18, 1997 128

Sports under EC Competition Law and US Antitrust Law 131

I. Introduction 131
II. Sport does not escape the reach of EC law 132
III. The significance of individual litigation in the EC system 134
IV. How special is sport? The window of opportunity opened in the *Bosman* ruling 135
V. Shaping the legal framework reflecting the special nature of sport 138
VI. Conclusion 141

The Helsinki Report on sport 143

Sports and Community law 143
The Helsinki Report on sport 146
Practices which do not come under the competition rules 148
Practices that are, in principle, prohibited by the competition rules 149
Practices likely to be exempted from the competition rules 149
Conclusion 153

Resisting the Pressures of 'Americanization': The Influence of European Community Law on the 'European Sport Model' 155

Introduction 155
The Appeal for Self-regulation in Sport 156
Bosman – the Road to Luxembourg 157
Bosman – What Did the European Court Decide? 158
Bosman and the Vigour of EC Law 159
Why Sport is Different 161
Commission Thinking in 1999 164
Some Outstanding Questions 169
Conclusion 173

'Fair Play Please!': Recent Developments in the Application of EC Law to Sport 177

1. Introduction 177

2. 'Sport is special' 178
3. Recent judgments of the Court 182
4. Recent decisions of the Commission 184
4.1. Football players' agents 185
4.2. Formula One 185
4.3. The '*Mouscron* case' 186
4.4. Multiple club ownership 186
4.5. Anti-doping rules in swimming 187
4.6. Ticket distribution for the 1998 Football World Cup 187
4.7. The player transfer system 189
4.7.1. *Bosman* remembered 189
4.7.2. Beyond *Bosman*: the Commission's agreement with the football authorities 190
4.7.3. Is the matter now closed? 192
4.8. Broadcasting 196
4.8.1. The economic context of sport and broadcasting 196
4.8.2. UEFA's rules on 'blocking' matches 197
4.8.3. Collective selling of broadcasting rights – the competing interests 198
4.8.4. Collective selling of broadcasting rights – legal straws in the wind 200
5. The structure of EC trade law applied to sport 202
6. The wider terrain of a policy on sport 207
6.1. The Commission's approach: a 'European Model of Sport' 207
6.2. The Treaties of Amsterdam and Nice: Declarations on Sport and their consequences 209
6.3. The several faces of 'sport' 211
7. Conclusion 212

Sport as Culture in EC Law 215

1. Introduction 215
2. Concessions made to the distinctive nature of sporting competition 216
3. Benefits claimed because of the distinctive nature of sporting competition: the player transfer system 219
(a) The transfer system before and after *Bosman* 220
(b) The 2001 agreement on the transfer system 221
(c) Outstanding legal questions 223
4. Benefits claimed because of the distinctive nature of sporting competition: collective selling of rights to broadcast matches 226
(a) Collective selling – the problems 226
(b) Collective selling – law and practice before Champions League 228
(c) Champions League 230
5. Burdens imposed because of the distinctive nature of sporting competition: 'protected' or 'listed' events 234
(a) 'Listed events' under the 'Television Without Frontiers' Directive 234
(b) Interpreting the Directive 237
(c) The purpose of the regime 239
6. Is there a broader cultural context? 242
7. Conclusion 246

Anti-Doping Rules and EC Law 249

Introduction 249
The background to the litigation 249

The judgment 250
What is a 'restriction' on competition? The judgment in *Wouters* 252
Wouters sidelined 254
A better approach-reinstating *Wouters* at the heart of the reasoning 256

Is the Pyramid Compatible with EC Law? 259

1. Introduction 259
2. EU sports law and policy – the constitutional background 259
3. EU sports law and practice 260
4. The autonomy of governing bodies in sport 263
5. The pyramid – its nature and purpose 265
6. The pyramid under challenge 267
7. Conclusion 271

The sale of rights to broadcast sporting events under EC law 273

1. Introduction – the constitutional context 273
2. The nature and purpose of an 'EC policy' 279
3. EC competition law 284
   3.1. The general purpose of competition law 284
   3.2. Competition law in Europe 286
   3.3. European Community Law of Cartels and Restrictive Practices 286
   3.4. Public and private enforcement of Article 81 288
   3.5. Control of the abuse of a dominant position: European Community Monopoly Law 291
4. The economic context of sport and broadcasting 294
5. Exclusive selling 298
   5.1. The scope of the prohibition 298
   5.2. Exemption 302
6. Collective selling of rights to broadcast matches 306
   6.1. The phenomenon of 'interdependence' in sports leagues 307
   6.2. Collective selling – law and practice 308
   6.3. Champions League – application to collective selling at national level 311
   6.4. Collective selling – unresolved questions about the place of 'solidarity' 314
7. Collective Purchasing 317
8. Blocking rules 321
9. Burdens imposed because of the distinctive nature of sporting competition: 'protected' or 'listed' events 321
   9.1. 'Listed events' under the 'Television without Frontiers' Directive 322
   9.2. The nature and purpose of the régime 325
10. What is the EC's 'policy' on the sale of right to broadcast sports events? 328
11. Conclusion 331

Anti-doping revisited – the demise of the rule of 'purely sporting interest'? 335

Introduction 335
The challenge of EC law and sport 335
The CFI's approach in *Meca-Medina and Majcen* 339
The appeal – setting aside the CFI's judgment 340
The appeal – rejecting the application for annulment 342
Why *Meca-Medina and Majcen* matters to the shaping of EC law on sport 345
Meca-Medina and Majcen and the future of sports litigation under EC competition law 346

The *Oulmers* case: putting *Meca-Medina* to the test 349
Conclusion 352

Concluding remarks by Ian S. Blackshaw 355

National and International Legislation 359

Table of Cases 363

Subject Index 369

LIST OF ABBREVIATIONS AND ACRONYMS

AG	Advocate General
BAF	British Athletics
C.M.L.R.	Common Market Law Reports
C.M.L.Rev.	Common Market Law Review
CAS	Court for Arbitration for Sport
CFI	Chamber of the Court of First Instance of the Court of Justice of the European Communities
CFO	Comité Français d'Organisation de la Coupe du Monde de Football
DG	Directorate-General
E.C.L.R.	European Competition Law Review
E.L.Rev.	European Law Review
E.T.S.	European Treaty Series
EBU	European Broadcasting Union
ECHR	European Convention on Human Rights
ECJ	Court of Justice of the European Communities
ECR	European Court Reports
ECSC	European Coal and Steel Community
EEA	European Economic Area
EEC	European Economic Community
EP	European Parliament
ESF	European Social Fund
EU	European Union
FFF	Fédération Française de Football
FIA	Fédération Internationale d'Automobile
FIBA	International Basketball Federation
FIFA	International Association Football Federation
FIFPro	Fédération International de Footballeurs Professionels
FINA	Fédération Internationale de Natation
Fn.	Footnote
IAAF	International Association of Athletics Federations
IIHF	International Ice Hockey Federation
IOC	International Olympic Committee
IRB	International Rugby Board
ITC	Television Independent Television Commission
J	judge
MEP	Member of the European Parliament
OJ	Official Journal
RPC	Restrictive Practices Court (UK)
s	section
SEA	Single European Act
UCI	Union Cycliste Internationale
UEFA	Union of European Football Associations
WADA	World Anti-Doping Agency
WLR	The Weekly Law Reports

INTRODUCTION

Stephen Weatherill*

I am immensely flattered and honoured that the Asser Instituut has undertaken to publish a collection of my writing in the area of EC law and sport, and I thank them most warmly for this generous mark of approval. I am delighted too to be given this opportunity to write a short Introduction designed to sketch just why I have always found this area to be intellectually rewarding. 'Sport and the law' is, for sure, something of a niche interest – though, thanks to Jean-Marc Bosman (and Jean-Louis Dupont too) it is a good less esoteric to claim an interest in sport and the law today than it was back in the distant 1980s when I first grappled with the complexities – but it is one that repays the investment of time and energy. Researching the field tells us something about sport, of course. But it tells us something about EC law too. Examination of the special character of sport when placed under EC law's microscope reveals the scope of EC trade law's adaptability to the particular context in which it is applied. And the story of EC sports law told through the case law illuminates the way in which EC law is exploited by actors as a lever to prise open sometimes long-established organisational patterns. Sport has in recent years become more commercialised and more juridified too. The challenges to its self-regulatory preferences have strengthened, and EC law plays a significant part in this narrative. But how to assess the *quality* of the EC's contribution? That has been an abiding concern for me.

Where lies the interest in 'EC sports law'?

The EC Treaty does not refer to sport at all. The EC is therefore not constitutionally competent to adopt *legislation* with the explicit aim of regulating sport. But the EC Treaty contains provisions that exert a broad control over the functioning of the whole economy. These include, most significantly, the provisions on free movement of persons and services (Arts. 39 and 49 EC) and the rules on competition (Arts. 81 and 82 EC). Since sport has an economic dimension, sporting practices fall within the broad scope of the EC Treaty. Therefore sporting practices must comply with these Treaty rules. In this way EC law has overlapped with 'internal' sports law.

It is this complex and ambiguous confluence that has long stimulated my interest in this field. How legitimate is the EC's claim to subject sporting practices to the rules of the EC Treaty given that the Treaty offers no guidance on the extent to which sport's distinctive features should inform the legal analysis? How legitimate are the frequent

* Stephen Weatherill is Jacques Delors Professor of European Community Law, Somerville College, University of Oxford, United Kingdom.

appeals of sports federations to be permitted autonomy from legal intervention given that their decisions frequently carry significant economic implications? In fact, the rapid increase in recent years in the commercial significance of the sports sector, driven in part by the technological and regulatory re-shaping of the broadcasting industry, has brought with it ever more intense scrutiny of the role of *law* in influencing the choices available to sports governing bodies.

My general feeling is that EC trade law should not be applied to sport in a way that neglects sport's undoubted special characteristics. For example, clubs in a professional League are not competitors of the type found in normal markets. Sports clubs need opponents – they need credible rivals. There is a pattern of interdependence among clubs in a League which marks out organised sport as culturally and economically distinct from sausage-making. Sport is, in some respects, a special case, and the law should respect that, or else suffer justified criticism for insensitive mishandling of the subject-matter. On the other hand I have never been able to accept that sport is quite as special as is sometimes claimed by sports federations. That is, I cannot accept that the mere fact that a practice with economic implications is located in the sports sector is sufficient to entitle it to immunity from legal control. Nor can I easily hide my occasional frustration at the airily uncritical claims of those engaged in sports governance that things are best done as they always have been done. So I have always favoured a model which embraces an inevitable intersection between the EC's legal order and sports governance – that is, one according to which sport is subject to EC law but in which sport's special features are relevant to the legal analysis. The interest for me then lies in deciding just where sport has a convincing claim to special treatment at law which recognises its special social and economic characteristics and where, by contrast, sports bodies are engaged in self-serving defence of a *status quo* which deserves no place in modern life. Sport *is* special. But *how* special?

The European Court sets the scene

Three major judgments of the European Court demonstrate an evolution in the Court's own depiction and understanding of the issues at stake. My writing is by no means confined to the practice of the Court, for the challenge of understanding EC law and policy as it affects sport necessarily demands that account be taken of the Commission and more generally of the range of public and private actors who exploit the EC tier of governance in order to promote their interests and who, in doing so, frequently induce adaptation in existing national, international and predominantly self-regulatory patterns of sports governance. But the Court's judgments serve to structure much of the debate and the analysis. And they illuminate the awkward tensions involved in shaping EC sports law and policy.

In *Walrave and Koch* v. *Union Cycliste Internationale* the Court treated the composition of national sports teams as unaffected by the EC Treaty's prohibition of nationality-based discrimination where their formation is 'a question of purely sporting interest and as such has nothing to do with economic activity'.[1] The result was understandable. There is simply no international representative football without restrictions on selection policies – a Dutch football team made up of Germans or Scots or Peruvians is no Dutch team at all. Rules relating to nationality define the very nature of the enterprise. But the Court, in showing respect for the nature of the sport, employed a poorly crafted legal formula. Its reference to 'a question of purely sporting interest' which 'as such has nothing to do with economic activity' is unhelpful. Clearly selection rules governing international representative football are of sporting interest. But – equally clearly, I think – such rules have plenty to do with economic activity. International football is big business – players enhance their profile and popularity, and therefore their earning potential, depending on their exposure as international footballers. In reality the spheres of sport and economics commonly overlap, for most sporting rules are of sporting interest and they also exert an economic impact. What is really at stake is not a group of sporting rules and a separate group of economic rules, but rather a group of sporting rules which carry economic implications and which therefore fall for assessment, but not necessarily condemnation, under EC trade law. This is the core of my thesis that EC law and 'internal' sports law cannot be kept separate.

Walrave and Koch introduced an unfortunate claim to a separation between the sporting and the economic sphere, while also accepting that sport's special expectations could be taken into account in the application of EC law. The second landmark decision, *Bosman*, is thematically similar.[2] The Court referred to the *problem* in drawing attention to 'the difficulty of severing the economic aspects from the sporting aspects of football'. But it did not offer a clear *solution*.

> '[T]he provisions of Community law concerning freedom of movement of persons and of provision of services do not preclude rules or practices justified on non-economic grounds which relate to the particular nature and context of certain matches.'

The Court is in general terms accepting there is an area of sporting autonomy free of interference by EC law, but the precise nature and purpose of these 'non-economic grounds' is not easy to discern. However, as in *Walrave and Koch*, the Court in *Bosman*, though unwilling to rule out the possibility in principle of sporting practices falling foul of the EC Treaty, was prepared to discover scope for the promotion of sport's special concerns. It stated that

> 'In view of the considerable social importance of sporting activities and in particular football in the Community, the aims of maintaining a balance between clubs by preserving a certain degree of equality and uncertainty as to results and of encouraging the recruitment and training of young players must be accepted as legitimate.'[3]

---

[1] Case 36/74 [1974] *ECR* 1405.

[2] Case C-415/93 [1995] *ECR* I-4921.

[3] Para. 106.

The EC Treaty offers nothing that points explicitly in this direction. It does not even mention sport. But the Court, while finding that the particular practices impugned in *Bosman* fell foul of EC law, showed itself receptive to an interpretative approach which in effect writes into EC law an active recognition of the special features of sport.

The third landmark case offers a clearer and intellectually more satisfying explanation of the relationship between sporting rules and EC law, while maintaining the thematic receptivity to sport's special concerns in the application of EC law. It is *Meca-Medina and Majcen* v. *Commission*, a decision of July 2006.[4] The applicants, professional swimmers who had failed a drug test and been banned for two years, had complained unsuccessfully to the Commission of a violation of the Treaty competition rules. The CFI rejected an application for annulment.[5] So did the ECJ. But whereas the CFI attempted to insist that anti-doping rules concern exclusively non-economic aspects of sport, designed to preserve 'noble competition',[6] the ECJ instead stated that 'the mere fact that a rule is purely sporting in nature does not have the effect of removing from the scope of the Treaty the person engaging in the activity governed by that rule or the body which has laid it down'.[7] And if the sporting activity in question falls within the scope of the Treaty, the rules which govern that activity must satisfy the requirements of the Treaty 'which, in particular, seek to ensure freedom of movement for workers, freedom of establishment, freedom to provide services, or competition'.[8] This abandons the notion of the 'purely sporting rule' which has an economic effect yet automatically falls out with the reach of the EC Treaty. The equivocation of *Walrave and Koch* is set aside. A practice may be of a sporting nature – and perhaps even 'purely sporting' in *intent* – but it must be tested against the demands of EC trade law where it exerts economic *effects*. But the Court did not abandon its thematically consistent readiness to ensure that in the application of EC law sport's special concerns should be carefully and sensitively fed into the analysis. It took the view that the general objective of the rules was to combat doping in order for competitive sport to be conducted on a fair basis; and the effect of penalties on athletes' freedom of action must be considered to be inherent in the anti-doping rules. The Court will not place such practices beyond the scope of judicial review as a matter of principle, but it is appropriately wary of questioning the expertise practised by sports federations in such sensitive realms. These are sporting rules – not *purely* sporting rules – and they are examined under an interpretation of EC law which is sensitive to sport's special concerns for *inter alia* clean competition.

I am not suggesting that this arrival at a model which embraces overlap between EC law and 'internal' sports law solves all problems. My argument is only that *Meca-*

4 Case C-519/04 P judgment of 18 July 2006.

5 Case T-313/02 [2004] *ECR* II-3291.

6 Para. 49 CFI.

7 Para. 27 ECJ.

8 Para. 28 ECJ.

Medina focuses attention in the right direction. Previous practice, initiated by *Walrave and Koch*, has tended to generate unhelpful arguments about whether a practice is purely sporting in nature, and therefore immune from challenge under EC law. I have never believed this to be a helpful starting-point. Better to accept that the vast majority of sporting practices have economic implications but then to apply EC law to them with appropriate respect for the particular sporting context in which they are used. In *Meca-Medina* the Court has taken a broad view of the scope of Community trade law, but having brought sporting rules within the scope of the Treaty it shows itself readily prepared to draw on the importance of matters not explicitly described as 'justifications' in the Treaty in order to permit the continued application of challenged practices which are shown to be necessary to achieve legitimate sporting objectives and/or are inherent in the organisation of sport. That, then, becomes the core of the argument when EC law overlaps with sports governance: can a sport show why prejudicial economic effects must be tolerated? As the Court put it in *Meca-Medina*, restrictions imposed by rules adopted by sports federations 'must be limited to what is necessary to ensure the proper conduct of competitive sport'.[9] This is a statement of the *conditional autonomy* of sports federations under EC law – an overlap between EC law and 'internal' sports law is recognised but within that area of overlap sporting bodies have room to show how and why the rules are necessary to accommodate their particular concerns – fair play, credible competition, national representative teams, and so on. The result of *Meca-Medina* itself demonstrates that the sporting expertise informing (*in casu*) anti-doping inquiries will not lightly be set aside by judges.

THE PAPERS CONTAINED IN THIS BOOK

In this vein a strong message of much of my work holds that sporting practices typically have an economic effect and that accordingly they cannot be sealed off from the expectations of EC law – but within the area of overlap between EC law and 'internal' sports law there is room for recognition of the particular needs of sport, which may admittedly differ from 'normal' industries. *Meca-Medina*, I think, conforms to this pattern, and I welcome it. But I have long sought to make a more general case in my writing that a claim to unconditional sporting autonomy under EC law lacks intellectual appeal, unless it can be shown that EC law's absence of sports-specific material in its Treaty has led to an insensitive application of the law which washes over sport's legitimate interests. I have not been able to detect this. Quite the reverse. In fact the Court and the Commission have been scrupulous in ensuring that the special features of sport play a part in their interpretation and application of EC law. Sometimes they are profoundly unimpressed by the arguments advanced by sporting bodies. Sometimes they accept their force in principle while rejecting their relevance in the particular circumstances. Sometimes they are open to persuasion. But never is sport treated like sausage-making by the institutions of the EU.

---

[9] Para. 47 ECJ.

I felt rather lonely when I wrote 'Discrimination on Grounds of Nationality in Sport'.[10] More than a decade had passed since the landmark decisions of the 1970s, *Walrave and Koch* the first of them,[11] which had established that the EC Treaty is in principle applicable to sport. *Bosman* was not even a speck on the horizon. Using EC law to challenge sports practices seemed to lack practical relevance. Who would risk taking the slow route to court and risk exclusion from the fast-moving world of sport? My interest in writing the article published in 1989 was largely driven by the appreciation that sport offers a testing ground for an oddity in the structure of EC trade law. That is to say, I was using sport to try and develop a better understanding of EC law, rather than taking sport as the main focus of inquiry. The legal conundrum centres on practices of private parties which create distortions in the labour market, in particular those that are discriminatory on grounds of nationality. They could be dealt with under (what is now) Article 39 EC. They could be dealt with under (what are now) Articles 81 and 82 EC. If dealt with under both provisions, how could one cope with the clashes between the distinct assumptions of competition law and free movement law? After all, in markets for goods, Article 28 controls the acts or omissions of public authorities (only), leaving Articles 81 and 82 to deal with private practices, so the labour market seems to be worryingly 'over-regulated' by EC law. My overriding concern was the scope of justification, which, as far as I could, see was different (and broader) under the competition rules than under the free movement rules. I did not advocate a demarcation between the two. Instead I argued that the restrictive labour practice is a curious creature which does not fit comfortably into the structure of the Treaty and I argued that a blended justification test should be devised.

Achieving this blend is, I think, more or less what the Court has subsequently done – though even now the matter lacks authoritative judicial guidance. I returned to the issue as recently as 2006, because in my view the *Meca-Medina* ruling on anti-doping is best understood against a background which assumes that practices of sports bodies that are necessary for the organisation of the game are legitimate and lawful whichever provision of EC trade law they are tested against.[12] Were it otherwise, the Treaty system would be exposed as incoherent.

My 1989 paper on Discrimination on Grounds of Nationality contains 'Concluding Remarks' which open with the observation that 'The organisation of football appears to be on a collision course with more than one area of the Treaty of Rome'. But I could hardly have imagined just how loud the collision would prove to be. The particular matter of discrimination in club football, which helped to structure the argument in my 1989 paper, allowed me to reflect on the extent to which such discrimination may be regarded as necessary to sustain professional leagues at national level. And

---

[10] 9 *Yearbook of European Law* (1989) p. 55 et seq.

[11] Note 1 above.

[12] See 'Anti-doping revisited – the demise of the rule of 'purely sporting interest'?', (2006) *ECL Rev.*, below.

the matter was, of course, vigorously addressed by the Court in *Bosman*,[13] the case that once and for all shattered the notion that EC law and sport mix in academic writing but never in practice.

The Annotation of the *Bosman* case[14] took as its purpose to reflect on the content of the judgment itself and to consider its impact from the perspective of both sport and EC law. The Annotation covers the litigation itself and the outcome of the case – the finding that the transfer system under challenge and nationality-based discrimination in club football were incompatible with EC law. It also (more ambitiously) seeks to look forward to outstanding issues, some of which had been aired already in my 1989 paper in the *Yearbook of European Law*, and to reflect on how much deeper into sporting autonomy EC law might be subsequently shown to reach. I considered the use of EC law to challenge transfer systems within a single Member State, reliance upon EC law by nationals of States that are not members of the EU and its invocation even in cases of players who are contracted to a club which they wish to leave, rather than players, like Bosman himself, who are out of contract. These issues have duly been the subject of litigation and consequent alteration in sporting practice. I concluded the Annotation in the *Review* by doubting that sport could or should be exempted from the scope of EC law. It has not been exempted, and I remain of the view that the case for such exemption lacks intellectual strength.

In 'European Football Law'[15] I took the opportunity to develop some of the ideas advanced in my Annotation of the *Bosman* case and to situate them in the broader structure of the development of EC trade law. It is also a piece in which, in the Conclusion, I am able to reflect on an abiding theme: aghast sports bodies commonly declare that litigation will destroy their sport. But it doesn't. The paper was based on the classes I gave on 'European Football Law' at the Summer Course of the European University Institute, on the hills outside Florence, and it allowed me an early opportunity to appreciate just how appealing the mix of sport and the law is to students. One reason, and from a sternly intellectual perspective not a very good one, is that sport is vivid and generates passion. A better reason, I think, is that sport presents unusual challenges for the law. It is 'special'. How special?

My piece on the sale of tickets for the 1998 Football World Cup was published as '0033149875354: Fining the Organisers of the 1998 Football World Cup'.[16] It reveals a case where in my view the Commission Decision consists of a proper refusal to find sports-specific justification. This was a case of nationality-based discrimination, a blatant violation of the basic principles of EC law. But even here, in an instance of egregious violation of a fundamental principle of EC law, the Commission imposed a penalty which reflected its concern to take account of the concerns of sport. By

13 Note 2 above.

14 33 *CML Rev.* (1996) p. 991 et seq.

15 Collected Courses of the 7th Session of the Academy of European Law (The Hague, London and Boston: Kluwer Law International, 1999) p. 339 et seq.

16 *ECL Rev.* (2000) p. 275 et seq.

imposing only a symbolic fine, amounting to € 1000, the Commission explained that it took the view that the circumstances were not adequately covered by existing practice, which had not directly concerned sporting events, and that therefore it would show leniency. My article reveals reasons for supposing that the Commission's own acquiescence in the unlawful practices might have contributed to its reticence to impose a heavier fine. It is not an edifying tale.

In 'Sports under EC Competition Law and US Antitrust Law',[17] I engaged in debate about the proper application of EC competition law to sport. *Bosman* famously involved the application of the free movement provisions to sport, and the Court carefully avoided examination of the Treaty competition rules. Advocate-General Lenz was not so reticent and nor was I in my Annotation of the case in the *Common Market Law Review* (*CML Rev.*), mentioned above. By the time this paper was written the Commission was faced with an increasing number of complaints about alleged anti-competitive practices in the sports sector and it was plain that there was a pressing practical need to understand how the special features of sport – organisational solidarity, scrupulous preservation of uncertainty as to result – affected the handling of Articles 81 and 82. The paper was presented to the Annual Conference on Competition Law held at Fordham University in New York, one of the most, if not the most, high-profile competition law events staged anywhere, which itself demonstrates how hot a topic the intersection of EC competition law and sport had rapidly become.

The 1999 Helsinki Report represents an important attempt by the Commission to step beyond the accidents of litigation and instead to shape a framework for understanding how and why EC law applies to sport. I wrote about it in 'The Helsinki Report on sport'.[18] A core aim of the Helsinki Report is to help to clarify the law. In that, it is not unsuccessful. In particular, its attempt to separate out categories of practices that are outside the reach of EC law (as 'the rules of the game') from those which are within its scope (though not necessarily incompatible with it) is a helpful starting-point. And the Report's assertion that 'the basic freedoms guaranteed by the Treaty do not generally conflict with the regulatory measures of sports associations, provided that these measures are objectively justified, non-discriminatory, necessary and proportional' is about right in my judgement, though of course it does not set aside the need to conduct detailed examination of just when one might find sporting practices to be supported by objective justification et al. The Helsinki Report did not stop at the Treaty competition rules. The Commission recognised the social and educational functions of sport and expressed concern that increasingly ferocious commercialisation of the sector may damage these virtues. It identified a 'European Model of Sport', based on *inter alia* vertical solidarity between sport's elite and the grass-roots, promotion and relegation, and, broader still, concern to improve health and to combat social exclusion, xenophobia and intolerance. I have at least two anxieties about the

[17] B. Hawk, ed., *International Antitrust Law and Policy: Annual Proceedings of the Fordham Corporate Law Institute for 1999* (Yonkers, NY, Juris Publishing 2000) Ch. 8, p. 113 et seq.

[18] 25 *EL Rev.* (2000) p. 252 et seq.

Commission's thinking. First, that to make such claims is to adopt a worryingly homogenous view of sport. Professional sport and recreational sport are very different in structure and motivation, and to bind them together as part of a single model may be an exercise in wishful thinking. Second, the EC lacks competence to develop law and policy in these broad fields. The Commission, adopting the discourse of cultural renewal, is in danger of generating expectations that it cannot meet.

In 'Resisting the Pressures of Americanization: the influence of European Community Law on the 'European Sport Model',[19] I sought to develop my thinking about the 'European Model of Sport' advanced by the Commission in the Helsinki Report. The paper focuses on the underpinning assumption that Europe is significantly different in its approach to sport from North America. From 'draft picks' to closed leagues to vast salaries, Europe has a long way to catch up – and the Commission strongly believes that not only should it not try to catch up it should not even seek to run the same race. The paper examines the legal issues at stake in these competing 'models' of sport. It concludes by reflecting that while the Commission is plainly concerned that EC law should not propel European law down the American path it lacks powerful tools to prevent moves in such a direction. Moreover, there are hints that some actors in European sport are tempted by American models. Whispers of 'breakaway leagues' are as common today as they were when this paper was written, and it is likely that the 'European Model of Sport' will come under increasing pressure in the years to come.

My paper 'Fair Play Please!: Recent Developments in the Application of EC Law to Sport'[20] was prepared at the invitation of the editors of the Review. It is designed as an overview of Court and Commission practice in the field of sport, and it attempts to provide a thematic account of the principal concerns that animate EC law- and policymaking in the field, against the familiar background acceptance that the EC Treaty is deficient in sports-specific material. Most of all, the article uses case law – on agents, on club ownership, on transfers, on broadcasting and so on – to explore that most basic of questions, that which asks how special sport really is. It also moves on to reflect on the 'wider terrain' of a policy on sport. Both the Commission, in its depiction of a 'European Model of Sport', and national political elites, in adopting the Amsterdam and Nice Declarations on Sport, display anxiety to make more of EU sports policy than economics alone. The problem which I identify lies in the absence of a comprehensive legal competence vested in the EC institutions to act in such broader realms. I doubt it is sensible for the EU to set itself up as an arena in which sport's wider social and cultural virtues can be comprehensively addressed when the constitutional reality is otherwise.

---

[19] S. Greenfield and G. Osborn, eds., *Law and Sport in Contemporary Society* (Frank Cass Publishing, London 2000) p. 155 et seq.

[20] 40 *CML Rev.* (2003) p. 51 et seq.

Is sport 'cultural'? I think it is. But what does this mean in law? In 'Sport as Culture in European Community Law'[21] I took the opportunity to develop further some of the thinking directed at 'sport' as a heterogeneous legal and cultural phenomenon that I had pursued in earlier papers mentioned above. This contribution to a book on EC law and culture critically examines the transfer system in football and the regulation of sale of broadcasting rights from the perspective of the claim that 'sport is special' and that it therefore deserves special protection from the normal assumptions of EC law. At stake is sport's claim to *benefits* consequent on legal immunity. The paper then examines the 'protected events' legislation – which affects the freedom of sports bodies to sell rights to the highest bidder where particularly high-profile events are involved. Here I find that sport is special in that it is asked to shoulder *burdens* which would not be imposed on a 'normal' industry. The rationale behind the 'protected events' legislation is obscure but it clearly reveals and reflects the unusual cultural prominence of sport. The paper concludes with further expression of my anxiety that the attempts of the EU's institutions, most prominently the Commission, to shape a policy for sport that is infused by social and cultural concerns tend to strain the outer edges of EC competence, and, in so far as the Commission lacks the legal and material resources to make good its promises, I find risks that the EU's legitimacy may be damaged.

'Anti-doping rules and EC Law'[22] criticises the Court of First Instance's decision in *David Meca-Medina and Igor Majcen* v. *Commission*. I mentioned the case above.[23] The CFI dismissed an application for the annulment of a Commission decision rejecting a complaint against the compatibility with EC trade law of doping controls practised by the International Olympic Committee. But in doing so it adopted an approach to the autonomy of sports federations which seemed to me to go far beyond the existing state of EC law and beyond what is wise. Most of all, the CFI took the view that anti-doping rules of an excessive nature would escape review pursuant to competition law provided that they remained limited to their proper object. This is contradictory in the sense that an excessive rule would by definition *not* be so limited. I developed the argument that a superior approach would be provided by reliance on the Court's decision in *Wouters*.[24] That is not a case concerning sport. But it is a ruling in which the Court insisted that a constraint on competition is unaffected by Article 81 EC where it is unavoidably required to sustain the functioning of an arrangement which is unobjectionable in the light of EC law. That, it seems to me, is the way to approach anti-doping rules. They have an economic effect. But are they necessary for the pursuit of sport? Yes – if confined to a basis for the imposition of proportionate sanctions. My broad concern was to connect EC competition law's application to sport to

21 R. Craufurd Smith, ed., *Culture in European Union Law* (Oxford University Press 2004) Ch. 4, p. 113 et seq.

22 *ECL Rev.* (2005) p. 416 et seq.

23 Case T-313/02 note 5 above.

24 Case C-309/99 *J.C.J. Wouters, J.W. Savelbergh, Price Waterhouse Belastingadviseurs BV* v. *Algemene Raad van de Nederlandse Orde van Advocaten* [2002] *ECR* I-1577.

general trends in EC competition law, rather than to follow the CFI's approach which produces a peculiar generous niche in which sporting practices can hide.

The organisational structure of football is shaped like a pyramid. I considered this in 'Is the Pyramid Compatible with EC Law?'.[25] FIFA, the world governing body, sits at the apex. Beneath FIFA lie the continental associations – in Europe, UEFA. On the next level down are found the national associations. And then come the professional clubs, along with other interested actors within individual countries, the 'grass roots' which include regional associations and amateur bodies. Clubs have a voice via their national associations. The richer clubs want a louder voice and a more direct involvement in the decision-making process. The tension that runs through this pyramid structure is created by the conflict of interest held by the governing bodies. The pyramid makes obvious sense as a means to arrange decision-making on the rules of the game. But it is a good deal more controversial in so far as commercially sensitive decisions emerge from the process. Consider setting the international fixture calendar or requiring the release of players for international duty. Clubs are increasingly frustrated by their perception that they have too little input into decisions of this type which have a direct impact on their business. And they are increasingly ready to go to law. The paper discussed the *Oulmers/Charleroi* case on player release, which has the potential to be the next high-profile sport-related decision of the European Court.[26] The issue at bottom is one of governance. Can the pyramid survive in its current form or will the law be used to require a redistribution of functions, involving a separation between regulatory and commercial activities of sports federations? I doubt the pyramid can be sustained unaltered. It allocates too much commercial power to the federations in circumstances of conflict of interest between their commercial and regulatory functions.

In writing 'The sale of rights to broadcast sporting events under EC law'[27] I was particularly concerned to take the opportunity to connect the important depiction of the detail of the law with the broader thematic literature about the possibilities and limitations of describing an EC 'policy' in a field where the Treaty does not provide a comprehensive mandate. The paper accordingly traverses important issues of competition law and policy pertaining to *inter alia* the permitted scope of sale of broadcasting rights on an exclusive basis and arrangements for collective buying and selling of broadcasting rights. The law develops with necessary appreciation of the extraordinary changes in the technological and regulatory structure of the broadcasting sector. When I first began to write about the application of EC law to sport I had no need to think about unbundling of packages to allow sale of internet rights, for example, nor

---

[25] 3-4 *International Sports Law Journal* (2006) p. 3 et seq.

[26] Pending Case C-243/06, lodged 30 May 2006 – *SA Sporting du Pays de Charleroi, G-14 GrOxford University Pressement des Clubs de Football Européens* v. *Fédération Internationale de Football Association (FIFA)*.

[27] 3-4 *International Sports Law Journal* (2006) p. 3 et seq.

indeed to think beyond traditional free-to-air media as the place to watch televised football. But the paper also reflects on how other areas of EC trade law, beyond sport, demand an infusion of concerns poorly mapped out by the Treaty. EC health care law, EC consumer law and EC labour law, for example, are shaped by the intersection of the rules of trade integration and the values promoted in these sectors by national policymakers. Sport is not intellectually unique in the challenge it presents to those seeking to understand how its special features affect the interpretation and application of EC trade law.

In 'Anti-doping revisited – the demise of the rule of 'purely sporting interest'?'[28] I addressed the ECJ's handling of the appeal in the anti-doping case, *Meca-Medina and Majcen*.[29] As explained above, the CFI's approach to anti-doping rules was to accept that there are rules concerning questions of 'purely sporting interest' which have nothing to do with economic activity. There are such rules. The offside rule, for example. But there are few such rules and they are hardly likely to provoke litigation. Most rules that are relevant to the organisation of sport also have direct and nowadays substantial economic implications. So it is with anti-doping rules. On appeal the ECJ set aside the CFI's decision. The ECJ dismissed the application for annulment of the Commission's Decision but it rejected the CFI's relatively generous approach to the scope of sporting autonomy to apply rules with economic effects. Sporting rules must be examined in their proper context, including recognition of their economic effect. The Court did not doubt that sport needs rules against doping. And it saw no reason on the facts of the case to interfere with the two-year ban imposed. EC law recognises the need to respect sporting expertise in such matters. But there is no special category of rules with an economic effect which are beyond review. This analytical formula will be put to renewed test in *Oulmers/Charleroi*.[30]

Concluding remarks

I believe that the practice of the European Courts and the Commission reveals a painstaking concern to piece together a sports policy of sorts at EU level. The Treaty does not help. It does not mention sport. Article 5(1) stipulates that the EC possesses a set of attributed competences, of which sport is not one, and so – one may argue – there is sports governance and there is EC law, and there is no overlap between the two. So one option was to refuse to apply EC law to sport. That would have sheltered a huge range of practices with economic impact from the assumptions of EC law, damaging the achievement of the objectives of the Treaty. It would have been deeply undesirable and the Court rejected that route *ab initio* in *Walrave and Koch*.[31] Another option would have been to apply EC law to sport as if it were a normal industry. That

[28] *ECL Rev.* (2006) p. 645 et seq.

[29] Note 4 above.

[30] Note 15 above.

[31] Note 1 above.

did not tempt the Court in *Walrave and Koch* either – rightly so, for sport is not an industry like any other. Instead the Court and Commission have taken a more ambitious, creative and yet realistic approach. That has demanded a significant investment of resources in making sense of the intersection between the demands of EC law and the aspirations of sport. The EU institutions necessarily proceed in an incremental manner. The opportunities to shape a 'policy' are constrained by the constitutional limitations on the matters to which they may pay attention. Article 5(1) stipulates that the EC possesses only the competences attributed to it. Its authority to supervise sporting practices derives from the broad functional reach of the relevant rules of EC trade law (free movement and competition law, most conspicuously), but it is denied any specific legislative competence in the field of sport. Incrementalism is also ensured by the accidental patterns of litigation, which may cause practice to develop according to unexpected, eccentric rhythms. These observations concern most prominently the Court and the Commission, both of whom are responsible for individual decisions applying the law, though the broader policy direction periodically offered by the Council, the European Council and the Parliament may also serve to embroider the tapestry. It is therefore of the highest importance to ensure that one does not over-state the possibilities of a systematic account of relevant EC law. On the other hand, this is not necessarily to concede that EC law is ripe for criticism. A qualitative account of its role is required. That the EC Treaty does not lends itself to the shaping of a comprehensive policy of the type that one would expect to find in a national setting does not entail that it is flawed, only that it is different. This is not a challenge that is in any sense unique. In fact, across a great many areas of EC law, policy and practice, one is confronted by the need to make some sort of sense of a set of laws and practices which are not constitutionally dedicated to dealing with the particular subject matter of concern and which are frequently lacking in detail and sophistication. So the EC has to shape a policy of sorts on all manner of things. Such is the *practice* of attributed competence, guaranteed as a *principle* of EC law by Article 5(1) of the Treaty. I hope that my work is thematically bound together by concern to explore how far the argument that 'sport is special' convincingly reaches, and to consider whether EC law is apt to reflect the aspirations of sport when it is shown to be truly special. My general conclusion is that the institutions of the EU have built an EC trade law which is respectful of sport's peculiarities.

DISCRIMINATION ON GROUNDS OF NATIONALITY IN SPORT*

I. Introduction

This paper is concerned with labour practices which are discriminatory on grounds of nationality and which are put into effect by private employers. The example chosen for the purposes of analysis is the discrimination against non-nationals practised by football clubs in most Member States of the Community, but it is suggested that the problem under investigation extends beyond football and indeed beyond sport, to discriminatory preferences which may be exercised by private bodies such as trade unions, professional bodies, employers, or employers' associations. The legal issue which appears to pose most difficulty in this area is the potential overlap between Articles 48 and 85-86 of the Treaty of Rome. It is suggested that the discrepancies which exist between these provisions are accentuated by the possibility that action to combat the discriminatory rules may be taken on two levels, at Community level and/or at national level, making use of national systems of remedies before national courts.

II. The discriminatory player restrictions

All the fifteen national football associations in the 12 Member States of the European Community[32] are members of UEFA.[33] European football's governing body, the headquarters of which are in Switzerland and which has over thirty member national associations. In most countries, limits are placed on the number of foreign players who are permitted to play for clubs in domestic fixtures, ostensibly in order to protect the well-being of the domestic game. The limits vary. In Italy, the maximum has recently been raised from two to three, and all leading clubs take advantage of this concession. In England, where in practice foreign players are relatively rare, clubs may not field more than three players who are not citizens of the United Kingdom or who have not been resident in the United Kingdom for a continuous period of five years. The first condition is an instance of direct discrimination on grounds of nationality; the second condition, a residence requirement, constitutes indirect discrimination on grounds of nationality. Both forms of discrimination are caught by Community law.[34] Within these limits, however, there are various anomalies and concessions. For example, in the English League, it is unsurprising that Scottish, Welsh, and Northern Irish play-

---

* 9 *Yearbook of European Law* (1989) p. 55 et seq.

[32] The numerical discrepancy arises because there are four associations in the UK.

[33] *Union des Associations Européennes de Football.*

[34] On indirect discrimination, see, e.g., Case 152/73 *Sotgiu* v. *Deutsche Bundespost* [1974] *ECR* 153. On objective justification for such discrimination, see below, Part III/B/(a).

ers are not classed as foreign for the purposes of football team selection; but neither are nationals of the Republic of Ireland. France has a special regime for Algerians, Portugal for Brazilians, By contrast, a small number of countries, including Scotland, impose no restrictions at all.

These limits, which appear discriminatory on grounds of nationality, are imposed by the individual governing bodies of the Football Leagues in each Member State, with the support of UEFA. Naturally, the clubs themselves are also involved in the application of these rules in declining to sign extra foreign players, in the performance of their contractual obligations to the national bodies. The precise legal nature of the limits imposed and the legal interrelation between the various bodies concerned is of considerable importance in identifying whether, and, if so, how, the limits may be susceptible to challenge.

The European Commission has taken the view that these restrictions contravene the principle of free movement of labour in the European Community, but talks aimed at removing the limits have broken down on a number of separate occasions over the last decade, most recently in 1987 when UEFA withdrew from negotiations. The Commission, stating that 1992, the intended date for the completion of the single internal market,[35] is the deadline for the elimination of these restrictions,[36] has indicated that it will support individual clubs wishing to initiate a legal challenge to the system.

UEFA's response has been to insist on the special situation of the football industry. It has announced the introduction of a new rule which will govern player eligibility in the three annual European club football competitions for which UEFA bears organizational responsibility.[37] This stipulates that in the three tournaments each club shall be restricted from the start of season 1988-1989 to four 'non-national' players.[38] A non-national player is one not qualified to play in international matches for the national representative team of the national association to which that club belongs. The basis of eligibility for such a national representative team is the link of nationality.[39] Obviously a French player in Italy or a Greek player in Belgium would be a 'non-national', but on a domestic note, it should be realized that for these purposes a Scot is to be regarded as a non-national in England and, vice versa and perhaps more pertinent-

[35] Art. 8A EEC, introduced by Art. 13 SEA.

[36] This should not be taken to suggest that the period up until the end of 1992 constitutes a new transitional period, during which the existing Treaty rules lapse – though cp. in this respect the concerns of Pescatore 24 *CML Rev.* 9-18 (1987). It is submitted that the 1992 date in this context has no formal legal significance and is instead merely a date chosen by the Commission in the exercise of its powers to enforce Community competition law.

[37] The three competitions are the European Cup the most prestigious, contested every year since 1956 by the national champions) the European Cup-Winners Cup, and the UEFA Cup.

[38] Art. 12(3) Regulations of the UEFA Club Competitions, 1989-90. A transitional period applies: a non-national registered prior to 3 May 1988, is excluded, i.e. is treated as a national, until the termination of the players registration with the club or the end of season 1990-1, whichever is earlier.

[39] The precise nature of the required link varies from State to State. The matter is particularly complicated in the UK, *supra* note 32.

ly given recent player transfer trends,[40] an Englishman is a non-national in Scotland.

The matter has also attracted the interest of a number of Members of the European Parliament, leading to the adoption by the Parliament of a Resolution approving a report drawn up by Mr Janssen van Raay on behalf of the Committee on Legal Affairs and Citizens' Rights.[41] This text places the issues raised by the practices prevailing in the football industry firmly in the general context of the individual worker's fundamental right of free movement within the common market.[42] The Parliament's Resolution uncompromisingly declares;

> 'the restriction on the number of foreign players entitled to play for a professional football team to be a proscribed discrimination on grounds of nationality, a contravention of freedom of movement pursuant to Article 48 of the EEC Treaty and a violation of Article 85 of the EEC Treaty, in so far as nationals of the Member States of the European Community are concerned'.

This paper will investigate these allegations. It will assess the applicability of Article 48 and Article 85, both of which are mentioned in the Janssen van Raay Report, and will consider whether infringements have occurred. Methods of enforcement of the Treaty rules will be examined. This is of particular importance given the fact that Community law is subject to 'dual vigilance'[43] and consequently its enforcement may be undertaken both by the Commission and by individuals pursuing litigation before national courts. It should be emphasized that the several issues raised illuminate areas of the application of Community law of a significance far more extensive than the football industry. It is submitted that some fundamental legal issues relating to the treatment of labour practices in the common market and to the enforcement of Community law are raised.

III. Is there a breach of the Treaty?

A. **Sport and the Treaty of Rome**

The European Community is not omnicompetent. Therefore it must first be established that sport falls within the ambit of the Treaty, before application of the rules of Community law to the discriminatory player restrictions can be considered.

---

[40] When Glasgow Rangers lost the 1983 Scottish FA Cup Final they had no English players; their team defeated in the 1989 Final contained 6 English players.

[41] Doc. A2-415/88, adopted 11 April 1989.

[42] The Report also considers the football transfer system unlawful: '[...] a latter-day version of the slave trade [...]' On English law and the transfer system, see the leading case of *Eastham* v. *Newcastle United* [1964] Ch. 413; for a historical survey, see Grayson, *Sport and the Law* (Butterworths 1988) 35-7, 260-8; for analysis in the legal context, see, e.g., Treitel, *The Law of Contract*, 7th edn. (Stevens 1987) 349. On a separate matter, the Report also declares 'without legal base and [...] contrary to the free movement of people' the exclusion of English clubs from European competition as a result of the tragedy at the Heysel Stadium, Brussels in 1985. On this point, see profound analysis by Evans 102 *LQR* (1986) 510-48.

[43] Case 26/62 *Van Gend en Loos* [1963] *ECR* 1 [1963] *CMLR* 105.

It has been clear that professional sport may fall within the Treaty since the European Court's decision in *Walrave and Koch* v. *Union Cycliste Internationale*,[44] a case considered more fully below. The Court declared that: 'Having regard to the objectives of the Community, the practice of sport is subject to Community law only in so far as it constitutes an economic activity within the meaning of Article 2 of the Treaty.'[45] 'Economic activity within the meaning of Article 2' is of such breadth that there can be no doubt that professional football, which represents a minor but genuine aspect of the market economy,[46] is subject to the Treaty rules designed to achieve a single market.

Which specific Treaty rules may be breached? There are two obvious candidates, already alluded to; Article 48, which provides for the free movement of workers within the Community and the abolition of discrimination based on nationality; and Articles 85 and 86, the Treaty rules on competition, which forbid activities by undertakings incompatible with the common market. Rules which seek to preserve a special status for footballers who are nationals of the State within which the particular League is situated appear prima facie to infringe both sets of provisions.

It may already be noted that the potential overlapping jurisdiction of Article 48 and Articles 85/86 is of especial interest. There are significant differences between the scope of the provisions and therefore the potential parallel application of the rules is capable of creating practical and theoretical difficulties. However, as a means of initiating the inquiry, the two provisions will be considered separately, first, Article 48, then Articles 85 and 86.

B. **Article 48 EEC**

Freedom of movement for workers shall be secured within the Community by the end of the transitional period at the latest. Such freedom of movement shall entail the abolition of any discrimination based on nationality between workers of the Member States as regards employment, remuneration and other conditions of work and employment [...]

Paragraph (3) of Article 48 proceeds to identify particular rights inherent in this general provision, including rights to accept offers of employment actually made and to move freely within the territory of Member States for this purpose.

Article 48 is an amplification in a specific area of the fundamental Community rule against discrimination on grounds of nationality found in Article 7 EEC:

> 'Within the scope of application of this Treaty, and without prejudice to any special provisions contained therein. any discrimination on grounds of nationality shall be prohibited.'

[44] Case 36/74 [1974] *ECR* 1405, [1975] 1 *CMLR* 320.

[45] Para. 4 of the judgment.

[46] The total 'live' audience (i.e., excluding television) for League football in England and Wales alone in season 1988-9 was 18,447,565 (Source: *The Football Trust)*.

Article 48 should also be read in conjunction with Articles 52 and 59, which apply parallel regimes to the freedom of establishment and the freedom to provide services in the Community. As a general proposition, these three sets of provisions should be read as a complementary package.[47] For the present purposes, analysis will be confined to Article 48, for it is plain that a professional footballer is a worker, rather than self-employed or the provider of services. It should however be noted that sportsmen and women competing in individual events such as golf and tennis may be covered by Articles 52 or 59, rather than 48 The same is true of sports teams.[48] Such cases would require careful investigation to determine whether they fall within the limited, anomalous areas under Articles 52 and 59 in which rules different from those applicable to workers under Article 48 reign.[49]

Finally, Article 48 is amplified by a range of secondary legislation, which elaborates the application of the rule against nationality-based discrimination in particular cases. Thus, for example, Regulation 1612/68 amplifies rights of equality in eligibility of employment in Title 1: and in Title II assures the migrant worker of equal treatment in respect of a range of conditions of employment, including the broadly-defined 'social and tax advantages'.[50]

The Treaty of Rome therefore outlaws discrimination in employment on grounds of nationality by dint of, in ascending order of specificity, Article 7, Article 48, and the range of secondary legislation which supports Article 48. Consequently, it may be thought that, prima facie, Article 48 and Regulation 1612/68[51] are infringed in the cases under consideration. One might compare *Commission* v. *France*, commonly referred to as the *French Merchant Seamen* case.[52] The French *Code du Travail Maritime*, as implemented by Ministerial Order, stipulated that the crew of French merchant ships should comprise at least three Frenchmen to each seaman of any other

---

[47] On the parallel interpretation of these provisions. see Case 48/75 *Royer* [1976] *ECR* 497, [1976] 2 *CMLR* 619, where the Court responded to questions referred under Art. 177 despite the fact that the national court had failed to specify whether the case was covered by Art. 48 or 52. It should also be noted in this respect that the Court in *Walrave and Koch*, *supra*, note 44, saw no need to determine whether a contract of service (Art. 48 or a contract for services (Art. 59) was in issue, because 'the rule of non-discrimination covers in identical terms all work or services' (Para. 7 of the judgment). The same approach may be identitied in *Donà* v. *Mantero*, below note 57.

[48] See Evans 102 *LQR* (1986) 510-48.

[49] See Wyatt and Dashwood. *The Substantive Law of the EEC*, 2nd edn. (Sweet & Maxwell 1987) 206-7. The most significant distinctions between the three provisions reside in the scope of the rights granted to beneficiaries by virtue of supporting secondary legislation. Most strikingly, Reg. 1612/68 applies only to workers under Art. 48, these falling within Arts. 52 or 59 must rely on the general rule against discrimination on grounds of nationality enshrined in Art. 7 EEC, the scope of which is inexplicit. This issue lies beyond the scope of the present analysis and is of no direct relevance to it, but compare, e.g., Case 795/83 *Gravier* v. *City of Liège* [1985] *ECR* 593, [1985] 3 *CMLR* 1; Case 39/86 *Lair* v. *University of Hanover* [1989] 3 *CMLR* 545; Case 197/86 *Brown* v. *Secretary of State for Scotland* [1988] 3 *CMLR* 403; Case 63/86 *Commission* v. *Italy* [1989] 2 *CMLR* 601.

[50] Art. 7(2) of the Reg. See Wyatt and Dashwood, *supra* note 49, 176-80; O'Keeffe 5 *YEL* (1985) 93.

[51] See particularly Arts. 1(2), 4.

[52] Case 167/73, [1974] *ECR* 359. [1974] 2 *CMLR* 216. See Goyder, *EEC Competition Law* (Oxford University Press 1988) 76: Wyatt and Dashwood, *supra* note 49, 175.

nationality. The European Court ruled that the legislation was discriminatory and unlawful under Article 48. However, the discriminatory football player restrictions are not legislative measures; nor are they connected with a central feature of the market economy such as shipping. Fuller analysis is required to support the submission that they should be held contrary to Article 48 in a manner similar to that applied in the *French Merchant Seamen* case.

(a) *Are the rules within the scope of the Treaty?*

A strict application of this rule against discrimination could give rise to some surprising results. Is there discrimination on the basis of nationality, contrary to the Treaty, if selection for the Italian national football team is limited to Italians? The answer is plainly in the negative and the reason can be discerned from the Court's statement in *Walrave and Koch*, alluded to earlier.[53] Professional sport falls within the Treaty when it constitutes an economic activity, but there are circumstances in which its rules fall outside the scope of this classification. In *Walrave and Koch*, the Court was prepared to accept the legality of discrimination against foreign participants 'for reasons which are not of an economic nature', citing as an example 'matches between national teams from different countries'. The discrimination inherent in the selection of a national representative team occurs for longstanding reasons of a purely sporting nature, rather than for economic reasons. The matter to which the rule relates falls outside the scope of the Treaty of Rome. Therefore, limiting eligibility for selection for the Italian national football team to Italian nationals is permissible under Community law, for it constitutes discrimination imposed without reference to economic motives or considerations. It is a matter of 'national pride and identity',[54] outwith the economic sphere.[55]

However, this does not lead to the conclusion that the several discriminatory rules in different Member States relating to League football are outwith the ambit of the Treaty and therefore permissible. Such special considerations advanced in the case of national teams appear inapplicable in the case of normal football League matches, since such fixtures are not in general played by distinctively representative teams. League football is an economic activity of some significance; English clubs are registered companies and one, Tottenham Hotspur plc, is listed on the Stock Exchange. The clubs are primarily businesses, rather than representatives, and their player selection policies reflect this fact.[56]

---

[53] See *supra* note 44.

[54] Consideration 10 of the Parliament's Resolution adopting the Janssen van Raay Report, *supra* note 41 which endorses the special status of national representative teams.

[55] This approach could also uphold discrimination in the selection of traditionally representative regional teams. Yorkshire County Cricket Club only selects Yorkshire-born players – it is the only one of the 17 first class counties to maintain this restriction. The discrimination is permissible, because it forms the means of preserving the uniquely representative nature of the team; it is not part of the economic structure or motivation of the club.

[56] This suggests that amateur clubs practising discrimination are not covered by the Treaty; *sed quaere* the possible relevance of Art. 7(2) Reg. 1612/68, *supra* note 50; see Ubertazzi (1976) *RTDE* 635, 644-7.

However, Advocate-General Trabucchi in *Donà* v. *Mantero*[57] appeared cautiously prepared to consider ordinary League clubs practising discrimination to be unaffected by the Treaty on the ground that they may qualify as national representatives in European inter-club competition; and that therefore their discriminatory practices exist for purely sporting reasons. It is submitted that this is an unwarranted curtailment of the scope of the Treaty. A club side is not a representative eleven analogous to a national selection. A club may be thought to represent a city and a country, but, exceptional cases apart,[58] the players themselves are not selected on such a basis – 'Die Person und die Herkunft der einzelnen Spieler bleibt im Hintergrund' – 'the identity of the individual player is of only background interest'.[59] Few leading club sides possess more than a minority of players native to the club's home city,[60] and even fewer successful clubs are without overseas representation in their ranks.[61] This is particularly true in England where it is common for club honours to be won by teams boasting a minority of English players.[62] There is no evidence that the clubs are deprived of local support and identity as a result of such player recruitment policies.[63] In the light of these practices, Advocate-General Trabucchi's suggestion that professional club football can be seen as representative and therefore pursuing discriminatory policies for purely sporting reasons must be rejected.

It must be admitted that the Court has on occasion shown itself receptive to the argument that rules which produce an effect which is discriminators on grounds of nationality may none the less fall outside the scope of the Treaty if the differentiation is explicable on objective grounds unconnected to nationality.[64] Thus, third party liability insurance required to register a motor car in Germany was generally available with the benefit of a 'no claims' bonus. However, this advantage was not offered in the case of cars with customs registration plates. It was argued[65] that this rule prejudiced car

[57] Case 13/76 [1976] 2 *CMLR* 578, [1976] *ECR* 1333.

[58] A small number of exceptions exists, where player selection is governed by local representativity criteria, e.g., in cricket, Yorkshire, *supra* note 55; in football, the Spanish League side Real Sociedad de San Sebastian, which finally surrendered its Basques-only policy at the start of season 1989-1990.

[59] Hilf, 'Die Freizugigkeit des Berufsfussballspielers innerhalb der EG', *Neue Juristische Wochenschrift* (1984) 517, 521 [the translation is the author's own]; cf. consideration 8 of the Parliament's Resolution adopting the Janssen van Raay Report.

[60] For example, for the 1989-1990 season, Liverpool's playing staff of 34 consisted of only 10 Liverpool-born players, 18 were born outside England *(Rothman's Football Yearbook. 20th Year*, Queen Anne Press). This pattern is typical of most English First Division clubs.

[61] Liverpool's first victory in the European Cup came in 1977 with a team including two non-English players. Since then, the only team to win the trophy with an entirely 'home-grown' 11 was Steaua Bucharest in 1986. The victory of Milan in 1989 was typical; they fielded 8 Italians and 3 Dutchmen.

[62] Three of the last live FA Cup winning teams (up to 1989) have fallen into this category. The last English team to reach the European Cup Final were Liverpool in 1985, when 9 of their 11 players were internationals of countries other than England.

[63] *Quaere* the value of such evidence, if adduced, as a means of escaping the ambit of the Treaty, the issue under consideration in this Part; or as a means of justifying such discrimination, cf. below, Parts III/B/(c), III/C/(c), IV/B/(b). Note also, issues of proportionality: is it permissible to subject all clubs to such rules even if evidence of some lost support exists?

[64] Schermers, *Judicial Protection in the ECs*, 3rd edn (Kluwer 1983) Paras. 89-94; Sundberg-Weitman, *Discrimination on Grounds of Nationality* (North-Holland 1977) 70-85, 109-11.

[65] Case 251/83 *Haug-Adrion* [1984] *ECR* 4277, [1985] 3 *CMLR* 266. See also Case 182/83 *Fearon* [1984] *ECR* 3677, [1985] 2 *CMLR* 228.

owners who were either not nationals of or not resident in the Federal Republic. Such owners would have a particular need for such plates, in view of their interests outside the Federal Republic. The system did not automatically advantage German nationals over nationals of other Member States; indeed, the complainant was a German national resident in Belgium. However, it was argued that the consequence in practice was indirect discrimination on grounds of nationality prohibited by the Treaty,[66] because the rule would mainly affect nationals of Member States other than the Federal Republic. The Court found no illegality. The system was based 'exclusively on objective actuarial factors and on the objective criterion of registration under customs plates'.[67] The indirect effect based on nationality was held purely incidental. There appears to be little scope for arguing that the rules of the English League, which are tied to citizenship and residence,[68] could be upheld on this basis, but one might argue that the rules of UEFA applicable to European club competition[69] are tied not to nationality *per se*, but to eligibility for national representative teams. Since such national teams are permissible under Community law.[70] The related rules in club football also acquire objective justification despite their indirect discriminatory effect. This argument possesses some force, but it is submitted that it should not be accepted. The flaw, put crudely, is the absence of causal link. Why should the composition of a club side be tied to the incidental fact of individual eligibility for national representative football? It is submitted that the preceding analysis of the practice of team selection demonstrates that a club is an entity independent of the identities of particular football players. Liverpool are no less an English club, or indeed a Merseyside club, when they field a majority of players unavailable for selection as England internationals.[71] There is no objective reason for supposing that the nationality of the playing staff of a club should reflect the identity of the State in which the club plays.[72]

It is therefore concluded that UEFA's requirement of eligibility for the national representative team is not susceptible to objective justification. At both domestic and European level, the rules are in fact a device to protect the health of the domestic game, by preventing an influx of overseas players who would be capable of denying opportunities for development to young home players. Without assessing the merit of this contention, it must, at this stage of the analysis at least, be rejected. The argument advanced is essentially a broad economic justification and cannot support a conten-

66 The insurance rules were State approved; this was not simply a case of horizontal direct effect, cf. *supra* Part III/B/(b).

67 Ibid., Para. 16. The Court did not expand on this view. The defendant had argued that cars bearing a plate are an increased insurance risk because the car is likely to be driven abroad in areas unfamiliar to the driver (see A-G Lenz's Opinion).

68 See *supra* Part II.

69 See *supra* Part II.

70 *Walrave and Kocht*, *supra* note 44.

71 See *supra* notes 60-62.

72 The rules of the English League, which make no distinction between English. Welsh, Scottish, or Irish players, offer strong support for this view. The UEFA rules, which make this distinction, can scarcely be objectively justifiable, given that the British association themselves see no need for such differentiation (see also note 96, below). The British case may be 'special', *supra* note 32, but it is submitted that in all Leagues, the identity of the club, not of the individual players, is the predominant concern.

tion that the rules under examination escape the ambit of the Treaty. Such arguments are relevant only to justification within the specific exceptions permitted by the Treaty – in this case, Article 48(3), considered below.

(b) *Are the Treaty rules horizontally directly effective?*

The discriminatory rules under consideration are promulgated by private bodies. It is necessary to establish that the personal scope of Article 48 is sufficiently broad to cover such institutions. Is Article 48 'horizontally directly effective' – that is, can it be invoked by private parties against other private parties?[73] It is generally[74] accepted that the answer is in the affirmative. Private bodies, as well as State bodies, are subject to the Treaty prohibition against discrimination in employment on grounds of nationality. The case in which this first became apparent was *Walrave and Koch* v. *Union Cycliste Internationale (UCI).*[75]

The UCI, an international body governing the sport of cycling, regulated the conduct of championship events for paced cycle racing. In this sport, a cyclist is assisted on long rides by a pacemaker on a motor cycle, whose lead the cyclist follows in order to obtain shelter and maintain a steady speed, often approaching 100 kilometres per hour. The UCI declared that from 1973 pacemaker and cyclist competing in the world championships must share the same nationality. Bruno Walrave and Noppie Koch, two leading pacemakers of Dutch nationality, had previously been accustomed to pacing cyclists of other nationalities, because of a dearth of top quality Dutch cyclists, and they were consequently perturbed by the implications of the new rule for their earning capacity. They challenged the UCI's ruling before a district court in Utrecht in the Netherlands, from which the matter was referred to the European Court under the Article 177 preliminary reference procedure. The Court first ruled that sport could fall within the ambit of the Treaty, as explained above. The Court was then obliged to consider whether the Treaty rules in question could be enforced against the UCI, a private body unconnected with any State. In this context, the European Court declared that:

> 'Prohibition of such discrimination [under Articles 7, 48, 59] does not only apply to the acts of public authorities, but extends likewise to rules of any other nature aimed at regulating in a collective manner gainful employment and the provision of services.'[76]

The European Court, having established that even the rules of a private sporting organization are in principle subject to Article 48, then left to the Dutch court the task of applying this finding to the facts of the case in order to determine whether the UCI's discriminatory rule could be seen as deriving from concerns of 'purely sporting interest' relating to the composition of a national team. This reflects the division of function between interpretation, the preserve of the European Court, and application, the

[73] 'Vertical direct effect' refers to the enforceability of rules between State and private individual. This is the phenomenon at issue on Case 167/73, *supra* note 52.

[74] See note 84-6, below.

[75] See *supra* note 44.

[76] Ibid., Para. 17.

province of the national judge, which is central to the structure of Article 177.[77] One might feel that the cyclist alone was the real competitor, that the pacer was not part of a 'national team', and that therefore the UCI's same-nationality requirement could not be upheld. However, the reality of effective extra-legal power intervened and, despite apparent probably success, Walrave and Koch declined to press for judgement by the court in Utrecht, because, it seems, the UCI had threatened to withdraw paced cycle racing from the world championship schedule.[78]

The assumption that Article 48 (and the other provisions relating to the free movement of persons) are horizontally directly effective and can therefore be invoked by private party against private party is also implicit in *Donà* v. *Mantero*,[79] a case concerning the discriminatory rules of the Italian Football Federation, a private body. The case involved an expenses claim by an agent who had attempted to recruit players from abroad, rather than a direct challenge to the rules by a frustrated foreign footballer. However, on the important point of principle, the European Court held that Article 48 should be applied to 'rules or a national practice, even adopted by a sporting organisation, which limit the right to take part in football matches as professional or semi-professional players solely to the nationals of the State in question.[80]

Burrows suggests that the direct effect of Article 48 is horizontal in so far as it covers 'collective action taken by bodies which, although not governmental, nevertheless in practice controlled the activities of the individual employers'[81] but that individual employers themselves are not caught. This would mean that both national football associations and UEFA (which affects the legal status of individuals within the Community even though its headquarters are situated outside the Community)[82] are within the scope of Article 48, but that individual clubs are not. Against this, it should be pointed out that the Court has never explicitly embraced such a distinction, and that the Opinion of Advocate-General Warner in *Walrave and Koch* declares that these provisions (Art. 59 and, 'in every material respect parallel' thereto, Art. 48) are 'apt to relate to restrictions imposed by anyone'. Moreover, Article 7(4) of Regulation 1612/68 refers to 'collective or individual' agreements which discriminate on grounds of nationality.[83]

---

[77] For analysis, and some scepticism as to the purity in practice of this distinction, see Hartley, *The Foundations of EC Law*, 2nd edn (Oxford University Press 1988) 278-80; Steiner, *Textbook on EEC Law* (Blackstone 1988) 233-4; Rasmussen. *On Law and Policy in the European Court of Justice* (Nijhoff 1986) 442-50; Schermers, *supra* note 64, Para. 611 et seq.; Weatherill 13 *EL Rev* (1988) 87, 100.

[78] Van Staveren, 18th Colloquy en European Law, *Sport and the Law* (Proceedings published by the Council of Europe, Strasbourg 1989) 67; Hilf, *Neue Juristische Wochenschrift* (1984) 517, 520, note 53.

[79] Case 13/76, *supra* note 57.

[80] Ibid., Para. 13.

[81] *Free Movement in EC Law* (Oxford University Press 1987) 131.

[82] The extension of Community competence to cover such bodies is implicit in *Walrave and Koch*, *supra* note 44. However, this is not an example of the controversial 'effects doctrine' of jurisdiction, being justifiable on normal territorial and nationality principles; see Para. 28 of the judgment in *Walrave*.

[83] Art. 7(l) Reg. 1612/68 also appears to assume this wider scope. Cf. also Art. 119 EEC (and supporting Directives) below note 89, 78.

Although the decisions of the European Court in *Walrave and Koch*[84] and *Donà* v. *Mantero*[85] point in favour of the horizontal direct effect of these provisions and although academic writing largely proceeds on that assumption,[86] there are nevertheless suggestions that as a matter of policy, drawn from the construction of the Treaty, this conclusion may be doubted.[87] It seems plain that Article 30 is not horizontally directly effective,[88] but that Articles 85 and 86 clearly are.[89] The role played by Article 48 is in this context rather obscure and remains unexplained by the Court. Specifically – if Article 48 *is* directly effective between individuals, how does it co-exist with Articles 85 and 86 in so far as the same subject matter may fall within the ambit of both provisions? This overlap may give rise to considerable difficulties both substantively and in relation to enforcement, whether by the Commission or by individuals. The status of Article 48 and whether its horizontal direct effect ought to be acknowledged in accordance with majority opinion will be reconsidered in Part VI/C/(a) below.

(c) *Justification*

The national rules appear plainly in breach of Article 48. There are however two areas of permissible restrictions on the free movement of workers found in Article 48. The first, Article 48(4). excludes 'employment in the public service' from the rule against discrimination; this is of no relevance to football. However, Article 48(3) justifies limitations on the right of free movement 'on grounds of public policy, public security or public health' and this derogation plainly requires assessment in the present context.

Supporting Community secondary legislation and the jurisprudence of the European Court have made it clear that these exceptions within Article 48(3) must be construed narrowly, because they are derogations from the basic principle of free movement in the common market. Specifically, recourse to these exceptions is only permissible if a threat to public policy, public security or public health is caused by the particular circumstances of an individual worker. Article 3(1) of Directive 64/221

---

84 See *supra* note 44.

85 See *supra* note 57.

86 Wyatt and Dashwood, *supra* note 49, 29-30, 205-6; Burrows, *supra* note 81, 240-1; Kapteyn and Van Themaat, *The Law of the ECs*, 2nd edn (Kluwer 1989) 377, 354, 414; Leleux in F. Jacobs, ed., *European Law and the Individual* (North-Holland 1976) 83; Barents 18S *CML Rev.* (1981) 271, 275; March Hunnings (1975) JBL 170: Sundberg-Weitman, *supra* note 64, e.g., 36. 163-4; *Halsbury's Laws of England*, 4th edn, 1986, Vols. 51-2, Paras. 3.05. 15.13. The Janssen van Raay Report, *supra* note 41, clearly assumes horizontal direct effect.

87 Evans, *supra* note 48, 510, 526.

88 For analysis and conclusion to this effect, see Quinn and MacGowan 12 *EL Rev* (1987) 163. For the Commission's similar view, see, e.g., Written Question 835/82 *OJ* 1983 C 93/1.

89 See below, Part III/C/(b). Analysis is not here devoted to Art. 119 EEC. This provision is also horizontally directly effective, which demonstrates that there is no reason in principle why Community rules forbidding discrimination should not be enforceable against private employers. Art. 119, however, appears in the Part of the Treaty setting out the Policy of the Community, in contrast to Art. 48, which is included in the Part entitled 'Foundations of the Community'.

demands that 'measures taken on grounds of public policy or of public security shall be based exclusively on the personal conduct of the individual concerned'. This narrow interpretation of the scope of available derogations is confirmed, and in fact yet further restricted, by the jurisprudence of the European Court.[90]

Article 48(3) does not justify general, preventative measures and, consequently, concerns about the harmful effects of imported footballers on the domestic game cannot justify a general policy of discrimination against players from other Member States.

A further, perhaps more fundamental, reason why the Article 48(3) exceptions may be unavailable to football authorities is that the construction of Article 48(3) appears to limit its use to the State, not private bodies.[91] The exception explicitly covers 'public' considerations. It is probable that such ends cannot be invoked by a private party and this view is supported by reference to Directive 64/221, which amplifies the Article 48(3) exception, and which refers in Article 2 only to 'measures [...] taken by Member States on grounds of public policy, public security or public health'. Essentially, Article 48(3) is concerned with protection of the interests of the State, not particular sectoral concerns. Legally, this indicates that Article 48(1) and (2) are horizontally directly effective; but that the Article 48(3) exceptions are not. Discrimination by a private employer against a national of another Member State could only be justified by State intervention in the shape of legislative or administrative action authorizing that discrimination. The State measure would then, of course, be subject to the need to relate that discrimination to the demands of a particular case in accordance with the normal rules relating to Article 48(3).

(d) *Discrimination internal to a single Member State*

The Treaty of Rome only operates to outlaw discrimination within its sphere of application. Just as discrimination for purely sporting ends is not caught by the Treaty,[92] discrimination within a Member State against nationals of that State is also not subject to the Treaty. Articles 7 and 48 do not forbid 'reverse discrimination'.[93] Consequently, rules may be enforceable within a State against nationals of that State where their enforcement against Community migrants would be impermissible.

This is of direct relevance to the new rules which UEFA is proposing to introduce to control the number of 'non-national' players who may appear in club sides in European competition. As explained, English clubs will be obliged to discriminate against Scottish, Welsh, and Northern Irish workers, just as against Danes and Ital-

---

[90] See, e.g., Case 30/77 *Bouchereau* [1977] *ECR* 1999, [1977] 2 *CMLR* 800. Wyatt and Dashwood, *supra* note 49, 186-95.

[91] Cf. similar arguments advanced in respect of Art. 36 by Quinn and MacGowan, *supra* note 88, 163, 176-7.

[92] See Part III/B/(a) *supra*.

[93] Case 175/78 *Saunders* [1979] *ECR* 1129. For analysis, see Greenwood 7 *YEL* (1987) 185, 193-205; *Halsbury's Laws of England*, 4th edn., 1986, Vol. 52, Para. 15.10. Cf. reverse discrimination and Art. 30, Cases 80 & 159/85 *Nederlandse Bakkerij* v. *Edah* [1986] *ECR* 3359, [1988] 2 *CMLR* 113.

ians. However, whereas players from other Member States will be able to invoke EEC law to counter such discrimination, Scottish, Welsh, and Northern Irish players will be unable to do so due to the absence of an EEC element in their case.[94] Their exclusion would be a matter purely internal to a single Member State and their remedies, if any, would be found only in national law.[95]

This difference in treatment will have particularly striking consequences for footballers qualified to appear for the Republic of Ireland. The rules of the English League treat such players as home players, on a par with Scottish, Welsh, and Northern Irish players; the new rules will however, be ineffective against them, as nationals of another Member State of the Community, while prejudicing Scottish, Welsh, and Northern Irish players.

It is small wonder that the proposed new UEFA rules have caused consternation among leading British clubs, who have traditionally made no distinction between English, Scottish, Welsh, or Irish players. However, British football, in declining to make such a distinction in club football while simultaneously maintaining four separate national representative sides possessed of one vote each on international governing bodies, here finds itself hoist by its own petard.[96]

C. **Articles 85 and 86 EEC**

Article 85 states:

> 'The following shall be prohibited as incompatible with the common market: all agreements between undertakings, decisions by associations of undertakings and concerted practices which may affect trade between Member States and which have as their object or effect the prevention, restriction or distortion of competition within the common market.'

Article 86 states:

> 'Any abuse by one or more undertakings of a dominant position within the common market or in a substantial part of it shall be prohibited as incompatible with the common market in so far as it may affect trade between Member States.'

---

[94] *Quaere* the case of a Scottish, Welsh, or Northern Irish player returning from employment in another Member State to play in England; see discussion by Greenwood, *supra* note 93.

[95] If an English court were to find the rules unlawful as being in restraint of trade, it seems that the court would be prepared to grant relief on terms which might require the domestic football authorities to refuse to obey the rules of the international governing bodies; see *Cooke* v. *Football Association*, *The Times*, 24 March 1972, discussed by Grayson, *supra* note 42, 206-7; cf. the more celebrated case relating to cricket. *Greig* v. *Insole* [1978] 1 *WLR* 302. NB: however, the immunity of an employers' association from the doctrine of restraint of trade, s 3(5) Trade Union and Labour Relations Act 1974; considered and held inapplicable in *Greig* v. *Insole*, ibid. 359-62.

[96] This separate status at international level does not however, constitute objective justification for tying eligibility to play for English clubs in European competition to eligibility for the English national team; the individual player is not a representative in his her own right in club football. See text, *supra* at note 59, 41.

Both Articles offer a non-exhaustive list of the types of conduct forbidden.

These two Articles form the core of the Treaty rules on competition, which are designed to prevent commercial undertakings partitioning the market along national lines. They thus complement Treaty provisions such as Articles 30 and 48, which prohibit State barriers to trade. Articles 85 and 86 possess distinct aims – Article 85 controls cartels, Article 86 monopolies – but they are clearly complementary provisions. This has been explicitly recognized by the European Court: '[they] seek to achieve the same aim on different levels'.[97] However, the extent to which Article 48, relating to free movement of persons, and the competition rules in Articles 85 and 86 may be seen as complementary or overlapping is considerably more problematic, in order to demonstrate this difficulty, the four headings considered in the previous section in relation to the application of Article 48 to the discriminatory player restrictions will now be considered in the light of the application of Articles 85 and 86.

(a) *Are the rules within the scope of the Treaty?*

Professional sport can constitute an economic activity and is therefore in principle subject to the competition rules of the Treaty of Rome. The Court has consistently affirmed that in principle Articles 85 and 86 regulate all sectors of the economy and that exclusion from the scope of these rules is only achieved by specific provision in the Treaty.[98] No such exclusion applies to sport.

There seems little difficulty in classifying clubs as 'undertakings' and football governing bodies[99] as 'undertakings' and, or 'associations of undertakings' within the meaning of Articles 85 and 86. The Court has chosen not to attempt to define exhaustively the meaning of the term 'undertaking',[100] but has preferred to indicate its broad scope through a series of judgments in which a wide range of entities have been accepted as 'undertakings' for the purposes of Articles 85 and 86.[101] Thus, for example, the concept embraces companies, partnerships, or sole traders; groups of companies or trade associations. The common feature of such bodies is, in a very general sense, their economic participation in the common market.[102]

---

97 Case 6/72 *Continental Can* v. *Commission* [1973] *ECR* 215, [1973] *CMLR* 199.

98 See, e.g., Cases 209-13/84 *Ministère Public* v. *Asjes* [1986] *ECR* 1425, [1986] 3 *CMLR* 173; Case 45/85 *Verband der Sachversicherer* v. *Commission* [1987] *ECR* 405; Goyder, *supra* note 52, 72-9.

99 Cf. *Ninth Report on Competition Policy*, Paras. 116-7.

100 The term is not defined for the purposes of the competition rules by the Treaty of Rome; cf. Arts. 52, 58 EEC; Art. 80 ECSC.

101 Goyder, *supra* note 52, 79-80: Korah, *EEC Competition Law and Practice*, 3rd edn. (ESC 1986) 14-15; Wyatt and Dashwood, *supra* note 49, 345-7: Whish, *Competition Law*, 2nd edn. (Butterworths 1989) 213-5; Bellamy and Child. *Common Market Law of Competition*, 3rd edn. (Sweet & Maxwell 1987) Para. 2.003; Green, *Commercial Agreements and Competition Law* (Graham and Trotman 1986) 229 et seq.

102 Cf. A-G Roemer in Case 32/65 *Italy* v. *Council and Commission* [1966] *ECR* 389; '[...] apart from legal form or the purpose of gain, undertakings are natural or legal persons which take part actively and independently in business and are not therefore engaged in a purely private activity [...]'

This approach probably excludes from the scope of the competition rules the discriminatory practices of national representative football teams. Such restrictions are inherent to the competitive, sporting composition of the team and are not imposed within the framework of the economic function or motivation of the activity. In this way, the ambit of Articles 85 and 86 runs parallel to that of Article 48 and covers club football, but not international representative football.[103]

Does 'trade' under Articles 85 and 86 cover footballers? EEC Competition law normally relates to restrictive practices concerning goods; it can also clearly cover agreements relating to services;[104] but it is submitted that there is no reason in principle why it should not also be interpreted to include restrictive practices concerning labour.[105] The free movement of not only goods and services, but also labour is fundamental to the concept of the creation of free trade within the common market.[106] The Treaty of Rome provides no explicit exclusion of labour practices from the application of the competition rules.[107] The Court, for its part, has consistently indicated that the notion of 'trade' is to be broadly interpreted.[108] Accordingly, private action in all these spheres which is contrary to the concept of the common market should fall within the ambit of the competition rules.[109] It is therefore submitted that there is no reason in principle why the discriminatory national football rules should not be considered in the light of the Treaty of Rome's competition rules.

It is a more complex task to decide precisely which arrangements fall within which prohibitions.[110] As explained above, Article 85 and Article 86 are complementary, but distinct in their spheres of application and, in certain important respects, they operate separate legal regimes. This is particularly apparent in the possibility of exemption under Article 85(3), which is formally unavailable under Article 86. This feature is considered more fully below, in Part IIIC(c).

There may be agreements of the type controlled by Article 85 between national clubs and their governing associations. A Football League might be considered an association of undertakings within Article 85, with the result that the player regula-

---

103 An alternative means of reaching the same result would be to deny that such rules concern 'trade' within Arts. 85/86.

104 See, e.g., Case 155/73 *Sacchi* [1974] *ECR* 409, [1974] 2 *CMLR* 177 (television broadcasts); Case 172/80 *Zeuchner* v. *Bayerische Vereinsbank* [1981] *ECR* 2021, [1982] 1 *CMLR* 313 (banking); for further examples, see Bellamy and Child, *supra* note 101, Para. 2.115.

105 Cf. Case 42/84 *Remia* v. *Commission* [1985] *ECR* 2545, [1987] 1 *CMLR* 1, Paras. 49-51 of the judgment, individual treated as an 'undertaking'; Commission Decision. *re Unitel OJ* 1978 L 157/39, [1978] 3 *CMLR* 30, where the implication is that the Commission intends to treat opera singers as 'undertakings'; it is submitted that footballers would not be so classified, because they must integrate into a team and therefore lack independent economic status in the sense of an 'undertaking' within Art. 85.

106 Arts. 3(a), 3(c), 8A EEC.

107 Contrast the position under English law, where restrictive labour practices are explicitly excluded from the scope of the statutory provisions – ss 9(6), 18(6) Restrictive Trade Practices Act 1976.

108 See, e.g., Para. 18 of the judgment in case 172/80, *supra* note 104.

109 Cf. Art. 119 EEC, which concerns labour and clearly covers private employers; cf. *supra* note 89.

110 Cf. Evans *supra* note 48, 540 et seq.

tions themselves could be characterized as decisions of an association of undertakings.[111] There may also be such agreements between the associations and European football's governing body, UEFA. Taking a broad view, these are in fact all part of the same cartel in the sense that all share the common overall aim of restricting players' free movement and distorting competition. More precisely, the agreements involving clubs and national associations may constitute unlawful agreements in respect of domestic fixtures; UEFA appear to become involved in the illegality when European inter-club fixtures are in issue.

Apart from the agreements covered by Article 85 which may be in operation, it seems conceivable that the discriminatory practices of national associations constitute an abuse of a dominant position contrary to Article 86 in respect of domestic fixtures, while UEFA are guilty of a similar breach of Article 86 in respect of international club fixtures. In this context, it should be noted that the European Court has accepted that both Article 85 and Article 86 may be infringed by a dominant undertaking which imposes restrictive agreements on its trading partners.[112]

To some extent, one may accept that there is no pressing need to define exactly what type of practices are in issue.[113] For example, it would seem to make little difference of substance whether the player regulations are held to be the decisions of an association of undertakings or the product of decision-making by several separate undertakings. In either event, Article 85 is in issue.[114] However, the precise nature of the various relationships will be of relevance in some important circumstances and it is therefore incorrect to content oneself with the adoption of a vague analysis. For example, if it is considered desirable to tackle the Leagues themselves, rather than or in addition to the individual clubs, it might prove more prudent to characterize the arrangements as the decision of an association of undertakings,[115] rather than decisions of undertakings. More fundamentally, it may be arguable that a more monolithic approach is appropriate; that the Leagues of each country should be seen as the holders of a dominant position in that territory, and that therefore their conduct should be as-

---

[111] See Goyder, *supra* note 52, Ch. 18; Green, *supra* note 101, Ch. 14; Whish, *supra* note 101, 220-1. On the rules of self-regulatory bodies in industry as agreements within Art. 85, see, e.g., four decisions adopted by the Commission on 10 December 1986, *OJ* 1987 L 19/18-30, [1989] 4 *CMLR* 287-308. Even non-binding advice given by trade associations has been held within Art. 85, Case 8/72 *Cementhandelaren* v. *Commission* [1972] *ECR* 977, [1973) *CMLR* 7; on Trade Associations, see Watson and Williams 8 *YEL* 121.

[112] Case 66/86 *Ahmed Saeed Flugreisen*, judgment of 11 April 1989.

[113] See, e.g., Goyder, *supra* note 52 et seq.; Bellamy and Child, *supra* note 101, Para. 2.031.

[114] Cf. the Opinion of A-G Lenz in Case 311/85 *Vlaamse Reisbureaus* [1987] *ECR* 3801, [1989] 4 *CMLR* 213, 228, Question (B)(a).

[115] See, e.g., Commission Decision 82/896 *AROW* v. *BNIC* [1983] 2 *CMLR* 240; fine of 160000 ECU's imposed on National Cognac Industry Board for minimum price fixing; cp. Cases 89/85 *et al. Ahlstrom and others* v. *Commission* (Woodpulp Cartel) [1988] 4 *CMLR* 901, Paras. 24-8, decision declared void in so far as it concerned a trade association (KEA).

sessed in the light of Article 86, to the exclusion of, or perhaps in addition to, Article 85.[116]

The fundamental problem resides in the extent to which a separation between the League and its individual clubs can be seen to exist. On the one hand, the clubs are companies which undertake independent economic activity in the sense that, for example, each sets its own price for admission to a stadium which, in most cases, is owned by the club. Furthermore, each club enters into contracts with its own employees, including, most importantly, players. This autonomy indicates that Article 85 is in issue. However, against this, it must be conceded that the clubs possess a range of common interests within the League structure. There is decision making of a necessarily collective nature, in respect of, for example, fixtures and rule making. The clubs cannot enjoy autonomy in such matters if the industry is to function effectively and therefore in this sense the clubs are all acting as one – to borrow a phrase common in United States anti-trust parlance, as a 'single entity'.[117] This would indicate the application of Article 86, rather than Article 85.

The tests for distinguishing the respective fields of application of Articles 85 and 86 are, perhaps inevitably given the diversity of conduct under review, imprecise. The European Court and the Commission have on several occasions been obliged to assess the practices of groups of firms and have shown themselves prepared to rule that even a legally binding contract under national law does not constitute an agreement within Article 85, if the deal is in reality simply a reflection of the allocation of functions within a single economic actor.[118] The test is one of 'economic independence',[119] which implies the necessity for an examination of corporate structure and control.[120]

It is submitted that, delicate though the application of these tests undoubtedly is, the football rules in question are more properly seen as falling within the Article 85 regime, rather than that of Article 86. The player restrictions are admittedly part of the governing structure of the League as a homogenous, regulatory entity, but they are the product of the independent input of each club and affect the independent business

---

116 For a challenge to a Commission decision on the basis that insufficient attention was paid to the distinct spheres of application of Arts. 85 and 86, see Case 9789 *Fabrica Pisana* v. *Commission*, lodged at Court Registry 22 March 1989 [1989] 4 *CMLR* 569. Note also the link between Arts. 85 and 86 exposed by the Court in Case 66/86 *Ahmed Saeed Flugreisen*, *supra* note 112.

117 For discussion in this context, see Goldman 'Sports, Antitrust and the Single Entity Theory', 63 *TUL L. Rev.* 751-97 (1989); cf. responses by Grauer, 64 *TUL L. Rev.* 71, Roberts ibid 117.

118 In English company law terms, the Commission will for these purposes 'pierce the corporate veil'; see Mann 22 ICLQ 35,48 (1973). A similar result is achieved In English cartel law by s43(2) Restrictive Trade Practices Act 1976.

119 Case 22/71 *Beguelin* [1971] *ECR* 949, [1972] *CMLR* 81; Case 170/83 *Hidrotherm Gerärebau* v. *Andreoli* [1984] *ECR* 2999; Case 30/87 *Bodson* v. *Pompes Funèbres*, 4 *MLR* 984 (1989); cf. the Commission's decision in *Christiani and Nielsen OJ* 1969 L 165/12, [1969] *CMLR* D36, See further, Whish *supra* note 101, 239-41; Wyatt and Dashwood, *supra* note 49, 353-4; Goyder, *supra* note 52, 82-3; Bellamy and Child, *supra* note 101, Para. 2.146; Green *supra* note 101, 231-4; Van Bael and Bellis, *Competition Law of the EEC* (CCH 1987) Para. 205.

120 Cf. the US S Ct decision in *Copperweld Corp* v. *Independence Tube Corp* 467 US 752 (1984); parent corporation and wholly owned subsidiary held legally incapable of conspiring with each other for the purposes of s 1 Sherman Act.

decision making of each club in player recruitment policy in the wider labour market.[121] The League is in this sense not to be described as a 'single entity'. In reality, the independence of the clubs precludes the dominance of the League as an autonomous governing body. The control exercised by the League as coordinator of the system is simply the consequence of an aggregation of power as a result of agreement between the clubs. It is therefore submitted that the League stands with the individual clubs as a party to an agreement covered by Article 85,[122] rather than constituting a dominant undertaking within Article 86.

In conclusion, it is submitted that prima facie breaches of Article 85 are established. The Football League rules constitute agreements concluded by the clubs and the League itself. At the level of the European club competitions. UEFA may be added as a party to the agreement. The applicability of Article 86 seems less likely, because these are instances of collusion rather than dominance. Finally, it should be noted that the competition rules only bite if an agreement has as its object or effect 'the prevention, restriction or distortion of competition within the common market'. This condition is satisfied in the case under review, for clubs are inhibited by the rules from recruiting players throughout the market without reference to the nationality of the worker. It might at this point be argued that the UEFA rules are in fact justifiable on objective criteria, being linked not to nationality *per se*, but to the composition of national representative sporting teams, a matter unaffected by the Treaty.[123] The Court has shown itself prepared to accept that an agreement which differentiates between different cases on objective grounds may be held to fail out with the scope of Article 85.[124] This is commonly known as the 'rule of reason' under Article 85.[125] This is a parallel argument to that discussed and rejected in relation to Article 48[126] and it is submitted that here too it must be rejected. There is no objective reason for imposing restrictions on eligibility for a club side which are based on eligibility for a national representative team. If the player restriction rules are to be upheld, it can only be by virtue of the more general economic justification found in Article 85(3).[127]

---

[121] It is submitted that this view accords with Goldman's 'Synthesis and Proposed Analysis' in the US context, *supra* note 117, 789-96. Note that if, in conformity with the arguments of Grauer and Roberts, *supra* note 117, considered under Art. 86, the League(s) would only have to justify the rules as a non-abusive if dominance is established: *quare* the relevant market for these purposes – football, sport, or entertainment generally.

[122] Cp KEA, which did *not* play a separate role in the agreement in Case 89/85 *et al. Ahlstrom and others* v. *Commission supra* note 115 with the result that the Commission decision was annulled in so far as it applied to KEA.

[123] *Walrave and Koch*, *supra* note 44.

[124] A striking example is found in the area of Selective Distribution, see Case 26/76 *Metro* v. *Commission* [1977] *ECR* 1875, [1978] 1 *CMLR* l (on which see Goebel (1987)24 *CML Rev.* 605).

[125] This has been the subject of extensive academic examination. For recent analysis, see, e.g., Whish and Sufrin 7 *YEL* (1987) 1; Green [1988] *ECLR* 195.

[126] Part III/B/(a) *supra*.

[127] Part III /C/(c) below.

(b) *Are the Treaty rules horizontally directly effective?*

There is no difficulty in establishing the horizontal direct effect of the competition rules. It is fundamental to the nature and purpose of these provisions that they bind private parties and this has long been recognized by the European Court:

> 'As the prohibitions of Articles 85(1) and 86 tend by their very nature to produce direct effects in relations between individuals, these Articles create direct rights in respect of the individuals concerned which the national courts must safeguard.'[128]

(c) *Justification*

Agreements which contravene Article 85(1) can none the less be exempted from the scope of the prohibition under Article 85(3).[129] This exemption provision contains, crudely, two 'positive conditions' and two 'negative conditions' for exemption, all of which must be satisfied. Under Article 85(3), exemption may be granted to an agreement [...]

> 'which contributes to improving the production or distribution of goods or to promoting technical or economic progress, which allowing consumers a fair share of the resulting benefit, and which does not:
> (a) impose on the undertakings concerned restrictions which are not indispensable to the attainment of these objectives
> (b) afford such undertakings the possibility of eliminating competition in respect of a substantial part of the products in question.'

On a strict reading, all commercial contracts could fall foul of Article 85(1), for the contracting parties, in binding themselves to each other, thereby restrict their freedom to contract with a third party in relation to the subject matter of the contract which they have concluded. This would be plainly absurd. Exemption under Article 85(3), the purpose of which is to permit restrictive but broadly beneficial arrangements, prevents such absurdity. There is no parallel justification provision under Article 86, but doubtless a similar result can be achieved by a dominant firm anxious to demonstrate the beneficial effect of its conduct by establishing that no 'abuse' has been committed.

It must be stated that the Commission alone is empowered to grant an exemption under Article 85(3). It derives this power from Regulation 17/62. Undertakings must notify agreements to the Commission to seek exemption and in the absence of such notification the agreement cannot be exempted even if theoretically meeting the Article 85(3) requirements.[130] No national football rules of the type under scrutiny

---

[128] Case 127/73 *BRT* v. *SABAM* [1974] *ECR* 51, 62; [1974] 2 *CMLR* 231, 271.

[129] Goyder, *supra* note 52, Ch. 8; Whish, *supra* note 101, 253 et seq.; Wyatt and Dashwood, *supra* note 49, 379 et seq.; Bellamy and Child, *supra* note 101, Ch. 3.

[130] Apart from the limited number of agreements covered by Art. 4(2) Reg. 17/62, which may be exempted without notification. The list in Art. 4(2) has no application to the discriminatory player rules under investigation.

have been notified and exemption is thus at present impossible. However, it is useful – for academic and practical reasons – to consider whether the football rules may be susceptible to exemption under Article 85(3); or whether they may be held to constitute non-abusive conduct under Article 86 on the part of the dominant football authorities.

It is immediately apparent on a reading of Article 85(3) that it is on its literal terms unsuited for application to an agreement restrictive of the movement of labour, rather than goods. However, it is submitted that the validity of the application in principle of Article 85 in such cases has already been established[131] and therefore due allowance in literal interpretation must be made. With that observation in mind, the following arguments may be advanced.

(i) The straightforward application of Article 85(3)

The agreements possess the necessary economic benefits to comply with the first positive condition in that they secure the long term future of the national game by encouraging large numbers of young players to commit themselves to a career in football, secure in the knowledge that places of employment will be available to them in the higher echelons of their national professions.

To turn to the second positive condition, there is significant consumer benefit[132] in that clubs are assured of a regular supply of young employees; football spectators gain by the continued existence of a large number of professional clubs, staffed by nationals attracted into the profession by the employment opportunities available at the highest level.

The first negative condition is, it may be submitted, satisfied, for the restrictions imposed are indispensable to the attainment of these objectives. Without the restrictions, secure employment opportunities would be reduced to such a degree that the supply of young players would be severely diminished. Some discussion of detail would doubtless revolve around the precise number of foreign players to be allowed, but a restriction to two or perhaps three seems proportionate to the objective in view.

Finally, competition for players will not be eliminated by the system. There remains a sufficient number of employers even at national level to ensure the maintenance of effective competition.

In relation to Article 86, it can be argued that no abuse has occurred and that the control exercised by the dominant bodies is in fact for the welfare of the industry and is designed to protect its proper status within the common market. This is plainly a similar, though less formalized, argument than that advanced in relation to exemption under Article 85(3).

In this manner, it is arguable that the restrictive rules do not in fact infringe the competition rules. The assumption is that the preservation of national restrictions,

---

[131] Part III/C/(a) *supra.*

[132] The word ‘consumer’ should not be construed narrowly to cover only the end user. The French word ‘ultilisateur’ possesses the broader meaning which more accurately reflects Commission practice in relation to the second positive condition.

contrary to the basic principle of the common market, must none the less be seen as permissible, for otherwise the national production of footballers and the long-term welfare of the game in each State will be detrimentally affected.

(ii) The straightforward application of Article 85(3) doubted

Such arguments would be of little weight if advanced to support discrimination on grounds of nationality in the production or supply of goods, as opposed to the use of labour. In *Coöperatieve Stremsel- en Kleurselfabriek* v. *Commission*[133] all Dutch cheese-making co-operatives had joined a co-operative which produced rennet used in the process of making cheese. The rules required members to purchase their required supplies of rennet from the co-operative, on pain of the imposition of fines and possible expulsion. The effect of the arrangement was that supplies of rennet were not acquired from outside the Netherlands. A breach of Article 85 was held to have occurred. This is closely analogous to the football rules, which limit opportunities for using labour, rather than goods, from outside the home State. The same approach applies to discrimination in conditions of supply as well as in methods of production. In its decision in the *Citroen* case,[134] the Commission was clearly of the view that Citroen was in breach of Article 85 by offering special deals only to consumers living in Belgium and Luxembourg. This constitutes discrimination on grounds of residence, but, as the Commission points out, the practice was likely to discriminate against final buyers according to their nationalities'; it was a case of indirect discrimination on grounds of nationality.[135] *Citroen* is an instance of discrimination practised against customers, rather than in respect of the means of production, but the illegality is in a general sense analogous to the Football League rules which favour nationals at the expense of Community migrants. In similar fashion, Article 86 has been held infringed by a dominant firm which seeks to discriminate on grounds of nationality.[136] A fundamental economic tenet of the common market is that if domestic production is harmed by the pressure of competition from industries in other Member States, then so be it. This is the nature of free competition and it is a means of promoting efficiency. The national resources should be reallocated to a use which is more suitable and valuable, in accordance with consumer demand and the market forces of traditional economic theory.

So, following the normal approach under Article 85(3), can it be argued that if an influx of foreign players is likely to harm the national game and opportunities for home players within it, so much the worse for the national game and for such players? It/they must compete or die!

---

[133] Case 61/80 [1981] *ECR* 851.

[134] [1989] 4 *CMLR* 338.

[135] Cf. *supra* note 34 and accompanying text on the subject of the restrictive rules of the English Football League. Note also that the residence requirement lacks objective justification; cf. *supra* note 66 and accompanying text.

[136] See, e.g., Case 7/82 *GVL* v. *Commission* [1983] *ECR* 483, [1983] 3 *CMLR* 645; Van Beal and Bellis, *supra* note 119, Para. 908, Bellamy and Child, *supra* note 101, Para. 8.060.

(iii) Making a special case for sport

The objection to this ruthlessly pro-competitive approach is derived from the nature of the sports industry and its role within the integrated common market. The logic of economic integration includes the withering away of the relevance of national boundaries in the conduct of the vast majority of manufacturing and service industries. However, the relevance of national boundaries in football cannot be dismissed so easily. They are not simply barriers to trade which impose arbitrary isolation on the market. Instead, they constitute an important aspect of the structure and attraction of the industry. In a sense, this is an extension of the 'non-economic' argument accepted by the European Court in *Walrave and Koch.*[137] The attainment of national superiority through competitive, sporting endeavour is the essence of the activity. In contrast to most industries, there is no compelling, economic reason for extending the industry throughout Europe. Indeed, the arguments run completely contrary to this integrative objective. The national identity of the League within an individual State is an important element in its economic function and definition. This is recognized in the Parliament's Resolution adopting the Janssen van Raay Report.[138] Recital D declares that: '[...] sport is an integral part of national culture and identity whose diversity adds to the richness of European culture and builds friendships among peoples'.

(iv) The special case for sport – the argument redefined

The core of the argument must be defined carefully. There are two issues. One is the existence of national Leagues access to which is limited to teams based in particular States. The other, separate question concerns access of players who are not nationals of a particular Member State to play without restriction in the League situated in that State. The arguments advanced above are sufficient to resist any attempt to apply EEC competition law to the maintenance of national leagues. The logic of market integration cannot be taken to mean that the rules of the Treaty of Rome possess the objective of the creation of a unified European (or at least EEC) League. National Leagues remain legitimate economic entities, being so comprised for essentially traditional, sporting reasons.[139] In the context of common market integration, they are a special case.

However, these arguments are much more problematic when deployed in favour of the perpetuation of the player restrictions within the national Leagues. It is incumbent on the football authorities to provide evidence as to why these are necessary to maintain the health of the domestic game. They need to demonstrate that the game will be harmed at the domestic level without these restrictions. The assumptions of market integration run contrary to such assertions. The arguments advanced above in relation to Article 85(3) to the effect that the restrictions are necessary in order to encourage

---

[137] See *supra* note 44.

[138] See *supra* note 41.

[139] Although certain minor anomalies exist; e.g., Berwick Rangers' home ground is in England, although they play in the Scottish League; Derry City's home ground is in Northern Ireland, although they play in the Republic's League of Ireland.

young players into the game are countered by pointing out that the removal of restrictions will in fact increase the attraction for youth, for the employment opportunities throughout the Community are multiplied several times over. This is the fundamental logic informing the creation of a European economic space and it is applicable to employment opportunities for labour as to marketing opportunities for goods. Similarly, just as the free movement of goods provides the consumer with a wider and more attractive choice of purchases, so too the free movement of labour improves the attraction of the 'product' on display each match-day. The Janssen van Raay Report declares that as a result of the lifting of the nationality-based restrictions 'there is every reason to expect that the game will receive a shot in the arm through the demonstration of a high level and, possibly, a different kind of footballing skill'.[140]

Yet there are grounds for supposing that an argument based on Article 85(3) to justify the player restrictions is not wholly implausible. Free movement of players may detrimentally affect both States which import and those which export players. In the case of the importing State, it has been argued that unfettered choice of players from all Member States would reduce incentives for promoting youth teams in the home State. This is not convincing, given the sheer number of players and clubs at all levels of the game. However, a more convincing case can be made in respect of the exporting State. The loss of leading players is likely to damage the health of the domestic game. There is admittedly a difficulty in the collection of empirical evidence, but it is submitted that there are genuine arguments that unrestricted free movement of players will seriously jeopardize the viability of national Leagues in the States where the football industry is economically relatively weak,[141] because of their inability to retain players of above-average ability.[142] Once one has accepted the legitimacy of national Leagues, as elaborated above, incidental rules to protect them may be justified, if proportionate. Consequently, the exporting State's industry is legitimately protected by imposing limits on demand in importing States by means of the player restrictions. In this fashion, the pattern of arrangements throughout the Community achieves a compromise between the special status of the football industry and the general objective of economic integration. The cartel is constituted by a Community-wide network of arrangements at the level of the national Leagues and justification under Article 85(3) is possible.

This paper has consistently rejected the view that the football authorities can claim objective justification for the application of nationality-based rules to the composition of club sides.[143] It is however, submitted that such rules, if directed to the maintenance of quality levels, may be supported, albeit by virtue of the justifications found in the Treaty, rather than the claim to objectivity. The quality of a club side and its

140 See *supra* note 41, Para. 16.

141 'To allow free movement of footballers would certainly have a devastating effect on the British game. Already clubs in France and West Germany and Belgium, quite apart from Spain and Italy, pay much higher salaries than our own [...] It is easy to foresee the departure of most of our leading players.' (Brian Glanville, *World Soccer*, May 1987, 22.)

142 See the Resolution tabled by MEPs Ephremidis, Adamou, and Alavanos, Doc B 2-1547/86, Annex IV to the Janssen van Raay Report, *supra* note 41; cf. Hilf, *supra* note 59, 521.

143 Parts III/B/(a), III/C/(a).

national League is a material consideration deserving protection, where the nationality of the individual players is not.

These are complex arguments, which do not appear formally to have been addressed, since the football authorities have never applied for exemption under Article 85(3). However, it is submitted that this analysis demonstrates that the applicability of Article 85(3) to the discriminatory player restrictions cannot be wholly discounted.

(d) *Discrimination internal to a single Member State*

Just as Article 48 is inapplicable to actions which discriminate in circumstances wholly internal to one Member State, without any Community element, so too Articles 85 and 86 are inapplicable to restrictive or abusive practices which produce effects purely internal to a single Member State. Articles 85 and 86 are only relevant where a connection with inter-State trade can be shown. On a superficial analysis, this appears to mean that practices, such as the new UEFA rule,[144] which restrict the movement of Scottish, Welsh, Northern Irish, and English players within the United Kingdom fall outwith the ambit of Community law.

This limited interpretation of the scope of Community law is, however, open to challenge. If a Scottish club is only allowed to play four British nationals who are not Scots in European club competition, then this will inevitably affect their readiness to purchase such players. The result will be that the club will look outside the United Kingdom to buy players, for the rules would be unlawful and therefore unenforceable as applied to, say, German players. It may also mean that English players will look to move outside the United Kingdom, where the restrictive rules are unlawful under Community law, rather than to move within the leagues in the United Kingdom. On this analysis, the UEFA rule, even as applied internally within the United Kingdom, distorts trade patterns within the Community, albeit indirectly, and therefore it falls to be considered under Articles 85 and 86.[145] It might be objected that the causal link between rule and trade distortion is not watertight. However, with regard to the burden of proof which is in this context borne by the Commission, the Court has declared that:

> 'Article 85(1) of the Treaty does not require proof that such agreements have in fact appreciably affected such trade, which would moreover be difficult in the majority of cases to establish for legal purposes, but merely requires that it be established that such agreements are capable of having that effect.'[146]

---

144 See *supra* Part II.

145 See the broad approach of the European Court in decisions such as Case 8/72 *Cementhandelaren* v. *Commission* [1972] *ECR* 977, [1973] *CMLR* 7 (conduct on the Dutch market alone had effects on other national markets within the Community). The requirement of an effect on inter-State trade is plainly not construed as a major obstacle to Community competence. For analysis, see Goyder, *supra* note 52, Ch. 7; Whish, *supra* note 101, 242-9: Wyatt and Dashwood, *supra* note 49, 375; Bellamy and Child, *supra* note 101, Para. 2.116 et seq.

146 Case 19/77 *Miller* [1978] *ECR* 131, Para. 15. See also Case 61/80 *Cooperatieve Stremsel- en Kleurselfabriek* v. *Commission* [1981] *ECR* 351, Para. 14, which refers to the need to show 'a sufficient degree of probability'. In both cases, the Commission discharged its burden. See further Bellamy and Child, *supra* note 101, Para. 2-119; Van Bael and Bellis, *supra* note 119, Para. 222; Green *supra* note 101, 238.

It is submitted that this test can be met in the present case.

It appears that a discrepancy in the scope of Article 48 and Article 85 has been exposed. In Part III.B.(d), the conclusion was reached that Article 48 was of no assistance in the 'internal' case under examination. Yet here it is suggested that Article 85 does cover the case. The discrepancy arises because of the broad interpretation given by the European Court to the effect on inter-State trade condition under Article 85, which has not been extended to Article 48.[147] It is possible that the European Court, provided with an appropriate opportunity by the accidents of litigation, will rule that the logic of the Treaty demands that Article 48 and Article 85 be interpreted in a parallel manner in such a case. This would mean that the UEFA rule could be attacked on the basis of both provisions, even as applied *prima facie* internally to the United Kingdom. Until such time as this occurs, a potential inconsistency between Article 48 and Article 85 exists.

D. **Conclusion**

The discriminatory player restrictions appear to fall foul of Article 48, with no possibility of justification. The only doubt concerns the question of the horizontal direct effect of Article 48, but it is submitted that an overwhelming weight of judicial and academic opinion has been assembled in favour of this attribute. The player restrictions are also caught by Article 85 (but probably not by Article 86), but there are genuine arguments of substance that exemption under Article 85(3) is a live possibility.

There is a significant difference between Article 48 and Article 85 because of this distinction in the nature of the exemption rules. In addition, other anomalies have been revealed, such as the apparent more flexible treatment of the condition that an effect on inter-State trade be shown under Article 85.

The focus of this article now turns to Enforcement of Community law in this area. In Part IV, close attention is devoted to the enforcement powers and practice of the Commission. In Part V, attention is paid briefly to the opportunities for enforcement by private individuals before national courts. A central theme will remain the anomalies between the use of Article 48 and Article 85.

IV. Enforcement by the Commission

A. **Article 48**

There are no means whereby the Commission can enforce Article 48 against private parties. It is, however, worth considering whether it would be possible for the Commission to initiate Article 169 infringement proceedings against all Member States requiring them to legislate against discrimination contrary to the Treaty occurring on their territory.

---

[147] Cf. Case 180/83 Moser [1984] *ECR* 2539 and discussion by Greenwood *YEL* (1987) 185, 199, 203.

Advocate-General Trabucchi in *Donà* v. *Mantero*[148] suggests that this possibility should not be allowed. He declares:

> 'I cannot accept the principle that the State should be made liable for activities carried out on its territory by individuals exercising their contractual autonomy solely on the ground that they have adopted measures which conflict with directly applicable Community rules.'

The Advocate-General contends that the State's duty does not extend beyond the duty to 'withhold legal recognition' from clauses which restrain sports clubs from signing foreign players. He supplements this view with the astute constitutional point that an acceptance of the propriety of the Article 169 action in these circumstances could distort the structure of legal obligations imposed by the Treaty. According to the Advocate-General, Article 48 is 'directly applicable'.[149] If a Member State were required to promulgate domestic legislation in order to force its nationals to comply with Article 48, then the true Community source of the legal rule would be obscured. This would introduce an uncertainty prejudicial to the integrity of the Community legal system.[150]

It is at least arguable that as a matter of law this is an unduly restrictive approach. The private bodies concerned have contravened Article 48 and should be subject to legal control; the States have committed a separate Treaty infraction by allowing parties within their jurisdiction to act in a manner contrary to Article 48. They are in breach of Articles 5 and 7 EEC by undermining the efficacy of Article 48, and this denial of the obligations of Community solidarity should be the subject of legal challenge under Article 169. By adopting this more rigorous approach, an effective solution may be achieved. Article 48 is made binding on private parties; national authorities are obliged to secure compliance.

However, this seems to go further than the European Court has been prepared to go in its view of the extent of Member State obligations in this area. A State must not support Treaty infractions committed by private parties by, for example, legislating purportedly to sanction or to encourage the illegality or by creating a legal environment within which the Treaty infringement is immune from challenge.[151] A national court's refusal to withhold legal validity from rules unlawful under Community law which are pleaded before it could also expose the Member State to proceedings under Article 169 for breach of Article 5 EEC. But there seems to be no State responsibility where the State is guilty of a simple omission to take steps against a private body acting in breach of the Treaty.[152]

---

[148] See *supra* note 57.

[149] Here is not the place for analysis of the debate about the distinction between 'direct applicability' and 'direct effect', see Winter 9 *CML Rev.* 425 (1972). *Quaere* whether the phrase is of value in relation to Articles of the Treaty, see *Halsbury's Laws of England*, 4th edn., 1986, Vol. 51, Para. 3.41.

[150] Cf. in respect or EEC Regulations. Case 39/72 *Commission* v. *Italy* [1973] *ECR* 101. See Hartley, *supra* note 77, 195 et seq. Contrast EEC Directives, which require domestic implementation (Art. 189 EEC).

[151] Cases 209-13/84 *Ministère Public* v. *Asjes* [1986] *ECR* 1425, [1986] 3 *CMLR* 173; Case 311/85 *Vlaamse Reisbureaus* [1987] *ECR* 3801, [1989] 4 *CMLR* 213. See Slot 12 *EL Rev* 179 (1987); Whish, *supra* note 101, Ch. 9(6).

[152] Cf. from the perspective of remedies, the Court's unwillingness to grant a 'mandatory injunction' against a State in Art. 169 proceedings; see Hartley *supra* note 77, 300.

Quite apart from these legal arguments against the use of Article 169, there are strong practical reasons for accepting the good sense of Advocate-General Trabucchi's desire to eschew Article 169 proceedings against the State in these circumstances. The real target is of course the private football organizations. To attack their illegality though the medium of the national State is both cumbersome and time-consuming. This is recognized in the Parliament's Resolution adopting the Janssen van Raay Report, which indicates that although such action against the State is 'theoretically possible',[153] it 'would not be appropriate'.

This being so, it is necessary to analyse the preferable course of action – proceedings against the football organizations directly. The next section, Part IV/B, examines such action brought by the Commission. Part V mentions opportunities for enforcement by private individuals.

B. **Articles 85 and 86**

(a) *The Commission's Enforcement Powers*[154]

In contrast to Article 48, the Commission is given specific and sophisticated powers of enforcement against private parties in relation to the competition rules. These are found in Regulation 17/62, which covers initiation of the procedure, the powers of investigation and the range of decisions from which the Commission may select as a means of disposing of the case.

The Commission has power to exempt a *prima facie* restrictive agreement under Article 85(3), but this power can only be exercised on notification of the agreement by the parties.

If the Commission takes the view that the football bodies are in breach of the competition rules, it has power to issue a decision requiring termination of the anti-competitive practice and, in addition, it may decide to impose a fine.[155]

(b) *Why has the Commission not initiated such proceedings?*

Hampered by scarce resources, the Commission's preference is for informal settlement. To save time and money and, as far as is possible, to preserve goodwill, it will usually decline to initiate formal proceedings if voluntary undertakings or informal remedial action can be extracted.[156]

It has endeavoured to pursue this course in relation to football. A cautious approach on the part of the Commission can be detected. In relation to the ban on English club

---

153 See the Report itself, *supra* note 41, Para. 11.

154 On enforcement, see Whish, *supra* note 101, Ch. 10; Wyatt and Dashwood, *supra* note 49, Ch. 16; Korah, *supra* note 101, 34; Kerse, EEC *Antitrust Procedure*, 2nd edn. (ELC 1988); Bellamy and Child, *supra* note 101, Ch. 12.

155 Arts. 15, 16, Reg. 17/62.

156 Van Beal 23 *CML Rev.* 61 (1986); more than 95 per cent of cases are terminated by 'settlement', the remainder by formal decision. See also Waelbroeck 11 *EL Rev* 268 (1986): Green, *supra* note 101, 304 et seq.

sides competing in European competitions, imposed in the aftermath of the Heysel Stadium tragedy of 1985, which is arguably unlawful under Community law,[157] the Commission, 'having regard to the very particular circumstances in which the ban in question was imposed by UEFA', has preferred to maintain a non-interventionist stance.[158]

In relation to the discriminatory rules of the national Leagues regarding foreign players, the Commission has been engaged in a policy of persuasion for over ten years.[159] It must now be conceded that this conciliatory strategy has not met with success. In this light, the Commission now finds itself urged to take more positive action in the exercise of its powers of administration of the competition rules. It is, however, of interest that even the Janssen van Raay Report, adopted by the Parliament,[160] supplements its call for action by the Commission under Article 85 with the suggestion that a gradual, rather than an immediate, increase in foreign players should be secured and that 'certain safeguards to allow clubs and spectators to identify with the teams' be elaborated. It is therefore plain that the Commission remains likely to use a subtle, measured approach. ideally with the objective of achieving a negotiated settlement.[161]

It is submitted that this, while admittedly legally inconclusive, is at least partial confirmation of the finding made in Part III/C/(c) that some protection may legitimately be claimed for the player restrictions by national Leagues on the basis of Article 85(3).

C. **Remedies against the Commission**

There is no direct method whereby an individual can bring proceedings against the Commission in respect of a Commission failure to initiate Article 169 proceedings against a Member State. An Article 175 EEC action for failure to act is unavailable because of the restrictive rules of *locus standi* under that Article.[162] The individual could launch an indirect challenge to the Commission's inactivity by bringing an action for damages under Article 215. In *Denkavit* v. *Commission*,[163] the applicants claimed to have suffered pecuniary loss as a result of the detention at the Italian

---

157 Evans, *supra* note 48.

158 Written Question 154/87 *OJ* 1988 C 46/7. The Commission's preferred inactivity does not exclude the possibility that the clubs may proceed before national courts on the basis that their directly effective Community law rights of free movement have been infringed. However, the only litigation pursued in this instance was based on English law and it failed; see Evans, *supra* note 48, 529.

159 Grayson, *supra* note 42, 211-2.

160 See *supra* note 41.

161 Cf. Resolution tabled by MEPs Ford and Stewart (Doc 2 – 1167/84, Annex I to the Janssen van Raay Report, *supra* note 41) '[...] demands that a full investigation [...] be undertaken before premature decisions are taken that might (a) damage further an industry in severe decline, and (b) damage national and Community prestige at large, hidden, economic cost.'

162 For analysis, see Schermers, *supra* note 64, Paras. 341-5, 434; Hartley, *supra* note 77, 300-2, 390-2.

163 Case 14/78 [1978] *ECR* 2497; see Hartley, *supra* note 77, 300-4, 464-5.

border of feeding stuffs which contained a potassium nitrate level exceeding that permitted under a regulation introduced as a matter of urgency by the Italian Minister of Health. Denkavit alleged that the Commission's delay in securing the repeal of this unlawful Italian regulation constituted a wrongful act yielding a right to compensation. Advocate-General Mayras, following the opinion of Advocate-General Warner in *Meyer-Burckhardt* v. *Commission*,[164] was plainly unreceptive to the idea of such a claim against the Commission,[165] but the Court adopted a rather more flexible position. While the Court declined to hold the Commission liable, it chose to do so on the basis that the Commission had not been guilty of a delay which could be considered wrongful in the circumstances. The Court appeared to regard the action as in principle available. Notwithstanding this apparent generosity, it is submitted that the difficulties in showing illegality on the part of the Commission and in satisfying the rules of causation, *inter alia*, make this an avenue of redress which should inspire little optimism in applicants.

The prospects of success are rather different in respect of Commission neglect to initiate enforcement proceedings against a private individual for breach of the competition rules.

Under Article 3(2) of Regulation 17/62 'natural or legal persons who claim a legitimate interest' may apply to the Commission to find that there is an infringement of Articles 85 and or 86. The 'legitimate interest' necessary to acquire standing to submit such a complaint under Article 3(2) has been broadly interpreted[166] and a footballer or a club would have standing to submit a complaint about the discriminatory rules to the Commission. The submission of the complaint then confers on the complainant a privileged status in the subsequent conduct of the investigation in respect of the following matters:

(i) if the Commission addresses a decision to the body under investigation, the complainant third party has sufficient standing to challenge the decision under Article 173(2);[167]

(ii) if the Commission declines to proceed with the investigation, it must inform the complainant of its reasons for this decision and it must offer the complainant an opportunity to submit further observations. This duty is imposed on the Commission by Article 6 of Regulation 99/63.

If the Commission adheres to its decision not to proceed despite these further observations, there follows no explicit legislative right vested in the complainant. On a strict reading of the legislation, it could simply be ignored. However, the Commission's practice is to issue a final letter to the complainant explaining why further action is not

164 Case 1/75 [1975] *ECR* 1171.

165 See *supra* note 163, 2515-6.

166 See, e.g., *Kawasaki* [1979] 1 *CMLR* 448, where the investigation was prompted by the complaint of an individual consumer.

167 Case 26/76 *Metro* v. *Commission* [1977] *ECR* 1875, [1978] 2 *CMLR* 1.

envisaged.[168] It is, however, submitted that apart from this practice there is in fact a legal right vested in the complainant to receive a final rejection decision.[169] This right must be implied in order to give effective content to the complainant's special status under Regulations 17/62 and 99/63, for otherwise the Commission could simply grant the hearing required under Regulation 99/63 and then ignore the complainant. This is not the intended legal role for the complainant. It is consequently submitted that there is a right to receive a final decision, enforceable under Article 175, and that the decision itself is reviewable under Article 173. Thus, the complainant is not entitled to a final decision on the infringement,[170] but is entitled to a final decision on the complaint.[171]

Finally, an Article 215 action against the Commission may be considered. This would amount to an allegation that the Commission's neglect to pursue the matter has caused loss to the applicant. However, it has already been suggested that although this type of action may be available in principle,[172] in practice the rules which are imposed in relation to liability under Article 215 are extremely restrictive and it is difficult to imagine that such an action would prove successful.

V. Enforcement by private parties before national courts

The *sine qua non* for enforcement of EEC law by private parties before national courts is the direct effect of the provisions concerned. In the case of the football restrictions, which are imposed by private parties, the matter concerns an action between private parties, with no element of direct State involvement, and therefore the *sine qua non* is horizontal direct effect. These issues have been discussed in Parts III/B/(b) and III/C/(b) and for the present purposes the horizontal direct effect of Articles 48 and 85/86 is assumed.

This indicates that the player restrictions could be challenged before national courts. Community law stipulates that it is for the national system to determine the procedural rules which apply and the remedies to be made available in litigation to vindicate rights derived from Community law,[173] subject to two qualifications:[174]

---

168 As in, e.g., Cases 142 and 156/84 *BAT and Reynolds* v. *Commission* [1988] 4 *CMLR* 24.

169 For fuller analysis, see Kerse, *supra* note 154, 60-6; Weatherill, 10 *The Company Lawyer* (1989) 47.

170 Case 125/78 *GEMA* v. *Commission* [1979] *ECR* 3173, [1980] 2 *CMLR* 177; and see Cases 142 and 156/84 *supra* note 168.

171 It should always be remembered that if the Commission refuses to act on the complaint, the aggrieved party may have recourse to the national courts, making use of the direct effect of the provisions in question.

172 Case 141/78, *supra* note 163; the issues are analogous even though the specific powers under Reg. 17/62, rather than the general powers under Art. 169 are in issue.

173 See Bridge 9 *EL Rev* (1984) 28.

174 First elaborated in Case 45,76 *Comet* v. *Produktsch.* [1976] *ECR* 2043, [1977] 1 *CMLR* 533; Case 3376 *Rewe* v. *Landwirtschaftskammer* [1976] *ECR* 1989, [1977] 1 *CMLR* 533, and since regularly repeated, see, e.g., Case 130/79 *Express Dairy Foods* v. *Intervention Board* [1980] *ECR* 1887, [1981] 1 *CMLR* 451. See Barav and Green, 6 *YEL* (1986) 55; Oliver 50 *MLR* 881 (1987).

(i) the remedy must be available on conditions no less favourable than those applied to a similar right of action in purely national matters; and
(ii) the conditions must not make it impossible in practice[175] to exercise the rights under Community law which national courts are under a duty to protect.

In English law, the judicial approach has been to regard the cause of action as breach of statutory duty;[176] breach of the duty under the European Communities Act 1972 to observe enforceable Community rights.[177] But what remedies are available?

A litigant could seek to establish the non-enforceability of the rules restricting the numbers of foreign players in a team on the basis of Article 48 or Articles 85/86, or both, by means of a challenge before the High Court. In accordance with the principle stated above, it is for the English system to determine the nature of the remedy and this immediately demands consideration of the legal nature of the League rules. The issue is the distinction between public law and private law; proceedings by way of judicial review under Order 53 of the Rules of the Supreme Court or by writ for an injunction and/or declaration. These are broad issues which cannot be tackled here. It is, however, submitted that despite the recent willingness of the English courts to look to the function of a body, rather than its form,[178] in determining its legal status for these purposes, a sports body, even though exercising a regulatory function, is properly regarded as a creature of private law and therefore susceptible to challenge by writ.[179] It is also submitted that a declaration and/or injunction could be sought even in the absence of existing contractual obligations, for example by a player against a national association.[180]

More intriguingly, a litigant might seek damages for loss suffered as a result of the discriminatory rules. There seems to be no reason in principle why the action should not be pursued in relation to breaches of both Article 48 and Article 85. Admittedly, it would prove difficult to demonstrate a quantifiable loss. However, it is conceivable that the remedy sought would take the form of an interlocutory injunction, thereby requiring the Court to assess the value of damages to the plaintiff at trial in accordance with the principles set out by the House of Lords in *American Cyanamid* v. *Ethicon*.[181] These several issues have been explored by the courts[182] and by academic

---

175 'Impossible in practice' [praktisch unmöglich] is the phrase used in *Rewe*, *supra* note 174. In Case 199/82 *San Giorgio* [1983] *ECR* 3595, [1985] 2 *CMLR* 658, the Court uses the phrase 'virtually impossible or excessively difficult' in the course of its judgment, but reverts to 'virtually impossible' in its ruling; *quaere* if this is intended to amend the formulation in Rewe.

176 See, e.g., the cases mentioned at below note 182.

177 S 2(1). The phrase may be taken to accord with the notion of directly effective provisions in the jurisprudence of the European Court; see Hartley, *supra* note 77, 239-40.

178 *R* v. *Panel on Take-Overs and Mergers, ex p Datafin* [1987] QB 815.

179 See *Law* v. *National Greyhound Racing Club Ltd* [1983] 1 *WLR* 1302; cf. Beloff, *Public Law* (1989) 95.

180 *Eastham* v. *Newcastle United* [1964] Ch. 413.

181 [1975] AC 396.

182 See particularly *Baurgoin* v. *MAFF* [1986] QB 716, [1985] 3 *WLR* 1027 (Art. 30); *Garden Cottage Foods* v. *Milk Marketing Board* [1984] AC 130, [1983] 3 *WLR* 143 (Art. 86).

writers[183] in relation to the action for damages before English courts for breach of Article 30 and Articles 85/86, and this exploration has revealed much complexity, largely arising, it seems, out of the application of the public private distinction to the availability of remedies. The introduction of Article 48 in this context cannot be investigated in depth within the confines of this paper. However, it is submitted that the implications of the direct effect of Article 48 and of Article 85 and their consequent availability to litigants before national courts render still more acute the problematic implications of their overlap in substantive scope. Briefly, one could imagine a case where a domestic litigant would be unable to attack a practice on the basis of Article 85, because Commission has acted, formally or even informally,[184] to 'protect' the practice under its Regulation 17/62 administrative powers, but where the same practice could be successfully attacked instead on the basis of incompatibility with Article 48. The discriminatory player restrictions may provide such an instance, given the earlier finding that they are more likely to be justifiable under Article 85 than under Article 48.

In this way, Article 48 could be used to circumvent obstacles to an action based on Article 85. This could be profoundly unsettling for the Community structure, in that Commission compromises under the competition rules could be upset as a result of domestic enforcement of Article 48. It is submitted that the enforcement of Article 48 before English courts requires deeper analysis than that which can be supplied in this article. At present, it can only be observed that the overlap of Article 48 and of Article 85 is a problem not just for the Community system, but also, by virtue of the direct effect of the provisions, for national systems.

VI. Concluding remarks

A. **General**

The organization of football appears to be on a collision course with more than one area of the Treaty of Rome. This should not occasion surprise. The industry is one which retains strong national identities, while at the same time operating, as it has for many years, internationally. European attitudes are beneficial to football, in that the sphere of attractive and lucrative competition is widened, but also constitute a threat to the game in the light of the fact that a continuing national identity within a national League remains a strong motive for continued spectator/customer support.

The arguments for giving special protection to the football industry are diverse. They have been alluded to earlier in this article[185] and will not be addressed in greater

---

[183] See, e.g., Barav and Green, *supra* note 174 (and see references at 96 note 175); Oliver *supra* note 174; Steiner 12 *EL Rev* 102 (1987); Davidson 34 *ICLQ* (1985) 178; Meade 37 *NILQ* (1986) 101; Picanol 2 *LIEI* (1983) 1; Goyder, *supra* note 52; Kerse, *supra* note 154 (and see references at note 93, 316).

[184] 'Comfort letters' are not binding on national courts, but may be taken into account; Case 253/78 *Guerlain* [1980] *ECR* 2327, [1981] 2 *CMLR* 94, on which see Korah 6 *EL Rev* (1981) 14.

[185] See Part III/C/(c) *supra*.

depth here. It will however, be noted that if free movement of players within the Commission is established, this will give a peculiarly disunified face to European football, for, presumably, in all other European States, in which the writ of the EEC does not run, restrictions will be enforceable. This reveals that the EEC is not a coherent organizational body in this sector of the economy. It is 'disfunctional', a criticism which may be attached to it in other rather more important spheres, including those impinging on the political.[186]

B. **The overlap between Article 48 and Article 85**

The central legal complexity which emerges from this article is that announced in the opening sentence – under which Treaty provision or provisions should action by private parties discriminating in employment against nationals of other Member State fall to be considered? and – how should such action be eliminated – by Commission action and/or individual litigation? This, of course, is a problem of relevance beyond the football related issues examined in this article and certainly beyond sport in general. One might consider the practices of a trade union, or, as referred to by Advocate-General Warner in *Walrave and Koch*,[187] those of an employers' association choosing employees on the basis of nationality.

One may begin with the submission that discriminatory labour practices in the private sector are in principle subject to both Article 48 and Articles 85/86. However, these provisions are not co-extensive. Several points of departure have been noted in the course of this analysis. It has been suggested that individual clubs may fall outwith the scope of Article 48, but not of Articles 85/86.[188] Article 85 seems to have a broader scope than Article 48 in that the notion of an effect on inter-State trade under the competition provisions allows practices *prima facie* internal to a single Member State to be caught by the prohibition.[189] The exemption procedures differ markedly under the provisions, that under Article 85 being significantly more likely to avail the football authorities than that under Article 48, for reasons of both material and personal scope.[190] Perhaps most fundamental of all, the enforcement procedures under the provisions are quite different.

These are essentially problems of coherence in Community law, but they become problems for national courts given that Articles 48, 85, and 86 are all directly effective. Consequently, these anomalies could confront a national court. The problem would arise in its most acute form where a litigant chose to base an action on one Article where the same set of facts litigated under a different, though in principle applicable, Article would not succeed, i.e. where the litigant is seeking to take advantage of the anomaly.

---

[186] Cf. President Gorbachev's plea for a 'common European home' and the instability of 'Eastern' Europe.

[187] See *supra* note 44, *ECR* 1425.

[188] Parts III/B/(b), III/C/(a).

[189] Part III/C/(d).

[190] Parts III/B/(c), III/C/(c).

To use the example elaborated in this article, a particular problem will arise if a player and or a club challenge the discriminatory rules before a national court on the basis of Article 48, even though the Commission has, formally or informally, decided to take no action to put an end to the practices, on the basis that the rules are compatible with Article 85, i.e., the use of Article 48 to circumvent obstacles to an action based on Article 85. This presents a risk of distortion of the Community legal structure.

C. **A solution**

Is there a solution? One could remove the overlap by establishing a demarcation at Community level between Articles 48 and 85. Or one could accept the overlap and leave its practical consequences to be dealt with as and when they arise. Which is best for the advancement of Community law?

(a) *Demarcation at Community level*

Two possible demarcations can be identified. Both centre on the 'troublesome' category which is the focus of this article – private sector barriers to the free movement of workers.

First, such rules could be exclusively dealt with by Article 48, by denying that the competition rules apply to restrictive practices concerning labour, i.e. that 'trade' under the competition rules covers goods (and services) alone, while acknowledging the horizontal direct effect of Article 48.

Second, they could be exclusively dealt with by Articles 85/86, by accepting that 'trade' within the competition rules covers labour as well as goods (and services), while denying the horizontal direct effect of Article 48.

Both approaches achieve demarcation; the first between rules and practices concerning goods (covered by Articles 30 and 85) and rules and practices concerning persons (Art. 48); the second between barriers imposed by the State in its legislative capacity (Arts. 30 and 48) and barriers imposed in the commercial sphere (Arts. 85/86).[191] That is to say, the first approach concentrates on what the rules apply to, the second on the applier of the rules.

However, it is submitted that, neat though both means of demarcation may seem, neither would make a valuable contribution to the coherent development of Community law. The first approach, which denies the application of the competition rules to labour practices, is unattractive. The competition rules apply to restrictive practices concerning goods and services. Their scope is to be interpreted broadly.[192] There is no indication in the Treaty that restrictive practices concerning labour constitute a special ease. Accordingly, it is not rational to suppose that labour practices can be excluded from the scope of a set of provisions plainly designed to control distortions relating

191 This may embrace the commercial activities of the State under Arts. 85/86 or, in the case of public undertakings, Art. 90. See Goyder, *supra* note 52, 80, 366-71; Whish, *supra* note 101, Ch. 9(6).

192 See Part III/C/(a); note 106 and accompanying text.

to any of the factors of production which are fundamental to the market economy referred to in the basic Treaty provisions such as Articles 2, 3, and 8A EEC.

The second approach would deny the horizontal direct effect of Article 48. It must be conceded that there are arguments against the horizontal direct effect of Article 48. If the derogations in Article 48(3) are unavailable to private parties, then it might seem logical that the prohibition in Article 48(1) should not bind private parties. More fundamentally, since the Commission cannot enforce Article 48 against private parties, such matters should be dealt with only under Articles 85/86, where the Commission is equipped with the sophisticated enforcement mechanism of Regulation 17/62.

However, it is submitted that it would be an unacceptable retrograde step for Community law to concede that Article 48 is not horizontally directly effective. Most jobs are in the private sector. In the light of this, the limitation of Article 48 to vertical direct effect would not simply produce anomalies and distort the structure of enforcement of Community obligations, it would also severely curtail the efficacy of Community law as a means of achieving the integrative objects set out in the basic Treaty provisions such as Article 2, 3, and 8A EEC.

There is in addition a substantial amount of evidence that the Court[193] and the legislature[194] of the Community regard the horizontal direct effect of Article 48 as inherent in the structure and purpose of the Treaty.

(b) *Accepting the overlap*

This, then, leads to the conclusion that the overlap must be tolerated. So the problems of substance and of enforcement procedure at Community and at national level must be confronted.

This is not a novel result for Community law. The Court has in the past been prepared to rule that the same practice may fall to be considered under two separate sets of Treaty provisions. In *Commission* v. *Italy*,[195] the Court held that a measure could be subject to scrutiny under both Article 92, concerning State Aids, and Article 95, which prohibits discriminatory systems of internal taxation.

Before looking more closely at judicial practice in eases of overlap, it is possible to deal with some of the problems of substantive overlap without great difficulty in order to preclude irrational anomalies between the scope of Article 48 and the competition rules. It is submitted that individual clubs are the subject of both provisions, notwithstanding the reservations on this subject expressed by some sources.[196] Furthermore. although the present state of the law indicates that the criterion of an effect on inter-State trade is interpreted more strictly in relation to Article 48 than Articles 85/86,[197] it is submitted that this apparent anomaly is simply the result of a paucity of Article

---

[193] See particularly Para. 19 of the Court's judgment in *Walrave and Koch*, *supra* note 44.

[194] Art. 7(4) Reg. 1612/68; see *supra* note 83.

[195] Case 73/79, [1980] *ECR* 1533. See further, Wyatt and Dashwood, *supra* note 49, 473-4; Bellamy and Child, *supra* note 101, Para. 14-32.

[196] See *supra* note 81, 56 and accompanying text.

[197] Part III/C/(d).

48 litigation on the point and that the European Court will, when presented with the opportunity, be ready to interpret the provisions in the same manner – in accordance with the broad approach already taken under Articles 85/86.

However, the differences between the justifications available under Article 48 in contrast to those under the competition rules[198] cannot be ironed out by a process of interpretation. These differences constitute an important distinction in the scope of the provisions. In the light of the fundamentally different enforcement procedures which attach to the provisions[199] these distinctions in scope confront not only the Community legal order, but also the national courts.

Should one follow the approach chosen in *Commission* v. *Italy*[200] with regard to Articles 92 and 95, with the result that conformity with both Articles 48 and 85 is demanded? Or should one provision take priority over the other, with the result that conformity with the former will suffice? On this second approach, one would suppose that Article 48 would be accorded priority. Because it forms part of the 'Foundations of the Community' in the Treaty of Rome; the competition rules are merely part of the Policy of the Community'.[201] Given the finding that the football rules are capable of justification under Article 85, but seem beyond redemption under Article 48,[202] the choice between these two approaches is of no moment. On either analysis, conformity with Article 48 is the difficult hurdle which must be crossed, but which the rules appear to be incapable of crossing.

This appears to rule out reliance on the arguments which have been advanced under Article 85(3).[203] In consequence, the Commission's formal powers under Regulation 17/62 and the informal strategy often preferred[204] become valueless. This does not seem satisfactory. The private party is locked into Article 48 with minimal opportunities for justifying the practices in question, given the strong indications that the derogations under Article 48 are intended to justify State action in the general interest, not private sector conduct.[205] The Article 85(3) justification is available in respect of restrictive practices concerning goods and services, but not labour. Restrictive labour practices in the private sector thus appear to be treated in an extremely harsh manner. Does this lure the analysis back to the attractions of demarcation, considered

198 Parts III/B/(c), III/C/(c).

199 Part IV

200 See *supra* note 195.

201 Cf. discussion of possible conflict between Arts. 30 and 85 in Wyatt and Dashwood, *supra* note 49, 5 12-3. See also in this respect Bellamy and Child, *supra* note 101, Para. 772; 'The Court in *Nungesser* [Case 258/78 [1982] *ECR* 2015] was clearly concerned that parties should not seek to retrieve by contract what would be prohibited under Articles 30 and 36'. See similarly, Case 58/80 *Dansk Supermarked* v. *Imerco* [1981] *ECR* 181, [1981] 3 *CMLR* 590, Para. 17 of the judgment. For analysis of these issues, see Turner 8 *EL Rev* (1983) 103.

202 Part III, *supra*, summarized at Part III/D.

203 Part III/C/(c).

204 Part IV, *supra*.

205 Part III/B/(c) *supra*. The problem of the inflexibility of Art. 48 is encountered even if an Art. 86 analysis of the status of the League is preferred, *supra* note 117, 90.

above?[206] One might argue that Article 85 alone should apply,[207] but the weight of legislative and judicial evidence against this is formidable. One might argue that Article 48 alone should apply, but this would emphasize even more clearly the anomalously harsh treatment of this category of practice.

It is submitted that a compromise solution should be sought. The restrictive labour practice is a curious creature which does not fit comfortably into the structure of the Treaty of Rome. This justifies a special regime. A strict application of Article 48 denies the genuine arguments of justification which can be made on the basis of Article 85(3). It is therefore suggested that a hybrid regime under which Article 85(3) arguments may be advanced should be devised. The Court has indicated an unwillingness to allow Article 85 to be used as a means of outflanking article,[208] but there seems no reason for adopting such a reluctant approach to the interrelation of Article 85 and Article 48. Unlike Articles 85 and 30, both Articles 85 and 48 are capable of applying to the same practice in the private sector and it is far from dear that the strongly integrationist nature of the provisions relating to free movement should override. A system whereby both provisions can be taken into account should be devised.

There is every likelihood that this matter will first be raised before a national court in litigation based on the direct effect of the relevant Treaty provisions. A national court could not decide for itself a complex matter of this nature relating to the structure of Community law. In the pursuit of the integrity and coherent development of Community law national courts are entitled to expect assistance in this difficult area.[209] However, it is far from clear what can be expected of either the European Court in the exercise of its Article 177 jurisdiction, or the Commission, in its administrative capacity, given the fact that these complexities emerge from the basic structure of the Treaty itself It is none the less submitted that the rules under investigation justify a radical approach with the objective of creating a regime more flexible than that available under Article 48 as normally interpreted.

It has frequently been asserted that the law is playing an increasing role in sport.[210] There is mutuality in this relationship. Sport can play an important role in developing the law. *Walrave and Koch*[211] is a long-standing example of this. It is submitted that the resolution of the issues discussed in this article could serve to illuminate some complex areas of Community law.

---

206 Part VI/C/(a).

207 Cf. Evans *supra* note 48, text at note 125.

208 See *supra* note 201. See especially Turner, *supra* note 201, 114-6, who concludes that 'Further discussion of the relationships between the different Treaty provisions would be worth while.'

209 This is not to suggest that a simple and satisfactory answer will be forthcoming; cf., e.g., the formidable (though, in comparison to the test, less fundamental) difficulties caused in national courts applying EEC competition law by the fact that Arts. 85(1) and (2) are directly effective, whereas Art. 85(3) is not; see, e.g., Greaves (1987) *ECLR* 256 and cf. *supra* note 184 on 'comfort letters' before national courts.

210 See, e.g., Grayson, *supra* note 42; Beloff, *supra* note 148.

211 See *supra* note 44.

EUROPEAN FOOTBALL LAW*

I. Introduction

> 'Tucked away in the fairyland Duchy of Luxembourg and blessed until recently with benign neglect by the powers that be and the mass media, the Court of Justice of the European Communities has fashioned a constitutional framework for a federal-type structure in Europe.'[212]

Eric Stein's famous words, which introduced one of the most influential academic surveys of the role of the European Court in the institutional and constitutional evolution of the EC, retain a resonance even today. The intensity of scrutiny of the attitudes of the Court has admittedly deepened over the years, in a manner already prefigured by Stein's insertion of the caveat 'until recently' into his observation, and the Court's approach has begun to attract an increasing level of comment and criticism. But it has remained largely true that the European Court is rather remote from and unfamiliar to the citizens of the European Union.

In December 1995 the Court's ruling in *Bosman* earned it more widespread publicity than it had ever before attracted.[213] Admittedly, much of the comment on the ruling was ill-informed. Nevertheless, for the first time, the application of EC law by the Court in Luxembourg became part of everyday discussion. Moreover, such are the far-reaching implications of the ruling that the Court's approach in *Bosman* is certain to command attention for many years to come. The ruling will alter the economic framework of football, the world's most popular sport and one which involves huge amounts of money. The European Championships, held in England in June 1996, attracted *profits* of £ 69 million, as a result of, *inter alia*, the sale of broadcasting rights (an increasingly competitive market), income from sponsorship and gate receipts. The impact of the European Court's ruling in *Bosman* on the position of the individual football player falls to be assessed in the context of the increasing wealth earned by the industry. The purpose of this paper is to examine the structure of the *Bosman* ruling and to explore its implications, which demand renovation of the structure of football. Although, on one level, this 'only' concerns football, the ruling has major economic implications for sport generally. *Bosman* is also of significance in the development of aspects of Community trade law. More generally, the saga offers an insight into the

---

* *Collected Courses of the 7th Session of the Academy of European Law* (The Hague, Kluwer Law International 1999) p. 339 et seq.

212 Stein, 'Lawyers, Judges and the Making of a Transnational Constitution', 75 *AJIL* (1981) 1.

213 Case C-415/93, *Union Royale Belge des Sociétés de Football Association ASBL* v. *Jean-Marc Bosman Royal Club Liègois SA* v. *Jean-Marc Bosman. SA d'Economie Mixte Sportive de l'Union Sportive du Littoral de Dunkerque, Union Royale Belge des Sociétés de Football Association ASBL, Union des Associations Européennes de Football Union des Associations Européennes de Football* v. *Jean-Marc Bosman*, judgment of 15 December 1995, [1991]*ECR* I-4837.

capacity of EC law to supply the individual with a means to disrupt the established and tenaciously defended self-regulatory patterns of an industry.

II. Jean-Marc Bosman

A. The Transfer System – the Road to Litigation

Jean-Marc Bosman was a Belgian national, born in 1964. He had earned a reputation in his youth as a footballer of some promise and he was sufficiently skilled to play at first division level in Belgium. He had been employed by RC Liège on a contract expiring at the end of June 1990 on an average salary of BFR 120 000 per month, including bonuses. In April 1990 the club offered him a new one-year contract at BFR 30,000 per month, the minimum permitted by Belgian rules, and a quarter of his previous salary. Bosman refused RC Liège's unattractive offer and was transfer listed, at a 'compensation fee' of 11,743,000 BFR fixed according to indicators based, in particular, on age and salary.

To some extent an awareness of the oddities of football in Europe is a precondition to appreciation of the significance of the ruling, and accordingly this paper includes explanation where necessary to ensure the intelligibility of the legal analysis.[214] Football is organized according to a hierarchical structure. Football clubs wishing to participate in official competitions must affiliate to national football associations. Each Member State of the European Union has its own national association, excepting the United Kingdom alone which has four associations, one for each home country, a pattern reflected at international level in the separate participation of England, Northern Ireland, Scotland and Wales in international tournaments. National associations are in turn members of FIFA, the world organizing body, which is based in Switzerland. FIFA is split into confederations for each continent. The European confederation is UEFA, also based in Switzerland, and the national associations of the EU Member States are members of UEFA and as such undertake to comply with its rules. At the bottom of this edifice are the players, contracted to the clubs and subject to rules set by the several national and international organizations. Players are in this manner subject to the rules of the industry which are decided at several levels within the hierarchy.

The rules which most intimately affected Bosman were those applicable to the transfer system. Players are unable simply to move freely between clubs once their employment contract comes to an end. A club is only able to field a player in an official match once it has secured the player's registration, held by the previous employer. That registration will be released only when the previous club is satisfied with the terms offered by the new club, which will typically involve payment of a fee. Fees over £ 1 million are commonplace, fees over £ 5 million are agreed several times a year and very occasionally fees have exceeded £ 10 million. A club which chose sim-

[214] A-G Lenz's Opinion contains an extensive and detailed examination. For useful collection of materials and some analysis, see R. Blanpain and R. Inston, *The Bosman Case: The End of the Transfer System?* (1996).

ply to field a player without complying with the requirements of the transfer system would find itself subject to heavy and immediate penalties imposed by national and transnational organizations.

US Dunkerque, a French second division club, contracted with Bosman to pay him a monthly salary of some BFR 100,000 plus a signing-on fee of some BFR 900,000. In July 1990 RC Liège and Dunkerque agreed a contract for the transfer of Bosman for one year only, at a price of BFR 1,200,000, including an option costing BFR 4,800,000 allowing Dunkerque subsequently to buy the player. Both contracts, RC Liège/Dunkerque and Bosman/Dunkerque, were conditional on the sending of a transfer certificate by the Belgian association to the FFF, the French association, in line with the rules governing the transfer system. It was worthless to Dunkerque to conclude a contract with Bosman without compliance with these transfer requirements, for they would have been unable to play him in official matches. Apparently RC Liège came to doubt Dunkerque's solvency.[215] It did not ask the Belgian association to send the certificate to the FFF. So neither contract took effect.

In accordance with the rules prevailing in Belgium, RC Liège suspended Bosman so that he could not play in the 1990/91 season. This prompted him to pursue redress before the courts. Initially, he sought, *inter alia*, an interlocutory order that the transfer rules did not apply to him. He was granted an interlocutory order in Liège in November 1990 ordering the club and the Belgian association to refrain from impeding his engagement. However, he was unable to secure employment with a leading club. As his case progressed through the courts, he was able to find only relatively small clubs in France and Belgium who were willing to offer him terms. RC Liège's readiness to cut his-wage so savagely in the summer of 1990, combined with the lack of interest in acquiring Bosman's services shown by major clubs at the time, may suggest that his ability to play top-level football was in any event in doubt, but it was widely suspected that Bosman was boycotted by leading clubs after 1990, despite the interim order in his favour.

The litigation initiated by Bosman was chequered by a remarkable series of delays and aborted references to Luxembourg. Other defendants were joined. There were interventions, *inter alia* by footballers' associations. During this period Bosman also attempted to rely on Articles 173 and 215 EC to challenge the Commission's approach to football before the European Court, but his application was rejected as inadmissible.[216] Eventually the matter reached the European Court in October 1993 by way of the Article 177 preliminary reference procedure. The questions asked by the Cour d'Appel, Liège were:

> 'Are Articles 48, 85 and 86 of the Treaty of Rome of 25 March 1957 to be interpreted as:
>
> (i) prohibiting a football club from requiring and receiving payment of a sum of money upon the engagement of one of its players who has come to the end of his contract by a new employing club;

---

215 Para. 33 of the Court's ruling.

216 Case C-1 17-91, *Jean -Marc Bosman* v. *Commission*, (1991) *ECR* I-4837; an application for interim measures was rejected in Case C.117/91R [1991] *ECR* I-3353.

(ii) prohibiting the national and international sporting associations or federations from including in their respective regulations provisions restricting access of foreign players from the European Community to the competitions which they organize?'

On 15 December 1995, the European Court felt able to provide answers to both questions referred to it by the Cour d'Appel. However, the Court was not prepared to answer those questions in the light of all the Treaty provisions mentioned by the referring court. The European Court instead confined itself to analysis in the light of Article 48 EC. By leaving aside discussion of the application of the Treaty competition rules to football, the Court left open a number of issues of significance for the future adjustment of industry structures. Some will be discussed in this paper, with reference to the Opinion of Advocate-General Lenz in *Bosman* which includes treatment of relevant issues arising under the Treaty competition rules.

B. Nationality Restrictions in Football

Although the first question referred to the European Court arises directly out of the obstacles that Bosman faced in his thwarted move to Dunkerque. The second question raises points of EC law which appear to be entirely irrelevant. The second question refers to rules which limit the ability of clubs to field 'foreign' players. Although the relevant rules have been altered periodically, recently restrictions have followed the model of the '3 + 2' rules, according to which clubs may field three 'foreign' players plus two 'assimilated' players.[217] For football purposes, nationality relates to qualification for the national representative side of that association, so on occasion football nationality is not the same as nationality at law.[218] National leagues were permitted to allow a higher number of non-national players, but the '3 + 2' restrictions were enforced mandatorily within the European club competitions organized by UEFA. These European club competitions complement national tournaments and, highly prestigious in sporting terms, they are extremely lucrative. The nationality rules plainly deterred acquisitions of players from other Member States, but they posed no problem for Bosman himself. Indeed, the whole point of his case was that he *was* in demand by a club in another Member State. Nevertheless, the Court decided that it did have jurisdiction on both the questions referred.[219] It repeated its longstanding view that in the context of the cooperative relationship between national court and European Court under Article 177 it is solely for the national court to determine in the light of the circumstances of the case both the need for a preliminary ruling in order to enable it to deliver judgment and the relevance of the question which it submits to the Court. This binds the Court in principle to give a ruling on questions submitted that concern the interpretation of Community law. The Court in *Bosman* was content to comment that- the national court felt the nationality rules could impede Bosman's employment

217 Assimilated players have played in the country of the relevant association for an uninterrupted period of five years including three years as a junior.

218 The UK provides a particularly odd example; there are four football nationalities in the UK.

219 Paras. 55-67.

chances and that it would not call that assessment into question. Looking behind the rather bland words of acquiescence in the ruling, one might surmise that the Court was eager to rule on the point to clarify the law. More-over, Advocate-General Lenz, whose observations on this point (as on others) were more revealing than those of the Court, supplemented an extended examination of the case-law with the comment that he could not see how the nationality rules could reach the Court in any way other than through individual challenge. He pointed out that there have been instances where clubs have been penalized for breaching the nationality rules, yet *still* have not gone to law. Although such a perception would seem formally irrelevant to an assessment of the Court's jurisdiction, one might realistically choose to identify it as a motivating force in the Court's decision to regard itself as competent to answer the national court's questions rather than to treat them as a misuse of the Article 177 procedure. This perception accords with an appreciation of the judgment as an instance of the individual using rights conferred by EC law to prise open an adhesive cartel whose participants had an incentive to accept the system rather than challenge it.

C. **Access to Justice in the Football Industry**

It would, however, mislead simply to proceed immediately to an examination of the structure of the Court's ruling. It is important not to underestimate the remarkable difficulty of obtaining effective access to justice in this industry. Acting collectively, the football industry is able to wield formidable economic power to shield itself from challenges by individual clubs or players prejudiced by the application of its rules. The industry is structured in such a way as to be able to impose immediate penalties of expulsion on clubs and players. Football is a sport based on annual competition, so there are disincentives for clubs to go to law to pursue a case that will take many years to resolve. Players' careers are relatively short; few players extend their careers much beyond the age of 30. Extended legal proceedings are unattractive. Even though suggestions by writers[220] and pressure from the European Parliament[221] had thrown a spotlight on unlawful practices within the game, football had been able to survive unscathed by legal challenge for many years. In particular, although the Court's ruling against the nationality restrictions amounts to a relatively unsurprising confirmation of its approach in *Walrave and Koch* v. *Union Cycliste Internationale* in 1974[222] and in *Donà* v. *Mantero* in 1976,[223] in the two decades that elapsed between those rulings

---

[220] E.g., M. Will, ed., *Sportrecht in Europa* (1993). Cf. also Hilf, 'Die Freizügigkeit des Berufsfussballspielers innerhalb der EG', *NJW* (1984) 517: Weatherill, 'Discrimination on Grounds of Nationality in Sport, 9 *YEL* (1989) 55.

[221] Cf. Nafziger, 'International Sports Law: A Reply of Characteristics and Trends', 86 *AJIL* (1992) 489, which examines *inter alia* the Olympic movement and litigation arising out of the 'America's Cup' yacht race, and Nafziger, 'International Sports Law as a Process for Resolving Disputes', 45 *ICLQ* (1996) 130, which considers *inter alia* litigation involving the runner 'Butch' Reynolds and ice-skater Tonya Harding.

[222] Janssen Van Raay report, PE DOC A2-415/88; Larive report, PE DOC A3-0326/94. The views expressed in both reports are close to the approach of the Court in *Bosman.*

[223] Case 36/74, [1974] *ECR* 1405.

and that in *Bosman* no case had reached the European Court involving a direct challenge to football's nationality-based discrimination. What is more, the Commission had given the green light to these practices. The '3 + 2' rules prevailing at the time of the judgment were the product of a compromise struck in 1991 between UEFA and the Commission, represented by Mr Bangemann.[224]

The *Bosman* ruling cracks open this cartel. Initially, it seems remarkable that an individual player was able to achieve this, when clubs, with greater resources and apparent incentives to challenge such restrictions on their economic freedom, did not. Yet, reading of the treatment meted out to Bosman, who at the time of the judgment was playing low-level football at the advanced age (for a football player) of 31, having endured alcohol-related problems caused by his plight, one may wonder whether the real impact of the judgment may be to warn potential litigants of the costs of challenging the game's structure. To this extent, the ruling confirms that UEFA, the European body, and FIFA, the world body, are not immune from legal challenge,[225] but highlights that they are remarkably powerful entities wielding global influence. Like other transnational sporting organizations, they are in practice frequently able to operate on the assumption that they enjoy a practical immunity from challenge. Sport is extraordinarily resilient to change. Walrave and Koch, the first litigants to assert EC law rights in the sporting arena, were denied probable success before the courts when they declined to press for judgment, apparently in the face of a threat by the defendant sporting body, the UCI, to withdraw paced cycle racing from the world championship schedule.[226] Even the ban on the participation of all English clubs in profitable European club competition imposed in the wake of the Heysel Stadium disaster in 1985 stimulated no challenge based on EC law, even though it was probably a disproportionate interference with economic freedoms guaranteed under Community law.[227] So, even though the game's governing bodies held an entirely misplaced expectation in the period before the *Bosman* ruling that the player would be induced to settle the matter out-of-court,[228] a false sense of security which prompted UEFA even to fail to submit relevant evidence on the alleged beneficial impact of the transfer system in accordance with procedural requirements of the European Court,[229] it cannot be excluded that even after *Bosman* the football industry will feel able to take its subjection to law rather less seriously than most industries.

---

224 Case 13/76, [1976] *ECR* 1333.

225 Essays by Karpenstein and Renz in M. Will, ed., *supra* note 220, examine the Commission's position.

226 Van Staveren, *18th Colloquy on European Law, Sport and the Law* (Proceedings published by the Council of Europe, Strasbourg 1989) 67; Hilf, *supra* note 220, 520. note 22.

227 Cf. Evans, 'Freedom of Trade under the Common Law and EC Law: the Case of the Football Bans', 102 *LQR* (1986) 510.

228 E.g., *The Guardian* newspaper, 4 April 1995, at 18.

229 In Paras. 52-4 of the ruling, the Court rejects an out-of-time request by UEFA for measures of inquiry.

III. Jurisdictional Questions

A. Is Sport Within the Scope of Application of Community Law?

Two general objections made by the football authorities confronted the Court, though neither was novel. To what extent is an economic motivation significant in fixing the scope of application of EC law to particular practices? To what extent is it relevant that the rules emanate from the private sector?

The Court had little difficulty in ruling that Community law is in principle capable of application to sport. This confirmed the approach taken in the 1970s in its well-known pair of 'sports law' rulings, *Walrave and Koch* v. *UCI*[230] and *Donà* v. *Mantero*.[231] The Court rejected submissions based on the alleged 'negligible' economic activity of smaller clubs. Nor was it persuaded by the argument that football is 'in most cases' not an economic activity.[232] Neither of these two points, even if perfectly well-founded, defeat the plain fact that in some of its manifestations sport belongs in the commercial sphere. As a matter of Community law, it is in principle subject to Community law in so far as it constitutes an economic activity within the meaning of Article 2 EC.[233]

Accordingly, the Court was unprepared to place sport beyond the reach of Community law. Indeed, despite the optimistic submissions of the football industry, one would not have supposed that the Court would have been prepared to place a particular industry uniquely beyond the jurisdiction of Community law. Although the Court was not unaware that its judgment could exert a profound impact on the football industry, it commented that 'this cannot go so far as to diminish the objective character of the law'.[234] In its ruling, its sole concession to the particular demands of football was a willingness to exercise its self-endowed power to limit the temporal effects of the judgment in relation to the transfer system. It ruled that the direct effect of Article 48 cannot be relied upon in support of claims relating to a fee in respect of transfer, training or development which has already been paid on, or is still payable under an obligation which arose before, the date of the judgment, except by those who have brought court proceedings or raised an equivalent claim under the applicable national law before that date. It made no such concession in respect of the nationality restrictions in spite of the fact that that regime had been applied with the blessing of the Commission.

The Court was also not persuaded to allow football an immunity from the application of the principles of Community trade law by the German government's submission that the subsidiarity principle dictated that public authorities' intervention in private commercial affairs should be limited to what is strictly necessary. This could not be accepted as a basis for permitting private associations to adopt rules which

230 *Supra* note 222.

231 *Supra* note 223.

232 Paras. 70 and 72, respectively.

233 Cf. overview by Zuleeg in M. Will, ed., *supra* note 220.

234 Para. 77.

restrict the exercise of Treaty rights conferred en individuals. This is not to say that football might not be able to show special interests which may deserve shelter from the normal assumptions of EC trade law. As will be explained, the Court was ready to acknowledge that sport may be marked by particular characteristics that entitle it to treatment in the light of Community law that is distinct from that meted out to 'normal' suppliers of goods and services. In particular, sporting leagues need to sustain a pool of realistic rivals in order to ensure the economic success of the 'product'. However, in *Bosman*, the Court was not prepared to offer sport any general insulation from the rules of Community trade law.

B. Application to Private Parties

The Court also drew on *Walrave and Koch* v. *UCI* and *Donà* v. *Mantero*, its twin sports law rulings of the 1970s, in insisting that Article 48 was applicable despite the private nature of sporting associations. Article 48 applies beyond the public sphere 'to rules of any other nature aimed at regulating gainful employment in a collective manner'.[235] This clearly embraces sporting associations where they fix terms which determine the capacity of professional players to engage in employment. The Court observed, as it had in *Walrave and Koch*, that, were it to confine Article 48 to the public sector, that provision would vary in its scope of application state-by-state in accordance with national choices about the reach of public regulation. The Court therefore confirmed the horizontal direct effect of Article 48, although that effect reaches only as far as collective regulation. There is nothing in the ruling which suggests that the Court would apply Article 48 in situations lacking the collective dimension present in cases such as *Walrave and Koch* and *Bosman*.[236] In the private sphere, where collective regulation is at stake, there is a potential overlap in the scope of application of Article 48 and the competition rules, although Advocate-General Lenz expressed the firm opinion that a violation of Article 48, a fundamental Treaty freedom, cannot be saved by reference to the Treaty competition provisions, in particular Article 85(3).

UEFA had sought to persuade the Court that it should not adopt such a broad interpretation of the personal scope of Article 48 for fear of anomalous consequences flowing from the scope of the rules on justification. It objected that the 'private' application of Article 48 would prejudice private individuals compared with Member States because of the inability of private parties to rely on the Article 48(3) grounds of public policy, public security or public health as justification for limiting rights. The Court decided that there was no such anomaly. It observed that private individuals too could rely on such grounds. Accordingly there was no variation in this respect between rules originating from public or private sources. There is a logical neatness attached to this approach, although it is not dear how the notions contained within Article 48(3) can be adequately re-shaped to suit the private sector. Indeed, there is some

---

[235] Para. 82.

[236] For discussion see Roth, 'Drittwirkung der Grundfreiheiten?' in Due et al., *Festschrift für Ulrich Everling* (1995); J. Handoll, *Free Movement of Persons in the EU* (1995) 135-6; Weatherill, Annotation, 33 *CML Rev.* (1996) 991, 1010, note 49.

risk that allowing private parties to invoke notions of 'public policy, public security or public health' may cause their over-stretching.

IV. The Nationality Restrictions

The Court found that the '3 + 2' rules, applied after negotiation with the Commission, limited the chances of employment of players. An obstacle to the free movement of workers was thereby established. Moreover, the rules were contaminated by nationality discrimination, albeit of an indirect nature *via* reliance on football rather than legal nationality. Such discrimination contradicts the fundamental assumptions of the EC legal order. The Court rejected several submissions presented in defence of the rules.

A. National Representative Football

The most significant issue related to the scope of the Court's view, first expressed in *Walrave and Koch*, that nationality discrimination may be permitted where it is based 'on non-economic grounds, concerning only the sport as such'. It is submitted that the basis of this permission lies in the scope of application of the Treaty. Nationality discrimination is not unlawful per se under EC law; it is unlawful where it occurs within the scope of application of the Treaty. So selection for a national representative side may be based on discrimination according to nationality, for the rationale for such choice lies in the function of the side as a representative of national pride, which is not a matter touched by EC law. Even though profits are doubtless made in the context of international representative sport and even though a player benefits financially from international status, the basis of team selection has no connection with economic objectives. So it is not incompatible with EC law for a national side to select only from a limited pool of players defined according to (football) nationality.

It is submitted that the crux is that such discrimination is lawful because it escapes the scope of application of the Treaty, not because it is 'justified'. Regrettably, the Court in *Bosman* improperly employed the language of justification in this context, which implies that the discrimination falls within the scope of the Treaty, but is permissible according to the standards of EC law. The legal source of any such justification would be elusive and it is submitted that the Court's terminology is inexact. Advocate-General Lenz adopted a more precise approach and referred to the limits of EC competence as the rationale for holding such nationality discrimination permissible. Although there is almost a temptation to retreat to Advocate-General Warner's blunt insistence in *Walrave and Koch* that the permissibility under Community law of national sporting teams is no more than a simple matter of common sense, it is submitted that Mr Lenz's orthodox jurisdictional reading of the approach employed in *Walrave and Koch* is to be preferred over the Court's drift into issues of justification.

B. Club Football

However, neither *Walrave and Koch* nor *Donà* v. *Mantero* offered the Court the opportunity to settle the issue that fell for resolution in *Bosman.* In *Walrave and Koch* the Court's ruling was delivered in the context of national representative teams. *Donà* v. *Mantero* involved nationality-based restrictions in the organization of Italian club football, but the Court scrupulously left the application of the law to the national court. The issue that was addressed in *Bosman* was the extent to which nationality discrimination counts as non-economically motivated (and thus escapes the scope of the EC Treaty) in the context of club football. This raises more nuanced questions about when the representative function that dictates a link between the identity of player and the status of team is exhausted. It was not settled in *Walrave and Koch* whether the national team was the *only* entity able to insist on selecting only a particular nationality. The Court ruled that the prohibition of nationality discrimination 'does not affect the composition of sport teams, *in particular* national teams, the formation of which is a question of purely sporting interest and as such has nothing to do with economic activity'.[237] The same formula is found in *Donà* v. *Mantero;* rules affecting national teams serve as an example of discrimination which is not forbidden by EC law, with the suggestion that the category might be rather wider. In both rulings,[238] however, the Court asserted that '[t]his restriction on the scope of the provisions in question must however remain limited to its proper objective'[239] and it is this perception which was tested in *Bosman.*

Advocate-General Trabucchi in *Donà* v. *Mantero* had suggested a rather generous approach to the ability of clubs to exercise discrimination in player selection without infringing EC law rights. He considered that it would be a matter of purely sporting interest, and therefore permissible, were a national association to limit the participation of foreign players in championship matches 'so as to ensure that the winning team will be representative of the State of which it is the champion team'. He added that this view was strengthened in the light of the fact that the champion club proceeds to represent the State at international level. These observations were not examined by the Court and they have not found favour in academic writing.[240] It is submitted that Mr Trabucchi mistakenly conflated the separate issues of whether a club may be taken to represent a country and whether that club's players possess any such representative function. The heart of the matter is whether a club side may be taken to represent the country in which it is based when it competes in club competitions organized by UEFA at transnational level, and whether *even if it does so* the discharge of that representative function also requires it to select a certain number of players of a particular origin. This issue was addressed directly in *Bosman.*

---

237 Emphasis added.

238 Para. 9 in *Walrave and Koch*, Para. 15 in *Donà* v. *Mantero.*

239 A strict application of the analysis offered in the text would question the Court's use of the noun 'restriction', since what is really at stake is definition of the scope of application of the provisions.

240 Weatherill, *supra* note 220, at 60-3; cf. also Renz in M. Will, ed., *supra* note 220.

The Court in *Bosman* confirmed the approach introduced in *Walrave and Koch*. Relevant provisions of Community law 'do not preclude rules or practices justified [sic] on non-economic grounds which relate to the particular nature and context of certain matches'.[241] It proceeded to reject the submission that the nationality restrictions contributed to a traditional link between club and country, important to the public in identifying with its favourite team. Nor was it prepared to accept that for clubs appearing at international level, it is important to secure representative status by limiting their ability to field 'footballing foreigners'. The Court was completely unpersuaded that reasons of sporting interest could dictate an enforced link between the location of a club and the origins of individual players. The Court stated that:

> '[A] football club's links with the Member State in which it is established cannot be regarded as any more inherent in its sporting activity than its links with its locality, town or region or, in the case of the United Kingdom, the territory covered by each of the four associations. Even though national championships are played between clubs from different regions, towns or localities, there is no rule restricting the right of clubs to field players from other regions, towns or localities in such matches.'[242]

The Court then extended this analysis on to the international plane:

> 'In international competitions, moreover, participation is limited to clubs which have achieved certain results in competition in their respective countries, without any particular significance being attached to the nationalities of their players.'[243]

The nationality of individual players is disassociated from the sporting identity of clubs. The governing assumptions about consumer attitudes towards the link between player nationality and identity of club are neatly captured by Advocate-General Lenz's comment that '[...] the great majority of a club's supporters are much more interested in the success of their club than in the composition of the team'. This could *not be* said in such terms of a national team, where selection of non-nationals would undermine the essence of the sporting endeavour.

If it could be shown that a particular club side selects its players on the basis of 'purely sporting interest', then discrimination on the grounds of nationality might exceptionally escape the scope of application of Community law.[244] However, the Court in *Bosman* has excluded any possibility of such practices applying generally within the game.

C. Residual Issues

The three remaining submissions on behalf of the football industry were treated by the Court as fundamentally unmeritorious. It was submitted that the rules were

---

241 Para. 76.

242 Para. 131.

243 Para. 132.

244 In any event, the practices of a single club would probably not fail within the scope of Art. 48, though this cannot be regarded as authoritatively settled cf. *supra* note 236.

needed to secure a sufficient pool of national players to allow the national team to flourish in all positions. However, according to the Court, even if the competitive labour market created by its ruling might diminish prospects for workers in their home State it ought to assist them finding work in other States. The assumption which underpins the Court's analysis on this point is that once nationality-based distortion is eliminated, the market will not shrink employment opportunities, but rather it will redistribute patterns of employment. In essence, this is an observation that places the football labour market on a par with all other markets affected by the evolving process of European integration. It was further submitted by the industry that the rules helped to maintain a competitive balance by preventing the richest clubs buying up the best foreign players. However, the Court commented that the current rules do not stop such clubs buying up the best national players and thereby undermining this alleged desirable balance. Finally, it was pointed out that the '3 + 2' rule had been drawn up by the football authorities in collaboration with the Commission. However, the Commission is not empowered to authorize practices which are contrary to the Treaty. Therefore this informal arrangement could not affect the Court's finding of a violation of Article 48.[245]

The Court concluded that Article 48 'precludes the application of rules laid down by sporting associations under which, in matches in competitions which they organize, football clubs may field only a limited number of professional players who are nationals of other Member States.'

D. Adjusting Practices in the Football Industry

The result is that all EU nationals must be treated as domestic players for the purposes of eligibility for selection for club matches. Clubs are therefore enabled to pursue more flexible recruiting strategies. The firmly expressed nature of the Court's conclusion suggests no loophole through which the game could seek to reintroduce adjusted schemes that prioritize particular types of player. For example, it is submitted that requirements for clubs to retain a minimum number of 'home-grown' players, without any explicit link to their nationality, would violate Article 48 as indirect nationality discrimination.[246]

The Court did not place any temporal restriction on this part of its judgment, which constitutes both a sharp warning of the fragility of a Commission green light for practices that violate primary Treaty provisions and also an implied rebuke to the Com-

245 According to A-G Lenz, even had the Commission formally exempted the industry's practices under Art. 85(3) EC (which he thought implausible in any event because of their disproportionately restrictive effect), this would not have overridden violation of Art. 48, as explained, the Court did not consider the application of Art. 85.

246 A-G Lenz's view that an Art. 85(3) exemption cannot save a violation of Art. 48 also rules out the practical utility of the argument that nationality restrictions may deserve exemption in order to preserve the viability of smaller national Leagues which would otherwise be plundered of all their leading players. The present author's suggestion, articulated *supra* note 220, at 76-8. 87-92, that violations of Art. 48 may be excused in circumstances where the Art. 85(3) conditions may be met by a labour practice, seems to have found no favour with A-G Lenz.

mission for its tolerance of unlawful discrimination. In principle, the Court's refusal to sanction any temporal restriction also required a change in practice in the middle of the 1995/1996 football season. This obligatory mid-term alteration provoked a mixed response in the football industry. Some domestic leagues, including that in England, promptly abandoned existing restrictions on EU nationals. Elsewhere, including in Germany, there were rumours that so-called 'gentlemen's agreements' had been struck under which clubs agreed to complete the competitions in season 1995/96 in accordance with pre-existing rules, notwithstanding the immediate effect in law of the *Bosman* ruling. UEFA's initial response to the ruling was to declare that the '3 + 2' nationality restrictions should continue to be observed in the European club competitions, which had at the time of the ruling reached the quarter-final stage. Although UEFA is in an unusual situation in the sense that its jurisdiction is Europe-wide and therefore broader than that of the EC, it is nevertheless clear that in so far as its practices are implemented within the EC it is subject to EC law.

It is submitted that such unwilling responses constituted violations of Article 48 as interpreted in *Bosman* in so far as they affected players with rights under EC law. However, no club chose to challenge either a national association or UEFA, a reluctance which corresponds to past trends of conformity with the industry's collective rules.

The Commission does not appear to possess powers to take action directly against a private association for violation of Article 48,[247] but it is submitted that the Commission could rely on its powers conferred by Regulation 17/62 to attack such associations for violation of the Treaty competition rules. For such 'gentlemen's agreements' amount to restrictive practices within the meaning of Article 85(1). With the threat of Commission intervention in the background, it was announced in February 1996 that UEFA. After discussion with the Commission, had abandoned the nationality-based restrictions for the following season's tournaments, beginning in August 1996. Even though there may have been unlawful practices persisting after the *Bosman* ruling until the end of the 1995/1996 football season, it seems highly improbable that they will generate any legal proceedings at either Community or national level. However, the cosy cartel based on discriminatory practices, agreed within the game and permitted by the Commission, has been dismantled. Football has been irrevocably changed.

V. The Transfer Rules

A. The Basis of the Court's Objection to the System

The rules governing transfer of footballers between clubs vary between different national associations. There is a transnational underpinning, which is fed by UEFA/FIFA regulations which are enforced at national level as regards relationships between players and clubs. In *Bosman* there was some dispute about precisely which rules were the relevant ones, but the referring court, the Cour d'Appel in Liège, considered that the FIFA regulations valid at the time applied.

[247] Cf. Weatherill, *supra* note 220, at 80-2, Karpenstein in Will, ed., *supra* note 220.

However, the approach taken by the European Court ensures that it is not necessary to pursue a detailed examination of the intricacies of each particular transfer system. All systems are underpinned by a refusal to accept that the expiry of a football player's employment contract should allow the player to go into the (labour) marketplace and conclude a new contract with another employer. A 'selling' club will not release the player's registration until satisfied with the terms offered by the 'buying' club, which typically involves payment of a transfer fee by buying club to selling club. No club will conceivably seek to conclude a contract with a player until such time as it has been able to satisfy itself that the registration will be released to it and that it will be permitted to field the player in official matches. It is this restraint on contractual freedom, characteristic of all national regimes, which is condemned by the Court's ruling.

The Court's focus on the perception that the transfer system inhibits player acquisition allowed it to take no account of the submissions in *Bosman* that the transfer system had recently been relaxed. The point that the transfer system in Europe had been widely adjusted to allow a fee to be fixed according to a defined formula based on age and previous salary without affecting the player's right to choose between clubs once the existing employment contract comes to an end was of no significance. This liberalized system may diminish the risk of a player being caught between two haggling clubs, but it in no way removes the basic feature to which the Court objects – that the buying club is deterred by the collectively agreed system of sanctions backing the player registration scheme from contracting with a player and that this therefore distorts players' opportunities for finding employment.[248] So, although there was some feeling in advance of the Court's ruling that it might choose to limit its ruling to the peculiarly restrictive Belgian transfer system of which Bosman had fallen foul, the Court instead adopted an approach that is in principle capable of application to any system under which the employee's freedom to sell labour on the expiry of a contract is restricted by collective arrangements between employers. This secures the wider importance of the ruling beyond football.

B. Players still under Contract

The explicit terms of the ruling in *Bosman* are focused solely on the situation arising at the end of a player's contract, when contractual freedom is subject to constraint exercised through the registration system. However, given that the essential feature to which the Court objected was the deterrence to acquisition and hence to player mobility caused by the collectively agreed and enforced player registration scheme, it is arguable that there is equally a violation of the player's Article 48 rights where the industry maintains systems designed to deter conclusion of a new contract even before an existing contract has expired. Where a player chooses to break a contract with club *a* in state *x* and signs to play for club *b* in state *y*, the current rules would dictate that club *b*, would be subject to penalties were it to attempt to field the player

248 Paras. 75, 101.

without satisfying club *a*, the holder of the registration. This collectively-enforced sanction, it is submitted, amounts to a deterrence to player mobility and constitutes as much a breach of Article 48 as the pattern of post-contractual restraint at stake in *Bosman* itself. It is therefore submitted that the impact of the *Bosman* ruling cannot be confined to the post-contractual situation in which Bosman found himself.

This appears to mean that the consequences of player mobility during the term of a contract would fall for determination solely in the light of relevant rules of private law. Plainly, a player (and perhaps the acquiring club) could be liable in private law in consequence on the contractual breach, in accordance with relevant provisions of national law (potentially with associated complications of private international law). The consequence of a finding that Article 48 precludes the industry from exercising control over player mobility both during and on the expiry of a player's contract of employment is that clubs can no longer rely on the transfer system to retain players or to extract a fee for them, but that instead they will have to turn to the private law to protect their commercial interests, by drafting appropriately worded contracts, in this, football clubs will be forced to negotiate terms with their employees in the same way as other employers. So, for example, one would assume that for marketable players with leading clubs the consequence will be that higher wages will be on offer, because money that previously circulated between clubs by way of transfer fee will now be released into the pot available for attracting employees.[249]

Clubs will be tempted to draft appropriate clauses in the employment contract which will allow the first club to secure compensation for its loss and/or which will induce players to stay with the club. The first category might include a clause in the contract requiring a player leaving before the expiry of a contract to repay sums spent on training,[250] although one would have to consider carefully the level at which such a sum could be fixed in order to ensure its enforceability at law. In English law, for example, in so far as a clause represents a genuine pre-estimate of the innocent party's likely losses (hard though they would be to quantify in such circumstances), rather than a means of terrorizing the other party into compliance and unconnected with actual loss, it would be enforceable. Under English contract law, at least, it would not be possible to re-introduce the vast transfer fees paid in the past under the guise of contractual terms, in the second category could be inducements to a player to stay by structuring the contract remuneration towards loyalty-payments falling due in the later stages of the contract's duration, including, perhaps, to options to re-sign. More generally, although there is an attraction to clubs to place younger players on long contracts at low wages, such strategies would require scrutiny against national standards of legal protection of employees, which, with regard to the risk of exploitation in a situation of imbalanced economic power, typically do not simply leave such matters entirely to private negotiation. Moreover, from a commercial perspective, acquiring players on longer contracts will be dangerous to the club's financial stability where those players fail to live up to expectations.

---

[249] In all instances, if clubs were to act together in drafting contracts they would be vulnerable to findings of violation of the Treaty competition rules; see further below.

[250] In practice, these might be paid directly or indirectly by an eager buyer.

C. Adjustments in the Game

It is plain that the climate of contract negotiation has been fundamentally altered by *Bosman.* Most obviously, a greater proportion of the money made by the industry will be diverted towards players' wages than has previously occurred. Even in advance of *Bosman* some players had been able to negotiate for themselves contracts which stipulated a maximum fee payable on transfer, in order to ensure that sums above that level, which would otherwise have formed part of the fee paid between the clubs, could remain available for salary negotiation. Such clauses were typically the preserve of the very best players, who were in a strong bargaining position as a result of their ability and who were able to extract unusually favourable terms from their own employers. *Bosman* greatly enhances the opportunities of players generally to claim a share of money that would previously simply have circulated between the clubs. This occurs at a time when the industry's money-making potential is higher than it has ever been, principally as a result of intensification of competition in the broadcasting market.

It is reported, for example, that Barcelona, one of Europe's richest and most successful clubs, have responded to the changes wrought by the Court's ruling by restructuring their employment practice post-*Bosman* in the direction of longer contracts for their players.[251] The wage bill at Tottenham Hotspur, one of the leading clubs in England, rose by 20 per cent to £ 10 million a year as a result of re-negotiation of contracts after the ruling.[252] Another leading English club, Manchester United, underwent an increase in its wage bill of £ 5 million as a result of new *longer-term* deals with players, which were struck in consequence on the ruling in *Bosman.*[253] This was in the context of a profit (excluding transfer fees) of £ 16.7 million made by Manchester United for the year ending in July 1996. These adjustments to the nature of the relationship between players and clubs have in turn forced alteration in the extent to which players can be treated as club assets for accountancy purposes.[254]

Simply extending players' contracts will not inevitably allow their retention, or their disposal only on payment of a transfer fee by the buyer, if the above submission that even industry restrictions on mobility of players under *existing* contracts violate Article 48 is well-founded. Nevertheless, as discussed above, clubs' may be able to protect themselves adequately through drafting appropriate clauses in such contracts. Moreover, commercial advantages may accrue from breeding employee loyalty. This process might incidentally provide football managers with greater security of tenure, for it will be harder (or at least more expensive) for a new broom to sweep clean where existing players are on long contracts.

Nevertheless, it seems that clubs have been engaged in a process of placing players on longer contracts in the expectation that the *Bosman* ruling has an impact only at the

---

251 *The Independent*, 28 September 1996, at 24. Two newly acquired players, Ronaldo, a Brazilian, and Baia, a Portuguese national, 'have signed for eight years'.

252 *The Independent*, 11 October 1996, at 22.

253 *The Independent*, 9 October 1996, at 22.

254 Cf. Morris, Morrow and Spink, 'EC Law and Professional Football: *Bosman* and its Implications', 59 *MLR* (1996) 893.

expiry of a contract and that in the meantime players cannot move without conforming with the requirements of the game's transfer system. Moreover, purchasing activities have continued on that same assumption that a player cannot move clubs while the contract remains in force unless a fee is paid to the satisfaction of the player's current club, indeed, the world record for a transfer fee was broken in the summer of 1996, some seven months after *Bosman*, when Newcastle United paid Blackburn Rovers £ 15 million to secure the services of Alan Shearer, the highest goalscorer in the European Championship tournament held in England in June 1996, who was under contract to Blackburn Rovers.[255] Several other expensive fees were also paid over the course of that summer. *Bosman*, it seems, is being read only according to its explicit terms. It seems plausible that the unwillingness of the clubs to seek to exploit the wider possibilities of the *Bosman* ruling is yet further testimony to the practical incentives to play within the rules of the football industry even where they may seem open in theory to legal challenge. For the time being, transfer fees for players in contract remain the norm, despite the apparent vulnerability of such a system to challenge based on Article 48.

VI. The Scope of the Law of Free Movement

The transfer system exerted a restrictive effect over the exercise of economic freedom. However, that is not of itself sufficient to bring a matter within the scope of application of Community law. In November 1993, the Court signalled a change in its approach to the deployment of Community trade law in circumstances where it perceives that the restriction on commercial freedom lacks an adequate inter-State element. In *Keck and Mithouard*, a case arising under Article 30,[256] the Court decided that French rules forbidding resale at a loss restricted commercial freedom, but that they did not exert the impact on cross-border trade required to allow a trader to invoke Article 30. This ruling was plainly part of a strategy designed to cut short ambitious attempts by traders, inspired in part by the Court's own jurisprudence,[257] to use EC trade law to impugn local regulatory choices unassociated with the imperatives of market integration and untainted by discrimination. The Court rejected Article 30 as a means of general supervision of restrictions on individual traders' commercial freedom. This respect for local regulatory choices is also apparent in rulings delivered in the same month as *Keck* in which the Court curtailed the capacity of Article 5 read with the competition rules to control State market regulation.[258] The Court declined to employ the competition rules in the light of a broad *effet utile* of securing undistorted competition.

---

[255] The situation was also distinct from *Bosman* in that it was 'purely internal', i.e. a British national not engaged in cross-border economic activity; see further below.

[256] Joined Cases C-267/91 and C-268/91, [1993] *ECR* I-6097.

[257] For a notorious overstretching of the reach of Article 30, see Case 45/88, *Torfaen Borough Council* v. *B & Q plc*, [1989] *ECR* 765, Case C-169/91, *Stoke-on-Trent and Norwich City Councils* v. *B & Q plc*, [1992] *ECR* I-6635.

[258] Case C-2/91, *Meng*, [1993] *ECR* I-5751; Case C-185/91, *Reiff*, [1993] *ECR* I-5801 and Case C-245/91, *Ohra*, [1993] *ECR* I-5851, judgments of 17 November 1993.

The ruling in *Bosman* is significant for the light it sheds on the nature of the change of direction piloted by the Court. For in *Bosman* the transfer system plainly imposed restrictions on the mobility of labour and, in the case itself, the problem arose in the context of a cross-border transfer. But the cross-border aspect was purely incidental. It would be imprecise to state that footballers were subject to exactly the same restrictions whether they wished to move between clubs within a single association or between clubs belonging to different associations, but such differences as did prevail formed no part of the Court's reasoning.[259] Restrictions of the same general type would have confronted Bosman had he wished to complete a transfer from RC Liège to another club in Belgium. In fact, Bosman's problem could compellingly be characterized as a problem of inhibited access to an employment market where the cross-border aspect was entirely incidental and of no material significance. That is, the problem he encountered was that the rules *existed*, not that they existed *in a particular Member State.* Given the equally restrictive effect felt by all footballers, one might question whether the problem called for resolution under the provisions on free movement at all. In so far as the problem arose because of private agreements within the game which distorted trade patterns without any taint of nationality discrimination, the correct basis for analysis might be thought to have been Article 85 EC. Nevertheless, despite the equal application of the rules in law and in fact to all players irrespective of origin or destination, the Court examined the matter with reference to Article 48. Indeed, its examination was conducted *solely* with reference to Article 48.

Brief comment only can be offered in the context of this paper, but it is relevant to explain how the Court came to the conclusion that the transfer rules should not be treated in an analogous fashion to the rules at stake in *Keck.* The Court determined that the transfer system represented an obstacle to free movement, the fundamental Treaty right involving a pattern of rights to enter and reside in another Member State and there to pursue an economic activity. The Court commented that rights of free movement would be rendered 'meaningless'[260] if the State of origin could prohibit the departure of an individual wishing to move to another State to pursue economic activity. The Court placed Article 48 alongside Article 52, referring to *R* v. *HM Treasury and Commissioners of Inland Revenue ex parte Daily Mail and General Trust.*[261] The Court's approach focuses on the direct impediment to market access which was suffered by Bosman as a trigger to the application of Community law of free movement. The equality in legal and factual application of the rules was insufficient to take them beyond the reach of Article 48.

The Court therefore decided that the factual circumstances in *Bosman* were simply different from those which arose in *Keck. Keck* was a case where the Court's insistence that Article 30 does not catch

259 A-G Lenz discusses possible discriminatory aspects, but he too prefers to rest his analysts on a wider treatment of Article 48 as a control over all restrictions on free movement, not simply a prohibition on nationality discrimination.

260 Para. 97.

261 Case 81/87, [1988] *ECR* 5483.

> 'the application to products from other Member States of national provisions restricting or prohibiting certain selling arrangements [...] provided that those provisions apply to all affected traders operating within the national territory and provided that they affect in the same manner, in law and in fact, the marketing of domestic products and of those from other Member States'[262]

was entirely comprehensible, in the sense that the rule *in the case* applied equally in law and in fact and exerted no impact antagonistic to the cause of completing the internal market. However, it seems that in recent rulings, of which *Bosman* is one, the Court has moved towards a rejection of a reading of *Keck* which limits examination of the challenged rules to the formal question of their equality of legal and factual application. Instead, the Court seems prepared to acknowledge that even factual and legal equality in application is insufficient to place a measure beyond the reach of the law of free movement where an impediment to direct access to the market of another Member State is shown (whereupon the regulator must show a justification recognized by Community law). In elaborating this post-*Keck* trend, the Court appears to be taking heed of the admonition of Advocate-General Jacobs in, *inter alia*, *Société d importation Edouard Leclerc-Siplec* v. *TFI Publicité SA and M6 Publicité SA*[263] that the test of equality of application is out of line with the objectives of the Treaty, principally the quest to establish a single market. Mr Jacobs commented: 'if an obstacle to inter-State trade exists, it cannot cease to exist simply because an identical obstacle affects domestic trade'. He felt that the appropriate test should be whether a measure exerts a substantial restriction on access to a part of the Community market.

In establishing a thematic linkage between the Treaty Articles on free movement and the cause of establishing and maintaining an internal market, allied to suspicion of the formalist character of the *Keck* ruling, *Bosman*, though distinct from *Keck*, has much in common with *Alpine Investments* v. *Minister van Financiën*,[264] a case arising under Article *59. Alpine investments* concerned Dutch rules placing a restriction on the practice of 'cold calling' potential consumers of financial services. The rule applied to all providers of services established in the Netherlands and restricted the opportunity to solicit business from customers both in the Netherlands and beyond its borders. In his Opinion in *Alpine Investments*, Mr Jacobs took the view that the question whether a rule restricts trade for the purposes of Article 59 'should be determined by reference to a functional criterion, that is to say, whether it substantially impedes the ability of persons established in its territory to provide intra-Community services.' This, he submitted, conformed to the notion of realizing the internal market more harmoniously than an approach based on discrimination. He thought the situation in *Alpine In vestments* involved a restriction within the scope of application of Community law, but he was receptive to justification. The Court declared that

262 Para. 16 of the ruling in *Keck*.

263 Case C-412/93, [1995] *ECR* I-179.

264 Case C-384/93, [1995] *ECR* I-1141.

> 'such a prohibition deprives the operators concerned of a rapid and direct technique for marketing and for contacting potential clients in other Member States. It can therefore constitute a restriction on the freedom to provide cross-border services'.

It neglected to observe that such restrictions were equally felt by domestic operators. The prohibition, the Court continued, is not analogous to the legislation at stake in *Keck.* Although the rule in *Alpine Investments* affected both domestic offers and offers made to potential recipients in another State, the Court found that it 'directly affects access to the market in services in the other Member States and is thus capable of hindering intra-Community trade in services'.[265] Nevertheless the Court found the rule justified. It would not accept that the Netherlands could claim jurisdiction to protect consumers in other States, even though it was forced to concede that a home State regulator is much better placed to achieve supervision than a target State regulator. But, viewing the Dutch rules from a different perspective in order to avoid treating them as extraterritorial in effect, it found that the protection of the reputation of Dutch firms in the sector could count as a justification for the rules.

In conclusion, it is submitted that although *Keck* was on its facts correctly treated as a case lying beyond the proper reach of the law of free movement, the ruling provides a perilous basis for a more broadly applicable principle, for it takes insufficient account of the dynamic process of opening up markets previously fragmented along national lines. *Bosman* stands with cases such as *Alpine Investments* in demonstrating adjustment towards a functional test, which takes account not only of factual and legal inequality of application as a basis for triggering the law of free movement but also of the imposition of a direct or substantial hindrance to the access of imported goods or services to the market of the regulating Member State as a sufficient, separate trigger for a measure to fall within the scope of application of Articles 30 and 59. The Court in *Bosman* asserted that the rules 'directly affect players' access to the employment market in other Member States and are thus capable of impeding freedom of movement of workers'. It will be observed that this formulation evades the point that 'direct' impediment to market access was also felt by those wishing to obtain access to the employment market in their home States.

Taken on to a still broader plane, *Bosman's* status as a judgment of general importance in the development of EC trade law is assured because of the Court's transparent concern to establish coherent principles which link the several Treaty provisions that constitute the law governing the creation and maintenance of the internal market.[266] The above discussion of *Bosman* locates that process of legal development in the context of fixing the threshold of application of the law of free movement. The *Bosman* ruling also reveals the same concern to create a common stream of free movement law, within which all relevant Treaty provisions flow, at the level of justification of national rules according to standards recognized by Community law. This is examined in the next section.

[265] Cf. the analysis of *Keck* provided by A-G Van Gerven in joined Cases C-69/93 and C-258/93, *Punto Casa SpA* v. *Sindaco del Comune di Capena et al.*, [1994] *ECR* I-2355.

[266] Nevertheless, the intrusion of Article 48 into the private sphere, discussed in Part III.B above, interrupts this process.

VII. Justification

A. Law

The Court stated that the industry's rules obstructed trade contrary to Article 48 EC subject only to the possibility of justification where the rules pursued a legitimate aim compatible with the Treaty and justified by 'pressing reasons of public interest', subject to conformity with the proportionality principle.[267] The assertion of this test of justification confirms the location of the ruling in *Bosman* in the category of those delivered by the Court which exerts general significance in the evolution of Community trade law. The Court, having drawn together the several Treaty provisions concerning free movement at the level of identification of trade restriction, also engaged on a process of drawing together those Treaty provisions at the level of available justification. *Bosman* stands alongside recent rulings such as *Dieter Kraus* v. *Land Baden-Württemberg*[268] and *Gebhard* v. *Consiglio dell'Ordine degli Avvocati e Procuratori di Milano*[269] as part of a process of extrapolating principles that are commonly identified as originating in a developed form in the famous *Cassis de Dijon* ruling[270] under Article 30 across the several Treaty provisions concerned with free movement. This points in the direction of the development of general principles of Community law governing the lawfulness of national measures that restrict the exercise of fundamental Treaty provisions. Non-discriminatory national measures that cross the threshold of a sufficient restriction on market access are compatible with EC law only provided that they are justified by mandatory requirements in the general interest; that they are apt to achieve the attainment of the objective which they pursue; and that they do not go beyond what is necessary in order to attain it.

B. Application to Football

The football industry has consistently sought to justify the transfer system on the basis that the restrictions on individual freedom are necessary to underpin the collective strength of the industry. The transfer system has been defended as a basis for the redistribution of income within the game. Smaller clubs are able to breed new talent and to earn money by selling players to bigger clubs. The transfer system is thus a source of income for clubs unable to survive merely by selling a product – the match – to their customers. This critical source of income would dry up were the transfer system to be abolished, allowing players to move freely between clubs on expiry of their contract (or perhaps even before that; Part V.B above). The loss of transfer revenue would remove the incentive for clubs to nurture young talent, thereby weakening the

---

[267] Para. 104.

[268] Case C-19/92, [1993] *ECR* I-1663.

[269] Case C-55/94, judgment of 30 November 1995, not yet reported.

[270] Case 120/78, *Rewe Zentrale* v. *Bundesmonopolverwaltung für Branntwein*, [1979] *ECR* 649. Earlier, less sophisticated traces of this test of justification may be identified in the rule of reason' in Case 8/74, *Procureur du Roi* v. *Dassonville*, [1974] *ECR* 837.

game's future health, and it would ultimately drive smaller clubs out of the professional game, thereby weakening its competitive structure and reducing the attraction of the product to the fan. In this sense the transfer system is designed to preserve a level of financial and competitive balance between clubs. UEFA attempted to present evidence of the economic impact of the transfer system to the European Court and in November 1995 UEFA asked the Court that an inquiry be launched to obtain fuller information on the role played by transfer fees in financing small or medium sized football clubs, evidencing a desire to show how income redistribution within the game was based on the transfer system. The request was rejected on procedural grounds, having been made when the oral procedure was closed and in the absence of any special circumstances applied.

The Court was prepared to accept that the football industry's arguments were in principle of significance.

> 'In view of the considerable social importance of sporting activities and in particular football in the Community, the aims of maintaining a balance between clubs by preserving a certain degree of equality and uncertainty as to results and of encouraging the recruitment and training of young players must be accepted as legitimate.'[271]

However, it is well established in EC trade law that both the ends pursued and the means employed by a restrictive measure must be justified. The Court regarded the means employed in the current football industry as inapt to achieve ends which might be capable of justification in principle. The Court did not consider that the transfer system acted as an adequate method of maintaining balance. The rules neither precluded richer clubs buying the best players nor prevented the 'availability of financial resources from being a decisive factor in competitive sport thus considerably altering the balance between clubs'. The Court agreed that a transfer fee system might act as an incentive to clubs to recruit and train new and young players, but it observed that because only a handful of young players will repay the investment by making the professional grade, it is impossible to predict the fees that will be obtained. In any event such fees will be unrelated to the actual cost of training all players. The current system is hit-and-miss, rather than a carefully constructed distributive mechanism. The Court concluded that 'the same aims can be achieved at least as efficiently by other means which do not impede freedom of movement for workers'.[272]

C. **Adjusting Football**

The Court's robust approach makes plain the need for radical change within the game if the alleged beneficial objectives of wealth distribution and nurture of young talent are to be secured through collective action, rather than simply left to market solutions. On the other hand, the Court has certainly left open the possibility that solutions could be put in place in the football industry which might not be tolerated elsewhere. The

[271] Para. 106.
[272] Para. 120.

Court was explicit in its view that football (and similarly structured team sports generally) possesses distinctive features which are not found in a normal manufacturing or service industry. In *Bosman* the Court's construction of a general test of justification in law occurs alongside its willingness to allow room for manoeuvre by a particular, unusual industry within the practical application of that test.

Since the Court accepted that 'the aims of maintaining a balance between clubs by preserving a certain degree of equality and uncertainty as to results and of encouraging the recruitment and training of young players must be accepted as legitimate',[273] but found that the current system, involving restrictions on player mobility, was inapt to achieve those permitted ends. It is now open to the football industry to devise alternative arrangements. It seems plain that a system of wealth distribution and support for youth training based on other instruments than those currently used via the transfer system may be permissible in the football industry. It is simply a question of finding means to the stated ends that are apt and proportionate and that are not incompatible with Article 48 or other provisions of EC law, especially Articles 85 and 86.

D. Fostering Competitive Equality

The European Court, in concluding that 'the same aims can be achieved at least as efficiently by other means which do not impede freedom of movement for workers',[274] referred to its Advocate-General for discussion of other means that may be available to the industry. Mr Lenz accepted that a system stopping rich clubs becoming ever richer and poor ever poorer could be justified. A viable professional league requires no glaring imbalance between the teams participating. This is a reason in the general interest which may justify the imposition of restrictions on free competition. Mr Lenz mentioned two particular alternative methods for preserving the financial and sporting balance between clubs that is vital to a healthy professional sports League.
First:

> 'it would be possible to determine by a collective wage agreement specified limits for the salaries to be paid to the players by the clubs'.

Shaping a *modus vivendi* for labour law and competition law is fiendishly complex. This is apparent from North American experience,[275] and although a small number of decisions of the European Court display a readiness to subject labour practices

---

[273] Para. 106.

[274] Para. 110.

[275] Cf. the June 1996 decision of the Supreme Court in *Brown* v. *Pro Football* 116 Sup Ct 2116, 135 L. Ed. 2d 521, in which the National Football League's fixing of salaries for players in a 'development squad' was ruled immune from antitrust liability. Analysis was devoted to the potential damage to industrial relations that could be wrought by allowing free rein to antitrust law, although the case arose in the context of salary fixing in response to an impasse reached in the collective bargaining process and Breyer J observed that the decision 'is not intended to insulate from antitrust review every joint imposition of terms by employers.'

introduced by public authorities to the control of the EC competition rules,[276] the application of Article 85 to private labour agreements would be complex. It is generally supposed that a collective agreement struck between both sides of industry would probably escape Article 85, for in circumstances concerning the structuring of industrial relations the parties would not be operating as 'undertakings' within Article 85(1), although the point cannot be regarded as definitively settled.[277] By contrast, a horizontal arrangement between employers would seem capable of falling within Article 85. It is possible that an agreed salary cap could be regarded as necessary to secure the (unusual) competitive structure of the industry and therefore untouched by Article 85(1), but it is more probable that the agreement would fall within Article 85(1) and therefore require exemption under Article 85(3). However, it is submitted that the legal and economic complexity that pervades this area serves as a deterrent to private arrangements such as collectively agreed 'salary caps'. Mr Lenz implies that he regards this route as thoroughly unappealing, for he spends little time in his Opinion in exploring it. It is plain that Mr Lenz regards his second proposed method as the more viable of his proposals. He stated:

> 'it would be conceivable to distribute the clubs' receipts among the clubs. Specifically, that means that part of the income obtained by a club from the sale of tickets for its home matches is distributed to the other clubs. Similarly, the income received for awarding the rights to transmit matches on television, for instance, could be divided up between all the clubs.'

As the Advocate-General asserted, 'each club needs the other one in order to successful'. The clubs in a professional league do not have the aim of driving their competitors from the market. Rivals are also partners. Professional sport is distinct from most industries because participants have incentives to share income out between themselves in order to maintain a balance within the league which is essential to its economic success.

Mr Lenz explained the availability of other means for achieving the objectives of the system – as defined by the football industry – as part of his unwillingness to find the current system capable of justification according to the standards of Community law. He has left open the possibility of justifying special, but adjusted, arrangements to reflect the unusual competitive relationship that prevails between football clubs. As Mr Lenz perceives, clubs have an economic incentive to avoid pure market-based solutions and instead to ensure that weaker clubs are sustained at a competitive level. It is now for the clubs within the industry to choose whether to put in place rational models of wealth distribution appropriate to their industry, relating to, for example, ticket receipts, sponsorship and television income, in fact, Mr Lenz mentions some existing patterns of distribution throughout the game of proceeds from the 'Cham-

---

[276] E.g., Case C-41/90, *Höfner* v. *Macrotron*, [1991] *ECR* I-1979; Case C-179/90, *Porto di Genova*, [1991] *ECR* I-5889.

[277] In favour of the inapplicability of Art. 85, see, e.g., R. Whish, *Competition Law* (1993) 187-90; V. Rose, ed., *Bellamy and Child's Common Markt: Law of Competition* (1993) 2.006. 2.007. 2.055. In Para. 274 of his Opinion, A-G Lenz also makes such a suggestion.

pions League', the most lucrative club tournament in Europe. At international level, the £ 47 million of the £ 69 million profit made on the European Championships 1996 (mentioned in the Introduction to this piece) was shared among the 16 countries which qualified for and participated in the Finals, but the remaining £ 22 million was allocated to a special UEFA fund for developing the game in the emerging nations of Central and Eastern Europe.

As European football contemplates the choices available to it in developing a strategy for wealth distribution as a means of securing competitive equality attractive to consumers, there is a fund of North American experience on which to draw. For example, the 'player draft', in essence, allows teams to pick graduating college (American) football players according to a hierarchy which is in inverse order to their on-pitch record during the preceding season. Major League Soccer', newly established in North America in 1996, is based on a comparable system that will allow weaker teams privileged access to leading college players, as a means for maintaining an adequate level of competitive equality between teams.

A direct transplant is improbable. These systems go far beyond anything envisaged in European football. Football in Europe does not enjoy the luxury of starting from scratch and such intense manipulation of the market is unlikely to find favour. In any event, the enforceability at law of such systems would be problematic. In North America, there has been judicial discussion of the draft's anticompetitive impact on the market for players' services weighed against its pro-competitive contribution to securing equality on the pitch.[278] Comparable problems would arise in Europe, although as is well known direct legal analogies are unwise given the different structure of the Sherman Act compared with Article 85 EC[279] and, moreover, any 'player draft' system would require scrutiny for compatibility with Article 48.

The structuring of an appropriate system of wealth distribution at national and international level involves a fascinating balance between the need for competition and the need for mutual support. An over-intrusive system reduces the pain of failure and undermines the will to succeed, but an unduly ungenerous system of distribution creates a risk that weaker participants will lose credibility with consumers. Ina study published in 1986, cited by Advocate-General Lenz in his Opinion in *Bosman*, Cairns, Jennett and Sloane expressed the view that prevailing arrangements for revenue sharing may be sub-optimal. They concluded that

> 'Conservatism and resistance to change have been evident both in North America and Europe, but the costs of such behaviour are probably greater in the latter case, where market conditions appear to be less favourable. Certainly, there is a whole range of issues to which sporting leagues need to give greater attention than in the past if they are to remain viable in an increasingly competitive leisure market.'[280]

---

278 E.g., *Smith* v. *Pro Football Inc*, 593 F.2d 1173 (1978), concerning the National Football League.

279 Cf., e.g., T. Frazer, *Monopoly, Competition and the Law* (1992).

280 Cairns, Jennett and Sloane, 'The Economics of Professional Team Sports: A Survey of Theory and Evidence', 13 *Journal of Economic Studies* (1986) 3, 71.

In the wake of *Bosman*, there is a clear need to revive discussion of appropriate models for professional sports leagues in Europe.[281] Cairns, Jennett and Sloane's (not uncontroversial) location of football in a leisure market than is wider than sport alone might lead one to anticipate that the incentives to eliminate sub-optimal arrangements would be rather strong. However, it seems probable that the extraordinary rise in income from the broadcasting market lately enjoyed by football, which is likely to be taken on to a new plane by technological advance in the area of 'pay-per-view' television, will reduce the industry's incentives to tackle any underlying inefficiencies.

In choosing the correct allocation of such incentives the industry, post-*Bosman*, is left to its own processes of internal regulation. The Court, and especially its Advocate-General, have limited their work in *Bosman* to ruling the current system unlawful – and to hinting at possible lawful routes to adjusting the industry's structure. The industry violates EC law by forcing players to bear the brunt of achieving the alleged objective of competitive equality between clubs through the haphazard trickle-down of wealth *via* the transfer system, but Community law does not in principle rule out wealth distribution between participants in sporting competition. Clubs may seek shelter from purely market-based solutions, subject to conformity with Article 85.[282]

E. **Encouraging Young Players**

The second justification for regulation of the industry which the Court accepted as permissible in principle was the need to encourage the recruitment of young players. Advocate-General Lenz suggested that *appropriate* transfer rules might be acceptable if based genuinely on costs of training. But, finding the present system irredeemably in violation of Article 48, he felt it unnecessary to explore the matter more fully. He commented that any system would have to cover costs incurred in training by the selling club. He expressed the view that this should only be the first club, which conforms to the pattern in France, where liberalization of the transfer system has progressed more rapidly than elsewhere. Nevertheless, this seems an irrational limitation, for it is not only the player's first club that may spend money in improving a player's capabilities. It is submitted that an adjusted system ought to take account of the costs actually incurred by the selling club, irrespective of its place in the player's career development. However, the essential point of the analysis offered by Advocate-General Lenz is that possible routes to achieving a restructured system that encourages the development of new talent are not foreclosed to the industry by EC law. Any fee must be

---

[281] Cf. Fort and Quirk, Cross-subsidisation: Incentives and Outcomes in Professional Team Sports Leagues', XXXIII *Journal of Economic Literature* (1995) 1265; Vrooman, 'A General Theory of Professional Sports Leagues', 61 *Southern Economic Journal* (1995) 971.

[282] Probably any such arrangements would have to be notified to the Commission in pursuit of exemption according to Art. 85(3), although it might be possible to view the arrangements as simply an indispensable element in the operation of the industry, reflecting the unusual interdependence of clubs, and therefore falling outwith Art. 85 entirely and not requiring notification (perilous though such an approach might prove in practice, for, if flawed, there would be no exemption and no immunity from fines). In any event A-G Lenz is firmly of the view that nothing in Art. 85 can detract from a breach of Art. 48; so grant of exemption under Art. 85(1) could not cure violation of Art. 48.

explicitly planned as compensation and not used to preclude the player's free choice, although it appears that the Court's shaping of Article 48 might allow justification of a renovated system even if it exerts an incidental impact on player mobility.

One way forward might involve some pooling of resources by clubs in the development of young talent, through a common, central fund built up through levies on all clubs and used to defray expenditure incurred by clubs shown to be successful 'breeders'. For example, levels of payment could be graded according to each year that a player has spent within the training system offered by the 'selling' club. The windfall profits that may accrue under the current system would be an available, but a successful nursery club might be in a position to enjoy a reliable and predictable source of income through a collectively agreed system of support. Such a system, unconnected with any restriction on players' contractual freedom, would seem a more sophisticated and reliable method than the transfer system for sustaining and improving the quality of youth training within the industry. Such change would involve a significant adjustment in the structure of the game, in particular in relation to the financial planning of smaller clubs. Smaller clubs may become part of a system where they are dependent on income from a central pool to which more successful clubs contribute; or perhaps they may become 'feeder' clubs for particular leading clubs. This may even form part of the institution of a 'player draft' system on the North American model, although it has already been suggested above that this may be culturally incapable of adaptation to European football. These are potential solutions to be considered within the industry itself, as clubs debate the economic rationales for mutual support. Naturally, the Treaty competition rules would have to be respected, although the special interests of organized sport would form part of the legal assessment.

VIII. A Transfer System within a Domestic League

A. **Reverse Discrimination**

The *Bosman* ruling was concerned with the application of Article 48 to a cross-border transfer. Nothing in the explicit terms of the ruling suggests that a purely domestic transfer would be subject to challenge derived from Community law and some national associations have asserted the continuing viability and, indeed, desirability of sustaining domestic transfer rules. Nevertheless, it seems improbable that any renovation of the system can be confined to the transnational system and it will instead have to involve a complete restructuring of the European, transnational and national system.

As a matter of Community law, it seems consistent with the Court's approach to assume that Article 48 would not avail a national of State A wishing to move between clubs in State A. Reverse discrimination by a State against its own nationals of this type has been regarded as lying beyond the scope of application of Community law. The Court in *Bosman* cited well-established case-law on the point.[283] However, a na-

[283] Para. 89, e.g., Case 175/78, *R* v. *Saunders*, [1979] *ECR* 1129.

tional of State A returning from another Member State after pursuit of activity falling within the scope of Community law is *not* necessarily in a purely internal situation and may be able to assert EC law rights against State A[284] and there would arise some marginal definitional problems in determining when a transfer of a national of State A from a club in State A to another club in State A via a club in State B would be a true cross-border transaction attracting a right to a fee-free transfer and when such a deal would be a sham, incapable of triggering protection under Community law.[285] On the other hand, the Court's refusal to sanction challenges to domestic rules by 'sham' migrants might not extend to a situation where the domestic rules in question, the transfer system, are not a comprehensive regulatory regime, but merely the tattered and anomalous remnants of a discredited system. But, notwithstanding the existence of such grey areas of economic activity, in principle purely national deals would remain unaffected by Article 48 as interpreted in *Bosman.* This, then, is a further reason, apart from the fact that the player was not out-of-contract (above, Part V.C), why the record-breaking £ 15 million transfer of Alan Shearer in summer 1996 was concluded in spite of *Bosman.*

B. Economic Pressures

The place of 'reverse discrimination' beyond the scope of application of the provisions on free movement will inject a peculiar distortion into the market. Purchasing an out-of-contract player from another State will be more attractive than buying a player of the same ability from another club in the same State, because no fee will be involved. Players too will have an economic inducement to cross borders, because in such circumstances no fee will be payable and money otherwise earmarked as transfer fee will, in part at least, be available as part of their salary package (assuming a competitive market for players). The better the player and the higher the fee payable would be, the greater the inducement to shop across borders and avoid the entanglements of the transfer system. Precisely this pattern could be identified over the summer of 1996. 'Out-of-contract' players were able to secure better deals by joining clubs in other Member States and obtaining pan of what would otherwise have been invested as a transfer fee payable to their previous club. For example, John Collins, a regular choice in the Scottish national representative team, moved from his club side, Glasgow Celtic, to Monaco in summer 1996, despite interest from English sides, he commented: 'I was going to cost an English team £ 3 million whereas Monaco could get me for nothing'.[286] A transfer between Scotland and England is cross-border in football terms, but it is not cross-border in the context of EC law. Collins's case, involving a transfer from the UK to France of a player who was out of contract, was on all fours with that of Jean-Marc Bosman.

---

284 Cf. Case C-370/90, *Surinder Singh*, [1992] *ECR* I-4265; Case C-19/92, *Dieter Kraus*, [1993] *ECR* I-1663.

285 Cf. Case 39/86, *Lair* v. *University of Hanover*, [1988] *ECR* 3161; in connection with regulation of legal persons, Case C-23/93, *TV 10 SA* v. *Commissariaat voor de Media*, [1994] *ECR* I-4795. Cf., under Art. 30 EC, Case 229/83, *Leclerc* v. *Au Blé Vert*, [1985] *ECR* 1.

286 *The Independent*, 9 October 1996, at 30.

As is plain from the answers given by the European Court to the second question referred in *Bosman*, national associations may not respond to trends in favour of cross-border movement by introducing limits on the number of EU nationals who may be imported in this way. Accordingly pressure will increase on national associations to remove the anomaly by agreeing to abandon fees altogether. In the longer term one would imagine domestic fees would be depressed in such a market, imbalanced in favour of cross-border acquisition. The unimpeded availability of cross-border purchasing opportunities makes the maintenance of a domestic system peculiar, perhaps even pointless. One would therefore suppose that pressure would grow for the eventual abandonment of domestic fees (perhaps in the context of a wholesale reorganization of systems of wealth distribution in the European game), even though such a requirement does not flow from the explicit terms of the *Bosman* ruling.

C. **Legal Issues**

Reshaping may be driven by litigation, not simply market forces. For the maintenance of a domestic system will affect inter-state trade patterns within the meaning of Article 85(1). The distortive effect on the wider market of a horizontal agreement between clubs relating to player acquisition brings it within the scope of application of Article 85(1).[287] Such practices are incompatible with the pursuit of 'the creation of a single market achieving conditions similar to those of a domestic market'.[288] Although the application of the competition rules to the football industry was left unexplored by the Court in *Bosman*, the issue is potentially highly significant. Indeed, there are existing decisions subjecting football to Article 85[289] and in his Opinion in *Bosman*, Advocate-General Lenz chose to discuss the application of Articles 85 and 86 EC to football. Article 86 was not relevant on the facts of *Bosman* because any collective dominant activity related only to the relationship between players and club, which Mr Lenz regarded as falling outwith the scope of Article 86. But he did not exclude the intriguing possibility that action taken by clubs as a group, for example to market television rights, could involve a potential breach of Article 86. Although Articles 85 and 86 were left out of account by the European Court in its ruling, despite explicit reference to those Treaty provisions in the preliminary questions referred to it by the Cour d'Appel in Liège, there are fertile fields for future litigation in this sphere.

An application for exemption of the transfer rules under Article 85(3) had not been made to the Commission in the context of the *Bosman* litigation, but even were

[287] Such labour-related agreements between employers are caught by Art. 85; the difficult question of whether collective agreements between employers and employees fall within Art. 85 does not arise. Cf. Part VII.D above.

[288] Case 26/76, *Metro-SB-Grossmärkte GmbH & CO KG* v. *Commission*, [1977] *ECR* 1875. Cf. also Case 22/78, *Hugin* v, *Commission*, [1979] *ECR* 1869. cited by A-G Lenz in *Bosman*.

[289] *OJ* 1992 L 326/31, distribution of package tours for the 1990 World Cup incompatible with Article 85; cf. also no dispute on application in principle of Art. 85 in Case T-46/92, *Scottish Football Association* v. *Commission*, [1994] *ECR* II-1039.

an application for exemption made it is probable that the system would be judged disproportionately restrictive and therefore ineligible for exemption. Advocate-General Lenz in *Bosman* expressed the firm opinion that a breach of Article 48 would not be excused by an Article 85(3) exemption. He also observed that a system that is disproportionately restrictive for the purposes of Article 48 should be regarded as disproportionately restrictive for the purposes of Article 85(3).[290] In particular, it is submitted that a domestic system imposes restrictions which are not indispensable to the attainment of the objectives of the system, contrary to the conditions in Article 85(3). Analysis used under Article 48 to show the incapacity of the transfer system to achieve the objectives attributed to it by the football industry, especially in relation to the haphazard nature of the patterns of wealth distribution, would be fatal to an Article 85(3) exemption, even though Article 48 is not formally relevant in the purely internal situation. It is entirely plausible that amended patterns of collective agreement within the industry, designed to distribute wealth in order to foster competitive equality and to underpin the development of young talent, could be compatible with the competition rules, but it is for the industry to devise such arrangements and to secure the approval of the Commission.

Vulnerable though current domestic transfer systems appear to a finding of incompatibility with Article 85, it is perhaps implausible that a sufficiently motivated football club or player will be forthcoming as the test litigant before a national court. A complaint to the Commission, envisaged under Article 3(2) Regulation 17/62, cannot oblige the Commission to proceed to a decision within the meaning of Article 189 on whether or not a violation of the competition rules has occurred.[291] The Commission's past record in the area of football bears witness to an unwillingness to pursue deep inquiry. Nevertheless, an inadequately reasoned rejection of a complaint made under Article 3 of Regulation 17/62 has been treated as susceptible to annulment in Article 173 proceedings brought by a complainant.[292] It is accordingly open to a complainant to seek to prompt the Commission to inquire into the compatibility of a domestic transfer system with Article 85 and to provide reasons for not pursuing a complaint, if that is the Commission's position. The Commission has set out its own priorities in a 1993 Notice on cooperation between national courts and the Commission[293] drafted in the wake of the important ruling of the Court of First Instance in *Automec Srl* v. *Commission, 'Automec II'*.[294] The Commission, in the exercise of its administrative discretion, is permitted to prioritize cases in accordance with the *Community interest*

[290] Cf. the Commission's inexplicit hint of a parallel between the proportionality test under Art. 36 and under Art. 85(3) in relation to permissibility of restrictions on World Cup ticket distribution for reasons of public safety, *supra* note 289.

[291] Case 125/78, *GEMA* v. *Commission*, [1979] *ECR* 3173.

[292] Case T-37/92, *BEUC and NCC* v. *Commission*, [1994] *ECR* II-285. Cf. Case T-7/92, *Asia Motor France* v. *Commission*. [1993] *ECR* II-669; Case T-74/92, *Ladbroke Racing* v. *Commission*, [1995] *ECR* II-115; Case T-548/93, *Ladbroke Racing* v. *Commission*, [1995] *ECR* II-2565. Bosman's challenge to the Commission before the European Court, *supra* note 216, was *not* treated as a complaint of this type.

[293] *OJ* 1993 C 39/6.

[294] Case T-24/90 [1992] *ECR* II-2223: Case T-28/90, *Asia Motor France SA and others* v. *Commission*, [1992] *ECR* II-2285.

in their pursuit. One aspect of this assessment involves the ability of the complaint to secure protection through proceedings at national level based on the direct effect of the relevant provisions. Paragraph 18 of the 1993 Notice cites the ruling in *Automec II* and states that

> 'there is not normally a sufficient Community interest in examining a case when the plaintiff is able to secure adequate protection of his rights before the national courts'.

In the few relevant rulings thus far delivered, the Court of First Instance has found no reason to impugn the Commission's view that it need not act because adequate national procedures were available to the complainant.[295] However, it is as yet far from clear whether the Commission is obliged to consider merely the availability *in principle* of adequate protection at national level, or whether it must undertake a more *practical* inquiry into the circumstances surrounding a particular complaint.[296] A player enmeshed in the domestic transfer system might he able to demand that the Commission, in evaluating the Community interest in pursuit of the matter, look beyond the theoretical possibility of an action before national courts based on Article 85 and take account of the practical probability that the player going to law would be sacrificing a large part of a short career. A separate issue relating to administrative priorities arises from the Court of First Instance's acceptance in *BEMIM* v. *Commission*[297] that the Commission had acted properly in declining to pursue a complaint relating to practices that were essentially confined to the territory of a single Member State, France. A domestic transfer system might be regarded as so limited – yet, as shown above, its very existence stimulates cross-border activity, and, moreover, a finding that one State's system is unlawful would have wider repercussions, as it is likely that national systems, despite their differences of detail, stand or fall together in the light of Article 85. So it may plausibly be maintained that a Community interest attaches to scrutiny of a single national system.

In conclusion, the Court's comments on the Treaty competition rules in *Bosman* were extremely brief:

> 'Since both types of rule to which the national court's question refer are contrary to Article 48, it is not necessary to rule on the interpretation of Articles 85 and 86 of the Treaty.'[298]

However, those Treaty provisions may provide the legal instrument for undermining even domestic transfer systems in the EC, thereby filling the gap caused by the Court's unwillingness to extend Article 48 to purely internal situations.

---

295 In *Automec II* itself and in Case T-114/92, *BEMIM* v. *Commission*, [1995] *ECR* II-147.

296 See discussion by Shaw, 'Decentralization and Law Enforcement in EC Competition Law', 15 *Legal Studies* (1995) 128; Brent, 'The Binding of Leviathan? – the Changing Role of the European Commission in Competition Cases', 44 *ICLQ* (1995) 255.

297 Case T-114/92, *supra* note 295.

298 Para. 138.

IX. Conclusion

> 'If a player could do just as he liked at the end of the football season, the wealthier clubs would at once snap up the best players' [...]

This observation is not drawn from *Bosman.* It is the reported submission of counsel for the football club in *Eastham* v. *Newcastle United*, the famous ruling of Wilberforce J in the Chancery Division of the High Court of England and Wales which led to the loosening of the system then applicable in the English game.[299] Under the rules of the football industry at the time, a club was able to place a player previously under contract to it on a so-called 'retained' list. For the club, this was an alternative to placing the player on the transfer list. The 'retained' player was then unable to play for another club. In practice the system was used to retain a player whom the club did not really wish to keep, because by 'retaining' him, often at a reduced wage, the club could then induce another club to offer a transfer fee for the player. The club would not necessarily achieve this objective by placing the player on the transfer list, because a player who had been placed on the transfer system, as distinct from the retained list, was able to apply to the League's management committee to have the stated fee reduced or even eliminated and also enjoyed the possibility of transfer to a club outside the league without any fee being paid.

The system of retaining players, instead of placing them on the transfer list, was brutal and even the manager of Newcastle United, appearing as a witness for the club, admitted that it operated harshly from the perspective of the player. The retain-and-transfer system was condemned by Wilberforce J as a rule in breach of common law rules governing the validity of clauses in restraint of trade.[300] The judge did not regard the transfer system alone, whereby a player after the termination of his contract can move to another club provided a fee was paid, as so objectionable. The restrictive effect of the transfer system was mitigated by the ability of the player to apply to have the fee reduced or eliminated and by the possibility of transfer to a club outside the league. Wilberforce J suggested that the transfer system alone could be regarded as a method for circulating money and, indeed, players within the game, but in *Eastham* he was not asked to rule formally on its compatibility with the common law. So although the combined retain-and-transfer system was condemned as an unjustifiable restraint of trade, the door was left open to a permissible adjusted transfer system.[301] English football abandoned the particular system condemned in *Eastham*, but a periodically modified transfer system has survived free of legal challenge thereafter.[302]

---

[299] [1964] Chancery 413.

[300] *Eastham* was applied by the High Court of Australia in *Buckley* v. *Tutty* (1971) 225 *CLR* 353, in which the system of retain-and-transfer in Rugby League was held an unreason restraint of trade.

[301] For discussion of the economics of the game pre- and post-*Eastham*, see Sloane, 'The Labour Market in Professional Football', 7 *British Journal of Industrial Relations* (1969) 181.

[302] It is, of course, possible that the domestic system which, as examined above, seems immune from challenge under Art. 48 but vulnerable to challenge under Art. 85, might be found to fall foul of the common law, as it evolves, were it be attacked on that basis to-day. Its application to out-of-contract players would seem especially vulnerable. Throughout the EC, the possibility of invoking national law, in addition to EC law, as a means of challenging the transfer system cannot be neglected.

The correspondence between the submissions made by the football industry in *Eastham* and those in *Bosman* is remarkable. The plea quoted at the start of this Conclusion was, in essence, repeated by the football authorities in *Bosman*, and received the same treatment in 1995 in Luxembourg that it had received from Wilberforce .J in 1963. The submission is fundamentally flawed: the *current* systems do not stop the wealthier clubs acquiring the best players. The system does not foster competitive equality.

Bosman is the latest stage in the process of forcing the football industry to respond to the perceived risk of undue domination by wealthy clubs by assessing the economic imperatives within the game and responding in a manner that does not burden the contractual freedom of players. Already in *Eastham* Wilberforce J considered explicitly the possibility of placing players on longer contracts, with staggered expiry dates so that a nucleus of key players remained available at the start of a new season. It is implicit in *Bosman* that such protection for individual clubs is available through contract negotiation – as in any other labour market. Naturally, the contractual negotiation process will be vastly altered, because clubs have now lost a major trump card in consequence on the demise of the transfer system and money is freed for circulation to players, not between clubs. More generally, at the collective level, agreed wealth distribution within the game remains plausible – but it is for the game to decide. Intriguingly *Eastham* was decided in 1963 at a time when the English game had just abandoned a maximum wage for players, and it is improbable that Advocate-General Lenz's suggestion in *Bosman* of a return to that device will be followed. But more attention is likely to be devoted to other forms of income sharing.

Eastham also corresponds to *Bosman* in the prophecies of doom emitting from the football industry. According to Wilberforce J:

> 'Hardaker [secretary of the English Football League], indeed, went further and said that if there were no retention system there would be complete anarchy in all world football, and the football-watching public in some parts of the country and in some parts of the world would quickly find themselves without a football club to watch.'[303]

The judge found this contention neither proved nor even plausible.

Hardaker's comments have been echoed by many sources within the game since *Bosman.* It is submitted that such criticism of *Bosman* is misplaced.

Football must change, but its special concerns have been accepted by the European Court and can be accommodated within the application of relevant Treaty provisions.

The possibility of a Treaty amendment to reflect the special status of sport bas been mooted. It is not implausible that a supportive Title in the Treaty comparable to that on Culture[304] could be devised to reflect the interest in sport throughout the Community,[305] but one could hardly envisage a broad exemption of sport from the

303 *Supra* note 299, at 435.

304 Art. 128 EC, inserted by the TEU.

305 For discussion in this direction, Palme, 'Das Bosman-Urteil des EuGH: Ein Schlag gegen die Sportautonomie?', *Juristenzeitung* (1996) 238. Cf. also Paras. 72, 78 of the ruling in *Bosman.*

basic assumptions of Community law. Nor should one. The *Bosman* ruling leaves the industry with leeway to renovate its structure and put in place a wealth distribution system, but it must not unlawfully restrict the exercise of fundamental economic freedoms guaranteed by EC law.

ANNOTATION [*BOSMAN* CASE]*

Case C-415/93, Union Royale Belge des Sociétés de Football Association ASBL v. *Jean-Marc Bosman; Royal Club Liégois SA* v. *Jean-Marc Bosman, SA d'Economie Mixte Sportive de l'Union Sportive du Littoral de Dunkerque, Union Royale Belge des Sociétés de Football Association ASBL, Union des Associations Européennes de Football; Union des Associations Européennes de Football* v. *Jean-Marc Bosman. Article 177 reference by the Cour d'Appel, Liège, on the interpretation of Articles 48, 85 and 86 EC. Judgment of the European Court of Justice of 15 December 1995.*

1. Introduction

The probability that a legal challenge would be launched against aspects of the regulatory structure of the football industry in Europe has grown steadily in recent years. There have been irregular murmurings about the lawfulness of the transfer system, which prevents footballers selling their labour freely to the highest bidder once their contract comes to an end. Doubt has also been cast on the permissibility of rules that restrict club teams to a specified number of foreigners. But suggestions by writers[306] and pressure from the European Parliament[307] had little practical impact. Football is evidently a tight cartel. Clubs appear to have weighed up their options and preferred to operate within the existing structure, deterred by the perils that await those that go to law to challenge the rules. UEFA, the European body, and FIFA, the world body, are remarkably powerful entities which, like some other transnational sporting organizations, have seemed on occasion to operate on the assumption that their global influence (and, typically, their base in Switzerland) renders them immune from legal control. Occasional suits demonstrate that such immunity may not be available as matter of law, but there are fiendishly complicated questions of jurisdiction, choice of law and recognition of judgments at stake, involving potentially conflicting decisions by national and transnational courts and sporting organizations.[308] In practice

* 33 *CML Rev.* (1996), p. 991 et seq.

306 E.g., Will, ed., *Sportrecht in Europa*, (Heidelberg, C.E Müller 1993). Cf. also Hilf, 'Die Freizügigkeit des Berufsfussballspielers innerhalb der EG', 1984/10 *NJW* 517; Weatherill, 'Discrimination on Grounds of Nationality in Sport?, 9 *YEL* (1989) 55.

307 Janssen Van Raay report, PE DOC A2-415/88; Larive report, PE DOC A3-0326/94. The views expressed in both reports are close to the approach of the Court in *Bosman*.

308 Cf. Nafziger, 'International Sports Law: A Reply of Characteristics and Trends', 86 *AJIL* (1992) 489, which examines *inter alia* the Olympic movement and litigation arising out of the 'America's Cup' yacht race, and Nafziger, 'International Sports Law as a Process for Resolving Disputes', 45 *ICLQ* (1996) 130, which considers *inter alia* litigation involving the runner 'Butch' Reynolds and ice-skater Tonya Harding.

litigants against sporting bodies are confronted by major obstacles to effective and prompt vindication of their rights. This is an important consideration in a fast-moving industry such as football, involving annual competition and relatively short playing careers.

Football clubs work together. The fact that a crucial challenge to the industry's regulatory structure was ultimately brought by an individual player, with some union support, serves as a demonstration of EC law's propensity for creating individual rights which may be employed as instruments for achieving the objectives of the Treaty. Jean-Marc Bosman, in asserting his own individual rights conferred by EC law, was simultaneously acting as a cartel-buster, just as Ms Defrenne acted both on her own behalf and as an instrument of anti-discrimination policy[309] and just as countless litigants have, by relying on EC law to claim individual rights, forced the abandonment of practices incompatible with the Treaty.

Bosman is the first occasion on which the fundamental patterns of a particular sport have been conclusively ruled incompatible with Community law by the European Court. Bosman's legal success will change football in particular and sport in general, but the ruling is also of major significance in the evolution of EC law. The purpose of this annotation is to explore the significance of the judgment to the general development of the EC legal order, and to outline some of the legal issues left unresolved by the Court which may generate litigation in the future. The author has largely resisted the temptation to immerse himself in the eccentric passions and statistical oddities that surround football in Europe, although some reference to the structure and the significance of the industry is provided where necessary to ensure the intelligibility of the legal analysis.[310]

2. The factual background

2.1. The structure of the football industry

Football is practised as an organized sport in clubs belonging to national associations. Each Member State of the European Union has its own association. The sole exception is the United Kingdom which has four associations, one for each home country, a pattern reflected at international level in the separate participation of England, Northern Ireland, Scotland and Wales in international tournaments.

National associations are members of FIFA, the world organizing body, which is based in Switzerland. FIFA is split into confederations for each continent. The European confederation is UEFA, also based in Switzerland, and the national associations of the EU Member States are members of UEFA and as such undertake to comply with

---

309 Case 43/75, *Defrenne* v. *SABENA*, [1976] *ECR* 455.

310 A-G Lenz's Opinion, which is splendidly well-informed about the football industry, contains an extensive and detailed examination. For a useful collection of materials and some analysis, see Blanpain and Inston, *The Bosman Case: The End of the Transfer System?* (Leuven, Peeters/London, Sweet and Maxwell 1996).

its rules. The *Bosman* litigation involves directly two national associations, URBSFA (Belgium) and FFF (France), as well as UEFA.

2.2. **The transfer rules**

The rules governing transfer of footballers between clubs are complicated and vary State by State. There is a transnational underpinning, which is fed by UEFA/FIFA regulations which are enforced at national level as regards relationships between players and clubs. There was dispute in *Bosman* about precisely which rules were the relevant ones, but the referring court, the Cour d'Appel in Liège, considered that the FIFA regulations valid at the time applied.

The key point is that a football player is not free to work his or her[311] contract through to its expiry and then go into the (labour) marketplace and conclude a new contract with another employer. Summarizing the essence of the industry's structure, the 'selling' club will not release the player's registration until satisfied with the terms offered by the 'buying' club, which typically involves payment of a transfer fee by buying club to selling club. Fees over £ 1 million are commonplace; fees over £ 5 million are agreed several times a year; very occasionally fees have exceeded £ 10 million. The redistribution of income within the game *via* the fee was defended in *Bosman* as a means of keeping smaller clubs solvent and as an incentive for nurturing young talent. Until the clubs have arranged the transfer of the player's registration, the buying club will be forbidden under the rules enforced by the relevant national association from fielding the player in any official match. Footballers, then, are not treated like plumbers, welders or University lecturers. The game's cartels constrain them from freely selling their labour in accordance with normal assumptions of contract law.

It was pressed on the Court in *Bosman* that recent liberalization within the industry had brought about a position in which the player would not be prevented from choosing between clubs once the existing employment contract comes to an end, with the fee then settled between the clubs according to a defined formula based on age and previous salary without affecting the player's right to play. However, the Court's ruling is clearly based on the recognition that the requirement imposed on the buying club to pay a fee to the selling club, backed by sanctions in the event of failure to pay, affects planning by clubs and therefore distorts players' opportunities for finding employment.[312] The ruling in *Bosman* is therefore directed at the general system which restricts post-contractual labour mobility in the EC, and is not confined to the (peculiarly restrictive) Belgian system of which Bosman fell foul. In this sense, nothing of fundamental legal significance turns on the intricacies of the several different systems operating in Europe.

---

311 There is very little women's professional football in Europe, but the *Bosman* ruling is plainly applicable to it.

312 Paras. 75, 101.

2.3. The nationality restrictions

Clubs were not free pre-*Bosman* to field any player they wanted. Associations have restricted the permissible number of 'foreigners'. For football purposes, nationality relates to qualification for the national representative side of that association, so on occasion football nationality is not the same as nationality at law.[313]

Restrictions in recent years have followed the model of the '3 + 2' rules, the product of a compromise struck in 1991 between UEFA and the Commission, represented by Mr Bangemann.[314] According to these rules, clubs may field three 'foreign' players plus two 'assimilated' players.[315] National leagues are permitted to allow a higher number of non-national players. In the English League, for example, the rules are more generous to clubs' flexibility in that British and Irish players all count as home players for these purposes. The '3 + 2' restrictions have been enforced mandatorily within the European club competitions organized by UEFA. This had a particularly noticeable impact in the United Kingdom, where clubs found themselves obliged to discriminate between different Britons, contrary to long-standing practice.[316] So in UEFA-organized competition, English clubs were forced to treat Scottish and Welsh players alongside Germans or Paraguayans as 'non-national', with a consequent market distortion in favour of purchase of English players by English clubs.[317]

2.4. Jean-Marc Bosman, the footballer

The Belgian transfer system was an unusually restrictive example of the genre. Perhaps this made *Bosman* an ideal test case, although, as mentioned, the ruling is not confined to the particular circumstances prevailing in Belgium at the time. Jean-Marc Bosman was a Belgian born in 1964. He had been employed by RC Liège, a first division club, on a contract expiring at the end of June 1990 on an average salary of BFR 120,000 per month, including bonuses. In April 1990 the club offered him a new one-year contract at BFR 30,000 per month, the minimum permitted by Belgian rules, and a quarter of his previous salary. This indicates that Bosman, a very promising

---

[313] The situation in the UK – four football nationalities, one nationality at law – is inevitably odd.

[314] Essays by Karpenstein and Renz in Will, ed., *supra* note 306, examine the Commission's position.

[315] Assimilated players have played in the country of the relevant association for an uninterrupted period of five years including three years as a junior.

[316] I refrain from an extended treatment of this issue; the impact may be measured by reference to the 1984 Liverpool side, the last British success in the European Cup, the leading club competition, which contained (including substitutes) international players from Scotland (4), Ireland (3), England (3), Wales (1), Zimbabwe (1) and one non-international. The introduction of restrictions may be regarded as no more than the corollary of the generosity of the world Football community in allowing the UK, a single state, uniquely to house four associations. This does not occur in e.g, the Olympic Games.

[317] 'One of the reasons that we got as much as £ 7 million for Andy Cole when he went to Manchester United was because he was English', Sir John Hall, Chairman of Newcastle United, *Independent on Sunday*, 10 December 1995, p. 30. A similar phenomenon could be observed in Scotland and, to a lesser extent because of the less radical break with history, in continental Europe too.

player in his youth, was by this stage not rated very highly.[318] He refused RC Liège's unattractive offer and was transfer listed, at a 'compensation fee' of BFR 11,743,000 fixed according to indicators based on age and salary. But Bosman was not without admirers. US Dunkerque, a French second division club, contracted with Bosman to pay him a monthly salary of some BFR 100,000 plus a signing-on fee of some BFR 900,000. In July 1990 RC Liège and Dunkerque agreed a contract for the transfer of Bosman for one year only, at a price of BFR 1,200,000, including an option costing BFR 4,800,000 allowing Dunkerque subsequently to buy the player. Both contracts, RC Liège/Dunkerque and Bosman/Dunkerque, were conditional on the sending of a transfer certificate by the Belgian association to the FFF, the French association, in line with the rules governing the transfer system. But RC Liège apparently came to doubt Dunkerque's solvency.[319] It did not ask the Belgian association to send the certificate to the FFF. So neither contract took effect. And RC Liège suspended Bosman so that he could not play in the 1990/1991 season.

2.5. **Jean-Marc Bosman, the litigant**

Bosman went to court. He sought interlocutory orders and other remedies, including an order that the transfer rules did not apply to him, and damages. He was granted an interlocutory order in Liège in November 1990 ordering the club and the Belgian association to refrain from impeding his engagement. Still only in his late twenties, he then found himself playing for ever smaller clubs in France and Belgium as his case progressed through the courts, which was itself a protracted saga involving a remarkable series of delays and aborted references to Luxembourg. The referring court mentioned clear grounds for suspicion that Bosman was boycotted by leading clubs after 1990, despite the interim order in his favour. Other defendants were joined; there were interventions, *inter alia* by footballers' associations. During this period Bosman also attempted to rely on Articles 173 and 215 EC to challenge the Commission's approach to football before the European Court, but his application was rejected as inadmissible.[320] Eventually the matter reached the European Court in October 1993 by way of the Article 177 preliminary reference procedure. The questions asked by the Cour d'Appel, Liège were

> 'Are Articles 48, 85 and 86 of the Treaty of Rome of 25 March 1957 to be interpreted as: (i) prohibiting a football club from requiring and receiving payment of a sum of money upon the engagement of one of its players who has come to the end of his contract by a new employing club (ii) prohibiting the national and international sporting associations or federations from including in their respective regulations provisions restricting access of foreign players from the European Community to the competitions which they organize?'

[318] Remarkably, in the light of his tenacity in the courts, the main reason for his declining fortunes on the football field was a perceived lack of aggression!

[319] Para. 33.

[320] Case C-117/91, *Jean-Marc Bosman* v. *Commission*, [1991] *ECR* I-4837; an application for interim measures was rejected in Case C-117/91R, [1991] *ECR* I-3353

It will be observed that the first question arises out of the obstacles that Bosman faced in his thwarted move to Dunkerque. The second question raises points of EC law, but appears to have nothing at all to do with the litigation. The nationality rules plainly deter acquisitions of players from other Member States, but posed no problem for Bosman himself; the whole point of his case was that he *was* in demand by a club in another Member State. Nevertheless the European Court felt able to provide answers to both questions referred to it by the Cour d'Appel.

3. The Opinion of the Advocate-General

The Opinion of Advocate-General Lenz is one of the more remarkable ever delivered. It covers no fewer than 113 photocopied pages, divided into 287 paragraphs containing 367 footnotes. It will be used by researchers as a quarry from which to extract references to a wideranging survey of judicial decisions and academic literature. In addition, the Opinion is peppered with references to football, from Kevin Keegan to Eric Cantona, TSV 1860 Munich to Blackburn Rovers.

The Advocate-General began by depicting the organization of the football industry in Europe, its transfer system shaped by the national and transnational associations and the rules restricting the selection of foreign players. He provided a full account of the facts of the case, placing emphasis on the economic significance of football and the importance of the case to players and fans alike. He found both questions referred admissible, although only after careful inquiry into the questions relating to restrictions on foreign players.

Mr Lenz referred to *Walrave and Koch* v. *UCI* and *Donà* v. *Mantero*,[321] the two well-known European Court decisions from the 1970s which established that sport is subject to the rules of the EC Treaty in so far as it constitutes an economic activity. He then moved to questions of the interpretation of Article 48. He chose to begin by looking at the rules on foreign players and found them discriminatory on grounds of nationality. He accepted that the rulings in *Walrave and Koch* v. *UCI* and *Donà* v. *Mantero* have correctly been interpreted to mean that selection for national or perhaps regional representative teams may be limited to those of a particular nationality without involving discrimination *within the scope of application of the EC Treaty.* But he was not prepared to extend this to matches in national leagues nor to European club competitions, where player choice is based on economics not sporting representation.

Mr Lenz then applied Article 48 to the transfer system. The main thrust of his argument was that Article 48, which he read in conjunction with Article 52, is developing beyond a discrimination rule towards a broader principle controlling restrictions on free movement, even where non-discriminatory, at least when the restriction relates to *access* to the employment market in other Member States rather than the *exercise* of an occupational activity.[322] The transfer rules fall within the scope of application of Ar-

321 Case 36/71 [1974] *ECR* 1405 and Case 13/76 [1976] *ECR* 1333 respectively.

322 Para. 205 of the Opinion, his emphasis. See this author's article. 'After *Keck:* Some thoughts on how to clarify the clarification', in this Review at 887-908.

ticle 48 and are to be considered lawful only if they are justified by imperative reasons in the general interest and go no further than is necessary to attain those objectives. Mr Lenz considered the most significant argument in favour of justification lay in the role of the rules in preserving a financial and sporting balance between clubs. But he doubted the system fulfilled that objective; and was sure other systems aimed at that objective could be devised with less or even no hindrance to the free movement of labour. Mr Lenz mentioned two alternatives in particular, a collectively agreed wage cap and planned distribution of income among the clubs. He also rejected the idea that the transfer system provided compensation for the costs of training incurred by a selling club. It was too hit-and-miss to be viewed in such a favourable light. He did not rule out the ability of the football industry to regulate itself in conformity with Community law and he acknowledged economic motivations for so doing, but he condemned the current pattern as irreconcilable with the rights of players under Article 48 EC.

Advocate-General Lenz then discussed the application of Articles 85 and 86 EC. A network of agreements covered by Article 85 operate within the football industry and indeed it had already been subject to some decisions based on Article 85.[323] The transfer system and the restrictions on foreign players are horizontal agreements between clubs which would fall foul of Article 85. Article 86 was not relevant because any collective dominant activity related only to the relationship between players and club, which Mr Lenz regarded as falling outwith the scope of Article 86. But he did not exclude the intriguing possibility that action taken by clubs as a group, for example to market television rights, could involve a potential breach of Article 86.

This provides no more than a brief overview of the main thread of the Opinion. Many of the arguments rejected in the Advocate-General's Opinion could be summarized as attempts by the football industry to insulate itself from the application of well-established general principles of Community law. Almost without exception these were rejected as unfounded[324] and they are not explored here in any depth.

Some of the issues examined at length by Advocate-General Lenz were not touched on by the Court. The most striking example is the competition rules, which the Court ignored in favour of reliance on Article 48 alone. Some of the issues neglected by the Court are, however, of enduring importance, including the role of the competition rules, and will be discussed below in Section 5. In other areas the observations of Mr Lenz were simply adopted by the Court without elaboration.

Explanation of these aspects will be provided in the discussion of the Court's own ruling.

---

[323] *OJ* 1992, L 326/31, distribution of package tours for the 1990 World Cup incompatible with Art. 85; cf. also no dispute on application in principle of Art. 85 in Case T-46/92, *Scottish Football Association* v. *Commission*, [1994] *ECR* II-1039.

[324] But see below, Part 5.1.1, on the interdependence of clubs.

4. The Judgment of the Court

4.1. The application of Article 48 EC to the transfer rules

4.1.1. *Sport and the Economy*

The Court ruled that Community law is in principle capable of application to sport, confirming the approach taken in the 1970s in *Walrave and Koch* v. *UCI* and *Donà* v. *Mantero*.[325] The Court rejected submissions based on the 'negligible' economic activity of smaller clubs, nor was it persuaded by the argument that football is 'in most cases' not an economic activity.[326] Neither of these two points, even if perfectly true, defeats the plain fact that in some of its manifestations sport belongs in the commercial sphere. It is subject to Community law in so far as it constitutes an economic activity within the meaning of Article 2 EC.[327]

One would not have supposed the Court would have been prepared to place a particular industry uniquely beyond the jurisdiction of Community law. Although the Court was not unaware that its judgment could exert a profound impact on the football industry, it commented that 'this cannot go so far as to diminish the objective character of the law'.[328] Its sole concession was a willingness to exercise its self-endowed power to limit the temporal effects of the judgment.[329]

4.1.2. *EC law and the private sector*

The Court bases its ruling firmly on Article 48 as creating a fundamental freedom within the Community Treaty system. So, for example, the German Government submitted that the subsidiarity principle dictated that public authorities' intervention in private commercial affairs should be limited to what is strictly necessary. But this could not be accepted as a basis for permitting private associations to adopt rules which restrict the exercise of Treaty rights conferred on individuals. The Court then pointed out that Article 48 applies beyond the public sphere 'to rules of any other nature aimed at regulating gainful employment in a collective manner',[330] again confirming its pair of sports law rulings delivered in the 1970s. The Court observed that, were it otherwise, Article 48 would vary in its scope of application state-by-state in accordance with national choices about the reach of public regulation.

UEFA had objected to the 'private' application of Article 48 on the basis that this prejudiced private individuals compared with Member States because of their inabil-

325 *Supra* note 321.

326 Paras. 70 and 72, respectively.

327 Cf. overview by Zuleeg in Will, ed., *supra* note 306.

328 Para. 77.

329 It ruled that the direct effect of Art. 48 cannot be relied upon in support of claims relating to a fee in respect of transfer, training or development which has already been paid on, or is still payable under an obligation which arose before, the date of the judgment, except by those who have brought court proceedings or raised an equivalent claim under the applicable national law before that date.

330 Para. 82.

ity to rely on the Article 48(3) grounds of public policy, public security or public health as justification for limiting rights. The Court simply observed that individuals too could rely on such grounds. Accordingly there was no variation in this respect between rules originating from public or private sources.

The Court concluded that Article 48 applies to rules laid down by associations which fix the terms on which professional sportsmen can engage in gainful employment.

4.1.3. *An obstacle to free movement*

After dealing with these relatively straightforward aspects of the role of Article 48, the judgment then moves on to a plane which ensures its significance in the general sweep of EC trade law, beyond the oddities of the football industry.

The Court identified an obstacle to free movement, the fundamental Treaty right involving a pattern of rights to enter and reside in another Member State and there to pursue an economic activity. Provisions restricting exercise of the rights constitute an obstacle to that freedom even if applied without regard to nationality. Rights of free movement would be rendered 'meaningless'[331] if the State of origin could prohibit departure of an individual wishing to move to another State to pursue economic activity. Here the Court placed Article 48 alongside Article 52, referring to *R* v. *HM Treasury and Commissioners of Inland Revenue ex parte Daily Mail and General Trust*,[332] signalling its concern to establish coherent principles which link the several Treaty provisions that constitute the law governing the creation and maintenance of the internal market.

There is, however, a difficult point lurking beneath the ready assumption that the transfer rules prevented Bosman from exercising his rights under Article 48 to leave Belgium to work in France. Had his putative new club been Belgian he would also have found himself subject to restrictions imposed by the transfer system. In such circumstances he would have remained equally dependent on RC Liège's willingness to release his registration. One might have thought that the equal application of the rules in law and in fact to all players irrespective of origin or destination would, by analogy with the well-known ruling in *Keck and Mithouard* relating to Article 30,[333] deny the player the opportunity to invoke the rules of free movement; and that, in so far as the problem arose because of private agreements within the game which distorted trade patterns without any taint of nationality discrimination, the correct basis for analysis should have been Article 85 EC. However, the Court asserted that the rules 'directly affect players' access to the employment market in other Member States and are thus capable of impeding freedom of movement of workers'. It will be observed that this formulation evades the point that that 'direct' impediment to market access was also felt by those wishing to obtain access to the employment market in their home States. The *Bosman* ruling stands with that in *Alpine Investments* v. *Minister van Finan-*

---

[331] Para. 97.

[332] Case 81/87 [1988] *ECR* 5483.

[333] Joined Cases C-267/91 & C-268/91 [1993] *ECR* I-6097.

ciën[334] as a clarification post-*Keck* that a restriction on market access which does not involve discrimination does not automatically escape the scope of application of Community trade law.[335]

4.1.4. *Justifying the rules*

The Court stated that the rules obstructed trade contrary to Article 48 EC subject only to the possibility of justification where the rules pursued a legitimate aim compatible with the Treaty and justified by 'pressing reasons of public interest', subject to conformity with the ubiquitous proportionality principle.[336] This seems to involve the importation of the familiar *Cassis de Dijon* principles into Article 48 and points in the direction of the development of general principles of Community law applicable to the internal market. The Court cited in this connection its rulings in *Diner Kraus* v. *Land Baden-Württemberg* and *Gebhard* v. *Consiglio dell 'Ordine degli Avvocati e Procuratori di Milano*,[337] both of which elaborate principles that govern the lawfulness of national measures that restrict the exercise of fundamental Treaty provisions. *Bosman* itself asserts the equal availability of justification (under Art. 48(3) and, wider, the 'Cassis' test) to both public and private parties subject to obligations drawn from Article 48, but, more generally, the ruling is part of a process of construction of general rules of justification for trade-restrictive measures in EC internal market law spanning, most noticeably, Articles 30, 48, 52 and 59.

The Court proceeded to consider whether the football industry was able to show sufficiently compelling reasons for maintaining its transfer system despite its apparent incompatibility with Article 48. It was submitted that the transfer rules are required 'to maintain a financial and competitive balance between clubs and to support the search for talent and the training of young players'.[338] There are, then, two limbs to the purported justification for the transfer system, the first relating to the need for dynamic equilibrium within the game, the second relating to the game's future playing resources. The Court acquiesced in the legitimacy of this potential source of justification: 'In view of the considerable social importance of sporting activities and in particular football in the Community, the aims of maintaining a balance between clubs by preserving a certain degree of equality and uncertainty as to results and of encouraging the recruitment and training of young players must be accepted as legitimate'.[339] However, it is well established in EC trade law that both the ends pursued and the means employed by a restrictive measure must be justified. The Court regarded the means employed in the current football industry as inapt to achieve ends which might be capable of justification in principle. The Court did not consider that

---

334 Case C-384/93 [1995] *ECR* I -1141.

335 These broader issues are addressed in a separate article in this Review, op. cit. *supra* note 322.

336 Para. 104.

337 Case C-19/92 [1993] *ECR* I-1663 and Case C-55/94 judgment of 30 Nov. 1995 nyr, respectively.

338 Para. 105.

339 Para. 106.

the transfer system acted as an adequate method of maintaining balance. The rules neither precluded richer clubs buying the best players nor prevented the 'availability of financial resources from being a decisive factor in competitive sport thus considerably altering the balance between clubs'. The Court agreed that a transfer fee system might act as an incentive to clubs to recruit and train new and young players, but it observed that because only a handful of young players will repay the investment by making the professional grade, it is impossible to predict the fees that will be obtained. In any event such fees will be unrelated to the actual cost of training all players. So '[t]he prospect of receiving such fees cannot, therefore, be either a decisive factor in encouraging recruitment and training of young players or an adequate means of financing such activities, particularly in the case of smaller clubs'.[340]

The Court concluded that 'the same aims can be achieved at least as efficiently by other means which do not impede freedom of movement for workers'.[341] The Court's rigorous application of the proportionality principle obliges the game to make radical changes, but the acceptance in principle that football might have objectives worthy of protection does not exclude the possibility that a restructured pattern of regulation could be devised in conformity with Community law. This is examined below (Section 5.1.1).

4.2. The application of Article 48 EC to nationality restrictions

4.2.1. *Trade restriction and nationality discrimination*

The Court found that the '3 + 2' nationality rules, and variants thereupon, limited the chances of employment of players. An obstacle to the free movement of workers was thereby established. Moreover, the rules were based on nationality discrimination, albeit of an indirect nature *via* reliance on football rather than legal nationality. Such discrimination contradicts the fundamental assumptions of the EC legal order.

4.2.2. *Jurisdiction under Article 177*

An oddity in *Bosman* was the Court's willingness to examine the nationality rules at all. In the abstract, their capacity to obstruct free movement and to contaminate the industry with nationality discrimination is plain. Yet Bosman, a Belgian, had in fact been offered employment by a French club. So answers to the questions referred appeared to meet no objective need for the purpose of settling the case. However, the Court decided that it did have jurisdiction on the questions referred.[342] It repeated its longstanding view that in the context of the cooperative relationship between national court and European Court under Article 177 it is solely for the national court to determine in the light of the circumstances of the case both the need for a preliminary ruling in order to enable it to deliver judgment and the relevance of the question which

340 Para. 109.

341 Para. 110.

342 Paras. 55-67.

it submits to the Court. This binds the Court in principle to give a ruling on questions submitted that concern the interpretation of Community law. As is well known, the Court has on occasion examined with some rigour the circumstances surrounding a reference. In *Bosman* it referred to its ruling in *Meilicke* v. *ADV/ORGA*[343] as an illustration of the principle that that it lacks jurisdiction where the problem is hypothetical and the Court does not have before it the factual or legal material necessary to give a useful answer to the questions submitted to it. Nor does the Court have jurisdiction where it is quite obvious that the interpretation of Community law sought bears no relation to the actual facts of the main action or its purpose.[344] Despite this limited willingness to inquire into the circumstances of a reference to check its own jurisdiction, the Court in *Bosman* was content to comment that the national court felt the nationality rules could impede Bosman's employment chances and that it would not call that assessment into question. The Court's approach has a distinctly 'hands-off' flavour. *Bosman* suggests that instances where the Court has decided it lacks jurisdiction to answer questions referred to it are exceptional and should not be seen as a consistent trend towards raising the threshold that the referring court must cross.[345] The Court's brevity in dismissing submissions that it lacked jurisdiction also provides a hint that the Court was eager to rule on the point to clarify the law.

Advocate-General Lenz was typically more forthcoming. He examined the case law at length, but supplemented his analysis with pragmatism. He could not see how the nationality rules could reach the Court in any way other than through individual challenge, pointing out that there have been instances where clubs have been penalized for breaching the nationality rules, yet *still* have not gone to law.[346] Such a perception would seem formally irrelevant to an assessment of the Court's jurisdiction. However, one might realistically identify it as a motivating force in the Court's decision to regard itself as competent to answer the national court's questions rather than to treat them as a misuse of the Article 177 procedure. This background emphasizes the role of the judgment as an assertion of the individual right-holder in EC law as an instrument for cracking open adhesive cartels whose participants have an incentive to accept the system rather than challenge it.[347]

343 Case C-83/91, [1992] *ECR* I-4871.

344 E.g., Case -143/94, *Furlanis* v. *ANAS*, judgment of 26 October 1995, nyr.

345 For an evaluation of the policy of the Court in rejecting references, see annotations by Arnull, 30 *CML Rev.* (1993), 613 and 31 *CML Rev.* (1994), 377. See also Anderson, 'The Admissibility of preliminary references', 14 *YEL* (1994), 179.

346 The most celebrated example is VfB Stuttgart's eventual elimination from the 1992-1993 European Cup by Leeds United, even though the German side won the tie on the pitch. The extra 'foreigner' in that instance was, however, not an EU national, so an EC law issue did not arise, subject to the argument presented below at Section 5.2.2. A-G Lenz mentions domestic matches in which penalties imposed for playing too many EU nationals were accepted by clubs.

347 Cf. Section 1 *supra*. Even the ban on English clubs' participation in (lucrative) European club competition imposed in the wake of the Heysel Stadium disaster in 1985 stimulated no challenge based on EC law, even though it was surely disproportionate; cf. Evans, 'Freedom of trade under the Common Law and EC law: the case of the football bans', 102 *LQR* (1986) 510.

4.2.3. *Defending the rules*

The Court addressed four points of differing cogency presented in defence of the rules.

It was argued that the nationality clauses 'are justified on non-economic grounds, concerning only the sport as such'. The Court's two pre-*Bosman* rulings in relation to sport,[348] had indeed shown a willingness to recognize that undoubted nationality discrimination might lie beyond the scope of application of EC law. The non-controversial example is a match between national sides. This is an economic activity in the sense that such matches generate vast sums of money and the players *inter alia* benefit financially directly and indirectly from inclusion in the team. However, the restriction of those available to a particular nationality (in footballing terms) is part of the sporting context in which the event is staged. National identity, not money, predominates. In *Bosman* the Court stated that relevant Community rules 'do not preclude rules or practices justified on non-economic grounds which relate to the particular nature and context of certain matches'.[349] It is submitted that this should be taken as confirmation of the Court's past approach, even though the Court's use of the word 'justification' is peculiar. Unless the Court is referring to a public policy justification under Article 48(3) – and it does not make explicit such a remarkable widening of its scope – the reason why refusal to select, say, Germans for the French national side is surely that it constitutes (non-economically motivated) discrimination which lies beyond the scope of application of Community law, and not that it is justified discrimination within its scope.[350]

The Court added that 'such a restriction on the scope of the provisions in question must remain limited to its proper objective'.[351] In *Bosman* the Court observed that the rules applied to all official matches; to uphold the rules would deprive Article 48 of its practical effect in this area. It was pressed on the Court that the restrictions contributed to a traditional link between club and country, important to the public in identifying with its favourite team; and that for clubs appearing at international level, it is important to secure their representative status by limiting their ability to field footballing foreigners. The Court was completely unpersuaded that reasons of sporting interest could require an enforced link between the location of a club and the origins of individual players.

> '[A] football club's links with the Member State in which it is established cannot be regarded as any more inherent in its sporting activity than its links with its locality, town or region or, in the case of the United Kingdom, the territory covered by each of the four associations. Even though national championships are played between clubs from different regions, towns or localities, there is no rule restricting the right of clubs to field players from other regions, towns or localities in such matches'.[352]

---

[348] *Walrave and Koch* v. *UCI* and *Donà* v. *Mantero*, cited *supra* note 321.

[349] Para. 76.

[350] A-G Lenz's approach, in contrast with that of the Court, is in line with this orthodox reading of *Walrave and Koch* v. *UCI*.

[351] Para. 76.

[352] Para. 131.

The Court logically extended this analysis on to the international plane:

> 'In international competitions, moreover, participation is limited to clubs which have achieved certain results in competition in their respective countries, without any particular significance being attached to the nationalities of their players'.[353]

The Court is firmly of the view that the nationality of individual players is entirely dissociated from the sporting identity of football clubs. The assumptions of this analysis are neatly captured by Advocate-General Lenz's comment that '[...] the great majority of a club's supporters are much more interested in the success of their club than in the composition of the team'.[354]

The three remaining submissions on behalf of the football industry were treated as unmeritorious. It was submitted that the rules were needed to secure a sufficient pool of national players to allow the national team to flourish in all positions. But, observed the Court, even if the competitive labour market created by its ruling might diminish prospects for workers in their home State it ought to assist them finding work in other States.[355] The Court's analysis here assumes that once nationality-based distortion is eliminated, the market will not shrink employment opportunities, but rather it will redistribute patterns of employment. In essence, this places the football labour market on a par with all other markets affected by European integration. It was further submitted that the rules helped to maintain a competitive balance by preventing the

---

353 Para. 132. This approach conforms to that proposed by the present author, *supra* note 306, 60-63; cf. also Renz in Will ed., *supra* note 306. The more permissive approach to restrictions in club competitions suggested by A-G Trabucchi in *Donà* v. *Mantero*, *supra* note 321, seems to be decisively rejected.

354 *Quaere* whether Art. 48 would apply to an *individual* club which chose only players of a particular nationality. The Court has consistently referred to Art. 48's role in regulating 'collective' labour regulation, and it is submitted that the application of Art. 48 to an individual club would go beyond what has previously been decided. It is submitted that such an extension should *not* be made. A supermarket can choose to sell only British goods without violating Art. 30: so too a club should he able to hire only British players without violating Art. 48. The analogy is admittedly not quite precise because Art. 48 catches collective private action, where Art. 30 does not, an unresolved anomaly. Moreover, one might submit that the personal nature of the Art. 48 right should dictate its deeper intrusion into private autonomy than occurs under Art. 30. Nevertheless, although the point remains finally unresolved, his submitted that private contractual autonomy should prevail where individual clubs' choices of players are concerned (subject to the possible application of domestic race equality laws). However, *were* an individual club held subject to Art. 48. it would presumably he able lawfully to discriminate only if it could go beyond showing a perceived commercial advantage showing from such discrimination (through attracting potential fans) and show instead that the origins of its players, unusually, were regarded as significant to the identity of the club – Yorkshire County Cricket Club's (now abandoned) policy of selecting only Yorkshire-born players might have provided an example. For a full discussion, including copious reference to academic writing, see Roth, 'Drittwirkung der Grundfreiheiten?', in Due, Lutter and Schwarze, eds., *Festschrift für Ulrich Everling (*Nomos 1995). p. 1231 et seq.

355 A-G Lenz looked at practice: the absence of any restrictions on foreign players in the Scottish league has not led to a shortage of players for the national side. He pointed out that an objection based on the poor performances of the Scottish national side over recent years did not carry weight in the tight of contemporaneously poor club performances. He added kindly that 'no doubt this will change again one day'.

richest clubs buying up the best foreign players. But, observed the Court, the rules do not now stop such clubs buying up the best national players and thereby undermining this alleged balance. Last and least, it was pointed out that the '3 + 2' rule was drawn up in collaboration with the Commission. But the Commission is not empowered to authorize practices which are contrary to the Treaty, and so the football authorities' informal arrangement with the Commission could not affect the Court's finding of a violation of Article 48.[356]

The Court ruled that Article 48 'precludes the application of rules laid down by sporting associations under which, in matches in competitions which they organize, football clubs may field only a limited number of professional players who are nationals of other Member States.' The result is that all EU nationals must be treated as domestic players for the purposes of eligibility for selection for club matches. The Court did not place any temporal restriction on this part of its judgment, which serves as a sharp warning of the fragility of a Commission green light for practices that violate primary Treaty provisions. The immediate application of the ruling from 15 December 1995 also required a change in practice in the middle of the 1995/96 football season. The mixed response of the football industry is traced below, Section 5.1.2.

5. Comment

5.1. **Bosman and the reorganization of the football industry**

5.1.1. *The transfer system*

Enforcing a system of wealth distribution between football clubs in Europe is not completely unfeasible as a result of the ruling in *Bosman.* The explicit terms of the judgment do *not* decide that it is unlawful for the football industry to establish its own system of regulation designed to shelter clubs from pure market-based solutions, only that that goal cannot be achieved through the current transfer system. The Court accepted that 'the aims of maintaining a balance between clubs by preserving a certain degree of equality and uncertainty as to results and of encouraging the recruitment and training of young players must be accepted as legitimate'.[357] It was incumbent on the football industry to demonstrate that the transfer system was an apt and proportionate means of achieving objectives which the Court is prepared to recognize as legitimate in principle; and that no other methods existed for achieving those objectives which are less restrictive of trade. In *Bosman*, the Court's application of the requirements of the proportionality principle was rigorous, in conformity with the well-rehearsed principle that exceptions to fundamental Treaty freedom must be

[356] According to A-G Lenz, even had the Commission formally exempted the industry's practices under Art. 85(3) EC (which he thought implausible in any event because of their disproportionately restrictive effect), this would not have overridden a violation of Art. 48. As explained, the Court did not consider the application of Art. 85.

[357] Para. 106.

construed narrowly.[358] The Court was unpersuaded that the system should be upheld.[359] For the industry, it is simply a question of finding means to the stated ends that are apt and proportionate and that are not incompatible with Article 48 or other provisions of EC law, especially Article 85.

The Court, in concluding that 'the same aims can be achieved at least as efficiently by other means which do not impede freedom of movement for workers',[360] referred to its Advocate-General for discussion of other means that may be available to the industry. Mr Lenz accepted that a system stopping rich clubs becoming ever richer and poor ever poorer could be justified. A viable professional league requires no glaring imbalance between the teams participating. This is a reason in the general interest which may justify the imposition of restrictions on free competition.

In rejecting the current system, Mr Lenz suggested two alternative methods for achieving the stated objective of achieving a balance between clubs. First, 'it would be possible to determine by a collective wage agreement specified limits for the salaries to be paid to the players by the clubs'. Mixing employment law and competition law brings legal and economic pitfalls, as experience from North America suggests,[361] and it is submitted that Mr Lenz was right to spend little time in exploring this route. Mr Lenz clearly feels that his second method is more viable:

> 'it would be conceivable to distribute the clubs' receipts among clubs. Specifically, that means that part of the income obtained by a club from the sale of tickets for its home matches is distributed to the other clubs. Similarly, the income received for awarding the rights to transmit matches on television, for instance, could be divided up between all the clubs.'

As the Advocate-General asserted, 'each club needs the other one in order to successful. For that reason each club has an interest in the health of the other clubs. The clubs

---

358 Although a small number of recent cases have been generous to public authorities. Contrast Case C-275/92, *Schindler*, [1994] *ECR* I-1039, Para. 61, where the Court explicitly allowed the State 'latitude' in its assessment of the means appropriate to achieve permitted ends in the context of the suppression of large scale lotteries; and cf. the result of *Alpine Investments*, *supra* note 334, where the Court did not rule the Dutch measures disproportionate even though other States, notably the UK, did not feel the need for a ban on 'cold-calling'. For discussion of trends see O'Leary and Fernandez Martin, 'Judicial Exceptions to the Free Provision of Services', 1 *European Law Journal* (1995) 308.

359 In November 1995 UEFA asked the Court that an inquiry be launched to obtain fuller information on the role played by transfer fees in financing small or medium sized football clubs, evidencing a desire to show how income redistribution within the game was based on the transfer system. The request was rejected on procedural grounds, having been made when the oral procedure was closed and in the absence of any special circumstances applied. It is no secret that UEFA's inaction was severely critized by its EU members; e.g., Rick Parry, Chief Executive of the English Premier League, '[...] UEFA put in what was really a very rudimentary analysis to try and support the maintenance of the transfer system, which obviously did not impress', proceedings of a seminar on the *Bosman* case held on 8 January 1996, published jointly by the FA Premier League and British Association for Sport and Law.

360 Para. 110.

361 Cf., e.g., Corcoran, 'When does the buzzer sound? The nonstatutory labor exemption in professional sports', 94 *Columbia L Rev.* (1994) 1045; Schneider, 'Unsportsmanlike conduct: the lack of free agency in the NFL', 64 *South Calif LR* (1991), 797. A survey of recent developments in basketball is provided by Greenberg, 'The NBA – A Model for Success', 3/3 *Sport and the Law Journal* (1995) 9.

in a professional league thus do not have the aim of excluding their competitors from the market?' Professional sport is distinct from most industries because participants have incentives to share income out between themselves in order to maintain a balance within the league which essential to its economic success. Football clubs need 'competitors' that will not be driven from the market: in commercial as well as in sporting terms, taking part is more important than winning.

On publication of his Opinion in September 1995, Advocate-General Lenz was the target of a torrent of abuse from the football industry for his alleged failure to grasp how the game works.[362] The criticism was misplaced. Mr Lenz found that the practices of the industry violated Article 48, a view confirmed subsequently by the European Court. In referring to the availability of other means for achieving the objectives of the system – as defined by the football industry – Mr Lenz left open the possibility of special arrangements to reflect the unusual competitive relationship that prevails between football clubs. Whether clubs will now choose to put in place rational models appropriate to their industry is not Mr Lenz's concern.[363] He has left it to the clubs to resolve precisely how much competition they feel is in the collective interest and to set up wealth distribution systems accordingly,[364] subject to conformity with Article 85.[365] His point is that the industry violates EC law by forcing players to bear the brunt of achieving the alleged objective of competitive equality between clubs through the haphazard trickle-down of wealth *via* the transfer system.

The second justification for regulation of the industry which the Court accepted as permissible in principle was the need to encourage the recruitment of young players. Advocate-General Lenz suggested that *appropriate* transfer rules might be acceptable if based genuinely on costs of training. But he felt it unnecessary to explore the matter more fully. He commented that any system would have to cover costs incurred in training by the selling club, which he thinks should only be the first club. This seems an irrational limitation, for it is not only the player's first club that may spend money in improving a player's capabilities.[366] However, one must presume that, once again, Advocate-General Lenz is simply offering the industry possible routes to restructure itself in pursuit of its declared objectives without falling foul of EC law. The play-

362 E.g.: 'We have no lessons to learn from somebody who, in a manner of speaking, doesn't even know that a football is round'. F. Meulemans. Vice President of the Belgian FA, quoted at p. 1 of Blanpain and Inston, *supra* note 310.

363 In fact, Mr Lenz mentions distribution throughout the game of proceeds from the 'Champions League', the most lucrative club tournament in Europe although he adds that club managements have not always behaved rationally. (Few football supporters would disagree.)

364 He refers at footnote 299 to Cairns, Jennett and Sloane, 'The economics of professional team sports: A survey of theory and evidence', *Journal of Economic Studies* (1986) 3. Cf. Carmichael and Thomas, 'Bargaining in the transfer market: Theory and evidence', 25 *Applied Economics* (1993) 1467.

365 Probably any such arrangements would have to be notified to the Commission in pursuit of exemption according to Art. 85(3), although it might be possible to view the arrangements as simply a reflection of the unusual competitive structure of the football industry and therefore falling outside Art. 85 entirely and not requiring notification (perilous though such an approach would be in practice, for, if flawed, there would be no exemption and no immunity from fines). In any event A-G Lenz is firmly of the view that nothing in Art. 85 can detract from a breach of Art. 48; so grant of exemption under Art. 85(3) could not cure violation of Art. 48.

366 It seems that the suggestion is derived from the French system.

ers rights under Article 48 must be respected in any such restructuring, so any fee must be explicitly planned as compensation and not used to preclude the player's free choice. The way forward might involve some pooling of resources by clubs in the development of young talent, through a common, central fund built up through levies on all clubs and used to defray expenditure incurred by clubs shown to be successful breeders. Such a system, unconnected with any restriction on players' contractual freedom, would seem more sophisticated and reliable than the transfer system. It is now for the clubs to decide whether to implement such a system in order to sustain and improve the quality of youth training. Here too obligations under Article 85 must be respected.

The Court in *Bosman* referred to its Advocate-General's Opinion in concluding that 'the same aims can be achieved at least as efficiently by other means which do not impede freedom of movement for workers'.[367] It did not endorse the extended discussion by Mr Lenz. Moreover the requirements of Article 85 in this context depend on the type of scheme devised by the industry;[368] Mr Lenz's observations cannot be conclusive of what is and is not allowed, and the Court, satisfied to find a breach of Article 48, did not address the relevance of Articles 85 at all. For the industry, then, there are many questions to resolve.

Meanwhile, after the removal of transfer fees for out-of-contract players moving between EC Member States, players (and their agents) who are in demand will presumably be able to negotiate higher wages from acquiring clubs able to raid the pot previously reserved for transfer fees. This occurs at a time of booming income for the football industry. There will be lively contract negotiations as clubs try to put young players on long contracts and old players on short ones, while the players seek precisely the reverse. But *Bosman*, by insisting that long-established patterns according to which individual contractual freedom was sacrificed to the collective interests of the industry's participants, will shake the game. Small clubs will no longer be able to live (or die) by speculative investment in youngsters who may or may not yield windfalls through transfer fees, but the Court has not ruled out the capability of big clubs to sustain small clubs in particular and youth training in general by other means. The ruling does not exclude some kind of income redistribution within the industry, though this must be developed independently of the player's right to move. Of course, there is no guarantee that leading clubs will feel an economic need to sustain *all* other current clubs in their League; some reduction in numbers of professional clubs is probable. Allegations that in the wake of *Bosman* clubs have no incentive to invest in training overlook the need for any firm to maintain a stream of quality employees. In any event, collective action to further youth training within the game seems possible; the clubs' professed concern for inducement of young talent must now be expressed without the ability to assert post-contractual control over workers.

---

[367] Para. 110.

[368] There is a fund of North American experience on which to draw, cf. *supra* note 361, although direct transplant is improbable since some aspects of regulation such as the 'player draft' (cf., e.g., *Smith* v. *Pro Football Inc.*, 593 F.2d 1173) go far beyond anything envisaged in European football.

5.1.2. *The nationality restrictions*

Wealth distribution in football may be resuscitated despite the collapse of the transfer system. However, the Court's ruling against the game's nationality restrictions seems uncompromising. The Court's judgment exposes the fallacy of supposing that the origin of a player is of any relevance to the club game as a whole. Decisions on hiring belong with individual clubs.[369] There is no suggestion in the ruling of a loophole through which the game could seek to reintroduce adjusted schemes that prioritize particular types of player. For example, it is submitted that requirements for clubs to retain a minimum number of 'homegrown' players, without any explicit link to their nationality, would violate Article 48 as indirect nationality discrimination. *Bosman* stands as a vigorous assertion of an individual right to non-discriminatory treatment.[370]

The emphatic nature of the Court's ruling is clear from its refusal to place any temporal restriction on this part of its judgment, even though the industry was applying the '3 + 2' rules with the approval of the Commission. Accordingly there was an immediate change to the rules of the game in the middle of the 1995/1996 football season. The English League promptly scrapped its restrictions on non-British and Irish EU nationals in December 1995 and several clubs took immediate advantage. As one would suppose, wealthy clubs in small countries were quick to welcome the increased flexibility the ruling allowed them in planning for European club competition.[371]

UEFA was faced by an odd result. Its membership is Europe-wide, so its rules remain enforceable beyond the scope of application of EC law.[372] This is the consequence of the limits of EC jurisdiction which are not coterminous with those of European football. UEFA's response was initially to refuse to change during the 1995/1996 season. It declared that the nationality restrictions should be observed in the European club competitions, which had at the time of the ruling reached the quarter-final stage. It is submitted that this is a clear violation of Article 48 interpreted in *Bosman* in so far as it affected players with rights under EC law. Unsurprisingly in the light of past practice, no club chose to challenge UEFA. After several meetings between the Commission and UEFA, it was announced in February 1996 that UEFA had abandoned the restrictions for next season's tournaments.

---

369 Subject to comments *supra* note 354.

370 A-G Lenz's view that an Art. 85(3) exemption cannot save a violation of Art. 48, *supra* note 365, also rules out the practical utility of the argument that nationality restrictions may be deserve exemption in order to preserve the viability of smaller national Leagues which would otherwise be plundered of all their leading players; cf. Weatherill, *supra* note 306, 76-78. An argument is made ibid. 87-92 for a 'softening' of Art. 48 in cases where the Art. 85(3) conditions may be met by a labour practice, but this proposal seems to have found no favour with A-G Lenz.

371 E.g., Glasgow Rangers in Scotland; football officials remained unpersuaded by the benefits, cf. Jim Farry, chief executive of the Scottish Football Association. quoted in *The Times*, 4 November 1996, p. 48, referring to Rangers: 'The big-fish-in-a-wee-pool syndrome could rapidly become a wee fish in a big pool' (wee = small).

372 Which may reach beyond the 15 Member States: see Section 5.2.2 below. Peculiar though it may seem, rules requiring discrimination by British clubs between different types of Briton would not violate Art. 48, for this would exert an impact purely internal to one Member State.

UEFA was not alone in its reluctance to alter its rules in mid-season. There have been murmurings that a number of so-called 'gentlemen's agreements' have been struck in competitions around Europe under which clubs will complete the current season's competitions in accordance with pre-existing rules, notwithstanding the immediate effect in law of the *Bosman* ruling. In so far as this amounts to persisting collective labour regulation in breach of Article 48, it would be open to challenge by private individuals. However, it would not be vulnerable to direct Commission intervention. The Commission has no power to initiate proceedings directly against private parties acting in breach of Article 48.[373] However it is submitted that such arrangements would fall foul of Article 85 and participants would be vulnerable in theory to the imposition of fines by the Commission. Perhaps the Commission will content itself with promises of compliance from the start of season 1996/1997, but this serves as a further reminder that the Court's exclusive focus in *Bosman* on Article 48 should not lead one to suppose that the competition rules are not potentially highly significant to the conduct of the football industry.

5.2. **The limits of the Bosman ruling and prospects for future litigation**

The explicit terms of the judgment do *not* decide that a system of transfer fees within a single Member State falls foul of Article 48, nor that non-EU nationals have any right to use Article 48 to escape from the constraints of the transfer system, nor that players whose contracts have not expired may evade the system. However, each of these aspects of the ruling has nuances that may lead to future litigation of importance to the football industry in particular and to EC law generally. What follows is simply a sketch of the possibilities.

5.2.1. *Domestic transfer systems*

Bosman wished to move Belgium to France and the explicit terms of the ruling deal only with cross-border matters in connection with Article 48, so nothing in the explicit terms of the judgment declares a transfer between two clubs located within the same Member State incompatible with Community law. Several national associations responded to the judgment by asserting its inapplicability to domestic transfers and confirming the maintenance of a transfer regime within their own League.[374] Such restrictions on contractual freedom seem to be subject to the supervision of national law alone.[375]

---

373 Cf. Weatherill, *supra* note 306, 80-82; Karpenstein in Will ed., *supra* note 306.

374 'At the moment no one's challenging our system. We hope it remains that way because it's an excellent one, without which many smaller clubs might not survive', English Football Association spokesperson, *The Independent*, 6 March 1996, p. 24.

375 One might ponder whether national judges might in practice be prompted by awareness that the cross-border transfer system has collapsed to adopt a more rigorous inquiry into the permissibility of domestic restrictions. The leading case in English law is *Eastham* v. *Newcastle United FC* [1964] Ch. 413; on the situation in Germany, Wertenbruch (1996) EuZW, 91; and, for comparisons, see A-G Lenz's Opinion in *Bosman.*

The Court conceded in *Bosman* that Article 48 is inapplicable to situations wholly internal to a single Member State, citing well-established case law on the point.[376] The Court seems reluctant to extend the scope of Community law to prohibit such 'reverse discrimination' by a State against its own nationals.[377] True, tricky situations may arise. One could envisage club A in State X wishing to acquire an out-of-contract player from club B also in State X. To avoid paying a transfer fee, club A arranges for its partner club in State Y to acquire the player without paying a transfer a fee in line with the *Bosman* ruling and then club A in turn acquires the player, also without paying a fee, from its partner. A national of State A returning from another Member State after pursuit of activity falling within the scope of Community law is *not* necessarily in a purely internal situation and may be able to assert EC law rights against State A.[378] One could imagine a lucrative trade in evading domestic transfers.[379] It is possible that such a system might be regarded as a sham cross-border transaction to which the Court might refuse to extend the right to rely on Article 48.[380] This would force the player to serve a period of uncertain duration as a 'genuine' economic migrant before returning to the home State. On the other hand, the Court's refusal to sanction challenges to domestic rules by 'sham' migrants might not extend to a situation where the domestic rules in question, the transfer system, are not a comprehensive regulatory regime, but merely the tattered and anomalous remnants of a discredited system.

However, there is a more fundamental problem that arises if cross-border transfer fees are outlawed, while domestic fees are permitted. Club F in State G needs a new striker; it will prefer to buy an out-of-contract player from State H rather than an equally good (or even superior) player available in State G, for the import will come free of the obligation to pay a fee. Naturally linguistic and cultural differences will in practice make it improbable that a team will ever be composed entirely of 'non-nationals', but the market will be distorted in favour of such cross-border acquisition. Purchase will not simply be driven by quality. One would suppose that fees payable within domestic Leagues will be depressed.[381] As is clear from the second question in *Bosman* national associations may not respond by introducing limits on the number of EU nationals who may be imported in this way, so pressure will increase on national associations to remove the anomaly by agreeing to abandon fees altogether. Moreover, it is plain that the successful institution of a proper wealth distribution system in

---

376 Para. 89, e.g., Case 175/78, *R* v. *Saunders*, [1979] *ECR* 1129.

377 Cf. on Art. 30, Weatherill, op. cit. *supra* note 322.

378 Cf. Case C-370/90, *Surinder Singh*, [1992] *ECR* I-4265; Case C-19/92, *Dieter Kraus*, *supra* note 337.

379 The fact that the Scandinavian season runs through the summer, while the major Leagues in Europe operates on an August–May model, may offer an opportunity for planning such a scheme without any break in the player's availability.

380 Cf. Case 39/86, *Lair* v. *University of Hanover*, [1988] *ECR* 3161; in connection with regulation of legal persons, Case c-23/93, *TV 10 SA* v. *Commissariaat voor de Media*, [1994] *ECR* I-4795, annotated by Wattel, 32 *CML Rev.*, 1257. Cf. under Art. 30 EC, Case 229/83, *Leclerc* v. *Au Blé Vert*, [1985] *ECR* 1.

381 The British anomaly persists; transfers between the English and Scottish leagues remain purely internal for EC law purposes.

Europe, as discussed in Section 5.1.1 above, would involve a removal of the anomaly between domestic and cross-border transfers, as part of a wholesale reorganization of the game's finances. To this extent, even though *Bosman* concerns only cross-border deals, it is likely to exert a wider impact on the football economy.

The unimpeded availability of cross-border purchasing opportunities makes the maintenance of a domestic system peculiar, perhaps even pointless. But there is a legal issue too. The type of market distortion outlined in the previous paragraph seems to be precisely that which is needed to trigger the application of Article 85. The juxtaposition of a domestic system requiring the payment of transfer fees and an absence of fees payable on cross-border deals affects inter-state trade patterns. The distortive effect on the wider market of a horizontal agreement between clubs relating to player acquisition brings it within Article 85(1).[382]

There is one twist only. The maintenance of a domestic system (only) induces clubs to buy players from outside their own State and players to move to clubs outside their own State. It will plainly *increase* cross-border trade. So one might submit that although the arrangement affects trade patterns between Member States it does not do so in a way capable of preventing the realization of a single market. As a purely pro-integrative arrangement it should be regarded as unaffected by the prohibition in Article 85(1). It is submitted that this approach should not prevail, and that a domestic system would be caught by Article 85(l). It has been plain since the seminal decision in *Consten and Grundig* v. *Commission*,[383] that a consequential increase in trade is no bar to the application of Article 85 to an agreement. Admittedly, that is not conclusive. The increase in trade in *Consten and Grundig* was accompanied by restrictions on parallel trade which tended to isolate the French market: so the increase in trade occurred in conjunction with action hostile to 'the creation of a single market achieving conditions similar to those of a domestic market'.[384] So a domestic transfer system which causes an increase in cross-border trade with *no* associated damage to market integration (indeed, with precisely the reverse impact) might fall beyond the ambit of Article 85(1). Admittedly, that submission seems irreconcilable with *Napier Brown/British Sugar*,[385] in which the Commission examined an abusive refusal to sell sugar which had led to a customer buying sugar from suppliers in other countries. This might seem pro-integrative, but the Commission considered that an artificial trade pattern had emerged and that Article 86 applied. Even this is not wholly conclusive; it was an Article 86 case where a structural test is more appropriate given the assumption in such cases of the need to tackle the structural problem of market dominance, but the Commission referred explicitly to *Consten and Grundig* in rejecting the idea

[382] As A-G Lenz remarks, there is no difficulty in catching such labour-related agreements between employers under Art. 85; the difficult question of whether collective agreements between employers and employees fall within Art. 85 does not arise. Cf. Weatherill, *supra* note 306, 68-73 and North American analogies, *supra* note 361.

[383] Cases 56 & 58/64, [1966] *ECR* 299.

[384] Case 26/76, *Metro-SB-Grossmärkte GmbH & CO KG* v. *Commission*, [1977] *ECR* 1875, Cf. also Case 22/78, *Hugin* v. *Commission*, [1979] *ECR* 1869, cited by A-G Lenz in *Bosman*.

[385] *OJ* 1988, L 284/41.

that an increase in trade could take the matter beyond the scope of application of the competition rules. Admittedly, the cross-border sugar buyer was forced to pay higher prices than at home, whereas the cross-border buyer of players buys for free, but it is submitted that this cannot affect the basic point that a trade distortion occurred.

To move to principle, what matters is the purpose of Article 85(1). It is submitted that that provision is not simply a vehicle of integration. Agreements that cause a hindrance to the inter-penetration of national markets are simply one particularly pernicious example of the type of market distortion at which Article 85(1) is targetted. It is concerned with addressing all distortions of competition, even where they are unconnected with the interpenetration of national markets, provided they affect trade between Member States. That is to say, Article 85 is concerned with both the single market's creation and its maintenance as an arena of undistorted competition. A football transfer system within a single State distorts the market by keeping domestic players' wages lower than they would be without the system and by artificially channelling competition between clubs. It has a structural impact on the market. It falls within Article 85(1).

It remains open to national authorities to apply for exemption under Article 85(3), although in the absence of such an application, the system cannot presently be maintained if it falls within Article 85(1).[386] Even were an application for exemption made it is probable that the system would be judged disproportionately restrictive. This seems to be the view of Advocate-General Lenz in *Bosman*. He is firm in his opinion that a breach of Article 48 would not be excused by an Article 85(3) exemption. He also observes that a system that is disproportionately restrictive for the purposes of Article 48 should be regarded as disproportionately restrictive for the purposes of Article 85(3).[387] In particular, it is submitted that a domestic system imposes restrictions which are not indispensable to the attainment of the objectives of the system, contrary to the conditions in Article 85(3). Analysis used under Article 48 to show the incapacity of the transfer system to achieve the objectives attributed to it by the football industry (Section 4.1.4 above), especially in relation to the haphazard nature of the patterns of wealth distribution, would be fatal to an Article 85(3) exemption, even though Article 48 is not directly relevant in the purely internal situation.

Although the Court's ruling, limited to Article 48, allowed it to evade the full implications of an approach based on Article 85, a domestic transfer system appears vulnerable to challenge based on Article 85. National associations may be driven to abandon domestic transfer fees in the wake of the tendency of their clubs to exploit the cross-market to acquire players without payment of a fee. One might suppose that these economic trends, combined with the peril of intervention based on Article 85, would drive national bodies to join transnational bodies in seeking alternative methods for achieving the objectives they claimed to pursue through the transfer rules. However, in practice, the *Bosman* saga suggests that it will take a brave player to test

[386] Art. 4(1) Reg. 17/62.

[387] Cf. the Commission's inexplicit hint of a parallel between the proportionality test under Art. 36 and under Art. 85(3) in relation to permissibility of restrictions on World Cup ticket distribution for reasons of public safety, *supra* note 323.

this point of law in the domestic arena if national associations remain obdurate in defence of their transfer systems.[388] Would a complaint to the Commission prompt it to examine potential breaches of Article 85 by national Leagues? The Commission has been reticent in the past to take on the football authorities and its image as guardian of the Treaties is tarnished by its agreement to practices exposed in *Bosman* as unlawful (Section 4.2). It is plain that the Commission, on receipt of a complaint, is not obliged to proceed to a decision within the meaning of Article 189 on whether or not a violation of the competition rules has occurred.[389] Nevertheless, an inadequately reasoned rejection of a complaint may be annulled in Article 173 proceedings brought by a complainant.[390] The Commission must take complaint-handling seriously. It has set out its own priorities in a 1993 Notice on cooperation between national courts and the Commission,[391] drafted in the wake of the important ruling of the Court of First Instance in *Automec Sri* v. *Commission* ('*Automec II*').[392] The Commission, in the exercise of its administrative discretion, is permitted to prioritize cases in accordance with the *Community interest* in their pursuit. One aspect of this assessment involves the ability of the complaint to secure protection through proceedings at national level based on the direct effect of the relevant provisions.[393] In the few relevant rulings thus far delivered, the Court of First Instance has found no reason to impugn the Commission's view that it need not act because adequate national procedures were available to the complainant.[394] However, it is as yet far from clear whether the Commission is obliged to consider merely the availability in *principle* of adequate protection at national level, or whether it must undertake a more *practical* inquiry into the circumstances surrounding a particular complaint.[395] Could a player enmeshed in the domestic transfer system demand that the Commission, in evaluating the Community interest in pursuit of the matter, look beyond the theoretical possibility of an action before national courts based on Article 85 and take account of the practical probabil-

---

388 Another professional sport, perhaps cricket, rugby or ice hockey, might breed a litigant.

389 Case 125/78, *GEMA* v. *Commission*, [1979] *ECR* 3173.

390 Case C-37/92, *BEUC and NCC* v. *Commission*. [1994] *ECR* II-285. Cf. Case T-7/92, *Asia Motor France* v. *Commission*, [1993] *ECR* II-669; Case T-114/92, *BEMIM* v. *Commission*. [1995] *ECR* II-147; Case T-74/92, *Ladbroke Racing* v. *Commission*. [1995] *ECR* II-115; Case T-548/93, *Ladbroke Racing* v. *Commission*, [1995] *ECR* II-2565. Bosman's challenge to the Commission before the European Court, *supra* note 320, was *not* treated as a complaint of this type.

391 *OJ* 1993, C 39/6.

392 Case T-24/90 [1992] *ECR* II-2223; Case T-28/90, *Asia Motor France SA and others* v. *Commission*, [1992] *ECR* II-2285. For comment, see Drijber, 30 *CML Rev.*, 1237; Shaw, 18 *EL Rev.* (1993), 427. See generally Vesterdorf, 'Complaints concerning infringements of competition law within the context of European Community Law', 31 *CML Rev.*, 77.

393 '[...] there is not normally a sufficient Community interest in examining a case when the plaintiff is able to secure adequate protection of his rights before the national courts', Para. 15 of the 1993 Notice, *supra* note 391, citing Case T-24/90, *supra* note 392.

394 In *'Automec II'* itself and in Case T-114/92, *BEMIM* v. *Commission*, *supra* note 390.

395 See discussion by Hutchings and Levitt, 'Concurrent jurisdiction', *ECLR* (1994) 119; Shaw, 'Decentralization and law enforcement in EC competition law', 15 *Legal Studies* (1995) 128; Brent, 'The binding of leviathan? – the changing role of the European Commission in competition cases', 44 *ICLQ* (1995) 255.

ity that the player going to law would be sacrificing a large part of a short career? A separate issue arises from the Court of First Instance's acceptance in *BEMIM* v. *Commission*[396] that the Commission had acted properly in declining to pursue a complaint relating to practices that were essentially confined to the territory of a single Member State, France. A domestic transfer system might be regarded as so limited – yet, as shown above, its very existence stimulates cross-border activity, and, moreover, a finding that one State's system is unlawful would have wider repercussions, as it is likely that national systems, despite their variety (Section 2.2 above), stand or fall together in the light of Article 85. So it may plausibly be maintained that a Community interest attaches to scrutiny of a single national system.

In conclusion, although the Court brushed over the competition rules in three lines by commenting that 'since both types of rule to which the national court's question refer are contrary to Article 48, it is not necessary to rule on the interpretation of Articles 85 and 86 of the Treaty',[397] they may be used to sweep away the last vestige of the transfer system in the EC, filling the jurisdictional gap caused by the Court's unwillingness to extend Article 48 to purely internal situations.

5.2.2. *Players who are not EU nationals*

The *Bosman* ruling is based on Article 48 EC, which confers rights only on nationals of EU Member States. Non-EU nationals have no rights under Article 48 to challenge the transfer rules or the nationality restrictions. So, for example, a fee system could be maintained for transfers of players from non-EU States.[398] That would seem peculiar, but would be a reflection of the limits of Community's jurisdiction and its lack of congruence with the remit of UEFA, in particular.

However, right-holders may extend beyond EU nationals. Players from Norway, Liechtenstein and Icelandic players are doubtless able to rely on Articles 28 et seq. of the Agreement on a European Economic Area, the parallel provisions to Article 48 EC, to defeat restrictions placed on their contractual freedom by the transfer system.

The Court has also been prepared to recognize that some provisions in agreements between the EC and third countries may generate effects in the EC legal order which are analogous to directly effective rights under the EC Treaty. So, for example, in *ONEM* v. *Kbizer*[399] the applicant, a Moroccan national resident in Belgium, was held able to rely on the 1976 Co-Operation Agreement between the Community and Morocco to secure a guarantee of non-discriminatory treatment on grounds of nationality in the field of social security on terms analogous to those applied to Community nationals by virtue of Regulation 1408/71. The Court conceded that the Association Agreement was less ambitious than the EC Treaty, which has been a basis for denying equivalence in substantive interpretation or constitutional impact between the Treaty

---

396 Case T-114/92, *supra* note 390.

397 Para. 138.

398 Subject, perhaps, to Art. 85 arguments similar to those presented in Section 5.2.1 above relating to the distortion that flows from having a system applicable to some players but not to others.

399 Case C-18/90, [1991] *ECR* I-199.

and other instruments even where textual comparability exists.[400] But on a true interpretation of the Agreement at stake in *ONEM* v. *Kbizer*, that reservation did not apply. A precise principle governing the legal status of an individual was concerned and interpretation in the light of Regulation 1408/71 was appropriate.

The Court has not always been so receptive to attempted reliance on such instruments by nationals of third countries. In *Demirel* v. *Stadt Schwäbisch Gmünd*[401] the Court found a provision of the EEC/Turkey Agreement insufficiently precise to confer directly effective rights on a Turkish national. By contrast, the Court in *Sevince* felt able to confer Article 48-type rights on a Turkish worker which were capable of vindication before the domestic courts of an EC Member State by virtue of Turkey's Association Agreement with the Community.[402] The well-known metaphor of 'concentric circles' underestimates the lack of geometric harmony in this area. The case law is not consistent or, at least, it has been generated by a rather varied selection of provisions and external agreements. Against this background, it is not easy to distil coherent principles for determining when the Court will regard a provision as capable of creating direct effective protection for the non-EU national.[403] But it is submitted that the basic right enshrined in Article 48 and interpreted in *Bosman* would allow at least a basis for a challenge to the transfer system by non-EU national players already resident within the EC. The Turkish situation has generated most of the case law, but there are avenues for other nationalities including players from Central and Eastern European countries linked to the EC by the 'Europe Agreements'.[404] It is beyond the scope of this paper to offer an exhaustive survey, but one may conclude that non-EU footballers may be able to secure an outcome comparable to that in *Bosman* by relying on the EC's external agreements.

5.2.3. *Players whose contract has not expired*

The *Bosman* ruling deals only with the position on the expiry of a player's contract. Nothing in the explicit terms of the judgment precludes a system whereby fees are required on the transfer of players currently under contract. Debate in the football industry since the ruling has focused on the temptation for clubs to sign players to

[400] E.g., Case 270/80, *Polydor* v. *Harlequin Record Shops*, [1982] *ECR* 329. The most remarkable example of this principle, albeit arising outside the sphere of litigation by an individual, is provided by Opinion 1/91, *Opinion on the draft agreement establishing the EEA*, [1991] *ECR* I-6079.

[401] Case C-12/86, [1987] *ECR* 3719.

[402] Case C-192/89, [1990] *ECR* I-3461. Both this decision and *Kziber* are criticized by Hailbronner for underestimating the more limited ambitions of the Association Agreements in contrast with the EC Treaty, in 'Third Country Nationals and EC Law', Ch. 9 in Rosas and Antola, eds., *A Citizens' Europe* (London, Sage 1995), p. 190.

[403] Cf. Peers, 'Towards equality: Actual and potential rights of third-country nationals in the European Union', 33 *CML Rev.*, 7.

[404] Cf. Cremona, 'Citizens of third countries: Movement and employment of migrant workers within the European Union. *LIEI* (1995) 87, especially 102 et seq.

longer-term contracts than has been past practice.[405] It has even been suggested that clubs might opt for 'rolling contracts', where the contract is for indefinite duration, subject to a notice period of, say, three years. The advantage would be that clubs would retain the services of their stars or, at least, could still expect to earn income cm transfer fees for those 'in-contract' players they chose to sell. Clubs would need to balance this against the disadvantage that they may be saddled with poor performing players for an extended period. Signing ten 16-year olds to ten-year contracts could bankrupt a club if all ten failed to mature into high quality, marketable players.

However, it is submitted that the logic of the judgment in *Bosman* may be extended to challenge a transfer system applicable to in-contract players too. Where a player wishes to switch from club A to club B while still under contract with club A, it would be as much a violation of the player's Article 48 rights for the industry to impose sanctions on club B if it fails to acquire the player's registration by paying a fee as it would were the circumstances to arise at the end of the player's contract. It is submitted that the principle asserted in the *Bosman* ruling suggests that rights under Article 48 to challenge rules laid down by sporting associations which require payment of a transfer fee should apply irrespective of the player's contractual relationship at the time with the club.

Naturally, if a player left club A for club B during the term of the contract, that player would be in breach of contract and could be sued by the club. The acquiring club might be liable too – in English law, for example, liability for inducing breach of the player's contract may form the basis of an action by club A against club B. The potential pattern of liabilities would depend on the applicable systems of national private law. The submission presented here is that action should be *confined* to the private law. If the industry attempts to add sanctions against the contract-breaker then it will violate that individual's Article 48 rights.

If this analysis is well-founded, there will doubtless be work for ingenious private lawyers in drafting contracts which will provide maximum protection for the (unwilling) 'selling' club. Placing players on longer term contract may yield higher damages in the event of breach, although quantification of loss suffered as a result of the breach would present awkward problems.[406] It might be possible to include a clause in the contract requiring a player leaving before the expiry of a contract to repay sums spent on training,[407] although one would have to consider carefully the level at which such a sum could be fixed in order to ensure its enforceability at law.[408]

405 'The simple answer for clubs is to extend the contracts of players they consider valuable, so that the out of contract situation never arises', Chairman's Notes, p. 8 of match programme for *A.F.C. Bournemouth* v. *Hull City, English League Division Two*, 23 December 1995, i.e., eight days after the *Bosman* ruling.

406 How could one cost an adequate replacement?

407 In practice, these might be paid directly or indirectly by an eager buyer.

408 English law, for example, would look to the distinction between liquidated damages and a penalty clause. A clause stipulating payment would have to be a genuine pre-estimate of the innocent party's likely losses, rather than a means of terrorizing the other party into compliance and unconnected with actual loss. This means that it would not be possible to re-introduce the vast transfer fees paid in the past under the guise of contractual terms.

A club might be better advised to induce a player to stay by structuring the contract remuneration towards loyalty-payments falling due in the later stages of the contract's duration, including, perhaps, to options to re-sign. More generally, although there is an attraction to clubs to place younger players on long contracts at low wages, such strategies would require scrutiny against private law standards that have over recent decades undermined classic, brutal notions of freedom of contract, even in markets that are notionally competitive such as that to sign young footballers.[409] Employment contracts fall outside the scope of application of the EC Directive on unfair terms in consumer contracts,[410] but that measure is no more than a first EC venture into private law terrain well explored at national level. National legal systems have developed an armoury of protection against unduly onerous employment contracts. In all instances, if clubs were to act together in drafting contracts they would be acting in violation of the Treaty competition rules.[411]

The author is constrained by both space and a lack of expertise in comparative private law in developing this discussion further. However, it is submitted that where a player wishes to move between clubs even while still under a contract, then Article 48 may be invoked to challenge restrictions introduced through the collective structure of the football industry. *Bosman* implies that the matter belongs in the realms of private law.

6. Conclusion

Football in particular and sport in general must change. The firmness of the Court's ruling, combined with aspects of the game's structure left unresolved by the ruling but presented in Section 5.2 of this paper as in danger of falling foul of EC law in the future, would indicate mat any successful reorganization within the game needs to be radical. Other aspects of the football industry beyond the transfer rules and the nationality restrictions may provoke litigation with implications for both the sport and for development of the law. Ticket distribution for major competitions and sale of broadcasting rights have typically been based on exclusive or restricted supply to national organizations, which raises questions of free movement and competition policy. The extent to which sporting bodies must observe rules of fair procedure where hey act as regulatory bodies, for example in the area of drug-testing or professional standards, asks questions about the scope and content of EC administrative law. Rights of supporters may generate concern, for example with regard to the citizen's access to information gathered and shared in the context of cooperation between States under Article K of the Union Treaty, the institutionally unsophisticated non-EC EU.

---

409 An important decision on the unenforceability of trade restraints in English law, *Schroeder Music Publishing Co Ltd* v. *Macaulay*, 1 *WLR* (1974) 1308, arose out of a contract agreed between an unknown composer and a music publisher active in a well-populated market.

410 Directive 93/13 *OJ* 1993, L 95/29.

411 Both Arts. 85 and 86 may be relevant. The assumption in this Section is that clubs acting alone would *not* be subject to control under Art. 48; cf. *supra* note 354.

However, sport seems extraordinarily resilient to change. Walrave and Koch, the first standard-bearers of EC law rights in the sporting arena,[412] were denied probable success before the courts when they declined to press for judgment, apparently in the face of a threat by the defendant sporting body, the UCI, to withdraw paced cycle racing from the world championship schedule.[413] Only a few months prior to the ruling in *Bosman* it was reported that feeling within the game's governing bodies was that the player would yet be induced to settle the matter out-of-court.[414] Moreover, the game has a successful track record in keeping the Commission at bay[415] and seems to have been able to shrug off the criticism of the European Parliament.[416] So, although the game was roundly defeated once it was drawn into court in Luxembourg,[417] one cannot discount the possibility that the industry will risk flying rather close to the legal wind in the expectation that many years may elapse before it is once again faced by an opponent as vigorous as Jean-Marc Bosman.[418]

The possibility of a Treaty amendment to reflect the special status of sport has been mooted. The Belgian Prime Minister Jean-Luc Dehaene, well-known as a football fan, was able to earn himself some doubtless valuable publicity in the aftermath of the judgment by calling for careful examination with a view to affording football some degree of protection under the Treaty.[419] However, although the political horse-trading that is characteristic of the process of Treaty revision has led to some rather trivial matters being placed beyond the fundamental norms of EC law,[420] it seems improbable that even a carefully cultivated campaign by the football industry would be sufficient to bring unanimous backing for a proposal to exclude it from Articles 48, 85 and 86 in such a way as to allow it to stick to its old ways. It is not implausible that a supportive Title in the Treaty comparable to that on Culture[421] could be devised to reflect the interest in sport throughout the Community',[422] but one could hardly envisage a broad exemption of sport from the basic assumptions of Community law. The *Bosman* ruling leaves the industry with leeway to renovate its structure (Section 5.1), but Jean-Marc Bosman's remarkable campaign precludes the sacrifice of the rights of individual football players on the collective altar.

---

412 *Supra* note 321.

413 Van Staveren, 18th Colloquy on European Law, *Sport and the Law* (Proceedings published by the Council of Europe, Strasbourg 1989) 67; Hilf, *supra* note 306, 520 note 22.

414 E.g., *The Guardian*, 4 April 1995, p. 18.

415 Section 2.3 above; also Sections 5.1.2. and 5.2.1.

416 *Supra* note 307.

417 Cf. *supra* note 359.

418 Even Bosman has not yet received compensation at time of writing. Lawyers would be intrigued by litigation relating to his ability to rely on the ruling in Joined Cases C-46/93 and C-48/93, *Brasserie du Pêcheur SA* v. *Germany* and *R* v. *Secretary of State for Transport, ex parte Factortame Ltd and others*, judgment of 5 March 1996, in order to secure compensation from the football authorities, but Bosman has surely taken more than his fair share of test cases!

419 Blanpain and Inston, *supra* note 310, pp. 27-30.

420 E.g., Protocol on the Acquisition of Property in Denmark, appended to the TEU.

421 Art. 128 EC, inserted by the TEU.

422 For discussion in this direction, Palme, 'Das Bosman-Urteil des EuGH: Ein Schlag gegen die Sportautonomie?', *Juristenzeitung*(1996) 238. Cf. also Paras. 72, 78 of the ruling in *Bosman*.

0033149875354: FINING THE ORGANISERS OF THE 1998 FOOTBALL WORLD CUP*

INTRODUCTION

On July 20, 1999, a year, a week and a day after France had defeated Brazil 3-0 to win the 1998 Football World Cup, the Commission adopted a decision finding that the organising committee for the tournament had violated Article 82 of the EC Treaty and Article 54 of the EEA agreement by applying discriminatory arrangements to the sale of tickets to the general public.[423] A fine of € 1000 was imposed. The purpose of this article is to consider why the investigation of such a high-profile violation of EC competition law culminated in a fine which the decision itself describes as 'symbolic'.[424]

THE FACTS

In 1992 the French football association, acting with the agreement of FIFA, the world governing body, established the Comité Français d'Organisation de la Coupe du Monde de Football (CFO) with the purpose of making the necessary preparations for the 1998 World Cup Finals, the organisation of which had been allocated to France by FIFA. In 1998, 32 teams participated in the Finals, which comprised 64 matches taking place in nine different French cities over a period of five weeks. The World Cup, the Finals of which are staged once every four years, is football's most prestigious and lucrative competition and attracts huge interest among spectators, not only those who watch matches on television but also those who wish to attend matches in person. Accordingly the arrangements for sale of tickets to matches, which was entrusted to the CFO subject to FIFA approval, were of keen interest to football fans. The majority of the total of the 2,666,500 available tickets was distributed to recipients such as national football federations, official tour operators and sponsors, but 28.12 per cent of tickets, some 749,700, were distributed by the CFO direct to the general public. This tranche forms the focus of this article, for this is where the violation of EC law was identified.

In 1996 and 1997 the CFO sold tickets for individual matches and tickets under the 'Pass France 98' system which guaranteed admission to matches played in a particular stadium. Until the draw for the Finals was made on December 4, 1997, purchases were made 'blind' in the sense that the date and venue of the match was known, but the identity of the teams was not. But sales were restricted to buyers able to provide a

* *ECL Rev.* (2000) p. 275 et seq.

423 Case IV/36.888, 1998 Football World Cup, Decision 2000/12/E.C, *OJ* 2000 L 5/55.

424 Para. 125.

postal address in France. Only from April 22, 1998 did the CFO alter its practice and sell tickets to members of the public able to provide an address within the EEA, but by then the large majority of direct sales to the general public by the CFO had already been concluded. Only 175,500 of the 749,700 tickets sold directly to the general public by the CFO, representing roughly 6.5 per cent, of the total available tickets for the tournament,[425] were sold in this way from April 22, 1998.

The decision

The Commission treats the matter as an abusive practice by a dominant firm in breach of the prohibition contained in Article 82 of the EC Treaty and Article 54 of the EEA agreement. In its definition of the relevant product market the Decision is notable for its explicit reliance on the 'SSNIP' test which plays an important role in the Commission's 1997 Notice on the Definition of the Relevant Market for the Purposes of Community Competition Law.[426] That is, a relevant product marker will normally be confined to a single product or service if a small but significant non-transitory increase in the price of that product or service (in the range of 5 to 10 per cent) does not lead to any measurable change in consumer demand in favour of substitutable products or services. Applying the SSNIP test, a North American import that is not inconsistent with the Court's case law although it represents a fresh packaging of it, the Commission concluded that an increase of at least 10 per cent in the price of match tickets would not have resulted in a significant switch in demand by the general public to competing products. The issue of market definition in the sports sector is potentially tricky, raising questions about the extent to which each sport can be treated as constituting a separate market or, at the other extreme, whether sport is merely part of a wider market for entertainment,[427] but for an event of the magnitude of the Football World Cup it is uncontroversial to regard the market for match tickets as standing alone from the consumer's perspective. The Commission did not find switching to other major sporting events likely; nor were other football tournaments likely to offer real substitutes. Supply-side substitutability of tickets, via national federations and tour operators, was not treated as providing a realistic possibility of constraining the CFO's conduct in the light of the initial patterns of distribution arranged by the CFO. The relevant product markets were the markets for the 'blind' sale in 1996 and 1997 by the CFO to the general public of 'Pass France 98' and in 1997 for blind tickets for available individual matches.

The relevant geographic market was 'at least all countries within the EEA'.[428] The CFO's preference for a market definition confined to France alone was based on the submission that in practice only locals would be interested in buying blind, but this was swiftly rejected as implausible in the light of the interest that the World Cup Fi-

425 This percentage is incorrectly given as 23.33 in Table 1 in Para. 12 of the Decision.

426 *OJ* 1997 C 372, Paras. 15, 17, 40 of the Notice.

427 For discussion see Beloff, Kerr and Demetriou, *Sports Law* (Hart Publishing 1999), Ch. 6.

428 Para. 77.

nals command, evidence of substantial direct (albeit by then not blind) sales to buyers outside France from April 22, 1998 and the proximity of some venues to borders with other Member States.

Given such a market definition a finding of dominance flowed ineluctably. This position of dominance created for the CFO a 'special responsibility' not to allow its conduct to impair undistorted competition, the scope of that special responsibility falling to be considered in the light of the specific circumstances of the case.[429] *In casu* it was incumbent on the CFO to offer tickets on a non-discriminatory basis to the general public throughout the EEA, despite the fact that demand from within France might be higher than from outside. Exceptions to the rule of non-discriminatory availability must be justified on an individual basis and must represent the means that are the least restrictive necessary to achieve the end in view. The requirement of a French postal address amounted to discrimination in practice against residents outside France. The CFO's conduct had the effect of imposing unfair trading conditions on residents outside France which resulted in a limitation of the market to the prejudice of those consumers.

The CFO submitted that conduct in breach of Article 82 must affect the structure of competition in the market to the detriment of the competitors of a dominant undertaking, denying that Article 82 is intended to operate as a direct protection for the interests of consumers. The Commission rejected this interpretation of the nature and purpose of Article 82. Citing Continental Can,[430] the Commission declared that Article 82 applies to situations in which a dominant undertaking's conduct directly prejudices the interest of consumers notwithstanding the absence of any effect on the structure of competition.

The Commission accepted that the CFO obtained no commercial advantage from its discriminatory practices. But this is not essential to a finding of abuse. This was discrimination on the basis of residence which constituted indirect discrimination on the basis of nationality which offends against 'fundamental Community principles'.[431]

In January 1998 the CFO informed the Commission that the condition of a postal address in France was designed to facilitate safe delivery of tickets but that neither indication of French nationality nor proof of residence in France was required. However, this gloss was not apparent from the documentation associated with ticket sales nor from the CFO's website, which explicitly distinguished between buyers accord-

---

429 Para. 85, citing Case T-83/91, *Tetra Pak II*, [1994] *ECR* II-755; Case 7/82 *GVL*, [1984] *ECR* 483.

430 Para. 100; Case 6/72 *Europemballage Corp. and Continental Can Co. Inc.* v. *Commission of the European Communities*, [1973] *ECR* 215.

431 Para. 102; also Para. 122. In fact, the commercial advantage was enjoyed by French residents, able during the Finals to take advantage of the excess of demand over supply by selling tickets for many matches to visitors at levels far above cost price. Michel Platini, a prominent member of the organising team, was quoted in *The Independent*: 'You have to defend those who pay their income tax in France and who allow stadium to be built or renovated' (June 9, 1998, p. 31). For Patrick Harverson and David Owen, writing in the *Financial Times* during the tournament (July 9, 1998, p. 25) 'so many French residents have made a killing from selling tickets that the event may well contribute to a further erosion of the country's traditional antipathy to the free market'.

ing to residence. Those resident outside France were directed to contact their national football federation or an authorised tour operator. Even had possession of a French postal address been the sole criterion It would have had the effect of favouring French residents in practice. The Commission concluded that the CFO's behaviour had the effect of discriminating against consumers on the basis of residence.[432] In June 1998 the CFO added that the obligation to hold a French postal address was designed to ensure tickets were sold only to 'neutral' spectators, a group which prior to the draw for the Finals in December 1997 the CFO treated as comprising all members of the public able to provide an address in France. The Commission regarded this as an inapt and disproportionately restrictive means of achieving the objective of effective crowd segregation.[433] The Commission accepts that security issues must be taken into account in organising ticket distribution.[434] However, the CFO itself informed the Commission of expert opinion that 'blind' tickets (that is, where the identity of the participating teams is not yet known) 'generally are purchased by peaceful spectators who do not present a specific security risk'.[435] Accordingly public security provides no sufficient basis for justifying the discriminatory practices. The Commission concluded that the obligation to supply a French postal address was 'excessive and failed to contribute in any material way to maintaining or improving security at football matches'.[436]

This left only the determination of the fine to be imposed. Notwithstanding the discrimination perpetrated by the CFO which violated 'fundamental Community principles',[437] the Commission chose to limit the fine to € 1000, which it explicitly describes as 'symbolic' in the concluding paragraph of the decision. It observes that the ticketing arrangements were similar to those adopted for previous World Cup Finals and that the issues raised 'are of such a specific nature as not to enable conclusions to be easily drawn from previous Commission decisions or case-law of the Court of Justice'.[438] The Commission concludes from this that the CFO was unaware that it was infringing EC law. The Commission also refers to formal and informal contacts made by the CFO with the EC and French competition authorities in order to ensure compliance of the arrangements with the law. The Commission also notes the CFO's willingness to respond to the Commission's request to make available the final tranche of 175,500 tickets in April 1998 to consumers throughout the EEA.

432 Paras. 88, 91.

433 It is in fact possible that the artificially restricted scheme of supply contributed to breakdown in segregation at some matches; cf. note 431 above.

434 Paras. 53-61, 105.

435 Para. 56; also Paras. 108, 109.

436 Para. 109.

437 See note 431 above.

438 Para. 123.

Comment

There are several refreshing aspects to this Decision. It is in the first place gratifying that the Commission declined to assert an absence of Community interest in pursuing this matter.[439] This would not have been a satisfactory outcome, for the circumstances of unlawful ticket distribution are not apt for effective control by individuals seeking to rely on Community law rights before nationals courts. Aggregate loss may be high, but it is spread among many individuals who will have little incentive to pursue the matter through the courts. Moreover, it was important to establish clearly that in future such discriminatory practices will not be tolerated. The deterrent value of the Decision may be thought negligible in the light of the tiny fine imposed, notwithstanding the parting shot in the Decision to the effect that such a lenient policy cannot be expected in future, but it is reassuring that ticket sales to the general public for the 2000 European football championships, to he held in Belgium and the Netherlands. have been conducted without any oven discrimination. This flows from the Commission's willingness to condemn the CFO's plainly discriminatory practices. It is well known that the Commission's current preoccupation with sport is in part provoked by the *Bosman* ruling,[440] which has sharpened awareness of the role of litigation in driving change in sports governance, but much more so by the close association between sport and the hugely significant broadcasting sector, which is changing with remarkable speed as the legal environment and the technological opportunities alter. These trends raise mans sensitive questions about the extent to which the business of sport deserves legal treatment which differs from that meted out to normal industries in recognition of its unusual characteristics, such as the inter-dependence of clubs participating in a healthy competitive league a team needs rivals!) and, more broadly, the social and educational function of sport. The Commission's December 1999 'Helsinki Report on Sport' addresses bur does not resolve some of these awkward matters.[441] But these intriguing debates about the extent to which the increasingly commercial world of sport should be permitted to retain autonomy in fixing its own rules free of the influence of EC law are not engaged by the blatantly unlawful practices pursued by the CFO, backed by FIFA. These constituted unacceptable discrimination. It is especially welcome that attempts to use the smokescreen of public security as an excuse for refusing to treat football supporters in the way that consumers of other products and services rightly expect under Community law were firmly rejected. Limits on supply justified by the demands of public security are not ruled out for the future but they must more carefully balance the risks involved. In short, the application of the proportionality principle helps to ensure the majority do not have to suffer because of the excesses of the minority of supporters.[442]

---

[439] For an example of this approach in the sports sector, set the 'Mouscron case', IP/991965, December 9, 1999.

[440] Case C-415/93 *Union Royal Belge des Sociétés de Football Association* v. *Bosman*, [1995] *ECR* I-4921.

[441] COM (99) 644, discussed by Weatherill, 25 *EL Rev.* (2000) 270.

[442] Cf. the disproportionate but unchallenged response to incidents of violence involving English football supporters during the 1980s discussed in A. Evans, 'Freedom of Trade under the common law and EC law: the case of the football bans', 102 *LQR* (1986) 510.

However, it is not clear why the Commission delayed until February 1998 before intervening. By the spring of 1998 a head of steam had built up and this led to the modest adjustment of practice relating to the final tranche of tickets sold in April 1998. In March 1998 the European Parliament adopted a Resolution in which it drew attention to the cultural significance of the event and condemned the emergence of a black market for tickets. It urged the Commission

> 'to initiate a formal infringement procedure without delay and to apply the necessary sanctions against Community competition rules so as to ensure that the CFO brings its sales system into line with these rules well before the start of the tournament'.[443]

A group of MEPs brought proceedings based on violation of EC law by the organisers before a French court before the start of the tournament but the action was treated as inadmissible by a court in Paris.[444] But the Commission's own belated interest effectively limited the possible courses of action to an *ex post facto* fine. According to the Decision, the arrangements that were notified to the Commission by the CFO in June 1997 provoked no objection. The Commission states that it was not then informed of the requirement to provide a French postal address and that in fact the CFO told it thatm'Pass France 98' would be accessible to all (although by the date of the notifications the batch of 'Pass France 98' aimed at the general public was already sold out).[445] The Commission appears not to deny that the CFO had at the time communicated to it information about arrangements falling outside the scope of the formal notification, but it states that it cannot be criticised for deciding subsequently to initiate proceedings in relation to arrangements on which it had not formally been invited to take a view.[446]

But the CFO's discriminatory website had been opened in May 1997. Ticket sales were then already well under way on a discriminatory basis. Acting in a personal capacity, I complained to the Commission about the incompatibility of the ticket distribution system with EC law by letter dated June 17, 1997.[447] The reply, dated September 25, 1997, states that the original CFO notification of June 11, 1997 caused the Commission to object to 'certain features', including the matter about which I had complained. The CFO had, it was written, then agreed to sell directly to customers outside France irrespective of nationality and residence. The letter refers explicitly to 'commitments made to the Commission' concerning sale of tickets to non-French customers. This account does not seem entirely consistent with that provided in the Decision imposing the fine. That these commitments were plainly not being adhered to, as a visit to the CFO website demonstrated, formed the subject of a follow-up letter which I wrote on October 14, 1997. On November 21, 1997 the Commission

443 *OJ* 1998 C 104/240.

444 I am grateful to Graham Watson MEP for information.

445 Para. 119.

446 Para. 120.

447 The live letters that passed between the author and the Commission are found at the end of this article.

replied, taking a different line from that adopted in the earlier letter of September 25, 1997. The Commission now considered that it would not take the matter further in the light of my ability to seek tickets from my national football association or from authorised operators even though it explicitly accepted that 'a certain allocation of tickets are sold only to French customers'. The commitments made by the CFO, on which the Commission's September letter to me was based, are not mentioned, even though the explanation provided in the November letter appears to contradict the information about the commitments previously communicated to me. My third letter of December 18, 1997, exploring the Commissions admission that discrimination had occurred, attracted no reply from the Commission. A follow-up email in February 1998, repeating my complaints, elicited an emailed reply in March 1998 to the effect that the Commission had on February 20, 1998 sent a warning letter no the CFO informing it that the Commission considered than a part of the system violated the competition rules. I sent a further encouraging email but secured no further information from the Commission before the start of the tournament in June 1998.

The small fine generated savage press criticism. 'The European Commission succeeded in lowering its reputation even further [...]', insisted one newspaper in summer 1999 when the amount of the fine was announced, making an explicit link with the Commission's resignation of March 1999.[448] The Commission's published guidelines on the method of setting fines[449] are not explicitly mentioned in the Decision. They involve establishing the 'basic amount' of the fine with reference to its gravity and duration. However, the Guidelines conclude by asserting that the Commission reserves the right to impose a symbolic fine of € 1000, which would not involve calculation based on duration or aggravating factors. Such fines are to be justified in the text of the decision. In the Decision under examination, the imposition of a merely symbolic fine is explained in the Decision's concluding paragraph as in part attributable to the 'specific nature' of the matter, in respect of which past Commission and Court practice yielded no conclusive view. It is true that the Decision finding infringements of EC law in the ticket distribution system for the 1990 World Cup held in Italy did not address this matter directly. It concerned impermissibly restrictive sales terms for tour packages.[450] No fine was imposed, because, it was explained, this was the first time the Commission had taken action in respect of ticket distribution for a sports event. Had the CFO's infringement in 1997 and 1998 constituted an amended version of the type of practice previously condemned, for which coherent arguments in favour of the compatibility of the adjusted arrangements with EC law existed, then the preference to limit the CFO's fine to a symbolic amount would have been understandable. But discrimination on the grounds of residence occupies no such grey area. This involved violation of 'fundamental Community principles', as the Decision itself makes clear.[451] Perhaps public security arguments might have been

---

448 French escape with 'derisory' fine, *International Guardian*, July 21, 1999, p. 16.

449 *OJ* 1998 C 9/3.

450 IV/33/384 and IV/33/378 Distribution of Package Tours during the 1990 World Cup, Dec. 92/521/EEC, *OJ* 1992 L 326/31.

451 See note 431 above.

thought to leave the result in balance but the Commission's analysis makes plain the inapt and grossly disproportionate nature of the CFO's system and it is significant that in the 1990 World Cup Decision to justifications related to public security were briskly rejected for similar reasons associated with the disproportionate nature of the restrictions.

The Commission also bases the symbolic nature of the fine on formal and informal contacts made by the CFO with the EC and French competition authorities in order to ensure compliance of the arrangements with the law. No information is supplied in the Decision on the reaction of those authorities to the CFO's approaches. Moreover, no mention is made of the commitments made by the CFO to eliminate discrimination to which communication received by the author refers. It is also significant that well into 1998 the CFO was still attempting to justify discriminatory practices.[452] In the Decision the Commission skates over the exact nature of its dealings with the CFO in June 1997, suggesting that there was more to the negotiation than was the subject of formal notification, but declining to specify what was at stake.[453]

The final stated reason for limiting the fine to a symbolic level lies in the CFO's willingness to respond to the Commission's request to make available the final tranche of 175,500 tickets in April 1998 to consumers throughout the EEA. This omits a significant episode in the saga. There are several references in the Decision to the opening of eligibility to buyers able to give an address in the EEA from April 22, 1998.[454] Indeed, in Paragraph 46 the Commission goes so far as to refer to its own intervention by letter dated February 20, 1998 which prompted the CFO to sell the remaining 175,500 tickets to the general public able to provide an address in the EEA rather than to maintain the arrangements favouring French residents which were previously in place. The Decision explains that from April 22, 1998 applicants whose addresses were located in one of the countries competing in the match for which an application was made were treated for reasons concerned with crowd segregation differently from those with no such association.[455] But the assumption on which the Decision is based is that otherwise French residents and residents of EEA countries other than France were on an equal footing from April 22, 1998.

This is flawed. The Commission, which began to pursue the matter in earnest in February 1998, initially pressed the CFO to make available the final tranche of tickets to non-French residents alone.[456] The CFO refused to discriminate in this way against French consumers.[457] But, contrary to the impression given in the Decision, even then the CFO did not treat French and non-French residents equally. Although tickets were made available to non-French residents from April 22, 1998, they were required

452 Paras. 44, 58.

453 Paras. 119, 120.

454 Paras. 12, 13, 24, 46, 59, 124.

455 Para. 59.

456 E.g., 'EU threat on World Cup ticket sales', *Financial Times*, March 13, 1998, p. 2.

457 E.g., 'Legal moves against World Cup organisers', *Financial Times*, March 24, 1998, p. 2; 'EU fans flames over World Cup tickets', *The Independent*, March 24, 1998, p. 1. See also *Agence Europe*, No. 7165, February 21, 1998, p. 6 and No. 2299, March 14, 1998, IV, p. 5.

to use a telephone number which was different from that used by French residents. The pattern of availability of operators meant that the chances of being connected to a salesperson were much higher for the French callers than for others.[458] This episode is not mentioned at all in the Decision.

Conclusion

It is hard to avoid the conclusion that the bafflingly low fine ultimately imposed on the CFO is at least in part explained by the lack of vigour with which the Commission pursued this matter and its inconsistent approach to the CFO's practices beginning in the summer of 1997. A strong Commission is vital in maintaining institutional balance within the EC Vigorous law enforcement is vital in achieving the commercial and consumer confidence in the viability of the internal market of which the Commission writes with such laudable enthusiasm in its documentation associated with market management.[459] The Commission's intervention in the arrangements for distribution of tickets for the 1998 World Cup represents a story of missed opportunities.

Letter from Stephen Weatherill to the EC Commission, June 17, 1997

I wish to complain that a breach of Article 85 EC has been committed by the football authorities responsible for the organisation of the football World Cup to be staged in France 1998. My complaint relates to ticket distribution outside France.

It is possible to buy tickets for matches in the tournament if one is a resident of France. It is possible to buy tickets if one is not a resident of France from national associations, but only in conjunction with packages including accommodation and travel. But – and this is my complaint – it is not possible to buy tickets for matches alone if one is not a French resident. To get tickets, the non-French consumer must buy extra services (accommodation, travel) from national operators, instead of having the choice of making his or her own arrangements. This is anti-competitive, it restricts consumer choice and it is a breach of Article 85 EC.

I know that the Commission published decisions which found breaches of Article 85 in the ticket distribution systems for the 1990 football World Cup and the 1992 Olympic games. The objection in those cases was that it was possible for buyers outside the territory of the State in which the event was staged to buy their packages from only one source. That was found to be a breach of Article 85. That

[458] Chaos as fans swamp World Cup ticket hotline', *Financial Times*, April 23, 1998, p. 1; 'French fans cash in on World Cup phone_line chaos', *The Independent* April 23, 1998, p. 1. The number was 0033149875354 (hence the title of this paper) and chances of a call from the UK being answered by a seller were estimated at 2 million to 1.

[459] E.g., Action Plan for the Single Market, Communication of the Commission to the European Council, CSE(97)1, final. June 4, 1997 ('The Single Market stands or falls on confidence'); see also the Commissions strategy for the internal market for the next five years, published on November 24, 1999 (COM (99) 642).

exclusive element is not present in the distribution system for the World Cup in France – there will be competition between suppliers of packages. But consumer choice is still restricted in breach of Article 85, because it is not possible for the non-French consumer to choose between buying a full package (tickets plus accommodation and travel) or simply buying tickets.

When I read the Commission decisions on the 1990 World Cup and the 1992 Olympics, it seems to me that the Commission correctly accepts that there may be restrictions on the distribution of tickets for sporting events where these are necessary to secure public safety. That means that tickets should he issued for particular parts of the stadium, and it would be lawful for a distribution system to make sure that a buyer in (for example) England could only get tickets for a particular part of the ground. But the additional requirement that a buyer must also buy accommodation and travel with a ticket does not contribute to public safety. It is an anti-competitive restriction which goes beyond what is necessary to achieve the objective of public safety and it is therefore in breach of Article 85. All the unlawful details about distribution can be found at http://www.fifa.com/france98/france98.tickets.html.

I hope that you will consider that there is a 'Community interest' in pursuing this complaint. The issue is of great relevance to many citizens of the Union, who would greatly benefit from Commission intervention. It is quite impossible in practice for a private consumer to challenge these unlawful practices before national courts. I look forward to receiving your response.

Stephen Weatherill

Reply from the EC Commission (DG IV – Competition) to Stephen Weatherill, September 25, 1997

Dear Mr Weatherill,

Thank you for your letter of 17 June 1997 concerning ticket distribution to the World Cup football 1998 in France.

The core of your complaint is that a separate ticket distribution system has been set up for France and that non-French residents are not allowed to buy tickets directly from France. Instead, you state, you are only able to buy tickets from accredited sources outside France.

The World Cup 98 ticket distribution system was notified to the Commission on 11 June 1997. After having examined the notification, my services found reasons to object to certain features thereof. One issue which was settled after discussions with the French Organising Committee was the same that you have complained about.

Thus, following the commitment made by the French Organising Committee, it should now be possible for all interested football supporters, irrespective of their nationality and place of residence, to buy tickets via the available sources in France.

After having received the required commitments from the organising committee concerning the ticket distribution system, the Commission cleared the system and issued a comfort letter on 30 June 1997.

For the reasons set out above I do not intend to investigate your complaint further should you not provide me with further evidence that the Organising Committee are refusing to sell tickets to customers from outside France on grounds of their nationality not being French, thereby not adhering to the commitments made to the Commission.

Failing a reply from you within one month, I consider your silence to mean that you have no further comments to make and the file will be closed.

Yours sincerely, Humbert Drabbe

Reply from Stephen Weatherill to the EC Commission, October 14, 1997

I write in reply to your letter of 25 September, in reply to mine of 17 June 1997. I cannot agree with your assessment.

I am pleased to hear that you have secured a commitment from the organising authorities to sell tickets directly to interested buyers who are resident outside France. But the organising authorities have not followed this commitment.

I refer you to the official Web sire of the organising authorities. This is at: http://www.FRANCE98.com/english/tickets. This explicitly distinguishes between sale of tickets inside France and sale of tickets outside France. And it is not envisaged that buyers outside France can buy from sources inside France.

The 'Questions and Answers' database is at http://www.FRANCE98.com/english/tickets/q_and_a.html. This begins by making clear that buyers outside France must approach their national authorities to buy tickets. They cannot buy directly from France. This is the very core of my original complaint of 17 June 1997.

It seems clear that the organising authorities are in breach of their commitments to you. (Of course, it is not adequate for the authorities to claim that in practice they will sell to buyers even outside France despite the information on the Web site. An administrative practice cannot be considered to save a breach of EC law, because otherwise legal certainty would be damaged).

French buyers will be able to buy tickets when sales re-open in November; and again in February. But it is clear from the Web site that this possibility is not available to buyers outside France. This is a breach of Article 85.

My rights as a consumer under EC law are under threat. I hope you will take action.

Stephen Weatherill

Reply to Stephen Weatherill from the EC Commission, November 21, 1997

Dear Mr Weatherill

I write in reply to your letter of 14 October 1997.

Let me first clarify some aspects concerning the object of your complaint and of my letter of 25 September.

At events such as the World Cup Football it is unavoidable that limitations occur both concerning the number of tickets available and also as to the way that those tickets are distributed, especially with a view to security aspects well known to the football world. It is natural that these limitations affect also the ticket distribution system for the 1998 World Cup in France.

The ticket distribution system of the World Cup 1998 is set up in a way which allow football supporters not resident in France to buy tickets via two sources. First, tickets are available through each country's national football association. Second, it is also possible to buy tickets from tour operators and travel agencies throughout Europe.

Concerning the latter option it is important to note that there are no limits imposed on the tour operators and travel agencies by the Organizing Committee of the World Cup with regard to countries in which the tickets may be sold. Furthermore, the tour operators and travel agencies are not obliged by the Organizing Committee to sell the tickets in packages, i.e. together with journey and accommodation.

Therefore it is for the tour operators and the travel agencies to decide how they sell the tickets to the public for example in the UK. Should the tour operators in the UK adopt anti-competitive business practices as part of their ticket sales you have the possibility to complain to the competent national authorities in your country.

Against the above background, I consider your rights as a consumer to be safeguarded by your options to acquire tickets from either your national football association or from tour operators or travel agencies located in any European country. This is not changed by the fact that a certain allocation of tickets are sold only to French customers.

For the reasons above I do not intend to investigate your complaint further. Failing new arguments from your side within one month, I consider your silence to mean that you have no further comments to make and the file will be closed.

Yours sincerely, Humbert Drabbe

Reply to the EC Commission from Stephen Weatherill, December 18, 1997

Thank you for your letter of 21 November, in reply to my letter of 14 October. I am happy that you now accept that the organising authorities for 'France 98' are refusing to treat consumers resident outside France in the same way as they treat consumers resident in France. However, in the light of that finding. I am very disappointed that you are not prepared to take my complaint further.

You mention restrictions on ticket distribution 'with a view to security aspects well known to the football world'. Of course, I understand this. As a British resident, I would not expect to be able to buy a ticket directly for the match between, for example, Scotland and Norway. There must be crowd segregation. But I cannot see any 'security' reason which should stop me from buying a ticket directly for (for example) Argentina v. Japan or Mexico v. South Korea. In fact, a British resident should he allowed to buy a ticket for these matches in the same way as a French resident – there are no special considerations. But, under the current rules for 'France 98', I cannot do this. So, in legal terms, the restrictions on distribution, which favour French residents, are disproportionate to achieve the objective of public security. They cannot he exempted under Article 85(3) EC because they are disproportionately restrictive of trade (and. if it were relevant, they could not be justified under Article 36 EC for the same reason).

With regard to the remaining points in your letter of 21 November, I have to say I cannot agree with your analysis. As you state, 'a certain allocation of tickets are sold only to French customers'. This very statement makes clear that this is a system which is discriminatory according to nationality, which is a breach of the fundamental principles of EC law. The fact that I might be able to obtain tickets through other, more difficult channels cannot alter the fact that I, as a British resident, am being treated less favourably than a French resident, because I cannot buy directly from the organisers in France. This fragments the market along national lines; it causes discrimination according to nationality; it is in breach of EC law.

I urge you to act to protect my rights both as a consumer under EC law and as a Citizen of the European Union.

Stephen Weatherill

SPORTS UNDER EC COMPETITION LAW AND US ANTITRUST LAW*

I. Introduction

As the paper presented by M. Pons makes very clear,[460] sport is on the Commission's agenda in a way which bears no resemblance to the sector's peripheral significance to the development of EC law and policy for most of the EC's lifetime. The 'commercialisation' of sport, most strikingly driven by the regulatory and technological transformation of the broadcasting sector, has been the major factor in changing the environment. In some respects, we are witnessing determined attempts to make sport in Europe – especially football – as lucrative as it is in North America. This is probably a realistic prospect, and it suggests that Europe will yet undergo further transformation in the structure and ownership of its professional sports, even if some of the features of North American sport (e.g. the 'draft pick' and team relocation) seem alien at present to the culture of European sport. The evolving debate has been sharpened by the European Court's remarkable 1995 ruling in *Bosman* – as remarkable for the very (act it was decided by the Court, rather than finessed into compromise by the governing authorities of football, as it is for the substantive content of the ruling. *Bosman* emphasised the peril attached to assuming that sport might in practice, if not in principle, live outwith the law – or at least outwith the law courts. And *Bosman* has radically altered the relationship between player and club, and with it the patterns of commercial planning in the industry.

In these circumstances, the Commission deserves credit for its attempts to provide a framework within which the application of EC law to sport may be predicted with a reasonable degree of reliability. Transparency, which M. Pons recommends, is much needed. The eagerly awaited Commission Communication in this area, trailed in a preliminary document in February 1999,[461] which summarised a fuller but confidential draft text, may resolve a great many open questions. Of course, the interpretation of the relevant legal provisions there offered by the Commission cannot prejudice the authoritative role in interpreting the law allocated to the European Court of Justice under the EC legal order. This hierarchy is necessarily accepted with consistency in the lengthening list of soft law instruments published by the Commission in recent years in its laudable attempt to make more transparent the application of competition policy.[462] However, I understand from the oral presentation of M. Pons that the con-

* B. Hawk, ed., *International Antitrust Law and Policy: Annual Proceedings of the Fordham Corporate Law Institute for 1999* (Yonkers, NY, Juris Publishing 2000), Ch 8, p. 113 et seq.

460 *Union Royale Belge des Sociétés de football association, Royal Club Liègeois et UEFA* v. *Bosman*, Case C-415/93, [1995] *ECR* 14921 (CJ).

461 IP/99/133.

462 See, e.g, Notice on market Definition, *OJ* C 372, ¶ 6(1997).

fidential draft prepared in February 1999 received a mixed response and that publication of a final version is now improbable in the short- or medium-term. In any event, both the Court and Commission can be expected to provide fertile material in the area of sports law in individual decisions expected in the coming months.

In my submission, study of the pattern according to which sport is subjected to the rules of EC law is unusually interesting. The matter is of profound practical importance for sports lawyers, but it is also intriguing to the specialist in EC trade law and in competition/antitrust law. Sport is *not* immunised from the supervision of EC law and neither is it simply another industry that must abide by the requirements of the EC legal order. Sport is a special case, but acute difficulty perennially afflicts attempts to trace how 'special' sport really is and how that special status is properly reflected in the shaping of the relevant rules of EC law.

II. Sport does not escape the reach of EC law

It is first pertinent to recall how and why sport cannot be immunised from the application of the basic rules of the EC legal order. In *Walrave and Koch* the Court rejected the submission that EC law operates only in the economic sphere and that sport lies beyond such realms.[463] The business of sport is an economic activity and does not escape the scope of application of EC law. This was confirmed with gusto by the European Court in *Bosman*, as is explained in the paper presented by M. Pons. It seems constitutionally inconceivable that this insistence on the subjection in principle of sport to the control of EC law could be overturned by anything short of an amendment to the Treaty. And it is important to appreciate that the setting aside of decisions of the Court via Treaty revision, though occasionally discussed as a live prospect, is in fact exceedingly rare – for several very good legal and political reasons, not least the requirement of unanimity for Treaty revision, which is difficult to attain and which tends to lend powerful support to the 'default setting' of the status quo under the Treaty as already interpreted by the European Court.

Equally, the basic constitutional principles of EC law closely circumscribe the scope for national systems to provide shelter from legal control for local practices in so far as these practices impinge en the field of application of EC law, which prevails over national law in the event of conflict. This conditions one's appreciation of the exemption recently allowed under German cartel law to central marketing of broadcasting rights for sports events.[464] Moreover, and as mentioned in M. Pons's paper, in July 1999 the UK's Restrictive Practices Court held that collective selling of rights to televised football was not contrary to the public interest under domestic competition law,[465] but the parties to the relevant agreements were promptly asked by the Commission to notify them in order to permit scrutiny according to the standards of EC law. If they fail the EC test, then in so far as the agreements exert an effect on inter-

463 Walrave and Koch, Case 36/74, [1974] *ECR* 1405 (CJ).

464 Gesetz gegen Wettbewerbsbeschraenkungen, s31, as amended with effect from 1 January 1999.

465 Currently available via www.courtservice.gov.uk/highhome.htm.

state trade patterns, they are void[466] and the decision of the UK Restrictive Practices Court cannot save them.

The Declaration on Sport attached to the Amsterdam Treaty, which entered into force on 1 May 1999, offers a good example of the way in which vague notions about the desire to 'protect' sport from the application of the law are difficult to convert into operational norms in the face of the clear-cut vigour and the wide reach of the basic EC Treaty freedoms. The Declaration asserts that:

> 'the Conference emphasises the social significance of sport, in particular its role in forging identity and bringing people together. The Conference therefore calls en the bodies of the European Union to listen to sports associations when important questions affecting sport are at issue. In this connection, special consideration should be given to the particular characteristics of amateur sport.'[467]

This is frankly rather feeble and far distant from the murmurs in the immediate aftermath of the *Bosman* ruling that a Treaty amendment might be drafted to set aside the impact of the Court's ruling on sport. Assembling unanimous support among the Member States for such a revision, which would have undermined the basic principles of EC law in one particular sector, was not feasible. The result is the anodyne Declaration. It has, however, bred initiatives at the political level, as sports ministers from the Member States have met, and it has prompted the Commission to seek to improve its dialogue with the sector. This is mentioned in the paper presented by M. Pons.

Moreover, any EC trade lawyer is familiar with the intense difficulty confronted by any party seeking to persuade the European Court that the matter at hand escapes the scope of application of EC law. The evolution of EC law is characterised by its outward spread. The EC Treaty confers defined competences on the Community, but it does not make explicit the residual areas of exclusive national competence. 'Protecting' such areas of exclusive national competence is accordingly awkward. Under the influence of both the political and the judicial institutions of the European Community, national systems have become gradually subject to EC incursion in ever wider fields.[468] There is no STOP! sign, although some blurred versions have emerged lately – for example, subsidiarity and, more worryingly, in the shape of explicit apprehensions about the role asked of them by national supreme courts in, for example, Germany and Denmark.[469] And in the extraordinarily rich decision in *Bosman* itself the quest to insulate football from the incursion of EC law was not helped by appeals to the principle of subsidiarity or by the declared anxiety to protect culture. The Court was not persuaded by the German government's submission that the subsidiarity principle dictated that public authorities intervention in private commercial affairs should be limited to what is strictly necessary. According to the Court, this could not be accepted as a basis for permitting private associations to adopt rules which restrict the

[466] EC Treaty, Art. 81(2).

[467] Amsterdam Treaty, Declaration on Sport.

[468] See Weatherill, *Law and Integration in the European Union* (1995) Ch. 2.

[469] See Weatherill and Beaumont, *EU Law*, 3rd edn. (1999) Ch. 12.

exercise of Treaty rights conferred on individuals. Once fundamental Treaty-based economic freedoms have been triggered, EC law applies. This is a classic example of the way the EC may lack explicit competence to regulate a sector, or else enjoy only very limited competence in a sector, and yet the cross-cutting effect of its rules, especially its economic freedoms, may greatly influence the conduct of actors in that sector (cf. culture, education). This is entirely consistent with the orthodox expectations of an EC lawyer, and once sport was forced to fight its battle on EC law's own playing field, its opportunity to make out a special case was severely confined.

Therefore, in conclusion, although the industry of sport continues to make occasional noises about its aspiration to secure a wholesale exemption from the rules contained in the EC Treaty, a much more realistic prospect is that the rules of the EC law game will continue to apply, but perhaps in a nuanced fashion in their application to sport in order to yield some (though doubtless not all) of the concessions sought through appeals to the special nature of the industry of sport.

III. The significance of individual litigation in the EC system

The previous section demonstrates how in principle sport is caught by EC law. However, a further pertinent element to this inquiry lies in the limit to which the Commission is able to control the flow of litigation. EC law is enforced at two levels: the so-called principle of 'dual vigilance' involving 'supranational' control in the hands of the Commission and, in principle an independent route, national-level control based on vindication before national courts of rights conferred on private parties. Accordingly, the preferences of the Commission, in the exercise of the discretion in the allocation of enforcement resources confirmed by the Court of First Instance in *Automec*,[470] to withhold active pursuit of alleged unlawful practices in the sport sector cannot prevent the matter being litigated by other means. So, to select a powerful example, the Commission's '3 + 2' compromise struck in the late 1980s with the European football authorities governing the number of non-national players allowed to represent football clubs was undermined by private litigation based on the direct effect of Community law before national courts. Bosman, acting to vindicate his EC law rights, was not dependent on the Commission to bring his case. The Court's ruling in his favour included a clear assertion that the nationality-based restrictions in European club football (as distinct from those applying to representative teams competing at international level) contravened the basic principles of EC law. The Court considered the matter so dear, notwithstanding the green light previously illuminated by the Commission in approving the '3 + 2' system, that it refused to grant any temporal restriction on this part of its ruling (in contrast to that applying to transfer fees). The nationality-based restrictions were required to be dismantled immediately. The result has been a dramatic change in the pattern of European club football, as many leading club sides are dominated by players of a nationality other than that of most of the club's supporters. This has led to persisting disquiet among football authorities.

[470] *Automec*, Case T-24/90, [1992] *ECR* II 2223 (CFI).

This is largely directed at perceived inadequate opportunities to blood young local talent but also at escalating wage bills caused by the other aspect of the *Bosman* ruling, the partial destruction of the collectively enforced transfer-fee system in football, which severely restricted labour mobility even on the expiry of an existing contract of employment. But, short of Treaty revision, representations aimed at the revival of nationality-based discrimination appear doomed in the face of the Court's firm ruling on the point in *Bosman.* The permanence of the Commission's choices in this area is accordingly confined not only by the dominant role of the European Court, but also by the potential for private litigation which may undermine Commission bargains. Litigants are, admittedly, few in the sports sector, because the time taken to win a case may be as long as an average career; but *Bosman* proves the potential vitality for this route.

IV. How special is sport? The window of opportunity opened in the *Bosman* ruling

The core of the current argument relates to the extent sport is able to work within the framework of EC law and to carve out a niche for itself in which its peculiar characteristics may be reflected and protected. This is the essence of the Commission's current work. The Commission is striving to identify a dividing line between rules that are inherent in the very nature of sporting competition – and which therefore escape control under Community law – and rules that are no more than the type of commercial restrictions that are apt for examination (though not necessarily condemnation) under 'normal' EC law, as would be the case in any sector. Ever since the Court in *Walrave and Koch* admitted that rules of 'purely sporting interest' (*in casu*, those concerning nationality requirements associated with national representative teams) escape Community law, which for Advocate-General Warner in the case was no more than a matter of 'common sense', we have known that there are limits to the intrusion of EC law into the 'rules of the game'. But we have remained sorely in need of an intellectual basis for making the distinction between rules that lie beyond the reach of the EC legal order and those that are subject to its demands, albeit perhaps with concessionary twists designed to reflect the unusual competitive environment prevailing in the organised sports sector. The location of this line allows choices to be made about how much autonomy sport is to be permitted in its selforganisation. To this extent, the debate is about *some*, but not absolute, room for manoeuvre for sport free of regulatory control. (Although, as outlined, the Commission's choices remain unreliable in the sense that the Court may take a different view, and that the flow of litigation is not controlled by the Commission alone.)

A brief rehearsal of *Bosman* is worthwhile, if only to observe that, contrary to some comment at the time, the Court in *Bosman* did not simply subject sport to EC law without recognition of any special features attached to the sector, but rather that the Court paved the way to acknowledgement of sport's special characteristics within the framework of EC law. It did not allow sport a blanket exemption from the application of EC trade law. But the Court did acknowledge that sport is *different.* Justification of its peculiar practices may be possible, albeit that justification must be presented in a manner recognised by EC law and acceptable to it.

With reference to the transfer system (which, it should be noted, is not a collective bargain of the type examined from the US perspective in Mr Goldfein's paper,[471] but rather a horizontal arrangement between employers), the Court in *Bosman* was willing in principle to allow the football industry to present two particular justifications for unusual practices that might not be tolerated in other 'normal' industries:

> 'In view of the considerable social importance of sporting activities and in particular football in the Community, the aims of maintaining a balance between clubs by preserving a certain degree of equality and uncertainty as to results and of encouraging the recruitment and training of young players must be accepted as legitimate.'[472]

However, it is well established in EC trade law that both the ends pursued and the means employed by a restrictive measure must be justified. As is mentioned in the paper of M. Pons, the Court regarded the means employed in the current football industry as inapt to achieve ends that might be capable of justification in principle. The Court did not consider that the transfer system acted as an adequate method of maintaining balance between clubs. The rules neither precluded richer clubs from buying the best players nor prevented the 'availability of financial resources from being a decisive factor in competitive sport thus considerably altering the balance between clubs'.[473] The Court agreed that a transfer fee system might act as an incentive to clubs to recruit and train new and young players, but it observed that because only a handful of young players will repay the investment by making the professional grade, it is impossible to predict the fees that will be obtained. In any event such fees will be unrelated to the actual cost of training all players. The system that was then applicable was hit-and-miss, rather than a carefully constructed distributive mechanism. The Court concluded that 'the same aims can be achieved at least as efficiently by other means which do not impede freedom of movement for workers'.[474]

It is of major significance that the Court bas built in a justification test to the application of EC rules. Moreover, it is a test which allows recognition of the perceived special concerns of the football industry. The Court, and especially Advocate-General Lenz, went so far as to comment on the types of internal regulation that might be allowed in football, though not in a normal industry, in recognition of its peculiar features. In his Opinion Mr. Lenz accepted that a system stopping rich clubs from becoming ever richer and poor ever poorer could be justified. He mentioned two particular methods for preserving the financial and sporting balance between participating clubs that is vital to a healthy professional sports League. His first suggestion

---

[471] See Ch. 7.

[472] *Union Royale Belge des Sociétés de football association, Royal Club Liègeois et UEFA* v. *Bosman*, Case C-415/93, [1995] *ECR* I 4921, at ¶ 106 (CJ).

[473] Id., ¶ 107.

[474] Id., ¶ 110.

was for a collective wage agreement capping salaries to be paid to the players by the clubs. His second – and apparently preferred -route involved the distribution of receipts from, for example, the sale of broadcasting rights and ticket sales among the clubs. Such internal taxation would probably be regarded as unlawful. In a 'normal' industry; indeed, there would rarely be an incentive to institute such a system. Participants in a sports league, however, are interdependent. The clubs do not have the aim of driving their competitors from the market. They need credible rivals. Neither Mr. Lenz nor the Court specify exactly what may lawfully be done in sport in order to attend to the special demands of the industry, but they open the door to the shaping of permitted arrangements designed to reflect the unusual competitive relationship that prevails between football clubs. The industry, post-*Bosman*, is left to select its own processes of internal regulation.

On the second of the special concerns of organised sport, the Court accepted as permissible in principle the need to encourage the recruitment of young players. Advocate-General Lenz went so far as to suggest that *appropriate* transfer rules might be acceptable if based genuinely on costs of training, which would exclude the multimillion pound deal. However, the Court does make not any such admission; rightly so, in my view. In Paragraph 114 of the Court's ruling in *Bosman* the Court states that Article 39 (ex 48):

> 'precludes the application of rules laid down by sporting associations, under which a professional footballer who is a national of one Member State may not, on the expiry of his contract with a club, be employed by a club of another Member State unless the latter club has paid to the former club a transfer, training or development fee'.[475]

There is no scope in that firm assertion for even a modest revamped transfer system (although Advocate-General Lenz is, as mentioned, less decisive on this point). Article 39 (ex 48) places a heavy emphasis on the key role of labour mobility and this severely restricts the scope for sport in Europe to devise special rules geared to, for example, player drafts or transfer restrictions. M. Pons suggests that some restructured form of reimbursement for nursery clubs may be feasible. I would agree, provided restrictions on labour mobility are not thereby implicated. For I cannot see any compelling reason for supposing that a football club is any less likely to train young employees because they might subsequently quit the company than a supermarket or a university would be. I would not entirely exclude the possibility that it could be regarded as legally permissible for football to devise an internal taxation system to transfer money into the hands of nursery clubs, as part of a scheme for sustaining a larger number of clubs than would survive in 'pure' market conditions. It is not inconceivable that public authorities may choose to intervene to require income to be used in order to support the 'grassroots' of the game as part of a broader project for improving social cohesion. But I find it difficult to believe football is truly as special as Advocate-General Lenz states. I am ready to accept only half of his argument. That is to say, the economics of football are special when it comes to preserving competitive

[475] Id., ¶ 114.

equality between clubs; the economics of football are much less obviously special when it comes to compensating and thereby encouraging the training of young players. And, of fundamental importance, I do not regard it as permissible in any event to pursue such ends via a system which impedes individual labour mobility.

V. Shaping the legal framework reflecting the special nature of sport

The emerging framework suggests that sport's interdependence of competitors and the need for uncertainty in results might justify special arrangements, but that this does not warrant automatic exemption from the competition rules of any economic activities generated by sport. This is plainly an intriguing agenda! It is also one that remains far from fixed. The notion of preserving 'uncertainty in results,' for example, demands economic analysis to help determine the true scope of its function in sustaining a viable product. Wealth distribution among clubs may breed more even and unpredictable competition but it may also remove incentives to press hard to succeed by dampening the pain of failure. Empirical analysis should be introduced. Potentially, however, the pursuit of uncertainty in results could provide a cover for a very wide range of interventionist devices.

The paper presented by M. Pons provides a very clear and very interesting discussion of the way in which these matters may be approached. There are several aspects of this programme that invite comment. In brief, the following appear to me to be among the more pertinent.

The use of the law of free movement, specifically Article 39 in *Bosman*, is a blip. It was always surprising that the Court in *Bosman* chose to decide the case exclusively on the basis of Article 39, neglecting entirely the impact of the Treaty competition rules. This was perhaps a hint that the Court realised the complexity associated with the application of Articles 81 and 82 to sport and that, by focusing on violation of the free movement rules alone, it preferred to leave consideration of competition law to another day and, perhaps better still from its perspective, to another institution. (Its hopes in this regard may be dashed; see the litigation mentioned in the paper presented by M. Pons). The Commission has now picked up the baton, and it seems plain that, *Bosman* notwithstanding, it is competition policy that will be the major battleground in the future elaboration of the application of EC law to sport.

Nevertheless, it must be appreciated that, first, the Court's deployment of Article 39 in *Bosman* was not problem-free in the context of the development of the law of free movement. There was no special *cross-border* problem to Bosman's plight, for he would have been confronted by (roughly) the same problem had he wished to change clubs inside Belgium. So the Court, trying to avoid the Treaty competition rules, stretched the law of free movement in its decision.[476] Second, and of more direct relevance to the present setting, the appreciation that Articles 81 and 82 were the dogs that did not bark in *Bosman* (though they may yet!) and that Article 39 has now become very much the underdog in the Commission's thinking should not detract

[476] See Weatherill, After *Keck*, 33 *CMLR* (1996) 885.

from the realisation that Article 39 remains relevant in the shaping of EC law in this sector. It affects the flexibility allowed to the Commission in applying Articles 81 and 82. Specifically, any concession granted to the industry must also comply with Article 39.[477] Furthermore, in so far as a revised system violates free movement rights, it may be challenged by a private litigant relying on the directly effective right contained in Article 39 even where the Commission is satisfied that the competition rules have not been infringed. Article 39 confers no absolute right of free movement. Instead it allows a form of public interest exception to the regulatory authorities subject to its personal reach (embracing both public and private sector), but it is perfectly possible that a practice may comply with Articles 81 and 82 but fall foul of Article 39. I have suggested above that this may be pertinent in the shaping of an adjusted system of transfer fees, where I submit that Article 39 injects a powerful strain of hostility to restrictions on labour mobility.

The *Bosman* ruling was explicitly directed at the status of players whose contract had come to an end. M. Pons explains that a violation of EC law may be established where transfers of players are blocked where those players have unilaterally terminated their contracts and fulfilled relevant obligations under local employment law. This would further slice into the persisting viability of what remains of the transfer system post-*Bosman.* I agree with M. Pons' view on this point (and, if I may be permitted to recall it, I made this case in my Annotation of the *Bosman* ruling[478]). The law of free movement forbids collectively-imposed sanctions on players wishing to escape agreed contractual obligations and pushes the consequences of such 'player power' into the realms of national private law, privileging astute contract negotiation with star players by an employer. This is normal in most industries, and in my submission the essence of the Court's approach in *Bosman* is that the football labour market should be organised in much the same way as any other labour market. The special demands of organised sport must be reflected other than through the imposition of extra burdens on players. Football may be different; footballers should not be. M. Pons approaches this issue from the perspective of competition law, and I believe that this route would achieve the same result as use of the free movement provisions in the EC Treaty.

The willingness to exclude some arrangements from Article 81(1) altogether on the basis that they are inherent to sport and/or necessary for its organisation represents the most malleable tool available to the Commission. This offers a new method for reflecting the special nature of sport, but the debate about which rules are properly treated as inherent to sport and necessary for its organisation and which, by contrast, constitute supplementary restrictions falling within Article 81 EC promises to reveal much about the perceived peculiar nature of the industry of sport and its subjection to EC law. What really are the 'rules of the game?' The supposed divide between a socially and culturally important core sporting agenda and other 'normal' economic interests and activities generated by sport is hard to fix and remains intellectually and commercially elusive.

---

[477] This is clear from *Bosman;* see especially A-G Lenz.

[478] See Weatherill, Annotation, 33 *CMLR* 991, (1996) 1028-1031.

I find the paper of M. Pons very illuminating on these points – not least because of his acceptance that the lines are very hard to draw in this area. He identifies a form of 'organisational solidarity' between clubs as a distinctive feature of sport in contrast to 'competition between industrial firms'. In sport there is interdependence among rivals. An uncertainty of outcome may be regarded as a means of improving the quality of the product, but, more than that, it may be treated as essential to the very conduct of sport in the first place. This may justify regulatory patterns that reflect the distinctive nature of sport. This might lead to the conclusion that the establishment of a 'solidarity fund' within a sport, to which wealthier clubs contribute from the proceeds of, *inter alia*, the sale of broadcasting rights and ticket income and on which poorer clubs may draw for financial support, may escape supervision under EC competition law. I concede, however, that this system may be attacked as an inapt and inefficient route to achieving the objective of workable competitive equality between clubs. On a rather different plane, M. Pons identifies 'socio-cultural' objectives. These are harder to pin down and offer a rather imprecise basis for allowing sport self-regulatory room to manoeuvre of a type that would be denied an undertaking in a 'normal' market.

I would not argue with the list of practices tipped to fall outside Article 81(1) supplied by M. Pons. The list does, of course, beg some intriguing questions – for example, relating to the status of rules forbidding multiple ownership of clubs, which could fall within the notion of 'Rules needed to ensure uncertainty as to results'. M. Pons mentions that such rules are now on the Commission's agenda. In addition, such rules might need to be examined from the perspective of their impact on free movement rights under EC law.

Rules that restrict competition within the meaning of Article 81(1) but that are in principle eligible for exemption under Article 81(3) constitute a separate category. These would include rules whose aim is to maintain the balance between clubs in a proportionate way by preserving both a certain equality of opportunities and the uncertainty of results and by encouraging recruitment and training of young players. As M. Pons makes plain, such rules may lie social and cultural in motivation, but they are economic too. Sport's special character is relevant to their assessment, hut that occurs at the stage of exemption. They do not by their very nature escape the Community's net. The dividing line between such rules and those of the type considered above is extremely hard to fix, because of the entanglement of cultural motivations with those of an economic character. The arrangements governing the 'solidarity fund' discussed above could legitimately be regarded as better analysed from the perspective of exemption under Article 81(3) rather than as falling outside Article 81 altogether. This is a key issue requiring the clarification of a formal Decision of the Commission.

Naturally, the choice of whether to place a practice outside Article 81 altogether or, rather, to exempt it under Article 81(3) has vital institutional consequences. Exemption currently remains the exclusive preserve of the Commission.[479] The institutional focus of supervision therefore depends at present on the scope allowed to Article 81(1).

479 Although this may alter; see the recent proposals for release of exclusivity in favour of a greater degree of national-level application discussed in Session III of this conference. See Ch. 10-17.

M. Pons provides helpful examples drawn from the broadcasting sector of how Articles 81(1) and (3) may be used to control the reach of exclusive rights, which, as is well known, may have ambiguous implications for the competitive structure of the market and similarly for collective selling. Although systems of wealth distribution that are internal to a sport may conceivably be regarded as part of the means for ensuring the uncertainty of results, which is essential in a League and therefore as lying beyond the control of EC competition law, I do not regard the point as settled. By contrast the collective selling of broadcasting rights exerts a direct impact on third party buyers. These arrangements are essentially economic in nature and therefore require exemption under the third paragraph of Article 81.

Finally, there are rules that are abusive within the meaning of Article 82. Use of Article 82 invites intriguing consideration of how markets for sporting events and activities may be defined, how market power is measured and what constitutes an 'abuse' of a dominant position in the market. Article 82 was used in condemning the ticket distribution system for the Football World Cup 1998, although I regard this affair as very far from being the Commission's finest hour in its supervision of the sports sector, for its intervention was belated and ineffective. The elision of the role of administration over a sport with that of marketer of commercial rights has attracted the Commission's examination through the lens of Article 82 especially in connection with Formula One motor racing.

VI. Conclusion

Is it possible to devise an intellectually coherent case in favour of allowing sports bodies an immunity from legal control? Certainly, sport possesses unusual features that mark it out from 'normal' industry. It has an unusually well developed pattern of globalised regulation. It has its own adjudicative tribunals, such as the increasingly prominent Court of Arbitration in Sport, based in Lausanne, which is involved with some of the issues that engage the Commission, such as UEFA's prohibition on football clubs belonging to the same owner participating in the same competition.[480] Sport has a need for healthy internal competition that is not the hallmark of 'normal' industry. Can a case be made that sport ought to be permitted to run its own affairs – self-regulation? Should the 'law' of international sporting bodies be treated as an autonomous system worthy of protection from disruption by state law or the law of transnational entities such as the EC? The intellectual case could be made that this is an internally coherent system, which responds to the special interests of sport, and which should not be invaded by differently motivated, alien systems. To treat decisions of sporting associations as 'law' in their own right, rather than as private acts subordinate to 'real law,' would argue for a differently conceived 'sports law' and would bring to mind questions surrounding choice of which legal order to apply in case of conflict. In the EC context, sporting bodies have enjoyed little success in mak-

[480] See *supra*, Section V.

ing this case. This is primarily because they have been obliged to fight the battle on the EC system's own terms, as explained above. Perhaps, of course, one could object to the characterisation of sporting rules as 'law' with reference to the (relatively) unrepresentative, unaccountable processes of decision making within the sector. Mr. Goldfein explains the need for bona fide arms length negotiation as a pre-condition to the applicability of the non-statutory labour exemption in the United States,[481] but in Europe such 'democratisation' (I simplify!) is largely absent from rule making, which remains predominantly based on a top-down model in which strong player unions are absent.

At a more practical level, the confrontational attitude of sporting associations to the incursion of EC law visible in *Bosman* appears to have been unwise. In practice, sporting associations would now be better advised to adapt their arguments in order to win autonomy for their role in fixing 'the rules of the game' while accepting subjection to the control of EC law in more obviously economic realms. This would, of course, leave space for debate about the precise location of the margin between the sporting and the economic category. They could improve their case by more sophisticated use of empirical evidence about the needs of organised sport. Both the Court's ruling in *Bosman* and evolving Commission practice exhibit readiness to acknowledge the special concerns of the sports sector, albeit not to the extent of conceding that its rules entirely escape the jurisdictional reach of the EC.

481 See Ch. 7.

THE HELSINKI REPORT ON SPORT*

In December 1999 the Commission issued a communication entitled 'The Helsinki Report on sport' (COM (1999) 644 and/2), designed for consideration by that month's European Council held in Helsinki. The purpose of this note is to examine the key features of the Report and to show the direction in which EC *policy on sport is likely to move in future. In order to achieve this, it is first necessary to sketch the history of* EC *involvement in sport, because much of the Helsinki Report can only be understood in the light of the incremental accumulation of material over time that has left the* EC*'s position on sports regulation uncertain and frequently (though not always fairly) criticised.*

Sports and Community law

In so far as it constitutes an economic activity sport falls within the scope of Community law. This was first established by the Court in a pair of rulings in the mid 1970s, *Walrave and Koch* v. *UCI* and *Donà* v. *Mantero.*[482] *Walrave and Koch* is perhaps best known for the Court's jurisprudentially imprecise concession that rules of 'purely sporting interest' escape the reach of Community law,[483] which has provided the legal basis for the assumption (which still holds good) that it is not forbidden to restrict selection for national representative teams to nationals of a particular Member State. However, in practice sporting organisations enjoy a formidable capacity to resist legal control. Potential litigants are deterred by the frustratingly slow progress of judicial proceedings compared with annual competition and short careers which are typical in sport. It is consequently no surprise that after the two rulings of the 1970s two decades passed in which the application of Community law to sport was periodically debated but formal legal action was minimal. It was the Court's ruling in *URBSFA* v. *Bosman*[484] which resuscitated interest in the vigorous application of Community law to sport. At one level *Bosman* merely confirmed the subjection of decisions of sporting associations to Community law. Much of the substance of the Court's ruling was not revolutionary as a matter of Community law. Anti-discrimination, the search for objective justification and proportionality are standard fare in Community law.[485]

* 25 *EL Rev.* (2000) p. 252 et seq.

482 Case 36/74, [1974] *ECR* 1405; [1975] 1 *CMLR* 320. Case 13/76, [1976] *ECR* 1333; [1976] 2 *CMLR* 578, respectively.

483 On this notion see S. Weatherill, 'European Football Law', in *Collected Courses of the 7th Session of the Academy of European Law* (European University Institute, Florence, Kluwer Law International 1999) pp. 339-382.

484 Case C-415/93 *URBSFA* v. *Bosman*, [1995] *ECR* I-4921; [1996] 1 *CMLR* 645.

485 The Court's readiness to find an obstacle to trade within the meaning of Art. 48 (now 39) EC even though the transfer system exerted no special cross-border hindrance was, however, surprising; see Weatherill. 'After *Keck:* Some thoughts on how to Clarify the Clarification', 33 *CML Rev.* (1996) 885.

Attempts to insulate sport from the control of Community law were found wanting according to rationales which will have raised no Community legal eyebrows, however, shocking they may have been to sports administrators. For example, the Court refused football an immunity from the application of the principles of Community trade law despite the German government's submission that the subsidiarity principle dictated that public authorities' intervention in private commercial affairs should be limited to what is strictly necessary. According to the Court, this could not be accepted as a basis for permitting private associations to adopt rules which restrict the exercise of Treaty rights conferred on individuals. More dramatically, the ruling represented an explicit and unavoidable finding that the collectively enforced transfer system then prevailing in Europe, which prevented player' from freely choosing a new employer even on the expiry of their existing contract, was incompatible with Community law. The Court added that nationality-based discrimination in European club football was unlawful, declining to find a 'purely sporting interest' in an enforced association between the origin of a player and the employing club and refusing to attach weight to the Commission's past preference to leave such rules unchallenged. The Court rested its ruling exclusively on Article 48 (now 39) EC, but. as is plain from the remarkably thorough Opinion provided in the case by Advocate-General Lenz, the Treaty competition rules are also capable of challenging cartels within football. What was truly remarkable in *Bosman* was the dogged determination of the litigant to pursue the matter all the way to Luxembourg, provoked by the astonishing insouciance of the European football authorities which caused them to totter to such a crushing defeat instead of settling the matter earlier out of court. Yet even Bosman's victory offers only qualified encouragement to crusading litigants. His contract expired in June 1990. Only in December 1995 did the European Court rule on the matter. He was not compensated until December 1998, when he received an out-of-court settlement of £ 312.000 from the Belgian football authorities.[486] He was then 34 years old, playing football at a very low level and his marriage had broken up under the strain.

Despite the relative absence of jurisprudential novelty, *Bosman* helped to change the climate. Law and sport came closer together. Within three years Directorate General IV of the Commission had more than 60 relevant complaints on its desk. It would wholly mislead to suppose that *Bosman* alone opened the floodgates. True, the Court's decision forced change in the governance of sport and, moreover, it reminded all concerned of the role of litigation as one part of the battle to restructure markets in sport. But during the 1990s the renovation of the broadcasting sector has exerted enormous influence. Acquisition of rights to broadcast sporting events is regarded as a key commercial ploy by new market entrants. Fierce competition has forced up prices for rights to club and international sports events (chiefly football in Europe) to unprecedented levels. Income generation through, for example, sponsorship and sale of merchandise (especially replica team kits) has accelerated. Compared to these manifestations of the commercialisation of sport, *Bosman* could fairly be regarded as a sideshow, although, of course, for professional sportsmen and women it ensured they would be better placed to claim their slice of the expanding cake.

[486] *The Independent*, December 23, 1998, p. 20.

The Commission placed on record the tensions it felt undermined the articulation of policy in this area in a Press Release issued in February 1999 summarising a confidential (but widely leaked) Commission draft communication on Community law and sport.[487] The breadth of interest in sport was emphasised by the fact that the release appeared under the name of three of the 15 Commissioners, representing competition policy (Van Miert), culture (Oreja) and social affairs (Flynn). Four main topics were to be the subject of wide consultation by the Commission: (i) the application of the competition rules, (ii) the development of a European sport model, (iii) sport as an instrument of social and employment policies and (iv) the fight against doping. The Commission made clear that it had no intention of acting as a regulator. But the Court's ruling in *Bosman* illustrates how readily Community law spreads into areas apparently out of its bounds. Although the Community may lack explicit competence under the Treaty to regulate a sector (this is true of sport), or else enjoy only limited competence in a sector (consider, for example, culture and education), nonetheless the encroachment of its rules, especially the economic freedoms at stake in *Bosman*, may greatly influence conduct in the sector. The challenge is to define this cross-over more clearly in order to provide a reliable basis for actors in the field. The Declaration on Sport attached to the Amsterdam Treaty provides no such thing, but rather merely reflects the sensitivity of the Community's incursion into the sports arena. As part of its quest to place practice on a more secure footing, the Commission pursued wide-ranging consultation in 1999, which included a 'European Union Conference on Sport' organised at Olympia, Greece, in May attracting representatives from, *inter alia*, governing bodies in sport, the media and interested public authorities. The conference generated a set of conclusions,[488] which included proclaimed adherence to a 'European sports model'. The model's features include the need for sport 'to keep its operational autonomy safe from any political or economic manipulation', which should involve preservation from 'over-commercialisation' tending to distort its values. Systems of sport governance in Europe, spanning clubs and national and international federations, ensure essential solidarity between different levels. The system of promotion and relegation is 'another identifying feature of European sport'. The balance that this has brought has allowed sport to flourish in Europe, but would be upset by clubs choosing to break away. The conclusions also warn that links between sport and television should not be used as a lever for damaging the way in which sports competitions are organised in pursuit of financial gain, and it is mentioned in this context that anxieties have been expressed about acquisition of clubs by broadcasters.

This agenda plainly challenges some actual and mooted trends in European sport (in football in particular).[489] But it is vital to appreciate that the Commission is neither competent nor anxious to impose solutions on sport. The point of the model is to identify common features of European sport with a view to, *inter alia*, ensuring that

---

[487] IP/99/133.

[488] The conclusions are available via DG 10's web site, http/europa.eu.int/comm/dg10/sport.

[489] See more fully Weatherill, 'Resisting the pressures of 'Americanization': the influence of EC law on the European sport model', in S. Greenfield and G. Osborn, *Sport and the Law* (London, Frank Cass 2000).

space is allowed by Community law for their maintenance. It is a permissive rather than a compulsory agenda. The decisions about whether the model will in fact endure belong to the business of sport.

The Helsinki Report on sport

It is identification of the divide between a core sporting agenda and distinct impulses towards (over-commercialisation which is central to the shaping of the legal regime. This emerged in *Walrave and Koch*, the first of the Court's rulings in the area, in the notion of a 'purely sporting interest'[490] and the Commission is now confronted by the need to assess how special the business of sport really is and how to reflect that peculiar character in the application of Community law.

The focus of the Commission's Helsinki Report is on safeguarding current sports structures and on maintaining the social function of sport within the Community framework, which were areas on which the Commission had been invited to report by the Vienna European Council of December 1998. The report begins with the ambitious assertion that it 'gives pointers for reconciling the economic dimension of sport with its popular, educational, social and cultural dimensions'. This is a daunting task and the Helsinki Report is understandably tentative. It contains more questions than answers.

The report announces that sport's 'social function', which is also asserted in the Amsterdam Treaty's Declaration on Sport, has lately been confronted by challenges including violence in stadiums, doping and 'the search for quick profits to the detriment of a more balanced development of sport'. The report maintains the Commission's identification of 'a European approach to sport based on common concepts and principles', which includes sport's role as 'an instrument of social cohesion and education'. Tensions have emerged between this function and the increasingly prominent economic motivations for sport. The Commission is plainly aware that it is touching on some of the most sensitive issues on European sport's agenda, such as the threat of a 'breakaway' European Football League established by a small group of leading clubs and divorced from traditional administrative structures which insist on, *inter alia*, distribution of some proceeds from the top of the game to the bottom, but the Helsinki Report is careful to do no more than advert to the tensions. It comments on 'the temptation for certain sporting operators and certain large clubs to leave the federations in order to derive the maximum benefit from the economic potential of sport for themselves alone. This tendency may jeopardise the principle of financial solidarity between professional and amateur sport and the system of promotion and relegation common to most federations'. This represents anxiety about damage to the 'European sports model', which is not based solely on wealth maximisation but rather also on sport's social and educational functions.

A link is made to the Commission's 1995 White Paper on teaching and learning[491] in search of methods for enhancing the educational role of sport, although the Com-

[490] *Supra*, note 482.

[491] COM (95) 590.

mission is naturally inhibited by the limited scope of Community competence in the field of education. Reference is also made to the Council of Europe's view that sport is an ideal platform for social democracy, and it is emphasised that 'existing Community programmes should make use of sport in combating exclusion, inequalities, racism and xenophobia'. This sustains the conviction displayed in May 1999 at Olympia that sport plays a role in protecting young people and in promoting democratic values, the integration of minorities and tolerance and fair play in society.

Violence at sporting events is to be the subject of increased co-operation between 'the relevant authorities' within the context of the pursuit of an area of freedom, security and justice, the catchphrase invented at Amsterdam and given legal shape in Articles 61-69 EC Doping is to be tackled by liaison between Commission and the Member States,[492] as well as through international co-operation involving the Olympic movement, although it is asserted that action will be fruitless unless 'the root causes of the rise in doping' are addressed. Presumably this serves as a reference to the claim made earlier in the Report that the prevalence of doping is in part caused by the lure of greater rewards for success consequent on increasing sponsorship combined with overloading of sporting calendars, which is presented as one manifestation of the damaging tensions between sport's social functions and its economic impact.

In a section entitled 'Clarifying the Legal Environment of Sport' the Commission contents itself with a relatively brief summary. The clarification referred to lies in the future. Pending disputes are merely mentioned with negligible elaboration, in particular those concerning the collective selling of television rights, the perceived failure post-*Bosman* to cope with the economic consequences of unrestricted player mobility, distortion caused by variation between relevant fiscal legislation in the Member States, monopoly powers over organisation of events held by federations and rules governing the multiple ownership of clubs. What is at stake is 'preserving the traditional values of sport, while at the same time assimilating a changing economic and legal environment'. The Commission calls on national authorities to clarify their rules as they apply to sport and sporting organisations too are invited to announce their missions more transparently, *inter alia* in connection with the promotion of amateur and professional sport and the integration of sport into society which are to be achieved by 'financial mechanisms of internal solidarity'. From the Community perspective, it is first asserted that although the sporting sector is not in principle excluded from the application of the Treaty, nevertheless its 'specific characteristics' should be taken into account. This is a concession familiar from *Bosman*, for, contrary to much of the ill-informed criticism hurled at that judgment by sporting organisations and administrators shocked at the intrusion of law on to their turf, the Court there accepted that in some respects sport has features which distinguish it from 'normal' industries.[493] With reference to the transfer system, the Court was willing to allow the football industry to present two justifications in law for unusual practices that might not be tolerated in other sectors:

---

[492] See already COM (99) 643, Community support plan in the combat against doping in sport.

[493] For comment see Weatherill, 'Annotation', 33 *CML Rev.* (1996) 991; O'Keeffe and Osborne, 'The European Court scores a goal, *International Journal of Comparative Labour Law and Industrial Relations* (1996) 111; Seche, 'Quand les Juges tirent au but', 32 *CDE* (1996)355.

> 'In view of the considerable social importance of sporting activities and in particular football in the Community, the aims of maintaining a balance between clubs by preserving a certain degree of equality and uncertainty as to results and of encouraging the recruitment and training of young players must be accepted as legitimate.'[494]

This leaves space in which to respect the autonomy of arrangements devised by sporting organisations provided they are designed to realise these objectives. However, applying the orthodox requirement of Community trade law that both the ends pursued and the means employed by a restrictive measure must be justified, the Court refused to accept that *this* transfer system could be defended. It was left to the industry to devise measures less restrictive of trade. The general notion that sport involves pursuit of at least two aims which distinguish it from normal industries, which in turn opens the door to sport-specific justification for restrictive practices, is absorbed by the Commission in the Helsinki Report. The Commission considers that there are three categories into which rules of sporting bodies might fall: practices which do not come under the competition rules, practices that are, in principle, prohibited by the competition rules and practices likely to be exempted from the competition rules.

Practices which do not come under the competition rules

These are rules to which Article 81(1) does not in principle apply because they are inherent to a sport's identity and/or necessary for its organisation. It is stated that. 'first and foremost', this would cover '[t]he rules of the game'. That football limits to 11 the number of players per team would not be challengeable, even though rugby league permits 13. The most widely cited example of a rule which may seem offensive to EC law yet which is treated as part of the sporting context within which competition is permissibly organised is provided by selection policies for national representative teams. The Danish national team may comprise only Danes without violating Article 12 EC This has always been taken as the consequence of the Court's notion of rules of 'purely sporting interest' adopted in the first of its sports rulings, *Walrave and Koch*,[495] and is readily absorbed by the concept of a rule inherent to the sport, employing the language of the Helsinki Report. It is immediately apparent how murky are the distinctions that are being drawn. International football is immensely lucrative for organising bodies. An international cap typically boosts a player's earning potential. Yet the very fact that there is traditional sporting competition between national representative teams carries with it, as an inherent element, selection policies which discriminate according to nationality. These lie beyond the scope of Community law. The Court in *Bosman* was wholly unpersuaded that rules requiring an association between the location of a club and a player's origins deserved similar respect. This was treated as discrimination with no necessary connection to the organisation of the game and therefore impermissible.

---

[494] Para. 106 of the ruling.

[495] Case 36/74 *supra,* note 482. Cf. also, pending before the Court, Case C-51/96 *Deliège* and Case C-176/96 *Lehtonen.*

Another type of rule close to the margin is one directed at maintaining the integrity of competition by excluding multiple ownership of clubs. UEFA's rules restricting multiple ownership of football clubs participating in European competition were examined in 1999 by the Court for Arbitration in Sport (CAS), an arbitral body established by the industry and based in Lausanne. CAS decided such rules were lawful, examining the matter from the perspective of both Community and Swiss law.[496] Having regarded the *Walrave and Koch* 'sporting exception' as unworkable, the CAS proceeded to find the rules did not appreciably restrict competition within the meaning of Article 81(1). Moreover, it treated the rules as necessary in any event to achieve the legitimate objective of securing a properly functioning and credibly competitive league and proportionate to that end, for the CAS was unpersuaded that *ex post facto* control over match-fixing (for example, by imposing criminal penalties) was adequate. This judgment does not preclude the matter being the subject of a different conclusion reached by a tribunal within the Community, although the parties responsible for bringing the case before the CAS acquiesced by adjusting their shareholdings in order to comply with UEFA's requirements. Subsequently the Commission issued its preliminary conclusion that the rule could fall outwith the Treaty competition rules, citing both the CAS decision and the Court's recognition in *Bosman* of sport's legitimate objectives although, in accordance with the orthodoxy of Community trade law, it requires further information to satisfy itself of the absence of less restrictive means of preserving the integrity of competitions in circumstances of multiple club ownership.[497]

Practices that are, in principle, prohibited by the competition rules

Among practices listed as likely to fall foul of the Treaty are restrictions on parallel imports of sports products, ticket sales which discriminate according to the residence of buyers,[498] sponsoring agreements that close a market by eliminating other suppliers without objective reason and the exclusion from the market by a sporting body for no objective reason of any economic operator which complies with justified quality or safety standards. The linking theme of a list which conflates Articles 81 and 82 is that these are practices of purely economic interest. They have no connection with the preservation of the special characteristics of sport. Community law therefore applies and such practices offend against basic expectations of non-discrimination and competitive markets.

Practices likely to be exempted from the competition rules

Citing *Bosman*, the Commission thinks it likely that exemption would be granted to agreements genuinely designed to achieve the objectives of maintaining 'a balance

496 CAS 98/200, *AEK Athens and Slavia Prague* v. *UEFA*, August 20, 1999. See generally on the CAS, Beloff, Kerr and Demetriou, *Sports Law* (Hart Publishing 1999), Chs. 8.101-8.108.

497 *OJ* 1999 C 363/2.

498 Cf. now Comm. Dec. 2000/12/E.C. *1998 Football World Cup*, *OJ* 2000 L 5/55.

between clubs, while preserving a degree of equality of opportunity and the uncertainty of the result, and to encourage the recruitment and training of young players'. It expresses a similarly favourable albeit tentative view of short-term sponsorship agreements involving transparent and non-discriminatory selection criteria.

It is the scope of this intermediate category of practices that are likely to be exempted from the competition rules that is the most intriguing and in need of clarification. Tricky questions of definition are inevitable, in particular at the margin between rules of the game or rules inherent in the organisation of sport, which escape the reach of Community law, and rules which are of an economic nature and which can accordingly survive only if exempted. Sporting organisations will doubtless press for a wider degree of autonomy for matters they choose to regard as 'the rules of the game' than the Commission will be prepared to concede. Even where it is determined that exemption is required, there is plenty of scope for controversy about the extent to which sport's special characteristics dictate a more generous approach to application of the Article 81(3) criteria than would prevail in a normal industry. Naturally, the choice of whether to place a practice outside Article 81 altogether or to exempt it under Article 81(3) has vital institutional consequences, for exemption currently remains the exclusive preserve of the Commission.[499] In making its choices the Commission runs the risk of being drawn into the role of the sports regulator it claims not to want to perform. Its caution may already be gauged by the much thinner feel to the analysis presented in the Helsinki Report compared with the February 1999 draft communication which now seems unlikely to mature into a final text, at least until the foundations of some key individual Decisions have been laid.

Resolution of the more sensitive points of demarcation must depend on the facts of individual cases, but it is topical and illuminating to consider arrangements governing wealth distribution within a sport. This involves pooling of (some proportion of) income received from commercial activities and re-allocation to financially weaker clubs. The purpose of such an arrangement is foreseen in the Court's key statement of sport's special characteristics in *Bosman:* it is designed to maintain 'a balance between clubs by preserving a certain degree of equality and uncertainty as to results'. Such concerns have no place in most sectors of the economy, but sports clubs are not business rivals in an orthodox sense. They are mutually dependent. It takes two to play a match and many more to constitute a worthwhile league. It is not inconceivable that such a system of wealth distribution could be treated as inherent to sport and therefore outside the reach of the competition rules altogether. After all, without a degree of planning aimed at controlling the breadth of the gulf between rivals, the keen competitive edge and (relative) unpredictability of outcome which distinguishes sport from forms of entertainment such as opera is lost. This, however, may be a difficult argument to sustain. There is certainly a degree of economic motivation for such rules, for internal wealth distribution is in part designed to make the sport more appealing to spectators. Who would watch a sporting foregone conclusion? It is to eco-

[499] This will change if the 'modernization' of competition policy proposed in the Commission's 1999 White Paper. *OJ* 1999 C 132/1 comes to fruition.

nomic analysis that one turns in designing an efficient model for wealth distribution which secures relative equality of opportunity for all participants without eliminating incentives to succeed.[500] This suggests that a sufficient degree of economic motivation is at stake for wealth distribution systems in principle to require exemption rather than to be treated as beyond the reach of the competition rules.[501] However, the ultimate outcome of regulatory supervision should not be crucially dependent on choice of classification. Exemption should be available. Without arrangements for wealth distribution, the vital need for uncertainty of outcome is lost to organised sport. Moreover, it is plain from the Helsinki Report that the Commission is minded to take a favourable view of such planning especially where wealth created in the upper reaches of the professional game is used to foster the grass roots. Although this might encourage sporting bodies to maintain a readiness to 'tax' richer clubs in order to foster deeply rooted 'organisational solidarity', they are doubtless mindful that it is precisely such intervention which provokes richer clubs to consider the merits of a breakaway. This provides an illustration of how the European sports model permits arrangements promoting solidarity but cannot require adherence to them, except in so far as departure constitutes a breach of EC law.

Anxiety to provide for distribution of wealth underpins sport's unusual treatment of broadcasting rights.[502] Aggressive competition to acquire rights to broadcast popular sporting events as a basis for the rapid development of new markets is a major reason for the recent increase in the 'commercialisation' of sport. It is also a key factor in the Commission's own interest in sport. The Commission is rightly anxious lest sport be used as a pawn to damage the flexibility of the restructuring occurring in the broadcasting industry in the wake of liberalisation and driven by dynamic technological change. It is accepted in the Helsinki Report that a degree of exclusivity may properly be granted to a broadcaster, especially where an investment is commercially risky because of, for example, use of innovative technology, but the Commission will carefully scrutinise the duration and scope of the grant of exclusivity lest it cause unacceptable market foreclosure. Questions of collective selling of rights are even more sensitive. Such cartels suppress the competition between clubs that would occur were they able to sell rights to cover matches separately. One would suppose that collective selling would raise prices paid by broadcasters and ultimately by consumers whose choice will also be reduced in so far as the package does not cover all matches. For the sports industry, by contrast, collective selling is typically defended as an essential mechanism for maximising revenue and then ensuring it is shared between all clubs in order to preserve the balance that is required for a competitive league. The matter has attracted the attention of national competition authorities. In Germany a legislative exemption was recently allowed to central marketing of broadcasting rights for sports

[500] See, e.g., from the American perspective, Quirk and Fort, *Pay Dirt: the Business of Professional Team Sports* (Princeton University Press 1997).

[501] In the USA some of these issues are played out against the different legal background of the 'single entity' thesis applicable to sports leagues and the rule of reason governing restrictions.

[502] See Beloff, Kerr and Demetriou, *supra* note 496. Ch. 6; Brinckman and Vollebregt, 'The Marketing of Sport and its Relation to EC Competition Law', *ECLR* (1998) 281.

events[503] and in July 1999 the United Kingdom's Restrictive Practices Court ruled that collective selling of Premier League rights was not contrary to the public interest under domestic competition law.[504] However, in so far as such agreements exert an effect on inter-state patterns, they must comply with Article 81 EC and, if they fail that test, then in accordance with the orthodox principles governing the relationship between Community and national law concessions made at national level cannot save them. The Commission ostentatiously made this point in 1999 by requiring notification of the agreements concerning rights to the English Premier League.[505]

Even though collective selling of broadcasting rights forms part of the strategy for maintaining competitive balance within a league, it is submitted that because of the direct impact on third party buyers it is inconceivable that it could be regarded as lying beyond the control of Community competition law. The arrangements are essentially economic in nature and therefore require exemption. A robust view would deny exemption. In so far as collective selling is designed to secure effective wealth distribution in a league. It is vulnerable to the criticism that it is not necessary to achieve that end. From this perspective, rights should be sold individually by clubs, allowing the price competition denied by collective selling, and only then should the proceeds be shared according to internal league rules, ensuring necessary organisational solidarity. That is to say, wealth distribution conducted within the game is proper, but systems that rig markets to require third parties to fund sport's special concerns seem indefensibly anti-competitive.

However, it is arguable that enforcing distribution in the absence of collective selling would be impractical,[506] and in the Helsinki Report the commission leaves the door to exemption ajar. It warns that any exemption would have to take account of the benefits for consumers and that restrictions must be proportionate to the end in view. It is observed that it is therefore appropriate 'to examine the extent to which a link can be established between the joint sale of rights and financial solidarity between professional and amateur sport, the objectives of the training of young sportsmen and women and those of promoting sporting activities among the population'. Even though the Commission expresses itself with great caution, this is an intriguing suggestion. It tends towards embedding the protection of the social and educational function of sport within the scope permitted to the lucrative practice of collective selling. The Commission, reflecting sport's special role in society, seems ready to override normal assumptions of competition in the market for broadcasting rights provided the proceeds accruing to the cartel are shared throughout the sport for the sake of its general health.[507] This could be taken as a hint that collective selling is impermissible if used merely as a tool of wealth maximisation, which might lead one to suppose that

---

[503] S.31. Gesetz gegen Wettbewerbsbeschraenkungen as amended with effect from January 1, 1999.

[504] *Re the supply of services facilitating the broadcasting on televsion of Premier League Football Matches* judgment of July 28, 1999, currently available via www.courtservice.gov.uk/highhome.htm.

[505] See also *UEFA Champions League*, *OJ* 1999 C 99.

[506] This was the RPCs view in the English context: see *supra* note 504.

[507] Approval of distribution of revenues outside the Premier League plays a part, albeit a minor one, in the RPC's decision, *supra* note 504, Para. 348 of the judgment.

a newly formed league that breaks away from traditional organisational structures in search of an increased slice of the financial cake would be denied an exemption for arrangements involving collective selling. Were this to occur, it would confirm the Commission's drift towards a significant role as the sports regulator it expresses a desire not to become, but the shaping of Article 81(3) in this manner offers the Commission a tempting device to give some shape to its 'European sports model'.

Conclusion

Sport cannot have it both ways. It cannot scoop up the fruits of commercialisation yet aspire to keep Community law entirely at bay. Nonetheless, as is plain from *Bosman*, there are aspects of the organisation of sport which either escape Community law or which, though subject to it, are examined with due recognition of sport's unusual features. The Helsinki Report betrays the complexity of the Commission's task in finding room for the special characteristics of sport within the overall framework of Community law. However, the Commission feels able to insist that 'the basic freedoms guaranteed by the Treaty do not generally conflict with the regulatory measures of sports associations, provided that these measures are objectively justified, non-discriminatory, necessary and proportional' and the report is clearly designed to leave space for sporting associations to abandon their confrontational attitude to the incursion of Community law on to their territory. Although it is not impossible that an exemption will be granted to sport on Treaty revision, the assembly of unanimous support for such a change among the Member States would represent an arduous task and frankly the sports sector has failed to present an intellectually convincing case as to why it deserves such unique treatment. For the time being, the only game in town is to play according to the Community's rules while seeking to exploit the clear acceptance of both Court and Commission that in some respects sport is special. Sports bodies need to adapt their arguments in order to win autonomy for their role in fixing 'the rules of the game' while accepting subjection to the control of Community law in more obviously economic realms.

It is particularly intriguing that whereas the Court's recognition in *Bosman* that sport is special was largely generated by perceived economic differences from normal industries, particularly clubs' need for credible rivals, the Commission's agenda is much broader. It is not prepared to surrender its concern for the social and educational functions of sport, nor for the preservation of sporting structures and ethics in the face of a changing legal and commercial environment. This requires consultation and partnership between interested levels of governance, including sports bodies, Member States, and European institutions. The Commission is explicit on the need to retain promotion and relegation as one of the characteristics of European sport. To this extent the caution of the Helsinki Report is embroidered by a bold opposition to some of the anticipated trends in the commercialisation of sport. But despite the intriguing possibilities of control over sport enjoyed by the Commission via, *inter alia*, its choice of what constitutes 'the rules of the game' with which it will not interfere and its approach to Article 81(3) exemption in the light of the need to secure a contribution to wider society from professional sport's economic clout. It remains plain that ultimately the Community's absence of explicit competence as a regulator in the field of sport ensures that the decisions about major changes in sport in the coming years will emerge from the boardroom.

RESISTING THE PRESSURES OF 'AMERICANIZATION': THE INFLUENCE OF EUROPEAN COMMUNITY LAW ON THE 'EUROPEAN SPORT MODEL'*

Introduction

Legal systems all over the world are increasingly confronted by the need to grapple with their impact on sport. Its accelerating commercialization has generated incentives to litigate. This in turn prompts questions about the extent to which the business of sport is properly treated as special and deserving of full or partial immunity from the application of normal legal rules. The European Community (EC) legal order is no different from others in its need to address these complex questions. But the purpose of this chapter is to enquire into the distinctive elements of the EC system of regulation. EC trade law is built around the pursuit of market integration and this conditions the application of the law of free movement and competition law to sport. Moreover, the institutional and constitutional characteristics of the EC system, relating in particular to the watchdog role allocated to the European Commission and the capacity of the individual to pursue violations before national courts, contribute to shaping a distinctive system. The European Court's *Bosman* ruling provides a high-profile illustration of the vigorous potential of EC law in driving change in the practices of sporting organizations, and the decision has brought to the fore many more intriguing issues, which will be discussed here. The chapter proceeds from the assumption that it is realistic to suppose that European sport, particularly football, will become ever more lucrative in the next few years in the wake of the media revolution, perhaps eventually to the extent that it compares financially with the dominant sports in North America, but that there are aspects of the American model that will prove unpalatable in Europe. It is significant in this context that the Commission has recently tentatively put forward a 'European Sport Model' and, in the light of the Commission's Helsinki Report on Sport of December 1999, this chapter assesses the viability of maintaining key aspects of the European tradition. Although the *Bosman* ruling has frequently been criticized as damaging to the fabric of European football, it is argued that the European Court in *Bosman* was, in fact, generous to sport's appeals for special treatment under the law. A series of legal issues, including the sale of broadcasting rights and transfers, is discussed. The chapter concludes with observations on how special sport should be taken to be as an industry, arguing that the mutual interdependence of clubs in a league demands a much deeper commitment to wealth distribution between clubs than has been visible in recent years, but that pleas to be allowed a form of renovated transfer system should be rejected as irrelevant to the true needs of restructured organized sport. The conclusion is that 'Americanization' of the European game is by

* S. Greenfield and G. Osborn, eds., *Law and Sport in Contemporary Society* (London, Frank Cass Publishing 2000), p. 155 et seq.

no means inevitable, and that EC law, too often misleadingly portrayed as a motor for change in circumstances where it is, in fact, the financial interest of clubs which is driving departures from traditional European preferences, in truth allows sport considerable autonomy to make the relevant key decisions about the shape of the game.

The Appeal for Self-regulation in Sport

As EC intervention in sport has increased in recent years, so too expressions of resistance by international sporting bodies as to what they perceive as inappropriate external interference in their affairs by ill-suited legal systems have become increasingly prominent. A selection of recent examples must suffice. Marcel Benz, a legal adviser to UEFA, is reported to have observed:

'We have our rules and our traditions. We are asking: Why should the EU interfere? The interests of sport are not necessarily best served by EU rules.'[508] Keith Cooper, FIFA's director of communications, commented that 'Football has always been remarkably successful at looking after its own affairs. It is difficult to understand why regulatory authorities feel they now have to become involved.'[509] The FIA, the governing body of grand prix racing, responding to the threatened application of EC competition law, stated that

> 'The Commission is being naive [...] The bottom line is that the FIA is not a European organization and if the EU tries in this unsubtle way to impose its regulations it will accentuate the trend to have more races elsewhere in the world.'[510]

In a similar vein the International Rugby Board sees itself as 'a governing body for the whole of world rugby and not simply the Unions within the jurisdictional area of the European Union'.[511]

Sport, then, seeks to maintain a pattern of self-regulation, perceiving its special character as being in danger of being misunderstood by 'normal' lawmakers; and as the third of these four quotations suggests, it is not afraid to allude in its own unsubtle way to its capacity to skip beyond the jurisdictional reach of interventionist regulators. Thus far the business of sport has failed to provide an intellectually convincing account of why it should be allowed a partial or total immunity from the application of legal rules to which normal industries are subject. The simple assertion of the adequacy and coherence of self-regulation cannot on its own suffice, for it is hard to imagine any industry which would not seek to make such a claim. The suggestion made in the third and the fourth of the extracts cited touches on the case that sport is a transnational, in some instances global, activity which should accordingly not be subject to the confining grip of national or regional laws. But, one might respond, a

508 *Financial Times*, 24 March 1998, 24.

509 Ibid., 23 January 1998, 2.

510 *Guardian*, 23 December 1997, 21.

511 *Independent on Sunday*, 7 June 1998, Sports Section, 17.

global cartel may be more, not less, pernicious than a domestic or regional cartel and may require supervision in the public interest by any and every available regulator. Sport possesses a number of unusual characteristics which set it apart from normal industries, but its accelerating commercialization has brought with it a sharpening of legal intervention and as yet its ruling bodies grope falteringly towards a framework which would legitimize their case for special treatment at law. As already observed, the EC legal order is no different from others in its need to address these complex questions. But this chapter will, first, explore the distinctive elements of the EC system and, secondly, test the extent to which European sport's adaptability and autonomy are conditioned by subjection to the rules of the EC legal order. As already suggested, the chapter develops the thesis that in so far as the 'European sport model' is being beckoned down the path of a form of 'Americanization', it is not EC law but rather the choices taken within sport that will be decisive. This case will be made by examining, first, the position of the European Court and then that of the Commission.

Bosman – the Road to Luxembourg

The European Court's dramatic ruling in *Bosman* is the unavoidable starting point in tracking the current pattern of EC law applied to sport. The facts of the case are now well known, but they deserve recapitulation not least, for the purposes of this chapter, to identify the elements of the judgment which underpin the subsequent rethinking about the viability of traditional regulatory structures within sport.

Jean-Marc Bosman was a Belgian national, born in 1964. He had earned a reputation in his youth as a footballer of some promise and he was sufficiently skilled to play al first-division level in Belgium. He had been employed by RC Liège on a contract expiring at the end of June 1990 on an average salary of BFR 120,000 per month, including bonuses. In April 1990 the club offered him a new one-year contract at a quarter of his previous salary. Bosman refused RC Liège's unattractive offer and was transfer-listed at a 'compensation fee' of BFR 11,743,000 fixed according to indicators based, in particular, on age and salary.

The transfer system then operating in football had a bewildering number of nuances, varying country by country and adjusted periodically over time. However, it operated by virtue of the hierarchical structure within the game. Football clubs wishing to participate in official competitions must affiliate to national football associations. National associations are in turn members of FIFA, the world organizing body, which is based in Switzerland. FIFA is split into confederations for each continent. The European confederation is UEFA, also based in Switzerland, and the national associations in the EU member states are members of UEFA and as such undertake to comply with its rules. No club is an island.

The rules which most intimately affected Bosman were those applicable to the transfer system. Players were unable simply to move freely between clubs once their employment contract had come to an end. A club was only able to field a player in an official match once it had secured the player's registration, held by the previous employer. That registration would be released only when the previous club was satisfied with the terms offered by the new club, typically involving payment of a fee. A club which chose simply to field a player without complying with the requirements of the transfer system would find itself subject to heavy and immediate penalties imposed by national and transnational organizations. Footballers, then, were not treated like ordinary employees. They were traded.

US Dunkerque, a French second-division club, contracted with Bosman to pay him a monthly salary of some BFR 100,000 plus a signing-on fee of some BFR 900,000. In July 1990 RC Liège and Dunkerque agreed a contract for the transfer of Bosman for one year only, at a price of BFR 1,200,000, plus an option allowing Dunkerque to buy the player subsequently. Both contracts, RC Liège/Dunkerque and Bosman/Dunkerque, were conditional on the sending of a transfer certificate by the Belgian association to the FFF the French association, in line with the rules governing the transfer system. It was worthless to Dunkerque to conclude a contract with Bosman without compliance with these transfer requirements, for they would have been unable to play him in official matches. It emerges from the Court's summary of the background that RC Liège came to doubt Dunkerque's solvency. It did not ask the Belgian association to send the certificate to the FFF. So neither contract took effect.

In accordance with the rules prevailing in Belgium, RC Liège suspended Bosman so that he could not play in the 1990/1991 season. This prompted him to pursue redress before the Belgian courts. He based his case on the alleged violation of Articles 48, 85 and 86 of the EC Treaty, which concern free movement of workers, control of anti-competitive agreements and prohibition of the abuse of a dominant position, respectively.[512] The matter ultimately reached the European Court in Luxembourg by way of the preliminary reference procedure.

Bosman – What Did the European Court Decide?

In a damning judgment,[513] the European Court rejected a series of submissions presented by the football industry in defence of its system and concluded that Article 48 governing worker mobility had been infringed (although it declined to examine the matter in the light of the EC Treaty's competition rules). The transfer system to which Bosman had fallen victim was incompatible with EC law. The Court added that the system of nationality-based discrimination applying to European club competition, which united the scope of clubs to select players eligible for national sides other than that of the association of which the club was a member, also violated the principles of EC law. Bosman himself was finally compensated three years after the judgment and

512 Since the entry into force of the Amsterdam Treaty on 1 May 1999, these provisions are renumbered as Arts. 39, 81 and 82 EC, respectively.

513 Case C-415/93 *URBSFA* v. *Bosman*, [1995] *ECR* I-4921. The decision has generated a substantial literature; see, for instance, at the time S. Weatherill, 'Annotation', 33 *CML Rev.* (1996) 991; D. O'Keeffe and P. Osborne, 'The European Court Scores a Goal', *International Journal of Comparative Labour Law and Industrial Relations* (1996) III; J.-C. Seche, 'Quand les Juges tirent au but', 32 *CDE* (1996) 355; M. Hilf, 'Das Bosman-Urteil des EuGH', *NJW* (1996), 1169; R. Blanpain, *Droit et Sport, L'Affaire Bosman* (Leuven 1996).

eight-and-a-half years after his transfer to Dunkerque had fallen through,[514] but his name will long remain associated with the renovation of football.

The Court's finding that the transfer system operated in violation of the EC Treaty liberated professional footballers from their peculiar status as employees not entitled to sell their labour to the highest bidder once their contract of employment comes to an end. Wage bills have increased overall, although distribution has doubtless not been even across all players in all divisions. If clubs want to retain their players, they must now use contracts not cartels. Players move into an especially strong position as they run into the final few months of a contract. Hence the prevalence of long contracts lately struck between big-name clubs and big-name players. Keeping a group of players together over an extended period may involve drafting contracts with generous loyalty bonuses payable in the later stages. None of these features are novel in a 'normal' industry. This is standard fare for employers seeking to retain the services of valued employees. Contract negotiation rules.

This has doubtless caused dismay among footballing traditionalists. It obliterates the caricature of the player whose loyalty is the greater, the tighter the legal tie to the club; whose toil is the more honest, the lower the wage. Yet this is to do more than to place footballers on a par with any other type of employee.

Bosman and the Vigour of EC Law

Bosman is a strong statement of individual rights deployed to challenge collective arrangements. The European Commission had been strikingly reluctant to intervene in sport, even declining to challenge the maintenance of nationality-based discrimination in club football. But individual suits based on EC law are not subject to Commission control. It cannot lock the floodgates. In this sense Bosman the litigant broke open, not simply a cartel within football, but also a cartel between the football authorities and the Community's regulatory authorities, thereby emphasizing the two routes to securing observance of EC law via, not only the European Commission, but also the vigilance of private parties concerned to assert their rights before national courts.

Moreover, the very existence of EC law as an 'extra' regulator diminishes the room for manoeuvre for national regulators. The basic constitutional principles of EC law dictate that it prevails over national law in the event of conflict. This conditions one's appreciation of the limited value of the exemption recently allowed under German cartel law to the central marketing of broadcasting rights for sports events[515] and of the July 1999 judgment of the British Restrictive Practices Court that the collective selling of rights to televised football was not contrary to the public interest under domestic competition law.[516] In so far as such agreements exert an effect on interstate

[514] *Independent*, 23 December 1998, 20; he received £ 312,000 in an out-of-court settlement by the Belgian football authorities.

[515] s.31 Gesetz gegen Wettbewerbsbeschraenkungen, as amended with effect from 1 January 1999.

[516] *Re the Supply of Services Facilitating the Broadcasting on Television of Premier League Football Matches* judgment of 28 July 1999; currently available via www.courtservice.gov.uk/highhome.htm.

trade patterns, they must comply with Article 81 EC and, if they fail that test, the concessions made at national level cannot save them.

More generally, the Court's ruling in *Bosman* emphasizes how readily EC law spreads into areas apparently out of its bounds. This in turn sharpens awareness of the difficulty of persuading the European authorities that they should leave sport alone. Although the EC may lack explicit competence to regulate a sector, or else enjoy only very limited competence, none the less the cross-cutting effect of its rules, especially the Treaty's economic freedoms which were at stake in *Bosman*, may greatly influence the conduct of actors in that sector.[517] The EC's competence under its Treaty to act as a regulator in the fields of, for example, culture or education is closely circumscribed. It is allowed no explicit competence in the sports sector. But rules in those sectors must comply with EC rules encroaching from elsewhere, most prominently from the realms of free movement. So the football industry in *Bosman* enjoyed no success in keeping EC law at bay by the argument that sport is not economic in nature. It is, subject only to an exception for amateur events where no economic motivation is at stake.[518] Nor can the impact of EC law be displaced by appeals to the principle of subsidiarity. The Court was not persuaded to allow football an immunity from the application of the principles of Community trade law by the German government's submission that the subsidiarity principle dictated that the intervention of public authorities in private commercial affairs should be limited to what is strictly necessary. According to the Court, this could not be accepted as a basis for permitting private associations to adopt rules which restrict the exercise of Treaty rights conferred on individuals. Moreover, the Court brushed aside the submission that the EC lacked jurisdiction as a matter of law over practices in the (transnational, global) sporting industry. The rather crude argument presented frequently by UEFA and FIFA, that they are based in Switzerland and therefore lie beyond the EC's jurisdiction, is as a matter of EC law plainly wrong.[519] Their rules are implemented on the EC's territory.

It seems highly implausible that the Court will ever be prepared to grant sport a blanket exemption from the application of the rules of the EC Treaty. It is very rare that matters with a transnational impact are treated as 'non-economic' for the purposes of the application of EC law. Activity in the industry of sport must comply with basic Treaty provisions such as those concerning the free movement of goods, persons and services and competition policy. This is not to say that EC law will necessarily condemn the rules of sporting bodies. Justifications in different form may be advanced, as explained below, but such justification fails to be assessed according to the standards recognized by EC law. These may be based on assumptions which differ from those of sport.

The Declaration on Sport attached to the Amsterdam Treaty, which entered into force in 1999, offers a powerful example of the way in which vague notions about the

---

517 S. Weatherill, *Law and Integration in the EU* (Oxford 1995) Chs. 2, 7.

518 This confirmed the approach taken by the Court in the 1970s in its well-known pair of 'sports law' rulings, *Walrave and Koch* v. *UCI* (Case 36/74 [1974] *ECR* 1405) and *Donà* v. *Mantero* (Case 13/76 [1976] *ECR* 1333).

519 Cases C-89/85 *et al., Ahlstrom* v. *Commission*, [1988] *ECR* 5193.

desire to protect sport are difficult to convert into operational norms in the face of the clear-cut vigour of the basic EC Treaty freedoms. The Declaration asserts that:

> 'The Conference emphasizes the social significance of sport, in particular its role in forging identity and bringing people together. The Conference therefore calls on the bodies of the European Union to listen to sports associations when important questions affecting sport are at issue. In this connection, special consideration should be given to the particular characteristics of amateur sport.'

This is frankly rather feeble and far distant from the murmurs in the immediate aftermath of *Bosman* that a Treaty amendment might be drafted to set aside the impact of the ruling on sport. Assembling unanimous support for such a revision, which would have undermined the basic principles of EC law in one particular sector, proved infeasible. And it is important to appreciate that the setting aside of decisions of the Court via Treaty revision, though occasionally discussed as a live prospect is in fact exceedingly rare, for several very good legal and political reasons, not least the requirement of unanimity for Treaty revision, the difficulty of attaining which tends to lend powerful support to the 'default setting' of the status quo under the Treaty as already interpreted by the European Court. The result at Amsterdam was the anodyne Declaration. It has, however, bred initiatives at the political level, as sports ministers have subsequently met. One cannot entirely rule out the possibility of unanimously agreed Treaty revision setting aside aspects of the *Bosman* ruling in future, but it would require an unusually high degree of political consensus about the special status of sport.

Why Sport is Different

The *Bosman* ruling has been widely, and perhaps deliberately, misread. Contrary to much of the misconceived criticism levelled at the European Court, the Court did not treat football as an industry like any other. True, it insisted that sport is an economic activity and therefore subject to EC law, and it applied the rules of free movement to the industry accordingly. But the Court did acknowledge that sport is different. Justification for its peculiar practices is possible – albeit on EC law's terms. With reference to the transfer system, the Court was willing in principle to allow the football industry to present two particular justifications that might not be tolerated elsewhere:

> 'In view of the considerable social importance of sporting activities and in particular football in the Community, the aims of maintaining a balance between clubs by preserving a certain degree of equality and uncertainty as to results and of encouraging the recruitment and training of young players must be accepted as legitimate' (Para. 106 of the ruling).

However, it is well established in EC trade law that both the ends pursued and the means employed by a restrictive measure must be justified. The Court regarded the means employed in the current football industry as inapt to achieve ends which might be capable of justification in principle. The Court did not consider that the transfer system acted as an adequate method of maintaining balance between clubs. The rules neither precluded richer clubs from buying the best players nor prevented the 'availability of financial resources from being a decisive factor in competitive sport thus considerably altering the balance between clubs'. The Court agreed that a transfer fee system might act as an incentive to clubs to recruit and train new and young players, but it observed that, because only a handful of young players will repay the investment by making the professional grade, it is impossible to predict the fees that will be obtained. In any event such fees will be unrelated to the actual cost of training all players. The system was hit-and-miss, rather than a carefully constructed, distributive mechanism. The Court concluded that 'the same aims can be achieved at least as efficiently by other means which do not impede freedom of movement for workers' (Para. 110 of the judgment).

It is of major significance that the Court has built a justification test into the application of EC rules. Moreover, it allows recognition of the perceived special concerns of the football industry. The Court, and especially Advocate-General Lenz, went so far as to comment on the types of internal regulation that might be allowed in football, though not in a normal industry, in recognition of its peculiar features. Mr Lenz accepted that a system stopping rich clubs from becoming ever richer and the poor ever poorer could be justified. He mentioned two particular methods for preserving the financial and sporting balance between participating clubs that is vital to a healthy professional sports league. His first suggestion was for a collective wage agreement capping the salaries to be paid to the players by the clubs. His second – and apparently preferred – route involved the distribution of receipts from, for example, the sale of broadcasting rights and ticket sales among the clubs. Such internal taxation would probably be regarded as unlawful in a 'normal' industry; indeed, there would rarely be an incentive to institute such a system. But participants in a sports league are interdependent. The clubs do not have the aim of driving their competitors from the market. They need credible rivals. Neither Mr Lenz nor the Court specifies exactly what may lawfully be done in sport in order to attend to the special demands of the industry; but they open the door to arrangements designed to reflect the unusual competitive relationship that prevails between football clubs. The industry, post-*Bosman*, was left to select its own processes of internal regulation. In line with the thesis of this chapter, EC law has admittedly foreclosed the option of the brutal transfer system under which Bosman himself suffered; but the autonomy of the industry to provide structures apt to realize its unique aspiration to maintain 'a balance between clubs by preserving a certain degree of equality and uncertainty as to results' has not been called into question. Quite the reverse. One might shrewdly note that since the *Bosman* ruling conspicuously little has been done in football to address by other routes the need for wealth distribution among clubs upon which such emphasis was placed in the pleadings of the football authorities in the case aimed at defending the transfer system.

I entirely agree that in sport the clubs are mutually interdependent and that, needing credible rivals, they properly support each other. But I am much less persuaded by the second of the perceived special concerns of organized sport: the need to encourage the recruitment of young players. The key paragraph of Mr Lenz's Opinion is 239, in which he suggests that an adjusted transfer system could be justified if, first, fees were limited to the costs incurred in training the player by the previous club (or previous clubs) and, secondly, provided the fee was payable only in the case of a first change of club where the previous club had trained the player. This would exclude the multimillion euro deal. There would also have to be a proportionate reduction for every year the player had spent with that club after being trained, since during that period the training club will have had an opportunity to benefit from its investment in the player. Even Mr Lenz cautiously concedes that such a system might not be sustainable in the light of the counter-argument that its objectives 'could also be attained by a system of redistribution of a proportion of income, without the players' right to freedom of movement having to be restricted for that purpose'. The associations, he noted, had not submitted anything to refute that objection. Nothing in the Court's judgment seems to support Mr Lenz's tentative embrace of a revamped transfer system. Paragraph 114 of the ruling seems to exclude it. It states firmly that Article 48 of the EC Treaty 'precludes the application of rules laid down by sporting associations, under which a professional footballer who is a national of one member state may not, on the expiry of his contract with a club, be employed by a club of another member state, unless the latter club has paid to the former one a transfer, training or development fee'. I find the whole notion that clubs need financial support when players move in order to sustain an incentive to train young players wholly unconvincing. I cannot see any compelling reason for supposing that a football club is any less likely to train young employees because they might subsequently quit the company than a supermarket or a university would be. Naturally, clubs assert the need to claw back costs and protest that they would abandon youth training were they not allowed to do so. No empirical nor economic evidence suggests any plausible basis for such claims. Quite the reverse; all employers need to train employees in order to take the benefit of their skills for as long as they are able to attract them to stay with the company. Football is no different. A club which neglected youth training would simply perform poorly. I would not exclude the possibility that it could be regarded as legally permissible for football to devise an internal taxation system to transfer money into the hands of nursery clubs, as part of a scheme for sustaining a larger number of clubs than would survive in 'pure' market conditions and to diminish gaps in economic strength between clubs.[520] But this should be regarded as part of the wider mission to maintain a degree of competitive equality and organizational solidarity within the sport, which may also embrace the anxiety to preserve viable national leagues even in smaller European countries. It should not be defended as a device that is necessary to induce clubs to invest in training. And, in line with the Court's strong assertion of free movement rights in its *Bosman* ruling, any such system must be wholly disassociated from residual restrictions on the ability of players to contract with their preferred employer. That is to say; the economics of football are special when it comes to preserving competitive equality between clubs; the economics are much less obviously special when it comes to compensating and thereby encouraging the training of young players.

520 On another level, it is not inconceivable that public authorities may choose to intervene to require income to be used in order to support the 'grassroots' of the game as part of a broader policy for tackling social exclusion.

In fact I would go even further. The *Bosman* ruling was explicitly directed at the status of players whose contract had come to an end. But I submit that a violation of EC law may also be established when transfers of players are blocked where those players have unilaterally terminated their contract and fulfilled relevant obligations under local employment law.[521] This would further slice into the persisting viability of what remains of the transfer system post-*Bosman*. The law of free movement forbids collectively-imposed sanctions on players wishing to escape agreed contractual obligations and pushes the consequences of such 'player power' into the realms of national private law, giving a privileged status to astute contract negotiation with star players by an employer.[522] This is normal in most industries, and, in my submission, the essence of the Court's approach in *Bosman* was that the football labour market should be organized in much the same way as any other labour market.[523] The special demands of organized sport must be reflected other than through the imposition of extra burdens en players. Football may be different; footballers should not be.

Commission Thinking in 1999

In February 1999 the European Commission published preliminary conclusions on the application of EC law to sport. This took the form of a press release summarizing a confidential (but widely leaked) Commission draft communication.[524] The breadth of interest in sport was emphasized by the fact that the release appeared under the name of three of the 15 Commissioners, representing competition policy (Van Miert), culture (Oreja) and social affairs (Flynn). Four main topics were to be addressed by the Commission: (i) the application of the competition rules, (ii) the development of a European sport model, (iii) sport as an instrument of social and employment policies, and (iv) the fight against doping.

This chapter is mainly concerned to examine the first of these topics, the application of the Treaty competition rules, but with special reference to its spill-over into the

---

521 Cf. Weatherill, note 6, 1028-31; M. Thill, 'L'arrêt Bosman et ses implications pour la libre circulation des sportifs a l'intérieur de l'U.E. dans des contextes factuels différents de ceux de l'affaire Bosman', *Revue du Marché Unique Européen* (1996) 89, 108-10.

522 It may even be argued that individual mobility would be unlawfully restricted by collective arrangements in the game even where local rules governing discharge of the employment relationship are not satisfied (that is, where the player is in breach of contract, in English law terms) and that the consequences of such action should be governed by national private law alone, not least because different jurisdictions in the EU adopt different approaches to such employee freedom.

523 Note also that, although *Bosman* concerned the transfer of an EU national between two member states, it is possible to argue, especially with reference to competition law (i) that non-EU nationals may be able to challenge the system; and (ii) that a player involved in a transfer which is purely internal to a single member state (which would include one between England and Scotland) may also be able to present a challenge. The *Bosman* ruling clearly exerts an impact beyond its formal limits. See S. Weatherill, 'European Football Law', *Collected Courses of the 7th Session of the Academy of European Law* (The Hague 1999) 339, 375-9; P. Spink, 'Blowing the Whistle on Football's Domestic Transfer Fee', *Juridical Review* (1999) 73; M. Beloff, T. Kerr and M. Demetriou, *Sports Law* (Oxford 1999) Ch. 4. Cf. also Case C-264/98 *Tibor Balogh* v. *Royal Charleroi Sporting Club* pending before the ECJ.

524 IP/99/133.

shaping of the European sport model. It is accepted in the February 1999 confidential draft that, following *Bosman*, sport's interdependence of competitors and the need for uncertainty in results might justify special arrangements, in particular, in the markets for the production and the sale of sports events. But this does not warrant automatic exemption from the EC Treaty's competition rules of any economic activities generated by sport. It is conceded that Commission practice is not yet sufficiently well developed to answer all the important issues on the agenda. Cited as pending issues are the principle that sports be organized on a national territorial basis, the creation of new sporting organizations, club relocation, the ban on organizing competitions outside a given territory, the regulatory role of sporting event organizers, the transfer systems applying to team-game players, nationality clauses, selection criteria for athletes, ticket distribution for the 1998 World Cup,[525] broadcasting rights, sponsorship, and the prohibition on clubs belonging to the same owner taking part in the same competition.

By way of preliminary conclusion the Commission identified four categories of practice which should be kept separate for the purposes of applying the EC Treaty's competition rules:

1. Rules to which Article 81(l) (ex 85(1)) does not in principle apply, given that such rules are inherent to sport and/or necessary for its organisation.
2. Rules which are in principle prohibited if they have a significant effect on trade between member States.
3. Rules which restrict competition but which are in principle eligible for exemption, in particular rules which do not affect a sportsman's [sic] freedom of movement within the EU and whose aim is to maintain the balance between clubs in a proportionate way by preserving both a certain equality of opportunities and the uncertainty of results, and by encouraging the recruitment and training of young players.
4. Rules which are abusive within the meaning of Article 82 (ex 86). The draft communication declares that it is not the power to regulate a given sporting activity as such which might constitute an abuse but rather the way in which an organization exercises such power. It would violate Article 82 (ex 86) to exclude from the market without objective reason any competing organizer or, indeed, any market player who, even meeting justified quality or safety standards, failed to obtain from the organizer a certificate of quality or of product safety.

This intriguing agenda attempts to provide a framework for analysis within which EC law will apply while showing sensitivity to sport's peculiarities. After discussion with the sports world in line with the Amsterdam Treaty's Declaration on Sport, the Commission planned to draw up final conclusions. For the purposes of discussion, a 'European Union Conference on Sport' was organized in Olympia, Greece, in May 1999 and attracted representatives from, *inter alia*, governing bodies in sport, public

525 See now Dec. 2000/12 *1998 Football World Cup, OJ* 2000 L 5/55 (fine of € 1000 imposed).

authorities and the media. This forum generated a set of conclusions.[526] The features of the European Sport Model agreed at the conference include the need for sport 'to keep its operational autonomy safe from any political or economic manipulation', which should involve preservation from 'over-commercialization' tending to distort its values. Systems of sport governance in Europe, spanning clubs and national and international federations, ensure solidarity between different levels, which is taken to mean both horizontal solidarity, meaning a balance between participants in the same competition, and vertical solidarity, whereby profits from major competitions should be reinvested in the promotion of sport, especially among young people. The system of promotion and relegation is 'another identifying feature of European sport'. It promotes equal opportunities for all participants, increasing the appeal of participation in competition. The balance that this has brought has allowed sport to flourish in Europe, but would be upset by clubs' choosing to break away from the established structure. The conclusions also warn that links between sport and television should not be used as a lever for damaging the way in which sports competitions are organized in pursuit of financial gain, and it is mentioned in this context that doubts or even outright opposition have been expressed about acquisition of clubs by broadcasters.[527] The role of sport in protecting young people is emphasized: so too, yet more ambitiously, its contribution to promoting democratic values, the integration of minorities and tolerance and fair play in society.

The European sports model, like its cousin the European social model, provides an exciting though slightly unstable springboard for debate, and a number of participants at Olympia were resistant to the Commission's perceived tendency to downplay differences between individual sports in its quest for a broadly applicable model. It should be noted that the model is not an attack on commercialism *per se*, for money has always played a significant role in professional sport even if income generation is more vigorously pursued today than in the past, but rather it is a quest to foster an environment within which commercialism will not undermine core sporting values such as uncertainty of result, integrity of competition and achievement based on merit. The Commission's European model is to an extent defined by what it is not: it is not an American model. The preference for promotion and relegation in Europe is explicitly contrasted with the closed league typical of North American sport, in which the autonomy of clubs from the league is typically less pronounced and investment doubtless more safely protected because of the absence of risk of loss of status.

It will be immediately apparent that several of these features of the European Sport Model have lately been called into question in Europe. The pressures are conveniently grouped under the rubric 'Americanization' because of the increasing perception that European sport, and most of all football, is steadily increasing its income generation by learning some lessons from North America. This does not mean that all aspects of North American sport are likely to be embraced in Europe. The draft pick,

---

[526] The conclusions are available via the Commission website http://europa.eu.int/comm/dg10/sport.

[527] This provides an intriguing link with the treatment under British domestic law of the BSkyB/Manchester United merger; see Ch. 12.

for example, is culturally wholly alien to the leading sports in Europe. In fact, it is a system which reflects the deeper commitment of North American sports leagues to managing competitive equality and uncertainty of results. However, some other typically American trends are plainly finding their way on to the agenda of some actors on the European stage – most of all, the richest football clubs. The removal of the 'uncertainty' of relegation and the elimination of the criterion of merit as the basis for qualification for the competition were at the heart of plots in 1998 by 14 leading European football clubs to create a league independent of the less lucrative structure offered by UEFA, the governing body. The mooted breakaway league would have been based on guaranteed membership for the elite group. It would have generated more revenue in absolute terms but, in addition, a much higher percentage of proceeds would have been retained by the participant clubs than under UEFA's schemes, which involved wealth distribution within the game.[528] The plans never came to fruition largely because of concessions made by UEFA. Its own most prestigious club competition, the Champions' League (formerly the European Cup), was expanded,[529] allowing increased revenue generation by the leading clubs at the cost of, *inter alia*, damage to traditional structures of national club competition.[530] UEFA's precarious hold over the governance of European club football leaves it vulnerable to further pressure from this group of 14 clubs to relax its traditional sporting rules. Rumours persist of, for example, attempts to broaden the elite group's eligibility for the major club competitions beyond qualification via placement in national leagues and to secure greater financial compensation for the release of players participating in international matches.[531]

By late 1999 it seemed that the Commission's ambitions to publish a final version of its February 1999 confidential draft communication had been put on hold, at least for the medium term, amid speculation about the high level of controversy the draft had aroused. The Commission now seems likely to pursue a clutch of *ad hoc* individual decisions in the sports sector, predominantly concerning EC competition law, before returning to the quest for an overall policy framework. It did, however, produce a less ambitious policy paper than its February draft in December 1999,

[528] See M. Bose, *Manchester Unlimited* (London 1999) Ch. 2. It might be noted that these financial motivations run parallel to those driving the establishment of the Premier League in England in 1992 as an organization separate from the Football League, although promotion/relegation between the two Leagues was not abandoned.

[529] In 1998/1999 the winner of the competition had to play a minimum of 11 matches; in 1999/2000, 17. The expansion was achieved partly by allowing more entrants; the tournament was conceived originally as open only to national champions, yet, entirely inconsistent with its renaming, some countries now contribute four entrants. The final in 1998/1999 was between Bayern Munich and Manchester United, neither of which had qualified as national champion.

[530] For instance, in 1999/2000 the dates of the English FA Cup were changed from those used for many decades and brought forward earlier in the season in order to make time for 'Champions League' matches which filled six of eight midweeks between early March and mid April 2000. In the event, one of the prime movers, Manchester United, did not participate in the 1999/2000 FA Cup, preferring instead to participate in a lucrative new tournament, the World Club Championship, staged in Brazil in January 2000.

[531] For instance, *The Times*, 4 February 2000.

when it published 'The Helsinki Report on Sport', designed for the consideration of the European Council held that month in the city.[532] The paper is strikingly less detailed in its treatment of the outstanding legal issues than that of February 1999. Instead, the focus of the Helsinki Report is on safeguarding current sports structures and on maintaining the social function of sport within the Community framework, which were areas on which the Commission had been invited to report by the Vienna European Council of December 1998.

The report begins with the ambitious assertion that it 'gives pointers for reconciling the economic dimension of sport with its popular, educational, social and cultural dimensions'. It maintains the Commission's identification of 'a European approach to sport based on common concepts and principles', which includes sport's role as 'an instrument of social cohesion and education'. It is suggested that tensions have emerged between this function and the economic motivations for sport which have increased in recent years. One example cited is

> 'the temptation for certain sporting operators and certain large clubs to leave the federations in order to derive the maximum benefit from the economic potential of sport for themselves alone. This tendency may jeopardize the principle of financial solidarity between professional and amateur sport and the system of promotion and relegation common to most federations.'

The Commission contents itself with a relatively brief summary of the legal environment, repeating the orthodox constitutional point that, although the EC lacks explicit competence in sport under its Treaty, nevertheless sports bodies must comply with Community law. Pending disputes are merely mentioned with negligible elaboration. The pattern according to which the Treaty competition rules are likely to apply is summarized in terms familiar from the February 1999 confidential draft, but less fully explained than in it. 'The rules of the game' will escape the scope of the competition rules. Other rules are in principle impermissible; for example, restrictions on parallel imports of sports products, ticket sales which discriminate according to the residence of buyers,[533] and the exclusion from the market by a sporting body, for no objective reason, of any economic operator who complies with justified quality or safety standards yet has been denied a certification document by the body. In between lie practices that are likely to be exempted from the competition rules, including exclusive rights to broadcast spotting events that are limited in duration and scope, and agreements within the game designed to achieve the two objectives recognized in *Bosman* as special to sport, namely preservation of competitive balance and inducement to develop young players.

The Commission asserts the value in preserving 'the social function of sport and therefore the current structures of the organization of sport in Europe', while assimilating a changing legal and commercial environment. This requires consultation be-

---

532 COM (1999)644 and /2. See S. Weatherill, 'The Helsinki Report on Sport', 25 *EL Rev* (2000) 282.

533 Cf. 1998 *Football World Cup*, note 525.

tween interested levels of governance – sports bodies, member states and European institutions. A partnership is presented as the way forward.

Some Outstanding Questions

Increasingly visible subjection to EC law flows naturally from the rising economic significance of sport. The February 1999 confidential draft, the Helsinki Report of December 1999 and a small collection of individual Decisions begin to reveal the Commission's concern to put flesh on the bones of the Court's acceptance in *Bosman* that the special characteristics of sport should be taken into account while subjecting it in principle to the rules of EC law. Several comments about the Commission's thinking are appropriate.

The use of the law of free movement in *Bosman* appears increasingly anomalous. It was always surprising that the Court in *Bosman* chose to decide the case exclusively on the basis of Article 39 (ex 48), neglecting entirely the impact of the Treaty competition rules. This was perhaps a hint that the Court realized the complexity associated with the application of Articles 81 and 82 (ex 85 and 86) to sport and that, by focusing on violation of the free movement rules alone, it preferred to leave consideration of competition law to another day and, perhaps better still from its perspective, to another institution. The Commission has now picked up the baton, and it seems plain that, *Bosman* notwithstanding, it is competition policy that will be the major battleground in the future elaboration of the application of EC law to sport. The appreciation that Articles 81 and 82 (ex 85 and 86) were the dogs that didn't bark in *Bosman* and that Article 39 (ex 48) has now been relegated in the Commission's thinking should not detract from the realization that Article 39 (ex 48) remains relevant in the shaping of EC law in this sector. It affects the flexibility allowed to the Commission in applying Articles 81 and 82. Specifically, any concession granted to the industry must also comply with Article 39 (ex 48)[534] and, in so far as a revised system violates free movement rights, it may be challenged by a private litigant relying on the directly effective right contained in Article 39 (ex 48) even where the Commission is satisfied that the competition rules have not been infringed. It is explained above that this may be pertinent in the shaping of an adjusted system of transfer fees, where I submit that Article 39 (ex 48) injects a powerful strain of hostility to restrictions on labour mobility. This insistence on individual economic freedoms fatally damages attempts to resuscitate a transfer system claimed to serve the collective interests of the game in so far as it involves burdens imposed on players direct.

The willingness to exclude some arrangements from Article 81(1) (ex 85(1)) altogether on the basis that they are inherent to sport and/or necessary for its organization represents the most malleable tool available to the Commission. This offers a method for reflecting the special nature of sport, but the debate about which rules are properly treated as inherent to sport and necessary for its organization, and which, by contrast, constitute supplementary restrictions of an essentially economic nature fall-

[534] This is plain from Bosman; see especially the Opinion of A-G Lenz.

ing within Article 81 (ex 85), promises to reveal much about the perceived peculiar nature of the industry of sport and its subjection to EC law. What really are the 'rules of the game'? The supposed divide between a socially and culturally important core sporting agenda and other 'normal' economic interests and activities generated by sport is hard to fix and remains intellectually and commercially elusive. The most widely cited example of a rule which may seem restrictive yet is treated as part of the sporting context within which competition is organized and therefore beyond the reach of EC law is provided by selection policies for national representative teams. The German national team may comprise only Germans without violating Article 12 (ex 6). This has always been taken as the consequence of the Court's notion of rules of 'purely sporting interest' adopted in the first of its sports law rulings, *Walrave and Koch* v. *UCI*.[535] The Court in *Bosman* seemed anxious not to kick wide open this concession to sporting bodies, for it showed itself completely unpersuaded that reasons of sporting interest could dictate an enforced link between the location of a club and the origins of individual players. The nationality of individual players is disassociated from the sporting identity of clubs, in contrast to that of national representative sides, and it was therefore necessary in law immediately to treat all EU nationals playing club football in the same way, irrespective of nationality.

It is submitted that the Court was correct in this finding, but it is plain that elusive distinctions are apt to present themselves in future. Rules that limit the number of clubs in a league to, say, 18 would not be open to challenge on the basis that 20 would allow wider access. These are 'the rules of the game' and they lie within the autonomous decision-making competence of sport's governing bodies. But once a practice is identified as lying within the scope of EC law – that is, because it possesses a sufficient economic element to constitute more than something which defines the core identity of the sport – it must be justified in accordance with the rules of EC law, albeit that sport's recognized special characteristics would at this stage be taken into account. In formal legal terms, exemption of a restrictive practice under Article 81(3) currently remains the exclusive preserve of the European Commission (although this may alter)[536] In fixing the margin between rules that escape the scope of EC law and rules that fall foul of it unless they can be shown to be justified. The EC's institutions – the Commission, supervised by the Court, and the Court itself in receipt of preliminary references from national courts[537] – are placed in a powerful position to shape the practical scope of decision-making autonomy allowed to sport. Many issues remain unresolved at the margin and there is an obvious peril that, in addressing them, the Commission will, in practice, stray close to assuming the function of sports regulator, which it conscientiously denies it could or should perform.

---

535 Case 36/74, [1974] *ECR* 1405. See Weatherill, note 438 above, 354-57.

536 See recent proposals for release of exclusivity in favour of a greater degree of national level application by courts and competition authorities discussed in the White Paper on Modernization, *OJ* 1997 C 132/1.

537 Case C-36/74 *Walrave and Koch*, note 518 and Case C-415/93 *Bosman*, note 513, were both preliminary rulings; see also Case C-51/96 *Deliège* and Case C-176/96 *Lehtonen*, pending before the Court.

Examples of the problem abound in connection with rules designed to maintain 'balance between clubs by preserving a certain degree of equality and uncertainty as to results', which the Court in *Bosman* conceded as a legitimate objective in sport. Systems of internal wealth distribution, designed to reflect the interdependence of clubs which is the peculiar hallmark of a sports league, might be treated as inherent to sport (and therefore outside the reach of the competition rules) or as economically motivated and therefore requiring exemption. An uncertainty of outcome may be regarded as a means of improving the quality of the product, but, more than that, it may be treated as essential to the very conduct of sport in the first place. The latter view might lead to the conclusion that the establishment of a solidarity fund within a sport, to which wealthier clubs are required to contribute from the proceeds of, *inter alia*, the sale of broadcasting rights and ticket income and on which poorer clubs may draw for financial support, may escape supervision under EC competition law. I concede that this system may be attacked as an inapt and inefficient route to achieving the objective of workable, competitive equality between clubs. This is an issue demanding analysis; removing the rewards of success and muffling the pain of failure by compulsory wealth distribution may damage the competitive edge, although this fear should not neglect the point that in organized sport it is much more than financial success alone that provides incentives to strive for supremacy.[538] But if such wealth distribution is treated as inherent to sport's need for a truly competitive base, then the relevant arrangements do not even need to run the gauntlet of EC competition law.

This tricky issue is relevant to legal treatment of the sale of broadcasting rights. The acquisition of rights to cover popular sporting events by media companies forms a central plank of strategy for the exploitation of new markets in the rapidly restructuring broadcasting sector. It is a major reason for the recent increase in the 'commercialization' of sport. In turn, these trends explain the Commission's own interest in sport, for acquisition of rights by media companies may imperil sustained flexibility in the broadcasting industry. As the revolution of media convergence gathers technological pace,[539] mergers between media groups and sports clubs may eventually come to be the subject of scrutiny at the European level as they already have at the national level,[540] but thus far such anxieties have emerged at the European level in connection with the sale of television rights. Article 81(1) and (3) may be used to control the reach of exclusive rights which, as is well known, may have ambiguous implications for the competitive structure of the market.[541] The Commission's 1999

538 For instance, P. Cairns, T. Jennett and P. Sloane, 'The Economics of Professional Team Sports: A Survey of Theory and Evidence', 13 *Journal of Economic Studies* (1986) 3. A-G Lenz's Opinion in *Bosman* also considers the matter. For economic analysis from a US perspective, see J. Quirk and R. Fort, *Pay Dirt: the Business of Professional Team Sports* (Princeton, NJ 1997).

539 See COM (1997) 623.

540 E.g., in the UK, BSkyB/Manchester United, note 20. The thresholds in Art. 1 of the EC Merger Regulation, Reg 4064/89 amended by Reg 1310/97, are set at a level which makes it improbable that the Commission will ever be able to claim jurisdiction over such mergers. leaving them to national authorities to examine.

541 See H. Fleming. 'Exclusive Rights to Broadcast Sporting Events in Europe', *ECLR* (1999) 143 and, more generally, D. Brinckman and E. Vollebregt, 'The Marketing of Sport and its Relation to EC Competition Law', *ECLR* (1998) 281; Beloff et al., Ch. 6.

documentation on sport properly accepts that a degree of exclusivity may be granted; but the Commission will carefully scrutinize the duration of the grant of exclusivity lest it cause unacceptable market foreclosure. Typically, the more speculative the investment (which might be the case if untried technology is involved), the longer the protection of exclusivity that is likely to be sanctioned. Questions of the collective selling of rights are still more complex. Clubs have an interest in acting collectively to sell rights to broadcast matches, rather than in making individual deals with separate broadcasters. This will typically be presented as a means of selling a coherent package covering an entire league programme and it also doubtless serves to simplify the task of sharing the proceeds from the central pool to all the participant clubs, which, in pursuit of competitive equality, typically involves some degree of support for the less successful or less attractive clubs. However, by reducing competition it will enable the clubs to keep prices (artificially) high. Broadcasters could complain that this is simply a price-fixing cartel which serves sport's internal requirement of 'organizational solidarity' through wealth distribution, but at a cost represented by the suppression of a market for rights involving many clubs and many potential buyers. This forces up prices and reduces consumer choice. A robust response would be to insist on the dismantling of collective selling, releasing a competitive market for purchase of rights to the advantage of third-party buyers, but to allow the sport in question, should it so choose, to adopt internal rules designed to underpin organizational solidarity requiring clubs able to extract high fees to share part of the income with clubs less favoured in the market place. It would need to be determined whether this alternative device for securing wealth distribution and competitive equality based on a type of internal taxation could, in practice, be reliably maintained once collective selling was ended.[542]

The Commission remains understandably cautious in this area but has left space for the possible exemption of arrangements for the collective selling of rights. In the Helsinki Report the Commission insists that any exemption would have to take account of the benefits for consumers and the proportionate nature of the restrictions in relation to the end in view. It is observed that it is therefore appropriate 'to examine the extent to which a link can be established between the joint sale of rights and financial solidarity between professional and amateur sport, the objectives of the training of young sportsmen and women and those of promoting sporting activities among the population'. This hints intriguingly at the use of the power to exempt restrictive practices as a lever for insisting that fostering the social and educational function of sport is a condition for giving a green light to collective selling. The cartel is permissible provided its proceeds are shared throughout the sport for the sake of its general health.[543] This suggests that collective selling designed solely as a tool of wealth

542 The perceived impracticality of alternatives in meeting the requirement of effective distribution of revenues was central to the UK's Restrictive Practices Court's finding that the system of collective selling in England be allowed to continue; set note 9.

543 In England the beneficial effects of distribution of revenues outside the Premier League was one element in the RPC's finding in favour of collective selling: see above, especially Para. 348 of the judgment.

maximization for the participants alone would not be exempted. So a 'breakaway' league of the type lately mooted in European football, may, by ridding itself of its roots in the wider organization of the sport, thereby surrender one commercially attractive opportunity, that of the collective sale of broadcasting rights. The 'European sports model' could in this way come to be defended by the Commission in deciding whether to grant exemption of restrictive practices under Article 81(3).

Rules designed to secure an uncertainty of outcome embrace not only general wealth distribution but may also be directed at maintaining the integrity of competition by excluding any whiff of match-fixing. The status of rules forbidding multiple ownership of clubs could fall within the notion of 'rules needed to ensure uncertainty as to results' which fall outwith legal control. UEFA's rules restricting multiple ownership of clubs participating in European competition have been examined by the Court for Arbitration in Sport (CAS), an arbitral body established by the industry and based in Lausanne. The CAS decided in July 1999 that such rules were lawful, examining the matter from the perspective of both EC law and Swiss law.[544] This judgment does not preclude the matter from emerging once again for decision by a tribunal within the EC, nor the possibility of a different conclusion on the matter being reached there. However, the commercial interests that brought the case before the CAS chose to adjust their shareholdings in order to comply with UEFA's requirements. And subsequently the Commission issued its preliminary conclusion that the rule could fall outwith the Treaty competition rules, although, in accordance with the orthodoxy of Community trade law, it requires further information to ensure that there are no less restrictive means of preserving the integrity of competitions where more than one club belongs to the same owner.[545]

Conclusion

Sport possesses unusual features which mark it out from 'normal' industry. It has an unusually well developed pattern of globalized regulation. It has its own adjudicative tribunals, such as the increasingly prominent Court of Arbitration in Sport. Sport has a need for healthy internal competition which is not the hallmark of 'normal' industry. There might be an intellectual case to be made that sport ought to be permitted to run its own affairs. One might contend that the 'law' of international sporting bodies be treated as an autonomous system worthy of protection from disruption by state law or the law of transnational entities such as the EC. After all, sport has already far transcended the rigidities of national political frontiers. Henri Delaunay was already far bolder than Jean Monnet; Jules Rimet a great globalizer more than half a century ago. This depiction of a system which responds to the special interests of sport, and which should not be invaded by differently motivated systems, begins to move towards art intellectually coherent version of the 'they don't understand. It's not their business' argument broached earlier in this chapter. To treat decisions of sporting associations

[544] CAS 98/200 *AEK Athens and Slavia Prague* v. *UEFA*, 20 August 1999.

[545] *OJ* 1999 C 363/2.

as 'law' in their own right, rather than as private acts subordinate to 'real law', would argue for a differently conceived 'sports law' and would bring to mind questions surrounding the choice of which legal order to apply in case of conflict.

In the EC context, sporting bodies have shown link interest in making this case. They have largely been able to rely on the relatively short span of a player's career and the regularity of annual competition contrasted with the stately progress of legal proceedings to scare off most would-be litigants.[546] However. on the rare occasions that litigation has reached the final whistle – such as *Bosman* – the case that sport is special has not been enough to secure victory. This is in part because sport has been obliged to fight the battle on the EC system's own terms, as explained above. Perhaps, of course, one could in any event object to the characterization of sporting rules as 'law' with reference to the (relatively) unrepresentative, unaccountable processes of decision-making within the sector. In the United States bona fide arm's length negotiation operates as a precondition to the applicability of the non-statutory labour exemption, which is a judicial creation designed to immunize collective bargains struck between both sides of industry from anti-trust law.[547] In Europe rule-making remains predominantly based on a top-down model in which strong player unions are absent and so, for example, attempts to introduce a 'salary cap' in Europe by appealing to American precedents deserve scepticism for the European version would be no more than a horizontal price-fixing cartel among employers, with the effect of loading the 'blame' for high costs on players and protecting inefficiencies elsewhere in the industry.[548] A budget cap, rather than a salary cap, might be more promising, though still legally problematic; but there are other avenues than the capping of spending down which sport in Europe could constructively seek to move in order to secure protection for its distinctive characteristics without falling foul of EC law, most of all involving more vigorous wealth distribution.

In practice, sporting associations, subject to individual litigation and the scrutiny of the Commission, would now be better advised to abandon a confrontational attitude and to adapt their arguments in order to win autonomy for their role in fixing 'the rules of the game' while accepting subjection to the control of EC law in more obviously economic realms. This would, admittedly, leave space for debate about the precise location of the margin between the sporting and the economic category. It was discussed earlier that rules designed to maintain a degree of competitive equality and uncertainty of results cover a wide spectrum, and though some may count as inherent to the organization of sport, others seem to sit more comfortably in economically-motivated realms. But even in the latter instance, the fact that rules fall within

546 Consider the (probably disproportionately restrictive) ban on all English football clubs from European competition in the 1980s: A. Evans, 'Freedom of Trade under the Common Law and EC Law: the Case of the Football Bans', 102 *LQR* (1986) 510. In *Bosman* itself UEFA, apparently believing until very late that litigation would not be pursued to the bitter end, failed even to submit within the time limit evidence about the economic impact of the system; see Paras. 52-4 of the ruling.

547 See generally P. Weiler and G. Roberts, *Sport's and the Law*, 2nd edn. (St. Paul, Westlaw 1998), especially Ch. 3.

548 Cf. Para. 275 of A-G Lenz's Opinion in *Bosman*.

the scope of EC law by no means inevitably deprives them of enforceability, for the Commission is clearly willing to consider exempting practices in recognition of the special characteristics of sport. The debate deserves to be entered into constructively on both sides. Both the Court's ruling in *Bosman* and evolving Commission practice, particularly in the generally conciliatory tones of the Helsinki Report, exhibit a readiness to acknowledge the special concerns of the sports sector, albeit not to the extent of conceding that its rules entirely escape the jurisdictional reach of the EC. Sporting bodies could improve their case by the more sophisticated use of empirical evidence about the needs of organized sport. Such submissions have been consistently absent from the plaintive cries of the industry in recent years. In its Helsinki Report on Sport, the Commission gently makes the fair point that sporting organizations could usefully clarify their missions and operate in a more transparent manner.

It is emphatically not the case that European sport is being propelled down the American road by the law of the Community. The Commission is keen to see the preservation of matters such as promotion and relegation. Nothing in the assumptions of EC law will necessarily disturb choices made in sport to protect vibrant competitive equality through arrangements for securing wealth distribution. *Bosman* explicitly allowed such planning, but conspicuously little advantage of this bas been taken by the game since its preferred, but evidently flawed instrument, the transfer system, was ruled offside.[549] It is possible to wonder how committed to competitive equality clubs really are once they discover that they are unable to place associated burdens on the shoulders of their employees. But the EC is a regulator of sport in only a limited sense. It judges decisions taken by sporting bodies. It does not impose its own decisions. As the Commission's European Sport Model makes plain, there are distinctive features of European sport which may legitimately be pursued within a permissive framework established by EC law. But the Commission cannot demand compliance with the European Sports Model, except in so far as departure from it involves a breach of EC law. That (some) of its features appear to be under threat in Europe, as part of a trend which may be labelled 'Americanization' in recognition of the lurking desire to eliminate traditional rules of the game (such as promotion and relegation) which may inhibit wealth maximization on a North American scale, is not to be blamed on the incursion of EC law into the autonomy of sport. If governance of the game based on national associations affiliated to a continent-wide ruling body is abandoned in (some) European sports, it will be as a direct result of the choice made in the market by the small number of entrepreneurs who control the continent's major sports clubs, especially football clubs. The damage that this is capable of wreaking on the European Sports Model should make one think hard about whether, far from allowing sport an exemption from the EC Treaty, instead what is urgently needed is a powerful regulator acting in the public interest and which should operate at a European level in order to be effective. League rules requiring transfers of wealth between clubs would not be permissible, but mandatory. Smaller leagues could be protected.

[549] This has not escaped the Commission's notice. In the Helsinki Report, note 437 above, it is commented that 'sporting federations [...] have not set up a new alternative system to the one condemned by the Court' in *Bosman*.

Criticism of EC law and of the *Bosman* ruling in particular, and talk of salary caps, intrusive player agents and a rejuvenated transfer system, obscures the central issues in today's organized sport, which do not concern the players but the shortsightedness of (some) clubs in pursuing commercialization without adequate respect for the nature and purpose of sport in society.

'FAIR PLAY PLEASE!': RECENT DEVELOPMENTS IN THE APPLICATION OF EC LAW TO SPORT*

1. Introduction

In the Official Programme published for the 2002 Football World Cup a full page plea appears under the title 'Help us to ensure Fair Play at the 2002 FIFA World Cup Korea/Japan™!'[550] At first glance one might expect the exhortation to be designed to encourage respect for opponents, both on and off the field, or perhaps to appeal to all participants to play according to both the letter and the spirit of the laws of the game. Not so. The page in question is in fact devoted to the phenomenon of 'ambush marketing'. It is explained that the 'Official Commercial Affiliates' of the tournament contribute greatly to its success, while other companies seek to promote their products by seeking to establish an association between them and the tournament without having paid FIFA for the privilege. Football spectators are encouraged to prevent such 'ambushes' by declining to bring commercially-branded material such as flags, banners, balloons and hats into the stadiums, even though they may commonly be cheerfully offered such free but unauthorized gifts on their journey to the match. Fair Play!

Sport has plainly become an industry of considerable commercial significance. Governing bodies are concerned with fair regulation of the game itself but also with effective exploitation of their commercial assets. No one would propose that the law has a valid role to play in dictating, for example, how many players there should be in a football team. Equally no one would deny that the law has a valid role to play in regulating, for example, price-fixing arrangements among suppliers of sports goods. But there is a more intriguing intermediate category of practices that may be peculiar to sport, but also carry direct commercial implications. Examples include the player transfer system and the sale of broadcasting rights for sports events. Typically the governing bodies of sport regard their proper sphere of autonomous decision-making competence as broader in scope than is admitted by public regulators. The style in which the argument is typically conducted is rather neatly captured by the anecdote at the beginning of this Introduction: sports bodies have a strong incentive to dress up a desire to maximize revenue streams in the clothes of 'Fair Play'. And sometimes they may be perfectly justified so to do. The broad issue that needs to be addressed is just how far it is proper to shelter arrangements in the sports sector from full or partial legal scrutiny and this inquiry demands as an essential preliminary a rigorous inquiry into what is really meant by the frequent claim that 'sport is special' – culturally, socially, economically. In Europe, this issue was catapulted on to the front pages of newspapers across the continent by the European Court's famous

* 40 *CML Rev.* (2003) p. 51 et seq.

[550] Korean/English edition, p. 122.

decision in 1995 in *Bosman*,[551] and since that time a cascade of opportunities has been presented to the Commission, in particular, and, less frequently, to the Court to clarify the treatment of sport under EC law. On 5 June 2002, a week after the World Cup began in Seoul, the Commission published a memorandum reporting on 'constructive discussions with sporting organizations' and listing a series of issues which the Commission considered to have been satisfactorily resolved after sports bodies had adjusted 'their sporting regulations to bring them into line with today's sporting, economic and legal requirements'.[552] The clear impression is that the Commission feels the time is right to call a halt to its vigorous enthusiasm of the last few years to employ the Treaty competition rules to scrutinize the professional sports sector. On the other hand, anxieties to show respect for the social and cultural benefits of sport may lately be identified in the practice of several institutions, including the Commission. This article surveys recent EC practice. It intends to take stock of how fair is the play in this field at present and it takes as a major theme the risk inherent in shaping a 'sports policy' that fails adequately to distinguish between professional sport and recreational/amateur sport.

2. 'Sport is special'

An insight into the peculiarities of economic power in professional sport may be derived from Scottish football. In April 2002, ten of the twelve clubs that compete in the Scottish Premier League announced their intention to resign. The 'breakaway ten' declared a plan to start a new League once the required notice period of two years had been served. The two clubs not involved were Glasgow Rangers and Glasgow Celtic, the so-called 'Old Firm', by far the most successful clubs in the history of Scottish football and also the clubs that attract by far the largest numbers of supporters. The 'breakaway ten' promptly informed Rangers and Celtic that the Glasgow duo would be welcome to join the new competition beginning in 2004, but only provided they accepted that major decisions would require the support of only 8 of the 12 participants in the League. The current arrangements dictate that 11 of the 12 must vote in favour. Plainly the ten smaller clubs plan to establish a structure that does not permit the two largest clubs to veto radical change and, in particular, they have in mind the adoption of systems of wealth distribution that will involve much more substantial transfers of revenue from the best supported clubs to the less well supported clubs than those which prevail today. Representatives of Celtic and Rangers reacted initially with dismay. Mr Ian McLeod, Celtic's chief executive, observed that the clubs that had announced their resignation 'appear to regard themselves as the oppressed ten when, because Celtic and Rangers generate 80 per cent of the revenue in Scottish football, they are actually being subsidized by the two biggest clubs'.[553] Presumably the figure of 80 per cent is a simple calculation based on size of gates at matches and it

[551] Case C-415193, *URBSFA* v. *Bosman*, [1995] *ECR* I-4921.

[552] MEMO/02/127, 'The application of the EU's competition rules to sport?', 5 June 2002.

[553] 'Celtic and Rangers to be kicked out as smaller clubs vote for new Scots league', *Financial Times*, 17 April 2002, p. 4.

is indeed true that in the (not untypical) season 2001/02, Celtic and Rangers attracted an average League attendance to home matches of 58,505 and 48,257 respectively while Aberdeen, the third-best supported club in the Scottish Premier League, could boast an average figure of only 13,938.[554] Celtic and Rangers are correspondingly far better supported away from home than any other Scottish club and their travelling fans therefore swell the income of teams playing at home to the 'Old Firm'. But Mr McLeod's comments overlook one important feature. Plainly the 'oppressed ten' make money as a result of their entanglement with the commercially dominant Glasgow clubs, but Celtic and Rangers also make their money because of the existence of their opponents. Rangers and Celtic far exceed the other football clubs in Scotland in the number of people who regard them as 'their team', but they depend on finding parties willing to supply that crucial extra element in the sporting bargain – opposition – to lend commercial and sporting purpose to their very existence. In this sense less popular teams in a professional league may have considerably more commercial leverage in their dealings with the 'bigger names' than one would suppose from a simple reading of turnover figures. In fact, one cannot carve up market shares in football the way one would in widget production. If smaller widget producers quit the market, the more powerful firms will typically simply cheerfully seize their market share.

In football, the 80 per cent market share claimed by Celtic and Rangers would not increase were their rivals to refuse to compete. Far from it. Exit by weaker parties ruins the game for the stronger. The two Glasgow clubs may seek new opponents by skipping the jurisdiction and playing in another League, most obviously in England, or they may feel obliged to strike a compromise deal in Scotland.[555] But for present purposes the tale reveals a key characteristic of professional sport which is not found elsewhere: there is an interdependence of interest between participants in sporting competition. In sport opponents are there to be beaten but the whole point of the endeavour is destroyed if opponents are, literally, beaten out of sight.

This understanding corresponds to the view adopted by the European Court in *Bosman*.[556] The Court famously stated that 'In view of the considerable social importance of sporting activities and in particular football in the Community, the aims of maintaining a balance between clubs by preserving a certain degree of equality and uncertainty as to results, must be accepted as legitimate'. This embrace of the notion of mutual interdependence in a sports league opens up the prospect of approval of rules that, for example, ensure the transfer of wealth from rich to poor clubs in pursuit of competitive equality and of rules that prevent multiple ownership of clubs in order to eliminate suspicions about fixed matches.

554 Source: Rollin and Rollin, eds., *Rothmans Football Yearbook 2002-2003* (London, Headline Book Publishing 2002).

555 The latter currently seems the more probable medium-term outcome because the former appears to hold insufficient commercial appeal to the English clubs who would be asked to act as hosts. The former option itself raises intriguing questions in so far as attempts by governing bodies to maintain the traditional structure of national Leagues in Europe by refusing permission for such cross-border moves collides with EC rules governing free movement (albeit not in the case of Anglo-Scottish adjustments, which are internal to a single Member State).

556 Case C-415/93, *supra* note 551.

In mapping a future co-existence between EC law and sport, the vital feature of *Bosman*, too often neglected in the popular debate, is that the Court admitted that football in particular, and sport in general, possesses unusual characteristics that distinguishes it from 'normal' commercial sectors. The Court insisted only that in principle the economic significance of sport is apt to secure its subjection to EC law and that those unusual characteristics should then be taken into account in shaping the application of the law.[557] The challenge for sport is to devise rules that serve these interests, which are peculiar to organized sport, without falling foul of EC law. In *Bosman* the European Court rejected attempts to demonstrate that two distinct existing practices in professional football were compatible with the Treaty provision governing the free movement of workers, Article 39 (ex 48) EC. Both the system governing the transfer of players between clubs and the rules requiring discrimination on the basis of nationality in European club football competitions were found to violate that provision. Adjustments have been made to the transfer system,[558] while the nationality rules have been abandoned in so far as they apply to EU nationals.

'Mutual interdependence' of participants is a feature that distinguishes sport from 'normal' industries. But key questions include: how much 'special' treatment does that feature justify? What other features are distinctive to sport, and how much special treatment do they justify? And how precisely is that 'special' treatment recognized within the framework of EC law? What is at stake here is an anxiety to connect the incentives at play in the sports industry, which generate unusual patterns of internal regulation designed to reflect *inter alia* the mutual interdependence of participants, with the application of orthodox legal rules to the chosen arrangements. Are 'legitimate' sporting practices outside EC competence entirely? Or are they merely capable of exemption from the basic prohibitions found in core provisions such as Articles 12, 39 or 81 EC? It is hem that the most awkward questions about the true character of the 'EC law of sport' arise, and the complexity of the inquiry is driven *first* by the eccentric cultural and economic nature of sport, *second* by the appreciation that sport is propelled by very different motivations in its professional context when contrasted to its recreational/amateur dimension and *third* by the constraints imposed on the relevant EC supervisory institutions by the fundamental constitutional point that the EC has no general Treaty-based competence to regulate sport.

Exposure of the intellectual challenge presented by the matter pre-dates *Bosman*. The European Court of Justice confirmed, in a pair of cases, decided in the 1970s that EC law is in principle capable of application to sport. In both *Walrave and Koch* v. *Union Cycliste Internationale*[559] and *Donà* v. *Mantero*,[560] the Court explained that insofar as sport constitutes an economic activity, it falls within the scope of applica-

[557] For comment at the time of the judgment see annotation by Weatherill, 33 *CML Rev.*, 991; O'Keeffe and Osborne, 'The European Court scores a goal', *International Journal of Comparative Labour Law and Industrial Relations* (1996) III; Seche, 'Quand les Juges tirent au but', 32 *CDE* (1996), 355. For general overview see Dubey, *La libre circulation des sportifs en Europe* (Berne, Staempfli 2000), Ch. 2.

[558] See further below, Part 4.7.2.

[559] Case 36/74, [1974] *ECR* 1405.

[560] Case 13/76, [1976] *ECR* 1333.

tion of Community law. Sport was not then and is not now a matter explicitly subject to supervision under the EC Treaty, but insofar as sport generates practices of economic significance it is affected incidentally by the principles of EC law. Sport offers an appealingly instructive case study of how the law of the EC may exercise a wider influence on the autonomy of public and private actors in the Member States than a formal inspection of the text of the Treaty may lead one to expect, primarily because of the extended reach of the rules governing the building of an integrated, competitive market.[561] However, the pair of cases from the 1970s also demonstrated the contortions forced on the Court as it struggled to accommodate sport's peculiarities within the orthodox framework of EC law. Faced with the alarming prospect that selection of players for national representative teams could be condemned as discrimination on grounds of nationality contrary to the rules of the Treaty, the Court in *Walrave and Koch* nervously concocted a category of practices which it described as of 'purely sporting interest' and having 'nothing to do with economic activity'[562] which lie beyond the scope of the EC Treaty. Nationality-based rules governing selection for national teams competing at international level fell conveniently into this category and could accordingly be applied without fear of challenge derived from EC law. Attempts to provide an intellectually satisfying explanation for this stance are awkward. Admittedly, the EC Treaty catches only 'economic' matters, but both the staging of international matches and the elevation of a player to the status of international have direct economic consequences, so it is unconvincing to argue that such rules escape the scope of the Treaty as in some way bereft of economic purpose or effect. Probably what is at stake is some elusive notion that the very structure of sport at the international level is founded on nationality discrimination and that this precludes disruption caused by the EC Treaty. In *Bosman* the Court, following the vigorous line pressed on it by Advocate-General Lenz, refused to extend this concession to nationality discrimination in *club* football, which it treated as incompatible with EC law, but it did nothing to rationalize the true jurisprudential basis of the so-called 'purely sporting interest' exception.[563] And probably there is no such clean-cut basis.[564] What is at

[561] Cf. for comparable narratives in other sectors, Scott, *Environmental Law* (Harlow, Longman 1998); Weatherill, *EC Consumer Law and Policy* (Harlow, Longman 1997). Much food for thought about, and examples of, this spillover may be digested from the essays contained in Craig and de Burca, *The Evolution of EU Law* (Oxford University Press 1999).

[562] Case 36/74 *supra* note 559, Para. 8. Cf. Case C-415/93 *supra* note 551, Para. 76.

[563] In fact, if anything it confused it, by referring to justification of such practices (Para. 76), which implies they in principle fall within the scope of EC law, whereas A-G Lenz took the more orthodox line of treating such practices as falling outwith the scope of EC law in the first place. See Weatherill, 'European Football Law', 339 pp., at p. 354 in *Collected Courses of the 7th Session of the Academy of European Law* (The Hague, Kluwer 1999).

[564] For an extended discussion see Dubey, *supra* note 557, Ch. 5, in which an ambitious case is made for the preservation of nationality discrimination at the higher levels of the club game (for comments, see my book review published at 39 *CML Rev.* (2002) 901-4). See also McCutcheon, 'Nationality Eligibility Rules after *Bosman*', in Caiger and Gardiner, eds., *Professional Sport in the EU Regulation and Re-Regulation* (The Hague, TMC Asser Press 2000) pp. 127-140. Pending before the Court is Case C-438/00, *Deutscher Handballbund eV* v. *Maros Kolpak* on the compatibility of nationality-based eligibility rules in handball with the EC/Slovakia Association Agreement; A-G Stix-Hackl delivered her Opinion on 11 July 2002.

stake here is sport as an oddity. The desirability of welding national markets into a wider more competitive European market may constitute the fundamental assumption of much of EC trade law and policy, but in sport national Leagues and national representative teams remain accepted building-blocks of the industry's structure. They are, in short, the 'rules of the game'.[565] EC law does not apply to sport in precisely the same way commonly accepted in other sectors, but this is not to say that satisfactory compromises cannot be found within which the 'objective character of the law', which in *Bosman* the Court ringingly insists must not be diminished,[566] can also recognize the objective character of sport. The question: is this being fairly and coherently achieved?

3. Recent judgments of the Court

Two judgments of the Court in April 2000 stand together as the most significant explorations of the friction-laden interface between EC law and sport since the *Bosman* landmark of 1995. They are *Deliège* v. *Ligue de Judo*[567] and *Lehtonen et al.* v. *FRSB*.[568] Both rulings are significant in the enduring quest to identify a satisfactory basis for determining when a measure exerts a sufficient impact on trade patterns to impose an obligation on the rule-maker to show justification on terms recognized by EC law. This aspect escapes the scope of this paper.[569] In both rulings the Court repeated the familiar principle that sport is subject to Community law only in so far as it constitutes an economic activity and confirmed that rules of sporting interest imposed for reasons that are not of an economic nature escape the reach of the EC Treaty.[570] It supplemented this observation with the insistence, already clear in *Bosman* and, before that, in *Walrave and Koch*, that such a restriction on the scope of application of EC law must not exceed its proper objectives and that it cannot be relied on as a basis for excluding the whole of a sporting activity from the ambit of EC law.

In *Deliège* the Court was asked by the referring national court to deal with matters of EC law pertaining to the selection of judokas for international competition by national judo federations. The matter was distinguishable from the rules at stake in *Walrave and Koch* and in *Bosman*. The selection rules at issue in *Deliège* did not determine the conditions governing general access to the labour market not did they contain clauses limiting the number of participating nationals from other Member States. Moreover, the rules did not relate to a tournament involving competition between national teams, but rather to a tournament in which, once selected, the athletes

565 This is explored in more depth and breadth in Part 5 below.

566 Case C-415/93 *supra* note 551, Para. 77 of the judgment.

567 Cases C-51/96 & C-191/97, [2000] *ECR* I-2549.

568 Case C-176/96, [2000] *ECR* I-2681.

569 On *Deliège* in particular see Van den Bogaert, 'The Court of Justice on the Tatami: Ippon, Waza-Ari or Koka?', 25 *EL Rev.* (2000), 554. For recent exploration, including a comprehensive collection of the cascade of comment, see Snell, *Goods and Services in EC Law: A Study of the Relationship between the Freedoms* (Oxford University Press 2002).

570 Paras. 41-43 of the judgment in *Deliège*, Paras. 32-34 of the judgment in *Lehtonen*.

then competed on their own account. The Court stated that although such selection rules

> 'inevitably have the effect of limiting the number of participants in a tournament, such a limitation is inherent in the conduct of an international high-level sports event, which necessarily involves certain selection rules or criteria being adopted'.[571]

It concluded that a rule requiring professional or semi-professional athletes aspiring to take part in competition to have been authorized or selected by their federations in order to participate in a high-level international sports competition, which does not involve national teams competing against each other, does not in itself constitute a restriction on the free movement of services prohibited by Article 49 (ex 59) EC, provided that it derives from a need inherent in the organization of such a competition. The final determination of whether the particular rule challenged by Ms Deliège fell foul of this test was left to the national court, which represents the orthodox division of function under the EC system of preliminary references found in Article 234 EC. The European Court in *Deliège* displayed a readiness to leave to sporting organizations considerable leeway in fixing rules governing participation in events.

Lehtonen concerned transfer rules in the sport of basketball. These rules are applied by national federations, under the supervision of the FIBA, the International Basketball Federation. In short, they provide for differential treatment of transferred players depending on the 'zone' in the world from which they are treated as having originated. The Court decided the case on the basis of Article 39 EC, the Treaty provisions that had formed the legal foundation of *Bosman*. The Court stated that the Treaty precludes the application of rules laid down by a sporting association which prohibit a basketball club from fielding players from other Member States in matches in the national championships where they have been transferred after a specific date, if that date is earlier than the date applicable to the transfers of players from certain non-member countries, unless objective reasons concerning only sport as such or relating to the position of players from a federation in the European zone and that of players from a federation outside the European zone justify such different treatment. The national court would be the ultimate judge of whether such justification was present. The Court in this way admits that EC law could be used as a basis for intervention in the conduct of sporting competitions. But the ruling in no way prohibits the possibility of devising acceptable even-handed transfer 'deadlines' during a season, after which no transfers are permitted. Such rules might restrict commercial freedom, but the Court in *Lehtonen* explicitly acknowledged the role of such deadlines in ensuring the regularity of competition. It shrewdly observed that transfers late in the season may upset competitive balance and damage the effective functioning of a championship, especially, where, as in the case itself, the national league is won on the basis of late-season play-off matches.[572] As in *Bosman*, so in *Lehtonen*; the rules under scrutiny *in casu* appeared inapt to achieve the ends claimed to be pursued, but adjusted

---

[571] Para. 64 of the ruling.

[572] See especially Paras. 53-56 of the judgment.

rules, designed more carefully to reflect the particular needs of organized sport, are by no means excluded by the Court in its interpretation of the application of EC trade law. This is not an exemption allowed to sport, but nor is it an insensitive subjection of sport to the 'normal' assumptions of EC law.

Both *Deliège* and *Lehtonen* assume that sports bodies are in principle permitted to set the parameters within which their sports shall be run and that the rules of the EC Treaty will not intervene, even if an incidental effect on the liberty of economic actors can be demonstrated. Insofar as the objective character of EC law is being developed with respect for the objective character of sport, then a judicial route towards Fair Play is being trodden.

4. Recent decisions of the Commission

Bosman itself, like *Walrave and Koch* and *Donà* v. *Mantero* twenty years earlier, drew attention to the difficulties in reconciling the assumptions of the sports industry with the imperatives of EC law. The Court had confined itself to the law of free movement in *Bosman*, and did so again in *Deliège* and *Lehtonen*, but the Commission has lately been confronted by the need to apply the Treaty rules governing competition in order to resolve most of its outstanding cases. These cases are examined in this Part. The Commission has had an unenviably ill-defined task as it found itself faced with a need to shape a policy on sport and to dear the backing of individual complaints. A broader assessment of its handling of the competition rules is provided in Part 5, before Part 6 surveys sport in a social and cultural context.

The Commission's brief memorandum of 5 June 2002 reports that

> 'Commissioners Monti and Reding in particular have engaged in constructive discussions with sporting organizations over the last two years. [...] As a result, the sporting organizations have put into effect very important changes to bring their rules into line with their legal obligations, bringing about better legal security to sport as a basis for future economic and sporting development, and a better deal for fans and consumers'.[573]

The memorandum records the Commission's satisfaction over the recent closure of a number of cases. In the sports sector, the Commission has been busier than the Court since *Bosman* and there is here a discernible feel that the Commission intends to draw a line under its adventures, and, moreover, with a sigh of relief. Neither Mr Monti nor Ms Reding, Commissioners for Competition and Culture respectively, have gathered much popular approval for their engagement with the sports sector and, at times of potentially radical institutional change within the Union s architecture, it would be unrealistic to suppose that such perceptions do not colour choice of priorities.

---

573 MEMO/02/t27. 'The application of the EU's competition rules to sports', 5 June 2002.

4.1. **Football players' agents**

Pursuant to its rules on football player agents, FIFA, the global governing body for football, had acted to prevent players employing agents not licensed by FIFA. This constitutes a classic anti-competitive barrier to entry to the market for supply of professional services. The Commission considered the matter worthy of investigation[574] but subsequently chose to recognize the need for FIFA to regulate the profession as long as access remains open and non-discriminatory. It accepted FIFA's adjusted requirements that an agent must pass a test and take out professional liability insurance, as well as agreeing to a Code of Professional conduct covering matters of transparency and honesty. In April 2002, the Commission expressed itself content that the contribution to raising standards and protecting consumers from unscrupulous operators allowed it to approve amended FIFA rules, albeit on an informal level.[575]

4.2. **Formula One**

A four-year Commission investigation into the Fédération Internationale d'Automobile (FIA) and the companies involved in Formula One motor racing as now been brought to an end. Notifications had been made in 1997,[576] and in 1999 the Commission had issued a statement of objections targeted in particular at the alleged over-mighty role of the FIA, which acted as regulator of the sport while also actively pursuing commercial exploitation. After long and occasionally public and acrimonious negotiations the FIA agreed to change its rules.[577] The agreed modifications ensure that the rule of FIA is limited to that of a sports regulator, and are designed to excise the risk of commercial conflicts of interest. Certain perniciously anti-competitive restrictions, designed to suppress the growth of new motor sports, have been abandoned, so that, for example, circuit owners hosting Formula One races will no longer be contractually restrained from staging other events that may compete with Formula One, nor will broadcasters be induced to commit exclusively to Formula One. FIA rules will not be used to prevent or impede new competitions unless justified on grounds related to the safe, fair or orderly conduct of motor sport. Appeal procedures against FIA have also been strengthened. The Commission announced its intention to take a favourable view of the new arrangements[578] and in October 2001 it did so, albeit at an informal level.[579]

---

[574] IP/99/782, 21 October 1999.

[575] IP/07/585, 18 April 2002.

[576] *OJ* 1997, C 361/7.

[577] Formula One, economically powerful and quick to threaten to move its operations beyond the EU's borders, has also been a tough nut for the legislature to crack; the Tobacco Advertising Directive, annulled by the Court in Case C-376/98 *Germany* v. *Council and Parliament* [2000] *ECR* I-8419, contained (now redundant) concessions to the industry. On the background see Khanna, 'The defeat of the European Tobacco Advertising Directive: a blow for health', 20 *YEL* (2001) 113.

[578] *OJ* 2001, C 169/5.

[579] IP/01/1523, 30 October 2001.

4.3. The 'Mouscron case'

A stadium owner in Lille, in France, had been refused permission by UEFA, football's governing body for Europe, to stage a UEFA Cup tie for which a Belgian side, Excelsior Mouscron, had been drawn as the home side. Presumably the prospect of increased revenue lay behind the desire to switch venues a short distance across a national border, but UEFA refused to depart from its rules requiring the match to be played in Belgium, the home side's country. The Commission rejected a complaint on the basis that this constituted a sporting rule that formed a necessary part of the organization of the competition. Home teams play at home. The rule was treated by the Commission as falling outside the scope of the Treaty's competition rules.[580]

4.4. Multiple club ownership

Rules forbidding a person owning more than one club participating in a particular tournament are directed at maintaining a sense of uncertainty of outcome and genuine competition that would be undermined by any whiff of collusion or match-fixing. UEFA's rules restricting multiple ownership of football clubs participating in European club competition were examined in 1999 by the Court for Arbitration in Sport (CAS), an arbitral body established by the industry and based in Lausanne. CAS decided such rules were lawful, examining the matter from the perspective of both EC and Swiss law.[581] Having regarded the *Walrave and Koch* 'sporting exception' as unworkable, the CAS proceeded to find the rules did not appreciably restrict competition within the meaning of Article 81(1). Moreover, it treated the rules as necessary in any event to achieve the legitimate objective of securing a properly functioning and credibly competitive league and proportionate to that end, for the CAS was unpersuaded that *ex post* control over match-fixing (for example, by the imposition of criminal penalties) was adequate. Subsequently the Commission issued a preliminary conclusion that the rule could fall outside the Treaty competition rules, citing both the CAS decision and the Court's recognition in *Bosman* of sport's legitimate objectives, although it required further information to satisfy itself of the absence of less restrictive means of preserving the integrity of competitions.[582] In June 2002 the Commission finally announced its termination of this investigation.[583] It recorded its view that the purpose of the rule was to guarantee the integrity of sporting competition and that the limitations on commercial freedom imposed by the rule did not extend beyond what was necessary to ensure the legitimate aim of preserving uncertainty about results. The Commission treated this as a case of a rule that undeniably interfered with commerce in the sector yet which, given its contribution to honesty in sports practice, fell outside the scope of the Treaty competition rules provided it was applied in a non-discriminatory manner.

580 IP/99/956, 9 December 1999, IP 99/956, 9 June 1999.

581 CAS 98/200, AEK *Athens and Slavia Prague* v. *UEFA*, 20 August 1999. See generally on the CAS, Beloff, Kerr and Demetriou, *Sports Law* (Oxford, Hart 1999), Chs. 8.101-8.108.

582 *OJ* 1999, C 363/2.

583 IP/02/942, 27 June 2002.

4.5. Anti-doping rules in swimming

In August 2002 the Commission rejected a complaint brought by swimmers who had been banned from competitions for doping offences by the International Olympic Committee and FINA, swimming s governing body.[584] The Commission emphasized the autonomy allowed to sporting organizations to ensure the integrity of their events. The anti-doping rules facilitated the smooth functioning of sporting competition; they were necessary to combat doping effectively; and their restrictive effects did not exceed those necessary to achieve this objective. Viewed in their proper context, they did not fall within the prohibition contained in Articles 81 and 82 EC.

4.6. Ticket distribution for the 1998 Football World Cup

This is a formal Decision which imposes a fine. The Commission condemned the CFO, the organizing committee for the 1998 World Cup football tournament, staged in and won by France, for violation of Article 82 of the EC Treaty and Article 54 of the EEA agreement.[585] Discrimination in the sale of tickets to the general public was at the heart of the abusive practices. The majority of tickets were distributed to recipients such as national football federations, official tour operators and sponsors, but 28.12 per cent of tickets, some 749,700, were distributed by the CFO direct to the general public. This bloc of tickets was first put on sale in 1996 but purchase was restricted to buyers able to provide a postal address in France. Only from 22 April 1998 did the CFO, under pressure from the Commission, alter its practice and sell tickets to members of the public able to provide an address within the EEA, but by then roughly three-quarters of the relevant bloc of tickets had been acquired by eager French buyers. Given the artificial structure of supply and demand imposed on this market, it is no surprise that in June 1998, during the tournament itself, games throughout France were typically preceded by heavy selling of match tickets by local residents to foreign visitors, often at prices far above those initially charged by the CFO.

The definition of the relevant product market in the Decision is notable for its explicit reliance on the 'SSNIP' test, which plays an important role in the Commission's 1997 Notice on the Definition of the Relevant Market for the Purposes of Community Competition Law.[586] This provides that a relevant product market will normally be confined to a single product or service if a small but significant non-transitory increase in the price of that product or service (in the range of 5 to 10 per cent) does not lead to any measurable change in consumer demand in favour of substitutable products or services. The Commission concluded that an increase of at least 10 per cent in the price of match tickets would not have resulted in a significant switch in demand by the general public to competing products. It considered that from the consumer's perspective the market for match tickets for the Football World Cup stands alone; and, moreover, supply-side substitutability of tickets, via national federations and

---

[584] IP/02/1211, 9 August 2002.

[585] Decision 2000/12 1998 Football World Cup *OJ* 2000, L 5/55.

[586] *OJ* 1997, C 372, Paras. 15, 17, 40 of the Notice.

tour operators, was not treated as providing a realistic possibility of affecting the CFO's conduct The relevant geographic market was 'at least all countries within the EEA'.[587] Consumers readily travel considerable distances to attend an event of such magnitude. Given such a tight market definition, a finding that the CFO possessed a position of dominance was inevitable. Accordingly, the CFO held a 'special responsibility' not to conduct itself in manner that would impair undistorted competition.[588] As a dominant supplier, the CFO was required to offer tickets on a non-discriminatory basis to the general public throughout the EEA,[589] and, since it had failed to do so, it was condemned for abusive conduct constituting the imposition of unfair trading conditions on residents outside France which resulted in a limitation of the market to the prejudice of those consumers.

Security issues are, of course, notoriously relevant in the planning of major football tournaments and spectator segregation may be required. So circumstances will arise where blocks of tickets could properly be limited to fans of a particular team. But the blanket discrimination practised by the CFO could not be justified as a targeted response to threats of disorder.[590] The Commission is to be congratulated on a rigorous application of the proportionality principle which ensures that the peaceful majority do not have to suffer because of the excesses of the minority of supporters.[591]

This was a case of discrimination on the basis of residence which constituted indirect discrimination on the basis of nationality. As the Commission makes explicit, this type of abuse offends against 'fundamental Community principles'.[592] Nonetheless, the fine imposed, described as 'symbolic'[593] was just € 1000. The Commission observed that the ticketing arrangements were similar to those adopted for previous World Cup Finals and added rather opaquely that the issues raised 'are of such a specific nature as not to enable conclusions to be easily drawn from previous Commission decisions or case law of the Court of Justice'.[594] This is not a convincing explanation. Admittedly, an earlier Decision finding infringements of EC law in the ticket distribution system for the 1990 World Cup held in Italy did not address the matter of ticket sales to the public directly. It concerned impermissibly restrictive sales terms for tour packages.[595] No fine was imposed. But it is hard to argue that discrimination on the grounds of residence, an accepted violation of 'fundamental Community principles', is truly an issue of 'a specific nature' such as to merit such

[587] Para. 77 of the Decision.

[588] Para. 85, citing Case T-83/91, *Tetra Pakt II*, [1994] *ECR* II-755, Case 7/82, *GVL*, [1983] *ECR* 483.

[589] The Commission cited Football World Cup in insisting on this principle in the (rather more important!) subsequent Decision 2001/892 *Deutsche Post OJ* 2001, L 331/40.

[590] See especially Para. 109 of the Decision.

[591] Cf. the disproportionate but unchallenged response to incidents of violence involving English football supporters during the 1980s discussed in Evans, 'Freedom of Trade under the common law and EC law: the case of the football bans', 102 *Law Quarterly Review* (1986) 510.

[592] Para. 102; also Para. 122.

[593] Para. 125.

[594] Para. 123.

[595] Decision 92/521 *Distribution of Package Tours during the 1990 World Cup*, *OJ* 1992, L326/31.

a small fine even if no Decision on the point in this particular sector has previously been recorded. It is hard to avoid the suspicion that the principal explanation for the mild sanction applied to such a blatant infraction rests in a degree of mishandling of the dossier by the Commission.[596] It is particularly perplexing that the Commission's intervention to press for elimination of discrimination came as late as February 1998, by which time the majority of the relevant tickets had long been sold in an abusive manner. The Commission had dealings with the CFO in June 1997, when it received a notification at a time when discriminatory practices were already being pursued. There was, it seems, more to the negotiation than was the subject of that notification, but it is left strikingly vague in the Decision whether the CFO misled the Commission or whether the Commission decided to turn a blind eye to what was happening.

The deterrent value of the Decision may be thought negligible in the light of the tiny fine imposed, notwithstanding the parting shot in the Decision to the effect that such a lenient policy cannot be expected in future, but it is reassuring that ticket sales to the general public of the EU for the 2000 European football championships, held in Belgium and the Netherlands, were approved by the Commission[597] and duly conducted without any discrimination rooted in nationality or residence.

4.7. **The player transfer system**

4.7.1. Bosman *remembered*

The transfer system in football, damaged but not eliminated by the ruling in *Bosman*, has mutated over the last century and may be found in different guises in different jurisdictions at different times.[598] However its essence is simply described. Players were unable simply to move freely between clubs in the exercise of their contractual freedom. Under rules enforced by football authorities across the world, a club is permitted to field a player in an official match only once it has secured the player s registration, held by the previous employer. That registration will be released only when the previous club is satisfied with the terms offered by the new club, which has typically involved payment of a fee. *Bosman* had fallen foul of the transfer system when he had found himself prevented from joining a French club because the Belgian club which held his registration refused to release it, even though *Bosman's* contract of employment with the Belgian club had come to an end.

The Court, having acknowledged sport's 'considerable social importance' and embraced as legitimate 'the aims of maintaining a balance between clubs by preserv-

---

[596] See Weatherill, '0033149875354: Fining the Organisers of the 1998 Football World Cup', *ECLR* (2000) 275 for discussion *inter alia* of inconsistency in the handling of my complaint to the Commission.

[597] IP/00/591, 8 June 2000.

[598] A-G Lenz's Opinion in *Bosman*, cited *supra* note 551, contains an overview. See also Blanpain and Inston, *The Bosman Case: The End of the Transfer System?* (Leuven, Peeters 1996); Greenfield, 'The Ties that Bind: Charting Contemporary Sporting Contractual Relations', Ch. 8 in Greenfield and Osborn, eds., *Law and Society in Contemporary Society* (London, Frank Cass 2000); Dubey, *supra* note 557, pp. 272-317, 569-583.

ing a certain degree of equality and uncertainty as to results and of encouraging the recruitment and training of young players',[599] nonetheless came to the conclusion that the transfer system in professional football constituted a violation of Article 39. The Court regarded the means employed in the football industry as inapt to achieve ends which might be capable of justification in principle. The Court did not consider that the transfer system acted as an effective method of maintaining balance between clubs. It did not preclude richer clubs buying the best players. Moreover, the Court observed that only a handful of young players repay clubs' investment in them by making the professional grade, so fees received are unpredictable and unrelated to the actual costs incurred. The system was hit-and-miss, rather than a carefully constructed distributive mechanism. The Court concluded that 'the same aims can be achieved at least as efficiently by other means which do not impede freedom of movement for workers'.[600]

4.7.2. *Beyond* Bosman*: the Commission's agreement with the football authorities*

The judgment required alterations to be made to the transfer system as it applied to players in *Bosman's* position, whose contract of employment had expired and who wished to exercise their right to migrate between Member States of the EU. Clubs have reacted to the judgment by seeking to like star players on longer (and more lucrative) contracts. Patterns of expenditure on players have altered. Transfer fees are still paid, sometimes at very high levels,[601] but wage increases have been more striking. Money that had previously been allocated to inter-club payments for transfers has been more likely to find its way into players' wages.[602]

It is readily arguable that the transfer system rested on even shakier foundations than the *Bosman* ruling itself suggested. In particular, although the Court in *Bosman* declined to consider the matter from the perspective of the competition rules in the EC Treaty, it seems highly probable that, had it addressed that matter, it would have condemned the practices as unlawful restrictions on trade in players imposed 'horizontally' between employers, involving also governing authorities in sport. This was clearly the view expressed in the case by Advocate-General Lenz. It is important to appreciate that the competition rules are lurking in the background, for they

599 Case C-415/93 *supra* note 551, Para. 106.

600 Para. 110 of the judgment; and see more fully (on this as on so many other things) the Opinion of A-G Lenz.

601 And sometimes to the dismay of investors; the potential conflict of interest between economic and sporting motivation was illustrated by disquiet expressed over Manchester United's purchase of Rio Ferdinand, then under contract to Leeds United, in summer 2002 for £ 28 million; e.g., 'Unappreciative investors cry foul at depreciating asset', *Financial Times*, 23 July 2002, p. 21: analyst Stephen Ford is quoted as suggesting that Manchester United shareholders 'may have preferred to see less money risked in player trading and more returned through the certainty of dividends'.

602 Cf. Dobson and Goddard, *The Economics of Football* (Cambridge University Press 2001) pp. 90-101 & Ch. 4; O'Leary and Caiger, 'The re-regulation of football and its impact on employment contracts', Ch. 16 in Collins, Davies and Rideout, eds., *Legal Regulation of the Employment Relation* (London, Kluwer 2000); Antonioni and Cubbin, 'The Bosman Ruling and the Emergence of a Single Market in Soccer Talent', 9 *Euro Int. Law and Econ* (2000) 157.

could readily be employed to strike at persisting remnants of the transfer system that would not be imperilled by the invocation of Article 39 EC. In particular, EC law was predictably susceptible to more vigorous deployment to slice away at transfer systems operating within a single State, to assist even non-EU nationals and to attack restraints imposed by the football industry on the mobility of players whose contract has not expired.[603] So it has proved, at least in part,[604] and some of the potential wider implications of *Bosman* have been instrumental in encouraging the shaping of a revised system.

The Court in *Bosman* ruled against the prevailing transfer system but, accepting the general argument that football is 'special', left space for the industry to choose how to re-arrange itself. And the transfer system lives on, albeit in modified and scaled-down fashion. In March 2001 it was announced that, after extended and sometimes acrimonious discussion, an agreement had been reached between the Commission and football's governing bodies for the world, FIFA, and for Europe, UEFA. The Commission went so far as to announce that the deal of March 2001 had been 'formalized' through an exchange of letters recorded in a Commission Press Release[605] between Mr Monti and the President of FIFA, Mr Sepp Blatter. In the aftermath of this legally ambiguous 'compromise' the International Federation of Professional Footballers' Associations, FIFPro, which had been heavily involved in the negotiation until at a late stage it walked away in dissatisfaction at what was being proposed and ultimately agreed in March 2001,[606] seemed a likely source of legal challenge to this deal. However, FIFPro's anxieties have been addressed[607] and in August 2001

---

[603] That, in any event, was the trio of prospects for future litigation that I identified in my Annotation of the ruling for this Review, cited *supra* note 557, 1019-1031. See also Thill, 'L'arrêt Bosman et ses implications pour la libre circulation des sportifs a l'interieur de l'U.E. dans des contextes factuels differents de ceux de l'affaire Bosman', *Revue du Marché Unique Européen* (1996) 89; Morris, Morrow and Spink, 'EC Law and Professional Football: *Bosman* and its implications', 59 *MLR* (1996) 893; Hilf, 'Das Bosman-Urteil des EuGH', *NJW* (1996) 1169; Spink, 'Blowing the whistle on Football's Domestic Transfer Fee', *Juridical Review* (1999) 73.

[604] On litigation, potential and actual, see Gardiner and Welch, 'Show me the money: regulation of the migration of professional sportsmen in Post-*Bosman* Europe', pp. 107-126 in Caiger and Gardiner *supra* note 564; McAuley, 'They think it is all over [...] It might just be now: unravelling the ramnifications for the European Football Transfer System post-*Bosman*', *ECLR* (2002) 331.

[605] IP/01/3 14, 'Outcome of discussions between die Commission and FIFA/UEFA on FIFA Regulations on international football transfers', 5 March 2001: 'formalisées' in French, 'formell besiegelt' in German, phrases which, like the English version, will perplex the EC lawyer. Cf. Egger and Stix-Hackl, 'Sports and Competition Law: a Never-Ending Story?', *ECLR* (2002) 81, 90-91.

[606] 'We don t accept this accord [...] It creates a new category of workers at European level – footballers who will not benefit like others from the same social protection', Laurent Dennis, FIFPro spokesperson, quoted in *The Independent*, 'New transfer system threatens stability of the game', 7 March 2001, p. 28.

[607] On discontinued proceedings before the Belgian courts, see Bennett, 'They think it s all over, [...] it is now! – How Extra Time was required to finally settle football's transfer saga', 9 *Sport and the Law Journal* (2001) 180. At EC level, a players' union brought an application claiming illegal failure to act on a complaint about the transfer system in Case T-42/01, *SETCA-FGTB* v. *Commission*, but the case was removed from the Court's register on 24 Jan. 2002, and the complaint (COMP/36.583) was rejected on 30 May 2002 as part of the Commission's closure of the investigation. Relevant documentation is collected at http://europa.eu.int/comm/sport/key_files/circ/a_circ_en.html.

FIFA and FIFPro were able to strike an agreement about FIFPro's participation in the implementation of the new rules, which entered into force on 1 September 2001.[608] Eventually, in June 2002, the Commission closed its investigation, declaring 'the end of the Commission's involvement in disputes between players, clubs and football organizations'.[609] Commissioner Monti stated: 'The new rules find a balance between the players' fundamental right to free movement and stability of contracts together with the legitimate objective of integrity of the sport and the stability of championships'.

The key features of this system that the Commission is prepared to treat as compatible with EC competition law and the law of free movement provide that in the case of players aged under 23, a system of training compensation should be in place to encourage and reward the training effort of clubs, in particular small clubs; that there should be the creation of solidarity mechanisms that would redistribute a significant proportion of income to clubs involved in the training and education of a player, including amateur clubs; that international transfer of players aged under 18 is to be allowed subject to agreed conditions; that there shall be created one transfer period per season, and a further limited mid-season window, with a limit of one transfer per player per season; that there shall be minimum and maximum duration of contracts of respectively one and five years; that contracts are to be protected for a period of three years up to age 28 and for two years thereafter; that the system of sanctions to be introduced should preserve the regularity and proper functioning of sporting competition so that unilateral breaches of contract are only possible at the end of a season; that financial compensation can be paid if a contract is breached unilaterally whether by the player or the club; that proportionate sporting sanctions may be applied to players, clubs or agents in the case of unilateral breaches of contract without just cause, in the protected period; that there shall be created an effective, quick and objective arbitration body with members chosen in equal numbers by players and clubs and with an independent chairman; that arbitration is voluntary and does not prevent recourse to national courts.

4.7.3. *Is the matter now closed?*

Under the new arrangements, collectively agreed and enforced restrictions en player mobility and associated sanctions imposed on contract-breakers are plainly to be reduced compared with past practice, but football will still be allowed to maintain arrangements that would not be tolerated in other industries. Is this lawful?

The Court has interpreted Article 81(1) to exclude agreements concluded in the context of collective negotiations between management and labour in pursuit of the improvement of conditions of work and employment.[610] Neither the method of its production nor its content brings the agreement en transfers within the sanctuary rec-

[608] See Dabscheck, 'The Globe al their Feet: FIFA's New Employment Rules', (as yet) unpublished paper on file with the author.

[609] IP/02/824, 'Commission closes investigations into FIFA regulations on international football transfers', 5 June 2002. The Commission does not propose to take the matter on to a formal plane.

[610] E.g., Case C-67/96, *Albany International* v. *Stichting Bedrijfspensioenfonds Textielindustrie*, [1991] *ECR* I-5751; Case C-219/97, *Maatschappij Drijvende Bokken BV* v. *Stichting Pensioenfonds*, [1999] *ECR* I-6121.

ognized by the Court. The level of collective involvement was inconsistent and fragmented; the effect is not to improve players' working conditions. It is submitted that there is no strong case in favour of an extended interpretation sufficient to confer such autonomy on the agreement, and that, in particular, residual restrictions en cross-border labour mobility within the ambit of Article 39 are inapt to benefit from the special treatment carved out by the Court for collective agreements between employers and employees.

But the fact that the matter is in principle subject to the rules of the EC Treaty does not mean it is unlawful. Sport has special features that deserve respect. In accordance with *Bosman*, it should be regarded as legally permissible for football to devise an internal taxation system to transfer money into the hands of nursery clubs, as part of a scheme for sustaining a larger number of clubs than would survive in 'pure' market conditions and to diminish gaps in economic strength between clubs. This would connect with the need to preserve a credibly competitive League, the most persuasive general rationale for permitting the sports industry autonomy to regulate itself in a more interventionist manner than would be permitted in other sector.[611] Similarly it is submitted that one could readily accept the permissibility under EC law of 'transfer windows', which typically prevent players being acquired and immediately fielded by a new club in the later stages of a competition, or rules that forbid a player appearing for more than one club during a particular competition. Doubtless such rules dampen the market for player acquisition and exert an incidental effect en patterns of player mobility, but, by restricting the ability of rich clubs to poach their rivals' star players at the sharp end of the season, they serve the legitimate purpose of ensuring the competition remains credible. *Lehtonen* already suggests judicial receptivity to such a model.[612] Insofar such devices constitute features of the agreement en transfers brokered by the Commission, it is my submission that they are capable of being treated as compatible with EC law as contributions to fulfilment of the wider mission to maintain a degree of competitive equality and a form of organizational solidarity within the sport.

Collective attempts to impose restrictions on the ability of players to contract with their preferred employer, even where that involves a breach of an existing contract, also feature in the 'compromise'. For example, up until the age of 28 a player must abide by a contract for at least three years or else suffer a suspension imposed by the game's governing authorities. This goes beyond the generally applicable 'transfer window' and instead envisages collective action designed to encourage observance of an individual contract rather than simply leaving the matter to applicable national law. It is submitted that this contribution to stabilizing club squads goes beyond the space allowed by the Court's acceptance in *Bosman* that in view of the 'considerable social importance of sporting activities and in particular football in the Community, the aims of maintaining a balance between clubs by preserving a certain degree of equality and uncertainty as to results [...] must be accepted as legitimate'. This, however, cannot conclude the argument. In the same sentence of *Bosman* the Court added that in view of the importance of sport 'encouraging the recruitment and training of

611 See generally Part 2 above.

612 *Lehtonen*, *supra* note 568.

young players must be accepted as legitimate'.[613] This separate aim may be advanced in defence of the supplementary collective intervention into contractual negotiation and compliance envisaged by the newly agreed system. It is indeed explicitly stated by the Commission in its publications of March 2001 and June 2002 that it accepts the need to 'encourage and reward the training effort of clubs, in particular small clubs'. But it is arguable that on this point the Court, and therefore the Commission, exaggerates the special status of sport. It is simply assumed that sport has an unusually pressing need to offer inducements to employers to train young workers. But where is the reason for supposing that a football club is any less likely to train young employees because they might subsequently quit the company than a bank or a University would be – and no transfer fee system applies in those sectors! All employers need to train employees in order to take the benefit of their skills for as long as they are able to compete successfully in the labour market to attract them to stay with the company. A transfer system doubtless encourages a higher level of investment in training than would otherwise occur but what is missing from the ruling in *Bosman* and the Commission's subsequent approach to the matter is any supplementary explanation why sports clubs should be treated as a special case on this point. Economic rationales may conceivably exist.[614] The ability of football players is immediately visible on the pitch, so clubs that invest in training quickly lose the advantage they enjoy in having more information than predator employees about an employee's developed skills. Perhaps that generates an unusually strong unwillingness to invest in training, although a similar rationale would apply to musicians or actors who are not currently subjected to a transfer system. For current purposes the point is simply that no such analysis has been conducted in the context of EU policy-making and that therefore the EU institutions since *Bosman* have proceeded on the unexplained assumption that sport, and in particular football, is 'special' in its need to protect incentives to invest in youth training.

From this perspective it is accordingly far from clear that the Commission's 'compromise' agreement with football governing authorities is fully compatible with EC law.[615] It is submitted that the insistence on individual economic freedoms that is driven by Article 39 EC, supplemented by, and in some factual situations extended by, Articles 81 and 82 EC, fatally damages attempts to resuscitate a transfer system claimed to serve the collective interests of the game in so far as residual restrictions on labour mobility apply, over and above permissible devices for income distribution and other schemes such as the 'transfer window' designed to stabilize the credibility of a competition.[616] But, as mentioned above, FIFPro, the association of players unions, is apparently not now minded to fund litigation designed to destabilize the compromise

---

[613] Case C-415/93, *supra* note 551, Para. 106.

[614] See, e.g., Feess and Muehleusser, 'Economic Consequences of Transfer Fee Regulations in European Football', 13 *European Journal of Law and Economics* (2002) 221.

[615] It may also be vulnerable to attack under national law, though this will vary State by State. E.g., for comment on the impact of German law, see Engelbrecht, 'New legislation on Fixed-Term Work: Impacts on the Discussion about a new FIFA-Transfer-Regulation' 5/6 *International Sports Law Journal* (2001) 49.

[616] Cf. Foster, 'Transfer Fees: still (il)legal after all these years?', *Singer & Friedlander Football Review 2000-01*, www.le.ac.uk/crss/sf-review/00-01/contents01.html.

arrangements, and a brave individual litigant may not be readily forthcoming. *Bosman*, after all, won his case, but his career was ruined by boycotts to which he was subject while his legal action was pending and fully eight years separated the initiation of litigation from an out-of-court payment made to him by the Belgian football authorities.

In closing the Commission's investigation in June 2002, Commissioner Monti, declaring 'the end of the Commission s involvement in disputes between players, clubs and football organizations', added that it 'is understood that EU law is able to take into account the specificity of sport, and in particular to recognize that sport performs a very important social, integrating and cultural function'.[617] Given the slender likelihood of litigation, combined with an admission that even the analysis above suggests that, at worst, the 'compromise' is only in limited respects vulnerable to a serious challenge based on EC law, one may be inclined to agree with this mood of all's well (more or less) that ends well (more or less). One may also readily appreciate Mr Monti's desire to trumpet the Commission's respect for sport's diverse strengths. There is little room for doubt that the background political mood played a rule in encouraging the Commission to find a way to terminate its dogged pursuit of this matter. Governing authorities in sport are often skilful in exploiting the fact that their games carry a value measured in newsworthiness that stands out of all proportion to their importance judged solely by turnover figures and balance sheets. Sport engages more than economics. In September 2000 Prime Minister Blair and Chancellor Schroeder were able to find time in their busy schedules to review the debate and, expressing the view that dismantling the current transfer system could imperil smaller clubs, they hoped that 'the Commission will take into account the special situation that exists in professional soccer [sic]'.[618] The slight to the Commission, by implication guilty of neglecting that special situation, is plain. It is doubtless appealing to politicians to grab cheap headlines by 'defending' football, especially where no financial commitment is involved. Subsequently, a letter written by UEFA to Prime Minister Goran Persson, at a time when Sweden held the Union Presidency, was conveniently leaked to journalists in early March 2001. It complained that Commission officials were almost impossible to deal with because of their unwillingness to accept the specific needs of the grass roots of the game' and 'out of sympathy with the expressed wishes of governments of their own member states and the recent [Nice] Declaration'.[619] In such an environment striving to close the file on the transfer system is not inconsistent with the formal independence guaranteed to and required of the Commission according to Article 213 of the Treaty but neither is it wholly disconnected from the practical politics of this sensitive matter.

617 IP/021824, *supra* note 609.

618 Press Release No 425/00 of the German Government, 10 September 2000, currently available at www.eng.bundesregierung.de/top/dokumente/Pressemitteilung/ix_17866.htm.

619 Quotes taken from 'UEFA fears for future as transfer talks reach impasse', *The Independent*, 3 March 2001, p. 26. See Part 6 below on the Nice Declaration.

4.8. Broadcasting

4.8.1. *The economic context of sport and broadcasting*

Bosman has been widely treated as a far more significant agent for change in sport in recent years than is realistic. Of course the judgment has brought to an end intra-EU/EEA nationality discrimination in club football, and, by generating curtailment of the scope of the transfer system, it has altered the nature of the relationship between player and club. But the dominating issue in professional sport over the last decade or so has been the transformation of the broadcasting sector. Sweeping deregulation and doses of privatization have combined with extraordinarily rapid technological change affecting the delivery of media services to convert broadcasting into a fiercely competitive and volatile sector. It is well known that broadcasting undertakings, and in particular new market entrants seeking to establish awareness of their presence among potential customers, have chased the acquisition of rights to transmit sports events with a zeal that reflects the intense appeal of sports coverage to viewers. Football and Formula One motor racing top the European tree. Media companies have vigorously pursued the acquisition of contractual rights and even in some cases have tried to secure a controlling interest in sports clubs themselves[620] or, at least, a lesser stake that increases their influence on decisions to sell rights.[621] Simple economics dictates that the explosion in the number of actors on the demand-side of the market combined with the relative difficulty in increasing the supply of truly attractive events leads to vast increases in the prices charged by the sports industry for broadcasting rights. Even if there are recent indications that the market is cooling down, at least in relation to demand for the sports events that, though not rated as top-level, were priced at frankly mysteriously elevated levels in this latest economic 'bubble',[622] it is nevertheless plain that rights to broadcast sports events, as a saleable commodity,

[620] E.g., in 1999 the UK competition authorities blocked a proposed merger between BskyB, a satellite broadcasting company, and Manchester United, a football club, on the basis that it would operate contrary to the public interest; cm 4305, 1999. Among other factors it was thought that competition in the market for acquisition of broadcasting rights would have been restricted by BskyB's more intimate involvement with the supply-side and that the gulf between rich and poor football clubs would be widened. For comment, see Tassano, 'Are Vertical Mergers Harmful?', *ECLR* (1999) 395; Harbord and Binmore, 'Toeholds, takeovers and football', *ECLR* (2000) 142, and on the broader background, see Bose, *Manchester Unlimited* (London, Texere 1999).

[621] E.g., in the UK the consequence of the blocking of the BskyB/Manchester United merger, *supra* note 620, has been the acquisition by media companies of minority but not insignificant stakes in football clubs; see Brown, 'Sneaking in through the back door? Media company interests and dual ownership of clubs', Ch. 8 in Hamil, Michie, Oughton and Warby, eds., *Football in the Digital Age: whose game is it anyway?* (Edinburgh, Mainstream Publishing 2000).

[622] Notoriously in 2002 the 72 professional English Football League clubs operating below the top tier, the Premiership (comprising the leading 20 clubs), found expected substantial income from sale of broadcasting rights would not after all be forthcoming when the buyer, ITV Digital, which had attracted far fewer viewers than planned, was placed in administration. Despite dire predictions no club has (yet) been forced to close as a result. The collapse of the Kirch empire in Germany also featured broken agreements to pay large sums for rights to broadcast football. Cf. *The Economist*, 'Passion, pride and profit: A survey of football', 1 June 2002.

have become sufficiently lucrative in recent years to transform the whole structure of professional sport as a commercial enterprise. Opportunities to sell branded merchandise, such as club shirts, have provided another explosion of revenue. The fan who pays at the gate is no longer the main source of revenue for sports clubs. The alteration of the transfer system post-*Bosman* is small beer compared with these developments.

So the prominence of EC law's intervention in sport in recent years is above all the consequence of the 'commercialization' of the sector, in particular as a result of its close association with the helter-skelter development of the broadcasting industry. In fact, much of the most economically significant sports-related material that cascaded into the Commission's in-tray in the late 1990s was concerned directly or indirectly with broadcasting. In some respects the Commission's recent preoccupation with sport has been driven by its need to monitor the much more important broadcasting sector, in which it is profoundly anxious to forestall practices that will facilitate existing incumbents anxiety to impede new entrants.

4.8.2. *UEFA's rules on 'blocking' matches*

In April 2001 the Commission issued a formal Decision concerning UEFA's 'blocking' rules.[623] These permit national football associations to prohibit the broadcasting of matches within their territory during a two-and-a-half hour period on a Saturday or Sunday corresponding to the normal time at which fixtures are scheduled in the relevant country. This, one would initially suppose, impedes the commercial freedom of broadcasters to conclude deals to show 'blocked' matches. On the other hand, it serves the rather differently calibrated value of encouraging spectators to attend matches 'live' and thereby to foster a vibrant atmosphere inside grounds. The Commission's market analysis led it to conclude that the rules do not appreciably restrict competition within the meaning of Article 81(1).[624] It explicitly states that it therefore need not assess the extent to which the televising of football exerts a negative impact on attendance at matches.[625]

Intriguingly, a different tune emerges from a reading of the Press Release concerning this matter. Mr Monti is quoted as observing that the decision 'reflects the Commission's respect of the specific characteristics of sport and of its cultural and social function'.[626] Admittedly the Decision is built on appreciation of the specific nature of the market for rights to broadcast football matches, just as all competition decisions take proper account of applicable market conditions, but Mr Monti's more ambitious claim that it reflects the Commission's respect for sport's 'cultural and social function' is disingenuous. It would be more accurate to state that market analysis conducted under Article 81 has led to a conclusion which preserves the autonomy of

---

[623] Comm. Dec. 2001/478, *OJ* 2001, L 171/12.

[624] Paras. 49-61 of the Decision. The Commission will monitor change in market structure, particularly in the wake of the 'Internet revolution', Para. 56.

[625] Para. 59.

[626] IP/01/583, 20 April 2001.

football governing bodies to choose to 'block' the broadcasting of matches. It is not the Commission's business to embark on an assessment of sport's cultural and social function, except in so far as it may be relevant under Article 81(3), and, even though the criteria governing exemption are not necessarily wholly incapable of influence by what may be loosely termed 'cultural factors',[627] such broader considerations are scrupulously excluded from the formal Decision, which is confined to Article 81(1) alone. The Commission may here be suspected of seeking to use its Press Release to build up credit for itself in the face of allegations that its application of EC trade law is liable to destroy the foundations of sport. Much as one may readily sympathize with the Commission for the more egregious attacks it has sustained from the sports industry and some prominent national politicians for its alleged meddling in matters that do not concern it, it is pertinent to wonder whether it may be storing up trouble for itself in making extravagant claims about its competence to cater for cultural and social matters in the application of orthodox EC trade law.

4.8.3. *Collective selling of broadcasting rights – the competing interests*

The decision on UEFA's 'blocking' system is explicitly stated not to prejudice assessment of collective selling of broadcasting rights to football matches under Article 81(l).[628] This more general issue awaits authoritative Commission treatment. It is truly intriguing.

Sport without uncertainty of result would be like opera. You would know who is going to die in the end. It might be entertaining; but it would not be sport. So the establishment of a 'solidarity fund' within a sport, to which wealthier clubs are required to contribute from the proceeds of, *inter alia*, the sale of broadcasting rights and ticket income and on which poorer clubs may draw for financial support, would probably escape supervision under EC competition law. It would not restrict competition within the meaning of Article 81(1); rather, it is a form of equalizing arrangement that is essential to sustaining vibrant inter-club competition in a professional sports league.[629] Doubtless a shrewdly-devised balance has to be struck between rewarding the successful and strengthening the unsuccessful,[630] but the key point for present purposes is that, by contrast, incentives to adopt such a strategy are completely absent from a typical manufacturing or service industry. The interesting questions in sport

[627] For a summary of the unclear scope of 'non-economic' aspects to Art. 81(3), see Whish, *Competition Law* (2001) 125-128. Neither Commission nor Court has yet offered satisfactory explanation of the impact of Art. 151(4) EC on Art. 81 EC, and the issue, which also engages *inter alia* the impact of Arts. 6 and 153(2), escapes the scope of this paper. For a taste, see Monti, 'Article 81 EC and public policy', 39 *CML Rev.*, 1057 esp. at 1069-78.

[628] *Supra* now 623, Para. 60 of the Decision.

[629] Cf. summary in Roth, ed., *Bellamy and Child's European Community Law of Competition*, Para. 4-150 (London, Sweet and Maxwell 2000). See also Part 5 of this paper, below.

[630] Much of the economic literature is North American in origin. For analysis, see Dobson and Goddard, *supra* note 602, especially Ch. 3. Cf. Rosen and Sanderson, 'Labour Markets in Professional Sports', 111 *The Economic Journal* (2001) F47, arguing US approaches to locating balance punish success while European approaches punish failure.

then surround the issue of how this peculiar economic status should be reflected in the legal regulation of practices that are presented as necessary to secure equality between clubs and uncertainty as to results. And this is the challenge presented by collective selling.

Collective selling arrangements typically offer prospective purchasers only the opportunity to compete for one package, comprising the league's entire output. Buyers are unable to conclude deals with individual clubs,[631] among whom there would otherwise be competition in selling.[632] As the Scottish excursion in Part 2 of this paper demonstrated, it is plain that clubs would have nothing to sell unless other clubs agreed to play against them. Fixtures cannot be arranged unilaterally – this is the nature of sport. But once clubs agree to play against each other, it is submitted the subsequent decision to sell rights to broadcast matches on a collective basis is capable of restricting competition within the meaning of Article 81(1). So collective selling of broadcasting rights should be carefully distinguished from arrangements internal to the game which reflect the peculiar economic interdependence of clubs because it exerts a direct external impact on third party broadcasters.[633] It restricts competition within the meaning of Article 81(1) EC, insofar as it has an appreciable effect on inter-State trade. It is unlawful unless it is exempted under Article 81(3). But here, at the stage of exemption, the peculiarities of organized sport may emerge. The fact that the collective system of selling has restricted supply will ensure that the price paid by buyers will be higher than the (aggregate) price that would have been paid for rights sold on an individual basis by clubs. So collective selling maximizes revenue which can then be shared between clubs in pursuit of the preservation of competitive equality and a more attractive spectacle. Moreover, raising revenue on a collective basis is a far more administratively convenient vehicle for the league to arrange for subsequent distribution between participant clubs than a model which insists on selling by individual clubs followed by some form of internal taxation. But how does the interest of sport in using collective selling to enlarge the pie and to make it easier to slice weigh against the interest of third party broadcasters, comprising both current incumbents and potential market entrants, in having a more competitive market for acquisition of rights?

---

[631] The precise nature of this 'right', typically comprising one of access to home matches, is dictated by national law cf. Beloff, Kerr and Demetriou, *supra* note 581, pp. 134-6, 153-6; Nitsche, 'Collective Marketing of Broadcasting Rights in Europe', *ECLR* (2000) 208; Van den Brink, 'EC Competition Law and the Regulation of Football', *ECLR* (2000) 359, at 360 and 420, at 422-23.

[632] The collectively sold package may be (and increasingly is) broken down into constituent units – live matches, recorded highlights, etc. – but this does not affect the basic issue, which is the suppression of sales by individual clubs. On the distinct question of exclusive sale see Fleming, 'Exclusive rights to broadcast sporting events in Europe', *ECLR* (1999) 143.

[633] Cf. Cave and Crandall, 'Sports rights and the broadcast industry', 111 *The Economic Journal* (2001) F4, especially at F18.

4.8.4. *Collective selling of broadcasting rights – legal straws in the wind*

The Commission has not decided how to answer this question. It is interesting, though naturally not decisive as a matter of EC law, that the permissibility of collective selling of broadcasting rights has been addressed at national level. In the United Kingdom a decision of the Restrictive Practices Court in 1999 found in favour of the legality of collective selling arrangements practised within the English (football) Premier League.[634] However, although the judgment is lucid in its identification of the gains for football flowing from collective selling, it is much less convincing in its measurement of the losses incurred by (existing and potential) broadcasters. The deficiency was not the Court's but rather that of the now-repealed statute under which the decision was taken, the Restrictive Trade Practices Act. That Act confined the Court to choosing between the public interest in maintaining the current arrangements and in having no restrictions al all, and, statutorily unable to weigh up more nuanced intermediate alternatives,[635] it preferred the former. In Germany, by contrast, collective selling was condemned by the competition authorities but, in a tribute to the lobbying power of football, it was subsequently granted statutory approval.[636] Of course, a green light under national law cannot displace the application of Article 81 in the territory of a Member State, so neither of these two distinct Anglo-German routes to preservation of collective selling can be treated as inevitably durable in so far as inter-State aspects to the arrangements are involved.

But how will the Commission judge collective selling? In July 2001 it sent a statement of objections to UEFA, European football's governing body, complaining that its arrangements for the sale of broadcasting rights to the 'Champions League', the principal European club competition, infringe Article 81.[637] UEFA sells rights collectively on behalf of all participating clubs and has preferred to sell to broadcasters on an exclusive basis, typically under arrangements covering a period of several years. The Commission considers UEFA's scheme constitutes a substantial restriction on competition, not least because of the foreclosure of the market to potential entrants into a sector capable of dynamic evolution, and that, although it in principle recognizes the need for wealth distribution and solidarity within the sport, it believes the UEFA arrangements go beyond what is necessary to achieve these legitimate ends. It is notorious that the rise of the 'Champions League' has coincided with a diminution in the percentage of revenue raised that is shared among clubs outside the game's elite. Moreover, the vast rewards on offer to the small pool of clubs able regularly to participate in the 'Champions League' may conceivably have made a significant

---

[634] *Re the supply of services facilitating the broadcasting on television of Premier League football matches*, [1999] UKCLR 258.

[635] E.g., in the form of a collectively-sold bloc of matches alongside which remaining matches could be made available on an individual basis. Cf. Szymanski, 'Hearts, minds and the Restrictive Practices Court case', Ch. 23 in Hamil et al., *supra* note 621; Spink and Morris, 'The battle for TV rights in professional football', p. 165 in Caiger and Gardiner *supra* note 564.

[636] Para. 31 Gesetz gegen Wettbewerbsbeschränkungen, as amended with effect from 1 January 1999.

[637] IP/01/1043, 20 July 2001.

contribution to weakening the competitive health of national league championships. One may accordingly suspect that the Commission, in seeking to apply Article 81 to break up collective selling of exclusive deals in the face of the sports industry's objection that such arrangements are essential to sustain internal organizational solidarity, has cunningly picked out the softest target. UEFA duly responded by proposing an amended system involving, in short, an 'unbundling' of the package of rights available for purchase. More operators, including internet content providers as well as more traditional public and private broadcasters, will be able to acquire a degree of involvement in the coverage of the Champions League. The Commission is favourably disposed to this plan for competitive diversification which, it considers, will benefit football fans while also assisting the growth of new technology in the media sector.[638]

In this case the Commission explicitly and scrupulously observes that it is not objecting to collective selling of sports rights as such.[639] But this case carries an echo of the Commission's intriguingly ambitious hint in its December 1999 'Helsinki Report on Sport',[640] that assessment of the compatibility of collective selling arrangements with Article 81 can legitimately involve analysis of the degree to which the revenues raised are shared throughout the sport. In the Helsinki Report, the Commission grouped features such as the notion of solidarity in sport, whereby the top of the professional game is connected to the humble 'grass roots', under the rubric of the 'European Sports Model'. The Commission commented that any possible exemption granted to collective selling arrangements would have to take account of the benefits for consumers and the proportionate nature of the restrictions in relation to the end in view. This is orthodox fare under Article 81(3) EC. It observed that it is therefore appropriate 'to examine the extent to which a link can be established between the joint sale of rights and financial solidarity between professional and amateur sport, the objectives of the training of young sportsmen and women and those of promoting sporting activities among the population'. In similar vein Commissioner Monti has cautiously suggested that 'financial solidarity between clubs or between professional and amateur sport' could be a relevant factor in assessing whether to grant an exemption to collective selling.[641] This is strikingly less orthodox as an articulation of the matters that are properly taken into account under Article 81(3). This line of thinking suggests use of the power to exempt restrictive selling practices as a method for insisting that sellers also take care to foster the social and educational function of sport by sharing proceeds throughout the sport.[642] So a 'breakaway' league of the type

---

638 IP/02/806, 3 June 2002; *OJ* 2002, C 196/3. So, e.g., in the UK live Champions' League matches were available only on ITV in 2002/03, but a greater number of live matches, screened by both ITV and Sky, will be available from 2003/2004.

639 'Background Note', Memo 01/271, 20 July 2001.

640 COM (1999) 644/1 and /2. See further below, Parts 5 and 6.

641 Speech delivered in Brussels at a conference on 'Governance in Sport', 26 February 2001, available as Speech/01/84 via http://europa.eu.int/comm/sport/key_files/comp/a_comp_en.html.

642 Support for this approach is expressed by the Committee of the Regions, Opinion on the European Model of Sport, *OJ* 1999, C 374/56, Para. 3.8.

lately mooted in European football,[643] may, by ridding itself of its roots in the wider organization of the sport, thereby lose one commercially attractive opportunity, that of collective sale of broadcasting rights.[644] The Commission may here be floating an idea that would exceed the proper scope of Article 81(3). It is, in entertaining this temptation, running the risk of allowing its desire to hold the line on the features of the European Sports Model which it cherishes to propel it into the position of general sports regulator which it insists it does not wish to fulfil and for which its constitutional credentials are lacking. The Commission is competent to do more than supervise the choices made within the industry for their compliance with EC law.[645] For the time being, the compatibility of collective selling of rights to broadcast sports events with EC law remains an intriguing but unresolved issue.

5. The structure of EC trade law applied to sport

The Commission issued 'The Helsinki Report on Sport' in December 1999.[646] In a section entitled 'Clarifying the Legal Environment of Sport' the Commission contents itself with a relatively brief summary, and it is the Treaty competition rules that are the centre of attention. In *Bosman* the Court notoriously avoided analysis of the matter from the perspective of the competition rules. *Balog*, which would have provided an opportunity to rule on the application of Article 81 to the pre-2001 version of the transfer system in litigation initiated by a non-EU (Hungarian) national, was withdrawn in the wake of a settlement of the dispute by the parties,[647] while in both *Deliège* and *Lehtonen* the Court concluded that the referral did not provide it with sufficient detail to allow it to provide an informed ruling on the interpretation of the Treaty competition rules.[648] Perhaps it is sound judicial technique to decide only matters that need to be decided for the purposes of disposal of the case at hand, but such judicial reticence has left plenty of space for debate, nurtured by the vigorous

643 'Project Gandalf', the European Football League, was notified to the Commission, *OJ* 1999, C 70/5, and though the breakaway has not (yet) been executed, the threat was enough to generate changes by UEFA that benefited larger clubs. See, e.g., van den Brink *supra* note 631, especially 364-65. The 'G-14' group of leading clubs met Commissioner Reding on 16 April 2002; see Commission 'Key Files', *supra* note 641.

644 On the very permissibility of such a League, if 'closed', under EC competition law, see van den Brink *supra* note 631, especially 364-8, 426; Hellenthal, *Zulässigkeit einer supranazionalen Fussball-Europaliga nach den Bestimmungen des europäischen Wettbewerbrechts* (Frankfurt, Peter Lang 2000).

645 Cf., however, note 78 above and the admittedly thoroughly ambiguous role of the *Querschnittsklausel* Art. 151(4) EC in shaping the ambit of Art. 81(3).

646 Cited *supra* note 640. See Weatherill, 'The Helsinki Report on Sport', 25 *EL Rev.* (2000) 282.

647 Case C-264/98, *Tibor Balog* v. *Royal Charleroi Sporting Club*, referred by the Tribunal de première instance de Charleroi under an order of 2 July 1998, removed from the Court's register on 2 April 2001. An Opinion by A-G Stix-Hackl, dated 29 March 2001, has not been made officially available (its hearing was 'cancelled', according to Court Press Release No 11/2001, 29 March 2001), but favours a finding of incompatibility with Art. 81; sustainable development has been secured by the recycling of the analysis in the unpublished Opinion in Egger and Stix-Hackl, 'Sports and Competition Law: A Never-Ending Story?', *ECLR* (2002) 81.

648 Deliège, *supra* note 567, Paras. 36-38 of the judgment; *Lehtonen*, *supra* note 568, Paras. 28-19 of the judgment.

Opinion of Advocate-General Lenz in *Bosman*, about the proper role of competition law in this field.[649]

In the Helsinki Report the Commission offers only a framework for analysis. It considers that, from the perspective of the Treaty competition rules, there are three categories into which rules of sporting bodies might fall:

(i) practices which do not come under the competition rules. These are rules to which Article 81(1) does not in principle apply because they are inherent to a sport's identity and/or necessary for its organization. The Commission states that, 'first and foremost', this would cover 'The rules of the game';

(ii) practices that are, in principle, prohibited by the competition rules. This category comprises practices that are motivated by economic interests, unassociated with the preservation of the special characteristics of sport. Orthodox Community law applies to forbid nationality-based discrimination outside the special case of representative teams and anti-competitive practices in, for example, distribution of sports goods;

(iii) practices likely to be exempted from the competition rules. The Commission draws on *Bosman* to express a favourable view in principle of agreements genuinely designed to achieve the objectives of maintaining 'a balance between clubs, while preserving a degree of equality of opportunity and the uncertainty of the result, and to encourage the recruitment and training of young players'. It is also ready to exempt 'an exclusive right, limited in duration and scope, to broadcast sporting events' and short-term sponsoring agreements based on clear and non-discriminatory selection criteria. Presumably such schemes that lack the beneficial features mentioned by the Commission are unlikely to enjoy exemption and, assuming the presence of an appreciable effect on inter-State trade, will be condemned as violations of Article 81(1).

It is certainly helpful to have this tripartite framework set out as a starting point. It is possible for those in the sports industry seeking to shelter their arrangements from intervention under EC law to adapt their arguments to the approach sketched by the Commission. But there is plenty of room for controversy about the proper location of particular practices on this ladder, not least because traditional sporting practices, viewed from within as, in short, 'rules of the game', carry inescapable economic implications which, moreover, may resonate more loudly as sport's commercial clout increases.[650] Disagreements at the borderline between categories (i) and (iii) and categories (ii) and (iii) seem especially likely to proliferate. And the Commission itself appears to waver on the matter of classification. Whereas the Helsinki Report locates

---

649 Cf. Hannamann, *Kartellverbot und Verhaltenskoordinationen in Sport* (Berlin, Duncker and Humblot 2001); Van den Brink, op. cit. *supra* note 631. See also sources, *supra* notes 603, 629.

650 Pons, Deputy Director General of (what was then) Directorate-General IV, confesses the difficulties involved in 'Sport and European Competition Policy', Ch. 6 in Hawk, ed., 1999 Fordham Corp. L. Inst. (2000), plus discussion ibid. in Ch. 9. For recent statements of practice by officials (including Pons), consult http://europa.eu.int/comm/sport/key_files/comp/a_comp_en.html; and see also Pons, 'La politique européenne de concurrence et le sport (1995-2002)', 2 *Revue du Droit de l'Union Européenne* (2002) 241.

arrangements designed to maintain a balance between clubs in category (iii), exemptable practices, it is at least arguable that such practices are necessary for the very organization of sporting competition, and that they accordingly belong in category (i), rules lying beyond the reach of Article 81(1). In a Press Release issued almost contemporaneously with the Helsinki Report the Commission, addressing this issue, appeared to slide on to the other side of the line in asserting that rules of sports bodies that are necessary to ensure equality between clubs, uncertainty as to results, and the integrity and proper functioning of competitions are not in principle caught by the Treaty's competition rules.[651] On this view, keeping a balance between clubs that prevents results being a foregone conclusion is an intrinsic feature of sport and systems for shaming out income that are indispensable to the maintenance of this balance would be capable of eluding Article 81 altogether even though hard currency is very obviously involved.

Locating margins between the Commission's three categories is evidently a delicate art, but it is important to assert that although this taxonomy is designed to supply a coherent framework for understanding how EC competition law applies to sport, it is not in itself divorced from the fundamental approach of EC competition law to any sector. Rules inherent to a sport's identity and/or necessary for its organization escape Article 81 altogether. This allows recognition of sport's particular characteristics. But the application of Article 81 is always conditioned by the particular context in which arrangements are struck. There must never be a lazy or mechanical assumption that a rule restricts competition within the meaning of Article 81(1). So an apparent constraint on competition that is in fact unavoidably required to sustain the functioning of an unobjectionable commercial arrangement is itself compatible with Article 81.[652] Not every agreement which restricts the freedom of action of one or both of the parties fails within the scope of the Article 81(1) prohibition.

> '[A]ccount must first of all be taken of the overall context in which the decision of the association of undertakings was taken or produces its effects. More particularly, account must be taken of its objectives [...] It has then to be considered whether the consequential effects restrictive of competition are inherent in the pursuit of those objectives'.[653]

This observation was delivered in the context of rules prohibiting multi-disciplinary partnerships between members of the Bar and accountants[654] but can readily be transplanted to underpin an argument that the overall context in which sports regulation occurs, built around pursuit of a broad objective of healthy equality of competitive opportunity, produces effects which though restrictive of competition are nonetheless inherent in the pursuit of those objectives. So restrictions indispensable to the proper

651 IP/99/965, 9 December 1999.

652 E.g., Case C-250/92, *Gottrup Klim* v. *DLB*, [1994] *ECR* I-5641. See also A-G Lenz in *Bosman*, *supra* note 551, Paras. 262-276.

653 Case C-309/99, *J.C.J. Wouters, J.W. Savelbergh, Price Waterhouse Belastingadviseurs BV* v. *Algemene Raad van de Nederlandse Orde van Advocaten*, judgment of 19 February 2002, nyr, Para. 97.

654 And is controversial in its application by the Court in that particular context; see annotation by Vossestein in 39 *CML Rev.*, 841.

functioning of a sports League lie in an arena of autonomous sporting regulation unaffected by the hot breath of Article 81. But the general jurisprudential point is that although sport receives 'special' treatment insofar as there is room for its economic peculiarities to be used as a reason for sheltering rules that may initially appear restrictive of competition from the Treaty, in fact all sectors are in principle permitted to invoke their peculiarities in this context. The issue is only that sport is unusually peculiar.

The cases set out and discussed in Part 4, above, can be slotted into the three categories to show how the Commission's practice has evolved. So, for example, the 'Mouscron case', concerning UEFA's 'home and away' rule)[655] illustrates an exercise of autonomous sporting regulation that does not in principle fall within Article 81 or 82 at all. This is category (i); so too anti-doping rules in swimming;[656] and the UEFA rules forbidding multiple ownership of clubs – correctly treated by the Commission as essential to preserving sporting competition as a real not a sham struggle for supremacy.[657] It is submitted that rules imposing a 'transfer window', which appear in the new transfer system[658] would be similarly treated. Such a restriction on buying and selling players amounts to a contribution to limiting the occasions on which money can talk and to focusing primary attention on clubs' abilities to succeed by astute deployment of existing playing resources.

Football World Cup fits comfortably into category (ii). These were ticketing practices of purely economic interest that contradicted the fundamental principle of EC law forbidding indirect nationality-based discrimination unless objectively justified.[659]

Other cases lately brought to an informal conclusion are not blessed by precise explanations of the Commission's position. Nor does the memorandum of 5 June 2002, though presented under the sweeping title 'The application of the EU's competition rules to sports', offer any more than a quick summary of recent practice.[660] What is really necessary for the organization of sport, and therefore beyond the reach of Article 81, is an invitation to debate rather than a clean-edged category. The two issues on which most attention is lavished in Part 4 above, the transfer system and collective selling of broadcasting rights, are particularly intriguing. The arguments do not bear repetition here; suffice to say that both practices can be regarded as elements in promoting wealth distribution that contributes to competitive balance in a league, but both are vulnerable to the powerful criticism that other devices for achieving this objective can be found that do not inflict damage directly on third parties, players and purchasing broadcasters respectively. It is therefore much harder to place them beyond the reach of the Treaty rules altogether, and, moreover, it is far from dear that the grant of exemption pursuant to Article 81(3) can be justified. A cautious Commission

[655] Part 4.2.
[656] Part 4.5.
[657] Part 4.4.
[658] Part 4.7.2.
[659] Part 4.6.
[660] Memo/02/127, 5 June 2002.

has declined to rule formally on the application of Article 81 to the transfer system, although it has informally suggested the conditions for exemption may be met by the system of collective sanctions against unilateral contract-breakers,[661] while it has explicitly avoided delivering any ruling on the general phenomenon of collective selling of broadcasting rights.'[662]

It matters, of course, whether a practice is placed outside Article 81 altogether or in need of exemption pursuant to Article 81(3), most prominently because exemption currently remains the exclusive preserve of the Commission.[663] So, tactically, sporting autonomy is best protected by a regime that takes a narrow approach to Article 81(1)'s net; conversely, Commission control is enhanced by a wide interpretation of that prohibition. This is standard fare for competition lawyers. But, in practice, the difference may be less profound than it may initially appear. The exclusion of practices from the reach of Article 81 is in any event conditional on those practices being shown to be necessary and proportionate, and accordingly in practice a degree of co-operation with the Commission is likely to be required of sports bodies, whatever theoretical preference one may entertain for the scope of Article 81(1).

Aficionados of *Bosman* may well inquire, in wounded tone: Whatever happened to Article 39? In fact, built into recent Commission practice is an assumption of convergence between the basic thrust of Articles 39 and 81/82, when applied to sport. Under the EC Treaty as interpreted by the Court, provisions governing persons cross over with the competition rules in away that the provisions on goods, which do not bind private parties directly, do not.[664] *Bosman* was directed at building into Article 39 an openness to sport's special characteristics and, seeking to avoid incoherence in the application of the Treaty rules, the Commission now appears ready routinely to build in the same formula in its treatment of sporting practices under Article 81. For example, in its communication dealing with UEFA rules on multiple ownership, the Commission invokes 'Article 39 reasoning' directly in the application of Article 81.[665] The Court in *Wouters* adopts a comparable assumption of convergence between Articles 39 and 81,[666] and both *Deliège* and *Lehtonen* contain material that is persuasive in this direction.[667] Rules intrinsic to the organization of sport are untouched by the Treaty

[661] Rejection of COMP/36.583 *supra* note 607.

[662] Part 4.8.4.

[663] This will change if the 'modernization' of competition policy initially proposed in a developed fashion in the Commission's 1999 White Paper, *OJ* 1999, C 132/1, comes to fruition.

[664] See Snell *supra* note 569, especially Ch. 3; Van den Bogaert, 'Horizontality', Ch. 5 in Barnard and Scott, eds., *The Law of the Single European Market: Unpacking the Premises* (Oxford, Hart 2002).

[665] *Supra* note 582. This feature of the Commission's approach provides Mortelmans with the springboard for a much wider exploration in 'Towards Convergence in the Application of the Rules on Free Movement and on Competition?', 38 *CML Rev.* (2001) 613. See also Stuyck, 'Libre Circulation et Concurrence: Les Deux Piliers du Marché Commun', in Dony, ed., *Melanges en Hommage à Michel Waelbroeck* (Brussels, Bruylant 1999), p. 1477.

[666] Wouters, *supra* note 653, Para. 122.

[667] *Deliège*, *supra* note 567, *Lehtonen*, *supra* note 568, in particular the Opinions of A-G Cosmas and A-G Alber respectively; and similarly the 'lost' Opinion of A-G. Stix-Hackl in *Balog*, *supra* note 648. See Mortelmans, *supra* note 665, especially 625-9.

rules despite their apparent restrictive effect on trade, and, at least at this level of analysis, Articles 39 and 81 run in parallel. Admittedly, it will frequently be tricky in individual cases to determine precisely which sporting rules meet this test.[668] And, of course, in contrast to its central role in the administration of competition policy the Commission has no powers to bring proceedings directly against private parties for violation of Article 39. But as a general proposition it seems correct that rules necessary for the basic organization of sport should be treated as equally immune from challenge whether reliance is placed on the Treaty provisions on free movement or those on competition. The Commission appears to have increased the probability in practice of parallel outcomes by informally treating aspects of the amended transfer system[669] and the amended FIFA rules on agents[670] as compatible with the Treaty rules governing free movement and, by analogous reasoning, also acceptable under Article 81(3) though not excluded from Article 81(1).

The Commission concludes its Helsinki Report on Sport by insisting that 'the basic freedoms guaranteed by the Treaty do not generally conflict with the regulatory measures of sports associations, provided that these measures are objectively justified, non-discriminatory, necessary and proportional'. This is very much the message which the Commission has sought to convey in its recent practice in dealing with individual cases. And, as a general claim, it is convincing. Sport has room to move under EC law. Fair Play!

6. The wider terrain of a policy on sport

Sport possesses unusual economic features. It is also culturally and socially significant. Attention has already been drawn above to instances of the Commission weaving together these distinct strands in its handling of eases, and it has been suggested that this regulatory ambition may be susceptible to criticism for its constitutionally unstable foundations.[671] The question of just how extensive should be an EC policy on sport now deserves more focused treatment.

6.1. The Commission's approach: a 'European Model of Sport'

The authorship of a Press Release issued in February 1999 draws attention to the Commission's broad horizons.[672] The document, which set out in brief the Commission's planned work agenda, appeared under the name of three of the fifteen Commissioners, representing competition policy (Van Miert), culture (Oreja) and social affairs (Flynn). As a general observation, sport doubtless deserves attention from all

668 The new transfer rules, which potentially attract the attention of both Arts. 39 and 81, would not meet it, in my view, see Part 4.7.2 above.

669 Rejection of COMP/36.583, *supra* note 607.

670 Part 4.1; Rejection of COMP/37.124, 16 April 2002.

671 See in particular Parts 4.7.3, 4.8.2 and 4.8.4.

672 IP/99/133, 24 February 1999.

these perspectives. But the scope of the EC's competence in each is quite distinct and, in different ways, limited. Already such a complex web of involvement within the Commission itself hints at inevitable tension in the quest to achieve coherent policy development.

The Commission organized a 'European Union Conference on Sport' at Olympia, Greece, in May 1999. This gathering attracted representatives from, *inter alia*, governing bodies in sport, the media and interested public authorities. It generated a set of conclusions,[673] which included proclaimed adherence to a 'European Sports Model'. This core notion duly re-appeared in the Commission's first major post-*Bosman* policy document, the 'Helsinki Report on Sport', considered above in connection with the application of the Treaty competition rules to sport.[674] The Helsinki Report begins with the ambitious assertion that it 'gives pointers for reconciling the economic dimension of sport with its popular, educational, social and cultural dimensions'. The Commission identifies 'a European approach to sport based on common concepts and principles', which includes sport's role as 'an instrument of social cohesion and education'. Tensions have emerged between this function and the increasingly prominent economic motivations for sport. The Commission mentions the threat of a 'breakaway' European Football League which may 'jeopardize the principle of financial solidarity between professional and amateur sport and the system of promotion and relegation common to most federations'.[675]

The breadth of the Commission's horizon is emphasized by further connections made to the Commission's 1995 White Paper on teaching and learning[676] in search of methods for enhancing the educational role of sport; to the Council of Europe's view that sport is an ideal platform for social democracy; and it is asserted that 'existing Community programmes should make use of sport in combatting exclusion, inequalities, racism and xenophobia'.

It is striking that whereas the Court's recognition in *Bosman* that sport is, in short, 'special' referred to its 'social importance',[677] it was in fact largely reasoned on the basis of economic differences from normal industries, particularly clubs' need for credible rivals. By contrast, the Commission's agenda is more wide-ranging. The Helsinki Report can persuasively be taken as a demonstration of the Commission's sensitivity to the charge that It is liable to under-estimate the wider social and educational functions of sport in its application of EC law. But it leaves the reader anxious lest too much is being asked of sport as an instrument for social progress and, moreover, lest too much is being asked of the EC, and of the Commission in particular, against a constitutional background of limited available competence and policymaking instruments in many of these fields of endeavour. The Commission may be in danger of raising inflated expectations of its regulatory competence. This is especially pertinent with regard to the Commission's stated anxiety to protect a 'European Sports Model''

---

673 The conclusions are available via http://europa.eu.int/comm/sport/index.html.

674 *Supra* note 640.

675 Cf. 'Project Gandalf' and the 'G-14 group', *supra* note 643.

676 COM (95) 590.

677 Case C-415/93, *supra* note 551, Para. 106 of the judgment. Cf. Part 2 above.

That model, dedicated to cohesion between the top flight and the grass roots, is plainly here constructed as a deliberate alternative to the 'closed league' system preferred in American professional sport.[678] But there is a tension between the Commission's preferred European vision and growing trends at the summit of European professional sport, especially football, enticed to look inquisitively at how money is made in North America. It was discussed above that the Commission is tempted to withhold exemption under Article 81(3) as a means of preventing the collective selling of broadcasting rights unconnected to adequate distribution of revenue to sporting grass-roots;[679] and it may be able to use Articles 81 and 82 to block the creation of 'closed' Leagues.[680] But the Commission will be ill-advised to offer any over-estimate of its ability to impede trends towards wealth maximization in professional sport. It is not a general sports regulator and it is not competent to impose a 'European Sports Model'.

6.2. The Treaties of Amsterdam and Nice: Declarations on Sport and their consequences

It is not only the Commission that has expressed high-minded sentiments about the value of sport in society. Pressure has been periodically exerted by the sports industry to exempt sport from the scope of EC law. This, as a Treaty revision, would require the unanimous support of the Member States. Sports bodies are modestly skilful at exploiting the media to broadcast their (usually unsubstantiated) allegation that they are better left to their own regulatory devices and an unusual combination of circumstances might deliver the unanimity required to rid the EC of this turbulent pest. But the assembly of unanimous support would represent an arduous task and frankly the sports sector has failed to present an intellectually convincing case as to why it deserves such unique treatment. The Declaration on Sport attached to the Amsterdam Treaty provides an illuminating insight into the failure of the sports sector to win the argument for exemption, but also displays the accompanying anxiety of the Heads of State and Government to be seen to be doing 'something' about sport – even if, in practice, that is not very much at all.

The Amsterdam Declaration provides that:

> 'The Conference emphasizes the social significance of sport, in particular its role in forging identity and bringing people together. The Conference therefore calls on the bodies of the European Union to listen to sports associations when important questions affecting sport are at issue. In this connection, special consideration should be given to the particular characteristics of amateur sport.'

The Commission can claim to have abided by the instruction to consult, not least through the Forum it organized in Olympia in 1999 as it undertook preparation of

---

678 See Weatherill, 'Resisting the pressures of "Americanization": The influence of EC law on the European sport model' in Greenfield and Osborn, eds., *Sport and the Law* (London, Frank Cass 2000).

679 Part 4.8.4.

680 *Supra* note 644.

what was to become the Helsinki Report on Sport. But otherwise this is an anodyne Declaration, far more important for what it does not do than for what it does. Most of all, it does not in any way challenge the basic point, made so vividly in *Bosman*, that the Treaty applies to sport insofar as it constitutes an economic activity. This was expressly acknowledged by the European Court in its treatment of the Amsterdam Declaration in *Deliège* and *Lehtonen*.[681]

The refusal to exempt sport, but the temptation to garland it with laurel, also marks the negotiations at Nice. A Declaration on 'the specific characteristics of sport and its social function in Europe, of which account should be taken in implementing common policies' was annexed to the Conclusions of the Nice European Council held in December 2000. This concedes the absence of any direct Community powers in the area, but asserts that the institutions of the Community must 'take account of the social, educational and cultural functions inherent in sport and making it special, in order that the code of ethics and the solidarity essential to the preservation of its social role may be respected and nurtured.[682] The Declaration calls for the preservation of 'the cohesion and ties of solidarity binding the practice of sports at every level', and, under a sub-title 'Amateur sport and sport for all', heralds sport as 'a factor making for integration, involvement in social life, tolerance, acceptance of differences and playing by the rules'. Sports federations are declared to carry 'special responsibilities' in the light of sport's social functions.

A process of dialogue endures. In October 2001 the 'European Sports Forum' was convened in Brussels in collaboration with the Belgian EU Presidency. The Forum included a working group on the follow-up to the Nice Declaration.[683] In its conclusions, the insistence on the value of a partnership between interested actors is sustained, alongside assertion of the social and educational function of sport, though the working group's most striking conclusion is its immodest claim that 'In the light of current international events, it is more than ever before essential to spread the message of peace and respect for others conveyed by sport'. A separate working group, dealing with 'sport and the social economy', concluded that sport should remain faithful to the values of the social economy, which 'is composed of people-centred organizations and enterprises based on democracy, solidarity and valorization of social, cultural and environmental resources'. It identified these as 'civic values [that] transcend the logic of profit-seeking interest'. In similar vein, a working group of the European Sports Forum held in Copenhagen in November 2002[684] called for promotion of 'ethical and social values' and lauded recent Commission decisions for reconciling 'respect for Community law and the unique nature of sport' in accordance with the spirit of the Nice Declaration. The text of a Portuguese proposal to con-

---

[681] Deliège, *supra* note 567, Paras. 41-42 of the judgment; *Lehtonen*, *supra* note 568, Paras. 32-33 of the judgment.

[682] This is duly quoted in the Commission's memorandum of 5 June 2002, *supra* note 552.

[683] Documentation is available via http://europa.eu.int/comm/sport/info/events/forum200_en. html.

[684] Working GrOxford University Press on 'Taking account of sport in Community policies and measures'. Documentation is available via http://europa.eu.int/comm/sport/info/events/forum2002_ en.html.

fer competence on the Community to develop a European sports policy is appended to the group's conclusions, although absence of unanimous support for this step is conceded. The Nice Declaration is also cited in the proposal for a Decision of the Parliament and Council establishing the 'European Year of Education through Sport' published by the Commission in October 2001.[685] This asserts sport's contribution to, *inter alia*, 'the all-round development of the person', 'counter[ing] school failure and head[ing] off social exclusion', 'fighting against racism' and serving as 'an excellent platform for social democracy'. This seems of itself vainglorious, but, mindful of the EU's limited constitutional and practical competence in these realms, such rhetoric is plain silly. The proposal concludes by describing professional sport as 'excessively commercialized' and its image 'tarnished', and declares it is time to 'restore the true Olympic ideals so that they can help to bring personal fulfilment'.[686] The Commission is on the wrong track by assuming there is 'bad' sport – which is professional – and 'good' sport – which is uncommercialized and educationally valuable. In truth, these are quite distinct phenomena, with different structures and objectives that call for more thoughtful discrete treatment. Nonetheless the Council reached a common position on adoption of a lightly amended version of the Commission's proposal in October 2002.[687]

6.3. The several faces of 'sport'

The thread linking Helsinki, Amsterdam, Nice and the Proposal for a European Year of Education through Sport is eager assertion of the EU institutions' awareness of sport's impact outside the purely economic sphere. I am anxious that this tends to over-state the EC's legal competence to act across the spectrum. And I am anxious too that this tends to over-state the proper scope of sport's claim to contribute to European society and culture. In particular, I am sceptical about use of the label 'sport' to describe a huge variety of practices and motivations. 'sport' is simply not a single social phenomenon and it is becoming increasingly apparent that it is fruitless, or perhaps worse, to attempt to develop a policy that will comfortably fit all the ambitions of those involved in sporting activity.[688] It is particularly pertinent to separate sport as an instrument of social cohesion from sport as a money-making enterprise. In fact, the vision of European sport as a pyramid, with the professional game at the apex, below which are nurtured semi-professional sport, amateur sport and, located at the base, purely recreational sport, offers a model glowing with instinctive normative attraction, yet increasingly hard to detect in reality. Professional sport has little to do

[685] COM (2001) 584, 16 October 2001.

[686] The Economic and Social Committee, endorsing the Proposal, gravely explains that 'The Olympic spirit is an unwritten law. A spirit cannot be codified or written down, and it eludes description. It must be experienced', SOC/092, 24 April 2002, Para. 1.6, citing a Greek Government website.

[687] *OJ* 2002, C 275E/70. A budget of € 11.5 million is envisaged.

[688] Cf. Parrish, 'Reconciling conflicting approaches to sport in the European Union', p. 21 in Caiger and Gardiner, *supra* note 564; and more generally Greenfield and Osborn, eds., *Regulating Football: Commodification, Consumption and the Law* (London, Pluto Press 2001).

with the social and educational function of sport mentioned in the Helsinki Report. Conversely recreational sport has no economic motivation. The notion of 'vertical solidarity', whereby revenue raised in the higher echelons of the professional game is used in part to sustain the grass roots, has not been abandoned entirely in Europe, but the commercial preferences of corporate sport, in particular football, are steadily loosening traditional vertical ties. In these circumstances parties engaged in top-level professional sport would be only too delighted to wrap their profit margins in the cloak of social and educational progress, the better to negotiate favourable legal treatment for their commercial practices.[689] But this is to concede too much to professional sport, which has frankly limited connection with high-minded values such as the promotion of a healthy lifestyle, tolerance and respect for others. In other manifestations, sport is socially and educationally beneficial. But, constitutionally, that is, in short, not the EC's business – or only peripherally is it so. There is much to be said for encouraging the drawing of more careful distinctions when the over-inclusive label 'sport' is used in association with social, cultural and educational virtues. One might conclude that if the structure of the EC Treaty causes its institutions to be primarily concerned with the economic aspects of sport, then that brings them neatly and appropriately into alignment with the dominant interests of those playing and governing professional sport.

7. Conclusion

Absence of an explicit Treaty-based competence in the field of sport has not prevented the EC institutions from crafting a brand of sports policy, primarily driven by the need to cope with the extended reach of the legal rules concerning the free movement of persons across national borders and the competition rules. But, against this constrained constitutional background, can there really be a suitably comprehensive EC policy on sport? Sports administrators would allege a bias rooted in an application of EC trade law to sport which reflects the market-making imperatives of the Treaty while failing to pay adequate respect to the economic peculiarities of sport and, in particular, they would object that EC law neglects sport's distinctive contribution to the realization of social and cultural objectives that are broader than economic gain alone.

---

[689] Admittedly this is not a one-way street. In 'Sport as Culture in EC Law', R. Craufurd Smith, (ed., *Culture in European Union Law* (Oxford University Press 2004) Ch. 4, p. 113 et seq., I argue that sport does not only invoke the cloak of culture to shelter itself from normal commercial assumptions (taking collective broadcasting and the transfer system as examples) but also, and under equally contestable assumptions, It may find itself required to make commercial sacrifices as a consequence of its cultural status ' the example being the 'protected events' provisions found in Directive 89/552, as amended by Directive 97/36, as well as under some national laws, which limit its ability to sell rights to broadcast some events to the highest bidder. See also on recent practice Craufurd Smith and Boettcher, 'Football and Fundamental Rights: Regulating Access to Major Sporting Events on Television', 8 *EPL* (2002) 107.

I do not accept these allegations, though one can readily identify the motivation of sporting interests, thirsty for enhanced autonomy, in making them. EC law has been shaped by the Court and the Commission in a way that permits the invocation of sport's peculiar economic characteristics, particularly that pertaining to the interdependence of clubs in a sports league. In fact, I have made a case that, if anything, the EC is *too* generous to sport. The Court's willingness to treat sport as peculiarly likely to suffer disincentives to invest in training in the absence of a transfer system has been criticized as inadequately explained.[690]

I also reject the allegation that EC law demeans sport's social, cultural and educational function. In fact, Commission policy documents are littered with references to respect for such issues. My anxiety is more that the Commission makes *too much* play of this dimension. This tends to obscure the constitutional limitations which apply to EC adventures in these realms, which, if neglected, may lead to the Commission exposing itself to legal rebuke for mistaking its competence in applying relevant EC rules.[691] Moreover, policy documents that sweep education and social inclusion into the Commission's sports bag tend to concede too much to *professional* sport. In fact, it is a theme of this paper that much professional sport is rapidly distancing itself from the social and educational context of recreational sport. I do not yearn for a golden age of sporting chivalry, but I do argue that essentially commercial practices be judged as such, and not enjoy protection provided by spurious claims to promotion of social inclusion.

In the cases that have been tidied up in the last few months I do not find instances of misapprehension by the Commission of sport's wider virtues. In fact, I would credit the Commission with having found largely sensible solutions against a legal background which is far from precise, both because the Treaty itself was not designed to cater for sport and because the Court has preferred to avoid giving guidance on the application of the competition rules to the sector. So the Commission's memorandum of 5 June 2002[692] carries a valedictory tone which gives a strong impression that the Commission, burdened by the task of supervising many economically more significant sectors while also seeking to engage in grand debates about the re-shaping of governance for an enlarged and, perhaps, constitutionally re-conceived European Union, feels it has devoted enough of its scarce resources to sport. But it is signing off on a relatively successful note. Fair Play!

And yet even though sport is increasingly anxious to improve the likelihood of resolution of disputes through mechanisms established within the industry[693] it is hard to believe the commercialization of sport will permit the EC institutions much peace. A case might arrive that the Commission deems irresistible; and there is plenty of

---

[690] Part 4.7.3.

[691] See in particular Parts 4.7.3, 4.8.2 and 4.8.4; and more generally Part 6.

[692] Memo/02/127, *supra* note 552.

[693] Cf. reference to the Court for Arbitration in Sport, *supra* note 581; also, e.g., Kaufmann-Kohler, *Arbitration at the Olympics – issues of fast-track dispute resolution and sports law* (The Hague, Kluwer 2001); Beloff et al., op. cit. *supra* note 581, Chs. 7 & 8.

scope for troubling the Court with individual litigation. Those involved in the sector periodically tantalize lawyers with their disingenuous assumptions about the special character of sport. For example, in May 2002 a spokesperson for the 'G-14' group of leading European football clubs,[694] referring to a commitment to agree a maximum ratio of turnover to player salaries and transfer costs, was reported to have identified as the first aim to reduce the competition between G-14 clubs as buyers: 'It is important to avoid auctions on a player because it has art effect of raising the prices'.[695] Restricting competition on the demand-side will presumably prove brightly effective in holding down prices, but this is the very heartland of the prohibition contained in Article 81 EC. Although true collective bargains escape the reach of Article 81,[696] horizontal arrangements between employers of this type do not, and one may anticipate that arrangements such as salary caps or other devices designed to foreclose clubs' opportunity to overspend, introduced by groupings of clubs or imposed by governing bodies, will offer rich pickings for lawyers in future.

694 Cf. *supra* note 643.

695 'Europe's football clubs hoping to curb costs', *Financial Times*, 16 May 2002, p. 8. The report adds to the reader's mirth by declaring this is 'the first time leading football clubs have unilaterally [sic] committed themselves to avoiding overspending'.

696 *Albany*, *supra* note 610.

SPORT AS CULTURE IN EC LAW*

1. Introduction

> 'Capital burns off the nuance in a culture. Foreign investment, global markets, corporate acquisitions, the flow of information through transnational media [...]. not that people want the same things, necessarily, but they want the same range of choices.'
>
> (Don DeLillo, *Underworld*, New York, Simon and Schuster 1997, p. 785)

My approach in this paper will be to inquire into aspects of the business of sport that are treated as different from 'normal' businesses; to inquire what legal devices reflect these special characteristics; and then to consider whether the distinct treatment is justified, which will involve not only consideration of the peculiar economic context of organized sport but also some assessment of the perceived 'cultural quality' of sport. Are sport's cultural properties being burned off by commercial growth?

I am particularly concerned to identify precisely what is al stake. It is commonplace to hear statements which assert that professional sport is a business but that it is 'special' in some respects. I accept this, but will endeavour to elucidate what this involves. It will be my submission that there is a general tendency to exaggerate the differences of professional sport from 'normal' commercial activity; and a consequent propensity to introduce or maintain distinctive self-regulatory and/or legal rules which may not be justified on close inspection. At the very least I argue that professional sport's perceived special status is frequently asserted and commonly accepted without adequate intellectual articulation of the true underlying issues. I propose to investigate this by looking at two distinct aspects in sport: first, circumstances in which sport claims immunities or exemptions from normal assumptions of legal control; and, secondly, circumstances in which sport is subjected to requirements that would not normally be imposed on other commercial activities. The first issue, where sport enjoys a benefit, will be illustrated with reference to two topics, those of player transfer fees and the collective selling of broadcasting rights. The second issue, where sport carries a burden, will be illustrated with reference to the so-called 'protected events' legislation, under which rights to broadcast some sport competitions may not be disposed of as freely as other such property rights.

I approach these questions full aware of the allegation of bias that is frequently aimed at the institutions of the European Community – principally the Court and the Commission – by representatives of sports federations. The Community lacks legislative competence in the field of sport. Indeed, even today, the word 'sport' is absent from the EC Treaty itself. But in so far as sport generates practices of economic

---

* R. Craufurd Smith, ed., *Culture in European Union Law* (Oxford University Press 2004), Ch. 4, p. 113 et seq.

significance, they are in principle subject to the control of EC law, most prominently the Treaty rules governing free movement and competition, as confirmed by the European Court in *Walrave and Koch* v. *Union Cycliste Internationale* in 1974[697] and *Donà* v. *Mantero* in 1976.[698] This approach was famously confirmed by the European Court in *Bosman.*[699] Sport, like other sectors such as education, environmental policy and consumer protection, demonstrates how the law of the EG may exercise a wider influence than a formal inspection of the text of the Treaty may lead one to expect, primarily because of the extended reach of the rules governing the building of an integrated, competitive market. The alleged bias manifests itself in an application of EC trade law to sport which reflects the marketmaking imperatives of the Treaty while failing to pay adequate respect to the economic peculiarities of sport. In particular, it is objected that EC law neglects sport's distinctive cultural context in society and its contribution to the realization of social and cultural objectives that are broader than economic gain alone. So, it is said, EC law does not understand sport. I am conscious of the strength of this feeling within sport. It is, among other things, the stimulus to periodic campaigns in favour of Treaty revision designed to have sport placed partly, or even wholly, outwith the ambit of EC law. And I intend to take seriously the anxiety that the EC institutions, applying the EC Treaty to sport, are hampered by constitutional limitations associated with the EC's limited competence in the field when invited to investigate the richness of its cultural contribution. But my task is to explore what these fine ambitions really mean, and how they are and should be reflected in the application of EC law to the systems of regulation found in sport. I entertain a suspicion that appeals to culture are being used in the sports sector as a cover for economic protectionism by business interests to the detriment of employees and consumers. I wonder too about the utility of treating 'sport' as a single phenomenon. I am particularly sceptical that high-minded sporting values and anxieties to promote a healthy lifestyle, tolerance, and respect for others have much to do with modern professional sport.

2. Concessions made to the distinctive nature of sporting competition

In *Bosman* the European Court found two distinct existing practices in professional football to be incompatible with the Treaty provision governing the free movement of workers, Article 39 (ex 48) EC. The system governing the transfer of players between clubs and the rules requiring discrimination on the basis of nationality in European club football competitions were both found to violate that provision. Adjustments have been made to the transfer system, while the nationality rules have been abandoned in so far as they apply to EU nationals.

The vital point for present purposes is that the Court did not deny that football in particular, or sport in general, possesses unusual characteristics that distinguish it

[697] Case 36/74, *Walrave and Koch* v. *Union Cycliste Internationale*, [1974] *ECR* 1405.

[698] Case 13/76, *Donà* v. *Mantero*, [1976] *ECR* 1333.

[699] Case C-415/93, *Union Royale Belge des Sociétés de Football Association ASBL* v. *Jean-Marc Bosman*, [1995] *ECR* I-4921.

from 'normal' commercial sectors. Rather, the Court insisted only that the economic significance of sport secured its subjection to EC law and that those unusual characteristics should then be taken into account in shaping the application of the law There is, then, room for acknowledging that 'sport is special', but that room exists within the jurisdiction of the institutions of the EC.

The exact nature of the Court's concession in *Bosman* requires examination. In Paragraph 106 of the ruling it remarked that:

> 'In view of the considerable social importance of sporting activities and in particular football in the Community, the aims of maintaining a balance between clubs by preserving a certain degree of equality and uncertainty as to results and of encouraging the recruitment and training of young players must be accepted as legitimate.'

The practices challenged in the case did not adequately contribute to these aims and they were judged to fall foul of Article 39 (ex 48) EC. But the Court's recognition in *Bosman* that sport has 'considerable social importance' and that it has two distinct legitimate aims set the scene for subsequent inquiry into exactly what type of practice might permissibly be pursued by governing bodies in sport in conformity with Community law in circumstances where 'normal' commercial actors would expect to be condemned for violation of the Treaty. Both the European Court and the Commission have been challenged to refine the contours of the acceptance that 'sport is – to some extent – special', and to elaborate the implications of this nuanced legal test in its application to particular sporting practices. I choose the player transfer system and the collective sale of rights to broadcast matches to illustrate the pattern of the intriguing evolving debate, but first I question the Court's wisdom in its 'twin-track' concession to the distinctive aims of professional sport. In fact, far from having failed to appreciate the unusual character of sport, of which it so often stands accused, the Court has, in my submission, adopted an inflated view of the distinct nature of sport as an economic activity.

In short, I agree with the Court that the aim 'of maintaining a balance between clubs by preserving a certain degree of equality and uncertainty as to results' is a matter that is peculiar to sport. I do not agree that the aim of 'encouraging the recruitment and training of young players' is distinctive to sport.

The legitimate aim of 'maintaining a balance between clubs by preserving a certain degree of equality and uncertainty as to results' reflects the unusual economic structure of sports leagues. In 'normal' industries one would not identify any economic basis for such mutual interdependence. The commercial undertaking covets its rival's market share with ferocity. It does not wish to sustain its rival's well-being. Monopoly power is a rational goal, for it brings potentially rich economic gains as a result of freedom from competition. This, of course, is precisely why market economies deploy legal controls to obstruct the acquisition of monopoly power and to supervise the conduct of actors that come to possess such economic might. But in football a single club is economically useless. It needs rivals to play against. And not just rivals who are routinely thrashed. The industry depends on the existence of credible competition in order to attract consumers, which encompasses the need for strong rivals so that results are not a foregone conclusion and the need to eliminate any whiff of suspicion about match-fixing or any other interference with the genuine nature of competition. Clubs in sports leagues enjoy a relationship of mutual interdependence which is not the norm in other spheres of commercial activity. So, for example, one would expect this economic rational notion of 'solidarity' to generate a degree of wealth distribution from strong to weak within the sport. Doubtless a difficult balance has to be struck between rewarding the successful and strengthening the unsuccessful.[700] North American sport, dominated by 'closed Leagues', is characterized by much more interventionism than European sport. But the key point for present purposes is that, by contrast, incentives to devise such a strategy are completely absent from a typical manufacturing or service industry. The interesting questions in sport then surround the issue of how this peculiar economic status should be reflected in the legal regulation of practices that are presented as necessary to secure equality between clubs and uncertainty as to results. I consider this below in connection with player transfer systems and collective selling of broadcasting rights.[701]

The aim of 'of encouraging the recruitment and training of young players' must also be accepted as legitimate, according to the European Court in *Bosman*, but I do not think this is correctly regarded as an issue that is in any way special to the nature of sport. In fact, I consider the Court is here overgenerous to the claims of sporting associations. Naturally, clubs protest that they would abandon youth training were they not allowed to maintain some system which compensates them for costs incurred when the employee moves on, but the question is whether this is in any way convincing. Surely a club that chose to neglect youth training would simply perform poorly in comparison with more far-sighted rivals? A transfer system doubtless encourages a higher level of investment in training than would otherwise occur, but what is missing from the ruling in *Bosman* and the Commission's subsequent approach to the matter is any supplementary explanation why sports clubs should be treated as a special case on this point. Supermarkets and universities train young employees even though they might subsequently quit the company, and expect no transfer fee as an incentive: so why is football different?

---

700 For economic analysis, see, e.g., P. Cairns, T. Jennett and P. Sloane, 'The Economics of Professional Team Sports: A Survey of Theory and Evidence', *Journal of Economic Studies*, 13 (1986) 3; J. Quirk and R. Fort, *Pay Dirt: the Business of Professional Team Sports* (Oxford and New York, Princeton University Press 1997); S. Dobson and J. Goddard, *The Economics of Football* (Cambridge, Cambridge University Press 2001); S. Rosen and A. Sanderson, 'Labour Markets in Professional Sports', *The Economic Journal* (2001) 111, F47; L. Buzzacchi, S. Szymanski T. and Valletti, 'Equality of Opportunity and Equality of Outcome: Open Leagues, Closed Leagues and Competitive Balance', 3 *Journal of Industry, Competition and Trade* (2003) 167. The home page of Stefan Szymanski is a rich mine: www.ms.ic.ac.uk/stefan.

701 On rules precluding multiple ownership of clubs, see the decision based on EC and Swiss law of the Court for Arbitration in Sport (CAS), an arbitral body established by the industry and based in Lausanne, in CAS 98/200, *AEK Athens and Sparta Prague* v. *UEFA*, 20 August 1999. The Commission subsequently chose to treat this as a rule that interfered with commerce yet which, given its contribution to honesty in sports practice, fell outside the scope of the Treaty competition rules provided it was applied in a non-discriminatory manner: COMP/37.806, *ENIC/UEFA*, IP/02/942, 27 June 2002.

I do not exclude the possibility that economic rationales may exist.[702] The ability of football players is immediately visible on the pitch, so clubs that invest in training quickly lose the advantage they enjoy in having more information than predator employers about an employee's developed skills. Perhaps that generates an unusually strong unwillingness to invest in training, although a similar rationale would apply to musicians or actors who are not currently subjected to a transfer system. But no such analysis has ever been conducted in the context of EU policy-making. The EU institutions since *Bosman* have proceeded on the unexplained assumption that sport is 'special' in its need to protect and promote youth training. Until this argument is supported by convincing evidence, football should be required to follow normal commercial practice, in which the method for retaining the services of valued employees is to offer them an attractive contract and keep them happy while they perform it. Admittedly, at a detailed level, contractual arrangements in football tend to take the shape of fixed-term deals, rather than contracts of indefinite duration with a notice period capable of exercise by either party, but this is not a difference which defeats the basic submission that the importance of recruiting and training young workers is a matter which in principle applies to all industries equally, and that it is not one which should be taken as justifying abnormal regulation within the sports industry.

I conclude that the economics of football are special when it comes to presenting competitive equality between clubs, but that the economics of football are not special when it comes to encouraging the training of young players. This conditions the analysis below of the proper legal approach to the transfer system and to the collective selling of broadcasting rights.

3. Benefits claimed because of the distinctive nature of sporting competition: the player transfer system

The transfer system in football, damaged but not eliminated by the ruling in *Bosman*, has mutated over the last century and may be found in different guises in different jurisdictions at different times.[703] However, its essence is simply described. Players are unable simply to move freely between clubs in the exercise of their contractual freedom. Employment as a footballer is different from employment as a plumber or professor. A club was – and is – able to field a player in an official match only once it has secured the player's registration, held by the previous employer. That registration will be released only when the previous club is satisfied with the terms offered by the

[702] See, e.g., E. Feess and G. Muehleusser, 'Economic Consequences of Transfer Fee Regulations in European Football', 13 *European Journal of Law and Economics* (2002), 221.

[703] A-G Lenz's Opinion in *Bosman* contains an extensive and detailed examination, see note 699 above. For a useful collection of materials and some analysis, see R. Blanpain and R. Inston, *The Bosman Case: The End of the Transfer System* (Leuven, Peeters 1996); also M. Beloff, T. Kerr and M. Demetriou, *Sports Law* (Oxford, Hart Publishing 1999), Ch. 4; S. Greenfield, 'The Ties that Bind: Charting Contemporary Sporting Contractual Relations', in S. Greenfield and G. Osborn, *Law and Sport in Contemporary Society* (London, Portland, Frank Cass 2000), Ch. 8; J-P. Dubey, *La libre circulation des sportifs en Europe* (Berne, Staempfli Editions 2000) pp. 272-317, 569-83.

new club, which typically has involved payment of a fee. A club which chose simply to field a player without complying with the requirements of the transfer system would find itself subject to heavy and immediate penalties imposed by national and transnational governing bodies.

(a) The transfer system before and after *Bosman*

Bosman had fallen foul of the transfer system when he found himself prevented from joining a French club because the Belgian club which held his registration refused to release it, even though *Bosman*'s contract of employment with the Belgian club had come to an end. The Court, having acknowledged sport's 'considerable social importance' and embraced as legitimate 'the aims of maintaining a balance between clubs by preserving a certain degree of equality and uncertainty as to results and of encouraging the recruitment and training of young players', nonetheless came to the conclusion that the transfer system in professional football constituted a violation of Article 39 (ex 48). It is well established in EC trade law that both the ends pursued and the means employed by a restrictive measure must be justified. The Court regarded the means employed in the football industry as inapt to achieve ends which night be capable of justification in principle. The Court did not consider that the transfer system acted as an adequate method of maintaining balance between clubs. The rules neither precluded richer clubs buying the best players, nor prevented the 'availability of financial resources from being a decisive factor in competitive sport thus considerably altering the balance between clubs'. Moreover, the Court observed that because only a handful of young players will repay the investment by making the professional grade, it is impossible to predict the fees that will be obtained. In any event such fees will be unrelated to the actual cost of training all players. The system was hit-and-miss, rather than a carefully constructed distributive mechanism. The Court concluded that 'the same aims can be achieved at least as efficiently by other means which do not impede freedom of movement for workers'.[704]

The judgment therefore required alterations to be made to the transfer system as it applied to players in *Bosman*'s position, whose contracts of employment had expired and who wished to exercise their right to migrate between Member States of the EU. But it is readily arguable that the transfer system rested on even shakier foundations than the *Bosman* ruling itself suggested.[705] The Court declined to consider the matter

[704] Para. 110 of the judgment at note 699 above; and set more fully the Opinion of A-G Lenz.

[705] For exploration, see, e.g., M. Thill, 'L'arrêt *Bosman* et ses implications pour la libre circulation des sportifs a l'interieur de l'U.E. dans des contextes factuels differents de ceux de l'affaire *Bosman*', *Revue du Marché Unique Européen* (1996) 89; S. Weatherill, Annotation of the *Bosman* ruling, 33 *CML Rev.* (1996) 991; P. Morris, S. Morrow and P. Spink, 'EC Law and Professional Football: *Bosman* and its Implications', 59 *MLR* (1996) 893; D. O'Keeffe and P. Osborne, 'The European Court Scores a Goal', *International Journal of Comparative Labour law and Industrial Relations* (1996) 111; J-C. Seche, 'Quand les juges tirent au but', 32 *CDE* (1996) 355; M. Hilf, 'Das *Bosman*-Urteil des EuGH', *NJW* (1996) 1169; S. Weatherill, 'European Football Law', in *Collected Courses of the 7th Session of the Academy of European Law* (The Hague, Kluwer Law International 1999), pp. 339-82; P. Spink, 'Blowing the Whistle on Football's Domestic Transfer Fee', *Juridical Review* (1999) 73.

from the perspective of the competition rules in the EC Treaty, but it seems highly probable that, had it addressed that matter, it would have condemned the practices as unlawful restrictions on trade imposed 'horizontally' between employers, involving also governing authorities in sport. This was clearly the view expressed in the case by Advocate-General Lenz. It is important to appreciate that the competition rules are lurking in the background, for they could readily be employed to strike at persisting remnants of the transfer system that would not be imperilled by the invocation of Article 39 (ex 48) EC. This is particularly relevant to challenges to restrictions imposed on non-EU nationals and to impediments applying to transfers which are purely internal to a single Member State (which would include one between England and Scotland). Moreover, seeking to exploit EC law still further beyond the fact pattern in *Bosman*, it is submitted that a violation of EC law may also be established where transfers of players are blocked where those players have unilaterally terminated their contracts and fulfilled relevant obligations under local employment law. This would further slice into the persisting viability of what remains of the transfer system post-*Bosman*. It may even be argued that individual mobility would be unlawfully restricted by collective arrangements in the game even where local rules governing discharge of the employment relationship are not satisfied (that is, where the player is in breach of contract, in English law terms), and that the consequences of such action should belong under national private law alone, not least because different jurisdictions in the EU adopt very different approaches to such employee freedom, ranging from liberal to restrictive. On this view, the law of free movement forbids collectively-imposed sanctions on players wishing to escape agreed contractual obligations and pushes the consequences of such 'player power' into the realms of national private law, privileging astute contract negotiation with top-quality performers by an employer. This is normal in most industries, and in my submission the essence of the Court's approach in *Bosman* is that the football labour market should be organized in much the same wav as any other labour market.

(b) The 2001 agreement on the transfer system

Bosman has prompted significant change in the practice of clubs in their dealings with players,[706] and some of the potential wider implications argued for above (though by no means all of them) have also been instrumental in inducing the shaping of a revised system. But the transfer system lives on, albeit in modified and scaled-down fashion. In March 2001 it was announced that, after extended and sometimes acrimonious discussion, an agreement had been reached between the Commission and football's governing bodies for the world, FIFA, and for Europe, UEFA. The Commission went so far as to announce that the deal of March 2001 had been 'formalised' through an

---

[706] Cf. S. Gardiner and R. Welch, 'Show Me the Money: Regulation of the Migration of Professional Sportsmen in Post-*Bosman* Europe', in A. Caiger and S. Gardiner, eds., *Professional Sport in the EU: Regulation and Re-Regulation* (The Hague, TMC Asser Press 2000) pp. 107-26; P. Antinioni and J. Cubbin, 'The *Bosman* Ruling and the Emergence of a Single Market in Soccer Talent', 9 *European Journal of Law and Economics* (2000) 157.

exchange of letters recorded in a Commission Press Release[707] between Mr Monti and the President of FIFA, Mr Sepp Blatter. In the aftermath of this legally ambiguous 'compromise' the International Federation of Professional Footballers' Associations, FIFPro, which had been heavily involved in the negotiation until at a late stage it walked away in dissatisfaction at what was being proposed and ultimately agreed in March 2001, seemed a likely source of legal challenge to this deal. However, FIFPro's anxieties were addressed,[708] and in August 2001 FIFA and FIFPro were able to strike an agreement about FIFPro's participation in the implementation of the new rules, which entered into force on 1 September 2001.[709] Eventually, in June 2002, the Commission closed its investigation, declaring 'the end of the Commission's involvement in disputes between players, clubs and football organisations'.[710] Commissioner Monti stated that '[t]he new rules find a balance between the players' fundamental right to free movement and stability of contracts together with the legitimate objective of integrity of the sport and the stability of championships'.[711]

The key features of this system that the Commission is prepared to treat as compatible with EC competition law and the law of free movement provide:

- that in the case of players aged under 23, a system of training compensation should be in place to encourage and reward the training effort of clubs, in particular small clubs;
- that there should be the creation of solidarity mechanisms that would redistribute a significant proportion of income to clubs involved in the training and education of a player, including amateur clubs;
- that international transfers of players aged under 18 are to be allowed subject to agreed conditions;
- that there shall be created one transfer period per season, and a further limited mid-season window, with a limit of one transfer per player per season;
- that there shall be minimum and maximum duration of contracts of respectively one and five years;
- that contracts are to be protected for a period of three years up to age 28 and for two years thereafter;

[707] IP/01/314, 'Outcome of discussions between the Commission and FIFA/UEFA on FIFA Regulations on international football transfers', 5 March 2001; 'formalisées' in French, 'formell besiegelt' in German, phrases which, like the English version, lack precise meaning under EC law. Cf. A. Egger and C. Stix-Hackl, 'Sports and Competition Law: a Never-Ending Story?', *ECL Rev.* (2002) 81, 90-91.

[708] On discontinued proceedings before the Belgian courts, see M. Bennet, 'They think it's all over, [...] it is now!-How Extra Time was Required to Finally Settle Football's Transfer Saga', 9 *Sport and the Law Journal* (2001) 180. At EC level, a players' union brought an application claiming illegal failure to act on a complaint about the transfer system in Case T-42/0l, *SETCA-FGTB* v. *Commission*, but the case was removed from the Court's regisrer on 24 January 2002, and the complaint (COMP/36.583) was rejected on 30 May 2002 as part of the Commission's closure of the investigation. Relevant documentation is collected at http://europa.eu.int/comm/sport/key.files/circ/a_circ_en.html.

[709] On how European law stimulates trans-national trade unionism, see B. Dabscheck, 'International Unionism's Competitive Edge', 58 *Relations Industrielles/Industrial Relations* (2003) 85.

[710] IP/02/824, 'Commission closes investigations into FIFA regulations on international football transfers', 5 June 2002. The Commission does not propose to take the matter on to a formal plane.

[711] Noted ibid.

- that the system of sanctions to be introduced should preserve the regularity and proper functioning of sporting competition so that unilateral breaches of contract are possible only at the end of a season;
- that financial compensation can be paid if a contract is breached unilaterally, whether by the player or the club;
- that proportionate sporting sanctions may be applied to players, clubs, or agents in the case of unilateral breaches of contract without just cause, in the protected period;
- that there shall be created an effective, quick, and objective arbitration body, with members chosen in equal numbers by players and clubs and with an independent chairman; and
- that arbitration is voluntary and does not prevent recourse to national courts.

Collectively agreed and enforced restrictions on player mobility and associated sanctions imposed on contract-breakers are plainly to be reduced compared with past practice, but football will still be allowed to maintain arrangements that would not be tolerated in other industries. Is this lawful? It requires testing against the demands of EC competition law and the law governing free movement.

(c) **Outstanding legal questions**

The Court has accepted that in some circumstances collective bargains designed to regulate conditions of employment may escape the scope of application of Article 81(1).[712] Neither the method of its production not its content brings the 2001 agreement on transfers within the sanctuary recognized by the Court. The level of collective involvement was inconsistent and fragmented; the effect is not to improve players' working conditions. I do not believe the relevant criteria for this concession are met by the new transfer deal. Nor should the criteria be stretched to confer autonomy upon it.

Assuming the arrangements are in principle subject to control pursuant to Articles 81 and 39 EC, the key issue surrounds the scope of justification. It is probable that the mode of justification runs roughly, and perhaps precisely, in parallel whether one examines the matter under the competition rules or the free movement rules in the Treaty.[713] The primary stated justification for this system is to be found in the Court's ruling in *Bosman*. It is encouraging the recruiting and training of young players. I have argued above that this represents a mistaken concession to the perceived special characteristics of professional sport and I take the view that the idea that this is a sport-specific issue would and should be demolished were it to be revisited by the

---

[712] E.g., Case C-67/96, *Albany International* v. *Stichting Bedrijfspensioefonds Textielindustrie*, [1999] *ECR* 1-5751; Case C-219/97, *Maatschappij Drijvende Bokken BV* v. *Stichting Pensioenfonds*, [1999] *ECR* I-6121.

[713] For much fuller investigation and defence of this thesis, see K. Mortelmans, 'Towards Convergence in the Application of the Rules on Free Movement and on Competition', 38 *CML Rev.* (2001) 613. Cf. S. Weatherill, '"Fair Play Please!": Recent Developments in the Application of EC Law to Sport', 40 *CML Rev.* (2003) 51, at 80-86.

European Court. However, even were one to accept at face value this aspect of the judgment in *Bosman*, it is difficult to defend the view that arrangements within the industry that envisage persisting collectively-enforced restrictions on player mobility, of a type absent from other industries, are compatible with EC law. That is to say, I do not think any transfer system of this nature can survive. The key paragraph of Mr Lenz's Opinion is Paragraph 239, in which he suggests that an adjusted transfer system could be justified if, first, fees were limited to the costs incurred in training the player by the previous club (or previous clubs) and, secondly, provided the fee was payable only in the case of a first change of clubs where the previous club had trained the player. This would exclude the multi-million euro deal. But even Mr Lenz cautiously concedes that such a system might not be sustainable in the light of the counter-argument that its objectives 'could also be attained by a system of redistribution of a proportion of income, without the players' right to freedom of movement having to be restricted for that purpose'. The football associations, he noted, had not submitted anything to refute that objection. Nothing in the Court's judgment seems to support Mr Lenz's tentative embrace of a revamped transfer system. Paragraph 114 of the ruling seems to exclude it. It states firmly that Article 39 (ex 48) of the EC Treaty 'precludes the application of rules laid down by sporting associations, under which a professional footballer who is a national of one Member State may not, on the expiry of his contract with a club, be employed by a club of another Member State unless the latter club has paid to the former club a transfer, training or development fee'. This strikes directly at attempts to impose restrictions on the ability of (particularly younger) players to contract with their preferred employer which feature in the 'compromise'. I would also be sceptical of the lawfulness of aspects which require a player to abide by a contract for at least three years or else suffer a suspension imposed by the governing authorities of football. The case of the unilateral contract-breaker is not covered directly by *Bosman*, but, as articulated above, I maintain that the EC rules are in principle equally applicable to restrictions imposed in this instance. This is collective action designed to encourage observance of an individual contract rather than simply leaving the matter to applicable national law. It is submitted that this contribution to stabilizing club squads goes beyond the space allowed to football by the Court in *Bosman*.

I therefore take the view that the compromise deal struck on transfers is incompatible with EC law.[714] In economic terms my submission is that the transfer system simply does not do what is claimed for it, as already exposed by the Court in *Bosman*. It is haphazard in its distribution of gains, and far from promoting competitive balance it instead strengthens the hand of clubs with deep pockets and tempts clubs to embark on financially imprudent adventures. In legal terms, the insistence on individual economic freedoms that is driven by Article 39 EC, supplemented by, and in some factual situations extended by, Articles 81 and 82 EC, fatally damages attempts to resuscitate a transfer system claimed to serve the collective interests of the game. The 'compromise' system would have been vulnerable to challenge by a private litigant relying on the directly effective right contained in Article 39 (ex 48) even had

[714] It may also be vulnerable to attack under national law, though this will vary state by state.

the Commission gone so far as to grant the revised arrangements an exemption under Article 81(3), a step which it has not taken. The Commission has been surprisingly triumphant in announcing that the deal had been successfully brokered. In closing the Commission's investigation in June 2002, Commissioner Monti, declaring 'the end of the Commission's involvement in disputes between players, clubs and football organisations', added that it 'is understood that EU law is able to take into account the specificity of sport, and in particular to recognise that sport performs a very important social, integrating and cultural function'.[715] This claim has no convincing connection with the transfer system, and the Commission's deal may yet be shown up as no more shrewd or enduring than its readiness to acquiesce in nationality-based discrimination in club football under the 'Bangemann compromise' of 1991, a cosy arrangement the basis of which was exploded by the Court in *Bosman*.[716]

I would not exclude the possibility that it could be regarded as legally permissible for football to devise an internal taxation system to transfer money into the hands of nursery clubs, as part of a scheme for sustaining a larger number of clubs than would survive in 'pure' market conditions and to diminish gaps in economic strength between clubs. Nor would I exclude the permissibility of 'transfer windows', which typically prevent players being acquired and immediately fielded by a new club in the later stages of a competition, or rules that forbid a player appearing for more than one club during a particular competition. These are a feature of the compromise agreement. Such rules doubtless dampen the market and exert an incidental effect on patterns of player mobility but, by restricting the ability of rich clubs to poach their rivals' star players at the sharp end of the season, they serve the legitimate purpose of ensuring the competition remains credible.[717] By contrast, the transfer system does no such thing. In conclusion, it is my submission that the wider mission to maintain a degree of competitive equality and a form of organizational solidarity within the sport may justify unusual forms of intervention by governing bodies, but that, in line with the Court's strong assertion of free movement rights in its *Bosman* ruling, any such systems must be wholly disassociated from any collective attempt to impose residual restrictions on the ability of players to contract with their preferred employer.[718] The case against even the revised transfer system is all the stronger if one accepts the view that the Court in *Bosman* was wrong to treat the interest in encouraging the training and recruitment of young players as peculiar to sport. Football may be different; footballers should not be.

---

[715] IP102/824, note 710 above.

[716] See Paras. 126 and 136 of the *Bosman* ruling, note 699 above. Cf. M. Will, ed., *Sportrecht in Europa* (Heidelberg, C F Mueller 1993); S. Weatherill, 'Discrimination on Grounds of Nationality in Sport', 9 *Yearbook of European Law* (1989) 55.

[717] Cf. Case C-176/96, *Jyri Lehtonen, Castors Canada Dry Namur-Braine ASBL* v. *Fédération Royale Belge des Sociétés de Basket-ball ASBL*, [2000] *ECR* I-2681, albeit that the system of 'windows' at stake in that case was tainted by unacceptable discrimination.

[718] Cf. K. Foster, 'Transfer fees: Still illegal After All These Years?', 01 *Singer & Friedlander Football Review* (2000), www.le.ac.uk/crss/sf-review/00-01/contents0l.html; R. Blanpain, *The Legal Status of Sportsmen and Sportswomen under International, European and Belgian National and Regional Law* (Dordrecht, Kluwer 2003), especially at p. 60.

4. Benefits claimed because of the distinctive nature of sporting competition: collective selling of rights to broadcast matches

The transfer system is defended largely and, in my view, unpersuasively on the basis of its claimed contribution to inducing the training and recruitment of young players. By contrast the issue of collective selling of rights to broadcast matches engages the first and, in my submission, more convincing limb of the Court's identification in *Bosman* of 'what is special about sport', the anxiety to sustain a degree of competitive equality between participant clubs. As explained above, I do not take issue with this distinctive feature of organized sport as a matter of principle. What is intriguing in the case of collective selling is the extent to which this desire to sustain the internal strength of the industry permits sport to pursue practices that impose costs on third parties.

(a) Collective selling – the problems

One would expect the peculiar economic interdependence of clubs to be reflected in rules which secure a certain equality between clubs designed to keep alive healthy competition. Systems of internal wealth distribution would not exist in 'normal' industries, but in sport they are indispensable, though, of course, fixing the desirable ambit of such intervention requires refined calculation.[719] One would suppose that the establishment of a 'solidarity fund' within a sport, to which wealthier clubs are required to contribute from the proceeds of, *inter alia*, the sale of broadcasting rights and ticket income, and on which poorer clubs may draw for financial support, would escape supervision under EC competition law. It would not restrict competition within the meaning of Article 81(1); rather, it is an arrangement that is inherent to the business of professional sport. And there are other matters that are agreed collectively between participants in a sports competition which are, loosely, the rules of the game, rather than restrictions on competition. Examples include fixing the numbers of players per team[720] and the scheduling of fixtures. Such arrangements do not fall within the scope of Article 81 at all.[721]

Collective selling of broadcasting rights is different. If rights are available only on a collective basis – so that a purchaser can buy only the output of the whole League

---

719 Cf. note 700 above.

720 Cf. Joined Cases C-51/96 and C-191/97, *Christelle Deliège* v. *Ligue Francophone de Judo et Disciplines Associées ASBL, Ligue Belge de Judo ASBL and Union Européene de Judo/François Pacquée*, [2000] *ECR* I-2549.

721 Cf. summary in P. Roth, ed., *Bellamy and Child's European Community Law of Competition*, 5th edn. (London, Sweet & Maxwell 2000), Para. 4-150; also J-F. Pons, 'Sports and European Competition Policy', speech given on 14 October 1999, available at http://europa.eu.int/comm/competition/speeches/index_theme_24.html, and S. Weatherill, 'Sports under EC Competition Law and EC Antitrust Law', in B. Hawk, ed., *International Antitrust Law and Policy: Annual Proceedings of the Fordham Corporate Law Institute for 1999* (Yonkers, NY, Juris Publishing 2000), Ch. 6, pp. 75-92, and Ch. 8, pp. 113-26, respectively. For recent statements of practice by Commission officials (including the above-mentioned Pons), consult http://europa.eu.int/comm/sport/index_en.html. Cf. also Mortelmans, note 713 above, especially at 628; Weatherill, note 713 above.

– then a market for acquisition of rights belonging to individual clubs (comprising access to their home games) has been suppressed. Broadcasters are forced to compete for one package and are unable to deal with individual clubs, among whom there would otherwise be competition in selling.[722] It is admittedly plain that clubs would have nothing to sell unless other clubs agreed to play against them. Fixtures cannot be arranged unilaterally – this is the nature of sport. But once clubs agree to play against each other, the subsequent decision to sell rights to broadcast matches on a collective basis is restrictive of competition.[723] And whereas it may well be convenient for sports leagues, and perhaps even for (some) broadcasters too, to arrange the sale of rights on a collective basis, it is by no means necessary to do so to make the league viable.[724] So collective selling restricts competition within the meaning of Article 81(1) EC, in so far as it has an effect on inter-State trade. It is unlawful unless it is justified.

As far as football is concerned, the principal justification is plain, and it is rooted in the notion of organizational solidarity which the European Court recognized as a legitimate concern of sport in *Bosman*. Resources raised from collective selling can be distributed within the game in a fashion which reflects not only relative success and popularity but also the need to sustain lively competition. So the stronger clubs – judged by on-field performance and off-field popularity – will receive more than the weaker clubs, but the league will devise a mechanism that ensures the gap will be less wide than it would be were the clubs to go to market on an individual basis. Moreover, in accordance with orthodox economic logic, the fact that the collective system of selling has restricted supply will ensure that the price paid by buyers will be higher than the (aggregate) price that would have been paid for rights sold on an individual basis by clubs. So collective selling allows proceeds to be shared between clubs on a more equitable basis than would prevail in the absence of such a system; but moreover, it ensures that the pie that is to be sliced up is larger than it otherwise would be.

The objection to this lies in the impact on third parties – the purchasing broadcasters. The restriction on competition caused by the collective agreement between clubs causes a diminution in choice and an increase in price. And although the system may

---

722 The collectively sold package may be (and increasingly is) broken down into constituent units – live matches, recorded highlights, etc. – but this does not affect the basic issue, which is the suppression of sales by individual clubs. Moreover, rights may be, but need not be, sold exclusively – exclusivity is a matter that is distinct from collectivity. See, on exclusivity, Fleming, H, 'Exclusive Rights to Broadcast Sporting Events in Europe', *ECL Rev.* (1999) 143.

723 The precise nature of this 'right' is dictated by national Law; cf. Beloff et al., note 703 above, pp. 134-6, also pp. 153-6; D. Brinckman and E. Vollebregt, 'The Marketing of Sport and in Relation to EC Competition Law', *ECL Rev.* (1998), 281; I. Nitsche, 'Collective Marketing of Broadcasting Rights in Europe', *ECL Rev.* (2000), 208. See also Paras. 118-124 of Decision 2003/778 *Champions League*, *OJ* 2003 L 291/25, considered more fully below. For comments on the position under English law by the Restrictive Practices Court, see Para. 219 of *Re the supply of services facilitating the broadcasting and television of Premier League football matches*, [1999] UKCLR 258, considered in more depth below.

724 Cf. M. Cave and R.W. Crandall, 'Sports Rights and the Broadcast Industry', 111 *The Economic Jounal* (2001) F4, especially at F18. See also Decision 2003/778 *Champions League*, note 723 above, considered more fully below.

indeed allow clubs to raise more revenue than would otherwise be possible, and may also permit them to make administratively convenient arrangements to distribute that income among clubs, the fundamental question is just why the sports industry should be permitted to improve its position at the expense of third parties, a category here covering both existing broadcasters and potential broadcasters kept out of the market by the restrictions imposed on supply. It is submitted that the orthodox approach under Article 81 would be to condemn collective selling as an unlawful restriction on competition between clubs and broadcasters, and to expect clubs to sell rights on an individual basis. Only then, once this has occurred, would the issue of sport's need for internal organizational solidarity be properly invoked It would be permissible for participant clubs to work together to distribute proceeds from these individual sales in a manner which reflects the collective need to sustain healthy competition. So popular, successful clubs would, in effect, be 'taxed' – according to the internal arrangements planned by the participants in the sporting competition – in order to assist clubs able to raise much lower sums of money from sale of broadcasting rights That is to say, the sports-specific anxiety to sustain an attractively competitive league would be reflected only after third party broadcasters have enjoyed the right to participate in a 'normal' competitive market for sale of rights. The question is whether there is any room for sport to argue that its special interests should prevail over those of broadcasters – that collective selling should be permitted, despite its detrimental impact on broadcasters, because sport is entitled to maximize its revenues and/or entitled to raise money collectively so as to facilitate its ready internal distribution.

(b) Collective selling – law and practice before Champions League

The matter is not the subject of an authoritative and final determination at EC level. It has, however, been the subject of inquiry at national level; and the issues have been approached increasingly actively at EC level.

Collective selling of rights has been the subject of examination *inter alios loci* in Germany and in England. Plainly a decision at national level does not in any way bind the institutions of the EC. But comparisons may illuminate both the law and the politics of the matter. In Germany, collective selling was condemned by the competition authorities but subsequently granted statutory approval.[725] This, of course, cannot displace the application of Article 81 in Germany. The matter was also examined at the some length by the UK's Restrictive Practices Court in its 1999 ruling which found in favour of the legality of collective selling arrangements practised within the English (football) Premier League.[726] Unfortunately, the decision of the Restrictive Practices Court is flawed as a model. The judgment convincingly identifies the advantages that accrue to the Premier League in particular and to football at all levels more generally from the collective arrangements governing sale of broadcasting rights The judgment

[725] Para. 31 Gesetz gegen Wettbewerbsbeschränkungen, as amended with effect from 1 January 1999.

[726] *Re the supply of services facilitacing the broadcasting on television of Premier League football matches*, [1999] UKCLR 258.

concludes that, were the current arrangements to be struck down, their replacement by forms of less restrictive coordination between clubs aimed at income sharing is, at best, an uncertain prospect. So ruling against the challenged arrangements would risk causing significant damage to the healthy balance of the competition. The problem with this approach is that it pays insufficient regard to the question whether the 'good of the game' in this sense should prevail over the interests of third party purchasing broadcasters in having the restriction on competition removed, or at least reduced, so that there emerges competition between selling clubs That would, one would suppose, diminish football's overall income, and perhaps also damage the effective distribution of wealth between clubs, but the broadcaster is entitled to the wry observation that the members of any dismantled cartel typically find that competition forces down the price their product can command. That is the point of cartel-busting. So why should parties outside the football industry be forced to subsidize internal peculiarities.

The problem is that the Restrictive Practices Court felt unable to explore the nuances of this matter. The decision was taken under the antiquated and subsequently repealed Restrictive Trade Practices Act. The court considered that the legislation confined it to choosing between the public interest in maintaining the current arrangements and in having no restrictions at all, and it preferred the former. The Court remarked on the difficulty it perceived in fashioning a reliable system of wealth distribution were the prevailing collective selling arrangements to be abrogated. But it did not – and felt it could not – assess the middle ground, in which a greater degree of competition could be injected into the market without adopting an entirely unconfined model of individual selling, for example by maintaining in existence a collectively-sold bloc of matches alongside which remaining matches could be made available on an individual basis.[727] The Restrictive Practices Court's failure to assess this type of method for meeting both the concerns of organizational solidarity in the sport and also the competitive nature of the market for broadcasting rights renders its analysis of the agreements unreliable, or – more charitably – of interest only to historians of the Restrictive Trade Practices Act but not to those wishing to identify the correct way to apply Article 81 EC. The Commission duly intervened and asked that the participants notify the agreements to it. Both the English and the German arrangements are now under investigation in the light of the anxiety that they lead to unlawful foreclosure of competing broadcasters.[728]

This is the key to the Commission's preoccupation with sport. It seeks to shape a policy appropriate to the rapidly changing needs of the broadcasting industry. Acquisition of rights to show popular sports events is a central strategy in the acquisition and retention of high market shares. Careful and cautious scrutiny is therefore inevitable. Of particular pertinence to this paper is the appreciation that the Commission is visibly conscious of the perception that the application of orthodox trade law may

[727] Cf. S. Szymanski, 'Hearts, Minds and the Restrictive Practices Court Case', in S. Hamil, J. Michie, C. Oughton and S. Warby, eds., *Football in the Digital Age: Whose Game is it Anyway?* (Edinburgh, Mainstream Publishing 2000), Ch. 23; also P. Spink and P. Morris, 'The Battle for TV Rights in Professional Football', in Caiger and Gardiner, note 706 above, pp. 165-96.

[728] England: IP/02/1951, 20 December 2002; Germany: IP/03/1106, 24 July 2003.

undervalue the distinct cultural and social contribution of sport. The core of the problem is how to judge whether this perception is reality; and, if it is, how, if at all, to shape the law accordingly.

A revealing example is provided by the Commission's Decision of April 2001 concerning a connected matter, UEFA's rules permitting national football associations to prohibit the broadcasting of football matches within their territory during a two-and-a-half hour period on a Saturday or Sunday corresponding to the normal time at which fixtures are scheduled in the relevant country. This, one would suppose, impedes the commercial freedom of broadcasters to conclude deals to show matches at designated 'blocked' times, but it serves the end of sustaining a lively atmosphere in stadia by encouraging spectators to attend matches 'live' rather than merely fester in front of a television set. The Commission concluded that the rules fall outwith the scope of application of Article 81. In the press release concerning this matter, Mr Monti is quoted as observing that the decision 'reflects the Commission's respect of the specific characteristics of sport and of its cultural and social function'.[729] However, the text of the formal Decision published by the Commission reveals a different, narrower story.[730] The Decision is in fact based on routine market analysis. The Commission finds that the UEFA rules do not appreciably restrict competition within the meaning of Article 81(1).[731] It explicitly states that it therefore need not assess the extent to which the televising of football exerts a negative impact on attendance at matches.[732] The Decision is, admittedly, built on appreciation of the specific nature of the market for rights to broadcast football matches, but it is to go too far to make Mr Monti's breezy claim that it reflects the Commission's respect for sport's 'cultural and social function'. Here one may suppose the Commission is seeking to build up credit for itself in the face of allegations that its application of EC trade law is liable to destroy the foundations of sport. And, while one may wonder whether the Commission may be storing up trouble for itself in making extravagant claims about its competence to cater for cultural and social matters, one may also sympathize with the Commission's anxieties, given the ill-informed ferocity of the attacks which it frequently faces from sports administrators and opportunistic national politicians.

(c) **Champions League**

The decision on UEFA's system of national 'blocked' periods is explicitly stated not to prejudice assessment of collective selling of broadcasting rights to football matches under Article 81(1).[733] In July 2001 the Commission sent a statement of objections to UEFA, European football's governing body, complaining that its arrangements for the sale of broadcasting rights to the Champions League, the principal European club

---

729 IP/01/583, 20 April 2001.

730 Comm. Dec. 2001/478, *OJ* 2001 L 171/12.

731 Paras. 49-61 of the Decision. The Commission will monitor change in market structure, particularly in the wake of the 'Internet revolution': Para. 56.

732 Para. 59, note 730 above.

733 Ibid., Para. 60.

football competition, infringe Article 81.[734] UEFA sells rights collectively on behalf of all participating clubs. It has preferred to sell to broadcasters on an exclusive basis, typically under arrangements covering a period of several years. The Commission is careful to observe that it does not object to collective selling of sports rights as such.[735] However, it states that it considers that UEFA's scheme constitutes a substantial restriction on competition, not least because of the foreclosure of the market to potential entrants into a sector capable of dynamic evolution, and that although it in principle recognizes the need for wealth distribution and solidarity within the sport, the UEFA arrangements go beyond what is necessary to achieve these legitimate ends.

The Champions League is a tournament that includes up to four entrants from each country that is a member of UEFA, and it represents a vastly inflated version of the 'European Cup' which it replaced some 10 years ago, to which only national champion clubs (and the winner of the previous season's competition, if not also national champion) gained access. There is a widespread assumption that UEFA expanded the competition under pressure from leading clubs eager for a higher number of more lucrative European matches and willing to break away from the governing body should their commercial ambitions be left unsatisfied.[736] It is notorious that the rise of the Champions League has coincided with a diminution in the percentage of revenue raised that is shared among clubs outside the game's elite. Moreover, the vast rewards on offer to the small pool of clubs able regularly to participate in the Champions League may conceivably have made a significant contribution to weakening the competitive health of national league championships. One may accordingly suspect that the Commission, in seeking to apply Article 81 to challenge collective selling in the face of the sports industry's objection that such arrangements are essential to sustain internal organizational solidarity, has cunningly picked out the softest target.

UEFA duly responded by proposing an amended system involving, in short, an 'unbundling' of the package of rights available for purchase. More operators, including Internet content providers as well as more traditional public and private broadcasters, will be able to acquire a degree of involvement in the coverage of the Champions League. The Commission expressed itself favourably disposed to this plan for competitive diversification which, it considered, would benefit football fans while also assisting the growth of new technology in the media sector.[737]

The Commission concluded its investigation by adopting a formal Decision in the *Champions League* case in July 2003.[738] It concluded that the collective selling arrangements restricted competition within the meaning of Article 81(1), but it exempted the deal pursuant to Article 81(3). The system created a single point of sale for defined 'packages' of matches, which the Commission considered generated efficiencies that were of a particularly significant magnitude as a result of the elimination of the need for broadcasters to deal with many different clubs subject to different

---

734 IP/01/1043, 20 July 2001.

735 'Background Note', Memo 01/71, 20 July 2001.

736 See M. Bose, *Manchester Unlimited* (London, Orion Business Books 1999) Ch. 2.

737 IP/02/806, 3 June 2002; *OJ* 2002 C 196/3.

738 Decision 2003/778, *OJ* 2003 L 291/25.

ownership structures in different jurisdictions throughout Europe. Transaction costs were kept relatively low. Moreover, the joint selling scheme tightened UEFA's grip on the competition's organization and allowed the commercially advantageous 'branding' of the Champions League as an unfragmented European product. Media operators would share in the advantages and they would be duly transmitted to consumers. The restrictions on competition were judged indispensable to provide these economic gains and competition would not be eliminated in respect of a substantial part of the media rights in question. The Article 81(3) criteria for exemption were satisfied. This important Decision will doubtless assume a high profile in future treatment of rights selling arrangements within national sports leagues under both EC and national competition law.

In pursuit of exemption UEFA also advanced an argument founded on solidarity.[739] It argued that raising revenue in this way enabled it to share income for the general benefit of the game. The Commission accepted the desirability of promoting a balance between clubs playing in a league. It also accepted the value in encouraging the supply of young players. These objectives may be realized by cross-subsidy from rich to poor. This, of course, loudly echoes *Bosman*. The Commission expressed itself in favour of the 'financial solidarity' principle, and referred to its endorsement in the Nice Declaration on Sport, examined further below. But – crucially – could such desiderata suffice to outweigh the restrictions on competition inherent in a system of collective selling? The Commission skipped clear of this point. It did not need to decide it. The criteria for exemption were already made out as a result of acceptance of the contribution of joint selling to delivering efficiencies, suppressing transaction costs, and improving the brand.

The issue avoided by the Commission is of great legal and political delicacy. It is one to which the Commission has been gently and cautiously drawing attention for some time. In its Helsinki Report on Sport, published in 1999,[740] the Commission sketched its view of the role of a 'European Sports Model'. This possesses a number of features, most prominently grouped around the contrasts drawn with North American sports practice.[741] For the Commission, European sport is characterized by, among other features, the notion of solidarity, stretching from the apex of the sport to the 'grass roots'. This has a direct connection with the question of the permissibility of collective selling of broadcasting rights. The Commission commented in the Helsinki Report that any possible exemption granted to collective selling arrangements would have to take account of the benefits for consumers and the proportionate nature of the restrictions in relation to the end in view. This is orthodox fare under Article 81(3) EC. It observed that it is therefore appropriate 'to examine the extent to which a link can be established between the joint sale of rights and financial solidarity between professional and amateur sport, the objectives of the training of young sports-

739 Paras. 164-167 of the Decision.

740 COM (1999) 644 and/2. For comment, see S. Weatherill, 'The Helsinki Report on Sport', 25 *EL Rev.* (2000) 282.

741 Cf. S. Weatherill, 'Resisting the Pressures of Americanization: the influence of European Community Law on the "European Sport Model"', in Greenfield and Osborn, note 703 above, pp. 155-81.

men and women and those of promoting sporting activities among the population'. In similar vein Commissioner Monti has cautiously suggested that 'financial solidarity between clubs or between professional and amateur sport' could be a relevant factor in assessing whether to grant an exemption to collective selling.[742] This is strikingly less orthodox as an articulation of the matters that are properly taken into account under Article 81(3). This line of thinking hints intriguingly at use of the power to exempt restrictive practices as a method for insisting that fostering the social and educational function of sport is a condition for giving a green light to collective selling. The cartel is permissible provided its proceeds are shared throughout the sport for the sake of its general health.[743] This suggests that collective selling designed solely as a tool of wealth maximalization for the participants alone would not be exempted. So a 'breakaway' league of the type lately mooted in European football[744] may, by ridding itself of its roots in the wider organization of the sport, thereby lose one commercially attractive opportunity, that of collective sale of broadcasting rights.

But although on this point the Commission's thinking has close similarities to the anxiety over support for the game's grass roots to which the Restrictive Practices Court paid heed in the Premier League case in applying the UK's now abandoned restrictive practices regime,[745] the Commission may here have floated an idea that would exceed the proper scope of Article 81(3). By cautious contrast, Champions League explicitly avoids addressing the relevance of horizontal financial solidarity (mutual support within a league) and wholly ignores the issue of vertical financial solidarity (apex to 'grass roots' base). Moreover, the approach to be found in the Commission's October 2003 draft guidelines on the application of Article 81(3) is committed to preventing any stretching of the criteria for exemption beyond those found in Article 81(3).[746] This seems to reveal a preference to barricade Article 81's walls against incursion by what may loosely be termed 'non-efficiency' factors. On this reading, if a practice is incapable of exemption pursuant to Article 81(3) it cannot be saved by reference to horizontal Treaty provisions such as Article 151(4). And if it merits exemption under Article 81(3), it cannot be denied it for neglect of other interests. This implies that the promotion of cultural objectives which are not congruent with decision-making orthodoxy under Article 81 is possible only under other Treaty provisions. It cannot yet be stated with confidence that the Commission has got this right, although this line of reasoning does bear some resemblance to the Court's at-

---

742 Speech delivered in Brussels on a Conference on Governance in Sport, 6 February 2001, available as Speech/01/84 via http://europa.eu.int/comm/sport/key_files/comp/a_comp_en.html.

743 Support for this approach is expressed by the Committee of the Regions, Opinion on the European Model of Sport, *OJ* 1999 C 374/56, Para. 3.8.

744 'Project Gandalf', the European Football League, was notified to the Commission, *OJ* 1999 C 70/5, and though the breakaway has not (yet) been executed the threat was enough to generate changes by UEFA that benefited larger clubs. See, e.g., P. Van Den Brink, 'EC Competition Law and the Regulation of Football', *ECL Rev.* (2000) 359, especially 364-5. The 'G-14' group of leading clubs has its own website: www.gl4.com/intro.htm.

745 Note 726 above.

746 Available via http://europa.eu.int/comm/competition/antitrust/legislation. See, especially Para. 38.

titude to the relevance of the horizontal provisions of the Treaty in the exercise of the competence to harmonize under Article 95. The conditions for recourse to Article 95 must first be satisfied before any question of the impact of the horizontal provisions can arise.[747]

5. Burdens imposed because of the distinctive nature of sporting competition: 'protected' or 'listed' events

Legislation governing 'protected' or 'listed' events is popularly supposed to have been introduced in order to ensure that particularly high-profile sporting fixtures are available to the general public without the need to pay a subscription to the broadcaster, but, at least in its EC dimension, this is in fact a misleadingly inflated view of the degree of legal intervention that exists. The relevant legislation at EC level is a good deal less interventionist, and a good deal more ambiguous, than the common misperception holds.

(a) 'Listed events' under the 'Television Without Frontiers' Directive

The so-called 'Television Without Frontiers' Directive, Directive 89/552, was amended by Directive 97/36,[748] and it is the latter Directive that provides the source of the relevant provisions. The Directives are based on the Treaty provisions governing co-ordination of laws in the establishment and services sectors,[749] and are accordingly measures of market integration, operative in a sector technologically well suited to trans-frontier growth. Because several Member States have regimes which, in differing ways, involve some degree of intervention into the manner of broadcasting major sporting events, it was decided that some attempt should be made to supply an EC-level framework for resolving the collision between such regimes and the quest for an integrated European market. This, of course, is a classic example of the endemic tendency of a policy of trade integration to spill over into other sectors. Because states have taken a stance on patterns of intervention designed to limit market freedoms, the EC, devising a regulatory framework for a broader European market, must respond by making its own choices about the content of the regime that shall be adopted at European level. So coordination and harmonization is much more than a technical process of fixing a framework of common rules for a common market instead it involves inevitable and sensitive selections of regulatory style and philosophy. So, in this instance, questions of sport and culture, in respect of which the EC lacks any general legislative competence, are nevertheless drawn on to its legislative agenda as a result of the wide-ranging functional impact of the programme of harmonization and

---

[747] Case C-376/98, *Germany* v. *Parliament and Council*, [2000] *ECR* I-8419 ('*Tobacco Advertising*').

[748] *OJ* 1989 L 298/23, *OJ* 1997 L 202/60, respectively. See generally on this regime, C.A. Jones, 'Television without Frontiers', 19 *Yearbook of European Law* (1999-2000) 299.

[749] Arts. 47(2) and 55 (ex 57(2) and 66) EC.

coordination of laws. In this vein, recital 25 of Directive 97/36 observes that Article 128(4) EC (now Article 151(4)) 'requires the Community to take cultural aspects into account in its action under other provisions of the Treaty'. Harmonization is permissible only provided a sufficient contribution to market-building is demonstrated, but in shaping the content of the harmonized regime it is perfectly proper for cultural policy to be taken into account, just as consumer policy and public health policy affect the shaping of market-integrative rules at EC level.[750]

So, offering a fine illustration of these regulatory ripples, the opportunity was taken on the amendment effected by Directive 97/36 to include new provisions on 'protected events' in the EC regime.[751] But, as one may have anticipated, given the sensitivity of the issues at stake, there is no question of the matter being dealt with exhaustively at EC level. In fact, the EC rules governing protected events are a very strange beast indeed. Of particular relevance to the current paper, they illustrate the point that the 'cultural' aspects of sport are extraordinarily ill-defined, although here the outcome of the shaping of legal intervention is that sport is subjected to unusual burdens, in contrast with the matters explored elsewhere which concern sport's modestly successful search for unusual benefits and immunities.

The relevant provision is Article 1(4) of Directive 97/36, which among other things provides for the insertion of a new Article 3a into Directive 89/552. Article 3a provides that

> 'Each Member State may cake measures in accordance with Community law to ensure that broadcasters under its jurisdiction do not broadcast on an exclusive basis events which are regarded by that Member State as being of major importance for society in such away as to deprive a substantial proportion of the public in that Member State of the possibility of following such events via live coverage or deferred coverage on free television.'

The anxiety is plainly that broadcasters to whom a fee must be paid by viewers to secure access to transmissions will acquire exclusive rights to major events with the consequence that the general population will be deprived of the opportunity to view such events for free,[752] but the word 'may', the fourth word in this extract, is vital to grasping the nature of the regime. There is no obligation imposed on Member States. The Commission has properly emphasized that this is a 'voluntary provision'.[753] The issue is national choices, not EC requirements. Article 3a of Directive 89/552 does not define more precisely the circumstances in which the power conferred may or should

750 Arts. 153(2), 152(1) EC. Cf. Case C-376/98, note 747 above; for discussion of the impact of this case on cultural aspects of harmonized laws, see Katsirea, I, 'Why the European Broadcasting Quota should be Abolished', 28 *EL Rev.* (2003) 190.

751 See R. Craufurd Smith and B. Boettcher, 'Football and Fundamental Rights: Regulating Access to Major Sporting Events on Television', 8 *EPL* (2002), 107.

752 Free television for these purposes means 'broadcasting on a channel, either public or commercial, of programmes which are accessible to the public without payment in addition to the modes of funding of broadcasting that are widely prevailing in each Member State (such as licence fee and/or the basic tier subscription fee to a cable network': recital 22).

753 Third Report on the application of Directive 89/552, COM (2001) 9, p. 8.

be exercised. Having introduced the notion of events of 'major importance for society', the provision proceeds simply to require a Member State that chooses to exercise this power to draw up a list of events which it considers to fall into this category and then to notify the Commission of measures taken or to be taken to protect them from falling into the hands of broadcasters who will act in such a way as to deprive a substantial proportion of the public in that Member State of the possibility of following such event on free television. These measures are to be scrutinized by the Commission and published in the *Official Journal*. A complementary transnational dimension is added by Article 3a(3) of Directive 89/552. This provides that Member States shall ensure that broadcasters under their jurisdiction do not exercise the exclusive rights purchased by those broadcasters in such a way that a substantial proportion of the public in another Member State is deprived of the possibility of following events which are designated by that other Member State as carrying major importance for society This is, of course, necessarily a mandatory rather than voluntary provision as far as Member State authorities are concerned; were it otherwise, one state's choices would be readily undermined by another's lack of concern in so far as broadcasters established in the latter state had acquired rights 'listed' by the former state.

The event of 'major importance for society' is a category which is amplified in the Preamble,[754] but which is nevertheless inevitably subjectively defined.

As one would have readily predicted, state practice varies. The majority of states have designated no events as carrying major importance for society pursuant to Directive 89/552. Those that have exercised the available power have made very different choices.[755] It comes as no surprise that no Member State apart from the United Kingdom reckons the televising of test match cricket to fall within the preferred scope of protection; nor that Italy alone lists the San Remo music festival. But there is wide variation even in connection with events which one would suppose would be of more or less equally powerful interest state by state. The finals of Football's World Cup, staged every four years and won by a European country as often as not, are 'listed' in their entirety in the United Kingdom, whereas as far as Germany, Austria, and Ireland are concerned only the final, semi-finals, opening match, and matches of the respective national team are included on the list, while Italy lists only the final and matches of the Italian national team. Moreover, the lists change. Denmark notified the Commission of its list in 1999 but withdrew this with effect from the beginning of 2002, and it now operates no list of the type recognized by Directive 89/552.

Commercially this legislation has the potential to be very significant indeed. Technological growth and, in particular, the rise of privately-owned broadcasting companies, a sector that has flourished since deregulation became fashionable beginning

---

754 They should be 'outstanding events which are of interest to the general public in the European Union or in a given Member State or in an important component part of a given member State': recital 21; recital 18 refers non-exhaustively to the 'Olympic games, the football World Cup and European football championship'.

755 The most recent consolidated list of measures may be found at *OJ* 2003 C183/03, and includes measures notified by Italy, Germany, Austria, Ireland, and the UK. For full list, see http://europa.eu.int/comm/avpolicy/regul/twf/3bis/implement_en.htm.

in the late 1980s, have injected a great many more players on to the demand-side of the market[756] and, with supply of major sporting events incapable of parallel increase because of consumer attachment to the existing small pool of established major events,[757] the cost of acquiring rights to major sporting events has accordingly increased dramatically in recent years. Indeed, it is well known that broadcasters seeking to enter new markets regard acquisition of exclusive sports rights as the preeminent method for rapid acquisition of a viable market share. This characteristic has further contributed to the race upwards in pricing. Traditional 'free' public broadcasters now find themselves operating in a much less cosy competitive climate than that which prevailed 20 years ago. In so far as this legislation governing 'protected events' involves a priority for such broadcasters it may be thought beneficial to consumers, for it improves the chances of popular events being available for free viewing. From the perspective of the sports industry, by contrast, direct or indirect interference wit the right to sell to the highest bidder is commercially alarming, and may call into question the opportunity fully to exploit an extraordinarily lucrative market.

(b) **Interpreting the Directive**

Given this huge, commercially sensitive issue, it is astonishing that the provisions of the EC Directive are so imprecise, yet that imprecision is testimony to the awkward issues that arise when sport as commerce and sport as hot topic in society merge. Once a state draws up the list of events that it perceives as being of 'major importance for society', it is entitled to take measures to ensure that broadcasters do not broadcast those events on an exclusive basis 'in such a way as to deprive a substantial proportion of the public in that Member State of the possibility of following such events via live coverage or deferred coverage on free television'. That may be interpreted to cover intervention that requires coverage on free television. That would plainly severely reduce the price that any other broadcaster would be willing to pay; exclusivity is worth a large premium to the commercial broadcaster eager to increase its portfolio of subscribers and interested advertisers. This would also involve a profound interference with the exercise of the property rights of sporting bodies.[758] But is the Directive properly interpreted in this way? Might it be that the public broadcaster is guaranteed access only to the bidding process on a non-discriminatory and transparent basis, so that there is a 'possibility' for the general population to have the opportunity of viewing the event on free television, but that it has no legal basis for complaint if exclusive rights are ultimately awarded to a broadcaster which a smaller audience and access to the services of which is dependent on payment by viewers? That would not simply be a question of price, for a free broadcaster may be able to promise a larger

---

[756] Set generally R. Craufurd Smith, *Broadcasting Law and Fundamental Rights* (Oxford, Clarendon Press 1997).

[757] On inelasticity of demand for major events, see Comm. Dec. 2000/400 *Eurovision OJ* 2000 L 151/18 (annulled, but not on the point of market definition, in Cases T-185/00 et al., *M6 and other* v. *Commission*, [2002] *ECR* II-3805); Comm. Dec. 2000/12 *1998 Football World Cup*, *OJ* 2000 L 5/55.

[758] Cf. Jones, note 748 above, 326-36.

audience, which may be more attractive to a sporting body aiming to enhance its long-term popularity and to satisfy its sponsors than the short term profit represented by a higher fee paid by a broadcaster whose services are not available free of charge to the viewer. But, admittedly according to this interpretation, economic gain, not access of the general population, would be the key factor in the awarding process.

There is no ruling of the European Court on this point. Litigation lawyers would lick their lips at these conundrums, and their appetite will be whetted further by inspection of the progress of litigation on the point before English courts. In *R* v. *Independent Television Commission, ex parte TV Danmark 1 Ltd.*,[759] the House of Lords took a fundamentally different approach to the interpretation of this regime from that preferred by the Court of Appeal. Of itself this confirms the ambiguous nature of the legal rules. The litigation arose against the background of Article 3a(3) of the Directive. The applicant, TV Danmark, a satellite television company newly established in England but targeting the Danish market, had acquired exclusive rights to broadcast World Cup football matches of the Danish national team, events that had been 'listed' under the Directive by Denmark.[760] TV Danmark had bought these rights on an exclusive basis after a bidding process in which they had, as part of a strategy to secure a presence in the market, beaten Danish public broadcasters who would have been able to broadcast the games to at least 90 per cent of the Danish population, the threshold laid down under Danish law and which TV Danmark would not be able to cross. This was, then, exactly the situation envisaged by Article 3a(3) of Directive 89/552, as amended by Directive 97/36. Under the UK's implementing legislation, in such circumstances the broadcaster was unable to screen the event without having secured the prior consent of the Independent Television Commission (ITC). The ITC, accepting that the rights had been bought by TV Danmark after a fair process and for a fair price, refused consent, taking the view that the Directive precluded it from granting consent in circumstances such as these, where the acquirer had refused to offer to free broadcasters the chance to share the rights on payment of a reasonable fee. An application for judicial review of the ITC decision failed at first instance but succeeded before the Court of Appeal, which held that the protection envisaged by the Directive was exhausted once a fair auction of the rights had taken place.[761] The House of Lords took a different view of the requirements imposed on the UK by the Directive. It found it necessary for the ITC to exercise its discretion so as to prevent the exercise by broadcasters of exclusive rights in such a way that a substantial proportion of the population in another Member State would be deprived of the possibility of watching a listed event on television. So their Lordships concluded, contrary to the view of the Court of Appeal, that it was not mandatory for the ITC to give consent to a broadcaster in TV Danmark's position, which had acquired the rights in a free and fair auction, and accordingly the ITC's original decision should stand.

The House of Lords decision, when contrasted with that of the Court of Appeal, plainly gives much greater respect to protection of the Danish choice about the im-

759 *R* v. *Independent Television Commission, ex parte TV Danmark 1 Ltd.*, 1 *WLR* (2001) 1604.

760 As mentioned above, Denmark has now abandoned its list.

761 The Court of Appeal decision is reported at 1 *WLR* (2001) 74.

portance of access to viewing the matches and correspondingly less to market forces and the interests of a non-Danish undertaking that had won a fair and open bidding process. Lord Hoffman, who gave the main speech, treated Article 3a(3) of the Directive as having carved out a defined circumstance in which market competition and unhampered enjoyment of contractual rights would not be permitted free rein. He rejected the Court of Appeal's view that the way in which the rights had been acquired was relevant. Instead he considered that Article 3a(3) of the Directive could not have been met if the general population could not watch the match when it was broadcast.

So, according to the interpretation of Directive 89/552 adopted by the House of Lords, the ITC does not have to grant consent to the holder of the exclusive rights even if the holder has won those rights in a free and fair competition. But would it ever be entitled to grant consent to a pay channel if free broadcasters do not have a share in the rights? Lord Hoffman seems to think not. He envisages that the exclusive right holder must always make an offer of a share – though plainly this will greatly affect the price which a channel in TV Danmark's position would be prepared to bid in the first place, for it is exclusivity which is the jewel. This seems to render the whole process commercially eccentric, even unviable, but it is, according to Lord Hoffman, exactly the interventionist model chosen by the EC legislature. But what price is expected of the free broadcaster? What if the free broadcaster offers a peppercorn for a share of the rights? Would the Directive then properly be interpreted to preclude a body in the position of the ITC from granting consent to the right-holder to broadcast the event on an exclusive basis to a small segment of the population of the listing Member State? This is to peer into a very awkward world of assessing 'fair' prices in a market already rigged by public intervention.[762] The European Court was not permitted the opportunity to explore this rocky terrain. The House of Lords, though a court of final instance and here overturning a contrary judgment of the court immediately below it in the judicial hierarchy, made no reference to Luxembourg under Article 234 EC. The Commission for its part has done no more than briefly mention this case in its fourth report on the application of Directive 89/552 in the context of a broad comment that application of Article 3a in the period under review had been 'satisfactory',[763] an approval repeated in the Discussion Paper released in April 2003 as part of the Commission's consultation exercise on the Directive.[764]

(c) The purpose of the regime

Enough of the detail. Why does this regime even exist? Why are sports events treated in this manner, which has such profound (albeit, in detail, uncertain) commercial consequences? A troublingly unbalanced 1996 Resolution of the European Parliament considers 'it essential for all spectators to have a right of access to major sports

---

762 Cf. Craufurd Smith and Boettcher, note 751 above, with particular reference to the controversial sale of rights to broadcast the World Cup Finals 2002 in the UK.

763 COM (2002) 778, p. 10.

764 Available via http://europa.eu.int/comm/avpolicy/regul/review-twf2003/consult_en.htm. As one might expect, the BBC response to the Commission is warmly supportive of the House of Lords ruling. See http://europa.eu.int/comm/avpolicy/regul/review-twf2003/contribution.htm.

events, just as they have a right to information' while paying no attention to the costs that right-holders incur as a result of the legal safeguarding of such a 'right'[765] Recital 18 to Directive 97/36 refers to a 'right to information' and to ensuring 'wide access by the public to television coverage' of events of major importance to society. Article 10 of the European Convention for the Protection of Human Rights and Fundamental Freedoms (ECHR) provides that the right to freedom of expression shall include the right to 'receive and impart information without interference by public authorities and regardless of frontiers'. This formulation is now also to be found in Article 11 of the EC Charter of Fundamental Rights of the European Union, proclaimed at Nice in December 2000,[766] which is to be interpreted to conform with the Convention.[767] True, Article 10 of the ECHR adds that states are not to be prevented from requiring the licensing of broadcasting or television enterprises, a proviso absent from Article 11 of the EU Charter. But in any event this seems to bear no relevance to the specific issue of 'protected events'.

So is the citizen's 'right to information', albeit that it is a right contingent on his or her Member State choosing to activate the power conferred by Article 3(a) of Directive 89/552, the key to understanding this legislation? Lord Hoffman began his speech in the TV Danmark case by asserting that the case concerned 'the right of the European Citizen to watch his national football team on television'. One might here detect a touch of the absurd, and one may well suppose that Lord Hoffman fully intends to jolt his audience into thinking critically about just what (in his perception) the EC legislature has chosen to do under this Directive. Can one truly consider that the watching of doubtless exciting and interesting sports events properly engages the language of fundamental rights? Such a proposition exceeds what is currently recognized as the scope of the right to information under the law of the European Convention.[768] One may go so far as to condemn such an approach as apt to demean the quality and dignity of rights discourse. And, moreover, the card of fundamental rights is a trump, but not one held by only one player. The rights to freedom of expression of broadcasters are in no small measure damaged by these interventionist provisions, whereas both the EC legal order and that of the European Convention recognize that commercial parties fall within the personal scope of this regime, albeit that their rights are not absolute.[769]

It is a strenuous effort to devise an intellectually satisfying and rational basis for this legislation. The Commission's April 2003 Discussion Paper understandably at-

765 Resolution on the broadcasting of sports events, *OJ* 1996 C 166/109.

766 *OJ* 2000 C 364/1.

767 Article 52 EU Charter.

768 Cf. more fully Craufurd Smith and Boettcher, note 751 above.

769 E.g., Case C-260/89, *ERT* v. *Dimotiki*, [1991] *ECR* I-2925; Case C-368/95, *Vereinigte Familiapress Zeitungs- and vertriebs GmbH* v. *Heinrich Bauer Verlag*, [1997] *ECR* I-3689; *Informationsverein Lentia and others* v. *Austria*, A No 276, 17 EHRR (1993) 93. See D. Wyatt, 'Freedom of Expression in the EU Legal Order and in EU Relations with Third Countries, in J. Beatson and Y. Cripps, eds., *Freedom of information: Essays in Honour of DGT Williams* (Oxford, Clarendon Press 2000); Craufurd Smith, note 756 above, especially Ch. 7.

tempts no such thing,[770] confining itself to seeking views on whether the procedures should be more tightly defined.[771] Several responses to the Discussion Paper advocated a clarification of the purpose of the system but most – again, understandably – exhibited a primary interest simply to defend their own interests. For example, both the BBC and ITV praised the regime, while by contrast UEFA criticized the legislative favouritism of one type of broadcaster over another.[772] In teasing out the intent of this legislation, the best guess is that some notion of a citizen's entitlement, albeit falling short of a constitutional right, to watch a national representative sporting team in action is at stake, although, admittedly, the events listed exceed this category. Perhaps part of the motivation for intervention is that national and international sports bodies, though typically in form creatures of private law, nonetheless in practice hold a form of general representative function, acting on behalf of the nation when a team is picked to play in international competition, and that accordingly a control over their commercial activities is justified in the public interest. This is capable of being combined with some notion of social solidarity in the nation generated by such events in order to find a rationale of sorts for the decision to create the category of events of 'major importance of society'. Participation even as a television viewer in a football World Cup or an Olympic Games, both of which are staged only once every four years, could be taken to contribute to the construction of a shared sense of identity and of history, and as an indispensable basis for social communication.[773] One may optimistically hope that, in so far as minority sections of a nation's population enjoy a disproportionately high representation among the cream of a country's sporting performers, the sight of the team or individual athletes in action may promote tolerance and respect for diversity in society. This appealing vision may be illustrated by the successful exploits of the multi-ethnic French national football side of recent years. But in response to every example of sport as a force for cohesion, it is not hard to paint a less agreeable picture. In 2001, two friendly football matches between countries with a troubled recent shared history, France and Algeria, and Portugal and Angola, were abandoned without reaching their allotted duration of 90 minutes as a result of violence among players and/or supporters. And in the uniquely odious case of the English national football team it is regrettably easy to reflect that scenes of young white men who travel in aggressive celebration of a deeply intolerant culture do nothing to foster social cohesion. Patriotism is too often transformed from allegiance to one's own country into disrespect or even hatred of other countries, and national representative sport has no special claim to be able successfully to achieve or promote the benefits of intercultural dialogue without suffering the burdens of sustained or deepened division.

---

[770] Note 764 above.

[771] A perspective doubtless in part inspired by pending litigation on its proper role: Case T-33/01, *Infront WM* v. *Commission*.

[772] Note 764 above.

[773] Cf. from the Australian perspective D. Fraser and K. McMahon, 'When Too Much Sport is Barely Enough: Broadcasting Regulation and National Identity', 1 *Entertainment Law* (2002) 1.

My conclusion is that the EC's legislation governing 'protected events' diminishes the commercial value of the rights to broadcast such events by interfering in the ability of the holder of the rights to extract the highest price the market would yield. The advantages generated by this intervention, and the rationales for legislating in this way, are remarkably under-explained. What is required is a balancing of the competing interests. If this has been done by the EC legislature then it has been kept very quiet. The impression is that, once more, sport is subjected to a 'special' regime without any sufficiently careful examination of what is and should be at stake.

6. Is there a broader cultural context?

In the Introduction to this paper, I observed that EC law is alleged to carry a bias which reflects the market-making imperatives of the Treaty while failing to pay adequate respect to the economic peculiarities of sport, and, moreover, that EC law suffers criticism for failure to pay due regard to the social and cultural contribution of sport. In fact, I consider that these are fundamentally different issues. The peculiar economic context of professional sport is distinct from the wider social and cultural place of sport in society, although both issues may find a home under the (perhaps unhelpfully broad) rubric of 'culture'.

The Declaration on Sport attached to the Amsterdam Treaty asserts that

> '[t]he Conference emphasises the social significance of sport, in particular its role in forging identity and bringing people together. The Conference therefore calls on the bodies of the European Union to listen to sports associations when important questions affecting sport are at issue. In this connection, special consideration should be given to the particular characteristics of amateur sport.'

At one level this is feeble. In particular, it is emphatically not subversive of the core of the *Bosman* ruling's firm application of the fundamental Treaty rules governing free movement law to sport. This was expressly acknowledged by the European Court in *Deliège* and in *Lehtonen*.[774] However, at a different level, the Amsterdam Declaration is rather bold. Whatever reservations one may entertain about the value of forging identity through sport, and however much one may wonder whether sport truly brings people together in any meaningful way, it is important that sport's 'social significance' is freely asserted precisely because the Treaty 'proper' allows no explicit room for account to be taken of such implications. So the Amsterdam Declaration is significant for peering beyond the limits imposed by the EC's attributed competence and appreciating a wider role for sport on society. And its reference to amateur sport is particularly illuminating, for it encourages us to make constructive strides towards re-thinking whether 'sport' makes sense as a single-issue definitional category.

The Commission's Helsinki Report on Sport was mentioned above in the specific context of collective selling of broadcasting rights.[775] It is of more general interest.

---

[774] Cases C-51/96 and 191/97, note 720 above, Paras. 41-42 of the judgment; Case C-176/96, note 717 above, Paras. 32-33 of the judgment.

[775] Note 740 above.

The Report is directed at safeguarding current sports structures and at maintaining the social function of sport within the Community framework, which were areas on which the Commission had been invited to report by the Vienna European Council of December 1998. The Report begins with the ambitious assertion that it 'gives pointers for reconciling the economic dimension of sport with its popular, educational, social and cultural dimensions'. It maintains the Commission's identification of 'a European approach to sport based on common concepts and principles', which includes sport's role as 'an instrument of social cohesion and education'. It is suggested that tensions have emerged between this function and the economic motivations for sport which have increased in recent years. One example cited is the temptation for certain sporting operators and certain large clubs to leave the federations in order to derive the maximum benefit from the economic potential of sport for themselves alone. This tendency may jeopardise the principle of financial solidarity between professional and amateur sport and the system of promotion and relegation common to most federations.

The Commission asserts the value in preserving 'the social function of sport and therefore the current structures of the organisation of sport in Europe' while assimilating a changing legal and commercial environment.

More fully than in the Amsterdam Declaration, one may observe in the Helsinki Report the strain that is placed on describing 'sport' as a single phenomenon and on developing a policy that will comfortably fit all the ambitions of those involved in sporting activity. This encompasses the regulated, from the summit to the grass roots of the game, and also the regulator, since different perspectives among relevant Directorates-General within the Commission doubtless create further fault lines. From any standpoint, the tension between sport as an instrument of social cohesion and sport as a money-making enterprise is all too clear. In fact, a realistic depiction of sport as a pyramid, with the professional game at the apex, below which are slotted semi-professional sport, amateur sport, and, located at the base, purely recreational sport, is increasingly hard to sustain. Professional sport has little to do with the social function of sport mentioned in the Helsinki Report. Conversely, recreational sport has no economic motivation. The apex and the base remain linked by their subjection in principle to the same set of rules governing conduct on the field. And the notion of 'vertical solidarity', whereby revenue raised through lucrative deals struck in the professional game is used in part to sustain the grass roots, has not been abandoned entirely in Europe. But, as the Helsinki Report confesses, the growth in commercialism in the professional game poses real and imminent threats to this model. The Commission, of course, has limited competence to act. Its mooted readiness to exempt collective selling of broadcasting rights only on condition that the proceeds are shared around the sport more widely is truly intriguing,[776] but to Europe's leading football clubs, plotting new arrangements that would free them of the irritation of having to hand over even a small percentage of their revenue to their weaker brethren and to the grass roots, this is a relatively peripheral anxiety. The Commission's vision for the protection of the 'European Sport Model' involves consultation between

[776] See Section 4 of this paper for discussion of the status of this view.

interested levels of governance – sports governing bodies, Member States, European institutions. A partnership is presented as the way forward. But, at least in the case of professional football, it is not clear that the leading clubs are interested.

A Declaration on 'the specific characteristics of sport and its social function in Europe, of which account should be taken in implementing common policies', was annexed to the Conclusions of the Nice European Council held in December 2000. This concedes the absence of any direct Community powers in the area, but accepts that in action taken under the Treaty the institutions of the Community must 'take account of the social, educational and cultural functions inherent in sport and making it special, in order that the code of ethics and the solidarity essential to the preservation of its social role may be respected and nurtured'. The European Council calls also for the preservation of 'the cohesion and ties of solidarity binding the practice of sports at every level'. Under a subtitle 'Amateur sport and sport for all', it is proclaimed that 'Sport is a human activity resting on fundamental social, educational and cultural values. It is a factor making for integration, involvement in social life, tolerance, acceptance of differences and playing by the rules.' The Declaration acknowledges the central decision-making competence of sports federations, but insists on their 'special responsibilities' in the light of sport's social functions.

A process of dialogue endures. In October 2001 the 'European Sports Forum' was convened in Brussels in collaboration with the Belgian Presidency of the EU. The Forum included, among other things, a working group on the follow-up to the Nice Declaration.[777] In its published conclusions, the insistence on the value of a partnership between interested actors is sustained, alongside assertion of the social and educational function of sport, though the working group's most striking conclusion is its shamelessly opportunistic claim that 'In the light of current international events, it is more than ever before essential to spread the message of peace and respect for others conveyed by sport'. A separate working group, dealing with 'sport and the social economy', concluded that sport should remain faithful to the values of the social economy, which 'is composed of people-centred organisations and enterprises based on democracy, solidarity and valorisation of social, cultural and environmental resources'. It identified these as 'civic values [that] transcend the logic of profit-seeking interest'. It is painfully difficult to avoid treating this as anything other than an exercise in self-parody, but through the haze of good intentions one can perceive once again the remarkably high-minded aspirations of sport – or at least the interest of sporting bodies in portraying themselves as equipped with a role that should be seen as more than merely commercially driven as an adept strategy designed to extract legal concessions.

The European Sports Forum was held in Copenhagen in 2002, at which Conclusions on *Taking Account of Sport in Community Policies and Measures* included a Portuguese proposal for a provision empowering action in the field of sport to be inserted into the Treaty. After years of periodic pleas to have sport partially or wholly excluded from the Treaty, it is intriguing that this nudge in the opposite direction was

[777] Documentation is available via http://europa.eu.int/comm/sport/info/events/forum2001_en.html.

enough to provoke the Convention on the Future of Europe to include sport in the Draft Constitutional Treaty released in July 2003. It is proposed that the Union shall have a competence to act in support of its Member States in the field of sport.[778] It shall contribute to the promotion of European sporting issues, given the social and educational function of sport.[779] In November 2003 the latest annual European Sports Forum took place in Verona. It hosted three working groups: 'Sport as a factor for social integration'; 'The role of European sport in un international context'; and, most bewildering of all, 'Sport and media literacy'.

So what is 'sport' today? And what challenge(s) does it present to regulators?[780] The leading football clubs, and operators in some other lucrative sports such as motor racing, are commercially ambitious and powerful companies. How they fulfil, and why they would fulfil, a role as contributors to the promotion of social, educational, and cultural values is increasingly difficult to identify. In fact, the sharp increase in the economic motivation for their activities is precisely the reason why they should, in principle, be accordingly subjected to the orthodox rules of EC trade law. The list of formal and informal Commission interventions duly grows ever longer.[781] Certainly the application of such rules should pay due regard to the peculiar characteristic of mutual interdependence which marks the relationship between participants in a professional sports league. This is a sports-specific issue, but it is perfectly capable of forming part of appropriately nuanced economic and legal analysis. After all, the application of Article 81 is always conditioned by the particular context in which arrangements are struck. The Court's fundamentally important decision in *Wouters* increasingly serves as the starting point in determining whether an apparent restriction on competition is properly pulled within the grip of Article 81(1).[782] The Court stated that

> 'account must first of all be taken of the overall context in which the decision of the association of undertakings was taken or produces its effects. More particularly, account must be taken of its objectives. [...] It has then to be considered whether the consequential effects restrictive of competition are inherent in the pursuit of those objectives.'

This observation was delivered in the context of rules prohibiting multi-disciplinary partnerships between members of the Bar and accountants, but it can readily be trans-

778 Art. I-16.

779 Art. III-182.

780 For general discussion, see K. Foster, 'How can Sport be Regulated?', in Greenfield and Osborn, note 703 above, Ch. 14; R. Parrish, 'Reconciling Conflicting Approaches to Sport in the European Union', and K. Foster, 'Can Sport be Regulated by Europe? An Analysis of Alternative Models', both in Caiger and Gardiner, note 706 above, pp. 21-42 and pp. 43-64, respectively.

781 Cf. Memo/02/127, 'The application of the EU's competition rules to sports', 5 June 2002, but the list has already lengthened, cf. nn 701, 727, and 737 above. For a survey, see Weatherill, note 714 above.

782 Case C-309/99, *J.C.J Wouters, J.W. Savelbergh, Price Waterhouse Belastingadviseurs BV* v. *Algemene Raad van de Nederlandse Orde van Advocaten*, [2002] *ECR* I-1577. Cf. Case C-67/96, note 712 above. Strains of this approach are evident in A-G Lenz's Opinion in *Bosman*.

planted to underpin an argument that the overall context in which sports regulation occurs, built around pursuit of a broad objective of healthy equality of competitive opportunity, produces effects which though restrictive of competition are nonetheless inherent in the pursuit of those objectives.[783] Only if a restriction on competition within the meaning of Article 81(1) is at stake does to inquiry move to the possibility of exemption pursuant to Article 81(3).[784]

This is sports law and sports economics, and it is central to deciding how to control governing bodies whose regulation of sport has a spill-over impact on commercial activities. But in so far as professional sport claims virtue in making a broader contribution to culture, one should be sceptical of what it seeks. In so far as the 'culture' of sport is simply 'the way things have always been done', one should not regard defence of 'culture' as a sufficient reason to find justification for practices perpetuated in sport. The transfer system provides a good example. Rarely, if ever, has the industry engaged with the need to demonstrate a rational basis for such collective intervention in contractual freedom. Rather the assumption has been that the rules are 'part of the game' – and should remain so. That is legally and intellectually inadequate. The vigorous application of EC trade law to generate modification of indefensible practices that maltreat employees is entirely appropriate.

Outside the realms of the wealth cascading into professional football and motor racing, sport has a rather different function. Wealth maximization is not the dominant concern. As the Amsterdam and Nice Declarations and the Helsinki Report assert, sport has an important and valuable social, educational, and cultural role. This deserves protection and promotion. But constitutionally this is not the EC's concern. And economically it does not seem to be a significant concern of major clubs. These are matters for public authorities in the Member States and for governing bodies in sport. Some of the most intriguing tensions in the years to come are likely to centre on the attempts of governing bodies to satisfy the commercial aspirations of the most powerful participants while also maintaining vertical solidarity within the sport and preserving the broader integrity of the character of the event.

7. Conclusion

> 'If religion is the opium of the people, tradition is an even more sinister analgesic, simply because it rarely appears sinister. If religion is a tight band, a throbbing vein and a needle, tradition is a far homelier concoction [...] the kind of thing your grandmother might have made.'
>
> (Zadie Smith, *White Teeth*, Penguin 2000, p. 193)

Professional football, in particular, has made much of the virtue of tradition, but in so far as it deploys its defence as a camouflage for the maintenance of inefficient or

[783] The Commission's decision in *ENIC/UEFA*, note 701 above, cites *Wouters*. For its invocation in relation to salary caps, see S. Hornsby, 'The Harder the Cap, the Softer the Law?', 10 *Sport and the Law Journal* (2002) 142.

[784] As in *Champions League*, note 738 above.

unfair practices in a world of increasing commercial exploitation of the sport's attractions, its subjection to EC trade law is entirely proper.

The transfer system provides an example of the imposition of burdens on players which, it is argued, is justified because of the sports-specific objective of inducing the recruitment and training of young players. I have argued that the EC rules of free movement are fatally damaging to any such system that involves persisting restrictions on player mobility and, furthermore, I have argued that in any event the notion that the need to encourage employers to recruit and train young players is peculiar to professional sport is misplaced. Sport is special in the need for internal organizational solidarity, and this provides an economic incentive to pursue, and a legal reason to authorize, the agreed distribution of wealth between participant clubs in a league. The issue of collective selling of broadcasting rights pitches this legitimate objective of sports clubs against the expectation of third party broadcasters that output shall not be restricted in this fashion. The Commission's apparent willingness, aired in its Helsinki Report, to link exemption of collective selling to wealth distribution throughout the sport, from top to bottom, represents a valiant attempt to offer inducements to sustain the pattern of vertical solidarity within a sport that it regards as characteristically European. However, its legal competence to insist on even this as a condition of exemption is far from clear and it has chosen cautiously to evade the issue in *Champions League*. More generally, the Community simply does not possess the regulatory competence to prevent professional sport in Europe mutating through breakaways from governing bodies, or through concessions extracted by large clubs by the threat of breakaway, towards the wealth-maximizing model typical of North American professional sport. In this vein, the EC regime governing protected or listed events may be regarded as a case of the biter bit. Sport, eager to extol its distinctive contribution in society when in pursuit of concessions from the application of orthodox legal regulation, here finds itself forced to suffer commercial detriment under a system which is driven by a wholly opaque notion of access to televised top-flight sport as a right of the citizen. This is a regime that urgently requires clarification, both with regard to its detailed application and, more fundamentally, its very purpose.

The EC in general and the Commission and the Court in particular possess limited competence in the field of sport. Elaboration of the social and cultural functions of sport belongs with the public authorities in the Member States and with sports federations. The Community's competence in these realms is lacking, but there is no compelling case for extending it. Below the professional level, EC action would add no evident value. In its economic manifestations, sport is subject to EC trade law. Given the burgeoning commercial significance of sport there is no convincing reason why this should not be so, provided that the peculiar economic interdependence of participants is taken into account – which it is, both by the Court and by the Commission. A wider 'cultural' aspect to professional sport is, however, hard to discern and such submissions by the industry deserve a sceptical hearing. 'Vertical solidarity' in European sport is under threat, but it is leading clubs, not the Court or the Commission, that are responsible. To end where this paper began, in so far as capital has burned off the nuance in sporting culture, it is professional sport that has embraced commercial growth and the institutions of the European Community have done no more than respond. And ultimately, sport in Europe today encompasses a great many different activities and motivations, to the point where pursuit of a 'Policy on Sport' may involve a misguided quest for uniformity.

ANTI-DOPING RULES AND EC LAW*

INTRODUCTION

In *David Meca-Medina and Igor Majcen* v. *Commission*[785] the Fourth Chamber of the Court of First Instance dismissed an application for the annulment of a Commission decision rejecting a complaint against the compatibility with EC trade law of doping controls practised by the International Olympic Committee (IOC). This note is not primarily concerned to quarrel with the outcome of the case, though it finds some flaws in the CFI's detailed reasoning. Its main purpose is to criticise the CFI's attempt to insist that anti-doping rules concern exclusively non-economic aspects of sport. In particular, the CFI's reluctance to use the formula in *Wouters*[786] as a basis for providing an intellectually satisfying explanation for the scope of autonomy allowed to sports federations under EC law is treated as a missed opportunity. The case is on appeal to the Court[787] and it is to be hoped that it will be used as a springboard to a clearer analysis of the limits of EC law and, in particular, that the CFI's disdain for orthodox competition law analysis as a means to deal with sporting practices will be set aside.

THE BACKGROUND TO THE LITIGATION

The background to the case is the doping control system overseen by the International Olympic Committee and implemented for swimming In that sport's governing body, 'FINA'. The applicants, long-distance swimmers representing Spain and Slovenia respectively, fell foul of the system after being tested in competition in Brazil in 1999.

FINA's Doping Panel suspended them for four years, a penalty confirmed on appeal by the Court of Arbitration for Sport (CAS). Subsequently scientific experiments showed that the identified prohibited substance, Nandrolone, can be produced naturally by the human body at a level above the permitted limit as a result of the consumption of certain foods such as boar meat *(la viande de porc mâle non castré*, in the fuller French version). FINA and the applicants agreed to rerefer the case to the CAS, which reduced the penalty to a suspension of two years.

In May 2001 the applicants filed a complaint with the Commission. They contended that the arrangements established by the relevant sports bodies interfered with

* *ECL Rev.* (2005) 416 et seq.

785 Case T-313/02, *David Meca-Medina and Igor Majcen* v. *Commission*, September 30, 2004, Fourth Chamber of the Court of First Instance.

786 Case C-309/99, *Wouters*, [2002] *ECR* I-1577.

787 Case C-519/04, pending.

competition[788] and the free movement of services.[789] Not just that: they took the view that the limits set were scientifically unfounded and could lead to the exclusion of innocent or merely negligent athletes. They added that the prevailing mechanism of strict liability and the establishment of tribunals responsible for the settlement of sports disputes by arbitration which are insufficiently independent of the IOC strengthened the anti-competitive nature of the arrangements.

The disputed decision was issued by the Commission in August 2002.[790] It concluded that that the rules did not fall foul of Arts 81 and 82 EC, and it rejected the applicants' complaint. The applicants sought annulment of the decision before the CFI. They failed.

THE JUDGMENT

The judgment in *David Meca-Medina and Igor Majcen* v. *Commission*[791] joins the string of sports-related decisions issued in Luxembourg over the last 30 years. In *Walrave and Koch*, the first case involving sport to reach the European Court,[792] the Court stated that 'the practice of sport is subject to Community law only in so far as it constitutes an economic activity within the meaning of Article 2 of the Treaty'. This, then, is a matter of competence. In principle, a sporting practice may be none of the EC's concern. *Walrave and Koch* involved nationality-based discrimination, which one would normally assume to fall foul of the Treaty's prohibition of such practices. However, the Court treated the composition of national sports teams as unaffected by the prohibition where their formation is 'a question of purely sporting interest and as such has nothing to do with economic activity'. In *Donà* v. *Mantero*[793] the Court held that the Treaty provisions governing free movement do not prevent practices that exclude foreign players from certain matches for 'reasons which are not of an economic nature' and which are 'of sporting interest only'. In *Bosman*[794] the Court, citing its judgment in *Donà*, again adopted this formula, but, reflecting the insistence found in the *Walrave* judgment and repeated subsequently that this 'restriction on the scope of the provisions in question must however remain limited to its proper objective', offered confirmation that the Court will patrol the limits of the autonomy granted to sports federations to set rules undisturbed by the demands of EC law. In *Bosman* the Court refused to accept that nationality-based restrictions in *club* football constituted legitimate rules of sporting interest only. It concluded that they fell within the scope of, and violated the requirements of, the EC Treaty.

In *Meca-Medina and Majcen* the CFI begins by repeating this orthodox judicial view that sport is subject to Community law only in so far as it constitutes an econom-

788 Arts. 81 and 82 EC.

789 Art. 49 EC.

790 COMP 38.158.

791 Case T-313/02, judgment of September 30, 2004.

792 Case 36/74, [1974] *ECR* 1405.

793 Case 13/76, [1976] *ECR* 1333.

794 Case C-415/93, [1995] *ECR* I-4921.

ic activity within the meaning of Article 2 EC.[795] It adds inelegantly that the Treaty provisions therefore 'apply to the rules adopted in the field of sport which concern the economic aspect which sporting activity can present'.[796] Cited case law reveals that this category includes rules governing the transfer of players between clubs,[797] rules governing the composition of club teams[798] and 'transfer windows' that vary according to the origin of the player.[799] These practices are placed in contrast to 'purely sporting rules, that is to say rules concerning questions of purely- sporting interest and, as such, having nothing to do with economic activity'.[800] These include rules on the composition of national teams,[801] rules relating to selection for high-level international competition,[802] and 'rules of the game in the strict sense' such as those fixing the length of marches or the number of players on the field. The CFI states that

> 'such regulations, which relate to the particular nature and context of sporting events, are inherent in the organisation and proper conduct of sporting competition and cannot be regarded as constituting a restriction on the Community rules on the freedom of movement of workers and the freedom to provide services'.[803]

The CFI concluded that in principle anti-doping rules fall within the category of practices which are of purely sporting interest and which consequently escape the Treaty rules. Nor did the CFI find any reason to alter its view when it examined the way in which this particular body of anti-doping rules was applied. It found no discriminatory targeting of particular athletes, which would have taken the rules beyond their proper object of preserving 'noble competition'[804] and would have exposed them to the Treaty rules. Nor did the CFI find the anti-doping rules excessive in their impact. Moreover even were the excessive nature of the rules to be established, this would not result in them ceasing to be purely sporting rules and therefore subject to scrutiny pursuant to EC competition law, provided that they remain limited to their proper object of upholding fair play.[805]

This is wonderful news for sports federations. But how should those interested in the clarity and coherence of the law react? I agree that in principle a properly structured system of anti-doping control should be regarded as compatible with EC law, even where it damages the livelihood of those found to have broken the rules. I have some difficulty with the CFI's attitude in this case to excessive rules against doping.

---

795 At [37].

796 At [40].

797 Case C-415/93, cited above at note 794.

798 Case C-415/93, cited above at note 794; Case C-438/00, *Deutscher Handballbund eV.* v. *Kolpak*, [2003] *ECR* I-4135.

799 Case C-176/96, *Lehtonen*, [2000] *ECR* I-2681.

800 At [41].

801 Case 36/74, cited above at note 792; Case 13/76, cited above at note 793.

802 Cases C 51/96 & 191/9 *Deliège*, [2000] *ECR* I-2549.

803 At [41].

804 At [49].

805 At [55].

It is the longstanding view of the Court, first found in *Walrave and Koch* and repeated in *Meca-Medina and Majcen* itself,[806] that any restriction on the scope of the application of the relevant Treaty provisions must remain limited to its proper objective. To hold – as the CFI does at [55] – that rules of an excessive nature would escape review pursuant to competition law provided that they remain limited to their proper object seems contradictory in the sense that an excessive rule would by definition *not* be so limited.[807] This may form the basis for exploration on appeal. But my principal concern with the ruling in *Meca-Medina and Majcen* is broader. It is directed at the unhelpful distinction that the CFI attempts to draw between 'sporting' practices and economic rules. There *are* distinctions that need to be drawn in this area. But they would be better drawn by reliance on more general practice in the field of EC competition law, rather than by concocting unhelpfully arcane sports-specific terminology.

What is a 'restriction' on competition? The judgment in *Wouters*

In Wouters[808] the Court stated that in applying Article 81(1) account must be taken of 'the overall context in which the decision of the association of undertakings was taken or produces its effects. More particularly, account must be taken of its objectives [...] It has then to be considered whether the consequential effects restrictive of competition are inherent in the pursuit of those objectives'. The case had nothing to do with sport. It concerned rules prohibiting multi-disciplinary partnerships between members of the Bar and accountants. But the statement of principle that the notion of a restriction falling within Article 81(1) must be assessed in context is readily capable of general application. One would in this vein employ *Wouters* to underpin an argument that the overall context in which sports regulation occurs, built around pursuit of a broad objective of fair competition, produces effects which though apparently restrictive of competition are nonetheless inherent in the pursuit of those objectives. Sport has its own admitted peculiarities, but in EC competition law the application of Article 81(1) is *always* conditioned by and receptive to the particular context in which arrangements are struck. What may appear to be a constraint on competition is unaffected by Article 81 where it is unavoidably required to sustain the functioning of an arrangement which is unobjectionable in the light of EC law.[809] In this sense there is no need for a wholly novel set of legal rules crafted for sport alone, and *Wouters*, though not on its facts concerned with sport, would provide a wholly adequate basis for legal assessment of the nature and purpose of anti-doping rules.

---

806 At [41].

807 The claim in the Commission Press Release (IP/02/1211, August 9, 2002) that the rules were applied in a proportionate manner is not matched by careful demonstration of this point in the decision proper. By contrast in the English courts an unsuccessful challenge to a suspension following a positive drugs test failed pursuant to a finding that the duration was appropriate: *Edwards* v. *BAF & IAAF*, [1997] Eu.L.R. 721.

808 Case C-309/99, *J.C.J. Wouters, J.W. Savelbergh, Price Waterhouse Belastingadviseurs BV* v. *Algemene Raad van de Nederlandse Orde van Advocaten*, [2002] *ECR* I-1577.

809 E.g., Case C-250/92, *Gottrup Klim* v. *DLB*, [1994] *ECR* I-5641. For an account of the nuances in the relevant case law see R. Whish, *Competition Law*, 5th edn. (Butterworths 2003), at pp. 115-128.

Traces of this need to adopt a sensitive approach to finding a 'restriction' appear in the famously lengthy Opinion of Advocate-General Lenz in *Bosman.*[810] So too in *Champions League* where the Commission accepts that football clubs are bound to co-operate in organising a league, so, for example, agreeing fixtures would not be a 'restriction' on competition, but where it concludes that recognition of this special relationship of interdependence does not justify treating an agreement to sell rights to broadcast matches in common as anything other than a restriction which can stand only if exempted according to the orthodox criteria set out in Article 81(3).[811] The Commission placed heavy reliance on *Wouters* in its *ENIC/UEFA* decision,[812] in which it concluded that rules forbidding multiple ownership of football clubs were indispensable to the maintenance of a credible competition marked by uncertainty as to the outcome of all matches. Seen in this context, any consequent restriction on commercial opportunity to acquire football clubs could not be regarded as a restriction falling within Article 81(1) EC. The *Wouters* formula has therefore been used to allow the peculiar features of sport to inform the application of the relevant legal rules. Commentators too have exploited this line of reasoning in debating whether 'salary caps' may be treated as restrictions on commercial freedom that are nonetheless necessary in the delivery of a viable sporting competition and therefore not restrictions within the meaning of EC trade law.[813]

In *Meca-Medina and Majcen* the Commission, applying Article 81 EC, states that it is necessary to determine whether, in the legal and economic context in which they are implemented, the object or effect of the rules is to restrict competition. It finds that this is not their *object.* The anti-doping rules may have the *effect* of restricting the athlete's freedom of action, but it finds that that such a limitation is not necessarily a restriction of competition within the meaning of Article 81 EC because it may be inherent in the organisation and proper conduct of sporting competition. Explicitly quoting the judgment in *Wouters*, the Commission concludes that the anti-doping rules are intimately linked to the proper conduct of sporting competition, that they are necessary to combat doping effectively and that the limitation of an athlete's freedom of action does not go beyond what is necessary to attain that objective. There is no breach of Article 81.

Given the scientific uncertainty about the body's production of nandrolone one might question whether the particular suspension at stake in the case of *Meca-Medina and Majcen* is a proportionate sanction. However, it is submitted that as a matter of principle this crafting of *Wouters* to offer potential shelter to an anti-doping regime from review founded on EC competition law is appropriate. And initially the CFI's judgment appears to agree. It states that

---

810 Case C-415/93, cited above at note 794, at [262]-[276].

811 Decision 2003/778, *OJ* 2003 L 29/125, at [125]-[131]. Exemption *was* granted on the facts. cf. generally M. Cave and R. Crandall, 'Sports Rights and the Broadcast Industry', 111 *The Economic Journal* (2001) F4 at F18.

812 COMP 37.806.

813 S. Hornsby, 'The harder the cap, the softer the law?', 10 *Sport and the Law Journal* (2002) 142; J. Taylor and M. Newton. 'Salary Caps – the Legal Analysis', 11 *Sport and the Law Journal* (2003) 158.

> 'regulations, which relate to the particular nature and context of sporting events, are inherent in the organisation and proper conduct of sporting competition and cannot be regarded as constituting a restriction on the Community rules on the freedom of movement of workers and the freedom to provide services'.[814]

This is important – and welcome – for the CFI's open acceptance that fixing the scope of EC law's control over sporting regulations is as valid for the provisions on freedom of movement as for those on competition.[815] More fundamentally still it is encouraging that the CFI does not here resort to sham demarcations based on the economic purpose of the rules. Instead it helpfully fixes on the idea that the application of the relevant Treaty provisions demands an assessment of the particular context of the sector in question. Speaking of 'restrictions' in the abstract is set aside in favour of examining what is inherent in the organisation of the sector itself. There could be no true sport without anti-doping controls, so automatically to treat suspensions of offenders as restrictions within the meaning of Articles 49 and 81 EC would be out-of-context formalism at its worst. This, it is submitted, is the very heart of the Court's message in *Wouters*.

Wouters sidelined

It is submitted that the CFI is right to conclude that in principle (properly structured and scientifically sound) anti-doping controls should be capable of application by sports bodies without interference rooted in EC law. There can be no sport without fair play. But having set out a coherent pattern of legal reasoning directed at this end founded on *Wouters* the CFI, abetted by the Commission, promptly resiles from it.

The CFI considered that *Wouters* concerned 'market conduct', an 'essentially economic activity, that of lawyers'. Anti-doping cannot be likened to market conduct without distorting the nature of sport, which 'in its very essence [...] has nothing to do with any economic consideration'.[816] It seems, then, that had the Commission decision been based squarely on *Wouters* it might not have survived the CFI's scrutiny. In the CFI's judgment it is reported that at the hearing, in reply to a question from the Court, the Commission stated that its disputed decision is based on *Walrave*, *Donà* and *Deliège*, and therefore on the 'purely sporting nature' of the anti-doping legislation at issue.[817] Examination under competition law in line with *Wouters* was performed 'in the alternative' or more 'for the sake of completeness'.[818] The CFI therefore decided

---

814 At [41].

815 *cf.* on this convergence K. Mortelmans, 'Towards Convergence in the application of the rules on Free Movement and on Competition', 38 *CML Rev.* (2001) 613; S. Weatherill, 'Fair Play Please!: Recent Developments in the Application of EC Law to Sport', 40 *CML Rev.* (2003) 51, at 80-86; R. O'Loughlin, 'EC Competition Rules and Free Movement Rules: An Examination of the Parallels and their Furtherance by the ECJ *Wouters* Decision', [2003] *ECLR* 62.

816 At [65].

817 At [62].

818 At [62].

that since the Commission's conclusion was based on the finding that 'the legislation is purely sporting legislation'[819] it would not disturb it.

It is submitted that in *Meca-Medina and Majcen* the CFI is in error to set aside *Wouters* and instead to place such faith in the notion that 'purely sporting legislation [which] may have nothing to do with economic activity' escapes the scope of application of the Treaty.[820] When it turns to the particular case of the anti-doping regime it begins its analysis by setting out enthusiastically on the wrong track. It declares that:

> 'It is appropriate to point out that, while it is true that high-level sport has become, to a great extent, an economic activity, the campaign against doping does not pursue any economic objective. It is intended to present, first, the spirit of fair play, without which sport, be it amateur or professional, is no longer sport. That purely social objective is sufficient to justify the campaign against doping. Secondly, since doping products are not without their negative physiological effects, that campaign is intended to safeguard the health of athletes. Thus, the prohibition of doping, as a particular expression of the requirement of fair play, forms part of the cardinal rule of sport.'[821]

This conclusion may be perfectly true – but an athlete subjected to an anti-doping ban faces immediate and dramatic economic hardship. Attempts to present the rules as 'sporting' and not 'economic' are unhelpful. They are both.[822]

The contortions forced on the CFI as it strives to separate our sport from the economy are vividly captured by [45] of the judgment.

> 'It must also be made clear that sport is essentially a gratuitous and not an economic act, even when the athlete performs it in the course of professional sport. In other words, the prohibition of doping and the anti-doping legislation concern exclusively, even when the sporting action is performed by a professional, a non-economic aspect of that sporting action, which constitutes its very essence.'

This puzzlingly opaque claim deserves a large red question mark scribbled in the margin. A similar impression that the CFI is groping desperately for a form of words that will make sense of this supposed gulf between sport and the economy is also found in [47]:

> 'The prohibition of doping is based on purely sporting considerations and therefore has nothing to do with any economic consideration.' Again, at [65], the CFI would have us believe that sport is not 'market conduct' and 'in its very essence [...] has nothing to do with any economic consideration'.

---

[819] At [66].

[820] At [41].

[821] At [44].

[822] The CFI draws on the Commission's Helsinki Report. COM (1999) 644, for support for the view that sport involves. *inter alia*, fair play and promotion of social cohesion which are remote from economic motivations. For criticism of lack of nuance in this account, and in particular its neglect of the deep differences between professional and recreational sport which should preclude a homogenous account of or policy towards sport, see S. Weatherill, 'Sport as Culture in European Community Law' in R. Craufurd Smith, ed., *Culture in European Union Law* (Oxford University Press 2004).

Of course the CFI has a point. The notion that there is in principle a separation between sporting rules (which escape the scope of application of EC law) and rules of an economic nature (which do not) reflects the nature of the EC as an institution possessing a set of attributed competences rather than a general regulatory competence.[823] But the reasoning deployed by the CFI in order to locate this margin is misguided. It is empty to claim that rules governing the composition of national sports teams or the conduct of anti-doping controls have nothing to do with economic activity. Such rules, which define the nature of sporting competition, are not primarily motivated by profit making but they visibly have economic repercussions. Players selected for national teams gain a higher profile and thereby obtain commercial advantage. Players excluded from eligibility for selection lose out. Similarly failing a doping control has enormous economic consequences for the athlete.

This type of rule may be of sporting interest but it has a commercial implication too. What is really at stake is not a group of sporting rules and a separate group of economic rules, but rather a group of sporting rules which carry economic implications but which are nevertheless necessary for the functioning of the sport and which therefore escape subjection to the normal assumptions of EC law.

So it is submitted that the heart of the matter is *not* that anti-doping rules are 'non-economic' but rather that they are part of the very core of the nature and purpose of the activity in question. And protecting that core is a task validly performed by sports federations. Regulation designed to meet that end is economic in the sense that those adversely affected by the application of the rules will be economically prejudiced. But, provided the rules remain within that core area, they are not undermined by the rules of EC trade law. The same point, delivered in slightly different vocabulary, is found in the Court's judgment in *Bosman* which accepts as 'legitimate' the perceived sports-specific anxiety to maintain a balance between clubs by preserving a certain degree of equality and uncertainty as to results and to encourage the recruitment and training of young players.[824]

A better approach-reinstating *Wouters* at the heart of the reasoning

How could the CFI's concerns be captured more elegantly and coherently than is permitted by its chosen but unsustainable divide between purely sporting considerations and economic considerations? By adapting the Court's formula in *Wouters*! The CFI's explanation that the rules at issue in *Wouters* concerned 'market conduct', while those in *Meca-Medina and Majcen* instead have 'nothing to do with any economic consideration' is flawed by the misguided assumption that the relevant compartments are watertight. The notion of the 'purely sporting practice' which escapes legal scrutiny is useful shorthand, but the CFI works it far harder in the service of precise legal analysis than it can possibly bear. In particular, the denial that such practices carry economic consequences is ill-founded. There is no profit in seeking to identify anti-

[823] Art. 5(1) EC, vigorously applied by the Court in Case C-376/98, *Germany* v. *Parliament and Council*, [2000] *ECR* I-8419, in finding the 'Tobacco Advertising' Directive invalid.

[824] Case C-415/93, cited above at note 794, at [106].

doping rules as sporting rules and not as rules of an economic or commercial nature. They are both. An individual who falls foul of an anti-doping regime is commercially damaged thereby. The more logical approach is to accept that the rules adopted by a sporting federation in order to regulate its competitions exert an economic impact, but to appreciate that *this is not of itself enough to justify the application of EC trade law.* The rules of the Treaty governing competition and free movement apply only where, after assessment of the overall context in which the decision was taken or produces its effects and after account is taken of its objectives, the consequential restrictive effects go beyond those inherent in the pursuit of those objectives. Or, seen from the other side of the coin, consequential restrictive effects of a sporting decision which cause economic hardship are not treated as restrictions for the purposes of application of Articles 49 and 81 EC provided they are inherent in the pursuit of those objectives. That is, of course, precisely the approach taken in *Wouters.* And it fits the business of sport perfectly well by leaving room for the particular concerns of sporting bodies – fair play, credible competition, national representative teams – to be advanced as part of an assessment of what is inherent in or necessary to the organisation of sport.

Admittedly there will always be arguments about where the margin lies between rules necessary for the running of a sport and more intrusive rules which are the subject of legal scrutiny. Patterns of litigation reveal that typically sports bodies claim a much wider sphere of necessary organisational autonomy than is judged appropriate by individual sportsmen and -women and by the Commission. The Court may ultimately be forced to adjudicate, as in celebrated cases such as *Walrave*,[825] *Bosman*,[826] *Deliège*,[827] and *Lehtonen*[828] and doubtless others to come.[829] But my claim is that such arguments will be conducted along the lines most likely to yield a coherent solution if one sets aside the unachievable quest to find the purely sporting rule which is devoid of an economic context. Once one openly acknowledges that sports rules have economic implications one can then focus on the key questions about which rules are truly necessary for the organisation of a particular sport and therefore sheltered from the impact of EC law even though they have economic implications. And the *Wouters* formula allows this to be done via the application of the general principles of EC competition law instead of seeking to invent mystical sub-categories of rules apt for EC law's regulation of sport. Sports federations can doubtless scarcely believe their luck when both the Commission and now the CFI permit sport to be lauded for its 'morally elevating role in society' in the absence of suitably careful distinctions between professional and recreational sport and without due regard for the immense commercial impact of some sporting activities.[830] However the European Court chooses to deal

825 Case 36/74, cited above at note 792.

826 Case C-415/93, cited above at note 794.

827 Cases C-51/96 & 191/97, cited above at note 802.

828 Case C-176/96, cited above at note 799.

829 Consider 'salary caps', at note 813 above.

830 See in particular [46] of the judgment in *Meca-Medina and Majcen.* The Declarations on Sport attached to the Amsterdam and the Nice Treaties are also vulnerable to the charge of woolly analysis, but at least nod to the separate character of amateur sport.

with the treatment at law of these particular anti-doping practices when it decides the appeal in *Meca-Medina and Majcen* it would provide a service to coherent legal reasoning were it to take the opportunity to insist on the use of the *Wouters* formula in determining the scope of autonomy properly left to sports federations. and on the abandonment of the unhelpful category of what the CFI describes as 'rules concerning questions of purely sporting interest [...] having nothing to do with economic activity'.[831]

[831] At [41].

IS THE PYRAMID COMPATIBLE WITH EC LAW?*

1. Introduction

The European Commission's Helsinki Report, which was published in 1999, includes the assertion that 'the pyramid structure of the organisation of sport in Europe gives sporting federations a practical monopoly. The existence of several federations in one discipline would risk causing major conflicts ?'.[832] Indeed it would create such a risk. It is not the purpose of this short paper to argue a case in favour of an injection of competition into the job of fixing the rules of the game. This contribution is instead driven by a concern that the pyramid structure, and its consequent attribution of monopoly power to sports federations, goes beyond what is required for the proper organization of European sport (in particular, football). A considerable degree of the monopoly power enjoyed by sports federations has profound commercial implications, and it is submitted that the currently constituted pyramid structure is inadequate to allow proper representation of and participation by all affected interests. Litigation is pending, and its potential impact is summarised. In particular, this paper makes a case in favour of allowing a more direct involvement in some aspects of decision-making by the major clubs than is permitted by the pyramid structure; and EC competition law is identified as a lever for achieving a re-shaping of the organisation of the game.

2. EU sports law and policy – the constitutional background

A brief inspection of the constitutional background is helpful in establishing an appreciation of the delicacy of the matter. According to Article 5(1) EC the European Community 'shall act within the limits of the powers conferred upon it by this Treaty and of the objectives assigned to it therein'. This principle of attribution or conferral insists that the EC may act only according to the limited mandate crafted for it by the Member States under the Treaty. Moreover, it is not open to the EC to extend the scope of that authorization from within the system. The Member States, acting at times of Treaty revision, are the constitutionally proper source of change.

Article 5(1) might initially seem to promise sport an immunity from the application of the rules of the EC Treaty. The EC has no explicit legislative competence in the field of sport provided by its Treaty. But sport as an economic activity is subject to the basic principles of EC law, including most prominently the Treaty provisions concerning free movement of labour and competition policy. This centrally important finding lies at the heart of the European Court's celebrated pair of sports law rulings

* 3-4 *International Sports Law Journal* (2005) p. 3 et seq.

[832] COM (1999) 644 and/2. For comment see S. Weatherill, 'The Helsinki Report on Sport', 25 *EL Rev.* (2000) 282.

of the 1970s. In *Walrave and Koch* v. *UCI*[833] and in *Donà* v. *Mantero*[834] the Court established that the functionally broad reach of the EC Treaty provisions governing the free movement of persons guarantees their application to sport in so far as it constitutes an economic activity – despite the absence of any explicit recognition in the Treaty of the subjection of sporting practices to the demands of EC trade law.

It took until the 1990s before the development of EC sports law became more than an esoteric backwater. *URBSFA* v. *Bosman*[835] was important as an expression of the European Court's persisting view that sport falls within the scope of the EC Treaty in so far as it constitutes an economic activity. The judgment was also significant for the Court's concern to grapple with the peculiar characteristics of sport, which in some respects is not an industry like any other. But most of all *Bosman* was a landmark in shaping EC law as a regime with capacity in practice to force significant change in the sporting status quo. *Walrave and Koch* and *Donà* v. *Mantero* mattered on paper. *Bosman* mattered on turf. The transfer system was radically amended and the system of intra-EU nationality discrimination in club football was abandoned as the direct and unavoidable consequence of the judgment.

3. EU SPORTS LAW AND PRACTICE

Since *Bosman* the body of 'EC sports law' has grown fat. One may readily cite important judgments of the Community judicature such as *Deliège* v. *Ligue de Judo*,[836] *Lehtonen et al.* v. *FRSB*,[837] *Deutscher Handballbund eV* v. *Maros Kolpak*,[838] *David Meca-Medina and Igor Majcen* v. *Commission*,[839] and *Igor Simutenkow.*[840] The Commission too has been actively engaged in assessing how EC law affects the autonomy of decision-makers in sport. One may readily cite richly illustrative decisions such as *UEFA/Mouscron*,[841] *FIA (Formula One)*,[842] and the formal Commission Decision published as *UEFA Champions League* giving a green light to collective selling arrangements[843] – and this is very far from an exhaustive list. The Commission's explorations have largely concerned Articles 81 and 82, the EC Treaty provisions governing competition law, rather than the free movement provisions which provided the cutting-edge for the Court's initial incursions into sporting autonomy. But, taken in the round, the basic approach to which both the rules on competition and those on

833 Case 36/74 *Walrave and Koch* v. *UCI*, [1974] *ECR* 1405.

834 Case 13/76 *Donà* v. *Mantero*, [1976] *ECR* 1333.

835 Case C 415/93 *URBSFA* v. *Bosman*, [1995] *ECR* I-4921.

836 Cases C-51/96 & C-191/97 *Deliège* v. *Ligue de Judo*, [2000] *ECR* I-2549.

837 Case C-176/96 *Lehtonen* et al. v. *FRSB*, [2000] *ECR* I-2681.

838 Case C-438/00 *Deutscher Handballbund eV* v. *Maros Kolpak* [2003] *ECR* I-4135.

839 Case T-313/02 *David Meca-Medina and Igor Majcen* v. *Commission*, judgment of 30 September 2004.

840 Case C-265/03 *Igor Simutenkow*, judgment of 12 April 2005.

841 IP/99/965, 9 December 1999, IP 99/956, 9 June 1999.

842 IP/01/1523, 30 October 2001.

843 Decision 2003/778 *UEFA Champions League*, *OJ* 2003 L 291/25.

free movement are wedded is the same – to what extent is sport able to show that it has distinctive characteristics and concerns which must be taken into account in the application of the rules of the EC Treaty?[844]

And this, in short, is the nature of the challenge facing the EC as it crafts a 'policy on sport'. Sport is an economic activity, as the Court has always insisted, but it is not simply an economic activity like all others. The institutions of the EC need to shape their approach to sport with due regard for its special characteristics, but the Treaty provides no explicit guidance on what these might be. And Article 5(1) EC looms large in denying the institutions of the EC an unlimited competence in regulating sport.

Visible points of thematic concern emerge from the case law. They represent threads that are gradually being woven into an EC sports law and policy. *URBSFA* v. *Bosman* was the launchpad for this intellectual quest. The European Court accepted that sport is, in short, special. It declared that:

> 'In view of the considerable social importance of sporting activities and in particular football in the Community, the aims of maintaining a balance between clubs by preserving a certain degree of equality and uncertainty as to results and of encouraging the recruitment and training of young players must be accepted as legitimate.'

So there are (at least) two features which in the view of the Court mark out sport as special – maintaining a balance between clubs and encouraging youth training. In a 'normal' industry a firm has no wish to see its rival prosper – quite the reverse. But in a football league each participant not only wants but needs credible rivals. Take away the competition and there is nothing left. So *Bosman* did not dismiss the special character of sport, despite frequent accusations in that vein – quite the reverse. The Court was simply unpersuaded that the practices that were challenged in the litigation were apt to achieve the objectives to which they were ostensibly dedicated. In particular the Court was disdainful of the argument that the transfer system of which *Bosman* himself had fallen foul was necessary to preserve the essential features of the game.

A decade of decisions of the Court and the Commission since *Bosman* have begun to piece together what is at stake in the notion that EC law applies to sporting practices but with due recognition of their peculiar characteristics. For example, preserving uncertainty of result is essential in sport, so rules preventing multiple ownership of clubs have been accepted as necessary to suppress suspicion of match-fixing.[845] Such restrictions on commercial freedom would not be found in a 'normal' industry – short of the threshold for merger control motivated by anxiety about acquisition of high levels of market power. Other instances – where sport is structured in a manner

---

[844] On this 'convergence' see K. Mortelmans, 'Towards Convergence in the application of the rules on Free Movement and on Competition', 38 *CML Rev.* (2001) 613; S. Weatherill, "Fair Play Please!": Recent Developments in the Application of EC Law to Sport', 40 *CML Rev.* (2003) 51, 80-86. Cf. also *David Meca-Medina and Igor Majcen* v. *Commission*, note 839 above Para. 42 of the judgment.

[845] CAS 98/200 *AEK Athens and Slavia Prague* v. *UEFA*, 20 August 1999; COMP/37.806, *ENIC/UEFA*, IP/02/942, 27 June 2002.

that would not ordinarily be encountered elsewhere – might include rules forbidding the relocation of clubs, transfer windows[846] and rules governing the selection of players for international representative competition. Occasionally of course practices in sport are condemned as anti-competitive in circumstances where there is no sport-specific context – consider the blatant discrimination in the distribution of 1998 football World Cup tickets.[847] And the CFI recently found that FIFA's rules governing agents concerned economic activity that was merely peripheral to the sporting context in which they applied – although the rules were not considered unlawful.[848]

More generally still, the Member States chose to add Declarations on Sport to the Treaties of Amsterdam and Nice. These (non-binding) texts assert the broader social, educational and cultural value of sport. The Commission too has engaged with the perceived need to set sport in a context that is broader than the merely economic. In its Helsinki Report on Sport, published in 1999,[849] the Commission sketched its view of a 'European Sports Model' which possesses a number of features, most prominently grouped around the contrasts drawn with North American sports practice.[850] For the Commission, European sport is characterised by, among other features, the notion of solidarity, stretching from the apex of the sport to the 'grass roots'. And the Commission lauds sport's role as 'an instrument of social cohesion and education'. One may readily entertain anxiety that these ambitious claims, albeit couched in a 'soft law' context, strain the bounds of the principle of attribution contained in Article 5(1) EC. Moreover I am suspicious that a discourse about a 'European policy on sport' suggests the imposition of an unsustainable homogeneity on a set of activities that carry very different motivations and implications in their amateur/recreational and in their professional manifestations.[851] Sport may have deep cultural resonance and it may also be 'big business' – but is a single stream of policy apt to accommodate this breadth of aspiration?

So EC sports law and policy amounts to a rather oddly shaped package. It has emerged out of the accidents of litigation and it is influenced by the constitutional constraints imposed on the EC by Article 5(1)'s principle of attribution and the absence of any expression of the sporting interest in the Treaty proper. But it is today entirely convincing to analyse the incremental growth of law and policy as something

[846] C-176/96 *Lehtonen* et al. v. *FRSB*, [2000] *ECR* I-2681.

[847] Dec. 2000/12 1998 Football World Cup, *OJ* 2000 L 5/55. For comment see S. Weatherill, '0033149875354: Fining the Organisers of the 1998 Football World Cup', *ECL Rev.* (2000) 275-282.

[848] Case T-193/02 *Laurent Piau* v. *Commission*, judgment of 26 January 2005.

[849] Note 832 above.

[850] Cf. S. Weatherill, 'Resisting the Pressures of Americanization: the influence of European Community Law on the "European Sport Model"' in S. Greenfield and G. Osborn, eds., *Law and Sport in Contemporary Society* (London, Frank Cass Publishing 2000) pp. 155-181.

[851] This is developed in S. Weatherill, 'Sport as Culture in European Community Law', Ch. 4 in R. Craufurd Smith, ed., *Culture in European Union Law* (Oxford University Press 2004). Cf. R. Parrish, 'Reconciling Conflicting Approaches to Sport in the European Union', pp. 21-42, and K. Foster, 'Can Sport be Regulated by Europe? An Analysis of Alternative Models', pp. 43-64, both in A. Caiger and S. Gardiner, eds., Professional Sport in the EU: Regulation and Re-Regulation (The Hague, T.M.C. Asser Press 2000).

a good deal more systematic than a random collection of fact-specific resolutions of disputes set against a background of loose political expressions of support for sporting values. There is today something recognisable as EU sports law and policy.[852] But it does not provide ready answers to the many questions that surround the debate about the future shaping of European sport. That is the intellectual fascination of EU sports law and policy – it is rich and open-textured. Much has changed in recent years; much will change in the years to come, under the pressure of potential or actual litigation. This paper reflects on one phenomenon that (it is submitted) is unlikely to endure in its current form – the pyramid.

4. The autonomy of governing bodies in sport

Within this evolving pattern of EU sports governance there can be no doubt that sporting organisations have the authority to set genuine sporting rules – that is, they may fix 'the rules of the game' or rules necessary for its organisation – and these escape control under EC law. Equally there can be no doubt that it is fiendishly difficult to identify what really are such rules that belong to the autonomy of sports federations and what are instead rules of a sufficiently commercial character to fall for inspection under the rules of the EC Treaty. This is what the Court in *URBSFA* v. *Bosman* described as 'the difficulty of severing the economic aspects from the sporting aspects of football'. Difficult indeed. One may go further. Is it even possible? Of course one may accept that in the abstract there must be a category of sporting rules which are essential for the very existence of the game – shape of the ball, size of the team, and so on. Such rules define the sport. And their fixing is not accompanied by any economic motivation. But they have economic effects. They are restrictive in the sense that they place some practices beyond the limits of what is permitted. It is frankly extremely difficult to imagine any 'sporting rule' which does not also have a commercial implication as a result of this restrictive effect. So there is a dividing line between sporting autonomy and the incursion of grubby commerce, but it will not be found by imagining the absence of an economic context, at least in so far as the debate is directed at the phenomenon of modern professional sport. Economic implications are everywhere.

The existing EC competition law acquis already accommodates the notion that a 'restriction' must be assessed in its proper context. In *J.C.J. Wouters, J.W. Savelbergh, Price Waterhouse Belastingadviseurs BV* v. *Algemene Raad van de Nederlandse Orde van Advocaten*[853] the Court observed that 'account must first of all be taken of the

[852] Cf. L. Halgreen, *European Sports Law: a Comparative Analysis of the European and American Models of Sport* (Copenhagen, Forlaget Thomson 2004); R. Parrish, *Sports law and policy in the European Union* (Manchester University Press 2003). For a useful collection of materials see R. Siekmann and J. Soek, eds., *The European Union and Sport: Legal and Policy Documents* (The Hague, T.M.C. Asser Press 2005).

[853] Case C-309/99 *J.C.J. Wouters, J.W. Savelbergh, Price Waterhouse Belastingadviseurs BV* v. *Algemene Raad van de Nederlandse Orde van Advocaten*, [2002] *ECR* I-1577. See similarly, e.g., Case T-112/99 *M6* v. *TF1*, [2001] *ECR* II-2159, Para. 76.

overall context in which the decision of the association of undertakings was taken or produces its effects. More particularly, account must be taken of its objectives. [...] It has then to be considered whether the consequential effects restrictive of competition are inherent in the pursuit of those objectives'. The litigation concerned Dutch rules prohibiting multi-disciplinary partnerships between members of the Bar and accountants which were defended as necessary to achieve the sound administration of justice, but the Court's appreciation of the need to analyse an agreement's effects that are restrictive of competition in the light of the objectives pursued can readily be transplanted to demand that the law's assessment of sports regulation must embrace fully the purpose of such rules in promoting a free and fair sporting event. So – for example – the suspension of a participant who has been found to have taken a banned substance is undeniably a restriction on that individual's commercial freedom. It may have a devastating impact on his or her career. It is clearly a matter with profound economic implications. But provided the rule is applied in a transparent, procedurally fair and proportionate manner it is submitted that it would not fall foul of EC law – not because it is a 'purely sporting rule' but instead, more precisely, because it is a rule that is essential to preserve the integrity of sporting competition.[854] Seen in that context, its economic implications do not deprive it of its character as an expression of the autonomy of federations to act in a transparent and proportionate manner in defence of the integrity of their sport. *Wouters*, applied to sport, should be taken to mean that the rules of the Treaty governing competition and free movement apply only where, after assessment of the overall context in which the decision was taken or produces its effects and after account is taken of its objectives, the consequential restrictive effects go beyond those inherent in the pursuit of those objectives. Or, seen from the other side of the coin, consequential restrictive effects of a sporting decision which cause economic hardship are not treated as restrictions for the purposes of application of Articles 39, 49 and 81 EC provided they are inherent in the pursuit of those objectives.

In this sense EC law admits that sporting bodies enjoy a conditional autonomy from its requirements. Provided the rules are shown to be necessary for the organisation of the sport, they escape control. But the border is patrolled with vigilance. In *URBSFA* v. *Bosman* the Court commented that 'a restriction on the scope of the [EC Treaty] provisions in question must remain limited to its proper objective. It cannot, therefore, be relied upon to exclude the whole of a sporting activity from the scope of the Treaty'.[855] So although it was pressed on the Court that the nationality of players matters in club football, the Court, led by Advocate-General Lenz, refused to accept this at face value – and rejected the assertions of the sports bodies. In similar vein, though the judgment in *David Meca-Medina and Igor Majcen* v. *Commission* is in

[854] It is submitted that the CFI in *David Meca-Medina and Igor Majcen* v. *Commission*, note 839 above has not helped the smooth development of the law by claiming to identify 'rules concerning questions of purely sporting interest ... having nothing to do with economic activity' (Para. 41). For criticism of flaws in that judgment, see S. Weatherill, 'Anti-Doping Rules and EC Law', *ECL Rev.* (2005) 416 et seq.

[855] Para. 76 of the judgment.

some respects flawed,[856] the assertion that 'regulations, which relate to the particular nature and context of sporting events, are inherent in the organisation and proper conduct of sporting competition and cannot be regarded as constituting a restriction on the Community rules on the freedom of movement of workers and the freedom to provide services' holds good – as, of particular present pertinence, does the supplementary admonition that 'That restriction on the scope of the above provisions of the Treaty must however remain *limited to its proper objective*' (emphasis added). And, in tune with *Bosman*, the Commission decision in *FIA (Formula One)*,[857] which required a separation of regulatory and commercial functions previously bundled together in the grip of the sports governing body, demonstrates that this is not just rhetoric. EC law has been used to enforce significant change within the governance of European sports. Though it is well known that it is intimidatingly difficult to challenge powerful sports bodies, individuals have (*Bosman*) and so has the Commission, and it is not at all the case that sports structures which have endured for a great many years can confidently predict a long life into the future.

5. The pyramid – its nature and purpose

So what of the pyramid? Is it simply an expression of the necessary organisational structure of sport? Or does it cross the line, and become a set of practices that are vulnerable to challenge under EC law?

The argument that is advanced in this paper holds that the pyramid represents an exaggerated view of what is necessary for the proper organisation of the sport of football in Europe. In particular, the exclusion of the major football clubs from formal participation in the taking of decisions that directly affect their commercial interests is not necessary in the governance of the sport, and is vulnerable to challenge under Article 82 EC. But what is the pyramid?

In football the pyramid places FIFA, the world governing body, at the apex. Beneath FIFA lie the continental associations – in Europe, UEFA. On the next level down the national associations are found. And then come the professional clubs, along with other interested actors within individual countries, the 'grass roots' which include regional associations and amateur bodies. The pyramid structure is based on the assumption that decisions about the game are taken after a more-or-less intense process of consultation, but the dialogue is formally limited to actors who are adjacent in the pyramid. So clubs have a voice via their national associations. Most famously of all, the 'G-14' group of leading clubs, established as a European Economic Interest Grouping and based in Belgium and comprising (18, not 14) members from seven EU Member States,[858] has been refused any formal recognised status by FIFA. Indeed Sepp Blatter, President of FIFA, has curtly dismissed G-14 as lacking any official

[856] Note 839 above.

[857] Note 842 above.

[858] www.g14.com/G14accueil/index.asp.

status.[859] As far as the governing bodies are concerned, the clubs are free to express views, and a degree of informal dialogue naturally occurs – rule-makers cannot be deaf to clubs as powerful as Milan or Real Madrid. But the major clubs' formal channel for influencing decisions is routed through their national associations, and then on up through the pyramid structure. And decisions taken about the running of the sport percolate downwards in the pyramid to continental and to national associations, and are then applied to the clubs participating in the several national and international competitions. Clubs that refuse to comply can be penalised – ultimately, they can be excluded from competition, an effective sanction which is not easily resisted, not least given that club football competitions typically operate on an annual basis whereas legal proceedings are rather less speedy.

It is no part of my argument that this structure is inappropriate for setting the rules of the game. I accept that the pyramid structure operates well as a basis for shaping the basic pattern of the sport. For example, I do not propose that clubs should have a greater input into deliberations about whether to change the offside rule. But a number of matters that are dealt with under the pyramid structure of sports organisation are much less obviously necessary elements in sports governance. Instead they contain a much more prominent commercial dimension. This leads one to question whether the exclusive grip of sports federations on the decision-making structure is truly justified in law.

Consider rules governing the release of players by clubs for international representative matches. These are contained in Articles 36-41 of the FIFA Regulations for the Status and Transfer of Players. Clubs must release players – their employees – for a defined period of time and for a defined group of matches so they can play for their country. Sanctions are envisaged in a case of non-compliance, which may include suspension of the club. The clubs receive no payment. They are explicitly stated to be responsible for the purchase of insurance to cover the risk that the player will be injured. Even if the player is not injured, he will arrive back at his club tired. Again – there is no question of compensation for the club. Remember too that there is an element of market competition at stake in these situations. International football tournaments are to some extent in the same market as club competitions when one considers potential interest from broadcasters and sponsors. So clubs are required to provide a free resource, the players, to an undertaking that is at least in part seeking to make profits from exactly the same sources on which the clubs would wish to draw. One would certainly not find this in a normal industry. Sport truly is special. But is this system lawful? In particular, from the perspective of EC law, is this an abuse of a dominant position within the meaning of Article 82 perpetrated by the governing bodies in football?

[859] A search against 'Sepp Blatter G-14' on www.google.co.uk will generate many references.

6. The pyramid under challenge

Litigation is underway. The 'G-14' group of leading clubs has lodged a challenge before the Competition Commission in Switzerland arguing that the mandatory player release system is unlawful. In separate proceedings in Belgium, Charleroi found that a highly promising young player, *Oulmers*, returned seriously injured in November 2004 from international duty with his home country, Morocco. Charleroi's fortunes on the field slumped without their young star. They were entitled to no compensation at all, despite the advantages enjoyed by Morocco in acquiring access to *Oulmers* on a mandatory basis. Here too litigation rooted in alleged violation of EC competition law is underway.[860]

To stand back, what are the pre-conditions for reliance by governing bodies on the notion that rules necessary for the organisation of the game may escape the scope of application of the EC Treaty? My summary of the criteria which shape the conditional grant of autonomy to governing bodies holds that the rules must be:

Transparent – Objectively justified – necessary – proportionate – and must allow appropriate levels of participation by those affected.

As explained above (and for the purposes of this short article here eschewing an extended exploration of the relevant material), I believe the case law of the Court (and, of a less authoritative legal nature, the practice of the Commission) can be distilled to these requirements. But I would support this view by supplementary reference to the soft law material pertaining to sport at EU level which has been a feature of the last few years. As the Court has made clear in *Deliège* and in *Lehtonen*,[861] this material is apt for citation in exploring the nature and scope of the relevant EC rules, and it is here submitted that despite the rather anodyne style of these texts, they operate in favour of the case that EC law forbids the current structuring of the player release rules.

The Declaration attached to the Amsterdam Treaty asserts that

> 'The Conference emphasises the social significance of sport, in particular its role in forging identity and bringing people together. The Conference therefore calls on the bodies of the European Union to listen to sports associations when important questions affecting sport are at issue. In this connection, special consideration should be given to the particular characteristics of amateur sport.'

The Declaration attached to the Nice Treaty includes consideration of the Role of sports federations.

> 'The European Council stresses its support for the independence of sports organisations and their right to organise themselves through appropriate associative structures. It recognises that, with due regard for national and Community legislation and on the basis of a

[860] 'La Fifa assignée!: La blessure de Majid *Oulmers* suscite réflexion et surtout reaction chez Abbas Bayat', La Dernière Heure, Jeudi 12 Mai 2005, Sports p. 7.

[861] Cases C-51/96 & 191/97, note 567 above, Paras. 41-42 of the judgment; Case C-176/96 note 495 above, Paras. 32-33 of the judgment.

democratic and transparent method of operation, it is the task of sporting organisations to organise and promote their particular sports, particularly as regards the specifically sporting rules applicable and the make-up of national teams, in the way which they think best reflects their objectives. It notes that sports federations have a central role in ensuring the essential solidarity between the various levels of sporting practice, from recreational to top-level sport [...] While taking account of developments in the world of sport, federations must continue to be the key feature of a form of organisation providing a guarantee of sporting cohesion and participatory democracy'.

In line with the thesis advanced above, these Declarations asserts a conditional recognition of the virtues of governing bodies, and the space allowed to their regulatory autonomy. In particular, sports federations are expected to operate 'on the basis of a democratic and transparent method of operation'; and they 'must continue to be the key feature of a form of organisation providing a guarantee of sporting cohesion and participatory democracy'. Insistence on the virtues of participation chimes with the broader agenda mapped by the Commission in its 2001 White Paper on European Governance.[862] It is perfectly possible to take these broad recommendations of good, transparent and participatory governance and to deploy them in a concrete legal setting. In this vein I would argue that the absence of such necessary levels of participation is a powerful reason for arguing that practices imposed on football clubs fall within the sphere of application of EC law, for it is not necessary for the federations to maintain such an exclusion of input from directly affected interests. The rule-maker occupies a dominant position within the meaning of Article 82 by virtue of the power conferred by the pyramid.[863] And the rules are abusive within the meaning of Article 82 EC.

The European Commission's 1999 Helsinki Report similarly expresses the view that – the basic freedoms guaranteed by the Treaty do not generally conflict with the regulatory measures of sports associations, provided that these measures are objectively justified, non-discriminatory, necessary and proportional'.[864] I think the pyramid as currently constituted is not entitled to be regarded in this positive light.

Moreover, were the Treaty establishing a Constitution for Europe, signed in October 2004, to enter into force (which is admittedly currently improbable) Article III-282(1)(g) would provide that Union action shall be aimed at

'developing the European dimension in sport, by promoting fairness and openness in sporting competitions and cooperation between bodies responsible for sports, and by protecting the physical and moral integrity of sportsmen and sportswomen, especially young sportsmen and sportswomen.'

Here is yet more rich material apt to nourish the argument that an absence of the cited 'cooperation between bodies responsible for sports' drives one to a finding that rule-

862 COM (2001) 428.

863 Cf. Case T-193/02 *Laurent Piau* v. *Commission*, judgment of 26 January 2005 (concerning FIFA's rules governing agents – no abuse was found in the case).

864 Note 832, p. 9.

making which shuts out the (directly affected) clubs is inconsistent with EC law.

My argument is not that clubs should be permitted to enjoy unfettered rights to decide whether or not to help the health of international representative football by releasing players. It is doubtless necessary that a system of players release to which clubs are bound be put in place, or else international representative football could not survive. I do not make a case designed to exterminate the World Cup. International representative football is part of the very structure of the sport – it is a distinctive feature of sport not found in other industries. But it does not follow that these rules, as currently constituted, are necessary elements of sports governance. Nor does it follow that the manner in which these rules are determined, within the pyramid and to the formal exclusion of the affected clubs, is necessary. Just as in *Bosman* one might have been able to defend a more sophisticated transfer system (perhaps of the type that has been subsequently introduced[865]) but could not defend that transfer system, so too here my submission is that a modified player release system could withstand challenge rooted in EC law – but the current system cannot. It may be perfectly true that exposure to a wider audience watching international representative football raises the value of the player to the club – but that is no reason for arguing for a system of mandatory and uncompensated release of the extreme type that currently prevails. The central legal point is that it is not necessary for the operation of international football to deny clubs compensation for the players they make available to national associations. Large profits are made through international football, and it is abusive for federations to enforce rules which allow them to take the benefit while imposing the burden of supplying players on the clubs. One could readily imagine an adjusted and potentially lawful system involving an obligation to release players imposed on clubs with corresponding obligations imposed on the governing bodies to provide compensation (*inter alia* to take account of the element of market competition for broadcasting and sponsorship money which is also at stake in this matter of regulation). Some national associations are doubtless too poor to compensate clubs. But federations could cope with this by establishing a revenue pool into which a slice of profits from international competitions could be paid before distribution to individual countries, and from which clubs could be compensated. Rich countries would subsidise poor countries from profits made through international football – at present clubs subsidise all countries despite taking no profits from international football.

Moreover there is a procedural dimension to the submission that the current arrangements violate Article 82 EC. It is not necessary to establish these arrangements to the formal exclusion of the participation of clubs. A committee representing a wider range of affected interests could readily be set up to determine the balance of rights and obligations in this matter. By formalising dialogue between transnational governing bodies and clubs this, of course, would challenge the pure lines of the pyramid, but this paper makes the case that the current pyramid structure is unsustainable. As explained, EC law admits that sporting bodies enjoy a conditional autonomy in

865 Cf. B. Dabscheck, 'The Globe at their Feet: FIFA's New Employment Rules', 7 *Culture, Sport and Society* (2004) 69.

setting rules to govern the game and ultimately, as the Court declared in *Bosman*, 'a restriction on the scope of the [EC Treaty] provisions in question must remain limited to its proper objective. It cannot, therefore, be relied upon to exclude the whole of a sporting activity from the scope of the Treaty'. The rules governing player release go too far, both in substance and in the exclusionary way they are agreed and administered. And their reform would be instrumental not in demolishing the pyramid according to which football is regulated but instead in confining the pyramid's scope of application to matters which are necessarily required for the organization of the game and in respect of which the clubs cannot reasonably expect to enjoy a right of direct participation – such as the offside rule!

The player release system is by no means the only set of practices that are vulnerable to challenge. Consider the setting of the international match calendar. It might seem that this is part of 'the rules of the game'. But at present the continental championships – in Africa, in Europe, in South America, in Asia – are scattered across the year, which maximises disruption for clubs forced to release players. There are naturally some reasons of climate for the selected dates, but this is not a total explanation. Part of the story is a desire to avoid competition between continental championships in order to maximise revenues from sale of broadcasting rights and luring of sponsors. So, as with the player release system, the planning of the match calendar has embedded within it an identifiable commercial dimension. And it is the clubs that suffer from staggered obligatory release of players. It is my argument that this economic context brings EC law into play, and that Article 82 controls the practices of sporting federations. The current pattern could readily be adjusted – in particular by aligning as many international tournaments as the weather will allow in the European summer – in order to re-balance a system currently loaded heavily against the clubs. Again, the establishment of a joint committee, in which the clubs have a direct voice, would be the obvious way forward. Another matter in which the common interests of the participants – clubs and governing bodies – could be represented in a manner that is more faithful to the economic context than is currently allowed by the pyramid is the management of the Champions League, the premier club competition in European football. The question of property rights in the League is a complex one. Article 295 EC provides that the Treaty shall not prejudice rules governing the system of property ownership in the Member States. However, this does not mean that issue of allocation of property rights can be kept off the agenda of the EC institutions. In its Champions League Decision concerning collective selling of television rights the Commission was forced to address such questions in the context of its examination of the application of Article 81 EC to the arrangements underpinning the organisation of the competition. UEFA argued it had set up the League and that it owned it – so, for the purposes of legal assessment, it was simply selling its own property to purchasing broadcasters and therefore Article 81 was not in issue. The Commission did not accept this. It observed that questions of ownership fall for determination under national law, and will not yield a uniform conclusion across the territory of the EU. However, it asserted that UEFA can 'at best be considered as a co-owner of the rights, but never the sole owner'.[866] Article 81 applied. Given that ownership patterns directly involve the clubs, it is accordingly arguable that they should be permitted a correspondingly more direct involvement in planning and managing the competition than they are currently allowed. In line with the theme on which this paper has touched on several occasions, the issue is that sports governing bodies currently claim a wider role in the name of regulation of the sport than is justified – they go beyond setting the rules, and occupy a monopoly position in determining matters of significant commercial impact.

7. Conclusion

What is at stake here is re-balancing authority within the game. There will always be arguments about where the margin lies between rules necessary for the running of a sport and more intrusive rules which are the subject of legal scrutiny. Patterns of litigation reveal that typically sports bodies claim a much wider sphere of necessary organisational autonomy than is judged appropriate by individual sportsmen and -women and by the Commission. The Court may ultimately be forced to adjudicate, as in celebrated cases cited in this paper such as *Walrave*, *Bosman*, *Deliège* and *Lehtonen*, and the proceedings involving the G-14 and *Oulmers/Charleroi* mentioned in this paper are potential new highlights. It is crucial that as a matter of EC law the international federations do not have autonomy to decide for themselves what is the nature of the sport and the rules necessary to protect and promote it. This paper does not seek to demolish the pyramid as an organisational paradigm for football. But it makes the case that the pyramid is currently too big – that too many decisions with direct and substantial commercial implications are taken by sports federations who disallow input from the clubs who are intimately affected by those decisions. Litigation is an unpredictable art, and there are plenty of subtle tactics that may be employed by both federations and clubs to get what they want without formal change or challenge, but there is in principle rich potential for EC law to be used to provoke a fresh process of change if not revolution in European sport and, in particular, to reduce the size of the pyramid.

866 Para. 122 of the Decision, note 843 above.

THE SALE OF RIGHTS TO BROADCAST SPORTING EVENTS UNDER EC LAW*

1. Introduction – the constitutional context

Although it may be intuitively appealing to assume that an integrated market for Europe inevitably brings with it an integrated regulatory strategy underpinning that market, the EC Treaty does not provide for this. Article 5(1) EC declares that 'The Community shall act within the limits of the powers conferred upon it by this Treaty and of the objectives assigned to it therein.' This is commonly referred to as the principle of 'attributed competence'. It is constitutionally fundamental. Accordingly the EC possesses no general regulatory competence and it cannot 'self-authorise' an increase in its own competence. It may act only in the areas in which the Member States have granted it a mandate. Extension of the grant rests with the Member States acting at times of periodic Treaty revision.

The principle, then, is that the EC possesses only limited powers. The practice, however, is that those limits are rather loosely drawn and tend to be stretched. The EC has a sphere of influence that extends considerably further than one may initially appreciate on an inspection of the formal text of the Treaty. This troubling trend is vividly captured by the catchphrase competence creep.[867] It is troubling because EU Treaty ratification is conducted in each Member State according to local constitutional requirements but it is performed everywhere on the basis that only a limited grant of power is being made to European level. Lawmaking excess at EC level represents a constitutionally illegitimate shifting of power to EU level which tends to weaken such controls over executive action as exist within national political cultures. So Article 5(1) does not state a technical rule. It states a rule that is fundamental to the chosen distribution of functions to different levels of democratic governance in Europe. Its violation is likely to induce protest from domestic constituencies such as national Parliaments and constitutional courts, and, perhaps in the long term most alarming of all, citizens are likely to suffer alienation from the complexity that flows from incremental drift in the growth of multi-level governance. Unwarranted or, at least, inadequately explained patterns of centralisation tend to generate resistance in

---

* 3-4 *International Sports Law Journal* (2006) 3 et seq.

[867] Cf. M. Pollack, 'Creeping Competence: The Expanding Agenda of the European Community', 14 *Journal of Public Policy* (1994) 95; S. Weatherill, 'Competence creep and competence control', 23 *YEL* (2004) 1.

any quasi-federal system.[868] This is why 'competence anxiety' emerged explicitly on to the reform agenda in the Treaty of Nice's Declaration on the Future of the Union and subsequently in the Laeken Declaration, and this is why the Treaty establishing a Constitution, endorsed by the Heads of State and Government in 2004 but unlikely now to be ratified, proposed to clarify and re-organise the Treaty rules governing competence, and additionally to freshen the system for monitoring the existence and exercise of competence by bringing in new actors from outwith the uncritical EU family – most of all, it is national Parliaments that are invested with the responsibility to stop creep according to a new ex ante monitoring system.[869]

Pending such reforms, we must make do with the current system. And currently the principal motor of competence creep is the ambiguity and functional breadth of the relevant Treaty provisions, underpinned by a perceived readiness practised by the EU's institutions to exploit textual ambiguity in order to extend their sphere of influence beyond that foreseen by the Treaty. The argument, then, is that there is a structural weakness in the EC Treaty which tends to promote rising centralization at the expense of local autonomy.[870]

As far as legal ambiguity is concerned, the principal issue is the poor way in which Article 5(1)'s principle of attribution is put into operation in the Treaty. The Treaty's general *modus operandi* is not to declare particular sectors off-limits the EC nor to reserve particular functions to the Member States. Instead Article 5(1) EC is made specific in its application to particular sectoral competences by a chaotic pattern of provisions granting legislative authority to the EC scattered throughout the Treaty. These provisions vary in scope and intensity and they vary in their impact on residual national regulatory autonomy. They are the confused and confusing consequence of incremental Treaty revision. It is disturbingly difficult to set out clearly an account of the nature of EC competence and its effect on State competence.[871] This is the fertile

868 For comparative inquiry, see e.g., K. Nicolaidis and R. Howse, eds., *The Federal Vision: Legitimacy and Levels of Governance in the United States and the European Union* (Oxford, Oxford University Press 2001) especially Ch. 3, J. Donahue and M. Pollack, 'Centralization and its Discontents: The Rhythms of Federalism in the United States and the European Union', and Ch. 4, D. Lazer and V. Mayer-Schoenberger, 'Blueprints for Change: Devolution and Subsidiarity in the United States and the European Union'; E. Young, 'Protecting Member State Autonomy in the European Union: Some Cautionary Tales from American Federalism', 77 *NYUL Rev.* (2002) 1612; D. Halberstam, 'Of Power and Responsibility: The Political Morality of Federal Systems', 90 *Virginia Law Rev.* (2004) 731.

869 Cf., e.g., S. Weatherill, 'Better Competence Monitoring', 30 *EL Rev.* (2005) 23; G. Davies, 'Subsidiarity: the wrong idea, in the wrong place, at the wrong time', 43 *CML Rev.* (2006) 63; I. Cooper, 'The Watchdogs of Subsidiarity: National Parliaments and the Logic of Arguing in the EC', 44 *JCMS* (2006) 281.

870 Cf., e.g., A. Von Bogdandy and J. Bast, 'The European Union's Vertical Order of Competences: the Current Law and Proposals for its Reform', 39 *CML Rev.* (2002) 227; A. Dashwood, 'The Relationship between the Member States and the European Union/European Community', 41 *CML Rev.* (2004) 355; D. Hanf and F. Baumé, 'Vers une Clarification de la Répartition des Compétences entre l'Union et ses Etats Membres', 38 *CDE* (2003) 135.

871 Cf. A. Von Bogdandy and J. Bast, op. cit., especially pp. 239-250; G. de Burca and B. de Witte, 'The Delimitation of Powers between the EU and its Member States', Ch 12, in A. Arnull and D. Wincott, eds., *Accountability and Legitimacy in the European Union* (Oxford, Oxford University Press 2002); F. Mayer, 'Die Drei Dimensionen der Europäischen Kompetenzdebatte', *WHI-Paper* 2/02 (Walter Hallstein Institut, available via www.whi-berlin.de); V. Michel, 'Le Défi de la Repartition des Compétences', 38 *CDE* (2003) 17.

soil of competence creep: it is hard to marshal operationally useful constitutional arguments against EC intervention. This is most of all true of two Treaty provisions in particular: Articles 95 and 308 EC. These are not sector-specific competences of the type typically added in recent bouts of Treaty revision.[872] They instead envisage a broad competence to act in pursuit of the Community's objectives. The limits that are imposed – in short, a tie to market-making under Article 95 and a tie to the EC's objectives under Article 308 – are limits that lack precision. And most significant of all they have been driven by a long-standing readiness among the Member States acting unanimously in Council to assert a broad reach to the EC's legislative competence. The growth of the programmes of consumer and environmental protection supply well-known examples of legislative activity pursued in the name of the harmonization programme and, in the latter instance, pursuant also to Article 308 (ex 235) at a time when the political will was firm, yet when the Treaty was deficient in explicit legislative competence to act in these realms.[873] The gulf between principle and practice in the assertion of legislative competence undermines the impression given by Article 5(1) EC of a sturdy defence of State autonomy from EC incursion beyond the limits authorised by the Treaty. It is Articles 95 and 308, the functionally broad legal bases, that lie at the heart of this intensification of regulatory ambition.

So EC law reaches further than Article 5(1) EC might lead one to expect because the 'limits' to EC powers on which Article 5(1) insists are in fact ill-drawn and, for those opposed to proposed EC action, hard to rely on. But there is more to 'competence creep' than simply legislative (over-)ambition. EC law exercises supervision over policy choices within the Member States not simply in circumstances where it has adopted secondary legislation but also where those policy choices conflict with the achievement of the objectives mapped out in the Treaty, most prominently those connected with the construction of an integrated trading space across the territory of all the Member States. The centrally important Treaty provisions in this context are those concerning free movement and competition. The basic structure of the law governing free movement is readily described. National measures which obstruct interstate trade are forbidden unless a justification for their continued application is shown to exist. This pattern is found in the EC Treaty – Articles 28/30 (goods), 39 (workers), 43/46 (right of establishment), 49/55 (services), 56/58 (capital) – but has been the subject of a vast body of case law in which the Court, while remaining true to this basic Treaty framework, has taken on the task of re-writing the law in terms that are far more elaborate than those found in the skeletal style of the Treaty. The competition rules are found in Article 81 and 82. They supplement the dedication of the free movement rules to the creation of an integrated trading space, while also serving to control other types of anti-competitive practices that stretch beyond market-partitioning. So Article 81, dealing with cartels and restrictive practices, and Article 82, dealing with

---

[872] Cf., e.g., Art. 152 on public health, Art. 153 on consumer protection, Arts. 174-176 on environmental policy.

[873] See S. Weatherill, 'Consumer Policy', in P. Craig and G. de Burca, eds., *The Evolution of EU Law* (Oxford, Oxford University Press 1999); J. Scott, *EC Environmental Law* (Harlow, Longman 1998).

dominant undertakings, control practices that tend to maintain the fragmentation of markets along national lines and other practices which harm the functioning of the market in other ways, such as price-fixing.

In reflecting on the EC's capacity to exercise an influence that is a good deal broader than Article 5(1) EC might suggest, the crucial point about these Treaty provisions is their functional breadth. What is at stake in the application of the free movement rules and the competition rules is the achievement of the Treaty's economic objectives. That is how the provisions are structured, and accordingly any field of national policymaking which tends to come into conflict with the quest for market integration is subject to review in the light of its impact on the EC rules on free movement or competition. So even though the EC may lack a legislative competence in a particular field does not at all mean that the matter rests in the province of national regulatory autonomy. The matter may perfectly conceivably be influenced by the EC Treaty's provisions directed at economic integration.

Accordingly internal market law has a wide functional sweep. For example the EC enjoys no general competence to legislate for the maintenance of press diversity or for a viable public health care system. Indeed, in the latter instance the relevant Treaty provision equipping the Community with a tightly confined legislative competence is explicitly deferential to Member State responsibilities to provide health care.[874] And yet in so far as national choices in such realms come into conflict with the drive to integrate markets, national measures fall within the scope of EC trade law and their permissibility falls for judicial determination pursuant to the Treaty.[875] National regulatory choices have to be assessed in the light of their impact on wider processes of integration. One might, of course, object to the values that the Court attaches to particular interests when it makes these decisions; additionally, one might choose to reflect on whether a judicial forum is the appropriate place to make such choices.[876] The deeper such case law intrudes into national practices that reflect sensitive cultural, moral and social choices the more acute such anxieties become. But, as a general observation, the case law offers the Court the opportunity to weed out unrepresentative and outdated manifestations of national-level decision making that are hostile to, and inappropriate in, an integrating European market of the type to which the Member States have committed themselves under the EC Treaty. And the fact that the EC lacks legislative competence in an area is absolutely no bar to it becoming the subject of radical reform under the influence of the prohibitions imposed by the Treaty provi-

[874] Art. 152(5) EC.

[875] On press diversity see Case C-368/95, *Vereinigte Familiapress Zeitungsverlags- und vertriebs GmbH* v. *Heinrich Bauer Verlag*, [1997] *ECR* I-3689; on health care see Case C-157/99, *B.S.M. Geraets-Smits* v. *Stichting Ziekenfonds VGZ, H.T.M. Peerbooms* v. *Stichting CZ Groep Zorgverzekeringen*, [2001] *ECR* I-5473; Case C-372/04 *ex parte Watts* judgment of 16 May 2006.

[876] Cf., e.g., M. Poiares Maduro, 'Striking the elusive balance between economic freedom and social rights in the EU', Ch. 13 in P. Alston, ed., *The EU and Human Rights* (Oxford, Oxford University Press 1999); R. Craufurd Smith, 'Community Intervention in the Cultural Field', Ch. 2 in R. Craufurd Smith, ed., *Culture and European Law* (Oxford, Oxford University Press 2004); P. Oliver, 'Competition and Free Movement: Their Place in the Treaty', Ch. 10 in P. Tridimas and P. Nebbia, eds., *European Union Law for the 21st Century – rethinking the new legal order* (Oxford, Hart Publishing 2005).

sions on free movement and competition law. Even in the few instances where the Treaty seems to guard against disruption of national autonomy, such as Article 295 which rules out prejudice to systems of property ownership in the Member States, the reality is that the influence of the Treaty rules governing economic activity has been sufficient to exert significant influence over State choices. Areas of truly exclusive State competence are few and, were it otherwise, the achievement of the core objectives of the Treaty would be gravely imperilled. The conclusion, then, is that for those who would wish to keep the EC at bay, Article 5(1) offers a good deal less comfort than may first appear likely. Most of all, the 'limits' to EC powers to which reference is made is Article 5(1) are limits that are remarkably loosely fixed.

The anxiety that Article 5(1) is taken less seriously in practice than its constitutional importance should demand is reinforced by appreciation of the surrounding institutional context. The current system of 'competence control' is founded on an assumption of *ex ante* restraint by the political institutions and ex post review by the Community judicature. So in principle an act should not be adopted if it trespasses beyond the scope of the mandate conferred by the Treaty and, if it is, it is susceptible to annulment by the Court. But the prevailing allegation is that the institutions do not offer a reliable checking mechanism. It has typically been Member State executives, acting in Council, that have been the primary actors in this centralising process of 'creeping competence'. Action has not infrequently been taken 'in Brussels' by national politicians as a rather convenient way to escape domestic constraints over policy reform – it is Article 5(1) EC and the very legitimacy of the EC that ultimately suffers from such opportunism. But neither Commission nor Parliament are regularly heard to raise audible voices of protest. The operational vagueness of Article 5(1) EC, and in particular the loose edges of the functionally broad competences provided by Articles 95 and 308, have been exploited by the EC's own institutions to strain the limits of the Treaty mandate. And did the Court adopt a disapproving tone? Rarely! Admittedly the vaguer the scope of an attributed competence, the tougher the Court's task in determining whether its bounds have been exceeded in the case of a particular challenged act but even so the 'competence sceptic' harbours deeper reservations about the Court's readiness to police the Treaty's limits. A dubious milestone is *Procureur de la Republique* v. *Adbhu*[877] in which the Court famously hailed environmental protection as 'one of the Community's essential objectives' at a time when only legislative practice, and not the text of the Treaty itself, could justify such a claim. The case law is admittedly not one-dimensional. In *Tobacco Advertising* – more properly, *Germany* v. *Parliament and Council*[878] – the Court for the first time annulled a Directive as lying beyond the competence attributed to the EC by the Treaty. The measure harmonised rules governing the advertising of tobacco products, but the Court found that it made an inadequate contribution to building the internal market and concluded that this was fatal to its validity as a measure of harmonisation. The judgment stands as an assertion of a constitutionalised reading of competence prevailing over purely

[877] Case 240/83, [1985] *ECR* 531.

[878] Case C-376/98, [2000] *ECR* I-8419.

political preferences. A connection should be made with Opinion 2/94 on Accession to the European Convention on Human Rights, in which the Court ruled that such accession falls beyond the current scope of the competence granted to the EC by its Treaty. This finding matches *Tobacco Advertising* for it too makes explicitly plain that there are judicially policed limits to the Treaty's functionally broad competences, *in casu* Article 308 (ex 235).[879] At their core these judgments assert fidelity to the principle of attributed competence in Article 5(1) EC. The legislature may not act in a manner that leads to amendment of the Treaty. But it is too soon to portray the Court as a consistently reliable guardian of 'State rights'. *Tobacco Advertising* establishes a test which is far from precise.[880] And in subsequent applications of the threshold test the Court has by contrast offered no relief to applicants seeking the annulment of measures in rulings including *Netherlands* v. *Parliament and Council*,[881] *R* v. *Secretary of State ex parte BAT & Imperial Tobacco*,[882] *Swedish Match*[883] and *Alliance for Natural Health*[884] – even though in some of these cases some powerful arguments were advanced against the validity of the adopted measures. The Court has also taken the opportunity in these rulings to emphasise that it will not lightly interfere with the exercise of legislative discretion in matters requiring complex assessment. So legislative harmonization is far from dead. *Tobacco Advertising* increasingly looks like a highly atypical case, and the recent case law deepens the concern that the Court cannot or will not effectively police the limits of legislative ambition in line with the dictates of Article 5(1) EC.

Equally, in the trade law field, the allegation is commonly made that the Court is very quick to assert the functional reach of the Treaty provisions on free movement and competition law, while very slow to accept that there is any case for insulating particular activities at national level from the supervision of EC law. The ruling in *ex parte Watts* encapsulates the Court's approach in a number of fields where EC trade law sweeps far beyond the limits of EC legislative competence:

> '– although Community law does not detract from the power of the Member States to organise their social security systems and decide the level of resources to be allocated to their operation, the achievement of the fundamental freedoms guaranteed by the Treaty nevertheless inevitably requires Member States to make adjustments to those systems. It does not follow that this undermines their sovereign powers in the field'.[885]

This has become a standard formula in cases where the achievement of economic integration collides with Member States powers to act in realms where the Com-

[879] Opinion 2/94, Accession by the EC to the ECHR, [1994] *ECR* I-1759.

[880] See for example use of imprecise adjectives and adverbs in the judgment such as genuinely, likely, probable, appreciable and 'remote and indirect' in Paras. 84, 86, 97, 108, and 109 of the judgment respectively. Cf. J. Usher, 'Annotation', 38 *CML Rev.* (2001) 1519.

[881] Case C-377/98, [2001] *ECR* I-7079.

[882] Case C-491/01, [2002] *ECR* I-11543.

[883] Case C-210/03, [2004] *ECR* I-0000.

[884] Cases C-154/04 & C-155/04, [2005] *ECR* I-0000.

[885] Case C-372/04, note 875 above, Para. 121.

munity is not competent to act as a substitute legislator. Social security is a common example;[886] taxation is another;[887] and even the maintenance of public order and the safeguarding of internal security have been revealed as matters of national competence that are nevertheless reviewable in so far as their pursuit impedes cross-border trade.[888] Free movement law stops States acting, in the absence of justification for chosen practices that impede cross-border trade. The Community cannot go further than this: it cannot set the ground rules for the organization of social security systems or taxation or for preserving public order. The EC does not become a substitute regulator, to the detriment of the autonomy of national choices, but it confines the exercise of that autonomy. Naturally one may argue that the Court is being disingenuous in declaring that the achievement of the fundamental freedoms requires legislative adjustment by the Member States while not undermining 'their sovereign powers in the field'. Surely the impact of free movement law is radically to circumscribe the scope of sovereign State choices? Perhaps so: and yet it is submitted that this is embedded deep in the structure of the Treaty. The Court is simply following the logic of the Treaty itself. The Treaty does not place particular sectors of economic activity beyond the reach of its basic rules. To interpret it in a way that manufactured such exclusions would subvert the whole aim of the Treaty. So, in order to make sense of the Treaty, the Court is correct to interpret the free movement and competition rules in an expansive manner. But those provisions do not automatically outlaw practices. Instead they put them to the test of justification. And it is in that process of justification that the Court is called on to recognize the particular features of each industry. This is where the Treaty often provides little help. It is here, then, where EC law intervenes in areas where the Treaty maps out no policy framework, nor even any legislative competence, where the need for an operationally useful 'EC policy' makes its sternest demands.

2. The nature and purpose of an 'EC policy'

The purpose of this paper's Introduction, which presents the constitutional background, is to provide an insight into just how challenging the depiction of EC law governing the sale of rights to broadcast sporting events under EC law really is. The EC has no general legislative competence in these realms. The rights in question are property rights, and they initially fall to be determined under national law. Certainly they will differ State by State within the EU. Article 295 EC goes so far as to provide that 'This Treaty shall in no way prejudice the rules in Member States governing the system of property ownership'. Does this place matters pertaining to rights to broadcast sports events off-limits the EC, so that, for example, anti-competitive agreements between right-holders would not be subject to EC competition law? Absolutely not! In the field of free movement the Court has consistently subjected national laws on

[886] Cf., e.g., Case C-512/03 *J E J Blankaert*, judgment of 8 September 2005.

[887] Cf., e.g., Case C-446/03 *Marks and Spencer* v. *Halsey*, judgment of 13 December 2005.

[888] Case C-265/95 *Commission* v. *France*, [1997] *ECR* I-6959.

property ownership to review in so far as they involve nationality-based discrimination. For example in *Albore*[889] exemption of Italian nationals from the requirement of obtaining an authorisation to buy a property in certain parts of the national territory led to unjustified discrimination against nationals of other Member States and an impermissible restriction on capital movements between Member States. In similar vein the capital provisions of the Treaty preclude the application of national rules requiring a mortgage securing a debt payable in the currency of another Member State to be registered in the national currency.[890] The lesson here is that Article 295's statement that 'This Treaty shall in no way prejudice the rules in Member States governing the system of property ownership' refers to the autonomy of the Member States to structure their own chosen systems of property ownership. But the way in which those systems are operated is subject to review for compatibility with the basic expectations of EC trade law.[891] This is symptomatic of the EC's claim to assert a very broad functionally-based review of national law and practice pursuant to the Treaty provisions on trade law. It means that practices pertaining to broadcasting rights are subject to the Treaty competition rules, notwithstanding the terms of Article 295 EC. And that in turn means that the particular context of the marketing of sports rights must be taken into account against a rather thin and unhelpful Treaty background.

For sport generally, the story of its subjection to EC law follows closely the narrative set out above. In short, the reach of EC trade law goes far beyond the limitations on the EC's legislative competence under the Treaty, and this brings in its wake the need to develop a 'policy' that is driven by the dictates of trade integration yet is also appropriately sensitive to the particular needs of sport. This is remarkably challenging- and frequently fiercely controversial. Famously the European Court confirmed in a pair of cases decided in the 1970s that EC law is in principle capable of application to sport. In both *Walrave and Koch* v. *Union Cycliste Internationale* in 1974[892] and *Donà* v. *Mantero* in 1976[893] the Court took the opportunity to explain that in so far as sport constitutes an economic activity, it falls within the scope of application of Community law. The Community lacks legislative competence in the field of sport. Indeed, even today, the word 'sport' is absent from the EC Treaty itself. But in so far as sport generates practices of economic significance, they are in principle subject to the control of EC law, most prominently the Treaty rules governing free movement and competition. This approach was triumphantly confirmed by the European Court in *Bosman*.[894] Sport, like other sectors such as education, taxation, environmental policy and consumer protection, demonstrates how the law of the EC may exercise

[889] Case C-423/98 *Albore*, [2000] *ECR* I-5965.

[890] Case C-222/97 *Trummer and Mayer*, [1999] *ECR* I-1661, Case C-464/98 *Westdeutsche Landesbank* v. *Stefan*, [2001] *ECR* I-173.

[891] Cf., e.g., E-M. Kieninger, 'Securities in movable property within the Common Market', 4 *ERPL* (1996) 41; J Rutgers, 'The Rule of Reason and Private law or the Limits to Harmonization', Ch. 9 in A. Schrauwen, ed., *Rule of reason: rethinking another classic of European Legal Doctrine* (Europa Law Publishing, Groningen 2005); U. Drobnig, H.J. Snijders and E. Zippro, eds., *Divergences of Property Law, an Obstacle to the Internal Market* (Sellier, Munich 2006).

[892] Case 36/74, [1974] *ECR* 1405.

[893] Case 13/76, [1976] *ECR* 1333.

[894] Case C-415/93, [1995] *ECR* I-4921.

a wider influence than a formal inspection of the text of the Treaty may lead one to expect, primarily because of the extended reach of the rules governing the building of an integrated, competitive market. This constitutional point underpins subsequent rulings of the Court in the field of sport and it also informs the Commission's batch of interventions into the sports field on the basis of the competition rules of the Treaty.

The EC's institutions have been firm on this point. The economic implications of sporting practices are enough to bring them within the scope of the Treaty, even if their purpose may be not be profit-making, and, with isolated unfortunate exceptions,[895] the main issues before the Court and Commission have concerned the question whether particular practices with an economic impact reflect permissible concern to secure the effective organisation of the game, rather than the question whether the EC can claim any jurisdiction in the first place. And therefore here too the EC has been forced to develop a means to understand how its trade law provisions – free movement and competition law – intersect with sport, an activity which is untouched by the explicit terms of the Treaty and for which the Treaty therefore offers no direction on how, and whether, to load in concern for its peculiar economic, social, and cultural features.

This is fascinating, but it is awkward and controversial too. The landmark ruling in *Bosman* delivered in 1995 is vividly emblematic. Although, as explained, the Court had twenty years earlier identified that sport is in principle subject to EC law, it was only in *Bosman* that EC law was seen to have practical force. Famously, the consequences of the ruling were that nationality-discrimination in club football had to be eliminated and the transfer system had to be radically amended. EC law did not stipulate what replacement transfer system should be introduced, if any – that would overstep its mandate – but it did require the elimination of existing unlawful practices.[896] Sport was accordingly forced to undergo significant adjustment as a result of the demands of EC law. The vital point for present purposes is that the Court did not deny that football in particular, or sport in general, possesses unusual characteristics that distinguish it from 'normal' commercial sectors. Rather, the Court insisted only that the economic significance of sport secured its subjection in principle to EC law and that those unusual characteristics should then be taken into account in shaping the application of the law. There is, then, room for acknowledging that 'sport is special', but that room exists within the jurisdiction of the institutions of the EC.

Is there an 'EC policy' to be discerned in such circumstances? The anxiety is that it may mislead to use a term such as 'policy' which suggests a degree of order and systematization that the EC may be constitutionally incapable of delivering. And yet it is not so misleading. In Paragraph 106 of its *Bosman* ruling the Court remarked that:

---

[895] In Case T-313/02, *David Meca-Medina and Igor Majcen* v. *Commission*, [2004] *ECR* II-3291 the Court of First Instance allowed itself to be lured down the misleading path of uncritically separating out sport from its commercial impact: see further S Weatherill, 'Anti-doping rules and EC Law', *ECL Rev.* (2005) 416. The case is pending on appeal before the Court: Case C-519/04 *David Meca-Medina and Igor Majcen* v. *Commission.*

[896] Cf. B. Dabscheck, 'The Globe at their Feet: FIFA's New Employment Rules', 7 *Culture, Sport and Society* (2004) 69; J.-C. Drolet, 'Extra Time: Are the New FIFA Transfer Rules Doomed?', 1-2 *International Sports Law Journal* (2006) 66. See also A. Egger and C. Stix-Hackl, 'Sports and Competition Law: a Never-Ending Story?', *ECL Rev.* (2002) 81.

> 'In view of the considerable social importance of sporting activities and in particular football in the Community, the aims of maintaining a balance between clubs by preserving a certain degree of equality and uncertainty as to results and of encouraging the recruitment and training of young players must be accepted as legitimate.'

The practices challenged in the case did not adequately contribute to these aims and they were judged to fall foul of Article 39 (ex 48) EC. But the Court's recognition in *Bosman* that sport has 'considerable social importance' and that it has two distinct legitimate aims set the scene for subsequent inquiry into exactly what type of practice might permissibly be pursued by governing bodies in sport in conformity with Community law in circumstances where 'normal' commercial actors would expect to be condemned for violation of the Treaty. The ruling in *Bosman* strongly supports the view that a policy of sports may be shaped in the application of the trade law provisions of the Treaty which is sensitive to the particular context and the particular sector of the economy which is involved. One might, of course, dispute the particular choices made by the EC's institutions, most prominently the Court and the Commission. But *Bosman* shows that the case law of the Court embraces a certain vision of the nature and functioning of sport.

So what is at stake in this paper is the exploration of an area of law in which the EC necessarily proceeds in an incremental manner. The opportunities for its institutions to shape a 'policy' is constrained both by the constitutional limitations on the matters to which they may pay attention – Article 5(1) looms large! – and also by the accidental patterns of litigation, which may cause practice to develop according to unexpected, eccentric rhythms. This concerns most prominently the Court and the Commission, both of whom are responsible for individual decisions applying the law, though the broader policy direction periodically offered by the Council, the European Council and the Parliament may also serve to embroider the tapestry. It is therefore of the highest importance to ensure that one does not over-state the possibilities of a systematic account of relevant EC law. The pattern of EC law cannot be systematic in the way that a national system may be, because of the limits set by Article 5(1), because of its inevitable entanglement with diverse national law and practice and also because of the accidents of litigation which rarely throw up the opportunity for the adjudicating institutions to handle easy cases that will make good law. On the other hand, this is not necessarily to concede that EC law is ripe for criticism. A qualitative account of its role is required. That the EC Treaty does not lends itself to the shaping of a comprehensive policy of the type that one would expect to find in a national setting does not entail that it is flawed, only that it is different.

There is accordingly a rich literature exploring the concept of EC sports law and policy.[897] It explores *inter alia* how the institutions of the EU seek to piece together

[897] E.g., R. Parrish, *Sports law and policy in the European Union* (Manchester University Press 2003); S. Greenfield and G. Osborn, eds., *Law and Sport in Contemporary Society* (London, Frank Cass Publishing 2000); H.-E. Meier, 'The Rise of the Regulatory State in Sport', conference paper available via http://regulation.upf.edu/ecpr-05-papers/hemeier.pdf (2005); L. Barani, 'The Role of the European Court of Justice as a Political Actor in the Integration Process: The Case of Sport Regulation after the *Bosman* Ruling', 1 *Journal of Contemporary European Research* (2005) 42; S. Van den Bogaert and A. Vermeersch, 'Sport and the European Treaty: a Tale of Uneasy Bedfellows' (31 *EL Rev.* (2006) 821-840).

a coherent approach to the regulation of sport against a Treaty background which is not at all dedicated to elucidating the peculiarities of sport; how diverse public and private actors, at national, European and international level, seek to exploit EC law to achieve their objectives or to keep it at bay in order to protect their privileges; and generally how EC law erodes the self-regulatory paradigm which has for so long been dominant in sports governance. This is not a challenge that is in any sense unique. In fact, across a great many areas of EC law, policy and practice, one is confronted by the need to make some sort of systematic sense of a set of laws and practices that are not constitutionally dedicated to dealing with the particular subject matter of concern. Take EC consumer law. This comprises the application of the free movement rules of the Treaty to control national measures that impede consumer choice in the wider market – including national measures, as famously in the *Cassis de Dijon* case,[898] that are themselves presented as measures of consumer protection; the body of measures that have promoted market integration by harmonising national consumer law and thereby creating a species of re-regulatory EC consumer law; a package of soft law measures and policy statements on the priorities to be pursued by EC consumer policy; and, last and certainly least, the tiny batch of binding EC measures that have been adopted under Article 153, the narrowly-drafted legislative authority granted to the EC in the specific area of consumer protection with effect from 1993 on the entry into force of the Maastricht Treaty. This package is not capable of being analysed as a pre-planned system of consumer law. For constitutional reasons, combined with reasons of political opportunism, the law has evolved in a much less rigorous fashion. But the product is not random. There are thematic connections that bind together the EC's interventions into consumer law. Commentators have debated the weight and merits of principles and techniques that pervade the acquis such as information disclosure, party autonomy and inquiry into substantive unfairness. They have sought to discover how much 'system' is at stake and to recommend ways to develop law and practice further.[899] This is typical of the search for an 'EC policy' in many areas. EC law and practice 'spills over' to provoke new academic sub-disciplines, as the 'Europeanisation' of many policy sectors that are in explicit terms subject to only a limited interventionist competence granted by the EC Treaty gathers pace.[900] The general lesson

[898] Case 120/78, *Rewe-Zentrale AG* v. *Bundesmonopolverwaltung für Branntwein*, [1979] *ECR* 649.

[899] E.g. – and by no means adopting the same outlook – S. Weatherill, *EU Consumer Law and Policy* (Cheltenham, Elgar 2005); N. Reich and H.-W. Micklitz, *Europäisches Verbraucherrecht* (Baden-Baden, Nomos 2003); S. Grundmann, W. Kerber and S. Weatherill, *Party Autonomy and the Role of Information in the Internal Market* (Berlin, de Gruyter 2001); H. Rösler, *Europäisches Konsumentenvertragsrecht* (Munich, CH Beck 2004); K. Riesenhuber, *Europäisches Vertragsrecht* (Berlin, de Gruyter 2003).

[900] E.g., on environmental law see J. Scott, *EC Environmental Law* (Harlow, Longman 1998), J. Jans, *European Environmental Law* (Groningen, Europa Law Publishing 2000), especially Chs. I and III; on labour market regulation and social policy more generally, see J. Kenner, *EU Employment Law: From Rome to Amsterdam and Beyond* (Oxford, Hart Publishing 2003), C. Barnard, *EC Employment Law* (Oxford, Oxford University Press 2000); on family law see E. Caracciolo di Torella and A. Masselot, 'Under construction: EU family law', 29 *EL Rev.* (2004) 32; on health care law see T. Hervey and J. McHale, *Health Law and the European Union* (Cambridge, Cambridge University Press 2004).

is that a programme presented as an exercise in securing market freedom inevitably involves a sustained commitment to rule-making within which a host of public and private actors jockey for position and influence.[901] And the EC has to shape a policy of sports on all manner of things. Such is the practice of attributed competence, guaranteed as a principle of EC law by Article 5(1) of the Treaty.

So now to consider the law governing the sale of rights to broadcast sporting events under EC law. The EC is not equipped with general competence in the field of property law. Nor is it so equipped in the field of sport. Here, then, is a gloriously illuminating case study into competence creep and policymaking in a constitutionally murky setting. What does it mean to speak of an 'EC policy' in such ambiguous realms?

My argument is that simply to present the law – or still worse the rules – is to mislead. The ground is less stable than would be the case in a typically national system. But nonetheless my argument is that the EC's institutions deserve respect for creating something that is a good deal more valuable, coherent and reliable than mere case-by-case dispute resolution. The free movement rules are not without significance, but most of all this has occurred in the shadow of the Treaty competition rules.

3. EC COMPETITION LAW

3.1. The general purpose of competition law

The market rarely functions perfectly. Producers and suppliers may be immunised from the discipline of competition and the consequent need to satisfy the consumer. As a general observation one may suppose that, in the absence of effective competition between producers and suppliers the 'invisible hand' of the market will be ill-directed. And, as an equally general observation, competition law is motivated by the objective of improving the functioning of the market as a whole.

In modern economies competition law and policy is typically directed at the suppression of practices on the 'supply-side' that the market system, supported by private law, cannot root out unaided. Under a general (though not unconditional) assumption that competition is a desirable process, competition law and policy is aimed at ensuring the market is reshaped into a competitive environment.

The restraints which would be removed by such laws could be behavioural or they could be structural. Behavioural restrictions would include cartels and restrictive practices agreed by producers and/or suppliers. Producers may prefer collusion to competition. Instead of trying to undercut each other's prices in order to increase sales, they may prefer to arrange a common selling price. This will make life altogether more comfortable for producers, but at a cost to the consumer: price competition will be suppressed. Such cartels appear antagonistic to the fundamental notion of the competitive market. Legal intervention may be justified as a method of correcting the imperfection introduced by producer collusion. Producers must be free to compete,

[901] M. Egan, *Constructing a European Market* (Oxford, Oxford University Press 2001).

but they are not free under the law to surrender that freedom. The regulatory authority charged with the supervisory task must therefore devise a legal response to the damaging effects of cartels on free competition. Horizontal agreements – those concluded between parties at the same stage of the production or distribution process, that is, firms who are supposed to be rivals – tend to be those which the law greets with most evident suspicion. Vertical deals tend to be far less pernicious and will often ostensibly improve distribution arrangements and, by injecting new sources of supply into a market, may frequently be pro-competitive (though careful case-by-case analysis is always required). So as a general proposition the law is much more permissive in its treatment of vertical agreements than it is of horizontal agreements. Here, however, is where sport may be special. 'The 'horizontal' relationships in organized sport are different in character from those which prevail – and are often anti-competitive – in 'normal' industries. Sports leagues are characterized by the unavoidable interdependence of the participants. This will be re-addressed below.

Structural impediments would include monopolies where the pattern of the market is not competitive, irrespective of the behaviour of firms. Put simply, in a monopoly the price and quality of what is produced are dictated by the choice of the producer, not the operation of the market dictated ultimately by the consumer. The law could be used to forestall the creation of monopolies (for example, by forbidding mergers) or to destroy existing monopolies (for example, by forcing large firms to sell off assets). The law would thus root out inhibitions on free competition. But the conventional approach to monopolies is to regulate them – a middle way between preventing monopoly power from coming into existence and destroying it once it has: to accept the existence of dominant economic power but to regulate the firm so that it cannot behave independently. For example, the firm may be subjected to price control or quality standards; it may be obliged to deal equitably with customers, existing or prospective. The essential point is that, once a firm has crossed a threshold of economic power which renders it in part immune from the pressure of competition, it becomes liable to act inefficiently and/or unfairly. There is then a rationale for exercising regulatory control which would not apply if it were economically weaker. In fact such controls in one sense mimic the results which would obtain were a competitive market in operation. In that case, an individual firm's prices would be controlled by reference to those set by rivals, but in a monopoly a regulatory authority may assume that function. The question of the precise level at which prices should be set (in the absence of guidance from the operation of the market) then becomes a point of detail, but one which is itself likely to be controversial.

In some areas, however, the purity of competition will not provide the best of all possible markets. Limits on competition may rationally be recognised as desirable. This compromise is often denoted by the comment that the law seeks 'workable' not 'perfect' competition. Desirable behavioural limitations on competition may include collaboration on research and development, where the pooling of resources may secure more effective research work carried out in common instead of duplication of superficial efforts. Desirable structural limitations may be observed in markets which are inappropriate for competition: 'natural monopolies' illustrate this phenomenon.

In these circumstances there is a place for competition law, but its function will not be to insist on competition. Instead, the law may be employed to permit beneficial agreements among firms. This implies a need for legal tests apt to distinguish between desirable and undesirable agreements and for institutions charged with the function of making the appropriate assessments.

3.2. **Competition law in Europe**

These general perceptions may be seen to underpin competition law throughout Europe. And they serve also to introduce the structure of Articles 81 and 82 EC, the twin pillars of EC competition law. In Europe competition law and policy have always held a high profile as part of the process of market integration and regulation. The first of the European Communities, the European Coal and Steel Community established in 1952 by the Treaty of Paris, included competition policy provisions. The European Economic Community came into existence in 1958 as the creation of the Treaty of Rome and was of much broader scope than the Coal and Steel Community. That Treaty also included a Chapter entitled 'Rules on Competition', comprising three sections, 'Rules applying to Undertakings', 'Dumping' and 'Aids Granted by States'. Enforcement powers were conferred on the Commission by Regulation. Some of the common policies of the Community emerged slowly over the later part of the twentieth century, with heavy reliance on the laborious development of secondary legislation; this is true of social policy and it is true of fields such as consumer policy and environmental policy. In sharp contrast, however, the fundamental principles of competition policy have always been firmly embedded in the very fabric of the Treaty. The main pillars are Articles 81 and 82 of the EC Treaty (ex 85 and 86), governing cartels and monopolies respectively. The competition rules act as a cornerstone of the activities of the EU, prominent among which remain the establishment of 'a system ensuring that competition in the internal market is not distorted'.[902] The European Court has gone so far as to describe Article 81 EC as 'a fundamental provision which is essential for the accomplishment of the tasks entrusted to the Community and, in particular, for the functioning of the internal market'.[903] For the EU, it should also be borne in mind that competition policy operates to regulate a market which is not integrated after the fashion of a national market. This lends to it a special, interventionist flavour not found in a national system.[904]

3.3. **European Community Law of Cartels and Restrictive Practices**

EC restrictive practices law is based on the overall perception that supply side collaboration carries the potential to damage the operation of the market. Article 81 (ex 85) is the relevant provision of EC law, which reads as follows:

---

[902] Art. 3(g) EC.

[903] Case C-126/97 *Eco Swiss China Time Ltd* v. *Benetton International NV*, [1999] *ECR* I-3055.

[904] See, e.g., A. Albors-Llorens, 'Competition Policy and the shaping of the Single Market', Ch. 12 in C. Barnard and J. Scott, eds., *The Law of the Single European Market* (Oxford, Hart Publishing 2002).

1. The following shall be prohibited as incompatible with the common market: all agreements between undertakings, decisions by associations of undertakings and concerted practices which may affect trade between Member States and which have as their object or effect the prevention, restriction or distortion of competition within the common market, and in particular those which:
   (a) directly or indirectly fix purchase or selling prices or any other trading conditions;
   (b) limit or control production, markets, technical development, or investment;
   (c) share markets or sources of supply;
   (d) apply dissimilar conditions to equivalent transactions with other trading parties, thereby placing them at a competitive disadvantage;
   (e) make the conclusion of contracts subject to acceptance by the other parties of supplementary obligations which, by their nature or according to commercial usage, have no connection with the subject of such contracts.
2. Any agreements or decisions prohibited pursuant to this Article shall be automatically void.
3. The provisions of Paragraph 1 may, however, be declared inapplicable in the case of any agreement or category of agreements between undertakings;
   – any decision or category of decisions by associations of undertakings;
   – any concerted practice or category of concerted practices;

   which contributes to improving the production or distribution of goods or to promoting technical or economic progress, while allowing consumers a fair share of the resulting benefit, and which does not:
   (a) impose on the undertakings concerned restrictions which are not indispensable to the attainment of these objectives;
   (b) afford such undertakings the possibility of eliminating competition in respect of a substantial part of the products in question.

Article 81(1) contains the basic prohibition. The application of Article 81(1) is based on the effects of an agreement. It does not matter what form the collaboration takes provided it has an effect which restricts or distorts competition (to summarise Article 81(1)). Article 81(2) contains the sanction for violation of the prohibition, namely the nullity of the agreement (though, as mentioned below, the perpetrators may also be fined). Article 81(3) sets out the criteria for exemption of an agreement falling within Article 81(1). It is here that the insight that not all collaboration is harmful is overtly reflected. Article 81(3) is more precisely drafted than a simple cost/benefit analysis, but its broad purpose is to permit the pursuit of agreements that, though restrictive of competition, are nevertheless beneficial. In practice, since the application of Article 81(3) solely through individualised decisions would be inefficient, the Commission has long found it prudent to issue Block Exemption Regulations. These govern particular categories of collaboration such as research and development[905] as well as

[905] Reg. 2659/2000, *OJ* 2000 L 304/7.

providing a more general shelter for vertical agreements (between traders at different levels in the distribution chain).[906] The content of the Block Exemptions is drawn from Article 81(3); in relation to particular deals, they constitute the concrete clause-by-clause expression of the abstract requirements of the criteria for exemption in that Article.[907] Strictly, there is no obligation to adhere to a Block Exemption Regulation: firms may draft a novel agreement and seek to show it falls within Article 81(3). However in practical terms, it is common to choose the convenient route of compliance with the Block Exemption where that is available.

At the institutional level within the EU, the administrative application of the prohibition on anticompetitive agreements affecting trade between Member States contained in Article 81 rests with the European Commission, specifically with the Competition Directorate General within the Commission. A supervisory jurisdiction is exercised, initially, by the Court of First Instance, with the possibility of an appeal to the European Court of Justice. The involvement of national bodies is also central to the practical administration of the rules. Both national courts and national competition authorities have responsibilities to apply the EC competition rules.[908]

3.4. **Public and private enforcement of Article 81**

All three paragraphs of Article 81 are susceptible to enforcement by both the Commission and national agencies. This has not always been so. Outside the sphere of Block Exemptions it used to be the case that the Commission enjoyed the exclusive right to decide whether or not to grant an exemption pursuant to Article 81(3). This meant that commercial parties were required to notify practices to the Commission in search of the protection of exemption. This was burdensome for all concerned. It made a bottleneck of the Commission. It was changed by Regulation 1/2003.[909] Exemption is no longer dependent on a Commission decision. Firms do not notify agreements to the Commission in the hope of securing exemption. Instead they make their own assessment of what is allowed and what is not. Mistaken choices are tackled *ex post facto*, by an investigation initiated by the Commission and/or in proceedings before national courts or tribunals who, thanks to Regulation 1/2003, are equipped with the competence to apply Article 81(3) which was denied them for the first 40 years of the lifetime of EC competition law. This system decentralises the application of EC competition law, and increases the number of responsible authorities.

The Commission's main preoccupation in devising the modernised system of decentralised enforcement recently instituted by Regulation 1/2003 has been to improve efficient use of enforcement resources. Exemption is no longer its task alone. It is able to rely on national agencies to judge whether the Article 81(3) criteria are satisfied. This allows the Commission to re-allocate the resources it previously spent on

[906] Reg. 2790/1999, *OJ* 1999 L 336/21.

[907] For a detailed examination, see R. Whish, *Competition Law*, 5th edn. (London, Butterworths 2003) pp. 168-174, Chs. 15 and 16.

[908] See for detail Whish note 907 above, Chs. 7 and 8.

[909] *OJ* 2003 L 1/1.

dealing with notification of (often benign, sometimes trivial) practices by firms in search of exemption. These resources will be re-routed to the front-line of the campaign to root out and eliminate hard-core hidden cartels, which would of course never have been notified anyway under the old system.[910] The Competition Directorate General in the Commission is powerfully equipped to pursue this quest. Powers conferred initially by Regulation 17/62, but now extended by and rooted in Regulation 1/2003, include powers to enter and to search premises and to seize documentation. Failure to co-operate may attract financial penalties which are independent of sanctions that may be imposed should a violation of the substantive rules come to light. The Commission also rules on whether a violation of Article 81 has occurred and is empowered to impose fines on the participants up to a ceiling of 10 per cent of the firm's world wide turnover.[911] The Commission enjoys a considerable discretion in fixing an appropriate fine, although it is directed by Article 23 of Regulation 1/2003 to consider in particular the gravity and duration of the infringement. Guidelines on the Commission's method in setting fines have been issued[912] and they are supported by a 'Leniency Notice',[913] which, by offering partial or total immunity from fines, is designed to encourage 'whistle-blowing' by participants in unlawful anti-competitive practices. Secret cartels are often best destroyed from within. Fines imposed by the Commission have exceeded £ 50 million on occasion and although the principle of proportionality ensures that most fines are much less severe, the availability of such powerful investigative powers combined with potential penalties of such magnitude mean that taking EC competition law lightly is not a practical option for business.

The principle of the direct effect of EC law has always meant that enforcement may be achieved through national courts in addition to activity by the Commission. This is blandly recited in Regulation 1/2003 which provides in Article 6 that 'National courts shall have the power to apply Articles 81 and 82 of the Treaty'. In principle the victim of a cartel incompatible with EC law could initiate proceedings at national level to secure an order that the practice should terminate. As a matter of Community law national courts must effectively protect Community law rights. The landmark ruling in *Francovich* v. *Italian State*[914] established that in appropriate circumstances this may include an obligation to order compensation in the event of loss suffered as a result of breach of EC law. The case concerned liability incurred by the State. In *Courage* v. *Crehan*[915] the European Court applied this principle in the sphere of competition law in a case involving two private parties. It observed that the practical enforcement of Article 81 would be promoted if it were accepted that an individual could claim

---

910 Cf., e.g., H. Gilliams, 'Modernisation: from policy to practice', 28 *EL Rev.* (2003) 451; J.S. Venit, 'Brave new world: The modernization and decentralization of enforcement under Articles 81 and 82 of the EC Treaty', 40 *CML Rev.* (2003) 545.

911 Art. 23 Reg. 1/2003.

912 *OJ* 2006 C 00/00, available via http://ec.europa.eu/comm/competition/antitrust/legislation/fines_en.pdf.

913 *OJ* 2002 C 45/3.

914 Cases C-6, C-9/90, [1991] *ECR* I-5357.

915 Case C-453/99, [2001] *ECR* I-6297.

damages for loss caused to him by a contract or by conduct liable to restrict or distort competition. The desire to maintain effective competition therefore prompted the Court to rule as a matter of EC law in favour of private actions for damages before national courts in the event of infringement of the Treaty competition rules.[916]

An action at national level may be initiated in parallel with a complaint to the Commission.[917] As part of that package the Commission has developed a policy of pursuing complaints only where there is a Community interest in doing so, leaving other matters to be pursued by the complainant at national level. This attempt to organise enforcement priorities and to promote decentralisation has secured judicial support.[918] The Commission is eager to rely ever more heavily on national-level enforcement. To this end, for example, it recently issued a Green Paper to promote discussion of how to facilitate private actions for damages for breach of the competition rules.[919]

Private enforcement of EC competition law before national courts is accordingly a practical feature of the system and although it used to be flawed by the inability of national courts to apply Article 81(3), that obstacle was lifted by Regulation 1/2003. National courts are now expected to apply Article 81 in its entirety. In this sense the ordinary courts of the Member States are also courts responsible for the application of EC competition law.

As explained, Regulation 1/2003 was directed at 'decentralising' enforcement of EC competition law, thereby to improve its effectiveness. Not only national courts but also national competition authorities are intended to form part of this scheme. National competition authorities are also enabled to apply Article 81 in its entirety.

The point of the pattern of enforcement crafted under Regulation 1/2003 is supposed to be that it will be tough to hide anti-competitive practices. There are many pairs of enforcement eyes and many places to challenge unlawful conduct. A solution had to be found for the risk of duplication of effort – or, worse, the risk that an agency in one Member State may go one way in enforcing the law, an agency elsewhere a different way and the Commission in a different direction again. The Commission, aware of these risks, has begun to establish a pattern of co-operation between responsible bodies pursuant to Articles 11-16 contained within Chapter IV of Regulation 1/2003. What is foreseen by these provisions is a 'network' of European competition agencies designed to encourage consistent application of the law within the newly decentralised system. The Commission has duly published a Notice on cooperation within the Network of Competition Authorities.[920] It is also explicitly provided that

---

916 Cf. A. Komninos, 'New prospects for private enforcement of EC competition law', 39 *CML Rev.* (2002) 457; G. Monti, 'Anticompetitive agreements: the innocent party's right to damages', 27 *EL Rev.* (2002) 282; and, more generally, C. Jones, *Private Enforcement of Antitrust Law in the EU, UK and USA* (Oxford University Press 1999).

917 Art. 7(2) Reg. 1/2003 confers standing for these purposes on 'natural or legal persons who can show a legitimate interest'.

918 Case T-24/90, *Automec* v. *Commission*, [1992] *ECR* II-2223.

919 COM (2005) 672.

920 *OJ* 2004 C 101/43.

where the Commission initiates proceedings this shall 'relieve the competition authorities of the Member States of their competence to apply Articles 81 and 82'.[921] So the Commission can, in effect, pull rank.

Moreover it is explicitly – and logically – stated that neither national courts nor competition authorities may take decisions which would run counter to a decision already adopted by the Commission.[922] In fact this makes concrete in a particular case the general consequences that flow from the European Court's celebrated insistence that within the scope of the EC Treaty EC law is supreme over national law and must accordingly be applied by national courts in preference to any conflicting national law.[923] Regulation 1/2003 also makes explicit the answer to the question whether a practice which may affect trade between Member States but which does not restrict competition within the meaning of Article 81(1) or which fulfils the conditions for exemption under Article 81(3) may be subject to prohibition based on national law. It may not.[924] So, in the particular context of competition law, the constitutional relationship between EC law and national law is such that it prevents Member States relying on domestic law to authorise practices which fall foul of Article 81 EC; and, moreover, it disallows stricter national approaches to practices that are within the jurisdictional reach of, but compatible with, Article 81. These constitutional rules have less overt practical significance than one might initially imagine, because in most parts of Europe domestic competition law today chooses to follow the EU's model,[925] not least in order to reduce the costs that would be incurred by business in complying with the layers of diverse regulation. So clashes are rare in practice.[926] But in so far as they occur the constitutional primacy of the EC rules is guaranteed. Therefore understanding the treatment of sale of broadcasting rights under EC law is absolutely vital to any national competition lawyer in Europe.

3.5. Control of the abuse of a dominant position: European Community Monopoly Law

Article 82 (ex 86) acts as the EC monopoly control provision, although the terminology used is prohibition of 'abuse of a dominant position'.

Any abuse by one or more undertakings of a dominant position within the common market or in a substantial part of it shall be prohibited as incompatible with the common market in so far as it may affect trade between Member States. Such abuse may, in particular, consist in:

---

921 Art. 11(6) Reg. 1/2003.

922 Art. 16 Reg. 1/2003.

923 The landmark decision was Case 6/64, *Costa* v. *ENEL*, [1964] *ECR* 585. In the competition law field the best-known decision is Case 14/68, *Walt Wilhelm*, [1969] *ECR* 1, although, as mentioned in the text above, Reg. 1/2003 has now addressed some relevant outstanding issues, Cf. Whish note 907 above, pp. 75-77.

924 Art. 3(2) Reg. 1/2003.

925 Cf. G. Dannecker and O. Jansen, *Competition Law Sanctioning in the European Union* (The Hague, Kluwer Law International 2004).

926 But see further below for different approaches to collective selling of broadcasting rights.

(a) directly or indirectly imposing unfair purchase or selling prices or unfair trading conditions:
(b) limiting production, markets or technical development to the prejudice of consumers;
(c) applying dissimilar conditions to equivalent transactions with other trading parties, thereby placing them at a competitive disadvantage;
(d) making the conclusion of contracts subject to acceptance by the other parties of supplementary obligations which, by their nature or according to commercial usage, have no connection with the subject of such contracts.

Any control system must devote careful attention to the proper definition of a monopoly. Products may be interchangeable. The sole producer of widgets is not in a monopoly in economically meaningful terms if there are available sources of gizmos, a product that is readily interchangeable with widgets. If the widget producer hoists prices, consumers can switch to gizmos. There is no rationale for treating the market as a monopoly enjoyed by the widget producer. More subtly, even where a producer is the single source of widgets, for which there is no other interchangeable product, there is no monopoly if other producers are capable of altering their techniques in order to enter the market for widget production. In such circumstances, consumers have no immediate alternative supply source, but prices should nevertheless be held down to competitive levels because the sole active producer knows that price rises will attract new firms into the market, offering lower prices and consumer choice. Markets should therefore not be assessed as static. They should not be treated as monopolistic where they are in fact 'contestable'. The need to define markets with care applies equally to geography as to product. The only British producer has no monopoly if the British market is open to external competition from sources of supply based in other countries. Monopoly law, like competition law generally, deals with the state of markets, so that where those markets change shape, the application of the law too must adjust.

These issues of market definition are critical in any policy of monopoly control. An underestimation of actual or potential competition will lead to an overestimation of market power. This in turn may prompt an intervention in the name of monopoly control where there is no monopoly. However, if a monopoly is identified, control may be judged appropriate in light of the potential damage caused by the absence of competition, ultimately to the detriment of the consumer.

The chief relevant piece of evidence that a firm has sufficient economic strength to render it subject to the Article 82 obligation not to abuse a dominant position is its ability to act in the market independently of normal competitive pressures. Article 82 applies to firms able to ignore the demands of 'competitors and customers and ultimately of consumers'.[927] In this matter careful economic analysis of the state of the market is vital, lest intervention be over-hasty or, at the other extreme, unduly

[927] E.g., Case 322/81, *Michelin* v. *Commission*, [1983] *ECR* 3461. See also Whish note 907 above, Chs. 1 and 5; W. Bishop and M. Walker, *The Economics of EC Competition Law: Concepts, Application and Measurement*, 2nd edn. (2002), especially Chs. 3 and 4.

reluctant. In practice the Commission's Notice on market definition, published in 1997, is helpful in explaining the factors which the Commission takes into account in determining whether the structure of the market is tainted by dominance and therefore properly subjected to public intervention in the name of controlling abuse of market power.[928] The Notice offers as a guideline a test based on inspection of consumer behaviour. If a 5-10 per cent non-transitory change in the price of a widget does not lead to consumers switching to buying a gizmo instead, then the widget is not regarded as forming part of the same market as the gizmo. They do not compete with each other. So for example in 1998 Football World Cup[929] the Commission applied this test and found that consumers of tickets for the Finals of the Football World Cup did not treat that product as interchangeable with tickets for other football or sports events or other forms of entertainment. This analysis led the Commission to the conclusion that there was a separate market for the supply of World Cup tickets alone. The competition organisers were free of effective competitive constraints on that market. They enjoyed dominant market power and, by applying terms that discriminated on the basis of nationality, they had unlawfully abused it.

Monopoly law is typically structured to tolerate the existence of monopolies while regulating the exercise of monopoly power. Article 82 bears precisely this stamp. Abuse is unlawful, dominance *per se* is not. The firm that is assessed to possess dominant market power is judged to fall under a 'special responsibility'[930] not to abuse that power. The organisers of the 1998 Football World Cup were fined not for holding monopoly power over distribution of tickets, but rather for using that dominant market power to discriminate in favour of purchase by French consumers. Dominant firms may not set unfair prices or act improperly to segregate the market. The most strikingly interventionist feature of Article 82 is that it may be applied in order to require a reluctant dominant firm to respond to consumer demand. In this vein, the Commission found a violation of Article 82 in *ITP, RTE, BBC*.[931] The three television companies printed separate guides to future programmes, using copyright which they held over their own listings to prevent the appearance of a single, integrated publication. A consumer of the information was thus forced to buy three separate guides. The Court of First Instance upheld the Commission finding that an abuse had occurred in *RTE, BBC, ITP* v. *Commission*[932] and the European Court subsequently dismissed appeals by two of the television companies.[933] The firms were obliged to make their listings available to third parties, subject to payment of a reasonable fee. The protection of the consumer interest is explicit in this decision, which imposes consumer choice on unwilling firms. Both courts observed that the companies had abused the economic power they enjoyed under their copyright by unjustifiably preventing the appearance

928 Commission Notice on market definition, *OJ* 1997 C 372/5.

929 Decision 2000/12/EC, *OJ* 2000 L 5/55. For comment, see S. Weatherill, '0033149875354: Fining the Organisers of the 1998 Football World Cup', *ECL Rev.* (2000) 275.

930 Case 322/81, note 927 above.

931 Decision 89/205, *OJ* 1989 L 78/43, 4 *CMLR* (1989) 757.

932 Cases T-69, T-70, T-76/89, [1991] *ECR* II-485, 535, 575.

933 Joined Cases C-241/91P and C-242/91P, *RTE and ITP* v. *Commission*, [1995] *ECR* I-743.

of a new product for which there was potential consumer demand. Admittedly the decision is exceptional. Were Article 82 routinely used to strip exclusivity out of the hands of holders of intellectual property rights, commercial incentives to invest in innovation would be diminished. This perception is plainer from subsequent case law. In *Oscar Bronner GmbH* v. *Mediaprint*[934] Oscar Bronner claimed that Mediaprint was acting in breach of Article 82 by refusing to include Bronner's newspaper in its home-delivery delivery service (for which Bronner was prepared to pay). It failed. It had not been established that it was economically unviable to create a second home-delivery scheme for the distribution of daily newspapers with a circulation comparable to that of the daily newspapers distributed by the existing scheme. Mediaprint was entitled to keep Oscar Bronner out of the distribution network it had itself built up, even if that might diminish the consumer's opportunity of gaining ready access to Bronner's product. The exercise of an exclusive right may, in exceptional circumstances, involve an abuse condemned by Article 82, but that had not occurred in Oscar Bronner. So Article 82 is an important provision but holders of monopoly power are not reduced to the puppets of regulators.[935]

Enforcement of Article 82 lies in the hands of the Commission and national courts and tribunals. Much of the comment above relating to Article 81 may be applied *mutatis mutandis* to Article 82. Violations of Article 82 tend to involve particularly large undertakings, and fines are commonly at the higher end of the scale. Article 82 is directly effective and may consequently be enforced before national courts at the suit of private individuals. And, consistently with the account given above of the constitutional relationship between EC and national law, it is not permitted that national law approve practices that are prohibited by Article 82. EC law must remain supreme over national law. However, a distinction from Article 81 applies here: whereas a practice which may affect trade between Member States but which does not restrict competition within the meaning of Article 81(1) or which fulfils the conditions for exemption under Article 81(3) may not be subject to prohibition based on national law, by contrast it is envisaged that a Member State may take stricter action against unilateral conduct which goes beyond that foreseen by Article 82.[936]

These provisions apply to the sale of rights to broadcast sporting events. The detail is explored more fully below, after a brief portrayal of the economic context.

4. The economic context of sport and broadcasting

Bosman[937] has been widely treated as a far more significant agent for change in sport in recent years than is realistic. Of course the judgment has brought to an end intra-EU/EEA nationality discrimination in club football, and, by generating adjustment of the scope of the transfer system, it has altered the nature of the relationship between

934 Case C-7/97, [1998] *ECR* I-7791.

935 See in similar vein Case C-418/01, *IMS Health*, [2004] *ECR* I-5039.

936 Art. 3(2) Reg. 1/2003.

937 Case C-415/93, note 894 above.

player and club.[938] But the dominating issue in professional sport over the last decade and a half has been the transformation of the broadcasting sector. Sweeping deregulation and doses of privatisation have combined with extraordinarily rapid technological change affecting the delivery of media and audiovisual services to convert broadcasting into a fiercely competitive and volatile sector.[939] It is well known that broadcasting undertakings, and in particular new market entrants seeking to establish awareness of their presence among potential customers, have chased the acquisition of rights to transmit sports events with a zeal that reflects the intense appeal of sports coverage to viewers (and to advertisers). Football and Formula One motor racing sit in a lucrative position at the top of the European tree. Media companies have vigorously pursued the acquisition of contractual rights – most of all, new entrants want exclusive rights to broadcast the most popular events, where, in some cases, consumers have a 'must see!' attitude.[940] In some cases media groups have even tried to secure a controlling interest in sports clubs themselves[941] or, at least, a lesser stake that increases their influence on decisions to sell rights.[942] Simple economics dictates that the explosion in the number of actors on the demand-side of the market combined with the relative difficulty in increasing the supply of truly attractive events leads to vast increases in the prices charged by the sports industry for broadcasting rights. Most recently the English Premier League was reported to have sold the rights to broadcast matches over a three-year period beginning in 2007 for a combined total of £ 1.7 billion. The cost to broadcasters of the three-year deal that stretched from 2004 to 2007 was only just over £ 1 billion.[943] It is plain that rights to broadcast sports events, as a saleable commodity, have become sufficiently lucrative in recent years to transform the whole structure of professional sport as a commercial enterprise. Opportunities to sell branded merchandise, such as club shirts, have provided another explosion of revenue, further enriched by the growing appreciation of the need to

---

[938] See, e.g., J.-P. Dubey, *La libre circulation des sportifs en Europe* (Bern, Staempfli/Brussels, Bruylant 2000).

[939] Relevant documents on the Commission's quest for 'modernisation' of the regulation of the sector may be accessed via http://ec.europa.eu/comm/avpolicy/reg/tvwf/modernisation/index_en.htm.

[940] On inelasticity of demand for major events see Comm. Dec. 2000/400, *Eurovision*, *OJ* 2000 L 151/18 (annulled, but not on the point of market definition, in Cases T-185/00, et al. *M6 and others* v. *Commission*, [2002] *ECR* II-3805); Comm. Dec. 2000/12 1998 *Football World Cup*, *OJ* 2000 L 5/55.

[941] E.g., in 1999 the UK competition authorities blocked a proposed merger between BskyB, a satellite broadcasting company, and Manchester United, a football club, on the basis that it would operate contrary to the public interest; Cm 4305, 1999. Among other factors it was thought that competition in the market for acquisition of broadcasting rights would have been restricted by BskyB's more intimate involvement with the supply-side and that the gulf between rich and poor football clubs would be widened. For comment, see F. Tassano, 'Are Vertical Mergers Harmful?', *ECL Rev.* (1999) 395; D. Harbord and K. Binmore, 'Toeholds, takeovers and football', *ECL Rev.* (2000) 142.

[942] E.g., in the UK the consequence of the blocking of the BskyB/Manchester United merger, *supra* note 941, has been the acquisition by media companies of minority but not insignificant stakes in football clubs; see A. Brown, 'Sneaking in through the back door. Media company interests and dual ownership of clubs', Ch. 8 in S. Hamil, J. Michie, C. Oughton and S. Warby, eds., *Football in the Digital Age: whose game is it anyway* (Edinburgh, Mainstream Publishing 2000).

[943] 'Sky retains Premiership title after £ 1.7 bn TV rights auction', *The Independent*, Saturday 6 May 2006.

protect and exploit image rights. The fan who pays at the gate is no longer the main source of revenue for sports clubs. The alteration of the transfer system post-*Bosman* is frankly a sideshow compared with this cascade of commercialisation.[944]

So the prominence of EC law's intervention in sport in recent years is above all the consequence of the 'commercialisation' of the sector, in particular as a result of its close association with the helter-skelter development of the broadcasting industry. In fact, much of the most economically significant sports-related material that tumbled into the Commission's in-tray in the late 1990s was concerned directly or indirectly with broadcasting. In some respects the Commission's recent preoccupation with sport has been driven by its need to monitor the commercially much more important broadcasting sector, in which it is profoundly anxious to forestall practices that will facilitate existing incumbents' anxiety to impede new entrants. And it is highly plausible that the pace of technological change will increasingly throw up new forms of rapid mass communication, generating intensified fragmentation in the pattern of supply of audiovisual services. This will fuel yet more demand for rights to broadcast sports events, and bring with it yet more challenges for EC competition law.[945]

It is Article 81 that has been the main area of activity. As the case involving ticketing for the 1998 World Cup,[946] the regulation of agents[947] and the ongoing *Oulmers* litigation[948] make clear one could certainly not exclude the possibility that Article 82 could play a role in review of sporting practices in cases of non-substitutable products and services. This is particularly pertinent in circumstances where a sports federation which enjoys monopoly power in making the rules that govern the sport makes decisions with direct commercial implications. This may apply in the case of sale of broadcasting rights. In FIA (Formula One) part of the Commission's objections related to rules that provided a financial disincentive for contracted broadcasters to show motor sports events that competed with Formula One.[949] The Commission was satisfied with a solution according to which the FIA retreated to a regulatory role, thereby releasing broadcasters to make their own commercial choices about which events to show. In principle then, the practices of sports governing bodies that have an impact on the broadcasting sector are subject to control under Article 82 EC where they go beyond what is necessary for the functioning of the sport. Put another way, in

[944] See generally, e.g., S. Morrow, *The People's Game Football, Finance and Society* (Macmillan 2003); Hamil et al., note 942 above; I. Blackshaw and R. Siekmann, eds., *Sports Image Rights in Europe* (Cambridge University Press 2003).

[945] Cf. D. Geradin, 'Access to content by new media platforms: a review of the competition law problems', 30 *EL Rev.* (2005) 68.

[946] Dec. 2000/12, note 929 above.

[947] Cf. Case T-193/02 *Laurent Piau* v. *Commission*, [2005] *ECR* II-000 (Art. 82 applicable in principle but no breach). An appeal against the CFI decision was dismissed in Case C-171/05P, *Laurent Piau* v. *Commission*, judgment of 23 February 2006.

[948] Pending Case C-000/06, referred to the European Court by Tribunal de Commerce de Charleroi in May 2006. For background, see S. Weatherill, 'Is the Pyramid Compatible with EC Law', 3-4 *International Sports Law Journal* (2005) 3.

[949] COMP 35.163, Notice published at *OJ* 2001 C 169/5.

such circumstances a sports regulator becomes (also) a commercial undertaking.[950] However, most of the relevant activity has focused on control of selling of rights pursuant to Article 81.

The selling of broadcasting rights in Europe takes many forms. One of the best known is the 'Eurovision' set of arrangements, which involve the collective buying and sharing of rights and which demonstrate the pressing commercial impetus towards cross-border collaboration in the European market for broadcasting services which has for regulatory, linguistic and cultural reasons long been fragmented along national lines. But how does Article 81 apply? The Eurovision system has been the subject of two favourable exemption Decisions by the Commission, both of which have been duly annulled by the Court of First Instance for want of accurate analysis.[951] This is doubtless rather embarrassing for the Commission, though the saga, which will be examined in depth below, is illuminating and emblematic of the complexity of the calculations at stake. However, as a general observation there is no automatic objection to such arrangements under the competition rules of the EC Treaty. In fact, it is entirely plausible that such arrangements are pro-competitive in so far as they group together operators who would not have the economic power to enter into the relevant transactions on an individual basis. However, the detailed way in which such schemes are structured, in particular in so far as they may damage the position of parties excluded from the arrangements, may generate anti-competitive concerns, and this has generated considerable activity at EC level. There are three issues which dominate the law governing the sale of broadcasting rights. First, exclusivity: what is the legal approach to the sale of rights to a buyer who acquires an exclusive right? Second, collective selling: what is the legal approach to the sale of rights in circumstances where the sellers join together, typically as members of a League operating collectively? Third, collective purchasing: what is the legal approach to the acquisition of rights in circumstances where the purchasers join together? There are also further issues concerning limitations on the disposal of broadcasting rights – by sports federations ('blocking rules') or by the EC regulator ('protected events' legislation). These matters are now examined in turn.

---

[950] Fixing the limits of the notion of the 'undertaking' for the purposes of determining the limits of the application of the Treaty competition rules is an awkward problem that extends far beyond sport: see, e.g., Joined Cases C-264/01, C-306/01, C-354/01 and C-355/01 *AOK*, [2004] *ECR* I-2493; Case C-222/04 *Cassa di Risparmio di Firenze*, judgment of 10 January 2006.

[951] Dec. 93/403 *Eurovision*, *OJ* 1993 L 179/23 granting exemption under (what is now) Art. 81(3) was annulled in Joined Cases T-528/93, T-542/93, T-543/93 and T-546/93 *Métropole Télévision and Others* v. *Commission*, [1996] *ECR* II-649; and the subsequent exemption granted by the Commission in Dec. 2000/400 *Eurovision*, *OJ* 2000 L 151/18 was annulled in Cases T-185/00 et al. *M6 and others* v. *Commission,* [2002] *ECR* II-3805. See further below.

5. Exclusive selling

5.1. The scope of the prohibition

Article 81 prohibits agreements which have as their object or effect the prevention, restriction or distortion of competition within the common market, subject only to the possibility of exemption in accordance with the criteria set out in Article 81(3). So one may suppose that where a seller agrees to supply a buyer with rights to broadcast sports events on an exclusive basis, Article 81 is engaged. After all, the exclusivity of the deal shuts out other would-be competitors who are unable to gain access to the content. And yet this would be to go too far. This approach, taken to its logical extreme, would mean any contract is subject to control under Article 81. This would be to extend the Treaty competition rules beyond their intended purpose. It is instead necessary to focus in a more economically informed manner on what should be the proper reach of Article 81. And simply because a seller grants exclusivity to a buyer of rights does not mean that Article 81(1) is automatically engaged.

One of the Court's most important early examinations of the issue arrived in *Nungesser* v. *Commission.*[952] The case involved the transfer of technical knowledge. The agreement conferred exclusive rights for Germany on Nungesser. The Court observed that a so-called open exclusive licence involved the owner undertaking not to grant other licences in respect of the same territory and not to compete himself with the licensee on that territory. Did this have the effect of preventing or distorting competition within the meaning of (what is now) Article 81 of the Treaty? The Court acknowledged that the grant of exclusive rights for a limited period is capable of providing a further incentive to innovative efforts. To prohibit an exclusive licence would cause the interest of undertakings in licences to fall away, which would be prejudicial to the dissemination of knowledge and techniques in the Community. So the Court concluded that 'the grant of an open exclusive licence, that is to say a licence which does not affect the position of third parties such as parallel importers and licensees for other territories, is not in itself incompatible' with the Treaty. So Article 81(1) does not automatically catch the sale of an exclusive right, even though such may initially appear to be a 'restriction' on trade. In fact it is no more than trade itself! But the implication is clear – this is not an unconditional exclusion of the application of Article 81. And in *Nungesser* the Court made clear that it would not countenance a licence which suppressed parallel trade: that is, one under which the parties to the contract propose, as regards the products and the territory in question, to eliminate all competition from third parties, such as parallel importers or licensees for other territories.

As suggested above, vertical deals generally have pro-competitive implications because they inject fresh competition into the market. They deserve, and typically receive, positive regulatory treatment, albeit not unconditionally so. Exclusivity is commonly a necessary element in a successful vertical deal. The grant of exclusivity is hugely attractive to the buyer, who may thereby be induced to invest much more confidently in the quality of the product – itself a clear consumer benefit.

---

[952] Case 258/78, [1982] *ECR* 2015.

In this vein the case law that has followed the Court's important lead in *Nungesser* is vast and is not usefully set out here at length.[953] *Coditel* should however be mentioned for its sector-specific relevance: it is one of the earliest cases in which the Court set out clearly that an exclusive licence for the distribution of films is not without more to be regarded as a violation of Article 81(1).[954] The important general point is that the Court is prepared to accept that some apparent restrictions on trade are immune from control under Article 81(1), provided that they are (loosely put) necessary as part of a package for securing the conclusion of desirable deals. Put another way, what may appear to be a constraint on competition is unaffected by Article 81 where it is unavoidably required to sustain the functioning of an arrangement which is unobjectionable in the light of EC law.[955] In this sense Article 81 must be interpreted in its true economic context. The Court of First Instance has helpfully captured what is at stake:

> '– it is not necessary to hold, wholly abstractly and without drawing any distinction, that any agreement restricting the freedom of action of one or more of the parties is necessarily caught by the prohibition laid down in Article 81(1) of the Treaty. In assessing the applicability of Article 81(1) to an agreement, account should be taken of the actual conditions in which it functions, in particular the economic context in which the undertakings operate, the products or services covered by the agreement and the actual structure of the market concerned?'[956]

In a similar vein of insistence on a realistic (and not unthinkingly broad) reading of Article 81(1) the Court of First Instance has recently explained that:

> 'The examination required in the light of Article 81(1) EC consists essentially in taking account of the impact of the agreement on existing and potential competition – and the competition situation in the absence of the agreement –, those two factors being intrinsically linked.'[957]

So, adopting this line of analysis, the sale of rights on an exclusive basis does not necessarily fall within the scope of Article 81. It may not be a restriction on competition. One should consider *inter alia* what would happen without the exclusive deal; if the answer is 'no deal at all' then the conclusion may be that far from restricting competition the exclusive deal in fact would have helped to inject fresh competition into the

---

953 See, for exhaustive treatment, Whish, note 907 above, Ch. 16. See also R. Subiotto and T. Graf, 'Analysis of the Principles applicable to the Review of Exclusive Broadcasting Licences under EC Competition Law', 26(4) *World Competition* (2003) 589.

954 Case 262/81, [1982] *ECR* 3381.

955 Cf., e.g., Case C-250/92 *Gottrup Klim* v. *DLB*, [1994] *ECR* I-5641; Cases T-374/94 et al. *European Night Services* v. *Commission*, [1998] *ECR* II-3141. For an account of the nuances in the relevant case law, see Whish, note 907 above pp. 106-131.

956 Case T-112/99, *Métropole télévision (M6), Suez-Lyonnaise des eaux, France Télécom* v. *Télévision française 1 SA (TF1)*, [2001] *ECR* II-2159.

957 Case T-328/03 O2 *(Germany) GmbH* v. *Commission*, judgment of 2 May 2006, Para. 71.

market. But unduly tight or lengthy restrictions will not escape subjection to Article 81 in this way. Nor would the Court countenance a licence which suppressed parallel trade. And an agreement conferring exclusive rights should be assessed in the context of any 'network effects' that are involved if that is relevant in the particular market – that means, an agreement's impact on competition must not be assessed in isolation if the economic reality is that the agreement is not an isolated transaction.[958]

So the sale of rights on an exclusive basis is not of itself subject to condemnation as a violation of Article 81(1). It depends on the precise terms and it depends on the particular market. This then translates into the detailed decision-making. Close attention to relevant market conditions is quite correctly the norm.[959] And this provides the key to determining what restrictions stretch beyond what is necessary for the protection of the seller's interests and what is therefore caught by the prohibition in Article 81(1).

How to apply these principles of law to the sports sector? As already sketched above, technological change and ubiquitous deregulation has combined to ensure that the market to acquire rights to broadcast sports events on an exclusive basis has become hugely commercially significant. Under the pressures imposed by this volatile situation, the Commission's preoccupation with the need to set out a tolerable clear indication of its approach was manifest in an important and influential paper published in 1998 by an official in the Competition Directorate-General, Anne-Marie Wachtmeister. In that paper, crisply entitled Broadcasting of Sports Events and Competition Law,[960] it is stated that 'Exclusivity is an accepted commercial practice in the broadcasting sector'. It maximises profitability for the buyer and is the key to building up a new audience. But 'duration, quantity and upstream and downstream market power need to be examined in order to assess whether the exclusivity seriously restricts competition'. Following the lead of the Commission's 1997 Notice on Market Definition,[961] the paper is significant and valuable for its insistence on the central function of proper market analysis for these purposes. This allows assessment of the foreclosure effect of the exclusive arrangement – it is this that determines whether Article 81(1) bites.

Appreciation of the structure of the demand-side of the market will condition the application of the rules. In *Champions League*[962] the Commission defined the market as one for the acquisition of television broadcasting rights for football events played regularly throughout the year. So international club competitions are part of the same market as national club competitions. Acquisition of exclusive rights to broadcast a

---

[958] Case C-234/89, *Delimitis*, [1991] *ECR* I-935; Case C-306/96 *Javico* et al. v. *Yves St Laurent Parfums*, [1998] *ECR* I-1983; and case C-214/99 *Neste Markkinoiniti Oy*, [2000] *ECR* I-11121.

[959] Although this is not to say that decision-making practice is completely internally consistent: cf. Subiotto and Graf note 953 above; H. Fleming, 'Exclusive Rights to Broadcast Sporting Events in Europe', 20 *ECL Rev.* (1999) 143.

[960] A.-M. Wachtmeister, *Broadcasting of Sports Events and Competition Law, Competition Policy Newsletter* (Brussels, European Commission, number 2 of 1998 (June), available via.http://ec.europa.eu/comm/competition/speeches/index_1998.html).

[961] Note 928 above.

[962] Dec. 2003/778, *OJ* 2003 L 291/25, Para. 79. See further below.

popular football competition may be handled differently from acquisition of rights to broadcast a sport of interest only to a minority of viewers such as weightlifting or bog-snorkeling. The markets are different: so, for example, a 5-year exclusive deal would, it is submitted, be highly unlikely to escape the application of Article 81 in the former case but may conceivably do so in the latter. Seven years of exclusivity was provisionally reckoned by the Commission to be too long in Dutch football.[963] Similarly in *FIA* (*Formula One*)[964] broadcasters had exclusive rights for the contracted territory that were too long in the Commission's estimation. The agreed solution was to cap the length of new free-to-air broadcasting contracts at three years, albeit with exceptional provision for five-year deals where a particular need to encourage investment is present. The fundamental issue is whether broadcasters can access other sources of material that will allow them to compete effectively. The less plausible this is, the more serious the foreclosure effect.

Some very popular events are, in the eyes of consumers, stand-alone events: they will not watch something else as a substitute. In such circumstances the supplier's market power is very strong.[965] An abiding regulatory concern in such circumstances is the damage done to the consumer by lengthy exclusive deals, which, moreover, have the capacity to shut the door on potential new competitors, who, though not in themselves the target of legal protection, are nevertheless important players in shaping a market that will fulfil the objectives of the Treaty. What this means in practice is that exclusive selling of rights to 'premium' sports events attracts close regulatory concern. The longer the grant of exclusivity, the more acute the regulator's scepticism. But this must be balanced against the perception that, as mentioned above, a grant of exclusivity is hugely attractive to the buyer, who may thereby be induced to invest much more confidently in the quality of the product – itself a clear consumer benefit. A balanced assessment of a deal is always vital.

Licensing on a territorial basis is common in the sale of sports rights. However, this is not of itself treated as artificial market-partitioning which would be condemned as a violation of Article 81. Rather it reflects reality. Tastes and preferences do show divergences when one crosses a frontier.[966]

Sub-licensing rights as a mitigation of an exclusive arrangement might be sufficient to win a green light.[967] The issue here is damage to competition: provision for sub-licensing lessens the risk. As ever, the assessment depends on the market conditions. In some circumstances, where the threat of market foreclosure is minimal, sub-licensing obligations will not be required. At the other extreme, where an exclusive deal threatens severe market foreclosure, even sub-licensing might not be enough to

963 IV/36.033, *KNVB/Sport 7*, *OJ* 1996 C 228/4.

964 COMP 35.163, Notice published at *OJ* 2001 C 169/5.

965 On inelasticity of demand for major sports events see Comm. Dec. 2000/400, *Eurovision*, *OJ* 2000 L 151/18 (annulled, but not on the point of market definition, in Cases T-185/00 et al. *M6 and others* v. *Commission*, [2002] *ECR* II-3805); Comm. Dec. 2000/12 1998, *Football World Cup*, *OJ* 2000 L 5/55. In the case of films, cf. Case IV/36.237 *TPS* 1, *OJ* 1999 L 90/6.

966 Cf. Case 262/81, note 954 above.

967 Cf. *Eurovision*, note 951 above, and more fully below in connection with collective purchasing.

haul the arrangement out of the grip of Article 81(1)'s prohibition. Wachtmeister summarises the position in the following terms: 'Sublicensing should not be regarded as a solution to all the competition issues which arise. In most cases it will be necessary and sufficient to deal with, for example, exclusivity which is of an excessive duration or scope'.[968]

The Commission has decided that Pay-TV constitutes a market that is separate from television funded by commercial advertising and public television financed through a combination of feed and advertising.[969] Because sources of funding are different the conditions of competition are different too. For advertising-financed television there is a direct commercial relationship between the supplier of the programme and the advertiser. On Pay-TV the relevant relationship is between supplier and viewer as subscriber. The point is that practices within one sector do not have an impact on the other, once one has concluded the absence of substitutability means that the markets are not the same, and that this therefore conditions the assessment under competition law. That means, more specifically, that anxieties about the acquisition of a high market share in one form of television by firm Z would not be alleviated by the fact that firm X has a high market share in another form of television.

5.2. **Exemption**

If an agreement does not fall within Article 81, it is immune from intervention based on the relevant EC rules. If an agreement does fall within Article 81, this does not mean it is automatically prohibited. Article 81(1)'s prohibition is supplemented by Article 81(3) which gives scope for exemption. So sale of rights to broadcast sports events on an exclusive basis could conceivably fall within Article 81(1), yet secure an exemption pursuant to Article 81(3).

Article 81(3) contains two positive and two negative criteria that must be satisfied by an agreement in order to secure entitlement to exemption. The practice must 'contribute to improving the production or distribution of goods or to promoting technical or economic progress, while allowing consumers a fair share of the resulting benefit'; and it must not 'impose on the undertakings concerned restrictions which are not indispensable to the attainment of these objectives', nor 'afford such undertakings the possibility of eliminating competition in respect of a substantial part of the products in question'.

In the case of sale of rights to broadcast sports events on an exclusive basis, one could readily imagine that the deal could be presented as a contribution to improving the production or distribution of goods or to promoting technical or economic progress because of the incentives created by the grant of exclusivity to penetrate new markets and to improve the quality of the product in order to increase market share – all of which is perfectly conceivably in the interest to consumers. The precise conditions of the deal would need to be scrutinized in order to be satisfied that it is not

968 Note 960 above.

969 Case IV/M469 *MSG Media Service*, *OJ* 1994 L 364/1; COMP/38.287 *Telenor/Canal+* (2004).

marred by restrictions which are not indispensable to the attainment of its objectives. It would also be necessary to ensure that the parties to the deal are not afforded the possibility of eliminating competition in respect of a substantial part of the products in question, which plainly requires careful examination of the structure of the particular market in question. The Commission's Notice on market definition is helpful and influential on this point.[970] In fact, in all cases careful examination of the prevailing market structure is essential in determining the application of not only Article 81(1) but also Article 81(3). Accordingly existing decisions can be no more than illustrative of general approach and in no sense reliable 'precedents'. However, as a general observation, one could readily envisage that sale of rights of an exclusive basis could in appropriate circumstances – in particular where the market remains sufficiently competitive despite the exclusive tie-up – secure an exemption pursuant to Article 81(3) even if it falls within the scope of Article 81(1).

There is little practice to report in the sports sector. On one of the very few occasions on which the Commission has entered these waters a 'comfort letter' expressing a favourable view of conformity with the requirements of Article 81(3) was issued in relation to a five-year exclusive deal to supply rights to broadcast football matches struck between *BBC, BSkyB and the English Football Association.*[971] A significant factor prompting the Commission's readiness to shine a green light was the concern to allow BSkyB, then a fledgling satellite broadcaster, a sturdy platform on which it could develop a durable presence in the market. Absent such special considerations which prompt benign regulatory scrutiny one would not normally expect to see such an extended period of exclusivity permitted in a market for such popular events.

In the Commission's Helsinki Report on Sport, published in 1999,[972] a list of practices declared to be likely to be exempted from the competition rules included the sale of an exclusive right, limited in duration and scope, to broadcast sporting events. Of course, in strict jurisdictional terms, such practices may not even fall within Article 81 in the first place, in which case there is no need to address the question of exemption – and indeed it would be improper to do so.[973] But if exemption is required the Commission has here sketched the conditions for a favourable attitude.

In law the key text is the Block Exemption Regulation on Vertical Restraints. This is Commission Regulation 2790/1999 of 22 December 1999 on the application of Article 81(3) of the Treaty to categories of vertical agreements and concerted practices.[974]

---

[970] Note 928 above.

[971] *OJ* 1993 C 94/6.

[972] COM (1999) 644 and/2. For comment see S. Weatherill, 'The Helsinki Report on Sport', 25 *EL Rev.* (2000) 282.

[973] Cf. Case T-328/03, note 957 above, Paras. 109-116: the CFI was unconvinced by the Commission's preference to treat such matters in the light of Art. 81(3) instead of Art. 81(1) and annulled the Exemption Decision. See similarly Cases T-374/94, note 955 above. Embedded in these detailed disputes is a larger issue about the precise relationship between analysis conducted under Art. 81(1) and under Art. 81(3): for recent exploration, see R. Nazzini, 'Article 81 EC between time present and time past: a normative critique of "restriction of competition" in EU law', 43 *CML Rev.* (2006) 497.

[974] *OJ* 1999 L 336/21.

Regulation 2790/99 is based on an assumption, amplified in its Preamble, that vertical agreements are apt to improve economic efficiency by facilitating better co-ordination between the participating undertakings. They tend to permit the reduction of transaction costs. Nonetheless such efficiency gains must be balanced against anti-competitive effects which may follow from agreed restrictions contained in vertical agreements. The cost-benefit calculation is heavily affected by the market power of the undertakings concerned: to what extent is their commercial freedom of action confined by competition from other suppliers? Article 3 therefore establishes a threshold based on market share.[975] The Regulation withholds the benefit of a block exemption from agreements where the share of the relevant market accounted for by the supplier exceeds 30 per cent. Below that crucial market share threshold of 30 per cent, exemption is permitted to vertical agreements falling within the scope of the Regulation – although even then, below the threshold, certain types of severely anti-competitive restraints are not granted the green light. Article 4 excludes from the scope of exemption vertical agreements which, directly or indirectly, in isolation or in combination with other factors under the control of the parties, have as their object:

(a) the restriction of the buyer's ability to determine its sale price, without prejudice to the possibility of the supplier's imposing a maximum sale price or recommending a sale price, provided that they do not amount to a fixed or minimum sale price as a result of pressure from, or incentives offered by, any of the parties;
(b) the restriction of the territory into which, or of the customers to whom, the buyer may sell the contract goods or services, except:
   - the restriction of active sales into the exclusive territory or to an exclusive customer group reserved to the supplier or allocated by the supplier to another buyer, where such a restriction does not limit sales by the customers of the buyer,
   - the restriction of sales to end users by a buyer operating at the wholesale level of trade,
   - the restriction of sales to unauthorised distributors by the members of a selective distribution system, and
   - the restriction of the buyer's ability to sell components, supplied for the purposes of incorporation, to customers who would use them to manufacture the same type of goods as those produced by the supplier;
(c) the restriction of active or passive sales to end users by members of a selective distribution system operating at the retail level of trade, without prejudice to the possibility of prohibiting a member of the system from operating out of an unauthorised place of establishment;
(d) the restriction of cross-supplies between distributors within a selective distribution system, including between distributors operating at different level of trade;

975 Art. 9 amplifies the method of calculation.

(e) the restriction agreed between a supplier of components and a buyer who incorporates those components, which limits the supplier to selling the components as spare parts to end-users or to repairers or other service providers not entrusted by the buyer with the repair or servicing of its goods.

Article 5 supplements this. Exemption is not available in the case of any of the following obligations contained in vertical agreements:

(a) any direct or indirect non-compete obligation, the duration of which is indefinite or exceeds five years. A non-compete obligation which is tacitly renewable beyond a period of five years is to be deemed to have been concluded for an indefinite duration. However, the time limitation of five years shall not apply where the contract goods or services are sold by the buyer from premises and land owned by the supplier or leased by the supplier from third parties not connected with the buyer, provided that the duration of the non-compete obligation does not exceed the period of occupancy of the premises and land by the buyer;
(b) any direct or indirect obligation causing the buyer, after termination of the agreement, not to manufacture, purchase, sell or resell goods or services, unless such obligation:
   - relates to goods or services which compete with the contract goods or services, and
   - is limited to the premises and land from which the buyer has operated during the contract period, and
   - is indispensable to protect know-how transferred by the supplier to the buyer, and provided that the duration of such non-compete obligation is limited to a period of one year after termination of the agreement; this obligation is without prejudice to the possibility of imposing a restriction which is unlimited in time on the use and disclosure of know-how which has not entered the public domain;
(c) any direct or indirect obligation causing the members of a selective distribution system not to sell the brands of particular competing suppliers.

So there are clauses in such agreements which EC competition law will simply not tolerate. In particular, deep-rooted anxiety about territorial segmentation in the European market is visible in these provisions.

There are several reasons – among them the rules concerning market share stipulated in Article 3 of the Regulation – why it will be abnormal for a contract for sale of rights to broadcast sports events on an exclusive basis to fit within Block Exemption Regulation 2790/1999. This does not mean that such arrangements cannot be exempted. An agreement that falls outwith a Block Exemption falls to be assessed on its own merits in the light of the criteria governing exemption contained in Article 81(3) EC. The approach found in the Block Exemption would, one would suppose, compare with the approach to assessing conformity with Article 81(3) on an individual basis.

After all, Regulation 2790/1999 makes concrete the application of the Article 81(3) criteria to a particular type of deal. But, as mentioned, there is little regulatory practice to report in the sports sector.

There might be an anxiety that the law is not very predictable. There is some truth in this. It has been suggested that a grant of three years' exclusivity should normally be permitted, even if the content is of premium quality.[976] This is probably about right. But markets differ and so therefore do legal assessments. 'Know your regulator' is good advice, although even here the elimination of the Commission's monopoly over the grant of exemption pursuant to Article 81(3) by the 'modernisation' Regulation 1/2003,[977] effective from 1 May 2004, means that proceedings before national courts and competition authorities are also features of the legal map where exemption is at stake.[978]

Ultimately it seems correct to conclude that the law governing exclusivity in the selling of rights to broadcast sports events is an application of general EC competition law. Sport is a little bit special, in the sense that acquisition of exclusive rights to broadcast the top events is doubtless of unusually great commercial importance, but in law it is not so very special. Market analysis is of central importance, as is true in all cases involving the grant of exclusive rights. The next issue for consideration is potentially rather different.

6. Collective selling of rights to broadcast matches

Rights to broadcast sports events are commonly sold on a collective basis. So it is typical, though not at all inevitable, that a sports league will sell rights to broadcast matches en bloc (perhaps on an exclusive basis, perhaps not), rather than leaving individual clubs to sell rights to broadcast individual matches. This is collective selling. It plainly raises questions about the application of the Treaty competition rules. Is this not a case of a restriction of competition? The collective arrangements replace the market that would otherwise exist for purchase of rights from the individual participants in the league. It is, in fact, a horizontal arrangement between operators at the same level of the market – the clubs, suppliers of rights to broadcast matches – and as explained above horizontal agreements are treated with great caution in orthodox thinking about competition policy.

And yet – as also suggested above – horizontal agreements in sport require careful appreciation. The relationship between clubs in a sports league is not precisely the same as the relationship between producers of sausages or makers of tractors. There is a necessary interdependence between clubs in a sports league. Each participant

[976] J. Taylor and A. Lewis, *Sport: Law and Practice* (Butterworths 2002) 414, Para. B2.290.

[977] *OJ* 2003 L 1/1.

[978] As mentioned above, Reg. 1/2003 foresees a pattern of co-operation within the 'network' of European competition agencies designed to encourage consistent application of the law within the newly decentralised system: see Arts. 11-16 Reg. 1/2003 and the Commission Notice on cooperation within the Network of Competition Authorities, *OJ* 2004 C 101/43.

needs the others to survive as credible rivals, against whom to compete. A market's sole producer of sausages or sole maker of tractors enjoys great economic power, for consumers have no choice. A solitary sports team is of no interest to anyone. It needs rivals. So in a sports league the horizontal relationship prevailing between the clubs is not that same as that which one finds in a normal market and the law must take account of that, or else risk mishandling the peculiar economic context in which the sports league operates.

6.1. **The phenomenon of 'interdependence' in sports leagues**

As a general observation, one would expect the peculiar economic interdependence of clubs in a sports league to be reflected in rules which secure a certain equality between clubs designed to keep alive healthy competition. Systems of internal wealth distribution would not exist in 'normal' industries, but in sport they are indispensable, though, of course, fixing the desirable ambit of such intervention requires refined calculation.[979] One would suppose that the establishment of a 'solidarity fund' within a sport, to which wealthier clubs are required to contribute from the proceeds of, *inter alia*, the sale of broadcasting rights and ticket income and on which poorer clubs may draw for financial support, would escape supervision under EC competition law. It would not restrict competition within the meaning of Article 81(1) EC; rather, it is an arrangement that is inherent to the business of professional sport. And there are other matters that are agreed collectively between participants in a sports competition which are, loosely, the rules of the game, rather than restrictions on competition within the meaning of the EC Treaty. Examples include fixing the numbers of players per team[980] and the scheduling of fixtures. A similar approach has been taken to rules forbidding multiple ownership of football clubs.[981] Eliminating any suspicion of match-fixing is indispensable to genuine sporting competition, and therefore any consequent restriction on commercial opportunity to acquire football clubs could not be regarded as a restriction falling within Article 81(1) EC. Such arrangements do not fall within the scope of Article 81 at all.[982] My own view is that this is given a per-

[979] For economic analysis, see, e.g., J. Quirk and R. Fort, *Pay Dirt: the Business of Professional Team Sports* (Princeton University Press 1997); S. Dobson and J. Goddard, *The Economics of Football* (Cambridge University Press 2001); S. Rosen and A. Sanderson, 'Labour Markets in Professional Sports', 111 *The Economic Journal* (2001) F47; L. Buzzacchi, S. Szymanski and T. Valletti, 'Equality of opportunity and equality of outcome: open leagues, closed leagues and competitive balance', 3 *Journal of Industry, Competition and Trade* (2003) 167.

[980] Cf. Cases C-51/96 & C-191/97, *Deliège* v. *Ligue de Judo*, [2000] *ECR* I-2549.

[981] COMP 37.806 *ENIC/UEFA*, IP/02/942, 27 June 2002.

[982] Cf. summary in P. Roth, ed., *Bellamy and Child's European Community Law of Competition*, 5th edn. (Sweet and Maxwell 2000), Para. 4-150; also J.-F. Pons, 'Sports and European Competition Policy' and S. Weatherill 'Sports under EC Competition Law and US Antitrust Law', Ch. 6, pp. 75-92, and Ch. 8, pp. 113-126, respectively in B. Hawk, ed., *International Antitrust Law and Policy: Annual Proceedings of the Fordham Corporate Law Institute for 1999* (Yonkers, New York, Juris Publishing 2000); K. Mortelmans, 'Towards Convergence in the Application of the Rules on Free Movement and on Competition', 38 *CML Rev.* (2001) 613. See also Parrish, note 897 above, especially Ch. 5 on competition law, building an analysis on a separation between 'a territory for sporting autonomy and a territory for legal intervention' (p. 3).

fectly coherent legal explanation by the adoption of the Court's Wouters formula. In *Wouters*[983] the Court stated that in applying Article 81(1) account must be taken of

> 'the overall context in which the decision of the association of undertakings was taken or produces its effects. More particularly, account must be taken of its objectives . [...] It has then to be considered whether the consequential effects restrictive of competition are inherent in the pursuit of those objectives'.

The case had nothing to do with sport. It concerned Dutch rules prohibiting multi-disciplinary partnerships between members of the Bar and accountants. But the statement of principle that the notion of a restriction falling within Article 81(1) must be assessed in context is readily capable of general application. One would in this vein employ *Wouters* to underpin an argument that the overall context in which sports regulation occurs, built around pursuit of a broad objective of fair and balanced competition, produces effects which though apparently restrictive of competition are nonetheless inherent in the pursuit of those objectives. That means that a sports rule which exerts a restrictive effect which goes beyond what is needed to achieve its objectives is subject to control under EC law.[984] But what may appear to be a constraint on competition is unaffected by Article 81 where it is unavoidably required to sustain the functioning of an arrangement which is unobjectionable in the light of EC law.[985]

6.2. **Collective selling – law and practice**

Collective selling of broadcasting rights is different. If rights are available only on a collective basis – so that a purchaser can buy only the output of the whole League – then a market for acquisition of rights belonging to individual clubs has been suppressed. Admittedly the precise nature of the legal right that is at stake is dictated by national law.[986] The Commission has tentatively decided to proceed on the basis that

---

983 Case C-309/99, *J.C.J. Wouters, J.W. Savelbergh, Price Waterhouse Belastingadviseurs BV* v. *Algemene Raad van de Nederlandse Orde van Advocaten*, [2002] *ECR* I-1577.

984 The CFI's failure to appreciate this is the principal source of my criticism of Case T-313/02 *David Meca-Medina and Igor Majcen* v. *Commission*, note 895 above. Para. 55 of the judgment is especially unfortunate.

985 A decision such as Case C-250/92, *Gottrup Klim* v. *DLB*, [1994] *ECR* I-5641 should therefore be seen as running in the same direction as Case C-309/99 *Wouters*, note 983 above. For an account of the nuances in the relevant case law see Whish, note 907 above, pp. 106-131; cf. also Nazzini, note 973 above. A-G Lenz's Opinion in *Bosman* carries traces of this approach, Case C-415/93, note 894 above, especially Paras. 262-276. Also relevant in insisting on a contextual appreciation of the scope of Art. 81(1) is Case C-67/96, *Albany International BV*, [1999] *ECR* I-5751 (especially Paras. 59-60). The Court accepts that a restriction of competition is inherent in collective agreements between organisations representing employers and workers, but is prepared to place the matter beyond the reach of Art. 81(1). The reason lies in the need to interpret the provisions of the EC Treaty as a whole. The social policy objectives pursued by such agreements and recognised by the Treaty would be seriously undermined if Art. 81(1) caught such arrangements.

986 Cf. M. Beloff, T. Kerr and M. Demetriou, *Sports Law* (Oxford, Hart Publishing 1999), pp. 134-6, 153-6; D. Brinckman and E. Vollebregt, 'The Marketing of Sport and its Relation to EC Competition Law', *ECLR* (1998) 281; I. Nitsche, 'Collective Marketing of Broadcasting Rights in Europe', *ECLR* (2000) 208; J. Taylor and A. Lewis, *Sport: Law and Practice* (Butterworths 2002) pp. 404-406. This aspect is also emphasised by Wachtmeister, note 960 above.

there is co-ownership of rights to broadcast matches held by a competition organiser and the clubs.[987] But the essential point is that even though EC law does not determine the ownership or content of such property rights, it does affect the way in which the rights are exercised. This illustrates the constitutional point made earlier that the Treaty competition rules have a much wider sweep than the EC's legislative powers. Sport escapes the latter but it does not escape the former.

Under the collective system, broadcasters are forced to compete for one package, and are unable to deal with individual clubs, among whom there would otherwise be competition in selling.[988] It is admittedly plain that clubs would have nothing to sell unless other clubs agreed to play against them. Fixtures cannot be arranged unilaterally – this is the nature of sport. But once clubs agree to play against each other, the subsequent decision to sell rights to broadcast matches on a collective basis is restrictive of competition. And whereas it may well be convenient for sports leagues, and perhaps even for (some) broadcasters too, to arrange the sale of rights on a collective basis, it is by no means necessary to do so to make the league viable.[989] So collective selling restricts competition within the meaning of Article 81(1) EC, in so far as it has an effect on inter-State trade. It is unlawful unless it is justified.

This preference normally to treat collective selling as a restriction falling within the scope of Article 81(1) is visible in the important Commission policy document published in 1998 under the name of Anne-Marie Wachtmeister and considered above.[990] This document connects the legal analysis to broader policy concerns by adding the warning that '[s]uch restrictions on output could in turn slow down the development of new broadcasting technologies at the national and cross-border levels'. And the subjection of collective selling to Article 81(1) is precisely the line of reasoning formally adopted by the Commission in Champions League, the most important decision dealing with collective selling of television rights (albeit not one that exhausts the interest in the matter for the future).

In July 2001 the Commission sent a statement of objections to UEFA, European football's governing body, complaining that its arrangements for the sale of broadcasting rights to the 'Champions League', the principal (and hugely lucrative) European club football competition, infringe Article 81.[991] UEFA sells rights collectively on behalf of all participating clubs. It has preferred to sell to broadcasters on an exclusive basis, typically under arrangements covering a period of several years. The Commission is careful to observe that it does not object to collective selling of sports rights as such.[992] However, it states that it considers that UEFA's scheme constitutes

[987] Paras. 118-124 of Dec. 2003/778 *Champions League*, *OJ* 2003 L 291/25, considered more fully below.

[988] The collectively sold package may be (and increasingly is) broken down into constituent units – live matches, recorded highlights, etc – but this does not affect the basic issue, which is the suppression of sales by individual clubs. Moreover, rights may be, but need not be, sold exclusively – exclusivity is a matter that is distinct from collectivity.

[989] Cf. M. Cave and R. Crandall, 'Sports Rights and the Broadcast Industry', 111 *The Economic Journal* (2001) F4, especially at F18.

[990] 'Broadcasting of Sports Events and Competition Law', note 960 above.

[991] IP/01/1043, 20 July 2001.

[992] 'Background Note', Memo 01/271, 20 July 2001.

a substantial restriction on competition, not least because of the foreclosure of the market to potential entrants into a sector capable of dynamic evolution, and that although it in principle recognises the need for wealth distribution and solidarity within the sport, the UEFA arrangements go beyond what is necessary to achieve these legitimate ends.

UEFA duly responded by proposing an amended system involving, in short, an 'unbundling' of the package of rights available for purchase. More operators, including internet content providers as well as more traditional public and private broadcasters, will be able to acquire a degree of involvement in the coverage of the Champions League. This is an important point with obvious thematic connections to the general attitude of the Commission to the importance of ensuring that deals have the minimum effect of foreclosing the possibility of entry into developing markets. So much restriction is tolerated – only so much. The Commission expressed itself favourably disposed to this plan for competitive diversification which, it considered, would benefit football fans while also assisting the growth of new technology in the media sector.[993]

The Commission concluded its investigation by adopting a formal Decision in the Champions League case in July 2003.[994] It concluded that the collective selling arrangements restricted competition within the meaning of Article 81(1). This was not a set of arrangements that were indispensable for the organisation of sport. Rather, this was a commercial choice, with significant implications for the competitive process. The Commission accepts that football clubs are bound to co-operate in organising a league, so, for example, agreeing fixtures would not be a 'restriction' on competition, but it concluded that recognition of this special relationship of interdependence does not justify treating an agreement to sell rights to broadcast matches in common as anything other than a restriction which can stand only if exempted according to the orthodox criteria set out in Article 81(3).[995]

So could the deal be exempted pursuant to Article 81(3)? According to the Commission – yes!

The system created a single point of sale for defined 'packages' of matches, which the Commission considered generated efficiencies that were of a particularly significant magnitude as a result of the elimination of the need for broadcasters to deal with many different clubs subject to different ownership structures in different jurisdictions throughout Europe. Transaction costs were kept relatively low. (Identification of this advantage was also a factor in the Commission's earlier favourable treatment of Eurovision[996]). Moreover, the joint selling scheme for the 'Champions League' tightened UEFA's grip on the competition's organisation and allowed the commercially advantageous 'branding' of the competition as an unfragmented European product.

993 IP/02/806, 3 June 2002; *OJ* 2002, C 196/3.

994 Dec. 2003/778, *OJ* 2003 L 291/25.

995 Dec. 2003/778, Paras. 125-131.

996 Note 951 above, and see more fully below on collective purchasing. The CFI annulled the Commission's Decisions in Eurovision but did not take issue with the identification of these economic benefits flowing from the arrangements.

Media operators would share in the advantages and they would be duly transmitted to consumers. The restrictions on competition were judged indispensable to provide these economic gains and competition would not be eliminated in respect of a substantial part of the media rights in question. The Article 81(3) criteria for exemption were satisfied.

In general *Champions League* demonstrates how the detailed application of Article 81 promotes the broader regulatory concerns of the Commission in its handling of the broadcasting sector. Collective selling has clear economic advantages, but it has costs too, specifically in the elimination of competition on the supply-side. At stake is a balance. The length of the contract is carefully scrutinised: the opportunities for new players to enter the market to acquire rights forms part of the assessment, especially where, as here, technological progress holds out the possibility of significant and rapid innovation that should yield benefits to the consumer.[997]

This important Decision was widely expected to assume a high profile in future treatment of rights' selling arrangements within national sports Leagues under both EC and national competition law. For example, Herbert Ungerer, a senior official in the Competition Directorate-General, used it as a blueprint,[998] providing a checklist of relevant factors emerging from the case. The Commission expects to see:

- An open tender;
- An unbundling of the offer to allow more than a single buyer;
- No excessive exclusivity – duration of the order of three years will often be acceptable;
- No automatic renewal, which is often just a disguised extension of the duration of exclusivity.

These are necessary elements in the quest to prevent vertical foreclosure, though Ungerer added that some markets may raise extra concerns where, for example, joint selling leads to excessive concentration in the downstream market. Where the single buyer can acquire the pool of matches, there may be regulatory concerns.

6.3. Champions League – application to collective selling at national level

The expected powerful influence of *Champions League* has become reality.

In fact, in advance of the Commission's Decision in 2003 on UEFA's arrangements for collective selling of rights to broadcast the Champions League, there had been some inquiry into selling by national leagues pursuant to national competition laws.

---

[997] On this aspect of Champions League in particular, see N. Petit, 'The Commission's Contribution to the Emergence of 3G Mobile Communications: an Analysis of Some Decisions in the Field of Competition Law', *ECLR* (2004) 429, 436-437. See subsequently the Commission report of 21 September 2005 into the provision of sports content over third generation mobile networks, available via http://ec.europa.eu/comm/competition/antitrust/others/sector_inquiries/new_media/3g/final_report.pdf.

[998] Speech delivered in Barcelona, 'Commercialising Sport: Understanding the TV Rights Debate', 2 October 2003.

In Germany, collective selling in the Bundesliga was condemned by the competition authorities but subsequently granted statutory approval.[999] The matter was also examined at the some length by the UK's Restrictive Practices Court in its 1999 ruling which found in favour of the legality of collective selling arrangements practised within the English (football) Premier League.[1000] It is, of course, perfectly possible that national competition law shall pursue different objectives from those mandated for EC law by its Treaty, for good or bad reasons. The UK's Premier League case was decided under the antiquated and subsequently repealed Restrictive Trade Practices Act, which had little in common with the effects-based EC system and which was vulnerable to the criticism that it lacked economic nuance.[1001] The UK has subsequently changed the law in order to establish a domestic model that is much more closely aligned with the EC model.[1002] Indeed, as mentioned above,[1003] in most parts of Europe domestic competition law is largely a replica of the EU's model. However, this paper is concerned to examine EC competition law, not domestic competition law. So although approaches taken within the Member States may be of interest for the purpose of comparative reflection, the key practical point focuses on the relationship between EC competition law and national competition law. This was explained above. Within the scope of the EC Treaty EC law is supreme over national law and must accordingly be applied by national courts in preference to any conflicting national law. A national court may not rely on national law to permit a set of arrangements which are contrary to the prohibition contained in Article 81. This, of course, reveals the limits of concessions made to sport under national law, whether in statutory form or through judicial decision-making. A practice that, for example, did not affect trade between Member States would lie outside the scope of Community competition law. It could therefore be dealt with as the State authorities please, even according to assumptions that contradict those underpinning EC competition law. But, as this paper has explained, in practice the EC's jurisdictional reach is broad. It will be relatively uncommon for matters with an economic impact to be of purely local concern. Not only international sports events but also the more popular national competitions provide a particularly good example of products with growing transnational appeal. And once the matter falls within the scope of the EC Treaty, the doctrine of supremacy dictates that EC law must prevail over national law in case of conflict.

So, notwithstanding the statutory approval granted to collective selling in Germany and the judicial green light allowed in the UK pursuant to the Restrictive Trade Practices Act, the Commission duly intervened and asked that the participants notify

[999] S31 Gesetz gegen Wettbewerbsbeschraenkungen as amended with effect from 1 January 1999.

[1000] *Re the supply of services facilitating the broadcasting on television of Premier League football matches*, [1999] UKCLR 258.

[1001] Cf. S. Szymanski, 'Hearts, minds and the Restrictive Practices Court case', Ch. 23 in Hamil, et al. note 942 above; also P. Spink and P. Morris, 'The battle for TV rights in professional football', in A. Caiger and S. Gardiner, eds., *Professional Sport in the EU: Regulation and Re-Regulation* (The Hague, T.M.C. Asser Press 2000) pp. 165-196.

[1002] The Competition Act 1998 is the key statute.

[1003] Cf. note 925 above.

the agreements to it. In law the application of Article 81 cannot be undermined by diverse national regulatory preferences.

In the case of the German Bundesliga commitments to loosen the prevailing form of collective joint selling were made legally binding by a Commission decision. Under the agreed new arrangements collective sale of broadcasting rights is not eliminated but it should occur in a manner which is open, transparent and non-discriminatory. In particular, the Bundesliga has undertaken to offer unbundled packages of rights for a duration not exceeding three seasons. The aim is plainly ensure that all rights are regularly offered to a large number of operators, in order to foster competition and choice in the market. Moreover, clubs are permitted to sell their own branded services to their fans, and there is provision for wider scope to sell new media products and services. This is plainly designed to stimulate innovation.[1004]

The Competition Commissioner Neelie Kroes's summary is illuminating in its depiction of the Commission's aspirations in the application of Article 81 in such circumstances:

> 'This decision benefits both football fans and the game. Fans benefit from new products and greater choice. Leagues and clubs benefit from the increased coverage of their games. Readily available premium content such as top football boosts innovation and growth in the media and information technology sectors. Moreover, open markets and access to content are an essential safeguard against media concentration.'[1005]

Joint selling of rights to broadcast matches in the English Premier League has similarly been handled in the light of Champions League. It was mentioned above that the English Premier League was reported to have sold the rights to broadcast matches over a three-year period beginning in 2007 for a significantly higher sum than that which it had extracted from broadcasting for the preceding three-year period – up from just over £ 1 billion to some £ 1.7 billion.[1006] From the perspective of Article 81, the most striking point concerns the identity of the buyer. Under the 2004-2007 deal (and earlier ones) the purchasing broadcaster was Sky, a subscription channel. Its determination to acquire exclusive rights to show live Premier League matches was firmly in line with the perception that broadcasters desperately need exclusive access to 'premium' sports events in order to build up a profit-making base of subscribers. This, however, contradicted the Commission's general policy preference for wider involvement in downstream markets for the acquisition of rights to broadcast sports events and, more specifically, the Commission declined to accept that such arrangements could continue in England in conformity with Article 81. A statement of objections was issued by the Commission in 2002, declaring the Commission's concern that the arrangements for joint selling restricted competition contrary to Ar-

---

[1004] COMP/C.2/37.214, *OJ* 2005 L 134/46.

[1005] IP/05/62, 19 January 2005.

[1006] 'Sky retains Premiership title after £ 1.7 bn TV rights auction', *The Independent*, Saturday 6 May 2006.

ticle 81. Eventually, after protracted and occasionally acrimonious negotiation,[1007] the Commission announced in March 2006 it had brought its investigation to an end, and that it had accepted binding commitments from the Premier League relating to future selling.[1008]

The core features of the agreed new system involve open and competitive bidding, and the availability of a wider range of rights, including those pertaining not only to television but also to mobile phones and the internet. For live television no fewer than six packages would be put on sale, with no buyer permitted to acquire all six. The anxiety to prevent a monopoly, albeit one limited in time, that will tend to make the market rigid is evident. In fact, Sky has retained its grip on the lion's share of matches, buying four of the six packages while two were acquired by an Irish based broadcaster, Setanta. It remains to be seen whether this system will really improve the consumer's lot.[1009] Do consumers really want choice and price competition in this newly fragmented downstream market or would they prefer, as in the past, to be able to get all available matches from a single source at a single price?

6.4. **Collective selling – unresolved questions about the place of 'solidarity'**

Champions League is an important but not exhaustive treatment of the legal issues at stake in the collective sale of rights to broadcast sports events. An open question is whether collective selling can be justified by reference to the need for organisational solidarity in sport. Consider resources raised from collective selling which are then distributed within the game in a fashion which reflects not only relative success and popularity but also the need to sustain lively competition – 'horizontal solidarity'. Broader still, consider the use of resources raised by collective selling of rights to broadcast professional sport to nurture the 'grass roots' of the game – 'vertical solidarity'. The basic point is that, in accordance with orthodox economic logic, the fact that the collective system of selling has restricted supply will ensure that the price paid by buyers will be higher than the (aggregate) price that would have been paid for rights sold on an individual basis by clubs. The losers are third parties – the purchasing broadcasters. From their perspective the restriction on competition caused by the collective agreement between clubs causes a diminution in choice and an increase in price. And although the system may indeed allow clubs to raise more revenue than would otherwise be possible and may also permit them to make administratively convenient arrangements to distribute that income among clubs and to the grass roots, the fundamental question is just why the sports industry should be permitted to improve its position at the expense of third parties, a category here covering both existing

[1007] E.g., 'Sky and Brussels at war over Premiership rights', *The Observer*, 11 September 2005 (Business Section, p. 1).

[1008] IP/06/356, 22 March 2006.

[1009] For criticism of the Commission's assumptions, see D. Harbord and S. Szymanski, 'Football Trials', *ECLR* (2004) 117; D. Geey and M. James, 'The Premier League-European Commission Broadcasting Negotiations', 4 *ESLJ* (2006), available via http://www2.warwick.ac.uk/fac/soc/law/elj/eslj/issues/volume4/number1.

broadcasters and potential broadcasters kept out of the market by the restrictions imposed on supply.

Champions League does not address this issue. In pursuit of exemption UEFA advanced an argument founded on solidarity.[1010] It argued that raising revenue in this way enabled it to share income for the general benefit of the game. The Commission accepted the desirability of promoting a balance between clubs playing in a League. It also accepted the value in encouraging the supply of young players. These objectives may be realised by cross-subsidy from rich to poor. This, of course, loudly echoes *Bosman*. The Commission expressed itself in favour of the 'financial solidarity' principle, and referred to its endorsement in the Nice Declaration on Sport, examined further below. But – crucially – could such desiderata suffice to outweigh the restrictions on competition inherent in a system of collective selling? In *Champions League* the Commission skipped clear of this point. It did not need to decide it. The criteria for exemption were already made out as a result of acceptance of the contribution of joint selling to delivering efficiencies, suppressing transaction costs and improving the brand.

The issue avoided by the Commission is of great legal and political delicacy. It is one to which the Commission has been gently and cautiously drawing attention for some time. In its Helsinki Report on Sport, published in 1999,[1011] the Commission sketched its view of the role of a 'European Sports Model'. This possesses a number of features, most prominently grouped around the contrasts drawn with North American sports practice.[1012] For the Commission, European sport is characterised by, among other features, the notion of solidarity, stretching from the apex of the sport to the 'grass roots'. This has a direct connection with the question of the permissibility of collective selling of broadcasting rights. The Commission commented in the Helsinki Report that any possible exemption granted to collective selling arrangements would have to take account of the benefits for consumers and the proportionate nature of the restrictions in relation to the end in view. This is orthodox fare under Article 81(3) EC. It observed that it is therefore appropriate 'to examine the extent to which a link can be established between the joint sale of rights and financial solidarity between professional and amateur sport, the objectives of the training of young sportsmen and women and those of promoting sporting activities among the population'. In similar vein Commissioner Monti has cautiously suggested that 'financial solidarity between clubs or between professional and amateur sport' could be a relevant factor in assessing whether to grant an exemption to collective selling.[1013] This is strikingly less

---

[1010] Paras. 164-167 of the Decision, note 994 above.

[1011] COM (1999) 644 and/2. For comment, see S. Weatherill, 'The Helsinki Report on Sport', 25 *EL Rev.* (2000) 282.

[1012] Cf. L. Halgreen, *European Sports Law: a Comparative Analysis of the European and American Models of Sport*, (Copenhagen, Forlaget Thomson 2004); S. Weatherill, 'Resisting the Pressures of Americanization: the influence of European Community Law on the "European Sport Model"', pp. 155-181, in Greenfield and Osborn, note 897 above.

[1013] Speech delivered in Brussels at a conference on 'Governance in Sport', 26 February 2001, available as Speech/01/84 via http://europa.eu.int/comm/sport/key_files/comp/a_comp_en.html.

orthodox as an articulation of the matters that are properly taken into account under Article 81(3). This line of thinking hints intriguingly at use of the power to exempt restrictive practices as a method for insisting that fostering the social and educational function of sport is a condition for giving a green light to collective selling. The cartel is permissible provided its proceeds are shared throughout the sport for the sake of its general health.[1014]

Is this sound as a matter of law? It is submitted that the orthodox approach under Article 81 would be to condemn collective selling as an unlawful restriction on competition between clubs and broadcasters and to expect clubs to sell rights on an individual basis. Only then, once this has occurred, would the issue of sport's need for internal organisational solidarity be properly invoked. It would be permissible and plausibly rational (in the service of an interesting competition) for participant clubs to work together to distribute proceeds from these individual sales in a manner which reflects the collective need to sustain healthy competition. One may also suppose that the clubs have some incentive to water the grass roots of the game with part of the income generated. That is to say, the sports-specific anxiety to sustain an attractively competitive league would be reflected only after third party broadcasters have enjoyed the right to participate in a 'normal' competitive market for sale of rights. The question whether there any room for sport to argue that its special interests should prevail over those of broadcasters – that collective selling should be permitted, despite its detrimental impact on broadcasters, because sport is entitled to maximise its revenues and/or entitled to raise money collectively so as to facilitate its ready internal distribution, is unresolved.

I am sceptical. The approach to be found in the Commission's 2004 guidelines on the application of Article 81(3) is committed to preventing any stretching of the criteria for exemption beyond those found in Article 81(3).[1015] Objectives identified elsewhere in the Treaty may play a part in the appreciation of whether an apparent 'restriction' really constitutes a practice falling within Article 81(1): what may appear to be a constraint on competition is unaffected by Article 81 where, analysed in its proper context, it is required to sustain the functioning of the activity in question.[1016] However, as explained above, collective selling may be appealing to those running a sports league but it is not an indispensable element in its functioning. As a restriction on competition it therefore falls within the scope of Article 81(1). This then places the focus on the possibility of exemption pursuant to Article 81(3). Arguments designed to justify the restriction on competition must be apt to be routed through one of the criteria set out in Article 81(3). The Commission's 2004 Guidelines seem to reveal a

[1014] Support for this approach is expressed by the Committee of the Regions, Opinion on the European Model of Sport, *OJ* 1999 C 374/56, Para. 3.8.

[1015] *OJ* 2004 C 101/97. See especially Para. 42. Cf. also Wachtmeister note 960 above who states that 'Competition law is not the right instrument for achieving cultural or regulatory aims' but also tentatively raises the same possibility in connection with solidarity as Commissioner Monti, note 1013 above.

[1016] Cf. discussion of Case C-309/99, *Wouters*, note 983 above; and also Case C-67/96, *Albany International BV*, note 985 above.

preference to barricade Article 81(3)'s walls against incursion by what may loosely be termed 'non-economic' factors. On this reading, if a practice is incapable of exemption pursuant to Article 81(3) it cannot be saved by reference to horizontal Treaty provisions such as Article 151(4). And if it merits exemption under Article 81(3), it cannot be denied it for neglect of other interests.[1017] This implies that the promotion of cultural objectives which are not congruent with decision-making orthodoxy under Article 81 is possible only under other Treaty provisions. It cannot yet be stated with confidence that the Commission has got this right, although this line of reasoning does bear some resemblance to the Court's attitude to the relevance of the horizontal provisions of the Treaty in the exercise of the competence to harmonise under Article 95. The conditions for recourse to Article 95 must first be satisfied before any question of the impact of the horizontal provisions can arise.[1018] My suspicion is that the defence of collective selling that falls within Article 81(1) by resort to arguments of solidarity (rather than the essentially economic arguments which prevailed in Champions League) is weak. Sport should find other means to promote solidarity which do not impose costs on third party broadcasters and ultimately on consumers, such as internally-arranged sharing of income.

7. Collective Purchasing

The matter of collective purchasing of rights also requires attention. As a general observation there is no automatic objection to such arrangements under the competition rules of the EC Treaty. In fact, it is entirely plausible that such arrangements deserve favourable treatment in so far as they group together operators who would not have the economic power to enter into the relevant transactions on an individual basis; and/or because they permit the economically efficient reduction of transaction costs. However, the detailed way in which such collective purchasing schemes are structured, in particular in so far as they may damage the position of parties excluded from the arrangements, may generate anti-competitive concerns, and this has generated activity at EC level.

One of the best known features of the European broadcasting sector is the 'Eurovision' set of arrangements. These involve both the purchasing and the sale of rights. This system has over time been handled rather awkwardly, even ineptly, by the Commission, but nevertheless it is possible to glean from the decision-making practice and its judicial scrutiny a tolerably clear impression of what is permitted and what it not.

The background to 'Eurovision' is provided by the European Broadcasting Union (EBU), an association of radio and television organizations set up in 1950 and based

[1017] For a summary of the unclear scope of 'non-economic' aspects to Art. 81(3) see Whish, note 907 above, pp. 125-128; see also O. Odudu, *The Boundaries of EC Competition Law: the Scope of Article 81* (Oxford University Press 2006), Ch. 7; E. Psychogiopoulou, 'EC competition law and cultural diversity: the case of the cinema, music and book publishing industries', 30 *EL Rev.* (2005) 838. Neither Commission nor Court has yet offered satisfactory explanation of the impact of Art. 151(4) EC on Art. 81 EC.

[1018] Case C-376/98, *Germany* v. *Parliament and Council*, [2000] *ECR* I-8419, *Tobacco Advertising*.

in Switzerland. It represents its members' interests in the field, including by the promotion of exchanges of radio and television programmes. Reflecting the history of the European broadcasting sector, most members had traditionally been public-sector organizations or bodies entrusted with the operation of a public service and commonly enjoying a monopoly. Times change: so too does technology. In 1984, the EBU for the first time admitted as a member a private television organization, the French company Canal Plus. In general the pattern of the sector began thereafter rapidly to change – to fragment – as ownership structures and regulatory patterns altered and technological development occurred. The tensions involved in these changes are visible in the interventions of the Commission, supervised by the Court of First Instance, into Eurovision.

Through 'Eurovision' itself, which has been in existence since 1954, the EBU organises the exchange of television programmes. Members offer to the other members, on the basis of reciprocity, their news coverage of important events and their coverage of current affairs and of sports and cultural events taking place in their countries. This, of course, is generally helpful in enabling all members to provide a high quality service in the relevant fields to their own viewers. And, as part of this scheme, members of the EBU are able to participate in a system of joint purchasing of television rights to international sports events, also embracing the sharing of rights once acquired.

Originally the benefit of the services of the EBU and Eurovision was exclusively reserved to their members. However, from 1988 the governing statutes envisaged that contractual access to Eurovision could be granted to associate members and non-members of the EBU.

The Commission's investigation into the Eurovision system began in the late 1980s, as the wave of change broke over the broadcasting sector. It was prompted in particular by complaints by third parties about their inability to extract sub-licences to broadcast material acquired by the collective action of the members of the 'Eurovision' scheme.

In 1993 the Commission issued its first Decision.[1019] It found that the joint purchasing arrangements struck between the members of EBU restricted competition within the meaning of Article 81(1). However, it concluded that the system yielded significant economic benefits. This was sufficient to persuade the Commission that an exemption pursuant to (what is now) Article 81(3) should be granted. Its duration was five years. The Commission's green light was conditional upon the acceptance of sub-licensing of rights to third party non-members as an element in the Eurovision scheme.

This, however, was an outcome that did not satisfy some third parties. The matter was brought before the Court of First Instance in search of annulment of the Commission Decision. The applicants before the CFI had, in differing ways and for differing reasons, found themselves unable to gain the level of access to the EBU's services that they desired. Their application was successful.[1020] The Court of First Instance

[1019] Dec. 93/403 *Eurovision*, *OJ* 1993 L 179/23.

[1020] Joined Cases T-528/93, T-542/93, T-543/93 and T-546/93, *Métropole Télévision and Others* v. *Commission*, [1996] *ECR* II-649.

focused in particular on the EBU's exclusion of purely commercial channels. In its Decision the Commission had found this to be a distortion of competition within the meaning of Article 81(1) which was nonetheless indispensable within the meaning of Article 81(3). But the Court considered the Commission had failed adequately to demonstrate that the EBU membership rules were objective and sufficiently clear so as to enable them to be applied uniformly and in a non-discriminatory manner. Therefore, in the absence of such analysis, the rules, as restrictions on competition, could not be deemed 'indispensable'.

The EBU reconsidered its position and prepared a revised set of rules. The Commission subsequently adopted a further exemption Decision in favour of Eurovision.[1021] It found a restriction of competition between members who would, without the collective purchasing scheme, have competed against each other to acquire rights, but it found that collective purchasing reduced the transaction costs that would have been associated with a plethora of separate negotiations. In general, the arrangements ensured that more sporting events were broadcast by a larger number of broadcasters. The Article 81(3) criteria were met.

This favourable treatment was based on significantly adjusted arrangements making the jointly purchased rights more readily available to non-members, including pay-TV operators.[1022] As the Commission recognises in its Decision this is a matter of huge commercial sensitivity given the surrounding environment of escalating prices of rights to broadcast major sports events.[1023] And accordingly the temptation to proceed once again to litigation was irresistible. The matter was once again the subject of judicial review initiated by broadcasters aggrieved at their position 'on the outside' of the EBU. Once again the Commission Decision was declared unlawful.[1024] The Court of First Instance objected to the rules governing the sub-licensing scheme and also to the thoroughly unhelpful way in which they were applied in practice. The Commission had contended that the sub-licensing scheme guaranteed that live transmission rights which were not used by EBU members would be made available to their non-member competitors. The CFI examined the system and it did not agree. This meant that the Commission's view that the sub-licensing scheme prevented the elimination of competition in the relevant market was not well-founded and that therefore the Commission had made a manifest error of assessment in the application of Article 81(3).

The background to this litigation is, of course, provided by the increasing ferocity of competition in the market for rights to broadcast major sporting events. What conclusions should be drawn from this saga about the expectations of EC law in the shaping of collective purchasing arrangements in the broadcasting sector? First

1021 Dec. 2000/400, *Eurovision*, *OJ* 2000 L 151/18.

1022 See Paras. 28-37, 106-110 of Dec. 2000/400, note 994 above.

1023 Paras. 50-58 of Dec. 2000/400, note 994 above.

1024 Cases T-185/00 et al. *M6 and others* v. *Commission*, [2002] *ECR* II-3805. For comment see A. Herold, 'Rules governing the acquisition by third parties of television rights for sporting events under Eurovision in breach of the European competition law', 7 *International Journal of Communications Law and Policy* (Winter 2002/2003) 1.

of all, accurate economic analysis is vital. It must be demonstrated that there is a violation of Article 81(1). This is not inevitable.[1025] In particular where individual operators would lack the necessary economic strength to enter relevant markets to purchase rights, a collective system may be viewed as a means to promote new competition and therefore, examined in its proper economic context, not as a restriction on trade within the meaning of Article 81(1) at all. Market analysis in the *Eurovision* cases revealed, however, that a sufficient degree of restriction of competition was the product of the collective purchasing scheme and that therefore in that case Article 81(1) was triggered. Even if a deal is caught by Article 81(1), it may be eligible for exemption pursuant to Article 81(3). This requires compliance with the four criteria, two positive, two negative, contained therein. It is perfectly conceivable that such criteria could be satisfied by a collective purchasing agreement – just as in *Champions League* the Commission came to the conclusion that collective selling generated economic benefits to the sellers in the shape of improved branding of the product and reduction of transaction costs.[1026] Collective purchasing, as a general observation, goes some way to tackling the costs generated by the fragmentation along national lines of much of the European broadcasting sector. As the Commission accepted in *Eurovision* – and on this point it was not contradicted by the CFI – collective purchasing is capable of reducing transaction costs by eliminating the need for multiple individual negotiation and it can promote the wider distribution of programmes. But any restriction on competition must be carefully scrutinised – in the terms of Article 81(3) it must be 'indispensable' to achieve the claimed economic benefits of the practice. The principal lessons of the Commission's travails in *Eurovision* involve understanding the importance of paying attention to the impact on third parties of the arrangements under scrutiny. It is here that objectionable anti-competitive features are most likely to arise. And the CFI twice refused to accept the Commission's view that as much as possible had been done to alleviate the damaging effect of the Eurovision scheme on the competitive position of non-members. So the Decision granting an Article 81(3) exemption was not upheld.

There is no necessary objection to membership rules per se. But they must be objective and sufficiently clear so as to enable them to be applied uniformly and in a non-discriminatory manner. Rules which do not meet these criteria cannot be treated as 'indispensable' and so cannot be exempted under Article 81(3). Moreover, sub-licensing arrangements are clearly treated as a necessary element in any possible exemption under Article 81(3), given the market power exercised by the members of the EBU acting collectively through Eurovision. The CFI insists that the rules governing sub-licensing as well as their practical management should form part of the examination into whether the Article 81(3) criteria are satisfied.

1025 See in particular Para. 64 of the judgment in Case T-185/00 et al., note 1024 above, citing the *seminal Case* 262/81, note 954 above.

1026 Dec. 2003/778, note 994 above.

8. Blocking rules

A Commission Decision of April 2001 addressed UEFA's rules permitting national football associations to prohibit the broadcasting of football matches within their territory during a two-and-a-half hour period on a Saturday or Sunday corresponding to the normal time at which fixtures are scheduled in the relevant country. This, one would suppose, impedes the commercial freedom of broadcasters to conclude deals to show matches at designated 'blocked' times, but it serves the end of sustaining a lively atmosphere in stadia by encouraging spectators to attend matches 'live' rather than merely fester in front of a television set. The Commission concluded that the rules fell outwith the scope of application of Article 81. In the Press Release concerning this matter Mr Monti is quoted as observing that the decision 'reflects the Commission's respect of the specific characteristics of sport and of its cultural and social function'.[1027] However, the text of the formal Decision published by the Commission reveals a different, narrower story.[1028] The Decision is in fact based on routine market analysis. The Commission finds that the UEFA rules do not appreciably restrict competition within the meaning of Article 81(1).[1029] It explicitly states that it therefore need not assess the extent to which the televising of football exerts a negative impact on attendance at matches.[1030] The Decision is, admittedly, built on appreciation of the specific nature of the market for rights to broadcast football matches, just as all competition decisions take proper account of applicable market conditions, but it is to go too far to make Mr Monti's breezy claim that it reflects the Commission's respect for sport's 'cultural and social function'. It would be more accurate to state that market analysis conducted under Article 81 has led to a conclusion which does not assert a basis for interference with the autonomy of football governing bodies to choose to 'block' the broadcasting of matches. It is not the Commission's business to embark on an assessment of sport's cultural and social function, except in so far as it may be relevant under Article 81(3), and, even though the criteria governing exemption are not necessarily wholly incapable of influence by what may be loosely termed 'cultural factors', as discussed above, such broader considerations are scrupulously excluded from the formal Decision on UEFA's blocking rules, which is confined to Article 81(1) alone.

9. Burdens imposed because of the distinctive nature of sporting competition: 'protected' or 'listed' events

Legislation governing 'protected' or 'listed' events is popularly supposed to have been introduced in order to ensure that particularly high-profile sporting fixtures are

[1027] IP/01/583, 20 April 2001.

[1028] Comm. Dec. 2001/478, *OJ* 2001 L 171/12.

[1029] Paras. 49-61 of the Decision. The Commission will monitor change in market structure, particularly in the wake of the 'Internet revolution', Para. 56.

[1030] Para. 59.

available to the general public without the need to pay a subscription to the broadcaster, but, at least in its EC dimension, this is in fact a misleadingly inflated view of the degree of legal intervention that exists. The relevant legislation at EC level is a good deal less interventionist, and a good deal more ambiguous, than the common misperception holds.

9.1. 'Listed events' under the 'Television without Frontiers' Directive

The so-called 'Television without Frontiers' Directive, Directive 89/552, was amended by Directive 97/36,[1031] and it is the latter Directive that provides the source of the relevant provisions. The Directives are based on the Treaty provisions governing co-ordination of laws in the establishment and services sectors[1032] and are accordingly measures of market integration, operative in a sector technologically well suited to transfrontier growth. Because several Member States have regimes which, in differing ways, involve some degree of intervention into the manner of broadcasting major sporting events, it was decided that some attempt be made to supply an EC-level framework for resolving the collision between such regimes and the quest for an integrated European market. This, of course, is a classic example of the endemic tendency of a policy of trade integration to spill over into other sectors. Because States have taken a stance on patterns of intervention designed to limit market freedoms, the EC, devising a regulatory framework for a broader European market, must respond by making its own choices about the content of the regime that shall be adopted at European level. So co-ordination and harmonisation is much more than a technical process of fixing a framework of common rules for a common market; instead it involves inevitable and sensitive selections of regulatory style and philosophy. So, in this instance, questions of sport and culture, in respect of which the EC lacks any general legislative competence, are nevertheless drawn on to its legislative agenda as a result of the wide-ranging functional impact of the programme of harmonisation and co-ordination of laws. In this vein, recital 25 of Directive 97/36 observes that Article 128(4) EC (now Article 151(4)) 'requires the Community to take cultural aspects into account in its action under other provisions of the Treaty'. Harmonisation is permissible only provided a sufficient contribution to market-building is demonstrated, but in shaping the content of the harmonised regime it is perfectly proper for cultural policy to be taken into account, just as consumer policy and public health policy affect the shaping of market-integrative rules at EC level.[1033]

So, offering a fine illustration of these regulatory ripples, the opportunity was taken on the amendment effected by Directive 97/36 to include new provisions on

[1031] *OJ* 1989 L 298/23, *OJ* 1997 L 202/60 respectively. See generally on this regime C.A. Jones, 'Television without Frontiers', 19 *YEL* (1999-2000) 299.

[1032] Ars. 47(2) and 55 (ex 57(2) and 66) EC.

[1033] Arts. 153(2), 152(1) EC. Cf. Case C-376/98 note 1018 above; for discussion of the impact of this case on cultural aspects of harmonised laws see I. Katsirea, 'Why the European broadcasting quota should be abolished', 28 *EL Rev.* (2003) 190.

'protected events' in the EC regime.[1034] But, as one may have anticipated, given the sensitivity of the issues at stake, there is no question of the matter being dealt with exhaustively at EC level. In fact, the EC rules governing protected events are a very strange beast indeed. Of particular relevance to the current paper, they illustrate the point that the EC's policy on sport is extraordinarily ill-defined to the point of challenging the very validity of the claim to constitute a 'policy' at all.

The relevant provision is Article 1(4) of Directive 97/36, which among other things provides for the insertion of a new Article 3a into Directive 89/552. Article 3a provides that

> 'Each Member State may take measures in accordance with Community law to ensure that broadcasters under its jurisdiction do not broadcast on an exclusive basis events which are regarded by that Member State as being of major importance for society in such a way as to deprive a substantial proportion of the public in that Member State of the possibility of following such events via live coverage or deferred coverage on free television.'

The underlying anxiety is plainly that broadcasters to whom a fee must be paid by viewers to secure access to transmissions will acquire exclusive rights to major events with the consequence that the general population will be deprived of the opportunity to view such events for free,[1035] but the word 'may', the fourth word in this extract, is vital to grasping the nature of the regime. There is no obligation imposed on Member States. The Commission has properly emphasised that this is a 'voluntary provision'.[1036] The issue is national choices, not EC requirements. Article 3a of Directive 89/552 does not define more precisely the circumstances in which the power conferred may or should be exercised. Having introduced the notion of events of 'major importance for society', the provision proceeds simply to require a Member State which choose to exercise this power to draw up a list of events which it considers to fall into this category, and then to notify the Commission of measures taken or to be taken to protect them from falling into the hands of broadcasters who will act in such a way as to deprive a substantial proportion of the public in that Member State of the possibility of following such event on free television. These measures are to be scrutinised by the Commission and published in the Official Journal. A complementary transnational dimension is added by Article 3a(3) of Directive 89/552. This provides that Member States shall ensure that broadcasters under their jurisdiction do not exercise the exclusive rights purchased by those broadcasters in such a way that a substantial proportion of the public in another Member State is deprived of the possibility of following events which are designated by that other Member State as carrying major importance for society. This is, of course, necessarily a mandatory

[1034] See R. Craufurd Smith and B. Boettcher, 'Football and Fundamental Rights: Regulating Access to Major Sporting Events on Television', 8 *European Public Law* (2002) 107.

[1035] 'Free' television for these purposes means 'broadcasting on a channel, either public or commercial, of programmes which are accessible to the public without payment in addition to the modes of funding of broadcasting that are widely prevailing in each Member State (such as licence fee and/or the basic tier subscription fee to a cable network', Recital 22.

[1036] Third Report on the application of Directive 89/552, COM (2001) 9, p. 8.

rather than voluntary provision as far as Member State authorities are concerned; were it otherwise, one State's choices would be readily undermined by another's lack of concern in so far as broadcasters established in the latter State had acquired rights 'listed' by the former State.

The event of 'major importance for society' is a category which is amplified in the Preamble,[1037] but which is nevertheless inevitably subjectively defined. As one would have readily predicted, State practice varies. The majority of States have designated no events as carrying major importance for society pursuant to Directive 89/552 (as amended). Those that have exercised the available power have made very different choices.[1038] It comes as no surprise that no Member State apart from the United Kingdom reckons the televising of Test match cricket to fall within the preferred scope of protection; nor that Italy alone lists the San Remo music festival. But there is wide variation even in connection with events which one would suppose would be of more-or-less equally powerful interest State by State. The Finals of Football's World Cup, staged every four years and won by a European country as often as not, are 'listed' in their entirety in the United Kingdom, whereas as far as Germany, Austria and Ireland are concerned only the Final, Semi-Finals, Opening Match and matches of the respective national team are included on the list, while Italy lists only the Final and matches of the Italian national team. Moreover, the lists change. Denmark notified the Commission of its list in 1999 but withdrew this with effect from the beginning of 2002 and it now operates no list of the type recognised by Directive 89/552.[1039]

As yet there has been little relevant litigation. In *Infront WM AG* v. *Commission* the applicant (formerly the Kirch Media Group) objected to the UK's list, which affected rights which it owned and which consequently affected its commercial position.[1040] However, the decision of the CFI casts no light on the regime generally. Infront challenged the letter sent by the Commission to the British authorities advising them that it had no objections to the notified measures. The CFI concluded that this letter was susceptible to judicial review because, by triggering the mechanism of mutual recognition foreseen by the Directive, it was endowed with binding legal effect and it also found the applicant to possess the necessary standing for the purposes of Article 230(4).[1041] The CFI then annulled the decision for procedural reasons. The College of Commissioners had not been consulted. The ruling demonstrates that access to the

---

1037 They should be 'outstanding events which are of interest to the general public in the European Union or in a given Member State or in an important component part of a given member State ...', Recital 21; Recital 18 refers non-exhaustively to the 'Olympic games, the football World Cup and European football championship'.

1038 The most recent consolidated list of measures may be found at *OJ* 2003 C 183/03, and includes measures notified by Italy, Germany, Austria, Ireland and the United Kingdom. This is, however, out-of-date. The Commission's Fifth Report on the application of the Directive reveals that in 2004 Belgium notified measures and in 2005 France did so: COM (2006) 49, Para. 3.3. For a full list, see http://ec.europa.eu/comm/avpolicy/reg/tvwf/implementation/events_list/index_en.htm.

1039 The list was an 'utter failure', Halgreen, note 1012 above, p. 131.

1040 Case T-33/01, judgment of 15 December 2005.

1041 The Commission has brought an appeal before the Court on this point: Pending Case C-125/06P *Commission* v. *Infront WM*, *OJ* 2006 C 108/7.

Community courts for disgruntled rights-holders is possible, but the decision reveals nothing about more profound questions concerning the willingness of the Community judicature to inquire into the Commission's role under Article 3a of the Directive and/ or the choices made by Member States. However, the Directive appears to establish a relatively loose set of discretionary rules. One would not imagine a court would lightly interfere with decisions taken within its framework, even though it is plain that the decisions in question are likely to have considerable commercial impact.

9.2. The nature and purpose of the régime

In commercial terms this type of legislation, introduced at national level and reflected in the EC's Directive, has the potential to be very significant indeed. Technological growth and, in particular, the rise of privately-owned broadcasting companies, a sector that has flourished since deregulation became fashionable beginning in the late 1980s, has injected a great many more players on to the demand-side of the market and, with supply of major sporting events incapable of parallel increase because of consumer attachment to the existing small pool of established major events,[1042] the cost of acquiring rights to major sporting events has accordingly increased dramatically in recent years. Indeed, as addressed earlier, it is well known that broadcasters seeking to enter new markets regard acquisition of exclusive sports rights as the pre-eminent method for rapid acquisition of a viable market share. This characteristic has further contributed to the race upwards in pricing. Traditional 'free' public broadcasters now find themselves operating in a much less cosy competitive climate than that which prevailed twenty years ago. In so far as this legislation governing 'protected events' enshrines a priority for such broadcasters it may be thought beneficial to consumers for it improves the chances of popular events being available for free viewing. From the perspective of the sports industry, by contrast, direct or indirect interference with the right to sell to the highest bidder is commercially alarming, and may call into question the opportunity fully to exploit an extraordinarily lucrative market. And this may diminish the level of investment in the quality of the product, which is likely to be to the detriment of consumers. So this is a complex situation. At the very least, one cannot avoid the conclusion that rules requiring the availability of sports events on 'free' television do not offer the consumer a free lunch.

An appetite for litigation is one likely outcome of this commercially sensitive yet loosely defined set of rules,[1043] but at a deeper policy level it is far from clear quite why this type of regime exists. Some – a minority[1044] – of Member States have chosen to adopt relevant legislation, and this, in Directive 89/552 (as amended), has then become the subject of 're-regulation' undertaken by the EC as part of the pro-

[1042] This is discussed above: on inelasticity of demand for major events see Comm. Dec. 2000/400 *Eurovision*, *OJ* 2000 L 151/18 (annulled, but not on the point of market definition, in Cases T-185/00 et al. *M6 and others* v. *Commission*, [2002] *ECR* II-3805); Comm. Dec. 2000/12 1998 *Football World Cup*, *OJ* 2000 L 5/55.

[1043] Case T-33/01, note 1040 above.

[1044] Note 1038 above.

cess of building an integrated EU-wide broadcasting market. But why protect sports events in this way? A troublingly unbalanced 1996 Resolution of the European Parliament considers 'it essential for all spectators to have a right of access to major sports events, just as they have a right to information' while paying no attention to the costs that right-holders incur as a result of the legal safeguarding of such a 'right'.[1045] Recital 18 to Directive 97/36 refers to a 'right to information' and to ensuring 'wide access by the public to television coverage' of events of major importance to society. Article 10 of the European Convention for the Protection of Human Rights and Fundamental Freedoms provides that the right to freedom of expression shall include the right to 'receive and impart information without interference by public authorities and regardless of frontiers'. This formulation is now also to be found in Article 11 of the EU Charter of Fundamental Rights of the European Union, proclaimed at Nice in December 2000,[1046] which is to be interpreted to conform with the Convention.[1047] True, Article 10 of the ECHR adds that States are not to be prevented from requiring the licensing of broadcasting or television enterprises, a proviso absent from Article 11 of the EU Charter. But in any event this seems to bear no relevance to the specific issue of 'protected' or 'listed' events.

Information is power and the discourse of fundamental rights is deservedly prominent in analysis of law and policy in the broadcasting sector.[1048] The promotion of pluralism in media markets has an immediate connection with sustaining the vibrancy of our democracies.[1049] Nevertheless it is a strenuous effort to devise an intellectually satisfying and rational basis for this particular piece of legislation. The Commission's April 2003 Discussion Paper[1050] understandably attempts no such thing, confining itself to seeking views on whether the procedures governing protected events should be more tightly defined. Several responses to the Discussion Paper advocated a clarification of the purpose of the system but most – again, understandably – exhibited a primary interest simply to defend their own interests. For example, both the BBC and ITV praised the regime, while by contrast UEFA criticised the legislative favouritism of one type of broadcaster over another.

What seems to be at stake here is some notion of citizen entitlements. But can one truly consider that the watching of doubtless exciting and interesting sports events properly engages the language of fundamental rights? Such a proposition exceeds what is currently recognised as the scope of the right to information under the law of the European Convention.[1051] One may go so far as to condemn such an approach

1045 Resolution on the broadcasting of sports events, *OJ* 1996 C 166/109.

1046 *OJ* 2000 C 364/1.

1047 Art. 52 EU Charter.

1048 See generally, R. Craufurd Smith, *Broadcasting Law and Fundamental Rights* (Clarendon Press, Oxford 1997).

1049 See, e.g., with particular emphasis on the EU context, M. Arino, 'Competition Law and Pluralism in European Digital Broadcasting: Addressing the Gaps', 54 *Communications and Strategies* (2004) 97.

1050 Available via http://ec.europa.eu/comm/avpolicy/reg/tvwf/modernisation/consultation_2003/index_en.htm.

1051 Cf. more fully Craufurd Smith and Boettcher, note 1034 above.

as apt to demean the quality and dignity of rights discourse. And, moreover, the card of fundamental rights is a trump, but not one held by only one player. The rights to freedom of expression of broadcasters are in no small measure damaged by these interventionist provisions, whereas both the EC legal order and that of the European Convention recognise that commercial parties fall within the personal scope of this regime, albeit that their rights are not absolute.[1052]

The obscurity of the regime's objectives is matched by its textual lack of lucidity. Given this huge commercially sensitive issue, it is astonishing that the provisions of the EC Directive are so imprecise, yet that imprecision is testimony to the awkward issues that arise when sport as commerce and sport as hot topic in society merge and, in the melee, public and private actors scramble to promote their particular interests. Once a State draws up the list of events that it perceives as being of 'major importance for society' it is entitled to take measures to ensure that broadcasters do not broadcast those events on an exclusive basis 'in such a way as to deprive a substantial proportion of the public in that Member State of the possibility of following such events via live coverage or deferred coverage on free television'. That may be interpreted to cover intervention that requires coverage on free television. That would plainly severely reduce the price that any other broadcaster would be willing to pay; exclusivity is worth a large premium to the commercial broadcaster eager to increase its portfolio of subscribers and interested advertisers. This would also involve a profound interference with the exercise of the property rights of sporting bodies.[1053] But is the Directive properly interpreted in this way? Might it be that the public broadcaster is guaranteed access only to the bidding process on a non-discriminatory and transparent basis, so that there is a 'possibility' for the general population to have the opportunity of viewing the event on free television, but that it has no legal basis for complaint if exclusive rights are ultimately awarded to a broadcaster with a smaller audience and access to the services of which is dependent on payment by viewers? That would not simply be a question of price, for a free broadcaster may be able to promise a larger audience which may be more attractive to a sporting body aiming to enhance its long-term popularity and to satisfy its sponsors than the short-term profit represented by a higher fee paid by a broadcaster whose services are not available free of charge to the viewer. But, admittedly, according to this interpretation, economic gain not access of the general population would be the key factor in the awarding process.

There is no ruling of the European Court on this point. In *R* v. *Independent Television Commission, ex parte TV Danmark 1 Ltd.*[1054] the English House of Lords concluded that a Member State in which a broadcaster is based is required to prevent

---

1052 E.g., Case C-260/89 *ERT* v. *Dimotiki*, [1991] *ECR* I-2925; Case C-368/95 *Vereinigte Familiapress Zeitungs- und vertriebs GmbH* v. *Heinrich Bauer Verlag*, [1997] *ECR* I-3689; *Informationsverein Lentia and others* v. *Austria* A No 276 (1993). See D. Wyatt, 'Freedom of Expression in the EU Legal Order and in EU Relations with third countries' in J. Beatson and Y. Cripps, eds., *Freedom of Information: Essays in Honour of DGT Williams* (Oxford, Clarendon Press 2000); Craufurd Smith, note 1048 above, especially Ch. 7.

1053 Cf. Jones, note 1031 above 326-336.

1054 1 *WLR* (2001) 1604.

the exercise by that broadcaster of exclusive rights in such a way that a substantial proportion of the population in another Member State would be deprived of the possibility of watching a listed event on television. Regrettably no reference to Luxembourg was made under Article 234 EC. The Commission for its part has done no more than briefly mention this case in its fourth report on the application of Directive 89/552 in the context of a broad comment that application of Article 3a in the period under review had been 'satisfactory',[1055] an approval repeated in the Discussion Paper released in April 2003 as part of the Commission's consultation exercise on the Directive.[1056]

My conclusion is that the combination of national and EC legislation governing 'protected events' diminishes the commercial value of the rights to broadcast such events by interfering in the ability of the holder of the rights to extract the highest price the market would yield. The advantages generated by this intervention, and the rationales for legislating in this way, are remarkably under-explained. What is required is a balancing of the competing interests. If this has been done by the EC legislature, then it has been kept very quiet. The impression is that sport is subjected to a 'special' regime without any sufficiently careful examination of what is and should be at stake.

10. What is the EC's 'policy' on the sale of right to broadcast sports events?

This paper began by situating the examination of the EC's treatment of the sale of rights to broadcast sports events not only in the wider context of EC law's treatment of sport and of broadcasting but also, broader still, in a context which questioned the extent which it is really helpful to discuss such matters under the ambitious label of a 'policy'. Given the constitutional limits of EC action, of which Article 5(1) EC represents the key assertion, and given, in addition, the incremental nature of the development of EC intervention in the field (principally involving the Court and the Commission presiding over the application and interpretation of the Treaty competition rules), one might be sceptical of any claim to a 'policy' which is even modestly coherent. The 'protected events' legislation simply adds to the impression of incrementalism. It is far from clear how, if at all, matters such as cultural concerns, and vertical redistribution of wealth – which form part of the European Model of Sport envisaged by the Commission[1057] – are properly seen as part of EC law's permitted concerns. This is the consequence of the EC's confinement to pursuit of objectives for which it is given authority by its Treaty, as well as use of only the means with which

[1055] COM (2002) 778, p. 10. The fifth – and most recent – Commission Report, note 1038 above, is similarly anodyne.

[1056] Available via http://ec.europa.eu/comm/avpolicy/reg/tvwf/modernisation/consultation_2003/index_en.htm. As one might expect, the BBC response to the Commission is warmly supportive of the House of Lords ruling.

[1057] See in particular the Helsinki Report, note 1011 above.

it is equipped by the Treaty. This, in short, is the effect of Article 5(1) EC. And it is the source of the criticism regularly levelled at the EC by those involved in sport: not simply that it 'doesn't understand sport' but that its Treaty constitutionally disables it from appreciating the breadth of sport's impact, concerns and activities.

I would accept that there are legitimate sources of concern here. And the institutions of the EU have attempted to bridge this perceived gap – in my opinion not always happily. Neither the Declaration on Sport attached to the Amsterdam Treaty nor the Declaration on 'the specific characteristics of sport and its social function in Europe, of which account should be taken in implementing common policies' annexed to the Conclusions of the Nice European Council would win awards for legal precision. Nor were they so designed. They are essentially political statements, with no pretence to subvert the Court's determination to apply the fundamental Treaty rules governing free movement and competition law to sport. Indeed this was expressly acknowledged by the European Court in *Deliège*[1058] and in *Lehtonen*.[1059] And yet such 'soft law' commitments, even drafted in the brittle style favoured at Amsterdam and Nice, carry weight. The lawyer should not discard such pronouncements without appreciating their capacity to generate a political dynamic to embed the discourse of a 'European Model of Sport' in institutional practice. It is here that the EU commits itself to a political recognition of the social and cultural virtues of sport which transcends its legal mandate; and it is here that one may identify how the evolution of policy (of a sort) is driven by a much broader pattern of sources than binding rules alone.[1060]

This is 'task expansion' or (more pejoratively) 'competence creep'.[1061] The problem is that in so far as such policy statements promise a good deal more than the EU can deliver, they may be damaging to the EU's legitimacy. If the EU is constitutionally unable to address matters lauded in the Nice Declaration such as respect and nurturing of 'the code of ethics and the solidarity essential to the preservation of' sport's social role and sport's contribution to 'integration, involvement in social life, tolerance, acceptance of differences and playing by the rules, and /or if lacks the material resources to promote such virtues, then it is unwise to raise citizens' expectations in this manner. The Commission's Helsinki Report on Sport might be vulnerable to similar criticism.[1062] After all, it begins by vaingloriously claiming that it 'gives pointers for reconciling the economic dimension of sport with its popular, educational, social and cultural dimensions'. Ultimately the problem is that there are severe constitutional limits on what the EC can achieve in defence of the 'European Sports Model' should the richer clubs choose to abandon all or part of it, and yet, by suggesting otherwise, the Commission is already setting itself up for criticism of its

---

1058 Cases C-51/96 and 191/97, note 980 above, Paras. 41-42 of the judgment.

1059 Case C-176/96, [2000] *ECR* I-2681, Paras. 32-33 of the judgment.

1060 This dealt with at some length by Parrish note 897 above, especially in Ch. 2 and, with particular reference to the Amsterdam Declaration, e.g., at pp. 15-16, 19, 104, 176, 196; cf. also Halgreen note 1012 above, pp. 56-64.

1061 Cf. note 867 above.

1062 Note 1011 above.

weakness should developments such as 'breakaway' closed competitions occur. And periodic support for initiatives such as the 'European Sports Forum' again lend an impression of a Commission ready to embrace the whole social and cultural baggage of sport despite its thin legal competence and its inadequate human and material resources. I think this is dangerous!

Is the EC really capable of adding value by developing general policies in this area? And in any event is 'sport' really a sufficiently homogenous phenomenon to attract a 'policy' anyway? Professional sport and recreational sport are different worlds. My case is not at all that it is irredeemably false to talk the language of an 'EC policy on sport', but my case is that one needs to be appropriately modest in choosing such a mode of discourse for fear that the gulf between breadth of the EU's stated political aspirations and its more limited legal competence and material resources generates disenchantment.[1063] After all, if the 'European Model of Sport' in football collapses under the pressure of the voracious commercial appetite of the major clubs it will not be the Commission's fault, so why court danger by embracing so vividly an endangered species which the Commission cannot protect?

However, in the particular case of the sale of broadcasting rights to sports events it is, in my view, appropriate to good deal more positive about the shape of EC law. I believe that the competition rules have been used in a sensitive way that meets the assumptions of EC law and the aspirations of sporting bodies and federations.

What are the relevant themes that help to understand the nature and purpose of the EC rules governing the sale of rights to broadcast sports events?

Sport is special in the need for internal organisational solidarity and this provides an economic incentive to pursue, and a legal reason to authorise, the agreed distribution of wealth between participant clubs in a league. The issue of collective selling of broadcasting rights pitches this legitimate objective of sports clubs against the expectation of third party broadcasters that output shall not be restricted in this fashion. The Commission's apparent willingness, aired in its Helsinki Report, to link exemption of collective selling to wealth distribution throughout the sport, from top to bottom, represents an attempt to offer inducements to sustain the pattern of vertical solidarity within a sport that it regards as characteristically European. However, its legal competence to insist on even this as a condition of exemption is far from clear and it has chosen cautiously to evade the issue in Champions League.[1064] As explained above, that Decision emphasises economic reasons for exempting collective selling arrangements based principally on reducing transaction costs. It chooses to circumvent the

[1063] I have made this argument in particular in S. Weatherill, 'Sport as Culture in European Community Law', Ch. 4, in R. Craufurd Smith, ed., *Culture in European Union Law* (Oxford University Press 2004) pp. 113-152. For general discussion, see K. Foster, 'How can Sport be Regulated?', Ch. 14 in Greenfield and Osborn, note 897 above; R. Parrish, 'Reconciling Conflicting Approaches to Sport in the European Union', pp. 21-42, and K. Foster, 'Can Sport be Regulated by Europe?' An Analysis of Alternative Models', pp. 43-64, both in A. Caiger and S. Gardiner, eds., *Professional Sport in the EU: Regulation and Re-Regulation* (The Hague, T.M.C. Asser Press 2000); S. Weatherill, '"Fair Play Please!": Recent Developments in the Application of EC Law to Sport', 40 *CML Rev.* (2003) 51. All the sources cited at note 897 above are relevant.

[1064] Note 994 above.

question of whether arguments founded on the promotion of (vertical or horizontal) solidarity are within the scope of Article 81(3) EC.

Certainly the application of such rules should pay due regard for the peculiar characteristic of mutual interdependence which marks the relationship between participants in a professional sports league. This is a sports-specific issue, but it is perfectly capable of forming part of appropriately nuanced economic and legal analysis. After all, the application of Article 81 is always conditioned by the particular context in which arrangements are struck. The Court's fundamentally important decision in *Wouters* should increasingly serve as the starting point in determining whether an apparent restriction on competition is properly pulled within the grip of Article 81(1).[1065] The Court stated that

> 'account must first of all be taken of the overall context in which the decision of the association of undertakings was taken or produces its effects. More particularly, account must be taken of its objectives. [...] It has then to be considered whether the consequential effects restrictive of competition are inherent in the pursuit of those objectives.'

This observation was delivered in the context of rules prohibiting multi-disciplinary partnerships between members of the Bar and accountants but can readily be transplanted to underpin an argument that the overall context in which sports regulation occurs, built around pursuit of a broad objective of healthy equality of competitive opportunity, produces effects which though restrictive of competition are nonetheless inherent in the pursuit of those objectives.[1066] Only if a restriction on competition within the meaning of Article 81(1) is at stake does the inquiry move to the possibility of exemption pursuant to Article 81(3).[1067] This is sports law and sports economics, and it is central to deciding how to control governing bodies whose regulation of sport has a spillover impact on commercial activities.

In sum, I consider that the EC's approach to the regulation of rights to broadcast sports events under EC competition law reveals an emphasis on market analysis which is not blind to the particular characteristics of professional sport.

11. Conclusion

Article 5(1) EC confines the Community to action 'within the limits of the powers conferred upon it by this Treaty'. It enjoys no explicit power to regulate sport. However, sporting practices may collide with the realisation of the EC Treaty's economic objectives, and accordingly the central trade law provisions, most of all those concerning competition law, have been used to induce significant change in European

---

1065 Case C-309/99 note 983 above. Strains of this approach are evident in A-G Lenz's Opinion in *Bosman*.

1066 The Commission's decision in *ENIC/UEFA*, note 981 above cites Wouters. For its invocation in relation to salary caps see S. Hornsby, 'The harder the cap, the softer the law?', 10 *Sport and the Law Journal* (2002) 142.

1067 As in Champions League note 994 above and in *Eurovision*, note 951 above.

sport. The functional breadth of EC law has as an inevitable consequence the shaping of a type of 'EC sports policy', within which a range of public and private actors, at national, European and international level, seek to exploit the possibilities provided by the existence of an EC tier of governance in order to achieve their objectives. EC law, in short, does not stipulate a form of governance into which sporting bodies must fit, but it does break open some of sport's often long-standing assumptions.

This interventionist capacity creates a complex mix and, given the constitutionally ambiguous background and the incremental pattern of decision making, it cannot be expected to yield a 'policy' that is wholly coherent or satisfying. One may indeed go further and wonder whether a European policy on sport is ever likely to display a compelling coherence, given the diversity of aspirations and structures that characterise sport in its professional, amateur and recreational forms. And yet there is a degree of order that one can identify in the EC's approach, and the case of the sale of rights to broadcast sports events offers an illuminating case study into the way in which EC law is able to secure the application of its fundamental economic law provisions without disregard for the sector-specific concerns of the industry subject to the rules.

Bosman[1068] remains centrally important. The Court ruled that existing practices in sport – the player transfer system and nationality-based discrimination in club football – were incompatible with EC law. It did not – it could not – dictate what should be introduced to replace the unlawful rules. That was a choice belonging to the sports authorities, acting in the shadow of the control exercised over their autonomy by the EC Treaty. But the Court did not simply treat football as an industry like any other. It accepted the salience of its legitimate interests in 'maintaining a balance between clubs by preserving a certain degree of equality and uncertainty as to results' and 'encouraging the recruitment and training of young players.'

This is the model used in this paper to examine EC law governing the sale of rights to broadcast sporting events. EC law does not require that private or public actors behave in a pre-determined manner. But its rules confine the scope of their permitted autonomy to arrange their affairs. So EC law, most of all EC competition law, has an impact on sporting practices, even without any explicit mandate to legislate granted by the Treaty. EC law governing the sale of rights to broadcast sporting events has four principal concerns. The first addresses the control of sale of broadcasting rights on an exclusive basis; the second addresses the collective selling of broadcasting rights; the third addresses the collective purchasing of broadcasting rights; the fourth deals with the restrictions that may be placed on sale of broadcasting rights by national governments, which are then reflected at European level in the 'protected events' provisions of Directive 89/552 (as amended).

With respect to the first of these concerns, this paper has made the case that the emphasis on market definition and market power which lies at the heart of the normal approach under EC competition law to assessing the compatibility of exclusive deals with Article 81 is perfectly appropriate in its deployment in the case of sale of rights to broadcast sports events. There are no issues which are unique to sport, though it is

1068 Case C-415/93, [1995] *ECR* I-4921.

certainly true that the Commission's sensitivity to the acquisition of exclusive rights to 'premium' events for an extended period reflects the profound concern about damage to market flexibility in the technologically and commercially volatile broadcasting sector which may be inflicted in such circumstances. With respect to the second of these concerns, the Commission in Champions League refused to accept the claim that collective selling is a necessary element in the organization of a professional sports league. Instead it treated it as a restriction on competition between suppliers of broadcasting rights. Rightly so, it is submitted. Collective selling is a commercial choice designed to strengthen the grip of suppliers at the expense of choice enjoyed by buyers. As is true of any restriction on competition caught by Article 81(1), exemption remains possible pursuant to Article 81(3) and the Commission's Decision in Champions League demonstrates that sport, like any other industry, is able to secure exemption provided that adequate consequent economic benefit is shown. Similarly, in dealing with the third of the concerns, the treatment of collective purchasing in Eurovision reveals that such arrangements will fall within Article 81(1) where they cause a sufficient degree of market foreclosure, but that their economic benefits may justify the grant of an exemption, albeit that effective provision for sub-licensing is likely to be a pre-condition to reliance on Article 81(3) for fear that otherwise there will follow an unacceptable elimination of competition in relevant markets.

The issue left untouched in Champions League is one that may in future test the receptivity of EC competition law to the special expectations of sport – could an agreement to sell rights on a collective basis, falling within Article 81(1), secure exemption pursuant to Article 81(3) even where economic benefits of the type identified in Champions League are missing but where the income is used to strengthen vertical and/or horizontal solidarity within the sport? I have doubts whether Article 81(3) can be stretched in this way. However, I consider that there are other ways in which sport can promote its interest in vertical and/or horizontal solidarity without the need to distort the market for sale of broadcasting rights by maintaining collective arrangements that fail to meet the criteria for exemption stipulated by Article 81(3). Most of all leagues could commit to more vigorous internal distribution of wealth. On the fourth and final concern of EC law in this area, that pertaining to restrictions to sale of 'protected' or 'listed' events, I confess that I find the relevant provisions hard to understand and generally unhelpful. In this instance the combination of interested national and European actors – most prominently headline-seeking politicians – has created an intervention that is hard to explain on any rational commercial or cultural basis.

ANTI-DOPING REVISITED – THE DEMISE OF THE RULE OF 'PURELY SPORTING INTEREST'?*

INTRODUCTION

On 18 July 2006 the European Court of Justice (ECJ) set aside the decision of the Court of First Instance (CFI) in *Meca-Medina and Majcen* v. *Commission.*[1069] Before the CFI the applicants, who are professional swimmers, had unsuccessfully applied for annulment of the Commission's decision to reject their complaint that bans imposed on them for violation of the sport's anti-doping rules contravened EC competition law.[1070] The swimmers also failed before the ECJ which, having set aside the CFI's judgment, dismissed the application for annulment of the Commission's Decision. However, the ECJ's ruling is significant for rejecting the CFI's relatively generous approach to the scope of sporting autonomy to apply rules with economic effects. In what may prove to be the most enduring phrase in the judgment, the ECJ ruled that 'the mere fact that a rule is purely sporting in nature does not have the effect of removing from the scope of the Treaty the person engaging in the activity governed by that rule or the body which has laid it down'.[1071] The ECJ's approach is in line with that suggested in this Review by the present author in a critical comment on the CFI's decision,[1072] but the purpose of this contribution is not simply to reflect on (what I consider to be) a helpful correction to the basis of interaction between EC competition law and sport, but rather also to look forward to future challenges. The practical effect of *Meca-Medina and Majcen*, as an authoritative statement of the limits of sporting autonomy under EC competition law, is to assert EC law's firm grip over the choices available to governing bodies, and this has important implications *inter alia* for the looming litigation arising out of FIFA's rules compelling football clubs to release their players for international representative matches.

THE CHALLENGE OF EC LAW AND SPORT

The straightforward fact pattern of the case illuminates the sensitive issues at stake when sport and the law collide. The swimmers were deprived of their means of making a living by the ban from competition which, after an appeal, was set at two years in duration. So the economic detriment of the action taken against them was plain. And yet this is clearly not only a matter of economics. Sport is based on fair play – it

* *ECL Rev.* (2006) 645 et seq.

1069 Case C-519/04 P, judgment of 18 July 2006.

1070 Case T-313/02, [2004] *ECR* II-3291.

1071 Para. 27 (ECJ).

1072 S. Weatherill, 'Anti-doping rules and EC Law', *ECL Rev.* (2005) 416.

is structured around rules which define the essence of the endeavour. Keeping out drug cheats has an undeniable economic context, but at the same time it is an existential choice: sport is only sport if there is a level playing field for competitors.

This, then, forms the heart of the conundrum. Sporting rules have an economic effect. But without some fundamental rules there is no sport. So how does EC law fit in?

The EC Treaty is not helpful. The EC Treaty does not refer to sport at all. The EC is not constitutionally competent to adopt legislation with the explicit aim of regulating sport. But its economic law provisions apply to sport because sport has an economic context. In Walrave and *Koch* v. *Union Cycliste Internationale*, the first case involving sport to reach the European Court,[1073] the Court stated that the practice of sport is subject to Community law 'in so far as it constitutes an economic activity within the meaning of Article 2 of the Treaty', an approach followed in *Donà* v. *Mantero*[1074] and vigorously confirmed by the European Court in *Bosman*.[1075] This is now settled law. What is at stake is a quest to develop a 'policy' that is driven by the dictates of trade integration yet is also appropriately sensitive to the particular needs of sport.

Sport, it is worth noting, is not alone in setting EC law such a challenge. In a number of areas the functionally broad reach of the Treaty provisions on free movement and competition collide with Member States powers to act in realms where the Community lacks competence under the Treaty to usurp national regulatory choices by acting as a substitute legislator. Social security provides a good a example of how EC trade law forces adjustment of national practices which obstruct inter-State trade in the absence of adequate justification;[1076] taxation is another;[1077] and even the maintenance of public order and the safeguarding of internal security have been revealed as matters of national competence that are nevertheless reviewable in so far as their pursuit impedes cross-border trade.[1078] The EC does not become a substitute regulator in these realms, but it confines the exercise of national autonomy in consequence on the consistently extensive interpretation applied to the rules governing the building of an integrated, competitive market. This perspective captures the Court's several rulings which assert the conditional autonomy of sporting bodies under EC law and it also informs the Commission's batch of interventions into the sports field on the basis of the competition rules of the Treaty. From this has grown a rich literature exploring the concept of EC sports law and policy, which explores how the institutions of the EU seek to piece together a coherent approach against a Treaty background which is barren of sports-specific material and reveals how EC law, by empowering a range of

[1073] Case 36/74, [1974] *ECR* 1405.

[1074] Case 13/76, [1976] *ECR* 1333.

[1075] Case C-415/93, (1995) *ECR* I-4921.

[1076] Cf., e.g., Case C-512/03 J E J Blankaert judgment of 8 September 2005; Case C-372/04 *ex parte Watts*, judgment of 16 May 2006, Para. 121.

[1077] Cf., e.g., Case C-446/03 *Marks and Spencer* v. *Halsey*, judgment of 13 December 2005.

[1078] Case C-265/95 *Commission* v. *France*, [1997] *ECR* I-6959.

actors, tends to erode the self-regulatory paradigm which has for so long been dominant in sports governance.[1079]

What precisely is this notion of 'conditional autonomy' under EC law to which governing bodies in sports can lay claim? This plainly matters in determining the basis and scope of legal challenge to penalties imposed for breach of anti-doping rules, but the need for a coherent legal framework goes much further and wider.

As mentioned, the ECJ has consistently placed sport within the scope of Community law 'in so far as it constitutes an economic activity within the meaning of Article 2 of the Treaty'; indeed this formula appears prominently in the ECJ's judgment in *Meca-Medina and Majcen*.[1080] So if sport is not an economic activity it falls outside the reach of the Treaty. How is this statement of principle elucidated in the case law?

Walrave and Koch[1081] involved nationality-based discrimination, which one would normally assume to fall foul of (what is now) Article 12 EC's prohibition of such practices. However, the Court treated the composition of national sports teams as unaffected by the prohibition where their formation is 'a question of purely sporting interest and as such has nothing to do with economic activity'. In *Donà* v. *Mantero*[1082] the Court held that the Treaty provisions governing free movement do not prevent practices that exclude foreign players from certain matches for 'reasons which are not of an economic nature' and which are 'of sporting interest only'. In *Bosman*[1083] the Court, citing its judgment in Donà, again adopted this formula, but, reflecting the insistence found in the Walrave judgment and repeated subsequently that this 'restriction on the scope of the provisions in question must however remain limited to its proper objective', offered confirmation that the Court will patrol the limits of the autonomy granted to sports federations to set rules undisturbed by the demands of EC law. In *Bosman* the Court refused to accept that nationality-based restrictions in club football constituted legitimate rules of sporting interest.[1084] It concluded that they fell within the scope of, and violated the requirements of, the EC Treaty.

In *Bosman* the Court also brought within the scope of the Treaty, and found incompatible with it, rules governing the transfer of players between clubs,[1085] while in Lehtonen it ruled against transfer windows that vary according to the origin of the

---

1079 E.g., R. Parrish, Sports law and policy in the European Union (Manchester University Press 2003); S. Greenfield and G. Osborn, eds., *Law and Sport in Contemporary Society* (London, Frank Cass Publishing 2000); L. Barani, 'The Role of the European Court of Justice as a Political Actor in the Integration Process: The Case of Sport Regulation after the *Bosman* Ruling', 1 *Journal of Contemporary European Research* (2005) 42; S. Van den Bogaert and A. Vermeersch, 'Sport and the European Treaty: a Tale of Uneasy Bedfellows', (*EL Rev.*, forthcoming).

1080 Case C-519/04P, judgment of 18 July 2006, Para. 22.

1081 Case 36/74 cited above, note 1073.

1082 Case 13/76 cited above, note 1074.

1083 Case C-415/93, [1995] *ECR* I-4921.

1084 See also Case C-438/00, *Deutscher Handballbund eV.* v. *Kolpak*, [2003] *ECR* I-4135.

1085 Case C-415/93 cited above, note 1083.

player.[1086] The Commission found discriminatory ticketing practices for the 1998 World Cup fell foul of Article 82, and imposed a small fine on the organisers.[1087] On the other hand, it is not only rules on the composition of national representative teams that have been allowed to continue undisturbed by the EC law.[1088] Rules relating to selection for high-level international competitions were similarly favourably treated.[1089] A similar approach has been taken by the Commission to rules forbidding multiple ownership of football clubs.[1090] Eliminating any suspicion of match-fixing is indispensable to genuine sporting competition, and therefore any consequent restriction on commercial opportunity to acquire clubs could not be regarded as a restriction falling foul of Article 81(1). More generally the Court in *Bosman* acknowledged that '[i]n view of the considerable social importance of sporting activities and in particular football in the Community, the aims of maintaining a balance between clubs by preserving a certain degree of equality and uncertainty as to results and of encouraging the recruitment and training of young players must be accepted as legitimate'.[1091] No adequate justification was forthcoming for the practices impugned in the case, but the Court here set out a framework for determining when sporting rules may be regarded as legitimate means to achieve such ends.

But why do some sporting rules escape condemnation under EC law? It is submitted that in very few cases is it because they have no economic effects. Normally it is because their economic effects are a necessary consequence of their contribution to the structure of sports governance. So nationality rules governing the composition of national representative teams do have an economic effect – by confining the opportunities enjoyed by players to choose which country to play for, by structuring international football in a way that appeals to spectators, sponsors and so on – but they serve to define the very endeavour of international competition, the character of which would be destroyed without such rules. In similar vein appropriately structured transfer rules and transfer windows might survive inspection against the requirements of the Treaty but not because they are devoid of economic effect. Such rules are not as a category outwith the scope of the Treaty, but provided they are shown to be necessary elements in sports governance the conclusion is that they do not fall foul of the network of provisions regulating trade under the Treaty.

The Court has not always been easy to read on this point. In Walrave and Koch the Court referred to 'a question of purely sporting interest' which 'as such has nothing to do with economic activity'. Perhaps there are some such rules which are beyond the reach of the Treaty – the detail of the offside rule perhaps, or the length of a match – but most rules of sporting interest are not purely of sporting interest, they also impinge on economic activity. In practice, the Court's consistent insistence that

---

1086 Case C-176/96, [2000] *ECR* I-2681.

1087 Dec. 2000/12 1998, *Football World Cup*, *OJ* 2000 L 5/55. For comment, see S. Weatherill, '0033149875354: Fining the Organisers of the 1998 Football World Cup', *ECL Rev.* (2000) 275.

1088 Case 36/74 cited above, note 1073, Case 13/76 cited above, note 1074.

1089 Cases C-51/96 & C-191/97, *Deliège*, [2000] *ECR* I-2549.

1090 COMP 37.806 *ENIC/UEFA*, IP/02/942, 27 June 2002.

1091 Para. 106 of Case C-415/93 cited above, note 1083.

any restriction on the scope of the Treaty provisions in question must remain limited to its proper objective has helped to contain inflated claims to sporting autonomy via this unhappy 'purely sporting interest' formula. But in *Meca-Medina and Majcen* the CFI fell into error by making improper use of the notion that a rule may be of sporting interest and therefore non-economic for the purposes of the application of EC law. The ECJ has corrected this error and, in particular through its embrace of the '*Wouters* formula' as a basis for reviewing sporting practices, it has provided a much more satisfying basis for understanding the treatment of sporting of rules which have economic effects under Article 81 EC. And, more profoundly still, its judgment is capable of being read as having extinguished the notion that EC law recognises and therefore leaves untouched the 'purely sporting rule', at least where such a rule has economic consequence. *Meca-Medina and Majcen*, then, is a landmark judgment.

The CFI's approach in *Meca-Medina and Majcen*

In *Meca-Medina and Majcen* v. *Commission*[1092] the CFI, declining to annul the Commission's decision rejecting the swimmers' complaint,[1093] twisted itself into knots as a result of failure clearly to grasp what the ECJ had astutely though evasively described in *Bosman* as the 'the difficulty of severing the economic aspects from the sporting aspects of football'.[1094] I have criticised the judgment already in this Review[1095] and will here do more than summarise the CFI's judgment for the purposes of proving a background to discussion below what the ECJ has now done on appeal.

In *Meca-Medina and Majcen* the CFI began by repeating the orthodox judicial view that sport is subject to Community law only in so far as it constitutes an economic activity within the meaning of Article 2 EC.[1096] It then attempted to insist that anti-doping rules concern exclusively non-economic aspects of sport, designed to preserve 'noble competition'[1097] and therefore outwith the scope of the EC Treaty. This led it into intellectually murky alleyways. At Paragraph 41 the CFI referred to 'purely sporting rules, that is to say rules concerning questions of purely sporting interest and, as such, having nothing to do with economic activity' and juxtaposed this to a description of 'regulations, which relate to the particular nature and context of sporting events, are inherent in the organisation and proper conduct of sporting competition and cannot be regarded as constituting a restriction on the Community rules on the freedom of movement of workers and the freedom to provide services'. But this is to conflate two different points. Perhaps there is a (small) category of purely sporting rules unassociated with economic activity, but regulations inherent in the organisation and proper conduct of sporting competition form a much larger

1092 Case T-313/02, [2004] *ECR* II-3291.

1093 COMP 38.158.

1094 Para. 76 of Case C-415/93, cited above note 1083.

1095 S Weatherill, 'Anti-doping rules and EC Law', *ECL Rev.* (2005) 416.

1096 Para. 37.

1097 Para. 49.

category in which economic effect is commonly present. Similarly at Paragraph 44 the CFI observed that the 'the campaign against doping does not pursue any economic objective'. That may not be true, for the CFI itself refers at Paragraph 57 to the economic value of a 'clean' sport to its organisers, but even if true, this is not of itself a reason for locating that campaign outside the Treaty. Anti-doping rules certainly have economic effects on those found to have contravened them. Attempts to present such rules as 'sporting' and not 'economic' are unhelpful. They are both.

True, the notion that there is in principle a separation between sporting rules (which escape the scope of application of EC law) and rules of an economic nature (which do not) reflects the nature of the EC as an institution possessing a set of attributed competences, of which sport is not one.[1098] But EC law has a broad functional reach because so few activities exert no economic impact. The CFI's attempt in Meca Medina to roll back this general trend in the special case of sport, though doubtless a source of delight to sports federations, was constitutionally deeply unconvincing. Rules governing the composition of national sports teams or the conduct of anti-doping controls may define the nature of sporting competition but they visibly have economic repercussions (for players most of all). What is really at stake is not a group of sporting rules and a separate group of economic rules, but rather a group of sporting rules which carry economic implications and which therefore fall for assessment, but not necessarily condemnation, under EC trade law.

The appeal – setting aside the CFI's judgment

On appeal, the ECJ took a significantly different and, it is submitted, superior approach. In *Meca-Medina and Majcen* v. *Commission* it dismissed the swimmers' application for annulment of the Commission Decision rejecting their complaint, but it corrected the legal analysis put forward the CFI.[1099] In doing so, it took no notice of an Opinion submitted on the very same day as the oral hearing by its Advocate-General, Mr Leger, which proposed dismissal of the appeal while adding reasoning even more unpersuasively convoluted than the CFI's. Mr Leger admitted that sport's commercial context endows anti-doping rules with an economic interest, but asserted that this is 'purely secondary' and cannot deprive the rules of their 'purely sporting' character.[1100] This is disappointingly impure reasoning.

The ECJ had no time for such intellectual self-bondage. It began by adding *Meca-Medina* to the list of cases in which it has asserted that 'sport is subject to Community law in so far as it constitutes an economic activity within the meaning of Article 2 EC'. It added that the prohibitions contained in Articles 39 and 49 EC 'do not affect rules concerning questions which are of purely sporting interest and, as such, have nothing to do with economic activity', citing Walrave and Koch. It then referred to

[1098] Art. 5(1) EC, vigorously applied by the Court in Case C-376/98, *Germany* v. *Parliament and Council*, [2000] *ECR* I-8419 in finding the 'Tobacco Advertising' Directive invalid.

[1099] Case C-519/04 P *Meca-Medina and Majcen* v. *Commission*, judgment of 18 July 2006.

[1100] Para. 28 of the Opinion delivered on 23 March 2006.

'the difficulty of severing the economic aspects from the sporting aspects of a sport' (which of course derives from *Bosman* though that is not cited in connection with this phrase), confirming its view that the free movement provisions 'do not preclude rules or practices justified on non-economic grounds which relate to the particular nature and context of certain sporting events', adding in line with long-standing judicial practice that such a restriction on the scope of the provisions in question must remain limited to its proper objective.

So 'the mere fact that a rule is purely sporting in nature does not have the effect of removing from the scope of the Treaty the person engaging in the activity governed by that rule or the body which has laid it down'.[1101] And if the sporting activity in question falls within the scope of the Treaty, the rules which govern that activity must satisfy the requirements of the Treaty 'which, in particular, seek to ensure freedom of movement for workers, freedom of establishment, freedom to provide services, or competition'.[1102]

The CFI was adjudged to have made an error of law in assuming that purely sporting rules which have nothing to do with economic activity and which therefore do not fall within the scope of Articles 39 EC and 49 EC equally have nothing to do with the economic relationships of competition, with the result that they also do not fall within the scope of Articles 81 EC and 82 EC. Instead the specific requirements of Articles 81 and 82 should be considered. In the absence of such analysis, the contested judgment was therefore set aside.

This part of the ECJ's judgment is brief and, in its broad message (if any), not easy to decipher, but it is probably best taken on its own limited terms, and not as a general rebuke to those who would argue for convergence between the provisions on free movement and the competition rules. Kamiel Mortelmans, for instance, has examined the current unsystematic state of the law and put forward the view that a degree of convergence should be recognised and welcomed, but that the provisions are not identical in their objectives and that therefore complete convergence is inappropriate.[1103] Renato Nazzini has argued that at the level of detail there is no convergence, although he accepts a methodological comparability in the general trend to allow a 'softening' of basic Treaty provisions by reference to factors other than those expressly set out in the derogations contained in the Treaty (Arts. 30, 46 81(3)).[1104]

My own view is that it would be unsatisfactory for a practice that is treated necessary for the organisation of sport under the free movement provisions then to be condemned under the competition rules – and it would be equally unsatisfactory for

---

1101 Para. 27.

1102 Para. 28.

1103 K. Mortelmans, 'Towards Convergence in the application of the rules on Free Movement and on Competition', 38 *CML Rev.* (2001) 613. Cf. S. Weatherill, '"Fair Play Please!": Recent Developments in the Application of EC Law to Sport', 40 *CML Rev.* (2003) 51, 80-86; R. O'Loughlin, 'EC Competition Rules and Free Movement Rules: An Examination of the Parallels and their Furtherance by the ECJ *Wouters* Decision', [2003] *ECLR* 62.

1104 R. Nazzini, 'Article 81 EC between time present and time past: a normative critique of restriction of competition in EU law', 43 *CML Rev.* (2006) 497.

a practice that is treated necessary for the organisation of sport under the competition rules to be found incompatible with the free movement provisions. In my view there is and should be an ultimate functional comparability between the inquiries conducted under these provisions in order to discover the scope of conditional autonomy properly allowed to sporting bodies – and accordingly in this paper I have placed little emphasis on whether case law arises under the rules on free movement or on competition (or both). If rules are shown to be necessary for the effective organisation of sport, then they are not incompatible with EC trade law, whichever provision is invoked. And, as a corollary, where the restrictive effect trespasses beyond what is necessary to achieve the rule's proper objective, the basic Treaty prohibitions bite. So, by insisting on viewing the sporting rules in their proper context, I argue here for 'convergence in outcome' between free movement law and the competition rules. Admittedly the ECJ in *Meca-Medina and Majcen* rebukes the CFI for failing to separate out the different detailed elements at stake in an analysis under Articles 39 and 49, on the one hand, and Articles 81 and 82, on the other, but I do not think the ECJ is doing anything more remarkable than drawing attention to the thinness of the CFI's analysis. The CFI did not even touch on possible differences between the provisions, which could encompass personal scope, need for market analysis, the role of 'internal situations', burden of proof and so on.[1105] The ECJ, in Paragraphs 32-33, is merely drawing attention to the inadequacy of Paragraph 42 in the CFI's judgment. It is not making any deeper normative criticism of the convergence thesis.

What is considerably more important than its brief finding that the CFI's analysis is inadequate is how the ECJ then proceeds itself to assess the claim for annulment of the Commission's decision rejecting the swimmers' complaint. Here, I submit, the ECJ puts the interpretation of Article 81 on the right track and should be taken also to have set a (convergent) course for the other economic law provisions in the Treaty that may affect sport.

The appeal – rejecting the application for annulment

The ECJ did not remit the case to the CFI. In accordance with Article 61 of the Statute of the Court of Justice, it felt it appropriate to give judgment on the substance of the appellants' claims for annulment of the Commission decision rejecting their complaint. And it rejected their application. That outcome is not of great interest beyond the facts of the case itself, but the most significant element of the ECJ's examination concerns the role of the judgment in *Wouters*.[1106] The way this is handled by the ECJ is of profound importance to the future treatment of sport under EC competition law and also – though this is less fully developed in Meca Medina – to the general question of where *Wouters* fits into the general law on Article 81(1) EC.

1105 Cf. Opinion of A-G Poiares Maduro in Case C-205/03P *Fenin* v. *Commission*, especially Para. 51.

1106 Case C-309/99, *J.C.J. Wouters, J.W. Savelbergh, Price Waterhouse Belastingadviseurs BV* v. *Algemene Raad van de Nederlandse Orde van Advocaten*, [2002] *ECR* I-1577.

In *Wouters* the Court stated that in applying Article 81(1) account must be taken of

> 'the overall context in which the decision of the association of undertakings was taken or produces its effects. More particularly, account must be taken of its objectives. [...] It has then to be considered whether the consequential effects restrictive of competition are inherent in the pursuit of those objectives.'

The case had nothing to do with sport. It concerned rules prohibiting multi-disciplinary partnerships between members of the Bar and accountants. But the statement of principle that the notion of a restriction falling within Article 81(1) must be assessed in context is readily capable of broader application. In the case of sport, the reasoning in *Wouters* invites an argument that the overall context in which sports regulation occurs, built around pursuit of a broad objective of fair competition, produces effects which though apparently restrictive of competition are nonetheless inherent in the pursuit of those objectives and therefore permitted.

In *Meca-Medina and Majcen* the Commission had explicitly quoted the judgment in *Wouters* in its Decision.[1107] It concluded that there could be no true sport without anti-doping controls and that accordingly there was no breach of Article 81.[1108] By contrast, the CFI had sidelined *Wouters* for reasons that were logical once it had chosen to analyse the anti-doping rules as 'purely sporting'. The CFI considered that *Wouters* concerned 'market conduct', an 'essentially economic activity, that of lawyers'. Anti-doping cannot be likened to market conduct without distorting the nature of sport, which 'in its very essence – has nothing to do with any economic consideration'.[1109] The Commission's reliance on *Wouters* was, however, not fatal to the validity of its Decision, largely because the Commission persuaded the CFI at the oral hearing that this was an analysis performed 'in the alternative' or more 'for the sake of completeness'.[1110] The core of the Commission's approach was to find anti-doping rules 'purely sporting' in nature, a conclusion of which the CFI approved. But in *Meca-Medina* this approach was not accepted by the ECJ in the part of the judgment that will carry most important long-term resonance.

The appellants' principal contention was that in rejecting their complaint the Commission wrongly decided that the anti-doping rules at issue were not a restriction of competition within the meaning of Article 81 EC. They submitted that the Commission misapplied the criteria established by the Court of Justice in *Wouters*. They argued that the rules were, contrary to the Commission's findings, not inherent in the objectives of safeguarding the integrity of competitive sport and athletes' health, but that they sought to protect the IOC's own economic interests. Second, in laying down a maximum level which did not correspond to any scientifically safe criterion,

---

1107 Cited above, note 1093, p. 10.

1108 Under a similar analysis, nor, in my view, would there be a breach of the free movement provisions.

1109 Para. 65 (CFI).

1110 Para. 62 (CFI).

the rules were criticised as excessive in nature and thus extending beyond what was necessary in order to combat doping effectively.

These, it will be noted, are distinct lines of attack. The first concerns the juridical basis of challenge pursuant to EC law. The second is concerned with the detail of the review. The appellants could conceivably succeed on the first point, but lose on the second. Roughly speaking, this is what happened.

The ECJ drew on existing case law in its interpretation of Article 81(1):

> 'the compatibility of rules with the Community rules on competition cannot be assessed in the abstract (see, to this effect, Case C-250/92 DLG [1994] ECR I>5641, Para. 31). Not every agreement between undertakings or every decision of an association of undertakings which restricts the freedom of action of the parties or of one of them necessarily falls within the prohibition laid down in Article 81(1) EC. For the purposes of application of that provision to a particular case, account must first of all be taken of the overall context in which the decision of the association of undertakings was taken or produces its effects and, more specifically, of its objectives. It has then to be considered whether the consequential effects restrictive of competition are inherent in the pursuit of those objectives (*Wouters and Others*, Para. 97) and are proportionate to them'.[1111]

So, in contrast to the CFI, the ECJ did not seek to attribute special magic to sporting rules. Anti-doping rules cannot simply be excluded from the scope of review pursuant to EC competition law by reference to their role in ensuring fair play. They must be examined in their proper context, including recognition of their economic effect. But placing the rules within the ambit of the Treaty does not mean they will be forbidden by it. The general objective of the rules was to combat doping in order for competitive sport to be conducted on a fair basis; and the effect of penalties on athletes' freedom of action must be considered to be inherent in the anti-doping rules. The Court considered that the rules did not constitute a restriction of competition incompatible with the common market, within the meaning of Article 81 EC, since they pursue a legitimate objective.[1112]

There is room for sporting autonomy – but it is a conditional autonomy. This is precisely in line with the general trend of the case law which had been mishandled by the CFI in its misplaced zeal to separate sporting rules from economic rules. And the ECJ helps us to see that *Wouters* is indeed capable of providing an intellectually sustainable basis for checking sporting practices against the demands of Article 81.

On the facts, the appellants failed. If penalties imposed on an athlete were ultimately to prove unjustified, adverse effects on competition prohibited by Article 81(1) could follow.[1113] Restrictions must be limited to what is necessary to ensure the proper conduct of competitive sport, and this relates to both defining the crime of doping and selecting penalties.[1114] I think the ECJ is cautioning sporting bodies against imposing draconian penalties that might severely damage athletes' livelihoods in par-

1111 Para. 42.
1112 Para. 45.
1113 Para. 47.
1114 Para. 48.

ticular where this is a device to achieve the economic objective of making the sport more appealing to sponsors and broadcasters. Here too some degree of proper procedure is probably also expected as a condition of finding anti-doping rules and associated penalties lawful, although the ECJ does not explore this in *Meca-Medina.*[1115] Generally, however, a court is understandably wary when invited to make detailed assessments which tend to undermine the expertise of sports administrators. How much nandrolone is too much? Why a two year ban, not three? The ECJ was able to escape these awkward matters of detailed assessment by concluding that the appellants had failed to establish that the Commission made a manifest error of assessment in finding the rules on quantities of permitted nandrolone to be justified. Nor, in the absence of pleading by the appellants, would it question the penalties imposed as excessive. So the swimmers lost. But it is crucial for the development of the law that they lost not because the rules were treated as 'purely sporting' in nature.

WHY *MECA-MEDINA AND MAJCEN* MATTERS TO THE SHAPING OF EC LAW ON SPORT

In this Review I asked that the ECJ adopt *Wouters* as the best way to handle this application for annulment.[1116] Consequently I welcome the judgment. The CFI's explanation that the rules at issue in *Wouters* concerned 'market conduct', while those in *Meca-Medina and Majcen* instead have 'nothing to do with any economic consideration' has been treated as flawed by the ECJ. Rightly so. But what does this mean for sport and for Article 81 generally?

At Paragraph 27 the ECJ states that 'the mere fact that a rule is purely sporting in nature does not have the effect of removing from the scope of the Treaty the person engaging in the activity governed by that rule or the body which has laid it down'. In its treatment of the substance of the application the ECJ does not even bother to mention the 'purely sporting' rule. A bold but sustainable interpretation of the ECJ decision in *Meca-Medina and Majcen* would hold that the so-called rule of 'purely sporting interest', originating in Walrave and Koch, has now been eliminated as a basis for immunising sports rules which have an economic effect from review under EC law. All that can be intended by the 'purely sporting rule' is a reference to the small category of rules which govern sport but which are devoid of economic effect – such as the offside rule and fixing the height of goalposts. In the unlikely event that such rules were to provoke litigation, they would be found to lie outside the scope of the EC Treaty.

The approach adopted by the ECJ in *Meca-Medina and Majcen* is to accept that the vast majority of rules adopted by a sporting federation in order to regulate its

---

1115 Cf. A. Van Vaerenbergh, 'Regulatory Features and Administrative Law Dimensions of the Olympic Movement's Anti-Doping Regime', IILJ Working Paper 2005/11 (New York University School of Law), available via www.iilj.org/papers/index.html, connecting sport to the general literature on 'global administrative law', on which see, e.g., N. Krisch and B. Kingsbury, 'Symposium: Global Governance and Global Administrative Law in the International Legal Order' 17:1 *European Journal of International Law* (2006) (Special Issue).

1116 Cited above, note 1095.

competitions exert an economic impact, but to appreciate that this does not of itself mean that they will be incompatible with EC law. Consequential restrictive effects of a sporting decision which cause economic hardship are not treated as prohibited restrictions for the purposes of application of Article 81 – nor, I would submit, Articles 39 or 49 – provided they are inherent in the pursuit of those objectives. This is *Wouters* absorbed by the ECJ in *Meca Medina*. It is conditional autonomy permitted under EC law: the key questions surround which sporting rules are truly necessary for the organisation of a particular sport and therefore sheltered from the impact of EC law even though they have economic implications.

As a matter of procedure, Article 2 of Regulation 1/2003 provides that the burden of proving an infringement of Article 81(1) shall rest on the party or the authority alleging the infringement.[1117] So those challenging sports bodies find that the *Wouters* formula is reversed: they must show that the consequential effects restrictive of competition go beyond what is inherent in the pursuit of the practice's objectives. Only then is there a violation of Article 81(1). This may be of some tactical value to sports bodies confronted by the prospect of litigation. However, the larger story of *Meca-Medina* is what sports bodies have lost. The CFI judgment was remarkably generous in its invitation to sports bodies to rest a successful case on the mere fact of a rule's sporting context, even where economic effects were also clearly at stake, but the ECJ has by contrast insisted on the need to review sporting practices which have economic implications. Sports bodies cannot keep out of court simply by asserting that sport is special.

And yet this does not mean that their interests will be ignored. Presumably, given the burden of proof, it is for the applicant, challenging a sporting rule, to demonstrate coherent alternative governance structures as a basis for arguing that there is evidence of a violation of Article 81(1), as interpreted by the ECJ in *Meca-Medina* in the light of *Wouters*. The examination would then permit sporting bodies to demonstrate how and why the rules are necessary to accommodate their particular concerns – fair play, credible competition, national representative teams, and so on. The key argument of this paper is that this is the way to ensure that EC law provides a proper environment for assessment of the interests at stake when sport intersects with the economic project mapped out by the EC Treaty. And the result of *Meca-Medina* itself demonstrates that the sporting expertise informing (*in casu*) anti-doping inquiries will not lightly be set aside by judges.

Meca-Medina and Majcen and the future of sports litigation under EC competition law

In its judgment the ECJ moves seamlessly between case law which insists that an agreed restriction on commercial freedom is not to be treated as a restriction on competition within Article 81(1) provided it is necessary to ensure that the relevant

1117 *OJ* 2003 L 1/1.

arrangements function properly[1118] and *Wouters* itself, where a restriction of competition is acknowledged but no violation of Article 81(1) is found provided those restrictive effects are inherent in the pursuit of legitimate objectives.[1119] Both approaches have important implications for the structure of Article 81: allowing practices to escape subjection to Article 81(1) curtails the importance of Article 81(3), which affects the way arguments about the economics of competition are loaded into Article 81 cases, as well as affecting more practical matters such as the burden of proof. In principle, however, these lines of case law are capable of being treated as analytically distinct.[1120] The fear generated by the second approach, but not the first, is that *Wouters* may cause the interpretation of Article 81(1) to become infected by all manner of obscure 'non-economic' values. The Court has not used Meca Medina to provide clear guidance on that broader debate about the future of Article 81(1), which has important descriptive and normative dimensions that will not be entered into here.[1121] Probably, however, *Meca-Medina* should not be read as favouring a wider application of *Wouters*. The Court has run together two analytically distinct lines of case law because in sport – but not necessarily more generally – they are functionally equivalent. The heart of the legal analysis asks whether the challenged rules, which exert a prejudicial economic effect on those excluded from participation by them, are necessary to achieve legitimate objectives. If so – but only if so – they do not infringe Article 81(1). In sports cases it does not matter whether one's conclusion is that there is no restriction of competition or that there is a restriction of competition which is permitted. Whichever line of analysis is followed, the result should be the same – context is all. In fact, in accordance with the 'convergence in outcome' thesis advanced above, the rules need to be assessed in the same contextually sensitive way whichever Treaty provision they happen to be attacked under, and their capacity to fall under Articles 49, 81 and 82 again reveals their unusual, if not quite *sui generis*, quasi-regulatory nature. *Wouters* is fit for the purpose of examining how the law should treat sporting rules that define the nature of the activity but have an impact on (would-be) participants,

---

1118 E.g., Case C-250/92, *Gottrup Klim* v. *DLB*, [1994] *ECR* I-5641, cited by the ECJ in Para. 42 of *Meca-Medina and Majcen*. In Case T-328/03, *O2* (*Germany*) v. *Commission*, judgment of 2 May 2006 the CFI treated that decision as a particular manifestation of a wider principle that insists that an agreement be considered in its true context: 'The examination required in the light of Art. 81(1) EC consists essentially in taking account of the impact of the agreement on existing and potential competition – and the competition situation in the absence of the agreement –, those two factors being intrinsically linked' (Para 71).

1119 Para. 42, set out above (text attached to note 43), also Para. 45.

1120 For an exploration of the nuances in the relevant case law, see R. Whish, *Competition Law*, 5th edn. (Butterworths 2003), pp. 115-128.

1121 See O. Odudu, *The Boundaries of EC Competition Law: the Scope of Article 81* (Oxford University Press 2006); also, with different emphasis, Nazzini cited above, note 1104; E. Loozen, 'Professional ethics and restraints of competition' 31 *EL Rev.* (2006) 28; A. Komninos, 'Non-competition concerns: resolution of conflicts in the integrated Article 81 EC', University of Oxford Centre for Competition Law and Policy Working Paper (L) 08/05, available via www.competition-law.ox.ac.uk/competition/portal.php; S. de Vries, Tensions within the Internal Market: the Functioning of the Internal Market and the Development of Horizontal and Flanking Policies (Europa Law Publishing 2006), especially pp. 189-198.

as it was fit for the purpose of dealing with rules of the Dutch bar association in the case itself. But this does not mean it is helpful as a general tool in the interpretation of Article 81 beyond cases involving rules established by non-State actors to govern the conduct of a profession.

For the time being sport alone offers plenty of testing grounds. Using *Meca-Medina and Majcen* one can conclude that there may be a restriction involved in the application of anti-doping rules, yet there need not be a violation of Article 81(1) when those rules are seen in their proper context as a guarantee of sport's pharmaceutical-free level playing field. So too, for example, agreeing fixtures in a league would not be a 'restriction' on competition, but rather essential to its organisation – though, by contrast, an agreement to sell rights to broadcast matches in common is not essential and so is a restriction which can stand only if exempted according to the orthodox criteria set out in Article 81(3).[1122] The Commission placed heavy reliance on *Wouters* in its ENIC/UEFA decision,[1123] in which it concluded that rules forbidding multiple ownership of football clubs suppressed demand but were indispensable to the maintenance of a credible competition marked by uncertainty as to the outcome of all matches. The *Wouters* formula has therefore been used to allow the peculiar features of sport to inform the application of the relevant legal rules. It fits! So for example this analytical framework can cope satisfyingly with rules governing selection of individuals for teams – restrictive but necessary[1124] –, rules framing transfer windows – restrictive but necessary to create the conditions for fair competition, especially in the later stages of a tournament,[1125] and rules limiting ticket sales for major events to particular nationals or residents – restrictive and unnecessary, so unlawful.[1126] There is scope too in debating whether 'salary caps' may be treated as restrictions on commercial freedom that are nonetheless necessary in the delivery of a viable sporting competition and therefore not restrictions within the meaning of EC trade law.[1127]

Wouters, absorbed in *Meca-Medina*, is, in short, a statement of the conditional autonomy of sports federations under Article 81. Moreover, as suggested above, it is capable of application in a functionally comparable manner to provide routes under other relevant provisions of EC trade law to ensure scope for continued application of proper sporting practices. I do not suggest it is simple to discover what rules are necessary for the effective organisation of sport, but I believe the *Wouters* line of analysis ensures the right questions are asked.

[1122] Dec. 2003/778 Champions League, *OJ* 2003 L 291/25, Paras. 125-131. Exemption pursuant to Art. 81(3) was granted on the facts.

[1123] COMP 37.806 cited above at note 1090.

[1124] Cases C-51/96 and C-191/97 *Deliège* v. *Ligue de Judo*, [2000] *ECR* I-2549.

[1125] Case C-176/96, *Lehtonen* et al. v. *FRSB*, [2000] *ECR* I-2681.

[1126] Dec. 2000/12 1998 *Football World Cup* cited above note 1087.

[1127] S. Hornsby, 'The harder the cap, the softer the law?', 10 *Sport and the Law Journal* (2002) 142; J. Taylor and M. Newton, 'Salary Caps – the Legal Analysis', 11 *Sport and the Law Journal* (2003) 158.

THE *OULMERS* CASE: PUTTING *MECA-MEDINA* TO THE TEST

Under FIFA's rules governing the release of players for international representative matches, clubs must release players – their employees – for a defined period of time and for a defined group of matches. The rules make no provision for the clubs to receive payment. The clubs, not the national association nor the international federations, are explicitly stated to be responsible for the purchase of insurance to cover the risk that the player will be injured when playing for his country. Even if the player is not injured, he will arrive back at his club tired. There is no question of compensation for the club. This system seems imbalanced. Is it lawful?

Litigation is underway. In Belgium, Charleroi found that a highly promising young player, *Oulmers*, returned seriously injured in November 2004 from international duty with his home country, Morocco. Charleroi's fortunes on the field slumped without their young star, while they continued to have to pay his wages. They were entitled to no compensation. They brought a case before the Belgian courts. They claimed damages from FIFA, alleging a violation of Article 82 EC. The case was the subject of an intervention supportive of Charleroi's case by the G-14 group of 18 (!) major clubs, who pay the highest wages and consequently have the largest incentive to procure adjustment of the current rules. FIFA, for its part, enjoyed the support of interventions from over 50 continental and national associations. In May 2006 the Tribunal de Commerce in Charleroi agreed to make an Article 234 preliminary reference to Luxembourg.[1128] It brushed aside a number of arguments advanced by football's governing bodies, some involving technical points of procedure, others of a more fundamental nature, some rooted in Belgian law, others arising under EC law. The Tribunal concluded that as a matter of Belgian public policy it would not defer to the jurisdictional exclusivity claimed by FIFA for the Court of Arbitration in Sport – doubtless an important finding on a point likely commonly to arise in such litigation. Of particular current relevance, the Tribunal was asked to treat the rules as purely sporting in nature. It considered the matter only briefly, and took the view that the complexity of the case law, combined with the transnational importance of the issue under examination, made this an appropriate case for referral to Luxembourg in search of an authoritative uniform interpretation of EC law.

That the Court in Charleroi refused to set aside the commercial implications of the rule, and proceeded to make a reference despite the 'sporting' context is doubtless of tactical value to the clubs. However, in line with the case advanced in this paper, this is not to make any assumption that the economic context overrides the sporting. The point is that both value systems are involved. The test will be to assess whether the player release rules survive being put to the test under EC law. If they do not, the damages claim will proceed – raising in its turn some fiendishly difficult questions of causation and quantification of loss in the context of an activity as unpredictable as football.

[1128] The ruling is available via the Tribunal's website: www.tcch.be. The case is Pending Case C-000/06, referred to the European Court by Tribunal de Commerce de Charleroi in May 2006. For background, see S. Weatherill, 'Is the Pyramid Compatible with EC Law?', 3-4 *International Sports Law Journal* (2005) 3.

And *Wouters* will surely supply the relevant framework for analysis in Luxembourg given its ready acceptance by the ECJ in *Meca-Medina*. Account must be taken of

> 'the overall context in which the decision of the association of undertakings was taken or produces its effects. More particularly, account must be taken of its objectives. [...] It has then to be considered whether the consequential effects restrictive of competition are inherent in the pursuit of those objectives'.

That needs to be adjusted to take account of the role of Article 82, but it is the consistent assumption of this paper that the same basic analysis does and should apply: that is, the essence of the inquiry asks whether the objectives pursued by the practice can be met by measures which exert a less prejudicial impact on affected parties. If so, the practice is unlawful – in Article 82 terms, it would not be proportionate, nor could it be held to be objectively justified.

EC law contains nothing that calls into question the legitimacy of international football, and there is nothing that would rule out a priori action taken by football governing bodies to protect and promote international football. Nevertheless such measures would be classic examples of measures taken for sporting reasons which also have economic effects for those clubs which get their players back in a state of disrepair. If clubs were free to choose whether to release players, international football would be reduced to a competition dependent on the whims of clubs. So mandatory player release seems indispensable if international football is to survive. But is this system of mandatory player release necessary to achieve that end? I suspect that just as in *Bosman* the Court was prepared to hold that a transfer system could be justified (perhaps of the type that has been subsequently introduced[1129]) but it would not accept the particular transfer system under attack in the case, so too in *Oulmers* the Court will conclude that a mandatory player release system is justifiable but that this one is not.

International football is extraordinarily lucrative, yet the clubs, who provide the players, their often highly-paid employees, as indispensable resources to adorn the major tournaments receive no direct financial benefit. Any advantage they receive arrives only indirectly, via proceeds transferred to the national association of which they are a member. Football's 'pyramid' structure of governance rules out any direct formal contact between clubs and international governing bodies, instead routing the representation of club interests through national associations. One may also note that there is an element of competition at stake. International football tournaments are to some extent in the same market as club competitions when one considers potential interest from broadcasters and sponsors. So clubs are required to provide a free resource, the players, to an undertaking that is at least in part seeking to make profits

[1129] A revised version has been subsequently introduced – see B. Dabscheck, 'The Globe at their Feet: FIFA's New Employment Rules', 7 *Culture, Sport and Society* (2004) 69 – though it too may be vulnerable to legal challenge, e.g., J.-C. Drolet, 'Extra Time: Are the New FIFA Transfer Rules Doomed?' 1-2 *International Sports Law Journal* (2006) 66.

from exactly the same sources on which the clubs would wish to draw. One would certainly not find this in a normal industry. Sport truly is special.

The crispest objection to the system is that mandatory player release is necessary – but not in a form that leaves clubs uncompensated. The arrangements can be treated as compatible with EC law only provided clubs are allowed to defray at least part, if not all, of the cost of paying their players while they are absent on international duty by being allowed access to the pot of gold accumulated by the organisation of international football tournaments.

I find this convincing. Admittedly, exposure to a wider audience watching international representative football raises the value of the player to the club, so clubs conceivably acquire an indirect benefit from international football. But that is no reason for arguing for a system of mandatory uncompensated release of the extreme type that currently prevails. It is merely a basis for considering whether players' wages need not be paid in full out of the proceeds of international football. Similarly, although it is true that international bodies, unlike the clubs, have responsibilities to nurture the game throughout the world by sharing money raised from international tournaments, it is submitted that this too seems a plausible reason for running a system in which clubs cannot raid the entirety of the income generated by international football, not a good reason for denying the clubs any share in the money.

An apparently more promising argument would assert that some national associations are too poor to compensate clubs. This would mean that such associations would simply not pick highly-paid players. Countries would field teams that would not reflect their true strength, and the pattern of international competitions would be distorted. However, one could respond that international governing bodies could cope with this by establishing a revenue pool into which a slice of profits from international competitions could be paid before distribution to individual countries, and from which clubs could be compensated. Rich countries would subsidise poor countries from profits made through international football – at present clubs subsidise all countries despite taking no profits from international football. Is this feasible? Are there impediments to making such arrangements? That would require close analysis of the way that the industry works, and could work. The point is that it is precisely this inquiry that would and should follow from the adoption of the *Wouters* formula, absorbed in *Meca-Medina*, as the basis for the legal investigation. That the (mandatory, uncompensated) player release rules are of sporting interest in no way immunises them from review. Demonstrating that their prejudicial economic effect is essential in order to preserve the activity of international football is the way to secure free rein under EC law.

Moreover there is a procedural dimension to the submission that the current arrangements violate Article 82 EC. There is support in EC law for the case that sporting bodies' conditional autonomy in setting rules to govern the game depends on something more democratic than the 'pyramid'. Soft law material pertaining to sport issued at EU level has been a common feature of the last few years and the Court has made clear in *Deliège* and in *Lehtonen*,[1130] this material is apt for citation in

[1130] Cases C-51/96 and 191/97 cited above at note 1124, Paras. 41-42 of the judgment; Case C-176/96 cited above at note 1125, Paras. 32-33 of the judgment.

exploring the nature and scope of the relevant EC rules. The Declaration attached to the Nice Treaty includes consideration of the Role of sports federations. It refers *inter alia* to the need 'for a democratic and transparent method of operation' and 'a form of organisation providing a guarantee of sporting cohesion and participatory democracy'. Insistence on the virtues of participation chimes with the broader agenda mapped by the Commission in its 2001 White Paper on European Governance.[1131] It is perfectly possible to argue that football's neglect of these broad recommendations of transparent and participatory governance serves as a powerful reason for arguing that practices imposed on clubs fall foul of EC law. It is not necessary for the federations to exclude direct input by clubs. A committee representing a wider range of affected interests could readily be set up to determine the balance of rights and obligations in this matter. By formalising dialogue between transnational governing bodies and clubs-as-employers this, of course, would challenge the pure lines of the organisational 'pyramid', an argument that has purchase in other contexts, such as the aspirations of the clubs to acquire a more direct role in the management of club tournaments such as UEFA's Champions League. It is no secret that the *Oulmers* litigation is an element in a broader political strategy pursued by richer clubs eager for a louder voice in the game's governance.

It is submitted that the rules governing mandatory uncompensated player release go too far, both in substance and in the exclusionary way they are agreed and administered. Large profits are made through international football, and it is abusive for federations to enforce rules which allow them to take the benefit while imposing the burden of supplying players on the clubs. One could readily imagine an adjusted and potentially lawful system involving an obligation to release players imposed on clubs with corresponding obligations imposed on the governing bodies to provide compensation (*inter alia* to take account of the element of market competition for broadcasting and sponsorship money which is also at stake in this matter of regulation). The gratifying point of this paper is that the ECJ in *Meca-Medina and Majcen* has prepared the ground for *Oulmers* to be decided with due recognition for both the sporting and the economic context of the player release rules, and has set aside the unhelpful separation between the spheres clumsily attempted by the CFI.

Conclusion

Using *Wouters* does not unlock the door to simple answers to the several conundrums that surround the application of EC law to sport. But it prevents intellectually wasteful arguments at the slippery margin between sport and the economy. The principal virtue of *Wouters* is that it brings the right questions centre-stage in the legal analysis. Most of all, *Meca-Medina and Majcen* seems to have brought to an end the practical value to sports bodies of arguing that their rules are of 'purely sporting interest'. This will be true only in trivial circumstances where one scarcely imagine litigation being pursued. Instead the emphasis will be on whether rules, carrying economic impact,

[1131] COM (2001) 428.

produce consequential restrictive effects which are inherent in the pursuit of their objectives. If so, but only if so, they escape prohibition under Article 81(1). The same point, delivered in slightly different vocabulary and in relation to Article 39 not Article 81, is found in the Court's judgment in *Bosman* which accepts as 'legitimate' the perceived sports-specific anxiety to maintain a balance between clubs by preserving a certain degree of equality and uncertainty as to results and to encourage the recruitment and training of young players.[1132] And in Deliège, an Article 49 case, the Court accepted that selection rules limited the number of participants in a tournament, but were 'inherent' in the event's organisation.[1133] Such rules are not beyond the reach of the Treaty, but they are not incompatible with its requirements. But, as *Meca-Medina* itself shows, there remains scope for sport to protect its right to assert internal expertise in taking decisions that have both sporting and economic implications. The ECJ has collapsed the idea that there are purely sporting practices unaffected by EC law despite their economic effect, but it has not refused to accept that sport is special. Its message to governing bodies – explain how!

1132 Case C-415/93 cited above at note 1083, Para. 106.

1133 Cases C-51/96 and C-191/97 cited above at note 1124, Paras. 64, 69.

CONCLUDING REMARKS

Ian Blackshaw*

At first sight, one may reasonably ask: what has sport got to do with the EU; and what has the EU got to do with sport? Any connection between the two might seem bizarre. Sport is a social and leisure activity, while the EU is essentially a single market for business, comprising some 450 million people (soon to increase with the imminent accession of Bulgaria and Romania). But apart from the social and health aspects, sport has an important economic dimension too.

Sport has become a global industry, representing more than 3 per cent of world trade and 2 per cent of the combined GNP of the 25 EU Member States; more than 2 million jobs have been created directly or indirectly in the sports industry. In the UK, for example, sport provides employment for some 500,000 people, and is worth more than £ 12 billion a year in consumer spending.

Although there was no specific provision in the founding EC Treaty of 25 March 1957 giving the European Union (EU) – as it is now known – any competence in the field of sport, the EU, since the *Walrave & Koch* v. *Union Cycliste Internationale* decision of the European Court of Justice in 1974 (Case 36/74 [1974] ECR 1405), has been ready to intervene in those cases in which 'the practice of sport [...] constitutes an economic activity'.

The developments since that landmark decision are faithfully charted and critically analysed and assessed in this collection of Papers, including the *Bosman* case, which started a revolution in the international football transfer market and spawned new Regulations on the subject by FIFA, the world governing body of football, and whose effects continue to reverberate in world sporting circles.

The European Commission and the Court of Justice have also intervened in ticketing cases involving major sports events, such as the Olympic Games and the FIFA World Cup. And, even Formula One, the brainchild and bastion of Bernie Ecclestone, has not been immune from a Commission Investigation, culminating in an agreed separation of the regulatory and marketing functions of the sport – the latter much to the financial benefit of Ecclestone, who is a billionaire!

* Ian Blackshaw is an International Sports Lawyer and Visiting Professor at several European Universities and also an Honorary Fellow of the ASSER International Sports Law Centre, The Hague, The Netherlands.

Again, the joint selling arrangements of the broadcasting rights to such leading football tournaments as the English Premier League – the richest national football league in the world – and the UEFA flag ship 'Champions League' have also come under the scrutiny of the Commission's anti-trust regulators. In both cases, changes have been made to these arrangements, which are worth billions of Euros, to open them up to competition in the business and economic senses. Indeed, UEFA, of all the International Sports Federations, has adopted a more positive and collaborative approach to the Brussels regulators and their attacks on the autonomy of these sports bodies, which they jealously guard and defend, by opening a 'liaison office' in Brussels, in order to engage, like other industries, in dialogue and lobbying activities. A smart move on the part of UEFA and one that is bringing its own dividends. Indeed, UEFA has been very much involved in the production and publication of the Independent European Sport Review (which, incidentally, started life as the Independent European Football Review and also known as the Arnault Report) in the Summer of 2006. This review is currently under consideration by interested groups and parties (see comments later). And, by the way, Prof. Stephen Weatherill is not a particular fan of this review!
The Summer of 2006 also saw the issue of another landmark decision of the European Court of Justice in the *Meca-Medina* case, which, according to some commentators, deprives Sports Bodies of justifying anti-competitive restrictions on the grounds of 'sporting interests'. In any event, this decision, in which Maitre Dupont acted for the appellants, certainly undermines – to some extent – the autonomy of Sports Bodies in regulating their sports where the rules concerned may also have commercial implications of an anti-competitive nature.

This book is not only testimony to the great scholarship and learning of Prof. Stephen Weatherill, based on his in depth knowledge, understanding and appreciation of EU Competition Law (as evidenced by his excellent and erudite book *Cases and Materials on EU Law*, which is now in its seventh edition!) and its application in the sporting arena, but also to the pragmatic and creative approach of the European Commission and the European Court of Justice to the regulation of sport within the Single Market of the European Union, even though there is no specific provision in the EC Treaty giving the EU competence in the field of sport. Despite that fact, in global terms, the European contribution to international sport far outweighs its relative geographical size, and not surprisingly, therefore, this fact is bound to attract the attention of the policy and law makers at the European Commission in Brussels and the European Parliament in Strasbourg, as well as the Judges of the European Court of Justice in Luxembourg, the guardians of the Treaty.

For, as Prof. Stephen Weatherill has argued on many occasions, and with which I would entirely agree, why should a major industry, like the sports industry, whose economic significance has already been noted, be treated any differently from any other major industry operating in the European Union? Nevertheless, major players, such as FIFA and the International Olympic Committee, will continue to press for some kind of sport protocol or special exemption for sport from EU Law in general and EU Competition Law in particular, to safeguard their independence and freedom of action.

Indeed, as noted above, since its publication, several major sports organisations have issued some interesting comments on the Independent European Sport Review. For example, the International Olympic Committee in a letter to the EU Commissioner, Jan Figel, who is currently consulting on a 'White Paper' on Sports, due to be published during the Summer of 2007, signed by the President, Jacques Rogge, and dated 22 September, 2006, has declared that:

> 'The report of Mr Arnault does not represent the Olympic and sports movement's view as a contribution to this consultation process.'

And added:

> 'We believe that the issue of governance is of the utmost importance for the sports movement [...] therefore, it does not fall within the EU's competence.'

FIFA Presidential Delegate for Special Affairs, Jerome Champagne, not surprisingly, shares the same point of view:

> 'The autonomy of sport is fundamental, as we need to protect it from political and economic interference. The issues related to sport must be dealt with by sport authorities globally, since they are world issues, not just European issues. We need legal stability in Europe to define what we accept in sport. Sport has specific characteristics on which autonomous rules should apply. For example, in the case of doping, this is why we have a World Anti-Doping Agency.'

Unease has also been expressed, following a meeting in Brussels on 20 September, 2006, by certain European Team Sports Federations, including, UEFA, FIBA Europe and the IIHF, in the following terms:

> 'The European Sports Model, including the pyramid structure and as defined in more detail in the Independent Sport Review, is currently under threat and must be preserved.'

No doubt, Prof. Stephen Weatherill will continue to chart these and other future developments in his further writings and analyses on the European Union and Sport, including the ground-breaking pending case against FIFA (Case C-243/06, lodged 30 May 2006 – *SA Sporting du Pays de Charleroi, G-14 Groupment des Clubs de Football Européens* v. *Fédération Internationale de Football Association (FIFA)*), dealing with claims for compensation for players injured on international duty in FIFA competitions, in which, once again, Maître Dupont is the lawyer for the football club and the G-14, the claimants in this case.

And, who knows, before too long, there may well be sufficient material for publishing a companion volume to this book!

NATIONAL AND INTERNATIONAL LEGISLATION

EC/EU Treaty

Art. 2	18, 26, 49, 59, 94, 251, 336, 337, 339, 340
Art. 3	49
Art. 3(a)	29, 286
Art. 3(c)	29
Art. 7 (now repealed)	18, 19, 23, 26
Art. 10 (ex art. 5)	40, 69
Art. 10(1) (ex art. 5(1))	12, 13, 256, 259, 261, 262, 273-278, 282, 284, 328, 329, 331
Art. 12	148, 170, 180, 337
Art. 17 (ex art. 8A)	16, 29, 49
Art. 26 (ex art. 28)	6
Art. 28 (ex art. 30)	25, 28, 48, 51, 69, 70, 72, 73, 95, 96, 275
Art. 30	275, 341
Art. 33 (ex art. 39)	1, 6
Art. 36	129
Art. 39 (ex art. 48)	15, 18-20, 23, 24, 26, 28, 29, 32, 38, 40, 41, 44, 45, 46, 47, 48-50, 55, 56, 59, 60, 63-70, 72, 73, 75, 77-80, 82, 83, 92-97, 99, 101-107, 109, 111-114, 91, 115, 137-139, 144, 158, 163, 169, 180, 180, 183, 190, 191, 193, 194, 206, 206, 207, 216, 217, 220, 221, 223, 224, 224, 264, 275, 282, 340, 341, 342, 346, 353
Art. 39(1) (ex art. 48(1))	26
Art. 39(3) (ex art. 48(3))	18, 23, 26, 49, 60, 95, 96, 99
Art. 40 (ex art. 49)	1
Art. 43 (ex art. 52)	19, 70, 92, 95, 96, 275
Art. 46	275, 341
Art. 47(2)	322
Art. 49 (ex art. 59)	19, 23, 24, 71, 72, 96, 183, 250, 257, 264, 275, 340 -342, 346, 347, 353
Art. 55	275, 322
Art. 56	275
Art. 58	275
Art. 77 (ex art. 81)	1, 6, 8, 10
Art. 81 (ex art. 85)	15, 18, 25, 27, 29, 30-32, 35, 38, 39, 41, 43, 44, 45, 46, 47, 48, 49, 50, 51, 55, 70, 75-78, 81-83, 91, 93, 95, 102-104, 106, 108-111, 115, 125-127, 138, 139, 149, 150, 152, 158, 160, 169, 170, 180, 187, 194, 197, 198, 200-202, 204-207, 209, 214, 223, 224, 226, 228-231, 233, 245, 250, 254, 257, 260, 264, 270, 271, 275, 286, 288-291, 294, 296-303, 307-309, 311-313, 316, 317, 321, 331, 332, 339, 342-348, 353

Art. 81(1) (ex art. 85(1)) 33, 38, 65, 76, 81, 108, 109, 139-141, 148, 149, 165, 186, 192, 197-199, 203, 204, 206, 207, 223, 226, 227, 230, 231, 245, 246, 252, 253, 287, 291, 294, 298-300, 302, 303, 307-310, 316-321, 331, 333, 338, 342-344, 346-348, 353
Art. 81(2) 287, 133
Art. 81(3) (ex art. 85(3)) 29, 32, 33-39, 41, 50, 51, 60, 76, 81, 82, 109, 129, 140, 141, 150, 153, 170, 171, 173, 198, 199, 201, 202, 205-207, 209, 225, 231-233, 246, 253, 287, 288, 290, 291, 294, 298, 302, 303, 305, 306, 310, 311, 315-321, 331, 333, 341, 347, 348
Art. 82 (ex art. 86) 15, 18, 25, 27, 29, 30-35, 38, 41, 43, 44, 45, 49, 50, 55, 75, 81, 83, 91, 93, 108, 115, 118-119, 138, 139, 141, 149, 165, 169, 187, 194, 205 , 206, 209, 224, 250, 260, 265, 266, 268-270, 275, 286, 289, 291-294, 296, 338, 341, 342, 347, 349-351
Art. 87 (ex art. 92) 49
Art. 90 (ex art. 95) 49
Art. 95 234, 275, 277, 317
Art. 141 (ex art. 119) 24, 29
Art. 151(4) 235, 322, 233, 317
Art. 152 275
Art. 152(1) 235, 322
Art. 152(5) 276
Art. 153 275, 283
Art. 153(2) 235, 322
Art. 174 275
Art. 175 275
Art. 176 275
Art. 213 195
Art. 226 (ex art. 169) 40-42
Art. 230 (ex art. 173) 44, 55, 82, 91, 110
Art. 230(2) (ex art. 173(2)) 43
Art. 230(4) 324
Art. 232 (ex art. 175) 42, 44
Art. 234 (ex art. 177) 23, 24, 51, 55-57, 91, 97, 98, 183, 239, 328, 349
Art. 249 (ex art. 189) 40, 82, 110
Art. 288 (ex art. 215) 42, 44, 55, 91
Art. 295 270, 277, 279, 280
Art. 308 275, 277, 278

European Convention for the Protection of Human Rights
Rome, 4.11.1950 (CETS No.: 005)
Article 10 240, 326

Treaty establishing the European Coal and Steel Community (ECSC),
24.7.1952 (expired on 23.7.2003)
Art. 80 28

Cooperation Agreement between the European Economic Community and the Kingdom of Morocco
Rabat 27/04/1976 (J.O. L 264) 111

European Economic Area (EEA) agreement
17.3.1993 (OJ L 1, 3.1.1994, pp. 3–36)
Arts. 28 et seq. 111
Art. 54 117, 118, 187

EC Charter of Fundamental Rights of the European Union
December 2000 (O.J. [2000] C 364/1)
Art. 11 240, 326
Art. 52 240, 326

Treaty establishing a Constitution for Europe
(OJ C 310, 16.12.2004, p. 474–474)
Art. I-16 245
Art. III-182 245, 268

COUNCIL DIRECTIVES

Council Directive 64/221/EEC of 25 February 1964 on the co-ordination of special measures concerning the movement and residence of foreign nationals which are justified on grounds of public policy, public security or public health (OJ P 056, 04/04/1964, pp. 850-857) 26
Art. 3(1) 25

Council Directive 89/552/EEC of 3 October 1989 on the coordination of certain provisions laid down by Law, Regulation or Administrative Action in Member States concerning the pursuit of television broadcasting activities (OJ L 298, 17/10/1989, pp. 23-30) 212, 234-236, 239, 322-325, 328, 332
Art. 3a 235, 236, 238, 239, 240, 323, 325, 328

Council Directive 93/13/EEC of 5 April 1993 on unfair terms in consumer contracts (OJ L 095, 21/04/1993, pp. 29-34) 114

Directive 97/36/EC of the European Parliament and of the Council of 30 June 1997 amending Council Directive 89/552/EEC on the coordination of certain provisions laid down by law, regulation or administrative action in Member States concerning the pursuit of television broadcasting activities (OJ L 202, 30/07/1997, pp. 60-70) 212, 234, 235, 238, 240, 322, 326
Art. 1(4) 235, 323

COUNCIL/COMMISSION REGULATIONS

EEC Council: Regulation No 17/62: First Regulation implementing Articles 85 and 86 of the Treaty (OJ P 013, 21/02/1962, pp. 204-211) 33, 41, 44, 46, 49, 50, 65, 289
Art. 3 82
Art. 3(2) 43, 82
Art. 4(1) 109
Art. 4(2) 33
Art. 15 41
Art. 16 41

Regulation No 99/63/EEC of the Commission of 25 July 1963 on the hearings provided for in Article 19 (1) and (2) of Council Regulation No 17 (OJ P 127, 20/08/1963, pp. 2268-2270) 44
Art. 6 43

Regulation (EEC) No 1612/68 of the Council of 15 October 1968 on freedom of movement for workers within the Community (OJ L 257, 19/10/1968, pp. 2-12)	19
Art 7(2)	19, 20
Art 7(4)	24, 49
Regulation (EEC) No 1408/71 of the Council of 14 June 1971 on the application of social security schemes to employed persons and their families moving within the Community (OJ L 149, 05/07/1971, pp. 2-50)	111, 112
Commission Regulation (EC) No 2790/1999 of 22 December 1999 on the application of Article 81(3) of the Treaty to categories of vertical agreements and concerted practices (Text with EEA relevance) (OJ L 336, 29/12/1999, pp. 21-25)	303, 306
Art. 3	304, 305
Art. 4	304
Art. 5	305
Council Regulation (EC) No 1/2003 of 16 December 2002 on the implementation of the rules on competition laid down in Articles 81 and 82 of the Treaty (Text with EEA relevance) (OJ L 001, 04/01/2003, pp. 1-25)	288-291, 306
Art. 2	346
Art. 3(2)	291, 294
Art. 6	289
Art. 7(2)	290
Arts. 11-16	290, 306
Art. 11(6)	291
Art. 16	291
Art. 23	289

NATIONAL LEGISLATION

Germany

Gesetz gegen Wettbewerbsbeschränkungen	
s 31	132, 159, 200, 228, 312

United Kingdom

European Communities Act 1972	
s 2(1)	45
Restrictive Trade Practices Act 1976	200, 229, 312
ss 9(6), 18(6)	29
s 43(2)	31
Rules of the Supreme Court	
Order 53	45

TABLE OF CASES

EUROPEAN COURT OF JUSTICE

Case C-26/62	Van Gend en Loos [1963] ECR 1, [1963] CMLR 105	17
Case C-6/64	Costa v ENEL [1964] ECR 585	291
Cases C-56 & 58/64	Consten and Grundig v Commission [1966] ECR 299	108
Case C-32/65	Italy v Council and Commission [1966] ECR 389	28
Case C-14/68	Walt Wilhelm [1969] ECR 1	291
Case C-22/71	Beguelin [1971] ECR 949, [1972] CMLR 81	31
Case C-36/71	[1974] ECR 1405	92
Case C-6/72	Europemballage Corp. and Continental Can Co. Inc. v Commission [1973] ECR 215, [1973] CMLR 199	28, 119
Case C-8/72	Cementhandelaren v Commission [1972] ECR 977, [1973) CMLR 7	29, 38
Case C-39/72	Commission v Italy [1973] ECR 101	40
Case C-127/73	BRT v SABAM [1974] ECR 51, 62; [1974] 2 CMLR 231, 271	33
Case C-152/73	Sotqiu v Deutsche Bundespost [1974] ECR 153	15
Case C-155/73	Sacchi [1974] ECR 409, [1974] 2 CMLR 177 (television broadcasts)	29
Case C-167/73	[1974] ECR 359; [1974] 2 CMLR 216	19, 20, 23
Case C-8/74	Procureur du Roi v Dassonville	73
Case C-36/74	Walrave and Koch v Union Cycliste Internationale [1974] ECR 1405; [1975] 1 CMLR 320	2-5, 12, 18, 20, 22-25, 32, 36, 47, 49, 51, 57, 59-63, 92, 94, 99, 115, 132, 135, 143, 146, 148, 149, 160, 170, 180-182, 184, 186, 216, 250-252, 254, 257, 260, 271, 280, 336-338, 340, 355
Case C-1/75	[1975] ECR 1171	43
Case C-43/75	Defrenne v SABENA, [1976] ECR 455	88
Case C-48/75	Royer [1976] ECR 497, [1976] 2 CMLR 619	19
Case C-13/76	Donà v Mantero[1976] 2 CMLR 578, [1976] ECR 1333	21, 24, 25, 40, 57-59, 60, 62, 92, 94, 99, 100, 143, 160, 180, 184, 216, 250, 251, 254, 260, 280, 336, 337, 338
Case C-26/76	Metro-SB-Grossmärkte GmbH & CO KG v Commission [1977] ECR 1875, [1978] 2 CMLR 1	32, 43, 81, 108
Case C-33/76	Rewe v Landwirtschaftskammer [1976] ECR 1989, [1977] 1 CMLR 533	44
Case C-45/76	Comet v Produktschap [1976] ECR 2043, [1977] 1 CMLR 533	44
Case C-19/77	Miller [1978] ECR 131	38
Case C-30/77	Bouchereau [1977] ECR 1999, [1977] 2 CMLR 800	
Case C-14/78	Denkavit v Commission[1978] ECR 2497	42, 44
Case C-120/78	Rewe Zentrale v Bundesmonopolverwaltung für Branntwein (Cassis de Dijon) [1979] ECR 649	73, 96, 283
Case C-125/78	GEMA v Commission [1979] ECR 3173, [1980] 2 CMLR 177	44, 82, 110
Case C-22/78	Hugin v Commission, [1979] ECR 1869	81, 108
Case C-175/78	R v Saunders, [1979] ECR 1129	79, 107
Case C-253/78	Guerlain [1980] ECR 2327, [1981] 2 CMLR 94	
Case C-258/78	Nungesser v Commission [1982] ECR 2015	298

Case C-73/79	Commission v Italy[1980] ECR 1533	49
Case C-130/79	Express Dairy Foods v Intervention Board [1980] ECR 1887; [1981] 1 CMLR 451	44
Case C-58/80	Dansk Supermarked v Imerco [1981] ECR 181, [1981] 3 CMLR 590	
Case C-61/80	Cooperatieve Stremsel- en Kleurselfabriek v Commission [1981] ECR 351	35, 38
Case C-172/80	Zeuchner v Bayerische Vereinsbank [1981] ECR 2021; [1982] 1 CMLR 313 (banking)	29
Case C-270/80	Polydor v Harlequin Record Shops, [1982] ECR 329	112
Case C-262/81	[1982] ECR 3381	299, 301, 320
Case C-322/81	Michelin v Commission [1983] ECR 3461	292, 293
Case C-7/82	GVL v Commission [1983] ECR 483, [1983] 3 CMLR 645	35, 119, 188
Case C-199/82	San Giorgio [1983] ECR 3595, [1985] 2 CMLR 658	45
Case C-170/83	Hidrotherm Gerärebau v Andreoli [1984] ECR 2999	31
Case C-180/83	Moser [1984] ECR 2539	39
Case C-182/83	Fearon [1984] ECR 3677, [1985] 2 CMLR 228	21
Case C-229/83	Leclerc v Au Blé Vert, [1985] ECR 1	80, 107, 277
Case C-240/83	Procureur de la Republique v Adbhu [1985] ECR 531	277
Case C-251/83	Haug-Adrion [1984] ECR 4277, [1985] 3 CMLR 266	21
Case C-795/83	Gravier v City of Liège [1985] ECR 593, [1985] 3 CMLR 1	19
Case C-42/84	Remia v Commission [1985] ECR 2545, [1987] 1 CMLR 1	29
Cases C-142 and 156/ 84	BAT and Reynolds v Commission [1988] 4 CMLR 24	44
Cases C-209-13/84	Ministère Public v Asjes [1986] ECR 1425, [1986] 3 CMLR 173	28, 40
Case C-45/85	Verband der Sachversicherer v Commission [1987] ECR 405	28
Cases C-80 & 159/85	Nederlandse Bakkerij v Edah [1986] ECR 3359 [1988] 2 CMLR 113	26
Cases C-89/85	Ahlstrom and others v Commission (Woodpulp Cartel) [1988] 4 CMLR 901	30, 160
Case C-311/85	Vlaamse Reisbureaus [1987] ECR 3801, [1989] 4 CMLR 213	30, 40
Case C-12/86	[1987] ECR 3719	112
Case C-39/86	Lair v University of Hanover, [1988] ECR 3161; [1989] 3 CMLR 545	19, 80, 107
Case C-63/86	Commission v Italy [1989] 2 CMLR 601	19
Case C-66/86	Ahmed Saeed Flugreisen	30
Case C-197/86	Brown v Secretary of State for Scotland [1988] 3 CMLR 403	19
Case C-30/87	Bodson v Pompes Funèbres, 4 MLR 984 (1989)	31
Case C-81/87	R v. HM Treasury and Commissioners of Inland Revenue ex parte Daily Mail and General Trust [1988] ECR 5483	70, 95
Case C-45/88	Torfaen Borough Council v B & Q plc	69
Cases T-69/89, T-70/89, T-76/89		293
	RTE, BBC, ITP v Commission [1991] ECR II-485, 535, 575	293
Case C-97/89	Fabrica Pisana v Commission [1989] 4 CMLR	30
Case C-192/89	Sevince [1990] ECR I-3461	112
Case C-234/89	Delimitis [1991] ECR I-935	300
Case C-260/89	ERT v Dimotiki [1991] ECR I-2925	240, 327
Cases C-6, C-9/90	[1991] ECR I-5357	289
Case C-18/90	ONEM v Kbizer [1991] ECR I-199	111, 112
Case T-24/90	Automec v Commission "Automec II" [1992] ECR II-2223	82, 110, 134, 290
Case T-28/90	Asia Motor France SA and others v Commission, [1992] ECR II-2285	82, 110
Case C-41/90	Höfner v Macrotron	76
Case C-179/90	Porto di Genova	76
Case C-370/90	Surinder Singh, [1992] ECR I-4265	80, 107
Case C-2/91	Meng	69
Case C-83/91	Meilicke v ADV/ORGA [1992] ECR I-4871	98
Case T-83/91	Tetra Pakt II, [1992] ECR I-4871; [1994] ECR II-755	98, 119, 188
Case C-117/91	Jean-Marc Bosman v Commission, [1991] ECR I-4837	55, 91
Case C-169/91	Stoke-on-Trent and Norwich City Councils v B & Q	69

Case C-185/91	Reiff	69
Cases C-241/91P	and C-242/91P RTE and ITP v Commission [1995] ECR I-743	293
Case C-245/91	Ohra	69
Cases C-267/91 & C-268/91		
	Keck and Mithouard [1993] ECR I-6097	69-72, 95
Case T-7/92	Asia Motor France v Commission, [1993] ECR II-669	82, 110
Case C-19/92	Dieter Kraus v. Land Baden-Württemberg and Gebhard v. Consiglio dell 'Ordine degli Avvocati e Procuratori di Milano [1993] ECR I-1663	73, 80, 96, 107
Case C-37/92	BEUC and NCC v Commission [1994] ECR II-285	82, 110
Case T-46/92	Scottish Football Association v Commission [1994] ECR II-1039	81, 93
Case T-74/92	Ladbroke Racing v Commission [1995] ECR II-115	82
Case T-114/92	BEMIM v Commission [1995] ECR II-147	83, 110, 111
Case C-250/92	Gottrup Klim v DLB [1994] ECR I-5641	102, 204, 252, 299, 308, 344, 347
Case C-275/92	Schindler, [1994] ECR I-1039	
Case C-23/93	TV 10 SA v Commissariaat voor de Media, [1994] ECR I-4795	80, 107
Cases C-46/93 and C-48/ 93		
	Brasserie du Pêcheur SA v Germany and R v Secretary of State for Transport, ex parte Factortame Ltd and others	115
Cases C-69/93 and C-258/93		
	Punto Casa SpA v Sindaco del Comune	72
Case C-384/93	Alpine Investments v Minister van Financiën [1995] ECR I -1141	71, 95
Case C-412/93	Edouard Leclerc-Siplec v TFI Publicité SA and M6 Publicité SA	71
Case C-415/93	Union Royale Belge des Sociétés de Football Association ASBL v Jean-Marc Bosman [1995] ECR I-4921	3, 4, 7, 53, 54, 56, 60-63, 65, 71, 72, 80, 85, 87, 121, 131-133, 135, 136 , 138, 143-145, 147-150, 153, 155, 157, 159, 160, 168, 171, 175,178-184, 186, 189-191, 193-197, 202-204, 206, 208, 210, 216, 216-221, 223-227, 232, 242, 245, 250, 251, 253, 256, 257, 260, 261, 263-265, 269-271, 280-282, 294, 296, 308, 315, 331, 332, 336-339, 341, 350, 353, 355
Cases T-528/93, T-542/93, T-543/93 and T-546/93		
	Métropole Télévision and Others v Commission [1996] ECR II-649	297, 318
Case T-548/93	Ladbroke Racing v Commission, [1995] ECR II-2565	82, 110
Case C-143/94	Furlanis v ANAS	98
Cases T-374/94	European Night Services v Commission [1998] ECR II-3141	299, 303, 299
Case C-55/94	Gebhard v Consiglio dell'Ordine degli Avvocati e Procuratori di	73, 96
Case C-265/95	Commission v France [1997] ECR I-6959	279, 336
Case C-368/95	Vereinigte Familiapress Zeitungsverlags- und vertriebs GmbH v Heinrich Bauer Verlag [1997] ECR I-3689	240, 276, 327
Cases C-51/96 and C-191/97		
	Christelle Deliège v Ligue Francophone de Judo et Disciplines Associées ASBL, Ligue Belge de Judo ASBL and Union Européene de Judo/ François Pacquée [2000] ECR I-2549	170, 182-184, 202, 206, 210, 226, 242, 251, 254, 257, 260, 267, 271, 307, 329, 338, 348, 351, 353
Case C-67/96	Albany International v Stichting Bedrijfspensioenfonds Textielindustrie [1991] ECR I-5751	192, 223, 245, 308, 316

Case C-176/96	Jyri Lehtonen, Castors Canada Dry Namur-Braine ASBL v Fédération Royale Belge des Sociétés de Basket-ball ASBL [2000] ECR I-2681	170, 182-184, 186, 193, 202, 206, 210, 225, 242, 251, 257, 260, 262, 267, 271, 329, 337, 338, 348, 329, 348, 351
Case C-306/96	Javico et al v Yves St Laurent Parfums [1998] ECR I-1983	300
Case C-7/97	Oscar Bronner GmbH v Mediaprint [1998] ECR I-7791	294
Case C-126/97	Eco Swiss China Time Ltd v Benetton International NV [1999] ECR I-3055	286
Case C-219/97	Maatschappij Drijvende Bokken BV v Stichting Pensioenfonds [1999] ECR I-6121	192, 223
Case C-222/97	Trummer and Mayer [1999] ECR I-1661	280
Case C-264/98	Tibor Balog v Royal Charleroi Sporting Club	164, 202
Case C-376/98	Germany v Parliament and Council [2000] ECR I-8419 ("Tobacco Advertising")	185, 234, 235, 256, 277, 317, 322, 340
Case C-377/98	Netherlands v Parliament and Council [2001] ECR I-7079	278
Case C-423/98	Albore [2000] ECR I-5965	280
Case C-464/98	Westdeutsche Landesbank v Stefan [2001] ECR I-173	280
Case T-112/99	Métropole télévision (M6), Suez-Lyonnaise des eaux, France Télécom v Télévision française 1 SA (TF1) [2001] ECR II-2159	263, 299
Case C-157/99	B.S.M. Geraets-Smits v Stichting Ziekenfonds VGZ, H.T.M. Peerbooms v Stichting CZ Groep Zorgverzekeringen [2001] ECR I-5473	276
Case C-214/99	Neste Markkinoiniti Oy [2000] ECR I-11121	300
Case C-309/99	J.C.J. Wouters, J.W. Savelbergh, Price Waterhouse Belastingadviseurs BV v Algemene Raad van de Nederlandse Orde van Advocaten [2002] ECR I-1577	10, 204, 206, 245, 249, 252, 254, 256-258, 263, 264, 308, 316, 331, 342-346, 348, 350-352
Case C-453/99	Courage v Crehan [2001] ECR I-6297	289
Case IV/36.237	TPS 1 OJ 1999 L90/6	
Cases T-69, T-70, T-76/89	[1991] ECR II-485, 535, 575	
Case IV/M469	MSG Media Service OJ 1994 L364/1	
Cases T-185/00	et al M6 and others v Commission [2002] ECR II-3805	237, 295, 297, 301, 319, 295, 297, 301, 319, 320, 325
Case C-438/00	Deutscher Handballbund eV. v Kolpak [2003] ECR I-4135	182, 251, 260, 337
Case T-33/01	Infront WM v Commission	241, 324, 325
Case T-42/01	SETCA-FGTB v Commission	191, 222
Cases C-264/01, C-306/01, C-354/01 and C-355/01	AOK [2004] ECR I-2493	297
Case C-418/01	IMS Health [2004] ECR I-5039	294
Case C-491/01	R v Secretary of State ex parte BAT & Imperial Tobacco [2002] ECR I-11543	278
Case T-193/02	Laurent Piau v Commission	262, 268, 296
Case T-313/02	David Meca-Medina and Igor Majcen v Commission [2004] ECR II-3291	4, 10, 299, 303, 335, 339, 249-250, 260, 281, 308
Case C-210/03	[Swedish Match [2004] ECR I-0000	278
Case C-265/03	Igor Simutenkow	260, 278
Case T-328/03	O2 (Germany) GmbH v Commission	299, 347
Case C-446/03	Marks and Spencer v Halsey	279, 336
Case C-512/03	J E J Blankaert	279, 336
Case C-205/03P	Fenin v Commission	342
Cases C-154/04 & C-155/04	Alliance for Natural Health [2005] ECR I-0000	278

Case C-222/04	Cassa di Risparmio di Firenze	297
Case C-372/04	ex parte Watts	276, 278, 336
Case C-519/04	Meca-Medina and Majcen v Commission	4, 12, 249, 260, 264, 281, 335, 337, 340, 335, 337, 339, 340, 342, 343, 345-353, 356
Case C-171/05P	Laurent Piau v Commission	296
Case C-000/06		296, 349
Case C-125/06P	Commission v Infront WM OJ 2006 C108/7	324
Case C-243/06	SA Sporting du Pays de Charleroi, G-14 Groupement des Clubs de Football Européens v Fédération Internationale de Football Association (FIFA) (Oulmers/Charleroi)	11, 267, 296, 271, 350, 352

COMMISSION DECISIONS

AROW v BNIC, Comm. Dec. 82/896 [1983] 2 CMLR 240	30
Napier Brown - British Sugar, Comm. Dec. 88/518/EEC, 18.7.1988, OJ L 284, pp. 41-59	108
ITP, RTE, BBC Comm. Dec. 89/205 OJ 1989 L78/43, [1989] 4 CMLR 757	293
Citroen, [1989] 4 CMLR 338	35
Distribution of package tours during the 1990 World Cup, Comm. Dec. 92/521/EEC, 27.10. 1992, OJ L 326, pp. 31-42	188
Football World Cup Comm. Dec. 000/12/EC, 20.7.1999, OJ L 005, pp. 55-74	187, 338, 348
UEFA/Mouscron IP/99/965, 9.12.1999, IP 99/956, 9 June 1999	121, 186, 205, 260
Eurovision, Comm. Dec. 2000/400, 10.5.2000, OJ 2000 L151, pp.18-41	295
FIA (Formula One) IP/01/1523, 30.10.2001	185, 260, 265
UEFA's "blocking" rules, Comm. Dec. 2001/478, O.J. 2001, L 171/12	197
Deutsche Post AG - Interception of cross-border mail, Comm. Dec. 2001/892/EC, 25.7.2001, OJ L 331, pp. 40-78	188
ENIC/UEFA IP/02/942, 27 June 2002	218, 246, 253, 261, 307, 331, 338, 348
Champions League, Comm. Dec. 2003/778, OJ 2003 L291/25 para. 79	260, 300

COURT OF ARBITRATION FOR SPORT (CAS)

CAS 98/200 AEK Athens and Slavia Prague v UEFA	149, 173, 186, 218, 261

AUSTRALIA

Buckley v Tutty (1971) 225 CLR 353	84

UNITED KINGDOM

American Cyanamid v Ethicon [1975] AC 396	45
Baurgoin v MAFF [1986] QB 716, [1985] 3 WLR 1027	45
Cooke v Football Association, The Times, 24 March 1972	27
Eastham v Newcastle United FC [1964] Ch 413	45, 84, 106
Garden Cottage Foods v Milk Marketing Board [1984] AC 130, [1983] 3 WLR 143	45
Greig v Insole [1978] 1 WLR 302	27
Law v National Greyhound Racing Club Ltd [1983] 1 WLR 1302	45
R v Independent Television Commission, ex parte TV Danmark 1 Ltd (2001] 1 WLR 1604	238, 327
R v Panel on Take-Overs and Mergers, ex p Datafin [1987] QB 815	45
Schroeder Music Publishing Co Ltd v Macaulay. [1974] 1 WLR 1308	114
Smith v Pro Football Inc., 593 F.2d 1173 (1978)	77, 104

UNITED STATES

Brown, v Pro Football 116 Sup Ct 2116, 135 L. Ed. 2d 521	75
Copperweld Corp v Independence Tube Corp 467 US 752 (1984)	31

SUBJECT INDEX

Advocates General
Jacobs 71
Leger 340
Lenz 8, 22, 54, 56, 57, 60, 61, 63, 64, 70, 75-78, 81, 82, 85, 88, 92, 93, 98-106, 108, 109, 136, 144, 162, 163, 171, 174, 182, 189, 190, 203, 204, 221, 224, 245, 253, 264
Mayras 43
Trabucchi 21, 40, 41, 62
Van Gerven 72
Warner 24, 43, 47, 61, 135
Agreement (*see also* **Contract**) 206
collective – 76, 82
horizontal – 76, 93, 108, 285, 306
vertical – 285, 288, 304
Ambush marketing 177
Antitrust liability
immunity from – 75
Arbitration 192, 223, 250
Arnault Report
Independent European Football Review 356
Athletes (*see also* **Player(s)**)
health of – 255, 343
physical and moral integrity of – 268
professional – 183
semi-professional – 183
Attribution
principle of – 259
British Athletics (BAF) 252
Bangemann Commission 58, 90, 225
Blatter, Sepp 191, 265
Block exemption 288, 304
Block Exemption Regulation on Vertical Restraints 287, 303, 305
Broadcasting 9, 11, 196, 203, 145, 266, 294, 345, 352
Canal Plus 318
European Broadcasting Union (EBU) 317, 318, 319
Eurovision 297, 310, 317, 318, 320
free broadcaster 239
free public broadcasters 325
free television 235, 237, 327
free-to-air broadcasting contracts 301
media revolution 155
pay-per-view 78
property rights 277
right to broadcast 11, 144, 151, 159, 165, 196, 197, 253, 273, 295, 298, 300
rights to transmit matches on television 102
– sector 144
television rights 81, 93

Broadcasting (cont.)
Television Independent Television Commission (ITC) 238
Television Without Frontiers Directive 234, 322
Broadcasting rights (*see also* **Right(s)**)
central marketing of – 151
co-ownership of – 309
collective sale of – 11, 132, 141, 147, 151-153, 159, 172-173, 198-202, 205-206, 209, 215, 217-219, 226, 228-233, 242-243, 247, 260, 270, 291, 297, 306, 308-317, 319-320, 330, 332
exclusive selling of – 298
sale of – 53, 114, 137, 155, 162, 171, 177, 270, 279, 284, 291, 294, 296, 297, 302, 305-307, 330, 332-333, 348
Burden of proof 342, 346
Business of sport
– an economic activity 18, 20, 28, 59, 92, 94, 95, 99, 132, 161, 180, 182, 217, 251, 255, 259, 262, 280, 337-339, 355
Cartels 30, 37, 58, 65, 98, 144, 151, 152, 159, 172, 229, 233, 275, 284, 286, 289, 316
adhesive 57
German cartel law 132, 159
global – 157
horizontal price-fixing – 174
Champions League (*see* **UEFA**)
Choice of law 87
Citizenship 22
Civic values 244
Club(s)
balance between – 74, 136, 171, 261
equality between – 138
interdependence of – 2, 78, 93, 140, 155, 165, 171, 179, 180, 199, 213, 217, 218, 226, 245, 247, 253, 285, 306, 307, 310, 331
legitimate interests 43
ownership of – 9, 140, 147, 149, 165, 173, 179, 186, 205, 206, 218, 253, 261, 307, 338, 348
relocation of – 165
Code of professional conduct 185
Cold calling 71
Collins, John 80
Comité Français d'Organisation de la Coupe du Monde de Football (CFO) 117-125, 187
Pass France 98 system 117, 118, 122
Commercial activities 215
Commission
1995 White Paper on Sports 146, 357
2004 guidelines on the application of Article 81(3) 316
April 2003 Discussion Paper 240, 326
enforcement Powers 41
Commissioners
Flynn 207
Monti 184, 191, 192, 195, 197, 198, 201, 222, 230, 233, 290, 315, 316, 321
Oreja 207
Reding 184, 202
Van Miert 207
Community law (*see also* **Freedom of movement**)
basic constitutional principles of – 7, 132

Community law (cont.)
EC policy on sport 143, 211, 212, 330
European Community Monopoly Law 291
EU sports law 260, 263
interpretation of – 98
misuse of the Article 177 procedure 98
objective character of – 184
– on sport 180, 345
soft law instruments 131
Treaty rules horizontally directly effective 23, 26, 33
Wouters formula 339, 348, 351
Community trade law
cross-border – 336
EC trade law 2, 13, 132, 155, 253
free market 119
Notice on market definition 118, 131
parallel imports of sports products 149, 168
principles of parallel trade 108, 144
restrictions on – 97
SSNIP test 118, 187
unfair trading conditions 119, 188
unlawful restrictions on – 190
Compensation 67, 144, 157
training – 192
Competence
– anxiety 274
attributed – 273
– creep 274-275, 277, 284, 329
regulatory – 273
sector-specific competences 275
system of – control 277
Consumers
consumer policy 286
consumer protection 275, 283
directive on unfair terms in consumer contracts 114
EC consumer law 283
Contract (*see also* **Agreement**)
breach of – 113, 192, 221, 223
freedom of – 104, 114, 106, 111, 219
minimum and maximum duration of – 192
stability of – 192
unilateral – breakers 206
Coordination and harmonization 234
Court for Arbitration for Sport (CAS) 141, 149, 173, 186, 213, 218, 249, 349
Decision-makers in sport
autonomy of – 260
Democracy
participatory – 268, 352
Discrimination (*see also* **Nationality**) 96, 143, 148, 187-189
discriminatory practices 121
intra-EU nationality – 260
nationality-based – 2, 6-7, 15-51, 61, 63, 64, 70, 92, 95, 97, 99, 105, 111, 119, 135, 144, 158, 159, 180, 182, 196, 203, 205, 216, 225, 251, 280, 281, 293, 294
– on grounds of residence 35
reverse – 79, 80
– rule 92
rule of non-discriminatory availability 119

Dominant position	158
abuse of a –	291, 292
dominant undertaking	119
Doping	114, 145-147, 164, 264, 335, 340
anti-doping controls	249, 254, 256, 343
anti-doping rules	4, 10, 12, 187, 205, 249, 253, 335, 337, 339, 340, 343-345
economic or commercial nature of anti-doping rules	257
nandrolone	249, 253, 345
– offences	187
Draft Constitutional Treaty	245, 268, 274
Draft pick	131
Dual vigilance	17
principle of –	134
EC competition law	335
Competition Act 1998 (UK)	312
Competition Directorate General	288, 289, 300, 311
national – authorities	290
competition rules	178, 190, 202-204
private enforcement of –	290
restrictions on free competition-	102
substantial restriction on –	310
Economic power	
abuse of –	293
Employment	
collective agreements between employers and employees	76, 81, 82, 108, 193
collective arrangements between employers	66, 159, 164, 221
collective bargains	75, 136, 174, 214, 223
collective intervention in contractual freedom	246
collective labour regulation	100, 106
collective negotiations between management and labour	192
collective wage agreement	75, 102, 137, 162
collectively-enforced restrictions on player mobility	224
– contract	66, 67, 89, 114, 135, 157, 159, 189, 190, 220
cross-border labour mobility	193
exercise of an cccupational activity	92
expiration of – contract	190
increase of wage	190
non-statutory labour exemption	142, 174
player mobility	147, 192, 193, 223, 247
predator employers	219
restraints on player mobility	191
residual restrictions on labour mobility	194
salary cap	76, 162, 174, 176, 214, 253, 257, 331, 348
social and employment policies	145
working conditions	193
Environmental policy	275, 286
environmental protection	275
European Coal and Steel Community (ECSC)	286
European dimension in sport	268
European Economic Area (EEA)	117, 118, 187
European Economic Interest Grouping	265
European Sports Forum	210, 244, 245, 330
European Sports Model	8, 145, 146, 151, 153, 155, 157, 164, 166, 173, 175, 201, 202, 207-209, 232, 243, 247, 259, 262, 315, 328, 329
European Union Conference on Sport	145, 165, 208
European Year of Education through Sport	211

Events
"protected" or "listed" – 215, 234, 235, 240, 247, 297, 321, 322, 325, 326, 328, 332, 333
free and fair sporting – 264
– of major importance for society 235-237, 241, 323, 327
Ex ante monitoring system 274
Exception
"purely sporting interest" – 12, 23,63, 146, 148, 182, 251, 339
sporting – 149, 186
Exclusion 298
Exclusive rights 227, 235-239, 294, 303, 306, 323
Exclusivity 297, 298, 300
Exemption 109, 215, 232, 247, 280, 288, 298, 302, 304, 311, 321, 332, 333
Fédération Française de Football (FFF) 158
Fédération Internationale d'Automobile (FIA) 156, 185, 296
Formula One 141, 185, 295, 296, 355
Fédération International de Footballeurs Professionels (FIFPro) 191, 194, 222
Fédération Internationale de Natation (FINA) 187, 249
Fines
method of setting – 123
symbolic – 123, 124
Fixed-term deals 219
Football 295
economic significance of – 92 governing bodies
autonomy of – 197
international representative football 269
– is special 191
professional – 216
professional footballer is worker 19
Free movement 13, 29, 9 69-73, 80, 2, 93, 95, 97, 114, 138, 155, 161, 169, 179, 207, 242, 247, 257, 264, 276-278, 275, 281, 336, 337, 343
– and competition law 329
law of – 184
obstacle to – 95, 97
Freedom of establishment 4, 19, 341
Freedom of expression 326
Freedom of movement for workers (*see also* **Employment**) 3, 4, 16-18, 24, 37, 47, 61, 74, 102, 104, 136, 158, 163, 165, 190, 192, 216, 220, 222, 251, 254, 259, 260, 265, 339, 341
Freedom to provide services 4, 19, 183, 250, 251, 254, 265, 339, 341
French Code du Travail Maritime 19
Fundamental Community principles 120, 123, 188
Fundamental freedoms 278, 279
Fundamental rights 240, 326
G-14 group 167, 214, 265, 267, 271, 349, 357
Game
essential features of the – 261
rules of the game 135, 142, 148, 150, 153, 168, 170, 182, 203, 259, 307
Goldfein paper 136, 142
Governance 352
multi-level – 273
participatory – 352
– rules 350
sport – 166, 283, 337:
systems of sport – 145
White Paper on European Governance 268, 352

Governing bodies in sport
autonomy of – 3, 31, 135, 249, 263, 277, 337, 344, 356
conditional autonomy of – 264, 269, 342
practical monopoly of – 259
Harding, Tonya 87
Harmonization
legislative – 278
Harverson, Patrick 119
Health
Alliance for Natural Health 278
general – 316
public health 95, 275, 276
Hearing 44
Helsinki Report on sport 8, 9, 143, 146, 148, 150-152, 155, 168, 169, 172, 175, 201-203, 207, 208, 210, 232, 242, 243, 246, 247, 255, 259, 262, 268, 303, 315, 328, 329, 330
Heysel Stadium disaster 42, 58
Horizontal direct effect of Article 48 25, 44, 48, 49, 60
Immunity 59, 87, 144, 215, 259
– from legal control 2
– from the application of normal legal rules 155
legal – 10
Income
redistribution of – 73
Injunction
mandatory – 40
Intellectual property rights 294
copyright 293
image rights 296
International Association Football Federation (FIFA) 11, 54, 58, 87, 117, 121, 156, 157, 177, 185, 191, 221, 265, 349, 355
regulations 266
rules governing agents 262
rules on agents 207
World Cup 7, 117, 165, 177, 187, 188, 293, 296, 355
International Association of Athletics Federations (IAAF) 252
International Basketball Federation (FIBA) 183, 357
International Ice Hockey Federation (IIHF) 357
International Olympic Committee (IOC) 187, 249, 343, 356
Olympic Games 90, 241, 355
Olympic ideals 211
Olympic movement 147
International Rugby Board (IRB) 156
Internet 231
Interventionism 218
Janssen van Raay Report 17, 21, 25, 36, 37, 41, 42, 57
Judgments
recognition of – 87
Jurisdiction 87, 98
Laeken Declaration 274
Leagues
breakaway leagues 9, 146, 151, 153, 166, 167, 173, 178, 201, 208, 231, 233, 247, 330
closed – 166, 209, 218
English (football) Premier League 228, 295, 312-313
German Bundesliga 312, 313
– legitimate economic entities 36
national identity of 36

Leagues (cont.)
property rights in – 170
Scottish Premier League 179
Legal intervention 157
Leisure market 78
Licensing
sub- 301, 319, 320, 332, 333
Locus standi
restrictive rules of – 42
Loyalty-payments 114
Market (*see also* **Community trade law**)
– distortion 90, 108, 109
– foreclosure 332, 333
– integration 155, 276
– share 179
Match
collective sale of bloc of matches 229
match-fixing 149, 179, 186, 218, 261, 307, 338
uncertainty of the result of – 150, 261
McLeod, Ian 178
Merchandise
branded – 197
sale of – 144
Migration 191, 221
Minorities
integration of – 166
Monopolies 217, 285
natural – 285
National courts
recourse to – 192
National identity 99
National measures
lawfulness of – 73
National regulatory autonomy 274
National representative teams 24, 61, 62, 181, 338
Nationality 3, 56, 61, 63, 90, 95, 170, 181, 264
3+2 rule 56, 58, 61, 64, 65, 90, 97, 101, 105, 134
EU nationals 107, 180, 216, 224
legal – 97
non-EU national 16, 26, 106, 111, 112, 164, 191, 202, 221
restrictions 56, 59, 63, 65, 90, 97, 105, 114
– rules 57, 92, 97-99, 180, 216, 338
-based discrimination (*see* **Discrimination**)
-based restrictions 62, 65, 134, 251, 337
Non-interventionist stance 42
Owen, David 119
Partnerships
multi-disciplinary – 204, 264
prohibition of multi-disciplinary- 343
Patriotism 241
Platini, Michel 119
Player draft system 77, 79
Player release
mandatory – system 267, 350, 351, 352
– system 266, 270
Player(s) (see also **Athletes** and **Football**)
acquisitions of 56
– aged under 23 192

Player(s) (cont.)
assimilated – 90
eligibility for selection of – 16, 256
foreign – 15, 42, 56, 90-93, 100, 101
home-grown 21, 64
in-contract – 113
mobility of 66-68, 75, 79
number of foreign – 17
numbers of – per team 307
out-of-contract – 80, 104, 107
recruitment and training of young – 136, 137, 138, 140, 161, 163, 165, 172, 256
right of direct participation 270
right to play of – 89
selection of – 143, 181, 182, 262
status of 164
young – 34, 37, 74, 75, 78, 96, 97, 101, 103, 104, 114, 136, 150, 152, 162, 168, 190, 194, 201, 203, 217-220, 222-226, 232, 247, 267, 268, 282, 315, 349
Player's agents 176, 185
Pons paper 131, 132, 133, 136, 138, 141
Practices
abusive – 187
Preliminary ruling 97
Price-fixing 177, 276
Professional liability insurance 185
Project Gandalf 233
Property law 284
Property rights 215, 279
Proportionality principle 73, 96, 97, 101, 121
Protectionism 216
Public interest 96
Public order 279, 336
Public policy 25, 26, 60, 61, 95, 99, 349
Public safety 126
Public security 95, 120
Racism 208, 211
Remedies 42, 45
Residence 22, 119, 120
discrimination on the grounds of – 123
residual restrictions 193
Restrictions
anti-competitive – 185, 356
Restrictive practices 284, 286
Restrictive Practices Court (RPC) (UK) 152, 172, 200, 228, 229, 233, 312
Restrictive Trade Practices Act (UK) 31, 29, 200, 229, 312
Revenue pool 269
Reynolds, "Butch" 87
Right(s)
collective selling of – 132
– of supporters 114
sale of – 300
– to information 240, 326
– to transmit 196
Sanctions (*see also* **Fines**) 57, 66, 158, 249
ban 345
draconian – 344
proportionate 10, 192, 253
suspension 193, 249, 264
system of collective – 206

Shearer, Alan 69, 80
Sherman Act (USA) 31, 77
Social cohesion 146, 241, 243, 262
Social exclusion 8
Social policy 286
Social security 111, 336, 278
Solidarity 145-147, 151, 152, 192, 193, 200, 201, 208, 210, 212, 218, 222, 225, 227, 229, 231, 232, 262, 268, 314, 315
– between professional and amateur sport 315
financial – 232, 233, 243, 315
fund 140, 198, 226, 307
horizontal – 166, 314, 331-333
organizational – 172
vertical – 166, 243, 247, 314, 331-333
Sponsorship 53, 76, 144, 147, 165, 352
sponsoring agreements 149
sponsors 266, 270, 345
Sport (*see also* **Business of sport** and **Football**)
amateur – 133, 178, 180, 232, 233, 242-244, 257
autonomy of 175
business of – 215
commercialisation of 131, 144, 145, 146, 151, 155, 157, 171, 197, 213, 296
cultural and social function of – 197, 215, 230, 321, 235, 262
distinctive nature of 140
economic dimension of – 1, 146
economic peculiarities of – 216
economic power in professional – 178
economic significance of – 180, 217, 281
economic value of a "clean" – 340
educational role of – 146, 208, 262
– for all 210, 244
global activity 156
global industry 355
– integral part of national culture 36
integrity of – 192, 222
international high-level – 183
international representative – 61
legal environment of – 202
legitimate objectives of – 149
nature of – 3, 343
non-economic aspects of – 249
North American professional – 218, 247
North American sports practice 232, 315
operational autonomy of – 145
peculiar characteristics of – 260
policy on – 178, 184, 248, 261
professional 213, 215-218, 221, 223, 226, 242, 243, 245-247, 295
purely sporting rules 4, 170, 251, 339, 345
pyramid structure of – 259
recreational – 178, 180, 212, 243
role of – 166
self-regulation in – 156
semi-professional 243
social importance of – 74, 96, 178, 179
– as social and leisure activity 355
social, cultural and educational function of – 121, 146, 152, 161, 168, 172, 210, 225, 242, 267, 316

Sport (cont.)
social importance of – 217, 220
social significance of –
special characteristics of – 153, 169, 230
special status of – 161, 194
specificity of – 2, 132, 177, 178, 195, 217, 219, 225
top-level professional – 212
traditional values of – 147
Sporting calendars
overloading of – 147
Sporting cohesion 352
Sporting competition
clean – 4
credible – 257
distinctive nature of – 226
equality between clubs 75, 101, 163, 219, 225, 226
equality of opportunity in – 150
fair – 343
fixtures 15, 197, 199, 226, 253, 307, 348
integrity of – 149, 186
noble – 251, 339
preservation of the integrity of – 264
unpredictable – 138
Sporting rules 178, 263, 340
economic effect of – 336
economic implications 3
Sports goods
distribution of – 203
suppliers of – 177
Sports law 141
State Aids 49
State autonomy 275
Statutory duty
breach of – 45
Strict liability 250
Subsidiarity principle 94, 144
Taxation 279, 336
Teams
identify with the – 42
relocation of – 131
Tickets
black market for – 122
blind sale of – 118, 120
distribution of – 114, 120, 123, 125, 126, 128, 141, 187
distribution of – 262
sale of – 102, 117, 119, 121, 137, 149, 162, 168, 188, 348
sale of – on a discriminatory basis 122, 338
unlawful distribution of – 121
Tobacco Advertising 277, 278
Tobacco Advertising Directive 185, 340
Tolerance and fair play 147, 166, 177, 184, 213, 255, 257, 335, 344

Transfer 9, 17, 155, 178, 180, 183, 190-195, 207, 214, 216, 251
2001 agreement on the – system 221
cross-border – 70, 79, 108
cross-border – fees 107
domestic – 83, 106, 107, 108, 109, 111

Transfer (cont.)
– fees 68, 69, 74, 106-108, 190, 194, 215
– fees system 97, 111, 135, 136, 139, 169
international – 192

ASSER INTERNATIONAL SPORTS LAW SERIES

Editors
Robert C.R. Siekmann and Janwillem Soek

ISSN 1874–6926

Basic Documents of International Sports Organisations, R.C.R. Siekmann and J.W. Soek, eds. (The Hague/Boston/London, Kluwer Law International 1998)

Doping Rules of International Sports Organisations, R.C.R. Siekmann, J.W. Soek and A. Bellani, eds. (The Hague, T.M.C.ASSER PRESS 1999)

Arbitral and Disciplinary Rules of International Sports Organisations, R.C.R. Siekmann and J.W. Soek, eds. (The Hague, T.M.C.ASSER PRESS 2001)

Professional Sport in the European Union: Regulation and Re-regulation, A. Caiger and S. Gardiner, eds. (The Hague, T.M.C.ASSER PRESS 2001)

Mediating Sports Disputes: National and International Perspectives, I.S. Blackshaw (The Hague, T.M.C.ASSER PRESS 2002)

The European Union and Sport: Legal and Policy Documents, R.C.R. Siekmann and J.W. Soek, eds. (The Hague, T.M.C.ASSER PRESS 2005)

Sports Image Rights in Europe, I.S. Blackshaw and R.C.R. Siekmann, eds. (The Hague, T.M.C.ASSER PRESS 2005)

The Court of Arbitration for Sport 1984–2004, I.S. Blackshaw, R.C.R. Siekmann and J.W. Soek, eds. (The Hague, T.M.C.ASSER PRESS 2006)

The Strict Liability Principle and the Human Rights of Athletes in Doping Cases, J.W. Soek (The Hague, T.M.C.ASSER PRESS 2006)

The Council of Europe and Sport: Basic Documents, R.C.R. Siekmann and J.W. Soek, eds. (The Hague, T.M.C.ASSER PRESS 2007)